Africa in Europe

Volume Two

Africa in Europe

Volume Two:

Interdependencies, Relocations, and Globalization

S<small>TEFAN</small> G<small>OODWIN</small>

LEXINGTON BOOKS

A division of
ROWMAN & LITTLEFIELD PUBLISHERS, INC.
Lanham • Boulder • New York • Toronto • Plymouth, UK

LEXINGTON BOOKS

A division of Rowman & Littlefield Publishers, Inc.
A wholly owned subsidiary of The Rowman & Littlefield Publishing Group, Inc.
4501 Forbes Boulevard, Suite 200
Lanham, MD 20706

Estover Road
Plymouth PL6 7PY
United Kingdom

British Library Cataloguing in Publication Information Available

Library of Congress Cataloging-in-Publication Data

Goodwin, Stefan, 1941–
  Africa in Europe / Stefan Goodwin.
     p. cm.
  Includes bibliographical references and index.
  ISBN-13: 978-0-7391-2765-0 (v. 2 : cloth : alk. paper)
  ISBN-10: 0-7391-2765-9 (v. 2 : cloth : alk. paper)
  ISBN-13: 978-0-7391-2766-7 (v. 2 : pbk. : alk. paper)
  ISBN-10: 0-7391-2766-7 (v. 2 : pbk. : alk. paper)
  eISBN-13: 978-0-7391-2995-1
  eISBN-10: 0-7391-2995-3
1. Africa—Relations—Europe. 2. Europe—Relations—Africa. 3. Europe—
Civilization—African influences. 4. Africans—Europe—History. 5. Africa—History. 6.
Africa—Civilization. I. Title.
  DT38.9.E85G66 2009
  303.48'2604—dc22   2008024523

Printed in the United States of America

♾™ The paper used in this publication meets the minimum requirements of American
National Standard for Information Sciences—Permanence of Paper for Printed Library
Materials, ANSI/NISO Z39.48–1992.

To all those who have drawn the inference from my words that Africa, as a continent, is somehow genetically inferior, I can only apologize unreservedly. That is not what I meant. More importantly, from my point of view, there is no scientific basis for such a belief.

JAMES D. WATSON
Molecular Biologist
Codiscoverer of DNA Structure
Nobel Laureate

Surely the day will come when color means nothing
    more than the skin tone,
when religion is seen uniquely as a way to speak one's soul,
when birth places have the weight of a throw of the dice
    and all men are born free,
when understanding breeds love and brotherhood.

JOSEPHINE BAKER
Entertainer and Human Rights Advocate
Heroine in the French Resistance
Chevalier of the Legion of Honor

Contents

Foreword

One of the great tragedies of the "racial worldview" that characterized so much of Western attitudes, beliefs, and values in the 19th and 20th centuries was the enormous distortion of world history and social realities that dominated all scholarship. Racial ideology required that the achievements of peoples of African ancestry in this country and elsewhere be demeaned and/or ignored. Examples of excellence among people of African ancestry were ignored, denigrated, or dismissed. Some scholars argued that Africans had no history worthy of mention, and scientists expended great efforts to demonstrate the inferiority of Africans. History was taught as if there had never been any interactions among Europeans and Africans before the slave trade brought ignorant Africans to labor for Europeans in the New World. Europeans were portrayed as superior peoples who naturally conquered and dominated what we now call Third World peoples.

In the mid-20th century we saw the beginnings of corrective histories, the recognition of facts about the peoples and cultures of Africa that had been hidden or ignored. Scholars began to reveal the true histories of Africa and its peoples. And, bit by bit, we have seen the retrenchment of racial bias in the writing of history and the revelation and incorporation of new information, including the now uncontested fact of the origin of the human species in Africa.

Stefan Goodwin's massive two-volume manuscript is a welcome attempt to bring together much of the information, newly acquired and/or restored over the past half-century, on the interaction between the peoples of Europe and Africa. He has pulled together enormous amounts of data that not only vindicate Africans but also demonstrate their productive and often outstanding roles in European cultures. Referencing the earliest documented records of the Roman conquests of parts of Europe (including England) with the use of African military units, he has shown the continuing presence of African peoples, both as individuals and as groups, in European lands and their full participation in the cultures of the ethnic groups among whom they settled.

We know now from vast archaeological evidence that dark-skinned people with crinkly hair were found throughout the Mediterranean world in ancient times. And Goodwin reminds us of the great phenotypic diversity found in Ancient Egypt, attesting without doubt to the intermixtures of people from southern Europe, southwestern Asia, and northern and eastern Africa. (I have touched the tight little braids of a mummy while in Egypt that could have graced the heads of many African Americans today.) The history of Egypt over the past four thousand years is in large part a history of the interaction among peoples from Africa, Europe, and southwestern Asia. Based on the written record, we know that much of the warfare of this region involved the use of mercenaries, many of whom were black Africans, and so were their leaders. The Roman conquest of north African territories led to more extensive interaction among Europeans and Africans, and Africans themselves became more involved with the affairs of Europeans, including through the growth of the Christian religion.

Africans were clearly involved with the spread of Islam to Europe; indeed, some individual Africans were participants in this new religion from the start. Those people known today as the Moors were originally consolidated as a movement in northern and western Africa after the Muslim conquest of Spain. The original site of their consolidation was a camp along the Senegal River where the leaders attracted many local people in an attempt to rejuvenate Islam. This leaves little doubt as to their black African identity and origins. Throughout the Muslim dominance of southern Europe, individual Africans played many roles, just as they did in Baghdad and other parts of the Middle East.

In the Middle Ages, both the Spanish and the Portuguese utilized Africans in their explorations of the New World and parts of Asia. It was information provided by Africans to the Portuguese, and their knowledge and abilities as sailors, that made success possible for these Europeans in their sailing ventures. Africans and people of part African ancestry were with virtually all of the explorers and conquistadors; their stories have yet to be fully told. During this time Africans traveled to Europe as ambassadors and merchants. Often their sons were sent to Europe to study in its universities. Many Africans were recruited to be interpreters and translators.

Individuals of African ancestry have indeed been creators of European cultural forms in ways that were out of proportion to their numbers. In the 16th century, one of the great patrons of the arts was Alessandro de' Medici who was appointed the first duke of Florence by Pope Clement VII. Alessandro's mother was an African servant, and it was widely believed that Pope Clement VII was his biological father. Alexander Pushkin is considered even today the greatest of the Russian poets. Alexander Dumas and his son Alexander Dumas fils are the French inventors of the romantic novel and adventure tales of enduring cultural significance. They were and are widely read around the world as exemplars of high French culture. Africans and their descendants in Europe were artisans, craftsmen, merchants, entertainers, musicians, military men, writers, poets, tailors, sailors, shoemakers, cooks, and many types of servants.

Until the 18th century there was no generalized negative status imposed on Africans. Not only did they hold diverse positions in European societies, they were assimilated into their various communities. Some held high positions in the government and the military, or they served in the courts of various kings as advisors, scribes, accountants, or diplomats. Some functioned as translators or entertainers whose skills were highly valued. Others were servants and/or slaves who served at the will of their masters in a world where large numbers of people of all colors were also slaves. Skin color had little or no social significance in this complex world where religious affiliation was the supreme signifier of identity. Interethnic conflict was widespread during the Middle Ages, and none of it had to do with skin color or the idea of "race," which had yet to be invented.

Goodwin has provided us a complex, yet nuanced and broad-ranging, portrait of the African presence in Europe, and he has done so in a comprehensive and compelling way. He has depicted important aspects of the political and economic histories of various European peoples as they competed with one another for power, wealth, and prestige and in the end did so by exploiting the peoples of the African continent. Additionally this study reveals new insights and fresh interpretations of events and circumstances surrounding the relationships between Africans and Europeans. Part of its value lies in how it reveals the contradictory trends manifest in the policies of many different European leaders as they struggled with the moral dilemma and economic enticements of slavery. It is clear that many Europeans knew Africans as people and accepted them as equals in their societies. It is also clear that, at least from the 18th century on, a process of racialization was at work that led to the dehumanization of Africans in the minds of many Europeans. At the same time, this study helps to explain why, despite some similarities, the experiences of Africans in Europe were quite different from those of Africans in the Americas.

This study is well documented with source materials not usually available in scholarly libraries. These materials reflect Goodwin's extensive experience in Europe and his long years of dedicated research on this topic. It is interdisciplinary in scope and reflects his many decades of teaching and study on an international level. The bibliography alone constitutes a gold mine for scholars who might want to conduct further research in this area.

With the publication of this work in two volumes, we have a major new reference for scholars in the future. It is essential reading for anyone interested in African studies, the history of slavery, the emergence of racial ideology, and the general history of Western civilization. It is the only study of its kind. I predict that it will soon become a classic. It will inspire other scholars to probe deeply into the archives of monasteries and private collections to reconstruct the history of African peoples everywhere. Finally, I suspect that this study will also help to transform the image of African peoples in world history.

AUDREY SMEDLEY

Professor Emerita
Anthropology and African American Studies
Virginia Commonwealth University

Preface and Acknowledgments

When we describe the Earth as divided among seven continents, we are engaged in compartmentalizing our planet simultaneously in complex and in simplistic ways. Overall, gene flow, cultural diffusion, and human history have not been channeled in accordance with such a schema. Through the ages, people have repeatedly changed how they have referred to large land masses, oceans, seas, and islands and the human lives that have unfolded thereon or nearby. Although this study focuses on Europe, the author is fully aware that people who inhabit Europe, Africa, Asia, and other parts of the world frequently interacted and influenced each other even extending back into prehistory.

Our concepts of Europe and Africa as places, like our concepts of Europeans and Africans as people, have evolved over time. At most, these are relative concepts. First, they are fluid; second, they overlap. The prehistoric radiation of people from Africa throughout the world overlapped with periodic movements of people back and forth between Africa and Europe as well as elsewhere. In addition to human connections between Africa and Europe that have been forged in direct ways, peoples of African and European descents are also related to each other through their encounters and exchanges that have occurred in scattered places around the planet.

Some parts of Europe lie much closer to Africa and Asia than to other parts of Europe. During most of history, there has been a tendency for people to interact more frequently and more intensely with people who lived nearby them than with people who lived in far distant places, regardless of whether they were considered to be located on the same land mass or not. Of course, mere access and proximity never completely accounted for human migrations or the density of human interactions whether on the same continent or across continents. Hence, people were never completely predictable in the ways that their destinies became linked or in the ways that they perceived and reflected on such linkages. In addition to climate, geography, pursuit of profits, and chance landings, numerous other factors have been instrumental in pulling people together while at other times pushing them away from each other. Even factors as varied as where relatives, strangers, friends, allies, and enemies lived as well as values concerning what was good, holy, beautiful, inferior, repulsive, threatening or boring or that offered the best prospects for prosperity.

An eventual revolution in seafaring technology began to make it possible for numerous peoples to engage in long-distance communication, commerce, and colonization. During much of the last six hundred years, Europeans were especially involved in global exploration, trade, and colonization. While this often resulted in a European presence far beyond Europe, it also accelerated the growth of an African presence in Europe and in places abroad that were under the control of Europeans. By the turn of the 20th century, a European "scramble for Africa" had virtually subjected the entire continent of Africa and all its inhabitants to the domination of one or another European power. This situation played a role in allowing Africa to be reduced in the minds of many Europeans to a place inhabited by people of deficiency and dysfunction. It also left many Europeans piously imagining that they had saved Africans from themselves through conquering, enslaving, and otherwise exploiting and oppressing them.

Such ways of treating and thinking about Africa and Africans by peoples of European descent coincided with the increasing popularity among Europeans of notions of African inferiority, docility, and passivity. Over time, such notions diffused around the world together with European colonization and Westernization. Such ways of treating and thinking about Africa were also buttressed by misconceptions that Europeans had about human variation in general and various delusions that they were superior and separate from other peoples in the world. Such thinking about Africans and Europeans involved much historical distortion, much twisting of science, and the diffusion of many myths. It would have been confusing and disturbing to many people of European descent had they been presented with contrary information about Africans and Europeans, including that Africans had a significant and continuing presence in Europe since antiquity. It would also have brought into question many European notions alleging European superiority and myths about their so-called racial purity. In large measure, Africa continues to be portrayed by many scholars and through mass media in ways more designed to perpetuate racist myths than to reflect reality.

Meanwhile, a revolution in electronic communications that involved certain mass media and the telephone eventually made it possible for people to interact selectively with people far away even while ignoring people in their immediate vicinities. Today's worldwide Web technology has further given masses of people the option to skip about the globe electronically on-line in ways that put them more in contact with global "others" than with people who reside nearby. That significant numbers of people are able to experience travel to virtual places while remaining physically stationery before monitors and screens is but one manifestation of globalization. Among others are an unprecedented dispersion of labor markets, capital, translocation of economic resources, and widely scattered bases of operation for a vast variety of multinational networks, organizations, and corporations. An additional manifestation of globalization may be seen in the considerable frequency with which masses of people physically move about the world and often settle, both officially and as undocumented migrants without benefit of legal authorization.

Although the two-volume work that is *Africa in Europe* primarily concerns Europe and Europeans, it is important that we avoid thinking of these labels in an essentialist way as something more than human-made constructs that have always been characterized by fluidity. In various periods and in various contexts, we have conceptualized many different Europes the same as we have variously conceptualized Europeans. Throughout history, our concepts of Europe and Europeans have continually been changing. This study documents that Europe is biologically, geographically, demographically, and socioculturally continuous internally as well as with neighboring continents, including Africa. No matter where one draws a line of demarcation for heuristic purposes, it is somewhat arbitrary.

Race, though real in the form of an array of social constructs, almost never has the biological significance that we so often ascribe to it. It is ironic that this non-race-centered approach to the study of Europe and Europeans across fields as varied as anthropology, social history, and migration is rather uncommon at a time when human beings globally are interdependent on each other more profoundly than at any time since we have been custodians of this planet. Many Europeans and Africans are, in fact, neighbors and close relatives of each other. While explaining how this is so, *Africa in Europe* encourages us to embrace a new way of thinking about who we are as a species. In the grips of globalization, our frequent inability to turn away from tribalism, racism, ideologies of intolerance, and the selfishness to consume as much of our finite resources for ourselves as possible, with insufficient consideration of our fellows at a time that we are more armed than ever, places our common survival as a species in jeopardy.

Because I feel myself in some ways at home everywhere and never fully at home in any one place, I am perhaps what Claude Lévi-Strauss has called *dépaysé* or a citizen of the world. Having such an identity however does not mean that I escaped from having any experiences that were disappointing, painful, or mystifying, Still my connections and bonds with Africa and Europe have helped me to pursue the topic of *Africa in Europe* with great passion, and with a realization that what is African and what is European do not need to exist in some type of natural opposition to each other. In fact, I remain fascinated by how much we human beings are similar, even with our many differences. As *Africa in Europe* was looking for an author and I was looking for a new challenge, my identity and background drew me to this undertaking with great passion.

I have fortunately been the recipient of considerable support, some of which I wish to acknowledge. The agencies involved include Northwestern University's Africa House, the National Science Foundation, the Ford Foundation, the U.S. Department of Education, and the U.S. Department of Defense for a grant to study Arabic. As I haunted bookstores, libraries, archives, and museums throughout Europe and elsewhere, I benefited from the assistance of numerous people who believed in the importance of my undertaking. Many sons and daughters of Europe, Africa, and others places opened their doors and the stories of their lives to me in ways that proved invaluable. I also wish to acknowledge some individuals.

David Dorsey, a scholar who has devoted much of his life to the study of ancient Greece and Rome, challenged me on many details and offered numerous suggestions for improving my manuscript, for which I am grateful. William J. Megginson, a historian and friend, time and again made himself available as a sounding board. In addition, he read several chapters of my manuscript offering me unvarnished critiques that I found very helpful. I owe a special debt of gratitude to Dean R. Wagner for years spent encouraging me to continue with this project, assisting me in some of my data collection, and for numerous hours reading and critiquing most of my many drafts. I am also in his debt for constantly reminding me that I was capable of meeting all the challenges that this undertaking placed before me.

In addition to numerous scholars such as these to whom I owe much gratitude, there were other people who assisted me with very specific questions. For example, helpful information on a work of art that intrigued and raised questions for me in Copenhagen came graciously from Jan Gorm Madsen, a curator of paintings and drawings at Denmark's Hirschsprung Collection. Lyn Sheppard, a friend in Switzerland, supplied me generously with much current periodical material and was kind enough to translate numerous items from German to English for me. He also was especially generous in his encouragement.

Jho Archer, the Haitian-born choreographer and singer, who after leaving New York in the early 1960s spent the last four decades of his life in Paris, provided me with many non-technical insights into French society from his perspective. My friend Robert Estrin, excited that my undertaking should succeed, surprised me on several occasions with titles that were rich in relevant information and opened new pathways in my thinking. Cornelius Goodwin, my father, loved the world that he knew as well as the world that he dreamed of knowing better, and he encouraged me from as early as I can remember to be inquisitive and informed about it. The favorite mantra of my mother, Dr. Helen Goodwin, was simply "Write, write, write!" I shall be forever grateful to all these people as well as to many others that I have not mentioned by name.

No work about the interactions and experiences of people of African descent in such a large area as Europe can ever be exhaustive, and I fully expect that other scholars will add new interpretations and supply many pieces missing and their own analyses and critiques as time goes on. Standing on the shoulders of scholars, archivists, and collectors, I posit this work as a new baseline from which others hopefully will find it difficult to retreat into some of the old and distorted ways of thinking about Africa vis-à-vis Europe as well as about the fallacy of race, which the anthropologist Ashley Montagu labeled mankind's "most dangerous myth."

Hopefully, *Africa in Europe* will contribute to its readers' awareness that we need to be critical and skeptical of mass media and official governmental sources with commercial and national interests to protect at a time when a wide-ranging informational war is underway to shape many of our values and our perceptions of the world. As a tactic in this war, some would confuse us with a combination of information and entertainment (sometimes referred to as "info-tainment") under the pretence that it is fact-based. Still others would do the same thing through brief and highly selective informational flashes that are propagan-distic, ethnocentric, crudely stereotypic, or based on pseudo-scientific racism.

It would be unfortunate and not intellectually productive for us to ignore this. *Africa in Europe* emerges out of a hope that in knowing more about our past and certain important challenges that confront us we shall be much better equipped to wisely navigate our future. I hope that this work will challenge us all to experiment with new and better ways of inhabiting our single global vil-lage for the common good.

Without reservations, I take full responsibility for any errors or misrepresen-tations that this work may contain.

Introduction

People across Boundaries

Europe, at the narrowest part of the Strait of Gibraltar, is only eight miles from Africa. On an especially clear day, it is sometimes possible to see from Africa to Europe across this waterway with the naked eye. It is likely that a tunnel between Morocco and nearby Spain will soon be a reality. After his election as President of France in 2007, Nicolas Sarkozy began advocating for the creation of a Mediterranean Union. A high-speed train system is scheduled to connect Tangier on Africa's Mediterranean coast with central Morocco in approximately two hours by 2013, and there is little doubt that it will eventually extend to the city of Marrakesh in the northern foothills of the Sahara. Assumptions that Africa and Europe are far apart are largely based on myths that take little account of the past, the present, and the future that is unfolding

The notion that so-called true Africans live only south of the Sahara desert and do not overlap in a significant biological way with Africans living further north on the same continent is also part of a mythical perspective. It is a perspective that ignores biological, social, and cultural continuities that have extended from parts of Africa to parts of Europe from prehistory to the present. During this age of globalization, when Europe struggles to reconcile with parts of itself that are largely African, this situation provides a convenient context to describe much about the human condition that is not widely understood but that deserves serious discussion and better understanding.

Around the world, human beings are more mobile than ever, and, as a consequence, our identities and boundaries are everywhere in flux. At the same time, xenophobia, competition over resources, status concerns, and territorialism contribute to periodic waves of discrimination, selective hostility against immigrants, and so-called ethnic cleansing or even genocide. A serious study of Africa in Europe provides a superb and challenging framework in which to examine how people loosely defined as Africans in a variety of ways have been received and integrated into numerous societies in Europe that are predominantly populated by Europeans. This study unfolds against the broad perspectives of anthro-

1

pology, social history, human geography, civilization, migration, and globalization. It sheds light on numerous issues and developments that are crucial to our survival as fellow inhabitants of a single global village.

This study challenges us to reexamine our unscientific thinking about human variation and human connections, including many outdated and distorted ideas about race. Our common biological status as human beings results from an evolutionary process along a single evolutionary path with eastern Africa especially important as a locus for much of this development. Known fossil evidence of Homo sapiens (the species to which we belong) dates back about 350,000 years. Fossil evidence for *Homo sapiens sapiens* (the subspecies to which all people belong) dating back over 100,000 years also has been discovered in some parts of Africa—in other words, considerably earlier than it is known in Europe.

Genetic evidence for a single cradle for the earliest human beings in Africa is confirmatory in the view of the vast majority of specialists in the study of human evolution. Many of these scholars even interpret certain genetic evidence involving mitochrondrial DNA as suggesting that a common female ancestor of all people plausibly lived in Africa as recently as 200,000 years ago. In addition to the part of our biological makeups that is genetic (i.e., our genotype), another part is physiological and morphological (i.e., our phenotype). While some surface features of the latter are visible to even a casual observer, this is not true of the genotype.

Human beings are members of a highly intelligent species accustomed to relying heavily on a good sense of vision that is stereoscopic and in color for taking in lots of information very rapidly. Unfortunately, however, we often overestimate the importance of what we can perceive visually and underestimate the importance of what is not readily apparent to us in a visual way. This means that we often attribute too much biological significance to a few surface features of our phenotypes as compared to equally important hidden biological traits, including many that are phenotypic and all of those that are genotypic. Even if it were possible to see all features of our phenotypes, they would not fully reflect our genotypes, as recessive parts of our genotypes, by definition, have no phenotypic expression.

While numerous surface differences obviously may be observed from person to person within our species, because they are largely superficial they can be misleading with regard to how we are biologically related to each other. Although no one with even a rudimentary understanding of science would choose to receive a blood transfusion or an organ transplant from another person based on surface features such as complexion or hair type, many people inconsistently assume that certain surface characteristics cause them to be biologically distinct from, and in some cases superior to, other people. In no area have we likely taken more wrong turns than in our thinking about human variation in terms that are racial. Racial thinking is pre-scientific in origin, and it typically incorporates many myths.

Scientists still understood so little about genetics as of 1900 that they had no idea why blood transfusions sometimes failed and at other times succeeded. Thanks to the phenomenal discoveries of Austria's Karl Landsteirner, it was around this time that they began to learn that there existed within our species differing distributions of A-B-O genes for blood and that these distributions were not race-based. Since this time, genetics has revolutionized our understanding of human biological variation, including in ways that often are at variance with what we perceive with our naked eyes. Since each person likely has between 50,000 to 100,000 genes, each of which involves a few thousand of base units of DNA, each of us carries an estimated three billion units of DNA in our chromosomes. Even if by some miracle we could see such genetic complexity, with their numerous levels of variation from individual to individual, we would be incapable of systematically cataloging it according to some small number of basic types.

Now that we can classify blood not only by the A-B-O system but also by the M-N system, by the Duffy factor, by the Rh factor, by the Kidd factor, by plotting frequencies of various hemoglobin genes, as well as in many other ways, it is not logical to attempt classifying all people biologically on the basis of just one, two, or three surface phenotypic characteristics. Although many people with dark skin in the world have tightly curled hair, there also exist other people with extremely dark or richly pigmented skin whose hair is very straight.

From a world perspective, there is no such thing as "black people's type of hair." Many dark-complexioned people of southern India, for example, have hair that tends to be very different from the tightly curled hair more common among dark people in many parts of Africa. Similarly, there is no one type of hair that is "white people's type of hair." For example, among the indigenous people of Australia, we sometimes witness hair that is curly at the same time that it is at times tawny or somewhat blond. Algerians from Kabyle, moreover, occasionally have hair and eyes that are rather lightly pigmented.

To some degree, all such surface features exist differentially in the eyes of various beholders in any case. Hair color is actually continuous like the vast majority of our phenotypic traits rather than existing in a few discrete varieties. Also, it can change over time. Hair color like many other surface features can in addition be changed cosmetically. We live in a world where we sometimes refer to blonds, brunettes, and redheads as though they are whole types of people with particular types of personalities and mental endowments when, in reality, natural hair color, eye color, and skin pigmentation in human beings are likely determined by at least three or four genes acting together in very complex ways.

In referring to the literature on people in Renaissance Spain, Casares (2005: 248-249) noted "descriptions of colour are arbitrary, inconsistent and sometimes even contradictory ('clear black', 'almost black', 'dark black', 'very dark black', etc.) since there is no such thing as 'pure black' or 'pure white.'" She further noted that the word *negro* (literally meaning "black") was sometimes used in Castilian Spanish in early modern documents to refer to people of at least seven different backgrounds. These included (1) sub-Saharan Africans, (2) Muslims of northern Africa, some of whom were enslaved and some of whom were free, (3) people born in the Iberian Peninsula but of ancestors from sub-Saharan Africa, (4) Moriscos, who were Spanish Muslims forced to convert to Christianity, (5) people indigenous to the Canary Islands off the coast of western Africa, (6) enslaved people from the subcontinent of India imported into Europe, and (7) people of appreciable African ancestry imported into Spain from colonial settings in the New World.

Delimiting any continent raises many problems, and Africa and Europe are not exceptions. Though geographers nowadays often encourage us to think of the Earth as divided into seven continents, they realize that such a conceptualization of our planet is far from neat. Physical geography and human geography do not always reveal parallel distributions of variation. Moreover, geology, demography, and culture are seldom concordant in a continental sense, and the association of islands with particular continents has always been large arbitrary.

Greenland, for example, is closely associated with Europe culturally and politically while it is geologically more closely associated with North America. The island nations of Malta and Cyprus are usually associated with Europe for cultural reasons although the former is further south than some northern fringes of nearby Tunisia and the former is much located much further east than any other landmass that is conventionally designated as European, except of course for Russia and perhaps occasionally Turkey. We typically consider the Russian Federation to be a European country although most of its territory lies in Asia, in fact, with some of it stretching even further east than China, Japan, and the Korean Peninsula.

In contrast, New Zealand, like many other parts of Oceania, is generally not considered to be a part of Asia or Australia. Since Hawaii joined the United States as a state in 1959, we often think of it as a part of North America although in terms of its indigenous culture it belongs to the subregion of Oceania known as Polynesia. Similarly, many people hardly realize that Israel lies in Asia, for they so strongly think of Jews as of European derivation or at least as having their strongest geopolitical ties nowadays with the so-called West, including with Europe and with North America.

Concepts such as the Far East, the Middle East, and the Near East are all predicated on viewing the world from a Eurocentric perspective, and while the last two mentioned terms used to have different referents, few people now consistently recognize a distinction between them. Both of these concepts, moreover, have very nebulous definitions and are frequently used differently even by scholars. Although Madagascar is a member of the African Union, an ancient infusion of at least some of its settlers from southeastern Asia means that from some perspectives its culture and some of its people are Afro-Asian. There similarly exist other so-called African countries in the Indian Ocean such as Mauritius and the Seychelles that could just as easily be considered Asian.

Africa has many diasporas, some ancient, some recent, and some in layers atop each other, as do also many other continents or peoples. Given the comings and goings of people from location to location and the diffusion of culture from place to place, the concept of continent is a relative one with fluid referents. Hence, when we refer to the Earth as divided among seven continents, we are engaged in compartmentalizing our planet both in complex and in simplistic ways. Throughout the ages and according to context, people have repeatedly changed how they have referred to large landmasses, oceans, seas, and islands.

Since our human ancestors radiated widely throughout the Old World, it has been impossible to find any period when people inhabiting Africa, Asia, and Europe were not continually interacting and influencing each other. A universal tendency in human intercourse throughout most of our history has been, all things being equal, that people interact more frequently and more intensely with their neighbors than with people in more distant places. However, some parts of Africa lie much closer to Europe and Asia than to other parts of Africa, and some parts of Europe lie much closer to some parts of Africa than to some other parts of Europe. Africa has always been in communication with the rest of the world. So it was during the long days of human prehistory, and so it is today. Neither diversity in Africa nor diversity beyond Africa should blind us to Africa's internal continuity and its continuity with neighboring continents. It should not surprise us therefore that boundaries between Africa and Europe have always been somewhat blurred.

Such concepts as Africa, Europe, African, and European emerge largely out of changing relationships that are geopolitical, social, cultural, psychological, emotional, mythical, and situational. These are not concepts with fixed or standardized definitions in the context of history or that of geography. Since at least the beginning of the Age of Global Exploration in the wake of the Iberian *Reconquistas* against so-called Moors and Saracens, most of whom arrived in Europe from nearby Africa, Europeans have tended to be more comfortable sometimes claiming that their dominion extended south of the Mediterranean Sea than in viewing Africa as extending north of the Mediterranean Sea. In this same spirit, European cartographers eventually classified the majority of islands in the Mediterranean Sea as parts of Europe rather than Africa, although the only continent that extends the full length of that sea is Africa.

Europeans had laid claim to a number of islands located off the coast of western Africa even before Columbus first headed westward across the Atlantic Ocean in search of India in 1492. European claims on Mauritania can be traced back to the Congress of Vienna in 1815 although it was only declared annexed along with Senegal in 1840. They began to lay claim to Algeria to 1830, on Djibouti by a treaty of 1862, to Eritrea as a colony in 1880, and on Tunisia and Egypt as so-called protectorates in 1881 and 1882, respectively. In the northern reaches of Africa alone, they followed this up with claims on Rio de Oro in 1884, to British Somalia in 1888, and to Italian Somalia in 1888 and 1889. After a conquest that lasted from 1895 to 1998, Sudan was declared an Anglo-Egyptian Condominium in 1899. Morocco was taken over in 1900 and declared a protectorate by the Treaty of Fez in 1912. Europeans used the Treaty of Lausanne in 1923 to declare Libya annexed, and they invaded Ethiopia in 1935, declaring it annexed to Eritrea and Italian Somalia as a part of Italian East Africa in 1936. This is only how Europeans invaded and declared their dominion over just a small part of Africa, and yet many people know little about how such undertakings as these also contributed to an African presence in Europe.

The French essayist Ferdinand Duchêne wanted his readers to think of the Mediterranean Sea as a "French lake" that divided France into parts. Claiming that the more beautiful half of France lay north of the Mediterranean, Duchêne suggested that it was the duty of inhabitants from the part of France in Algeria to visit the other half (Gosnell 2001: 161). Stating as its rationale that the Portuguese reached the Indies and Columbus reached the so-called New World, a caption at the German Historical Museum as of 2007 literally claimed that "the borders of Europe expanded." By the time the so-called European "scramble for Africa" was entering into its most active phase around the time of the Conference of Berlin in 1884-1885, some Europeans claimed at times that Africa only began below the Sahara desert or even further south.

Continuity within Africa, as well as between Africa and Europe, is underscored by the fact that hardly more than 10,000 years ago, some parts of the Sahara desert contained fishing villages. Some parts of it were as well a rich ecological magnet that attracted large game animals and foragers who hunted them. Zartman, Desanges, Murdock, and numerous other scholars have pointed out that the Sahara region within the heartland of Africa during a very long period functioned as much like a highway as like a barrier.

As recently as the period between 1848 and 1879, a number of European writers who visited the area of the central Sahara around Fezzan in Libya reported a preponderance of "blacks" speaking mainly Hausa living in the region although Hausa-speakers nowadays are concentrated much further south, largely in Niger and northern Nigeria. According to Murdock (1959: 131-132), verification of "black" Hausa-speaker among residents in the Fezzan came from Richardson (1848), Duveyrier (1864), and Chavanne (1879). Similarly, the Mediterranean Sea has since antiquity served much like a highway between Africa and Europe. Such truths however are still resisted by masses of people who find great comfort in myths that allow them to believe that humanity is fundamentally divided according to so-called races, races that are separated from each other by physical barriers deemed to be largely impenetrable.

Many stereotypes attach to such words as African, European, "black," and "white" that greatly complicate our ability to understand how the peoples referred to by these terms are related to each other and have historically interacted with each other. Thanks to continuous gene flow resulting from sexual intercourse and reproduction among human beings in ways that produce offspring, people in all parts of our planet remain united as a single species. Sexual reproduction automatically shifts genetic material around somewhat randomly whenever we produce a new offspring. The variation in our species also increases through the operation of mechanisms such as natural selection, mutations, genetic drift, and sexual selection.

We live in a world where so-called black people are sometimes lighter in complexion than so-called white people and where "white" people sometimes have "black" people as one of their parents or grandparents and vice versa. Given this reality, it should be readily apparent that the people labeled in such ways often overlap and are continuous with each other. Any hypothesis that there exist human breeding populations that correspond with nonoverlapping or pure races is completely disproved.

The concepts of Africa and Africans, on the one hand, and Europe and Europeans, on the other, are fluid concepts. They have evolved over a long period of time and they continue to evolve, sometimes as extensions of each other as well as in distinction from each other. Even before the Punic Wars began to be fought in 264 B.C., Europeans were involved in Africa, and this involvement continued under Roman imperialism, Hellenistic imperialism, and Byzantine imperialism. It further continued during the age of the Crusades, during Napoleon's entry into Egypt in 1798, and during France's entry into Algeria in 1830.

One can hardly gaze at the name plaques on the streets or at the names of various metro stations in Paris without being reminded how much the French honor various sons who carried the French *tricoleur* or flag into various colonies abroad. So important did investments in African slavery become to the economic elite inhabiting Bordeaux that even at present almost all the major streets and many of the most important buildings in this third largest of French cities are named for men who grew wealthy from the African slave trade (Pétrissans-Cavaillès 2004: 43-117). In the port of Marseille, which is the second largest city in France, the names of many streets and neighborhoods continue to evoke France's colonial links with Algeria, which is located nearby in Africa (Blanchard and Boëtsch 2005: 14).

Europeans tend to glorify their expansion beyond Europe, including their various thrusts into Africa. On the other hand, many Europeans nowadays view the growing presence of Africans in Europe as problematic or as an anomaly. Complicating this situation is a very distorted, stereotypic, and sensationalized treatment of the enslavement of African peoples as though it evolved largely apart from the enslavement and serfdom of other peoples, including Europeans. In many parts of the Old World (in contrast to the New World), the reality was that it was often common for Europeans, Africans, and others to be enslaved alongside each other under rather similar conditions.

Undoubtedly much of this contrastive way of thinking about Europeans in Africa and Africans in Europe has to do with territorialism coupled with racism. Many people mistake the "race" categories about which they are taught or that they conceptualize into being for actual units of reproduction and heredity. Some people, including some scholars, have set hurdles in the way of our understanding the complex ways in which we humans are related to each other. They sometimes postulate the existence of race divisions as givens and then attempt to reconstruct the past in terms of how such entities (really stereotypic mental and cultural abstractions) are thought to have interacted with each other from remote antiquity until the present.

"Race," Ruth Benedict (1968: 56) once said, "is an abstraction even as it is defined by a geneticist; as it is defined statistically by a physical anthropologist it is even more of an abstraction. It is not the *race* which copulates and reproduces." It is individuals. Our species overflows with variation, and few individuals within it can make any claim to being more or less biologically identical to any other. Despite the sometimes necessary use in this work of the terms "mulatto," "miscegenation," "black," and "white," given the continuous nature of human variation that all anthropologists claim to recognize nowadays, such usages represent compromises of convenience and should not be assumed to be technically exact in some biological sense.

In his *Europe, A History: A Panorama of Europe, East and West, From the Ice Age to the Cold War, From the Urals to Gibraltar*, Norman Davies (1998: 221) made the following observation. "Certainly, racial purity is a non-starter when applied to the European peoples in historic times. The population of the Roman Empire contained a strong admixture of both north African negroids and west Asian semitics. . . . Language, culture, religion, and politics have been more powerful determinants of ethnicity than race."

It was ironic that, after arguing in *The Myth of Continents: A Critique of Metageography* that continental and region studies sometimes involve environmental determinism and the politics of space, Lewis and Wigen (1997) then argued in favor of their own system of regional classification that was highly reliant on religion and race. In fact, people can change their religions several times in a lifetime, and the mechanism of gene flow that operates along with human reproduction is not restricted by our attributions of names to places.

Human races, conceptualized as mutually exclusive or nonoverlapping groups, exist only in myth. Because breeding populations are sometimes referred to in scientific literature on human biology as "genetic isolates," some people are unfortunately led to the incorrect conclusion that some parts of the human race may have been isolated from all other parts in some absolute sense until quite recent times. There exists no scientific evidence to support such a view. According to Ferraro, Trevathan, and Levy (1994: 142), so-called races never existed, at least in the forms most of us imagine them to. According to them, although "races" remain pervasive social concepts, they have no validity as biological concepts, and to discuss races as biological concepts is scientifically unacceptable and incorrect. In the same vein, Ashley Montagu (1974) has noted that race is a dangerous myth associated with the false assumption that social and cultural grouping of people is determined by biology.

Similarly, Audrey Smedley (2007) has been emphatic that race constructs are cultural inventions produced through folk ideologies as ways of justifying attributions of inequality and are not scientifically deduced from biology. Quite apart from biology, some human diversity is social, cultural, and ethnic. Variation at these levels is conceptualized differently in different time periods, in different places, and by different people. We have no standardized terminology by which to refer to these types of diversity. In part, this is because of their complexity. It is also because of their overlap and because they are inconsistently perceived. Biological variation among humans at neither a genotypic nor phenotypic level mimics, or is consistently parallel with, human diversity that is social, cultural, or ethnic.

Adding to the complexity of referencing social, cultural, and ethnic types of human diversity, people in everyday conversation are content to attribute social, cultural, and ethnic identities to the people around them using very simplistic and conflicting nonscientific typologies. In a global and confusing way, racial concepts often conflate human variation that is partly phenotypic, partly social, partly cultural, partly linguistic, partly religious, and partly geographical. Racial concepts also tend to be very inadequate in accounting for numerous ways in which we overlap in our numerous differences.

Although the genes of people belonging to all breeding populations operate in the same ways, how people are identified and allowed to assimilate in different social settings can differ considerably from place to place as well as in different time periods. Depending on the sociocultural setting, numerous types of factors sometimes impact such situations. Among these factors are the following: residential status, citizenship status, nationality status, kinship rules, state of health, perceived state of health, age, dependency status, employment status, gender, physical appearance, place of residence, length of residence, mode of dress, place of birth, perceived place of birth, marital status, marital status of parents, social status of one or both parents, economic status, language use, educational status, political orientation, and religious affiliation. Social settings also differ with respect to the degree to which they are open and closed due to xenophobia and racial and religious prejudice as well as such other structural features.

In the Netherlands, Belgium, and Austria, for example, an additional issue is pillarization (a situation existing in certain societies that are divided into semi-autonomous vertical "pillars," with each such pillar providing many basic social institutions for an affiliated group). In some European societies, Islamic affiliation shows signs of evolving along this line and tends to be more pronounced even where Muslim women are concerned than with regard to Muslim men. In part, this gender difference for Muslims in Europe may be related to some female dress coupled with various degrees of observance of Sura 5.5 of the Quran, which most Muslims interpret as proscribing mixed marriage across religious lines for Muslim women but not for Muslim men.

As is apparent in France, where since *l'affaire du voile* in 1989 there has recently arisen much conflict over the wearing of headscarves in schools by Muslim females, this tendency toward Islamic pillarization can be especially explosive in a society that in some respects has a quasi-assimilationist tradition in matters relating to immigration. Further evidence of pillarization in some other European societies in association with Islam is perhaps apparent in so-called honor killings of Muslim women, which various members of their families have sometimes justified because the victims made marital or life-style choices that their families deemed to be shameful to them. The fact that the victims of these so-called honor killings are universally females, rather than males, demonstrates the existence of higher hurdles for the assimilation of Muslim females into European societies.

The relative importance of such factors as these greatly impacts the possibilities for acceptance and assimilation within various European social settings, and such factors obviously can differ a great deal over time. Given the interplay of such factors at numerous different levels, many of which can change at various times and places, there is little uniformity in how people of appreciable African descent are received in European societies. Complicating this situation further, as a child matures, he or she may self-identify with one or the other parent in ways that are different from those of other people. In addition to the fact that social rules change over time, it is not uncommon for members of complex societies to have divergent experiences, outlooks, and opinions about themselves and others even during a single period based on a wide range of variables.

Various social settings differ with each other in the degree to which they afford security, acceptance, and opportunity to people in the process of being assimilated. Taking such issues as these into account, it will become obvious in the course of this work that the notion of Africa in Europe has multidimensional implications that extend far beyond the boundaries of biology. These implications can have different meanings for different people, and they are continually in a state of flux.

In 1969, the British historian Victor Kiernan originally wrote his *The Lords of Human Kind: European Attitudes Towards the Outside World in the Imperial Age*, a work that since has been reproduced in at least two other editions. In this work, he undertook to produce a history of attitudes held by Europeans toward "others" in the 19th century, attitudes that with few exceptions were infamously ethnocentric, racist, and based on false notions. In a conclusion that this Marxist historian appended to the 1995 edition of his work (p. 336), Kiernan perhaps correctly suggested a connection between such attitudes and Europe's "long crisis of doubt and self-distrust that owned much to declining confidence in its position in the world, and deepening uncertainty about what the world thought of it."

Kiernan's considerable interest in European imperialism also led him to suggest that Europe's crisis of doubt, self-distrust, and declining confidence factored into its embrace of Fascism in the mid-20th century in part in "a convulsive effort to shake off this mood, to restore the legend of virility by hysterical and suicidal violence." While Kiernan may have been correct on this issue, he was most certainly not correct in contributing to a legacy of distortion where even erudite Europeans have tended to join ranks in diminishing the role of Africa in Europe. As Kiernan (1986: 195; 1995: 335) dismissively put it: "Europe itself had a sprinkling of Africans, besides the many assimilated into the population of southern Portugal where their influence on the physical type still struck visitors in the nineteenth century." Although Kiernan earned a distinguished reputation for himself teaching in India and at the University of Edinburgh long before he wrote this statement, considering that his work on the history of Eurocentrism in which it is contained has influenced a generation of historians, cultural critics, and laypeople, it is part of an outlook and belief system that requires a corrective.

Although all people increasingly find themselves as inhabitants of a global village, we—consciously or unconsciously—often rely on mountains of misconceptions about who we are as part of the human family and how we have interacted with each other in arriving where we are. These types of misconceptions not infrequently lead us to use the past in ways that are inappropriate for making wise decisions regarding how we can best live together. One of these misconceptions is that Europeans are more evolved from a primordial primitive state than are Africans. A second misconception that has found much support in Western literature relying heavily on odd interpretations of legends, myths, and pseudo-scientific racism is that the presence of Europeans in Africa has a long and extensive history while the presence of Africans in Europe is only shallow and recent. Much of our confusion about human connections existing between Europeans and Africans results from misinformation about biology and voids about social history. Wherever we have attempted to use race as a meaningful biological construct, as a factor to determine what territory people should control, or whether some people should have a greater right to live and prosper than others, it has not served us well.

Considering how extensively European imperialists eventually dominated Africa even to its southernmost extremity, it is remarkable that the world remains largely ignorant of the important roles that Africa and Africans have played in Europe. Although most wealthy countries in the world attract many immigrants nowadays who are undocumented, *Africa in Europe* raises many additional issues. Waves of Africans now flock to Europe seeking advantages in much the same ways that Europeans earlier flocked to Africa seeking gold, diamonds, land, enhanced status, and virtually free labor while exercising considerably more brutality toward the indigenous peoples than anything that is now occurring in Europe. That globalization and porous border controls have enabled waves of "others," many of whom Europeans associate with Africa and other places they view as problematic, gives great urgency to the need to understand aspects of human connections that have been ignored or greatly distorted.

Many people of appreciable African ancestry have been absorbed rather easily through assimilation over long periods of time into the great mainstreams of European populations. By contrast, some have achieved this only against great odds. Still others survive mostly from an underground economy and on the peripheries of societies where they lack opportunities to succeed and where they grow increasingly alienated, as has been pointed out by Ribbe (2007) among many others. Many people who identify strongly as Europeans, or as being primarily of European descent, are on record as assuming that people of African origin cannot be Europeans in the same way as so-called white people. This includes some people who have never resided in Europe and know little of European history and civilization but who nonetheless consider themselves honorary Europeans and are so accepted by other Europeans as such for reasons considered to be racial. On the other hand, some European citizens of African descent find themselves sometimes being treated as virtual foreigners in their own countries on the very continent where they reside also for reason considered to be racial. Such thinking about racial and diasporic commonalities increasingly comes into conflict with rules having to do with shared citizenship that supposedly are not race-based.

An African and quasi-African presence in Europe that extends from antiquity until the present can no longer be airbrushed out of serious studies of European history and civilization, nor should it. The record needs to be corrected. If as a result of this work people in general learn to navigate the present and the future in ways that honor our interdependencies and make it easier for us to inhabit the same global village, this work will have served its purpose. This writer presumes that there is urgency in our turning away from misconceptions about our past and present in order that we may work for a larger common good in an Age of

Globalization. What sometimes terrorizes us the most is the gathering together of all our relatives for a family portrait or seeing our real selves in a mirror that shows us without distortion.

Volume 1 of this work has focused on Europe's African presence from antiquity into the 16th century. The main focus of volume 2 will be the period from the 1640s through the early years of the 21st century. In Britain, the 1640s coincided with the beginning of civil war known as the "Great Rebellion." By 1689, this struggle had definitely established the supremacy of the British Parliament over the monarch. The 1640s also coincided with the last years of Cardinal Richelieu tenure as the chief minister of a France obsessed with aggrandizement and absolutism and his succession by Cardinal Mazarin shortly before the Thirty Years' War ended. It is within this last-mentioned context of French absolutism that I now return to the theme of Africa in Europe.

Chapter One

Absolutism, Status, and Dominion

1640s to 1770s

By the 15th and 16th centuries, piracy had a long history in and around the Mediterranean Sea and along the western coasts of Europe, and it had also reached the Atlantic coast of Africa. As if ignoring this long history, many Europeans reacted to sometimes being victimizing by pirates from northwestern Africa by referring to the Mediterranean coastline of that region as the "Barbary Coast." In fact, Europeans were as involved in piracy as were the people operating out of northwestern Africa. Although many pirates preferred to target victims whom they deemed not to be of their same religion, they did not always follow this preference, as piracy was an opportunistic activity that first and foremost produced profits. Moreover, as many pirates were renegades who had changed their religious affiliations and political alliances several times, it was not always a simple matter to classify an individual pirate as Muslim, Christian, European, or African in a particular situation.

By around 1640, European involvement in the trading and kidnapping of slaves from along the coast of western Africa intensified in large measure because opportunity and technological superiority on the part of certain Europeans made this possible around the same time as there was an expansion of European-dominated sugar plantations in Brazil and the Caribbean. The capture and exploitation of people whose largely free labor could be used by their various masters were not uniquely European specialties motivated by budding racism in some physical sense, at least in the Old World. In many of the larger cities of northwestern Africa around this same time, between 10 and 20 percent of the population consisted of slaves, many of whom had once been the captives of pirates. Although this situation lacked a quantitative equal in Europe, the activities of European pirates and slave traders were as barbarous as those whose bases of operation lay in northwestern Africa.

Although this remained a time in Europe when slavery continued to have more than a superficial presence, including especially in such southern areas as Spain, Portugal, Italy, Malta, and France (Earle 1970: 82, 122, 125; Goodwin

13

2002: 39-42), those enslaved were neither of some single physical type or religion nor where they from any single region of origin. In the 1630s and 1640s, in fact, a large proportion of the corsair ships raiding the coasts of England came from Salé in Morocco, piloted through the English Channel by Irish or English captives or renegades. Morat Rais, a Dutch renegade working for Africans in 1631, for example, raided the Irish town of Baltimore, and pirates from Salé took 500 English people captive, which led to a retaliatory raid on Salé by English Captain William Rainsborough the following year (Clissold 1977: 140-141, 146-147). Seventeenth-century Livorno was one of the largest of all the slave markets in Europe.

In the slave quarters of northern Africa, it was not uncommon for enslaved people originally from Africa and from Europe to serve in bondage side by side with each other. While many of the Africans involved had been transported from further south in Africa, including especially across the Sahara desert, Arabs and Berbers also not infrequently fell into the hands of European slavers and pirates. Considerably more has been written in the West about the welfare institutions that were preoccupied in northern Africa with captive Europeans than about welfare institutions in Europe that were concerned with captive Africans, and this has led many people to presume falsely that there was no African presence in Europe apart from Iberia during the period under discussion in this chapter.

In fact, Paul Cardinal Burali d'Arezzo, who was ordained as a Catholic priest in the Congregation of Cleric Regular in 1558 and was later ordained the archbishop of Naples in 1576, founded the Congrega dei Catecumeni that was later joined with the Congrega della Doctrina Cristiana. This association of priests and laymen arranged for the baptism of numerous African slaves held captive in Naples beginning in the 16th century. Around the same time that Pope Paul III in 1537 undertook, not with a great deal of success, to excommunicate all Catholics engaged in the slave trade, the Jesuits or Society of Jesus was founded by Saint Ignatius of Loyola in Spain shortly after the triumph there of the *Reconquista* over Islam and had as its primary objective to convert Muslims to Christianity. Nearby Africa and Africans served as an early focus of chauvinistic Jesuits wishing to expand Catholicism at the expense of other religions. In fact, Jesuits eventually targeted for extermination the Protestant Reformation as well.

Already between 1603 and 1624, Father Pais of the Jesuits was engaged in missionary work in the Tigre area of Abyssinia. From 1623 to 1629, the Jesuits also operated a training college for the missions in Kongo. Already by this time, however, a Jesuit congregation for African slaves had been founded in the southern Italian city of Naples, and the Jesuits used the slaves held in captivity there to learn African languages that they intended to use in their evangelization both among African slaves held in Europe and on the mainland of Africa. In 1726, a Jewish convert to Catholicism from Aleppo named Father Paul Israel, who was attached to the Augustinians, even allegedly founded a college for captured African slaves in Naples. It would continue to function until Napoleon installed his brother as King of Naples in 1805 apart from a short period after 1773 when an aged Pope Clement XIV reacted to pressure from the Bourbon kings of France and Spain, as well as the autocracy of Portugal, by suppressing the Jesuits by means of his bull *Dominus ac Redemptor* (Debruner 1979: 88; Freeman-Grenville 1973: 99, 103, 133).

This was also a period when many Europeans found themselves taken into bondage by Turks and by Africans living near the Mediterranean Sea. In some cases, the captives were even sold to Muslims by fellow Europeans intent on making a profit. Irrespective of the exact places of origin of such captives or even of their religions, many people became ensnarled in a network of piracy and enslavement that was far-reaching, especially on the Mediterranean Sea, an area where both European and African pirates were very active. Christians, Muslims, and Jews were sometimes involved, both as victims and as agents involved in helping to bring about various transactions. In addition to the numerous people from Europe and Africa who were entrapped into bondage in northern Africa in these ways, others were similarly entrapped in Europe and eventually distributed rather widely throughout the European continent.

The majority of people who served in various types of bondage in Europe during the period under discussion were native-born Europeans, including both slaves and serfs most of whom were not kidnap victims. Although serfdom at least in western Europe declined during the 15th and 16th centuries, it still had not disappeared. Even Christian slaves could be found in Portugal as late as the 16th century. Well into the period under discussion here, a non-Christian of any complexion or ethnicity was considered fair game for being enslaved in Iberia (Rout 1976: 10). Serfdom existed legally in England into the 1600s, and it existed to some extent in France until the French Revolution in 1789. In Scotland, some native-born coal miners even in their homeland remained serfs until finally being emancipated in 1799. While on the Mediterranean and along the western coast of Africa some pirates operated entirely as free agents, others had the support of their governments and in some cases religious sanction in the form of papal bulls.

Although the government of France was not itself involved in importing Africans from western Africa as of the end of the 16th century, some people of African descent were in France. People of African descent had been entering France for centuries. In addition to the fact that African ambassadors traveled freely through France, France also had an African presence for other reasons. There were direct crossings of the Mediterranean Sea by Africans, sometimes as free people and sometimes in bondage or quasi-bondage. Africans were also sometimes present in France as a result of the country's close proximity to Iberia, where people of African descent were somewhat numerous. Others arrived largely as a result of close relationships that existed among Frankish, Bavarian, and Lombardi nobles who not infrequently used Africans in various types of service. Many European adventurers (led by the Portuguese) had been involved in explorations and periodic kidnappings of people down the Atlantic coast of Africa during much of the previous two centuries. Between 1540 and 1578, some 200 or so French ships left Norman ports on the Channel, heading for western Africa.

Among these were the French traders from Dieppe who in 1558 traveled inland along the Senegal River to Podor, the ancient capital of Tekrur, in order to initiate commercial relations. By 1626, the *Compagnie libre de Dieppe et Rouen* was formed to facilitate commerce between France and western Africa (Lucas 1894: 62). Between 1626 and 1688, the Compagnie was still controlling French trade along the Senegal River, an area where the commerce that took place eventually included the annual acquisition of about 100 slaves a year. At least some of these slaves were presumably sent to the French city of Dieppe (Debrunner 1979: 73), although some were likely shipped off to Saint-Christophe (now Saint Kitts), which the French began colonizing in 1625. There was much fluidity in this situation. For example, when in 1571 some "black" Africans were placed on sale in southwestern city of Bordeaux, the court of that city called the *parlement* ordered them freed on the grounds that slavery was not a recognized institution in France.

In contrast to Britain's emphasis on a strong parliamentary system that provided good representation for at least a portion of citizens as well as to prevailing governance in a number of multi-ethnic European nations that were emerging largely by accretion, in France the tendency in governance was toward absolutism. As the middle of the 17th century approached, a drift in France and nearby Navarre (located largely south of the Pyrenees in a Basque area of Spain) toward absolutism was largely the result of policies supported by Henry of Navarre. He had become King Henry IV in 1589, and, by later policies supported by Richelieu and then Mazarin during the Thirty Years' War, movement in the direction of absolutism continued.

Reflective of the growing concern with absolutism and dominion in France around 1604, Marie de' Medici, the wife of King Henry IV who enjoyed strong family ties to reigning dukes in northern Italy, decided to put up in honor of her husband an equestrian statue in Paris on Pont Neuf, a new bridge that was shortly to be constructed across the Seine. For the statue, she awarded the commission to Giambologna (also known as Jean Boulogne and Giovanni da Bologna), who had executed two major equestrian statues in Florence, one of Ferdinand I and one of Cosimo I. Le Pont Neuf was to be the first bridge that would connect the Right and Left Banks of Paris without being cluttered with houses and shops in the manner of a number of ancient bridges in Europe. In addition to reflecting the grandeur of France at this point in time, the statuary project on which Giambologna worked was also intended in part to reflect prevailing French attitudes toward the larger world, a world in which piracy and slavery involving both Europeans and Africans were commonplace. In fact, people of African descent were by no means nonexistent in France, and they were beginning to be reflected more often in works of art in keeping with current events.

In 1608 before Giambologna completed his execution of the statue intended for Paris, he died, and work on the project passed to Pietro Tacca. Already in 1607 Pietro Tacca had begun to make wax models of African and Turkish captives he observed in the holding facility in Livorno known as the bagno when they were not engaged in the exhausting work of rowing giant vessels through the Mediterranean Sea (Seelig 2005: 199; Goodwin 2006: 107-108, 112). Eventually in 1613, when the statue was completed and inaugurated on August 23, the queen commissioned Cabrai-born Pierre Francqueville (also known as Pietro

Francavilla), who had also been one of Giambologna's most brilliant pupils in Florence and had been invited to work at the court of Henry IV in Paris, to design a pedestal for the statue.

This commission for the equestrian statue of King Henry IV came as a new wave of representations of Africans in sculpture was becoming common in the work of several Flemish and Italian artists. The bas-relief figures on the pedestal that Francqueville designed depicted three captives with their hands firmly bound behind their backs with rope in a manner that was very much in keeping with the spirit of the age. At around the same time that Francqueville was working on this commission, he was also working on another pedestal of a similar spirit for a monument of Grand Duke Ferdinand de' Medici I in Livorno's Piazza della Darsena, which was to be called the "Four Moors." In contrast to the pedestal in Livorno, only one of the four captives on the pedestal for the statue of Henry IV in Paris definitely evoked Africa. Another captive, in fact, seemed to represent peoples of northern Europe. As the figures on the pedestal were of contrasting ages they seemed also to represent the ages of man as well as a theme of world domination by France where Africans were merely included among others.

Although Francqueville died in 1615, the pedestal of Henry IV commissioned by Marie de' Medici was finally completed three years later by Francesco Bordoni, the son-in-law and pupil of Francqueville (Seelig 2005: 199-203). That in 1635, the same year that the completed equestrian statue of Henry IV was set in place on the Pont Neuf, the oldest standing bridge crossing the Seine in Paris, French settlers from the Caribbean Island of Saint-Christophe (now Saint Kitts) began to settle the nearby islands of Martinique and Guadeloupe was destined to intensify only gradually France's focus on sub-Saharan Africa as a source of enslaved settlers for these islands. Although absolutism in France would run a course of a century and a half before this equestrian statue of Henry IV on the Pont Neuf in Paris would be destroyed during the frenzy shortly after the French Revolution in 1792, the figures designed for its pedestal are on display at the Louvre.

As King Henry IV was in general a rather weak king, the absolutism that prevailed during his reign was less the result of his strong hand than the ambitious policies pursued by the French noble, statesman, and bishop named Richelieu,who in 1622 was elevated to the rank of a cardinal. Richelieu, was Henry IV's secretary of state for foreign affairs from 1616 and head of his royal council as prime minister from 1624. Firmly believing in the divine right of kings, Cardinal Richelieu, who was also a duke, gave his support to internal consolidation while at the same time aggressively insisting upon the aggrandizement of French power in Europe. In pursuing this policy, Richelieu indulged a major contest with the Austrian-based Hapsburgs and with Spain. In addition to rebuilding the Sorbonne and helping to found the French Academy, Richelieu supported the French navy and pushed for the colonial involvement of France in Africa and the Caribbean. Largely through Henry IV's attempts to contain internal religious conflict, Henry contributed to internal consolidation that was to continue under the succeeding reign of King Louis XIII, his son with Marie de' Medici.

Nowhere in Europe was cultural and political absolutism achieved with more splendor than in France, especially after the Thirty Years' War had left it as the most powerful state in Europe. It would be especially under Louis XIV, born in 1638 as the first son of King Louis XIII and Anne of Austria, however, that absolutism would reach its apex. If during his minority it was Anne of Austria, his mother, who was regent in theory, it was strong-willed Jules Cardinal Mazarin (a naturalized Frenchman of Italian origin who earlier had worked in service to Richelieu) who functioned essentially as the ruler of France.

Much more than is generally realized, the era of the larger-than-life Louis XIV was characterized both by an important African presence in Europe and by an intensification of relationships between Europeans and Africans, and these were not limited to people from western Africa. An African named Zaga-Christ, who presented himself (apparently falsely) as the son of Yacoub, then the Solomonic emperor or *negus* of Abyssinia, arrived in Paris after having spent several months in various Italian cities, including Turin. There, he had been a guest of the Duke of Savoy. This was at a time that Richelieu was heading the royal council of Louis XIII as France's prime minister. Zaga-Christ eventually died at Rueil in 1638 while a guest of Cardinal-Duc de Richelieu. It was around this same time that the emperor of Abyssinia sent ten of his subjects to France with a present of horses and elephants (McCloy 1961: 15).

By the time that the reign of Louis XIV began in 1643 when he was but five years old, France's considerable appetite for overseas trade caused it to focus considerable attention on Africa and Africans. During Holy Week in 1644 while the Peace of Westphalia was being negotiated in the German city of Münster to end the Thirty Years' War, for example, le comte d'Avaux, the French ambassador, arrived at the cathedral with a retinue of 140 Africans in attendance. When shortly thereafter three Spanish envoys arrived to attend the same service, they felt themselves sufficiently upstaged that they departed to worship elsewhere (McCloy 1961: 12; Rogers 1952: 145). Despite the Peace of Westphalia signed at Münster and the Treaty of Aix-la-Chapelle, also known as Auchen, in 1668, Louis XIV was not finally constrained from his attempt to capture the Spanish Netherlands until the end of the Franco-Dutch War of 1672 to 1678 by which time a number of European powers had joined in several coalitions to prevent further French aggrandizement in Europe. Still strongly wedded to French absolutism, these developments also contributed to France's growing attention to the Caribbean and Africa.

According to Jules Michelet, a head of the Historical Section of the French National Archives in the 19th century and author of the monumental *Histoire de France*, which took him more than three decades to write, Anne of Austria even provided Philippe I, duc d'Orléans (her younger son and the brother of King Louis XIV) with a "black" chambermaid as a mistress. In 1661, however, Philippe I married Henrietta Anne Stuart, who was his and Louis XIV's first cousin as well as the sister of Charles II of England. Having provided Charles II in an effort to end his support of the Netherlands against a French takeover, Louis

XIV of France was in fact on good terms with Charles II during what the British now refer to as the Restoration Period. Reflective of a royal connection with Africa around this same time, when a Frenchman named De Beaufort returned from a trip to northern Africa in 1663, he brought back as a gift to Marie Theresa, daughter of King Philip IV of Spain and queen consort of Louis XIV, a young "black" African lad who thereafter was in frequent attendance to her as a retainer.

By 1665, the wasteful excesses of Louis XIV had pushed France so close to bankruptcy that the king appointed Jean-Baptiste Colbert comptroller general of finance in hopes that Colbert would put the country on a sound financial footing. Attempting to increase France's share of international trade was a major policy adopted by Colbert, and in 1668 King Louis XIV additionally appointed him as state secretary for his very marginal navy. France had sent indentured servants to its Caribbean colonies of Guadeloupe, Saint Christophe or Saint Kitts, and Martinique, to the last of which King Louis XIII had already authorized the introduction of African slaves in 1642 virtually at the end of his regime. In a bold attempt to strengthen the French economy, Jean-Baptiste Colbert lost little time in founding the *Compagnie des Indes Occidentales* to replace the *Compagnie des Cent-Associés* to chase away rival Dutch interests and to better exploit French holdings in the Caribbean, and by extension also in Africa.

By the mid-17th century, Portugal and Spain no longer dominated the oceans, and the French were among the European peoples who remained deeply involved in piracy and increasingly involved in the slave trade. As the captured slaves were transported in various directions, some of them reached Europe directly, whereas others reached Europe after having first been transported to the Americas. Even as these developments took place, Africans continued to travel long distances on various diplomatic and trade missions, which, in addition to Europe, sometimes took them in other directions. In the 1640s, King Garcia II Nkanga a Lukeni a Nzenze a Ntumba of Kongo, for example, dispatched a number of trade missions to Brazil, including a northern portion that was occupied by the Dutch. Portraits of some of these BaKongo ambassadors drawn in Brazil by the Dutch painter Albert Eeckhout are now in the collection of the Danish National Museum in Copenhagen. At least one of these missions from Kongo subsequently proceeded to the Netherlands. This was around the same time that a brother of the chief of Rio Sanguin in Liberia also lived in Europe for three years before returning to his homeland, conversant in fluent Dutch (Debrunner 1979: 76).

In the 17th century, a number of the princes of the Temne kingdom in Sierra Leone were educated in Jesuit colleges in Portugal, including Serenkombo and a son of King Borea the Great, who ruled between 1665 and 1680 with the name of Philip II. Between 1672 and 1688, the Royal African Company sponsored 249 voyages to Africa and transported approximately 90,000 to 100,000 slaves from western Africa to the Americas, with many of them branded with the initials RAC on their chests. Between 1680 and 1686 alone, the Company transported an average of 5,000 African slaves a year. Solely in an effort to facilitate its taking of slaves from western Africa, the Royal African Company established a school for teaching English to a limited number of African boys living on the British Gold Coast in 1696. After this school collapsed soon afterward, the Company sometimes sent a few African boys to England to be trained in English and as craftsmen. Sir Dalby Thomas, who was agent general of the Royal African Company from 1703 to 1711 and governor of the British Gold Coast from 1701 to 1708, favored sending 20 boys annually to London for the purpose of learning English. As this undertaking was very expensive, however, it probably did not last much longer than a decade (Debrunner 1979: 74, 77).

Against the wishes of the directors of the Royal African Company, the British Parliament yielded to the demands of rival English merchants in 1698 by passing legislation in 1698 that dissolved the monopoly in the slave trade of the Company. The ending of the monopoly of the Royal African Company was advantageous for merchants in Bristol, such as Edward Colstonn, many of whom had already been involved in the Company in any case. Of greater importance, the dissolution of the monopoly of the Royal African Company allowed all Britons wishing to participate in the slave trade to do so without restrictions. However, it was not until Britain's repeal of its Ten Per Cent Act in 1712 by which private ships from ports other than London trading in African slaves had to pay a special levy that the ending of the monopoly of the Royal African Company caused the number of African slaves being transported in English ships to increase dramatically.

Ironically, one of the most prominent stakeholders in the Royal African Company had been the influential English philosopher John Locke, who died in 1704. Although he had opposed aristocracy and slavery in some of his later major writings, he cared much more about the liberty and property rights of European capitalists, including those who were owners of African slaves, than in the rights of human beings generally. In fact, Locke considered the African slaves, so brutally captured from their homeland by the Royal African Company from which he personally profited, as mere property and prisoners taken in "just war." Locke's professed concern with "government with the consent of the governed" had essentially no relevance during his lifetime for masses of people he deemed to be of African descent. Even in later life while Locke was secretary to the wealthy and politically powerful Anthony Ashley Cooper, eventually the Earl of Shaftesbury, and no longer associated with Oxford University, he participated in drafting the *Fundamental Constitution of the Carolinas*, which provided for a feudal aristocracy and absolute power of slavers over the enslaved.

Meanwhile in addition to ambassadors, the sons of African chiefs, and "mulattoes," most of whom were the children of European traders in western Africa, who were present in Europe in the 17th and 18th centuries, some other Africans were in Europe as the result of accompanying their owners as servants and in some cases as slaves, including by individual traders who were not connected with the official trading companies (Debrunner 1979: 78). In 1658 when King Toxonu or Tohonou of Ardra of a small coastal state in what is now the country of Benin wished to attract additional European trade to his country and win more independence from the nearby state of Whidah, for example, he sent a diplomatic mission to Madrid. Led by an ambassador named Bans, who was accompanied by a servant, the members of the party were received by King Philip IV. After being instructed in Christianity, both were baptized there, the ambassador as Felipe and his servant as Antonio. Although King Toxonu was especially interested in an increase in commerce with Europeans, his ambassador only returned in 1659 with a group of Spanish Capuchins as missionaries. Those of the Spanish missionaries who had survived the climate departed Arda or Allada in 1661 (Debrunner 1979: 66-67).

Hoping to rekindle European relationships with Arda after the departure of these Spanish Capuchins in 1669, France's King Louis XIV dispatched two envoys there on a goodwill mission to Houegbadja, the *ahosu* or king of Dahomey (in what is now the African country of Benin). While one of these envoys was a German adventurer named Sieur Herik Carolof, the other was Delbée, the commissioner of the French navy. In reciprocity for this mission, King Houegbadja dispatched a mission headed by Don Matteo Lopez to Louis XIV the following year. That the African who headed the mission was named Don Matteo Lopez likely resulted from his previous contacts with the Spanish Capuchinis who had previously lived in Arda. Accompanied by Herik Carolof and Delbée, the diplomatic party of Matteo Lopez included his three wives, three of his sons, a trumpeter, and four valets. Perhaps in an effort to impress these Africans, their hosts provided them an opportunity to travel to across the Atlantic to the French colony of Martinique on their way to Europe. On arriving in the Caribbean they were received with dignity and perhaps shielded from some of the worst horrors of the racist slave system that prevailed there.

After returning from across the Atlantic Ocean, they eventually arrived in the French port of Dieppe on December 3, 1670. Lopez's party then departed immediately to meet French officials. As the result of negotiations that Lopez had at Versailles, he gave assurances that the *Compagnie des Indes* would receive preferential treatment and protection in his homeland. In a formal Parisian reception that included Lopez's reception by King Louis XIV, large bodies of troops paraded on the grounds of the Tuileries adjacent to the Châteaux du Louvre (Ly 1993: 100-103). Based on information reported on by Debrunner about an etching of Lopez supposedly executed by d'Armessin while Lopez was in France, one may assume that the French anticipated using this undertaking as a pretext for craftily seizing the assets of Arda. According to Debrunner (1979: 69-70), this etching made of Lopez while he was in France was eventually labeled "Don Matteo Lopez, ambassador of the king of Arda, one of those in Guinea, to the most Christian King Louis XIV, in the year 1670, to whom he offered on the part of his master all his lands, harbors, and all that depended from him."

In accordance with Colbert's policy of attempting to increase France's stake in international trade, he devoted considerable attention to making France an important maritime power for the first time. It was in this connection that the works and arsenal of Toulon were reconstructed, port facilities established at Calais, Dunkerque, Brest, Le Havre, and Rochefort, as well as naval schools founded at Rochefort, Dieppe, and Saint Malo. While France established an Atlantic fleet that was made up of sailing ships, its Mediterranean fleet consisted of galleys that were powered by numerous oarsmen. In contrast to the French Atlantic fleet, which relied heavily on professional sailors, the French Mediterranean fleet relied heavily on criminals, political offenders, Protestants, Jews, and even Slavonic slaves from Russia, Turks, and Africans for oarsmen, most of whom were Arabs and Berbers. In 1679, France's *Compagnie du Sénégal* provided 227 Senegambian slaves for working on French galleys in the Mediterranean. After sixty-eight of the Senegambians put to work as oarsmen fell sick and another eighteen died soon after from disease and exhaustion, however, France turned again to its more traditional sources for this arduous work of being chained in place while being forced to row huge galleys through the Mediterranean Sea.

In addition to founding a new company to undertake trade with northwestern Africa in 1665, French dominion reached a very new stage when in this same year King Philip IV of Spain died. It was at this time that France acquired the western half of the island of Hispaniola, which it named Saint-Domingue (where the country of Haiti is now located). Within a short time, this newly acquired French colony of Saint-Domingue became France's largest and most profitable Caribbean colony. In keeping with Colbert's policies of increasing France's share of international trade, France also granted a charter to *Compagnie des Indes Occidentales* to specialize in exporting slaves to the Caribbeans, and it seized a number of factories from the Dutch on Gorée Island and nearby Senegambia as early as 1672. It was also in this connection that France offered a bounty of 10 *livres* for every slave who would be transported to the French West Indies.

While Nantes had emerged as the first French port on the Atlantic Ocean to become heavily involved in the African slave trade, it was joined in 1672 by Bordeaux. It was at this time that a boat outfitted to capture slaves with the name of *Saint-Etienne-de-Paris* and armed by the *Compagnie des Indes Occidentales* departed Bordeaux for Africa. French preoccupation with African commerce was growing so rapidly that the following year it chartered *Compagnie du Sénégal* (Pétrissans-Cavaillès 2004: 24). From Commenda, an area located on the western coast of Ghana near what is now Côte d'Ivoire, a chief named Amoysy sent ambassadors to Louis XIV in 1672 and in 1686. Based on agreements arrived at as a result of these missions, the French gained territory in the area of Commenda in exchange for a promise to construct a fort there that could be used for helping to maintain Amoysy power against any competing interests, whether European or African. Feeling threatened by this agreement, the Dutch, who were established nearby, soon attacked Commenda and killed Amoysy. Despite this unfortunate manner in which the life of Amoysy ended, African ambassadors continued to be a feature of life in Europe. Several rulers or their ambassadors from what is now the country of Ghana, for example, were entertained by the Elector Brandenburg in Berlin in 1683.

In a competition between the French and the British to gain favor with John Corantee, an African chief of Anomabu, a town inhabited in the 1700s by people of Fanta ethnicity located in what is now Ghana, each of these European countries hosted one of his sons in Europe. After the first son had been graciously received in France by King Louis XIV and eventually sent back home with many gifts, the British hosted his brother, William Ansah, in England, who arrived there after traveling first to Barbados on what he anticipated would be a grand adventure to see more of the world. Sometimes referred to in England as "Cupid" and at other times as "the Royal African," he was accompanied there by another young man from his town named Frederick who had traveled from Africa to Barbadoes to secure his freedom. After being hosted quite royally in England during the year 1736, William Ansah and his friend Frederick returned to their homeland (Debrunner 1979: 66-69).

Meanwhile, in the domain of European art new works on the Adoration of the Magi theme depicting one or more Africans continued to be produced during this period. At least one such work produced by Jean Tassel is in the Louvre while a variation of the work resides in the Museo de San Telmo in San Sebastian, a largely Basque city along the coast of northern Spain. Quite apart from this Magus theme, much other European art produced during the 17th century testifies to Europe's increasingly broadening and diversifying focus on people of African descent.

A Louvre work titled "Jesus Christ Instituting the Eucharist," painted around 1664 or 1665 by Gerard de Lairesse, though religious, differed considerably from the traditional works on the Magus theme in that a "black" figure in the lower-left corner of this painting appears to be a servant who is pouring perhaps water into a tub. A smaller version of this painting is in the Rijksmuseum in Amsterdam. These works mark a definite shift from many of those that included people of African descent in religious settings during the previous century and a half that tended to depict people of African descent only in rather lofty ways and side by side with European figures. In the same vein, a painting at the Louvre by Frans Mieris (also known as Mieris the Elder) of Leyde executed in 1678 is titled "A Woman Doing Her Toilette Assisted by Her Black Servant."

Another way in which Africans are increasing portrayed in art from this period is as soldiers. A 17th-century painting in the Danish National Gallery in Copenhagen by Karel van Mander III called "A Moor Wearing a Turban and Armor," showing a "black" man is illustrative of such treatments. An oval painting of a "black" man, by the same Dutch painter, that is contained in a metal frame of gold color with a glass cover is presently in the same museum. Since the portrait fills the entire oval case, it is devoid of background or context. Dated between 1625 and 1670 and titled "Head of a Negro," it is about three inches in maximum length and an inch and a half in maximum width.

Also showing Africans in 17th-century military settings is a series of works painted between 1700 and 1720 by Georg Philipp Rugendas that focuses on Europeans military victories over Turkish forces in Europe. Two such paintings are currently at Berlin's German Historical Museum. One of these, "The Relief of Vienna on September 12, 1683" commemorates the battle of Kahlenberg after a two-month Turkish seize of Vienna. As shown in this painting, a "black man" is prominent among the Turkish troops. The other of these paintings is "The Taking of Buda, 1696," now a part of Budapest, Hungary. It depicts European allies breaking the hold of the Turks after 140 years. Among the Turkish troops at least one "black" soldier is shown, both documenting an African presence and suggesting a tendency by some Europeans to view Africans and Muslims as "others" by this time.

Still, diversity of physical features was perhaps more readily accepted in many parts of metropolitan Europe during the 17th and 18th centuries than diversity in association with religion. One begins to gain some insight into the complexities of these situations by focusing on the Edict of April 23, 1615, promulgated by King Louis XIII, which forbade Christians under the penalty of death and confiscation of their property to shelter Jews or even to converse with them at a time when violent anti-Jewish riots were taking place in Provence. These riots forced many Jews to migrate from southeastern to northern France. Louis XIV later considered banishing Jews from Alsace and Lorraine (near what is now Germany), when those areas were acquired. After first extorting from Jews all the wealth he could obtain, Louis XIV changed his mind and in 1675 granted them letters of patent that afforded them a measure of special protection instead. Still, the king remained religiously intolerant and explicitly expelled Jews from his newly acquired colony of Martinique in the Caribbean only eight years later.

Although in metropolitan France courts were continuing to uphold the principle that when slaves touched French soil in Europe they were immediately free, some royal impatience with the *parlement* of Paris apparently on this freedom principle likely played a role in Louis XIV's taking away the right of *remonstrance* from the *parlement* in 1673. This right of *remonstrance* enabled any of the twelve *parlements* in France to review and register various decrees and edicts. Where a *parlement* objected or felt that revision was required, it sometimes refused to register and enforce the decree. As the *parlement* of Paris had jurisdiction over approximately one-third of the territory of France, including the capital of Paris and the court of Versailles, it was by far the most important in the country and was obviously using its right of *remonstrance* in ways that were not in keeping with the spirit of royal absolutism (McCloy 1961: 14-16, 43; Peabody 1996: 15, 18).

In 1679, eighty-five "black" Africans arrived at the French port of Marseille aboard a frigate that was under the command of a Captain Bonneau, which had weathered a storm off the coast of Portugal and was in need of repairs. Around the same time, a "black" youth who had been given by an African prince to Louis Phélypeaux, marquis de Phélypeaux and chancellor de Pontchartrain, was baptized at Fontainebleau in 1681. That Maria Theresa of Spain, also known as Marie Thérèse of Austria, who was the queen consort of King Louis XIV, was his godmother and the comte de Brienne his godfather suggests that, despite brutal forms of racist oppression prevailing in the colonies, Africans were arriving and being assimilated into metropolitan France in the 17th century (McCloy 1961:15).

Another European country with a keen interest in commerce with western Africa in the 17th century was the Dutch Republic. It had been exploring for new routes to Africa, Asia, and America since early in the century when it had established the Dutch West India Company. When France under King Louis XIV inherited Lorraine in 1667, the United Provinces of the Dutch Republic were under Johan de Witt as their grand pensionary of Holland. With its strong navy, the Dutch Republic (also known as the United Provinces) around this time established a relationship with the African state of Agona along the Gold Coast of western Africa. In this connection at Senya Beraku in the vicinity of Agona, the Dutch constructed a lodge, and eventually a fort called *De Goede Hoop* (meaning "Good Hope"), where its agents dealt in gold, ivory, and slaves. Three decades after France and Britain overthrew De Witt, the Orange faction, which was very much opposed to him, came to power in the Dutch Republic.

Also heavily invested in trade with western Africa at this time was England. Once the Stuart family retook the English throne in the English Restoration of 1660, it chartered a slaving company led by James II, Duke of York and the brother of Charles II, that was initially known as the Company of Royal Adventurers Trading to Africa. At first the company was mismanaged, but in 1663 it was reorganized with its newly stated objective being clearly set forth as engaging in the slave trade. Because of war with rivals in the Dutch Republic, this company largely collapsed in its early years. From 1672 when the Company of Royal Adventurers Trading in Africa was re-established as the Royal African Company, however, the British Parliament once again granted it a monopoly of the slave trade and with a manifest raison d'être being to gain control of as many captive Africans as possible, irrespective of the brutality involved.

In 1660 and again in 1663, moreover, England enacted Navigation Acts that specified not only that African commodities brought into England be transported in English ships but that trade between its colonies pass first through England. Further, in 1672 an additional Navigation Act was passed to reinforce the previous two. This was a period during which British laws were designed to support a trade in slaves sanctioned by the Crown and Parliament, and, since a decision by the solicitor general in 1677 stated that "Negroes" ought to be "esteemed goods and commodities with the Trade an Navigation Acts" (Walvin 1986: 32), it may be inferred that many of these also passed through England. In addition to making it clear that English law at this time viewed slaves as less than fully human, this ruling permitted slave owners to use property law with regard to their slaves "to recover goods wrongfully detained, lost or damaged" as they would any other property. Another Navigation Act was passed in 1692 to prevent abuses of the first three suggesting that not everyone obeyed the earlier ones. Such navigational acts passed during this period undoubtedly helped to increase the numbers of enslaved Africans entering England in the late 17th century.

Many people of African ancestry in Europe around this time were not slaves, and those who were slaves tended to be treated not distinctly different from others who were serfs and lower-class residents there. In some cases where Europeans of African ancestry had well-to-do or noble patrons or relatives, they were in many respects treated much better than most other Europeans. As people in 17th- and 18th-century Europe became increasingly aware of the oppressive and racist treatment of "blacks" and "mulattoes" in European colonies, however, this sometimes impacted attitudes toward people of African descent present in Europe.

In contrast to the somewhat permissive attitudes toward most people of African descent in metropolitan France in the late 17th century, proof that this did not mirror the situation for enslaved Africans in French colonies is obvious from an undertaking for Louis XIV by Jean-Baptiste Colbert that began in 1681. It was at this time that Colbert began working on an elaborate document to codify relationships between slaves and their masters in French colonies located in the Caribbean. Hardly one to empathize with the lower classes and the oppressed anywhere, Jean-Baptiste Colbert had reimposed the much hated *corvée* system from a much earlier era on French peasants and allowed religious discrimination against Frenchmen who were not Roman Catholic to remain unchecked.

Although there were still serfs in France as of this time (Peabody 1996: 31), prevailing policies in metropolitan France did not target them in the same racist way as the *Code Noir* that Colbert was drafting for the French-controlled overseas colonies would target enslaved people of African ancestry vis-à-vis their "white" masters. That Protestants, Jews, and Africans resident in metropolitan France were not targeted to the same degree was very significant in terms of how race thinking was evolving in France as a justification of colonial exploitation by this time (Pétrissans-Cavaillès 2004: 19).

Though Jean-Baptiste Colbert actually died shortly before completing the infamous sixty-article *Code Noir* or Black Code of 1685, the code was finalized by his son, Jean-Baptiste Antoine Colbert, marquis de Seignelay. While this code or royal edict enshrined in law intolerance against non-Catholics in areas under the control of the French monarch, its primary objective was to regulate the status of people of African descent in Caribbean colonies under French control (Boulle 2006: 21). So pleased was Louis XIV with this Code Noir that he signed it in 1689, around the same time he also designated Jean-Baptiste Antoine Colbert, its final author, as the new French secretary of state for the navy.

Article 1 of the new code was blatantly anti-Jewish in explicitly setting forth its intent to extend the Edict of April 23, 1615, whereby all Jews were to be chased from the islands in question. As specified in articles 2, 3, and 4, the code reflected total intolerance of any religion other than Roman Catholicism. While article 9 sought to discourage sex between "blacks" and "whites," articles 16, 32, 34, 36, 38, and 42 provided for the corporal punishment of slaves and in some cases for their execution (e.g., on a third escape attempt). Slaves were deemed to have no possessions, as everything belonged to their masters, and article 28 further specified that slaves could not inherit from each other even among close relatives.

That slaves were not legal persons was provided for in articles 30 and 31, as they could not give testimony in court. Article 21 made clear that slaves needed a written ticket from their masters to move about, and articles 38, 39, and 40 provided harsh penalties for aiding fugitive slaves. As articles 4 and 40 of the *Code Noir* specifically referred to *nègres* (meaning "blacks") and articles 44, 45, and 46 defined slaves as *"meubles"* and *"choses mobilaires"* (meaning fixtures, furnishings, and moveable objects), the code left room for mistaking neither the identity of its main targets nor that it considered them subhuman. Although Sahlins (2004: 182) is on record as claiming that the *Code Noir* of 1685 permitted the manumission of slaves and their exemption from the *droit d'aubaine* "provided that they converted to Catholicism," this is not true. Although according to Loisel's *Institutes coutumières* of 1608 a slave in France needed to be baptized a Christian before being manumitted (Peabody 1996: 30-31), this did not require that he be manumitted, and in principle all the slaves in France's Caribbean colonies had been forced to convert to Catholicism in any case.

Among the main influences on Louis XIV's undertaking, for the first time in France, such a broad conflation of racism and slavery through the force of law were (1) the economic crisis in France, (2) appeals from French colonists living in Saint-Domingue (now Haiti), and (3) theorizing about race in French scholarly circles that was heavily tinged with racism. As the *Code Noir* was applicable only in the colonies, French slaves who touched French soil in Europe were technically free. That "black" people sometimes profited from emancipation through relocation from the French West Indies or Antilles to Europe cannot be doubted. The French father of Alexandre Dumas *le père*, for example, realized this in eventually bringing his "mulatto" son from Saint-Domingue to metropolitan France. Although the racist *Code Noir* that had been drawn up by the Colberts for Louis XIV was intended to regulate life for people of color living under colonial rather than metropolitan conditions, at least indirectly it had an impact that was felt widely in Europe as well.

In the mid-1680s even before the *Code Noir* was finalized, France became involved in disputes with Morocco, Algiers, and Tunis, where both Europeans and Africans were not infrequently enslaved. Around the same time, there also took place an upsurge in France's interest in establishing posts in western Africa. It was in this connection that it founded a new trading company, the *Compagnie française de Guinée*. In keeping with this upsurge of interest in western Africa, some French Dominicans on their way to the French West Indies aboard a ship of this new company arrived at Assinie in what is now Côte d'Ivoire or the Ivory Coast and by no coincidence very near the Gold Coast. When, shortly thereafter, France sent a second expedition to Assinie in Côte d'Ivoire under André Ducasse that also involved French Dominicans and traders to Assinie, its members were received more warmly than before. King Zéna, the ruler, even agreed to let a Father Henri Serzier remain there with five French traders. The king also agreed to allow two local lads, one named Banga and one named Aniaba, to travel back to France with André Ducasse to visit with King Louis XIV.

The *Code Noir* of 1689, together with developments surrounding this lad Aniaba, gives us considerable insight into the status of people of color, both enslaved and free, living under French control. As André Ducasse introduced Aniaba to the French as a prince and heir to the Assinie, the two young African men after meeting the king and his court were put in the care of the Dauphin and under the tutorship of Bishop Bossuet. Aniaba, of whom we know much more than Banga, was even baptized in 1691 with King Louis XIV as his sponsor. Although French intelligence had learned by the next year that Aniaba was not an actual prince, the French continued to pamper him in the hope that he might later be used as a pretender to the throne of Assinie. When later it was time for

Aniaba to be instructed for his Communion, he received his religious instruction from no lesser a figure than the Cardinal of Noailles, the Archbishop of Paris.

French law did not define citizens as rights-bearing persons so much as it defined them as subjects of the king excluded from limitations that would otherwise have been placed on them through the king's exercise of his right known as the *droit d'aubaine*. Except where foreigners and slaves had been included individually or collectively exempted from the *droit d'aubaine* by the French monarch, no such exclusion applied to them. Because of the royal *droit d'aubaine* in the case of the former, they lacked any right to pass down property in France to heirs unless those heirs were French, and were similarly not permitted to inherit property from Frenchmen.

During the late medieval period around the first half of the 15th century, foreigners in France had accumulated civil disabilities in that they were usually barred from holding political offices and religious benefices. They were also made subject to special judicial constraints and occasional taxes that prevented them from undertaking some types of economic activities or entering certain professions. Over the course of time, these disabilities or incapacities also became incorporated into France's so-called *droit d'aubaine*.

Despite the spirit of competition that often divided European powers and the rather allied policies that had been pursued by France and Turkey against the Hapsburgs, when in 1683 the Ottomans led an assault against Vienna, at least for a short while, even the French closed ranks with other Europeans powers that were Christian against this Muslim super power. No lasting pan-European sense of identity based on this development and religion came to be, however. As Turkish forces had included numerous African troops, when the Hapsburgs's successfully repulsed this assault the Hapsburgs had hundreds of Africans as prisoners of war.

An additional disability that distinguished some people in France as noncitizens was their status as "others," which sometimes included non-Catholics, Roma, and slaves. When however a pair of "black" enslaved stowaways made it safely to France in 1691 from the French-ruled colony of Martinique, Pontchartrain, secretary of state for the navy, brought this to the attention to Louis XIV. Although the king, in conformity with France's freedom principle, declared them free and allowed them to remain in France, that the ship's captain was fined indicates that the king was not happy about their arrival and did not wish to see similar cases in the future (Peabody 1996:12).

When in 1691 many European powers again cooperated with each other against Ottoman Turkey and managed to again conquer Transylvania in what is now Romania, additional African prisoners of war fell into their hands. Within a short time, quite a few of these prisoners found themselves relocated to France as prisoners of war where they were made to serve in the French military. Although Africans may have been considered exotic in France during the reign of Louis XIV, they were not rare. Louis Phélypeaux (also known as chancellor de Pontchartrain), who in 1690 became the French secretary of the navy, even issued a declaration that enslaved Africans brought into France would be considered free upon their arrival. This declaration was strongly opposed by French

sued a declaration that enslaved Africans brought into France would be considered free upon their arrival. This declaration was strongly opposed by French
colonial planters, however, as they not infrequently brought slaves of African
heritage to metropolitan France to use as servants who they wished eventually to
return as slaves to various French-controlled colonies. For some so-called
people of color it was not unusual to spend considerable time going back and
forth in this manner between Europe and the colonies before eventually settling
permanently either in Europe or abroad.

The Duke of Burgundy, who was the grandson of King Louis XIV through
his son Louis le grand dauphin, had been reared with François de Fénelon as his
aristocratic tutor. For the young duke Fénelon had written the novel *Télémaque*,
first published in 1699. While this novel had Ulysses as its hero, it was also full
of animadversions about the material wealth, great wisdom, philosophy, and
justice of the Egyptians (Bernal 1987: 169), anticipating a new awakening in
some parts of Europe to the northeastern corner of Africa, which was increasingly being thought of by some Europeans as part of a part of the world they loosely considered a part of the Orient. At the same time that Egypt was presented as
a model of a well-governed state, this novel presented a nameless African interior as wild, uncouth, and largely deficit in civilization (Haavik 2001: 129).

That the year that *Télémaque* was published Louis XIV dispatched an emis-
sary named Poncet to travel overland from Cairo to Abysinnia demonstrates that
France was becoming directly interested in northeastern Africa during this period. It is further confirmed by the fact that only two years later the French government contracted to pay the travel expenses to France of an African "prince"
from Alexandria. This so-called prince, in fact, traveled by boat to Marseille,
then by coach to Paris, where he created quite a sensation and was feted accor-
dingly (McCloy 1961: 17).

Meanwhile the charade having to do with western Africa, whereby Aniaba
was alleged to be a royal heir to the king of Assinie, continued to play itself out.
Louis XIV even appointed Aniaba to the rank of captain in the French cavalry.
In February 1701, moreover, Aniaba was installed as a member of the knightly
Order of the Star of Our Lady in the grand Notre Dame Cathedral in the presence of the French court and Bishop Bossuet, with Cardinal de Noailles officiat-
ing. Although Aniaba had sired children in France by a number of French wom-
en and, along with his French guardian named Dumesnil, had accumulated numerous debts, shortly after the king of Assinie died both the French and Aniaba
deemed it an appropriate time for him to return to Africa as French-backed
claimant to the throne.

With Aniaba back in western Africa by 1701, however, a number of complicating factors arose concerning him, making it impractical for France to press
his claim to the throne. Disappointed over this turn of events, Aniaba turned into
an implacable foe of the French, eventually even turning away from Christianity. Illustrating that the presence of Africans in Europe and the presence of Europeans in Africa were often parts of the same story, the Aniaba affair and the lack
of suitable harbors in Côte d'Ivoire largely discouraged further French settlement in the area of Assini until well over a century later when they established

During 1701, a British vessel carrying 300 "black" Africans was captured by the French near Ile du Prince off Africa. Later, during the same year, the French captured two other ships, one British and one Dutch, both laden with "blacks" (McCloy 1961: 19). By this time, an elderly Louis XIV was attempting to gain control over a great Bourbon empire that would include Spain. When Charles II of Spain died in 1700 without leaving a male offspring, this whetted Louis XIV's appetite to gain control over a great Bourbon empire that would include Spain at the expense of the Hapsburgs. Far from going unchallenged, efforts on the part of Louis XIV to accomplish this caused the War of Spanish Succession to erupt between 1702 and 1713. In some ways, this war anticipated that France (who had the longest-ruling monarch in European history) was close to experiencing succession problems of its own.

In 1711 when King Louis XIV was quite elderly, his son Louis le grand dauphin died. Contributing to the complications of this loss for France's Bourbon dynasty, Louis, titular Duke of Burgundy, the grandson of Louis XIV and brother to King Philip V of Spain, died the following year. This posed an additional threat to the continuity of the Bourbon dynasty.

By the time the War of the Spanish Succession ended, bringing rivalry between the Bourbons of France and the Hapsburgs in Spain to an end, Sicily had a large Muslim population, largely from Africa. In part, this was because Savoy, which was technically subsumed into the kingdom of Sicily, was a place where corsairing and piracy brought many Africans into Europe even as Europeans continued to be enslaved in Africa.

In various parts of Europe, life for people of appreciable African ancestry continued to be varied and fluid. By contrast, in European colonies in the New World, which depended on the exploitation of slave labor for their survival as the Native American population fell sharply, notions of race began to acquire rigidity at an earlier time. In addition to giving Europeans a greatly enlarged sense of dominion for themselves, colonization of the New World involved thinking and behaving in racial categories as soon as decisions had been made to use African peoples as a oppressed, despised, and exploited caste of laborers that would be treated as sub-humans. Under these conditions it did not take long for race thinking and blatant discrimination to be transformed into racism that operated to the detriment of all who could be deemed African and/or black. Despite the fact that some European colonists arrived in the New World as settlers who were not fully free, these Europeans seldom labored under the social and physical disabilities comparable to those of the enslaved Africans.

Although social interactions between enslaved masses of people largely of African ancestry and a master class of European colonists who considered themselves superior had its impact in Europe, the impact across Europe was not uniform. Differences in how a master class of Europeans interacted with enslaved Africans and "mulatto" Afro-Europeans also differed from place to place and from one period to another. Similarly, there were differences in how various Europeans powers interacted with their overseas colonies in general. Under French absolutism, for example, there was less room for colonial autonomy in governance than in most of the English colonies of the New World. Even in Europe, France had not developed as many checks and balances on its monarchy as in England, where a strong parliamentary system had emerged.

Also, the languages of Europe were impacted by practices of slavery associated with colonial settings where people of African descent were held captive in large numbers. During the mid- and late 1600s in France, for example, the race construct gradually came to be much more associated with what people were perceived to look like and their cultural and political backgrounds than at any previous time. Still as compared to the French colonies, it was only gradually that race as a rather rigid quasi-biologic construct came into existence in metropolitan France (Peabody 1996: 76-77, 141n).

That "mulatto," a term most commonly taken to refer to the offspring of a so-called black and so-called white person, had made its initial appearance in the Oxford English Dictionary in 1595 and "quadroon" appeared in the same work in 1707 leaves little doubt that such people were neither rare nor considered anomalies. As late as the 17th century in Europe, race remained for many Europeans a vague concept referring loosely to people sharing common lineage, not greatly different from an extended family, a tribe, a nation, or a collective of closely related nations. Most thinking by Europeans about human variation in that century still remained sufficiently in accord with the Bible, such that rather few Europeans openly doubted monogenesis, which is to say, that all people were much more closely related to each other than to any other living animals and had a single origin. In some European colonies, however, race thinking began earlier than elsewhere to follow along other paths, including some that seemed to lack consistency from one situation to another.

As recounted by Saint-Simon and others, King Louis XIV was very fond of a female of at least partial African ancestry—sometimes called the Mooress of Moret and sometimes the Negress of Moret—who in 1695 left the royal household to enter a convent in Moret. The nun of Moret received an annual allowance from the Louis XIV throughout his lifetime, which apparently continued after his long reign came to an end in 1715. That throughout her life she was considered somewhat more assured of herself than the other sisters in the nunery where she resided, and that shortly before her death in 1732 she was visited by Marie Leszczyńska, who in 1725 had become the wife of France's King Louis XV, lends plausibility to the belief of many of her contemporaries that she was a "mulatto" offspring or other close relative of France's Sun King (McCloy 1961: 13-14; Rogers 1967: 251; Debrunner 1979: 97-98). This nun believed herself to be the daughter of Louis XIV, a belief shared by Voltaire, and she was visited periodically at her convent by Madame de Maintenon, whom Louis XIV secretly married in July 1683 around six months after the death of Marie Thérèse of Austria. Louis XIV, it is interesting to recall, sired a number of children out of wedlock most of whom were never legitimized.

Toward the end of his life, however, Louis XIV did legitimize two of his sons by his former mistress, Madame de Montespan, who were later reared by Madame de Maintenon. Two of these out-of-wedlock sons eventually were even given titles, whereupon they became the Duke of Maine and the Count of Toulouse. Still, when the long reign of Louis XIV finally came to an end in September 1715, only his five-year-old great-grandson—the son of the Duke of Burgundy (as well as eventually the Dauphin) with Marie Adelaïde of Savoy—had the requisite legitimacy to succeed him.

Extravagances extending back to Louis XIV, coupled with debts that France incurred in numerous wars during and after his reign, such as the country's rush to reconstruct its navy under the Duke of Choiseul (Dull 2005: 245-247), reduced France to surviving on the edge of insolvency under the youthful Louis XV. Still, France's absolutism remained unchecked. With Philippe II, duc d'Orléans, as the regent, the aristocracy and upper bourgeoisie seemed determined to increase their power at the expense of the masses at home and, even more so, at the expense of the slaves under the country's control. It was against this background in 1716 with "blacks" increasing in France at a very fast rate that a new law was enacted, clarifying the position of slaves by allowing masters from overseas colonies to maintain them in bondage even in metropolitan France.

This was a time when in England as well as in France there had come into being an activist and outspoken group of people who were opposed to marriages between so-called blacks and whites. With respect to France, one such person was Gérard Mellier, intendant for Nantes and its eventual mayor. It was no mere coincidence that Nantes at this time was one of the most important French ports with ties to the overseas slave interests. Of 75 French vessels that transported 11,833 Africans to Martinique between 1714 and 1721, for example, 59 had departed from the French port of Nantes (McCloy 1961: 19). In addition to being an apologist for the enslavement of "blacks" in French colonies, Mellier held blatantly racist views of "blacks" in general and was opposed to their permanent settlement in France (Boulle 2006: 21-22).

Various *parlements* of this period in France, which were really courts, until 1673 had a right of remonstrance, which enabled them effectively to resist enforcing certain laws to which they objected by neglecting to officially register them. The broad policies that determined how France functioned vis-à-vis Africa and people of African descent were evolving haltingly when the racist policies advocated by Mellier found their way into the Edict of October 1716, which was promulgated by France's Royal Council of State (McCloy 1961: 25). By this time, the *parlements* had regained their right of *remonstrance* that allowed they to criticize and delay royal edicts that Louis XIV had taken away in 1673. That the *parlement* of Paris, which was the most influential *parlement* in France, did not recognize the legitimacy of the Edict of 1716 was highly significant. Despite this, however, racism was becoming an outstanding feature of the regency government of Louis XV that was headed by Philippe II, duc d'Orléans, nephew of the late Louis XIV.

Quite apart from assimilation as a social fact and an extra legal process, a series of administrative circulars during 1717 and 1718 began to bring some clarity to the legal issue of how the *droit d'aubaine*, which was to be applied to non-indigenous Frenchmen living in France's growing colonies, especially in North America and the Caribbean. Non-enslaved foreigners in the colonies were to be subjected to the *droit d'aubaine*, and slaves held by such foreigners who died in the colonies were to be considered "movables," subject to the *droit d'aubaine*. But in metropolitan France, as of the last decade of the rule King Louis XIV, there existed many exemptions to the *droit d'aubaine* with respect to some national groups, most often because of certain international treaties or because they resided in territories over which the French king maintained some kind of claim (Sahlins 2004: 48-49).

In 1720, Sicily was traded to Austria for Sardinia and Savoy (whose capital was Turin), while much of the northern Italian Peninsula was given to the kingdom of Sardinia. Turkey, a long-time ally of of France in opposition to the Hapsburgs, was aware that these changes might provide it with an opportunity to interfere, especially as France was under the control of only a regency government. Also carefully watching these developments, however, was France waiting to see if they might cause Turkey, still a thorn in the side of Russia's Peter the Great, to react. Contributing to the machinations and tensions of this period, Maltese corsairs focused almost exclusively on areas of northwestern Africa under the suzerainty of Turkey at the same time Turkey was frequently at odds with the knights of Malta.

Turkey was greatly involved in the enslavement of people of many colors and ethnic backgrounds in Europe, in Africa, and in Asia. In addition to its involvements with slaves from all these areas, it also had relationships with people from these areas who were not enslaved. It follows therefore that Turkey played a major role in circulating people of many diverse backgrounds and statuses around the Mediterranean, including into and out of Europe, during the period under discussion. Although Turkey was greatly invested in slave trading and slave holding, that in 1722 it requested that Malta liberate all its slaves (Wettinger 2002: 26, 293) had less to do with its attitude toward slavery than with the fact that numerous of the slaves in Malta were Muslims.

One African who around this time likely passed through Turkey's network handling slaves was a young African probably from what is now the country of Eritrea. Known in history as Abram, he eventually ended up in the service of Tsar Peter in 1705, that is, only a couple of years after the tsar had commissioned the construction of Saint Petersburg on the delta of the Neva River at the east end of the Gulf of Finland as a "window to the West." While retaining the name of Abram, he was permitted to use Petrov as his surname after that of the tsar, which was Petrovich, One reason that we know so much about Abram is that when he was baptized as Abram Petrov in the Russian Orthodox Church at Vilnius in 1707, Peter the Great was his godfather and Christina, the wife of the Polish King Augustus II, was his godmother. As Abram was both Peter's godson and valet, he accompanied the tsar often and was provided with a good education, especially in mathematics.

When during the period from 1716 to 1723, as part of the tsar's policy aimed at developing Russia and opening it to new ideas from the West, Peter selected especially gifted Russian students to pursue advanced studies in Paris at government expense, he included Abram among those he selected. In accordance with Tsar Peter's desire that Abram become specialized in military engineering, Abram joined the French Army as part of his training and in that force was

eventually promoted to the rank of lieutenant. While in France, Abram continued his military education in Metz in 1722 before being ordered home to Russia
the following year. Though Philippe II, duc d'Orléans, who was at that time
nearing the end of his term as the regent of King Louis XV, tried to persuade
Abram to remain in France, Abram returned home to Russia instead. One of the
best-educated people in his adopted country at the time, Abram returned with a
library of some four hundred books that included many French classics (Blakely
1986: 13-14, 20-25; McCloy 1961: 18).

It was also in 1723 that Tsar Peter I, also known as Peter the Great, converted Russian household slaves into house serfs. Throughout the remaining
years of his reign, by contrast, Peter made certain that Abram was assigned to a
number of high-ranking positions. Even when Peter II succeeded Catherine in
1727, this tsar for whom Abram had once been a mathematics tutor continued to
insist that he remain away from Saint Petersburg. After Catherine the Great,
wife of Peter, arranged for his assassination by poisoning in 1729, perhaps per-
ceiving Abram as a threat after her ascension to the throne, she had him stationed away from Saint Petersburg. It was only in 1730 when Tsarina Anna succeeded Peter II that Abram was allowed to settle again in the capital of Saint
Petersburg. Probably to remove himself from any suspicion of being a factor in
palace intrigues, it was during the 1730s that Abram changed his surname from
Petrov to Hannibal. It was also during the 1730s that he married two times. His
first marriage was to the reluctant and unfaithful daughter of a Greek sea captain
by whom he had a daughter. Before their divorce could become final, however,
Abram contracted a second marriage to the daughter of a German army officer;
with this second wife he fathered eleven children.

Meanwhile when Tsarina Elizabeth succeeded Ivan VI to the Russian throne
in 1741, Abram Hannibal found himself again in enough royal favor that he was
given the rank of major general, a number of estates in Pskov and Petersburg
provinces, and control over thousands of serfs who worked the land. A number
of prestigious posts to which he was appointed at various times included commandant of the city of Reval and major general of fortifications. As the family
of Abram Hannibal continued along its path of assimilation into the elite of Russian society, several of his sons had careers that ranged between respectable and
distinguished. Nadezhda, the daughter of his son Osip, even married into the
aristocratic Pushkin family and in 1799 gave birth to Alexander Sergeyevich
Pushkin, the single most celebrated writer of Russian literature (Blakely 1986:
13-14, 20-25). Pushkin in 1827 published the biography of Abram Hannibal, his
mother's father's father, a work that he called *Arap Petra Velikogo*, usually
translated in English as *The Negro of Peter the Great* or *The Moor of Peter the
Great*.

The Dutch were still active along the Gold Coast around 1703 when they
captured an African infant about four years of age from the Axim region and
transported him back to the Low Country. The Dutch West India Company (or
WIC) placed this infant in the care of three German brothers of the Brunswick-
Wolfenbüttel family who were dukes, Anton Ulrich, Wilhelm August, and Ludwig Rudolp, and shortly thereafter the infant was baptized with the name of An-

Wolfenbüttel family who were dukes, Anton Ulrich, Wilhelm August, and Ludwig Rudolp, and shortly thereafter the infant was baptized with the name of Anton Wilhelm Rudolph Amo. Under the protection of these three aristocrats, Amo resided in a royal castle in Lower Saxony and was educated as a nobleman. This involved his mastering Latin, Greek, Hebrew, French, German, and English. After completing his classical education, which included religious training at the Wolfenbüttel Ritter-Akademie and the University of Helmstedt, Amo qualified for postgraduate studies.

Proud of his origins, he preferred the name of Antonius Guilielmus Amo, Afer of Axim (the last part meaning "African of Axim"). In October 1730, Amo earned a doctorate of philosophy in law from the University of Halle with a dissertation on the subject of the rights of Africans or "Moors" in Europe. Continuing his education at the University of Wittenberg, he earned a second doctorate in 1733, this time in medicine. After teaching as a professor in Europe at the universities of Halle, Wittenberg, and Jena, this scholar of the Enlightenment chose eventually to return to his homeland in western Africa where he lived out the rest of his life (Blakely 1993: 253; Debrunner 1979: 97, 106-108).

Although in France slave trading was not occurring in public to the degree that it was in Britain, there remained much legal confusion in both countries about whether slaves imported into Europe became free on their arrival. According to documents filed with the French government by French planters who brought slaves of African ancestry into Europe in the early 1700s as apprentices, the males were most often being trained as barbers, wigmakers, coopers, tailors, cooks, painters, carpenters, bakers, and not infrequently as saltmakers and plow makers. The females most often were being trained in tailoring and wardrobe keeping. Not all Frenchmen were in favor of people of African or quasi-African descents being allowed to marry "whites" while studying as apprentices in Europe (McCloy 1961: 20-23, 29).

Meanwhile in France in 1723 when Louis XV turned 13, the *parlement* of Paris declared that he had reached his age of majority, and at least technically the regency was ended. Showing little interest in governing on his own at this time, however, the youthful king left Cardinal Dubois as first minister, at least until the cardinal's death in August of that same year. Adding further instability to the regime of the youthful monarch, Philippe II d'Orléans, in charge of state affairs, died four months later in December. Still reticent to personally seize the reins of government, Louis XV then appointed as the prime minister, his cousin the Duke of Bourbon and Prince of Condé. It was while the duc of Bourbon was in this position that the *Code Noir de Louisiane* or Black Code of Louisiana was adopted in 1724 with fifty-five articles that made it in many respects similar to the *Code* that had been promulgated for the French Caribbean colonies in 1685.

In fact, however, some of the articles of the new *Code* were even more oppressive. In contrast to the last fifty articles that were exceedingly racist, the first five articles of *Code Noir louisiane* were more about religious intolerance of anybody who was not Roman Catholic, including Jews. In fact, the *Code Noir* of 1685 contained no provision for manumission of slaves or their exemption from the *droit d'aubaine* simply because of their conversion to Catholicism (Sahlins

2004: 182). Though never enforced in earnest, article 6 as modified forbade marriage as well as sexual cohabitation of "whites" and "blacks" in the colonies, under the pain of imprisonment and fine.

In 1726, Louis XV had dismissed the very unpopular Duke of Bourbon as his first minister, who was preparing a war against Spain and Austria. It was at this time that the king appointed Cardinal André Hercule de Fleury, who had been made his tutor in 1717 and with whom he had a close relationship, to replace the duc de Bourbon. As in 1725, Louis XV had already married Marie Leszczyńska, daughter of Stanislaus I of Poland, the toppled king of Poland. And he found himself in 1733 intervening in the War of Polish Succession in an attempt to restore his father-in-law to the Polish throne. While in the wake of the Seven Years' War there was no chance that France could restore Stanislaus to the throne of Poland, France shortly after the war embarked upon an invasion of Lorraine, located between France proper and French Alsace and where Stanislaus held the title of the Duke of Lorraine. It was in this way that a basis was established for France to eventually inherit Lorraine on the death of the father-in-law of Louis XV.

Meanwhile in 1738, a new edict relevant to mainland France more racially restrictive than the one of 1716, was promulgated. Among the racist provisions of this later edict was a ban on marriage of enslaved people of African descent while in metropolitan France even in cases where they had the consent of their owners. It decreed moreover that "black" slaves could not stay in France more than three years; otherwise they were subject to being confiscated by the Crown (possibly for work on the royal navy's galleys). Though Frenchmen were clearly not of a single opinion with regard to the racist edicts discussed here, they did receive considerable support from "white" colonists as well as from people living in metropolitan France with financial interests in the colonies. While the modifications contained in this edict were not intended to curtail the number of slaves coming into France, it was intended to more strictly control their movements and actions. As had earlier occurred in 1716, the *parlement* of Paris refused to recognize the legitimacy of the Edict of 1738 that was promulgated under Louis XV. That a number of ordinary French citizens who were considered "white" also were not supportive of it seems apparent from the fact that in 1738 a French woman living in Bordeaux named Nancy Draveman married a "mulatto" (McCloy 1961: 26-27; Pétrissans-Cavaillès 2004: 36).

Privateers and pirates introduced people of Africa descent into France throughout the 1700s, including the fifteen captives that the pirate Dulain turned over to the French government at Nantes in 1729. France's mediation in the war between the Austrian empire and the Ottoman Empire led to the Treaty of Belgrade in September 1739, which ended the war in favor of the Ottoman Empire, a traditional ally of France against the Hapsburgs, thereby bringing additional ambiguity and confusion to how Frenchmen were during this period thinking about what it meant to be European.

On the death of Emperor Charles VI of the Holy Roman Empire, and the death soon after by Emperor Charles VII in 1745, Maria Theresa, Archduchess of Austria, Queen of Hungary, Bohemia, Croatia, and Slavonia, managed to win the title of Emperor of the Holy Roman Empire for her husband Francis I (also known as Franz Stefan) who was already the Duke of Lorraine. As in this way, Maria Theresa became the de facto power at the helm of the Holy Roman Empire and even sometimes styled herself as its Empress. In so doing, she gave new life to the War of Austrian Succession, which had begun in 1740 when her father, Charles VI died intending that she should succeed him despite being a female, to flare up again. Already in 1741, France had entered this seven-year conflict by allying itself with Prussia this conflict was occurring at a pivotal time in French history, for the year after France became involved in it, Cardinal Fleury died and Louis XV, then 33 years old, decided to rule himself without again appointing a chief minister. In addition to France, people of African descent were present in numerous countries of Europe by this time, and although their numbers were often small, they became involved with considerable frequency in many of the conflicts that erupted across the continent, including this one.

During the War of Austrian Succession when Maurice, comte de Saxe, was but a lieutenant general at the head of a French army division sent to invade Austria, he also seized Prague during the night before the forces defending the city were even aware of his presence. This stunning success made him famous throughout Europe and eventually led to his being promoted to Marchal of France. Historians have been considerably less generous in explaining that somewhat late during the War of Austrian Succession Maurice de Saxe recruited an all-Muslim and predominantly African regiment that consisted completely of free men who were already living in France, who eventually became popularly known as Saxe Volunteers.

Though resident in France, these soldiers traced their origins to Madagascar, Guinea, Senegal, Congo, Saint-Domingue, and French Guyana or were Arabs. The head of this regiment of Saxe Volunteers was led by Jean Hitton, a general who claimed to be the son of an African chief. They particularly distinguished themselves in a battle of the war that occurred in 1748. Moreover, their regiment was the last that returned to France from Flanders at that war's end.

After later being stationed for some years at Saint-Denis, this regiment was later stationed at Chambord, where on November 28 of each year King Louis XV, his family, and certain other members of the court customarily visited it as it performed its exercises. Over time many of these soldiers took European wives without any restrictions because of color or ethnicity being imposed. So strong was the connection between Marshal Maurice de Saxe and this regiment that when he died in 1750 his body was first embalmed and kept for a while at the Château de Chambord before being taken to Strasbourg for burial on January 8, 1751 (McCloy 1961: 87-88; Debrunner 1979: 126).

That throughout the 18th century rulers in numerous parts of Europe, including France, decreed the expulsion of Jews as well as Roma or Gypsies from their realms with much greater frequency than Africans suggests that Europeans as of that time had no universal concept of how "otherness" was defined. As of August 29, 1742, for example, Tsarina Elizabeth ordered the expulsion of all Jews from Russia. To the extent that Europeans assumed there existed races of people prior to the 1700s, they were not accustomed to thinking of them in precise numbers or of conceptualizing various interrelationships among them in rigid ways.

In the mid-18th century, a number of "black" African rulers sent their sons to France to be educated. One African king in 1746, for example, sent his son to Bordeaux in the custody of a French captain named Delzollies for such a purpose (Pétrissans-Cavaillès 2004: 36). Between 1746 and 1747 the French also captured a number "blacks" who were imported into France through the port city of Le Havre. Meanwhile, a second so-called Treaty of Aix-la-Chapelle that was concluded in 1748 finally brought the War of Austrian Succession that had begun in 1740 to a conclusion. By this time in France, some people of appreciable African descent were entering the country independently of their own volition while others already in France sometimes departed for other European destinations at their own expense (McCloy 1961: 36-39).

In 1756, François Antoine, a highly skilled but enslaved "mulatto" surgeon from New Orleans who was captured by the British while en route to the French port of La Rochelle, was carried to Portsmouth where he was required to work in a hospital. Only two years later was he allowed to proceed to the French port of Calais, on the other side of the Channel from Dover. As the result of the complexity and individual differences involved in such situations, French courts were many times during the 18th century called upon to make rulings concerning the status and rights of people of appreciable African ancestry in France, including especially those who were seeking to escape from slavery (McCloy 1961: 36-39).

The Seven Years' War, which lasted largely from 1756 to 1763, involved fighting from as far west of Europe as the Americas and as far east of Europe as India and the Philippines. The war involved such contestants as Louis XV of France, Frederick the Great of Prussia, George II and George III as kings of the United Kingdom of Great Britain and electors of Hanover, Elizabeth and Peter III of Russia, Maria Theresa, Archduchess of Austria, Queen of Hungary, Bohemia, Croatia, and Slavonia, Augustus III of the Poland-Lithuanian Commonwealth and an elector of Saxony, and eventually Ferdinand VI of Spain, and by extension his empire that included the Two Sicilies and Spanish America (Dull 2005: 206-217). Whereas at the beginning of the war France was by far the most powerful country in Europe and Portugal and the Dutch Republic were in decline as colonial powers, it ended with France's navy decimated and with Louis XV having lost much of his colonial empire, including French Canada (Dull 2005: 218-243). As he had governed without a prime minister between 1743 and 1758, Louis was very much at the helm when this war erupted and hence could blame no one else for his country's humiliating defeats. People of African descent were involved as fighters on all sides during the Seven Years' War (Debrunner 1979: 125).

Beginning in 1758, well-to-do European landowners in Saint-Domingue who had enriched themselves from the labor of multitudes of African slaves brought about legislation that also discriminated against so-called people of color or mulattoes, forbidding them from taking up certain professions, from marrying "whites," from wearing European-style clothing, from carrying weapons in public, and from even attending social functions where their "white" relatives were present. Despite such blatant discrimination, however, a considerable number of mulattoes living in Saint-Domingue managed to accumulate considerable wealth. As many of these French planters insisted on a more brutal exploitation of their slaves coupled with greater reliance on racism, they often found sympathetic allies among government officials in Europe. At times, it even became difficult to separate the racism that was emanating from the colonies from the racism that was homegrown in France, and was in some important ways impacting life for Frenchmen of color residing in their homeland.

One far-reaching development in France during the Seven Years' War was the 1762 case of Louis, a "mulatto" slave imported into France by his master, who, though living in Paris, refused to recognize Louis as free. Even more noteworthy than the Court of the Admiralty's eventual ruling that Louis should be free was the lengthy report that the Guillaume Poncet de la Grave, the Royal Procurator, assembled for this case. In addition to the fact that it is very revealing of prevailing conditions for people of African ancestry in France as of the time, the report is reflective of some general attitudes in France having to do with race. Irrespective of the law, Poncet noted that numerous Parisians had "black" slaves who were often thrown into prison on no other ground than the whim of their masters. He also claimed that "blacks" were entirely too numerous in Paris and therefore "dangerous for society" and, in a further nod in the direction of racism, noted with regret that so many of them were free and expressed his fear that, because of the presence in France of so many people of African ancestry, one might "soon see the French nation disfigured."

These attitudes notwithstanding, Louis was ordered to be set free and overdue compensation was paid to him for certain work that he had performed while in France. Essentially at the same time of this decision, however, the government passed an ordinance bearing the date of March 31-April 3, 1762, that incorporated much of the language of the judicial ruling with respect to the attitude that people of African descent were too numerous in France and were a danger to society. This ordinance moreover was distributed to all Admiralty offices nationwide and mandated the immediate registration of all "blacks" and "mulattoes" in France regardless of whether they were enslaved or free. On June 30 of the following year, the government of France sent out letters to officials in its colonies that no "blacks" should be allowed to embark for France regardless of whether they were enslaved or free. It further stipulated that all slaves in France would be returned to the colonies by October 1 to stop the mixing of blood and the debasement of French culture (McCloy 1961: 44-46).

In accordance with the 1763 Treaty of Paris, which along with the Treaty of Hubertusburg ended the Seven Years' War, overwhelming British colonial dominance outside of Europe was established most especially at the expense of France, although Spain also lost Florida. Whereas France lost essentially all of French Canada, and all of North America east of the Mississippi River except for the island of New Orleans, it recovered the West Indian islands of Guadeloupe, Martinique, and Saint Lucia by agreeing to British control of Dominica, Grenada, Saint Vincent and the Grenadines, and Tobago. Although France already had captured Senegal and had recovered the strategic island of Gorée off the coast of Senegal, in the wake of the Seven Years' War it had to agree to British interference along the Senegal River valley. Further humiliating France, the Treaty of Paris even referred in two places to the British monarch as "the King of France."

Although the Seven Years' War was not primarily about Africa or people of African descent, it nonetheless occurred when the destinies of Europeans and Africans were becoming increasingly entwined in ways that posed a range of new challenges. Among these challenges were efforts to reconcile European involvement in slavery abuses, abuses of colonial exploitation, and concerns about abolitionism. In 1757, or the same year of France's defeat in the disastrous Battle of Rossbach early during the Seven Years' War, France had forbidden the publication of the *Encyclopedia* out of a concern that it was too revolutionary with respect to certain attitudes expressed that were critical of slavery. Voltaire, the grand figure of the Enlightenment, for example, mocked those who call themselves "whites but. . . ." He mocked the Church of Rome for accepting slavery. He mocked slavery in *Candide* (1759). He also criticized slavery in his *Dictionnaire philosophique* in 1764 (Thomas 1997: 464-465). Jean-Jacques Rousseau, more extreme than any other well-known writers of the Enlightenment in France with regard to slavery, insisted even during the Seven Years' War that the essence of the institution of slavery was its dependence on force. In his *Discours sur l'origine et les fondements de l'inégalité*, published in 1755, he condemned slavery absolutely, describing it as the final manifestation of the degrading and idiotic principle of authority. Similarly in his *Du contrat social*, published in 1762, Jean-Jacques Rousseau stated that however one looks at slavery, it is null and void (Thomas 1997: 466).

Although devastated by the Seven Years' War, France's only pretense to being an important colonial power lay in its control of colonies predominantly populated by people of African descent, impacting French attitudes concerning race and dominion in important ways. Saint-Domingue was by far the most lucrative colony that the French possessed in the Caribbean at this time. Hoping not to lose any additional colonies, France adopted policies that were more sympathetic to the planters than to the slaves on whose labor the colonial economies depended. As many of these French planters insisted on a more brutal exploitation of slaves coupled with greater reliance on racism, they often found sympathetic compatriots who were government officials in Europe. In fact, it was not uncommon for Europeans to discriminate against even their own offspring, pretending that they were so-called people of color rather than relatives who were also partially of European ancestry.

As France attempted to hold onto its colonies, French slave ships traveling to western Africa that averaged one or two a year until 1740 increased between 1763 and 1778 to about seven annually (Pétrissans-Cavaillès 2004: 25-26). France's invasion of Lorraine shortly after the end of the Seven Years' War was a further demonstration of its tendencies to become involved in war while it was struggling with fiscal insecurity and attempting to establish an empire. As these tendencies compounded each other, they caused issues that revolved around so-called race to become magnified at a time that revolutionary fervor was beginning to sweep the country. Since the middle of the 18th century, France's continuing absolutism, weak economic foundation, and the incongruity of its heavy involvement in the brutalities of race-based slavery alongside increasing rationalization of social contracts was pushing the country in the direction of a revolutionary conflagration.

Because some people of African descent present in 18th-century Europe blended in rather easily with masses of Europeans in terms of their appearances, not a great deal is known as to how they were received or the numbers in which they were present. By contrast, a considerable amount is known about those who stood out because of their darker complexions, tightly curled hair, or status as less than totally free people. As Great Britain was a European power with a vast overseas colonial empire in the 18th century, and most especially after 1763, examination of its history is key to understanding much that is important about the entry of people of African descent into Europe during this period as well as about conditions for such people already resident in Europe.

Although in Britain it was people of more or less obvious African ancestry who were more likely to encounter periodic displays of racism, the fact that even most of such victims of racism recoiled at the idea of being sent, or in some cases returned, to British colonies in the New World suggests that whatever problems they encountered in Europe paled in comparison to those they would have faced under colonial conditions. To this generalization, the author is aware of one major exception. Born on the British-controlled island of Jamaica in 1700, Francis Williams, a man of appreciable African ancestry, managed to pursue higher education in Europe. After studying at Cambridge University, he eventually returned to Jamaica of his own free will, where he operated a school in the early capital at Spanish Town.

By the time this was occurring, there was ample evidence of racism on both sides of the Atlantic; still, race and racism in the overseas colonial settings controlled by Europeans did not evolve in ways that exactly mirrored developments in Europe itself. In the countries of Europe, for example, societies never became stratified into castes that were deemed racially different from each other, and the assimilation of Africans into the European societies where they resided ensued in less sensationalized ways than in colonial settings. Our immediate concern is to focus particular attention on some of the ways that racism as manifested in Europe increasingly became conflated with colorism, ethnocentrism, and xenophobia in the 18th century and beyond. To be certain, there still existed considerable ambivalence among Europeans about how Africans, or at least "black" Africans who looked more or less like those being exploited as slaves in the New World, should be treated in Europe.

In some respects, one is left to wonder about the extra legal stages of assimilation through which people of appreciable African ancestry living in France were gradually winning acceptance as Frenchmen. Quite apart from assimilation as a social fact and an extra legal process, a series of administrative circulars during 1717 and 1718 casts some light on the legal issue of how the *droit d'aubaine* was being applied to non-indigenous Frenchmen living in France's growing colonies, especially in North America and the Caribbean. Non-enslaved foreigners in the colonies were subjected to the *droit d'aubaine*, and slaves held by such foreigners who died in the colonies were considered "movables," subject to the *droit d'aubaine*. The various Black Codes promulgated by France specified that anything a slave may have thought that he or she owned actually belonged to the master involved, including even in most cases the children of the slave and any right to give consent to the marriage of an offspring of the slave.

The power of the slaveholder over the slave mirrored in many respects the *droit d'aubaine* that was recognized as inherent in the power of the monarch over foreigners in France. As of the last decade of the rule King Louis XIV, however, there existed many exemptions to the *droit d'aubaine* with respect to some national groups (Sahlins 2004: 48-49). Still, the *droit d'aubaine* in metropolitan France in many respects paralleled the de facto *droit d'aubaine* of the slave masters.

The statuses and experiences of so-called black people in 18th-century Europe were quite diverse. While some were enslaved or worked more or less as bounded servants, others were totally free. In a number of British port towns, many "black" males worked as sailors, including as members of the Royal Navy, and lived rather ordinary lives with their families. Also whereas some were essentially Europeans of appreciable African ancestry in stages of assimilation, others were temporarily or even clandestinely in Europe and almost invariably dwelled on the margins of society. A few, however, were visitors with statuses such as merchants, members of diplomatic missions, and simply people who had seized the opportunity of being in Europe to obtain education or develop and publicize their talents.

This was a period during which the statuses of people of African descent in Europe were diverse, as were European attitudes toward their presence. In 1725, Marivaux, the most important French playwright of that century mocked slavery in the one-act play "L'Ile des escalves" (Thomas 1997: 464). In 1738, the English *Weekly Miscellany* published an article that declared that if Africans were to seize people from the coast of England, one could easily imagine the screams of "unjust" that would be heard (Thomas 1997: 468). A letter written by a certain Mercatus Honestus that England's *Gentleman's Magazine* published in 1740 addressed "the Guinea merchants" of Bristol and Liverpool by declaring that men were born with a natural right to liberty and that they could only forfeit this right by taking away property that did not belong to them (Thomas 1997: 468).

Reflecting contrary European views during the same period, a Royal Declaration in France dated December 15, 1738, tightened certain clauses in the Royal Edict of October 1716 while arguing that "most of the Negroes contract [in France] . . . habits and a spirit of independence which could have unfortunate results . . . and that [among those who remain in France] . . . there are some who are for the most part useless and even dangerous." Henceforth, masters to whom slaves were to be apprenticed were to be named in the owner's declaration at arrival, and their time of residence in metropolitan France was limited to three years. Marriages were prohibited, and infractions no longer led to the slave's freedom, but to his confiscation, "to be employed on our labors in the colonies" (Boulle 2006: 22).

Many people of African ancestry living in Britain during the 18th century were baptized as adults in hopes that this might spare them from perpetual enslavement, proving both that oppression awaited some people of African descent living in Europe and that such oppression was not totally based on physical features or places of origin. As attitudes regarding Africans became more rigidly oppressive in a racial sense, Sir Robert Walpole's attorney general and solicitor general, Sir Philip Yorke and Mr. Charles Talbot, in 1729 overturned the decision of 1706 by ruling in a case brought by West Indian planters that a slave in England was not automatically free and that baptism did not "bestown freedom on him, nor make any alteration in his temporal condition in these kingdoms" (Thomas 1997: 474).

In the same vein, English courts in 1734 reversed an opinion of law officers of the Crown that had said slaves became free by being in England or by being baptized. Though in 1755 Britain's Bishop Thomas Hayter, who was eventually to become chancellor of Virginia's College of William and Mary, preached a sermon against the slave trade, his view was not reflective of general concern on the part of the British public, and it did nothing to slow European involvement in the thriving business of human trafficking. In fact, far more slaves were transported across the Atlantic from Africa in the 18th century than in any other.

Although many of the people largely of African ancestry who lived in Europe in the 1700s were there in some type of bondage, including some who were considered "black," many others were not slaves, including some who despite being free were handicapped by poverty, discrimination, and colorism or negative attitudes toward dark complexions that had been evolving among many Europeans for several centuries. On the other hand, at least some Europeans were genuinely attracted to the dark complexions of Africans for what they considered its sensuality, smoothness, and beauty. In addition to these persons, numerous elite Europeans sought out Africans of especially dark complexion in order to draw attention to what they considered to be their own contrasting fairness and power within a cultural and linguistic milieu where dark and black for arbitrary reasons quite independent of logic often had negative connotations and attributions while light and white conjured up numerous ideas deemed positive or praise worthy. Associated with this behavior in many cases was the flawed notion that people considered white were somehow more pure and less tainted than other people.

Much myth and overgeneralization surround the subject of the status of people of African descent in Europe during the period under discussion and rather complicates our ability to understand much about the conditions of life for such people already resident in Europe. Reflecting nationalist arrogance more than reality, the boasts of John Rushworth and William Cowper that England was somehow a land that was too good for slaves was without any foundation in fact. As Rushworth had put it in a 1569 judicial decision, English air was "too pure . . . for slaves to breathe in." Similarly in 1672 Edward Chamberlayne falsely wrote in *The Present State of England* that "Foreign slaves in England are none since Christianity prevailed. A foreign slave brought into England is, upon landing, ipso facto free from slavery but not from ordinary service" (Thomas 1997: 473). William Cowper echoed denials and misrepresentations in the tradition of Rushworth and Chamberlayne in "The Task": "Slaves cannot breathe in England; if their lungs Receive our air that moment they are free" (Woodard 1999: 138). In 1679 England approved a Habeas Corpus Act on which much later Granville Sharp based his arguments opposing the kidnapping of "blacks" in England, testifying to the obvious existence of slavery in England.

Adding to this confusion, though the Court of King's Bench and the Court of Common Pleas both had previously found that slaves could be reclaimed in England, Chief Justice Sir John Holt ruled in the case of Smith v. Brown and Cooper in 1706 that "one may be a villein in England, but not a slave" (Thomas 1997: 474-475). This demonstrated sufficient confusion surrounding the slave status of some people in England at this time, seeing as a court was required to intervene. Similarly in France where there existed similar confusion, the French had a legal adage that held, "There are no slaves in France," a belief that some constitutional theorists in France had held at least since the 16th century (Sahlins 2004: 23; Peabody 1996: 13). Given that some French people returning from French colonies to France during the 18th century occasionally gave people of color as gifts to friends and relatives in Europe, there can hardly be any question that the people handled in this way were less than free (McCloy 1961: 42). Some people of African descent in Europe who sometimes were in bondage at one stage of their lives did not necessarily remain unfree throughout their lives.

In the general area where southeastern Liberia meets southwestern Côte d'Ivoire, a male orphan came into the hands of the Dutch officer named Jacobus van Goch and was given the name of Capitein. Capitein was brought to Europe in 1728 when he was around ten years of age and was provided lodging with his master's family in The Hague. Capitein received Christian instruction and eventually asked to be allowed to study theology. In addition to being fluent in Dutch, Captein took private lessons that included German, Latin, Greek, Hebrew, and Biblical Aramaic. While attending the Latin School in The Hague. Capitein developed into quite a good poet, and when he was baptized in 1735 with the name Jacobus Elisa Joannes Capitein, a poem composed for the occasion (perhaps by Capiein) compared the occasion to the baptism of the Ethiopian recounted in Chapter 8 of the Book of Acts in the Bible.

Thanks to financial support from the so-called Hallet Fund, Capitein continued his education at the University of Leyden from 1737 to 1742, where he specialized in divinity. On the occasion of his graduation, the printed program prepared contained dedicatory poems by fellow students, twelve poems of his own in Latin, his portrait, and some biographical notes. After his ordination in the United Provinces of the Dutch Republic (as the Kingdom of the Netherland was then called), he was appointed as chaplain to Elmina Castle near his homeland, a position of that caused him to rank immediately below the governor. That three years after his return to Africa Capitein married a young Dutch woman named Antonia Grinderdos, who was sent out to him from Europe by the Dutch West India Company, or WIC, for that purpose (Debrunner 1979: 80-81), suggests that certain Europeans as of that time considered his religious identity to be more important than his identity based on physical features or place of origin.

Although in the early 1600s the Dutch navy of the United Provinces was among the most powerful in Europe and WIC had already been established in 1621 in order to usurp as much Spanish trade as possible, including that involving slaves, race for the Dutch still retained in part a significant religious component at least into the next century. The WIC was not greatly involved in the slave trade until the 1630s, however, the Dutch conquest of northern Brazil coupled with the Dutch ousting of the Portuguese from Elmina in the Gold Coast transformed them into major participants. As the result of English-Dutch rivalry and some Dutch rivalry with the English in an alliance of convenience with the French intermittently between 1652 and 1674, De Witt was overthrown in the Dutch Republic thereby allowing the Orange faction to come to power in the Dutch Republic. Although the original WIC went bankrupt, a new Dutch West India Company or WIC was organized, which beginning in 1675 operated an *asiento* whose major focus was on delivering African slaves to the Spanish colonies in the New World. As Spain lacked a navy capable of supplying its colonies with the slaves it needed in sufficient numbers, it relied heavily on the Dutch in this regard. As the WIC lost this monopoly in 1734, however, it was at most only tangentially involved in slave trading by the time that Capitein returned to his homeland. Unlike many Dutch privateers who remained involved in capturing and transporting slaves, this did not much involve WIC. Although WIC continued to exist until 1791, it had almost no involvement in the slave trade after 1735.

Capitein died in Elmina in 1747, around the same time that the British began to expel the Dutch from what is now the country of Ghana. Only four years after Capitein's death, in fact, a Reverend Thomas Thompson, who was an Anglican, arrived at Ghana's Cape Coast as castle chaplain. In the following year, 1752, a contingent of missionaries of the Church of England mission organization that had been founded in 1701 as the Society for the Propagation of the Gospel in Foreign Parts, or SPG, also arrived. On a trip that Thompson made back to Britain two years before his final departure in 1756, he took with him three Africans to be trained as missionaries in Britain. Although two of these youths died in Britain of various medical problems, Philip Quaque, the third, eventually became the first African to be ordained by the Anglican Church.

Reverend Quaque's training was completed in Britain in 1765, and he departed for his homeland with his English wife at the end of that year. By the time that he arrived back in his homeland the following February, he had forgotten so much of his mother tongue that he would be dependent on translators during the many years that would remain of his successful ministry in the Gold Coast. Unlike Reverend Thompson, the mentor who had taken him to Britain and who supported slavery, Reverend Quaque, as quoted by a witness testifying before a select committee of the House of Commons in 1790, was decidedly opposed to it (Debrunner 1979: 81-82; Freeman-Grenville 1973: 128). In contrast, Latewi Awuku, an African slave trader from Anecho, in a part of what is now Togo close to the Gold Coast, was in England around 1750. Also, Ezakle Akuete, his son, visited England in the late 1700s (Debrunner 1979: 78-79).

In addition to the Portuguese, the Dutch, and the British, and the Swedes, the Danes also had a rather early presence in the Gold Coast, which is now the counry of Ghana. Even before the ouster of the Portuguese from Christiansborg Castle in 1683 the Danes had driven the Swedes out of all their Gold Coast trading lodges in 1657. The Danish Castle School founded at Christiansborg, in fact, was the first school in the country to offer education in a European language when it was established in 1722, and with only a few interruptions it continued to operate until 1850, catering especially to the children of privilege and to "mulattoes." It was from this Danish Castle School in 1727 that two African boys were taken to Denmark by Reverend Elias Svane, who was completing his term of duty there as its director. While Christian Jakob Protten was from a prominent African family, Frederik Pedersen Svane was the son of a Danish father and an African mother from Christiansborg-Osu. Both had been chosen by the governor of Danish Guinea to receive additional education in Denmark (Debrunner 1979: 82-83).

When Protten and Svane were baptized in Denmark, it was King Frederick IV, the king of Denmark and Norway and Queen Anna Sophie Reventlow, his consort although Frederick had never divorced his first wife, who served as their godparents. While both Protten and Svane would from this time forward alternated between living in the Gold Coast and living in Denmark, the majority of their remaining years were spent in the latter. Although Protten attended a Danish University, he never earned a degree. He did, however, become fluent in German and Danish, and taught for quite a few years at the Danish Castle School at Christiansborg. Protten eventually married another "mulatto," in fact, from the Danish Virgin Islands who, like him, had strong religious ties to the Moravian Brethren. Named Rebecca Freundlich, his wife was the widow of a Dane who had been missionary in the Caribbean. Among Protten's close European friends was a Danish count named Zinzendorf (Debrunner 1979: 84-85, 108-109).

Sometimes also known by the Latin name of Fredericus Petri Svane Africanus, Svane was admitted to Copenhagen University in 1732 and graduated two years later with a bachelor's degree. Although he married a Danish woman named Maria Badsch, with whom he had a son, many of the European settlers at Christiansborg thought it inappropriate that a "mulatto" should be married to a "white" woman when they returned to Gold Coast, suggesting that some concept that Europeans were, or should be, racially "pure" was beginning to gain ground at least among Danish colonial settlers in the Gold Coast by the mid-18th century. After his wife and son were, as a consequence sent back, to Denmark, it took Svane approximately ten years before he was allowed to join them there, perhaps also suggesting that Danish settlers in Africa were beginning to object to some sense of racial mixing in a physical more than in a religious sense between 1736 and 1746 when Svane was attempting to reunite with his wife and son in Denmark and that they were willing to use bureaucratic impediments to delay his reunification with his family. Except for those difficult years, Svane never again lived in Africa. Although he eventually died a poor man in Denmark, he had a career there as a deacon and teacher and was an acquaintance of Baron Holberg as well as of Count Plessen (Debrunner 1979: 84-85). It is significant that the creeping discomfort of Danish colonists in Gold Coast around "miscegenation" was apparently much more pronounced than in Denmark itself around the same time.

In 1773 Pope Clement XIV in response to heavy pressure placed on him by the absolutist Bourbons ruling in France and Spain (with quasi-dependencies in Naples and Parma) and by the autocratic royal house ruling in Portugal eventually issued his Brief of Suppression against the Jesuits, which happened to coincide with the waning of Portuguese influence in several areas of Africa. As Portuguese influence waned in some coastal areas of western Africa, for example, that of the British grew. During this transitional period, the British developed a great dependence on "mulatto" descendants of European traders to act as translators. Some of those in this category had been educated in Europe, for example—Tom Osiat, who had spent time in Ireland, and Edward Barter, who had resided in England and even married a European wife (Debrunner 1979: 74, 76-77). Far from suggesting that Europe was free of racism, the brazenness with which Europeans sometimes used Africans as tools to help them more efficiently maintain systems of exploitation that were essentially racist merely reflected the complexity and fluidity of racism that was continuing to evolve.

To illustrate that racism was used in ways broad enough to even sometimes target "white" people based on religion or ethnicity, one need look no further than Henri, comte de Boulainvilliers, whose life straddled the 17th and 18th centuries. The only true "French" people, according to him, were descendents of the Franks, the legitimate aristocracy of the nation and rightful rulers, and could not include the people living in France who were descended from the Gauls, as they were merely present there as a conquered Romano-Celtic people. Other examples of racism against "whites" may be seen north of the Channel between England and France around the same time. Here, many people felt essentially on the grounds of racism that pro-Catholic Stuarts had to be dethroned at all cost in order that England would not become a Catholic country. The religious wars in England, Scotland, and Ireland led to a religion-based descent into anarchy so dire that it still has as part of its living legacy the highly controversial annual march of the Order of the Orange in Northern Ireland that is intended to remind Irish Catholics of their defeat by people who sometimes deem themselves to be superior.

Even as Europeans moved in the direction of creating a set of more strongly centralized states that could contain such occurrences, what Michel Foucault referred to as a "politico-historical discourse of race struggle" had emerged in the world in a way that social dominance could be used in attributing place and position to people in terms of one's own vested interests or worldview. At least in Europe, this was a race struggle that in some respects was as likely to pit some Europeans against other Europeans as it was to pit so-called white people against people deemed to be non-white. Ironically, this was occurring as novel rationalizations of race and racism were about to unfold alongside revolutionary campaigns that would focus on social contracts and freedoms. Although demands for such freedoms would be rationalized for people of European background as God-given or as intrinsic to being born human beings, people of European backgrounds were about to find it increasingly difficult to advance such rationalizations seriously in European-dominated colonial settings, where color even more than religion was increasingly becoming the principal axis around which social stratification and privilege revolved. It was exactly in these colonial settings that the plights of people of African and other non-European descents were in some respects about to worsen.

Chapter Two

Geopolitics, Revolution, and Racism

1760s to 1815

The period roughly from the end of the Seven Years' War in 1763 through the Congress of Vienna in 1815 held at the end of Napoleonic Wars was filled with many complexities. Important among these complexities were revolutions, conflicts over colonies, attempts to expand empires, and much contradictory rhetoric relating to democracy, freedom, race, slavery, and the abolition of the slave trade. The primary focus of this chapter is how the American Revolution, French Revolution, and Napoleonic Wars impacted life for people of African descent in Europe, and to some extent in European colonies. It will conclude with a brief discussion of how geopolitical opportunism took precedence over issues of human rights by the Great Powers and began to be a factor in Western thinking about race and racism, both in connection with attitudes toward so-called Orientalism and in connection with attitudes toward bondage especially in the form of slavery. How people of European descent should respond to slavery, Orientalism, and the decline of the Turkish Empire (sometimes called "the Eastern Question") were central in Western social thought around this same time as racial thinking in the West was becoming increasingly racist. This was also a time when notions of "otherness" based on what was deemed to be biologic or physical not infrequently became more pronounced than notions of "otherness" tied to religion although both types of racism helped to drive Western imperialism.

With respect to the two major revolutions that dominated the period under discussion, one occurred in British North America and the other in France, and by extension in some French colonies. Despite certain similarities in these revolutions, such as a major colonial loss for Britain in North America and a major colonial loss for France in the Caribbean, there also were important differences. For example, while the French Revolution unfolded largely in Europe and the American Revolution largely in North America, the French Revolution eventually became much more fundamentally intermixed with a struggle against racism and slavery than did the American Revolution. The fact that the Caribbean took on central importance in this struggle against racism and slavery that was part of the French Revolution had no parallel in North America.

Although in the Seven Years' War that began in this period Britain triumphed especially over France and Spain, that war ended without leaving any of the major participants fully content. While the colonial empire of Britain greatly expanded largely at the expense of France, the war left both countries saddled with enormous debt. Whereas the debt of Britain at the war's beginning, for example, was £74.5 million, its debt at the war's end was £133.25 million. Britain's efforts to pay off its large debt largely by raising taxes on its North American colonies backfired by encouraging British colonists in what is now the Eastern Seaboard of the United States to rebel. As these developments were unfolding, an Industrial Revolution that began in Great Britain contributed to ongoing Anglo-French competition as each country tried to control ever larger empires. During the instability that would follow the French Revolution, this Anglo-French competition reached a crisis level as Napoleon Bonaparte undertook to establish a greatly expanded French empire in Europe and as both Britain and France competitively pursued policies of establishing large empires abroad. The Congress of Vienna in 1815 that finally convened at the conclusion of the Napoleonic Wars was an attempt by European powers to impose some order on these developments. Despite some lip service that the participants at the Congress of Vienna paid to ending the bondage of people who were not Europeans, this Congress neither took decisive action against slavery nor placed any restrictions on European imperialism abroad, imperialism that was increasingly rationalized on the basis of racist thinking.

When in an effort to reduce British debt remaining from the Seven Years' War the Parliament in London unanimously passed a Stamp Tax of 1765 that was meant to raise revenue from North American colonists, American opposition to this measure was so great that the tax was repealed the next year. This coincided with the beginning of the tenure of William Pitt the Elder as British prime minister. In keeping with Pitt's concern to replenish his country's treasury, he chose Charles Townshend as chancellor of the exchequer, whose job it was to manage and collect revenues. Townshend quickly moved to address the problem of the remaining huge war debt with his so-called Townshend Acts. These acts provided for North American colonists to pay duties on such common items as lead, paint, tea, glass, and paper.

As colonial opposition to these acts grew, one "white" colonist wrote a letter to the Boston *Gazette* that was published in 1771 comparing the general plight of British colonists to those of slaves. It is ironic that this letter was written at a time when the economies of most of the colonies depended largely on the exploitation of multitudes of people of African descent who were really being abusively exploited as slaves. This irony brings to mind a statement by the eminent British poet, essayist, biographer, and lexicographer Dr. Samuel Johnson, who by this time was in his early sixties: "How is it that we hear the loudest yelps for liberty among the drivers of negroes?" (Johnson 1977: 454).

As the voices of colonists unhappy with the colonial status quo grew louder, a group of rebellious British subjects in the New England region in 1773 held their so-called Boston Tea Party to protest recent revenue-raising acts imposed on them, especially as they also lacked representation in the British Parliament at Westminster. Into the next year, armed skirmishes erupted among colonists in Massachusetts, most notably at Lexington on April 19 and at Bunker Hill on June 17. Among the free Americans participating in these conflicts were "black" and "white" colonists who fought side by side.

For the purpose of suppressing incipient rebellion in its North American colonies by military means, Britain selected four generals: Sir William Howe, Sir Henry Clinto, John Burgoyne, and a little later Charles Cornwallis. In order to counter this action, representatives from twelve of Britain's North American colonies met to form an Association under a Continental Congress to more effectively organize their ongoing protest. Among the decisions that this Congress reached in 1774 was to no longer trade with Great Britain, including with respect to slaves. That the issue of slavetrading became central had little to do with colonial empathy toward actual slaves. However it had a great deal to do with how the representatives of the rebellious colonies thought they could most impressively retaliate economically against the mother country.

Meeting later the same year at Philadelphia, the Continental Congress appointed George Washington—a charismatic planter with vast land holdings in Virginia, the largest of the colonies, and a veteran of the Seven Years' war—to head its so-called Continental Army. At Cambridge on July 3, 1776, General Washington officially took command of his forces, and on the following day, Britain's rebellious colonists in North America issued their Declaration of Independence.

Here, people rebelling in order to demand freedom for themselves although many were still slaveholders managed through lofty mental gymnastics to state in their Declaration of Independence: "We hold these truths to be self-evident, that all men are created equal, that they are endowed by their Creator with certain unalienable Rights, that among these are Life, Liberty, and the pursuit of Happiness." Not only was Thomas Jefferson a member of a Committee of Five who drafted the Declaration of Independence for the Continental Congress, he was in fact its principal author and himself an owner of slaves. Still, he tried to have incorporated in the document a statement that condemned the English Crown for having introduced slavery into its North American colonies. Such a statement however was eventually removed at the request of delegates from South Carolina and Georgia.

Despite the precedents of American rebels pursuing a common purpose across so-called racial lines that had been established at Lexington and Bunker Hill, as Washington was a slave-owning man apparently uncomfortable with seeing the kinds of people he had mostly known as slaves in roles comparable with those of men he deemed his racial equal, he made a decision to no longer enlist "blacks" in the Continental Army. The New York victory of the rebels at Saratoga in 1777 involving over 8,000 British soldiers and German mercenaries attracted much attention in the West Indies and across Europe, including from a number of European countries that were still bitter over the outcome of the Seven Years' War. Many colonial planters in Jamaica and on other islands of the

British West Indies were sympathetic to the independence cause of the American rebels. Since on several of these islands these colonials were outnumbered by their slaves of predominantly African descent by as much as six to one, however, they thought it more in the interest of maintaining slavery to continue their dependence on Britain.

While during the American Revolution most European countries chose to remain officially neutral in the manner of Russia, Sweden, Denmark, Spain, the Netherlands, then known as the United Provinces or Dutch Republic, and France moved to support it. The United Provinces, for example, lent funds very liberally to the Continental Congress and Spain dispatched Bernardo de Galvez to British Florida where he occupied every fort. The support of Louis XVI of France and Charles, comte Vergennes, his prime minister, would be especially crucial, both diplomatically and on the battlefield. Having already recognized the rebellious colonists as independent from Britain on December 17, 1777, France throughout the war sent weapons, ships, and manpower. While the central role of Frenchmen such as Marie Joseph, marquis de la Fayette, Comte François de Grasse, and Jean Baptiste, comte de Rochambeau, in the American War of Independence or Revolutionary War is well known, often overlooked is the fact that among the French subjects who came to the military assistance of the rebellious colonists in a crucial battle at Savannah, Georgia, was a contingent among French forces that included between some 545 and 900 men of color from Saint-Domingue.

In response to a call from Count d'Estang, these "blacks" and "mulattoes" enlisted to participate in a French expedition that was to fight against the British in a crucial Savannah battle in 1779. Known as *Chasseurs-Volontaires* de Saint-Domingue and sometimes as *Légion de Fontages*, these men are seldom mentioned by American historians. Among members of this contingent specifically named in a variety of sources however are André Rigaud, Louis-Jacques Beauvais, Julien Raimond, Henri Christophe, Alexandre Pétion, Jean-Baptiste Mars Belley, Martial Besse, Jean-François l'Eveille, Vincent Ollivier, Vilatte, Beauregard, and Lambert (Clark 1980: 356-366; Steward 1904: 46; McCloy 1961: 65, 91; Debrunner 1979: 126). Also much overlooked by many historians of this war are the multitudes of African-Americans who played important roles in this war.

This American War of Independence began at a time when people of appreciable African descent constituted between one-fourth and one-fifth of the entire population of the British colonies that were in rebellion. As a great many of these people remained enslaved, Britain tried to win their support by making extravagant promises of emancipation to certain male slaves among them if they would fight along with the Tory cause as British loyalists. Lord Dunmore, the British governor in Virginia, first issued this appeal to African-Americans in a proclamation in November of 1775 by calling on slaves to desert their masters who were in rebellion against King George III (Conlin 1984: 130). Although perhaps no more than 800 African-Americans eventually joined Dunmore's so-called Ethiopian Regiment, his proclamation inspired multitudes of other "blacks" to take sides in a bid to obtain freedom from enslavement.

"Colonel" Tye, an escaped bondman from a Quaker master in New Jersey, emerged as perhaps the best known of the "black" loyalists. At times, this warrior commanded as many as 800 troops, including "blacks" and "whites," whose guerrilla tactics were especially effective against the American rebels in New York and New Jersey. Another loyalist of color was Boston King, an escaped slave who, though wounded in battle, later rejoined in fighting rebellious Americans in South Carolina. In reality, the British were no more vested in obtaining freedom for people of African descent than were the Americans. They merely wished to maintain their huge colonial holdings in North American in the face of a major rebellion and found "black" people residing in America convenient tools that they hoped would help them achieve this result.

In October 1781 when rebel forces, aided by the French, surrounded Cornwallis's men at Yorktown in Virginia, for example, the British sacrificed the lives of their "black" allies liberally in hopes of saving their own. That the British offered freedom only to adult male slaves, billeted them in segregated camps, and put those who fell sick in segregated hospital tents or offered no medical treatment at all is clear proof of the British lacking any genuine interest in the general welfare of "black" people in their colonies. This is further indicated by the fact that the British often court-martialed "black" loyalists who supported their cause at great risk of their own lives even for such minor infractions as petty theft, not infrequently giving them from 500 to 1,000 lashes.

Despite such abusive and discriminatory treatment, tens of thousands of sons of Africa opted to support the British side in hopes of winning freedom from enslavement (Fryer 1984: 191). Though "blacks" fought on both sides of the American War of Independence, detest of the horrors of slavery led many more of them eventually to fight as loyalists than for those in rebellion. Although free "blacks" and "whites" committed to the cause of independence from Britain had fought side by side at Lexington and Bunker Hill, Washington as head of the American war effort later banned them from such roles. It was only in the face of a desperate need for additional manpower that he eventually reconsidered his position, again allowing "black" Americans to enlist and fight for American independence (Robinson 1971: 111-130; Thomas 1997: 481). An estimated 100,000 American residents of African ancestry escaped, died, or were killed during the American War of Independence. Still, neither the American victors nor the defeated British demonstrated much enthusiasm for insisting on freedom for their "black" allies as the war was nearing its end.

When on November 12, 1779, nineteen slaves of African ancestry petitioned the state of New Hampshire House of Representatives for freedom on the basis of ideals of liberty plainly stated in the American Declaration of Independence, their petition was rejected. In the wake of a series of losses to the American rebels in the South, the British undertook a process of evacuation from that region in 1782, making essentially no provision for evacuating the "black" loyalists who had previous been their allies. When in the face of this British evacuation from such ports as Charleston and nearby Savannah frightened "black" loyalists made desperate efforts to swim out to British boats that were departing, in many cases the departing British merely hacked away at their arms with cutlasses in order to speed their own departure to the city of New York, which was the last British stronghold near the end of the war. In fear of their lives and in fear of being enslaved again, numerous "black" loyalists made their way to New York still seeking a means to escape slavery and retribution prior to what appeared to many to be an impending British departure. While some eventually reached New York on horseback and by boat, some reached there on foot greatly exhausted after much ducking and dodging of American rebels against whom they had fought.

When after the war a final peace was being arranged so the Treaty of Paris could be signed in September 1783, most American leaders, including Washington, considered the slaves to whom the British had promised emancipation American property that the defeated British should leave behind. The British, though ambivalent, tended to feel somewhat differently. While some of them wished to ship most loyalists of African descent to their colonies in the West Indies where they could be sold for profit, others felt that Britain was at least somewhat bound to respect certain promises that it had made to them. Since London failed to devise a general policy in conformity with its earlier promises of emancipation, it fell to commanders in the field to make *ad hoc* decisions on this issue.

Sir Guy Carleton (later to be Lord Dorchester), the acting commander of British forces, sought for a means to ease the human catastrophe as thousands of "blacks" who reached New York desperately sought to document their service as loyalists. It was in this connection that Brigadier General Samuel Birch, British commandant of the city of New York, created a list of claimants known as "The Book of Negroes." While many of these terrified "black" loyalists were abandoned to their fate, some managed to board ships for the Caribbean (where they probably again were enslaved). Between 3,500 and 4,000 boarded ships for Nova Scotia and Quebec. Still others sailed directly for Europe and the land they had truly earned the right to call their mother country. About these and others who reached Great Britain after first going to Nova Scotia or Quebec, more will be said later.

Great Britain's "black" population swelled considerably after 1784 as the result of the arrival there of many loyalist soldiers who had supported the Crown in America's War of Independence. Many of these landed in Liverpool. Perhaps as many as 4,000 ended up in London, where, despite the lavish promises that had been made to them during the war, many were eventually reduced to surviving as destitute beggars, including especially in the poor northern city fringes of Seven Dials and in the dockside areas of Ratcliff and Limehouse. One such loyalist veteran of the lost British cause was Shadrack Furman, formerly a slave in Virginia. During the war, he had given food and information to British troops and had been captured, flogged, and left blind and crippled by the American rebels. After eventually ending up in England, his only support until 1788 came from playing the fiddle in the streets of London.

Eventually given a pension of £18 a year in 1788, Furman's was the most generous settlement award made to any of the "black" veterans from North America, in contrast to "white" loyalists from America who were typically compensated with lump-sum payments of no less than £25. Although twenty "black" claimants received tiny sums ranging from £5 to £20, in keeping with prevailing British racism, the vast majority of "black" veterans received no payments at all from the British government. By mid-1786, there were at the very least 1,144 "black" loyalists from America living in London, most of whom were penniless due to British government neglect (Fryer 1984: 193-194).

Unhappy about the presence of numerous poor "black" loyalists in Britain in the wake of its losing war in North America, the British government began seeking a means by which it could permanently resettle some of them in Africa and perhaps in that process also establish an allied colonial beachhead on African soil. From an English botanist who recently had visited the coast of western Africa to study plant life, the government learned of an area that he considered favorable for farming and began using its influence with abolitionists to launch a so-called Sierra Leone plan. In an effort to make the plan attractive to a number of abolitionists, the British government contacted a number of businessmen and abolitionists, including in this latter category Olaudah Equiano and Granville Sharp.

Already by this time, Olaudah Equiano, a "black" Londoner, was one of the most prominent abolitionists in Great Britain. At around the age of ten when Equiano had been sold to an officer in the Royal Navy called Michael Pascal, Pascal gave him the name of Gustavus Vassa, after a 16th-century Swedish nobleman who had been involved in leading the Swedes out of a sort of slavery from the Danes. Although Olaudah Equiano worked cooperatively with Granville Sharp, the most prominent "white" English abolitionist from 1765, it was Olaudah Equiano, who in his best-selling abolitionist autobiography entitled *Interesting Narrative of the Life of Olaudah Equiano or Gustavus Vass, The African, Written by Himself* that was published in 1789, became the first abolitionist in England to assert as a principle that slaves had a moral duty as well as a moral right to resist enslavement. By the time this work was published, William Wilberforce had succeeded Granville Sharp as the best known "white" abolitionist in Britain. Olaudah Equiano still remained the best known of numerous London-based abolitionists of African descent. If the trade in African slaves by Britain was at its apogee by the 1780s as suggested by Thomas (1997: 494-495), this was only because Britain, like France, was becoming more interested in empire building, which in many cases could be equally as abusive and racist.

Various British businessmen attracted to the Sierra Leone undertaking were seeking to make money from the undertaking. One early supporter of the project was the Committee for the Relief of the Black Poor chaired by a Jonas Hanway who was on record for his dislike of "unnatural connections between black persons and white; the disagreeable consequences of which make their appearance but too frequently in our streets." Even Granville Sharp, at least in part, supported it as an idealistic scheme in social engineering. Almost from the beginning, by contrast, the majority of "blacks" in Britain viewed the undertaking with suspicion and distrust, with Olaudah Equiano being among them (Fryer 1984: 196; Emmer 2005: 90-92; 112-115; 139-141).

Despite considerable reluctance by Olaudah Equiano to become involved with the Sierra Leone resettlement scheme, he eventually consented in November 1786 to accept an appointment as its commissary of provisions and stores. Almost from the beginning, the undertaking was troubled. Hanway chose recruiters who put considerable pressure on poor "black" Londoners to participate in a scheme that many feared would leave them vulnerable to enslavement in a distant land where they had never personally lived. Also, his committee appealed to the public to stop giving alms to poverty-stricken "blacks." Adding to distrust of the undertaking, London's lord mayor ordered city marshals and constables to arrest any "black" begging on the streets so they could be relocated in Africa (Fryer 1984: 199).

Although the government had originally planned for the departure of 750 persons, that only 411 passengers were on board the first three ships that made the initial voyage was reflective of some major disinterest and distrust on the parts of "black" Londoners. For each passenger whom the British government could interest or pressure into leaving for Sierra Leone, it contributed £12 per African toward the cost of transport. Even before departure, Equiano discovered gross negligence and embezzlement of government resources intended for the settlers by the government agent in charge of procurement, and when Equiano complained to government authorities about this he was removed from his position and criticized as being turbulent, discontented, and for having a spirit of sedition (Fryer 1984: 105-106).

Of those people who had signed up to leave for Sierra Leone, some 400 did not show up, and another 50 died of cold and disease on board before the three ships, the *Atlantic*, the *Belisarius*, and the *Vernon*, could even depart. When these three ships, accompanied by the war sloop *Nautilus*, were driven by gale-force winds into the harbor of Portsmouth shortly after their departure, some local magistrates were so upset at hearing about these passengers walking around near the harbor and fearful that some might be left behind that the Navy Commissioners told Captain Thomas Boulden Thompson of the Royal Navy to prevent them from any longer coming ashore even temporarily. When on April 9, 1787, these ships finally exited British territorial waters carrying among others a considerable number of "black" loyalists who had fought for King George III in the American War of Independence hoping that this would ensure them freedom, the ships carried an inadequate quantity of beds, clothing, and other provisions. While many died en route, on arrival in Africa, some survivors were even sold into slavery to Frenchmen nearby (Fryer 1984: 196-206; Thomas 1997: 497-498; Makannah and Bailey 1994: 299; Padmore 1955: 30-32; Equiano 1988: 162-166).

Britain was not the only European destination to which some African-Americans yearning to be free traveled after the American War of Independence. During the war, the ruler of Hesse-Kassel became infamous for selling certain of his subjects as mercenaries to Britain to fight in North America against the revolutionaries in order that he could maintain an opulent lifestyle. After American independence was established and many of these Hessian mercenaries returned to Europe, some of them brought "blacks" from America with

these British "loyalists" ended up exploited in Germany. In fact, Duke Frederick II of Hessen-Kassel settled a number of them at Wilhelmhohe, where they made up the population of an entire village (Coquery-Vidrovitch 2007: 15; Mazón and Steingröver 2005: 1).

Near this area of settlement in Germany, Samuel Thomas von Soemmerring, a scholar much interested in studying human variation from a racial perspective, had been engaged in studying the corpses of Europeans, including some foundlings from a local institution. Soemmerring had studied medicine at Göttingen from 1774 to 1778, receiving instruction from professors who included Johann Friedrich Blumenbach, and he had worked for a short time thereafter with Peter Camper in the United Provinces or Dutch Republic, with John and William Hunter in England, and with Alexander Munro Secundus in Scotland as he prepared to become a professor of anatomy and surgery at Collegium Carolinum in Kassel. Soemmerring immediately saw in the arrival of African Americans an opportunity to study their customs and anatomies. As some of these African American veterans died within a couple of years of their arrival in Germany, Frederick II of Prussia's Hohenzollern dynasty, also known as Frederick "the Great" and who reigned until 1786, allowed Soemmerring to dissect their bodies for the purposes of his research.

Based largely on observations of these African American loyalists in the baths as well as on his dissection of their bodies after they died, Soemmerring in 1784 published in Mainz his *Über die körperliche Verschiedenheit des Mohren vom Europäer* in which he compared the anatomy of so-called Moors and Europeans. In the first edition of this work, he was unequivocal that all people were of the same species and that the "Moors" were in no way inferior. When however he expanded and revised this publication for its Frankfurt publication, some important changes more in keeping with pseudo-scientific racism were present. In addition to substituting in its title the word "Negers" for the word "Mohren" (meaning "Moors") that he had used in the first edition, he reached the conclusion that while "blacks" were entirely human that they were "still somewhat nearer [than Europeans] to the race of apes," a conclusion more reflective of contemporary prejudices prevailing among his mentors and collaborators (Soemmerring 1785: 77-78; Fryer 1984: 167-168).

Among scholars with whom Soemmerring remained in close contact during the five years that he remained in Kassel was Johann Friedrich Blumenbach. It was, in fact, from Soemmerring that Blumenbach received a number of the skulls is his collection of some sixty that he eventually used in theorizing that humanity was divided into a number of different races (Hopkins 1996: 28n). For the numerous African American loyalists of the British Crown who had sacrificed so much to fight for their freedom, including even having to flee their American homeland at the war's end, it came to pass that even in Europe they were exploited inhumanely in ways that sought to prove them racially inferior. Such anti-African racism in Europe was by no means limited to the two countries of Britain and Germany.

Already in 1710 when Eusèbe de Laurière published a new edition of Loisel's *Institutes coutumières* of 1608 in Paris, he argued in it that being baptized and setting foot on the soil of metropolitan France were not sufficient grounds to guarantee freedom in the case of slaves of African descent who had been resident in France's New World colonies (Peabody 1996: 31). Adult slaves from the Caribbean encountered even more difficulties than some children who were received in France more or less like living trinkets directly from Africa shortly before the outbreak of the French Revolution.

For example, when Chevalier Stanislas de Boufflers, the Governor of Senegal, brought as a present for Queen Marie-Antoinette a Senegalese lad to France around 1787 to whom he had given the name Jean Almicar, the status of Jean seems to have been like that of an exotic attendant and toy. Baptized in Notre Dame de Versailles in the year of his arrival, this young boy of about six years of age was housed on behalf of the queen by a certain person named Beldom who hoarded some of the funds given him for this purpose because of his own financial difficulties. The same Chevalier de Boufflers brought a teenage Senegalese girl named Ourika to France the following year as a present to the family of Marshal de Beauvau, who legally adopted her. Although both of these young Senegalese would survive the turmoil that would be associated with the revolution, both would die young but not without winning a warm place in the hearts of the French. Around this same time, young children of African descent were also being exploited as living status symbols or toys in some other parts of Europe—for example, like Sambo, who was in the service of Elizabeth Cudleigh, the Duchess of Kingston in England (Debrunner 1979: 89, 99-101).

Of course this was not by any means the principal way in which the African presence in Europe was manifested in the 18th century. In fact, people of African descent were also present in Europe in significant numbers as students, as sailors, as soldiers, as military officials, as ambassadors, as secretaries, as priests, and in many other capacities. By contrast to situations in the Americas where large-scale colonial economics were concerned and where great powers of Europe provided for more limited ways of allowing people of African descent to be employed such that they did not view as threatening the maintenance of their overseas systems of exploitation (Debrunner 1979: 87), social roles for "blacks" and "mulattoes" were more diverse in Europe.

The situation for the assimilation of Africans within Portuguese society followed a somewhat different course than in 18th-century Britain and France, however, although France, like Portugal, was also mired in absolutism. In Portugal, the 18th century belonged to the Pombaline Era because of its increasingly dictatorial rule by Sebastião José de Carvalho e Melo, Marquis of Pombal. This rule posed some special problems for people of African descent in Portugal. Even before a massive earthquake that hit Lisbon in 1755 killed approximately one-third of its population, Portuguese control over its empire in Brazil and in Asia were more in decline than in Portuguese-dominated parts of Africa. In the wake of this earthquake, moreover, the Marquis of Pombal mobilized military forces to prevent able-bodied survivors from fleeing so that they could be pressed into clearing the ruins thereby increasing Portugal's dependence on its residents of African descent although racism was becoming more pronounced in metropolitan Portugal around this time.

Even as the Marquis of Pombal moved to create several companies and guilds by which to regulate every commercial activity in Portugal and end, for example, many forms of discrimination against non-Catholic Portuguese Christians, he in 1761 prohibited the importation of additional Africans allegedly to protect free labor. There can be little doubt that he was greatly influenced by racism associated especially with the colonies as he sought to bring all aspects of domestic economic and social policy under his control. In contrast to France and Britain, Portugal had a larger African presence, and the failure of the Marquis of Pombal to insist on the incorporation of people of African descent into the guilds that he was establishing caused Africans in Lisbon to be more openly targeted for discrimination in a racist way than was common at the same time in some other parts of metropolitan Europe (Debrunner 1979: 88). In colonial settings under various European powers, and most especially where the colonials were considered to be non-Europeans, racism led to broadly practiced discrimination.

In 1784, free "mulattoes" of Saint-Domingue dispatched Julien Raimond, one of their number, to France to campaign for an amelioration of their lot. Said to be "an octoroon" married to "a quadroon," Raimond had many more European than African ancestors. Although he had been born rich and free, and had even inherited a large fortune and thirty-seven slaves on the death of his father, even he could not escape many of the handicaps of colonial racism (McCloy 1961: 65). Already by the time of his arrival in France, there was growing revolutionary fervor in the air. This notwithstanding, it had yielded essentially no results even for well-to-do free "mulattoes" on Saint-Domingue and even less for the masses of slaves there, virtually all of whom were "black."

In Paris, in February 1788, however, a group of very prominent Frenchmen founded *La Société des Amis des Noirs* (The Society of the Friends of Blacks). Founded largely at the initiative of a lawyer named Jacques Pierre Brissot, this organization of the privileged was never intended as one that would attract the masses. One of the early members was Honoré Gabriel Riqueti, comte de Mirabeau, a writer, popular orator, and statesman; another was Marie Joseph, marquis de la Fayette, a friend of George Washington celebrated for his gallantry in assisting the Americans win their War of Independence against their former British overlords. Étienne Clavière, at one time one of the democratic leaders of the Geneva Republic, where he was born, became a friend of Jacques Pierre Brissot while exiled in London and he joined *Les Amis* early as a result of later relocating to Paris, where he became prominent as a financier and politician.

Henri Grégoire (also known as Abbé Grégoire), managed to reconcile a strong devotion to religion, to the cause of abolition, and to the cause of revolution. Étienne Charles de Loménie de Brienne, at one time a cardinal and exponent of abolition, would eventually die shortly after being arrested during the height of the French Revolution even after he had repudiated Catholicism. Still another cleric who was an early member of this society was Abbé Sieyès. Also known as Emmanuel Joseph Sieyès, he was also a statesman and a pioneer in the social sciences. In fact, Sieyès coined the term "*sociologie*" (meaning sociology) a half century before it was first used by Auguste Comte, who is usually considered the father of that discipline. Other early members included Antoine-Laurent de Lavoisier, the father of modern chemistry, Nicolas de Caritat, marquis de Condorcet, a philosopher, political scientist, and mathematician, and Constantin-François Chasseboeuf, a historian, a traveler, and an early Orientalist in France as well as eventually a count. Also affiliated were Jérôme Pétion de Villeneuve, Jean-Louis Carra, Dominique de la Rochefoucauld, and Léger-Félicité Sonthonax, the last mentioned of whom would eventually be destined to have the most direct impact on France's involvement with race-based slavery, at least in its colonies (Mazauric 2006; Thomas 1997: 496).

Despite the fact that most of these people eventually would become Republican leaders involved in the French Revolution, *Les Amis des Noirs* was hardly a radical group of people on the issues of racism and slavery in the sense that they campaigned for rapid change in society. Its members, in fact, wished first to work in favor of an international accord to abolish the slave trade and then to establish a plan whereby over two or three generations slavery in the colonies would be abolished. Even these modest goals were bitterly opposed by another French organization called *Club Massiac*, after the Hôtel de Massic, which it used as its headquarters, at least until it was forced out of existence in 1792 (McCloy 1961: 66-67). When the prominent British abolitionist Thomas Clarkson visited *Les Amis des Noirs* in Paris in 1789, he claimed that this French abolitionist movement was more radical than the one then existing in Great Britain. Assuming his assessment to have been accurate, the European establishment in the late 18th century was not receptive to the abolition of slavery in any absolute or immediate sense despite the work of some exceptional individuals.

Spain, in fact, had been intensifying the reliance on racism and slavery in its colonies even as the War of Independence in North America and the French Revolution unfolded. For example, King Carlos IV in 1789 promulgated his *Código Negro Español*, based largely on the earlier *Código Carolino* of 1783 of King Carlos III and the infamous French *Code Noir* of 1685 (Thomas 1997: 505). Even when King Carlos IV ascended the Spanish throne in 1788, he sought to justify such laws by explaining that he hoped the new slave-trade law would help increase agricultural and mineral production in his American colonies (Sharp 1976: 118-119). In the same spirit, he approved more liberal slave-trade laws in 1791 to facilitate larger-scale shipping of African captives directly from Africa to such places as New Granada (now Colombia and Panama).

As racism targeting "black" people reached unprecedented levels in many areas of the world dominated by people of European ancestry, masses of "white" people in North America and France, many of whom had investments in the enslavement of "black" people, were demanding new and extravagant rights for themselves. Consistent with such contradictions, George Washington, a slaveholder, on April 30, 1789, became the first president in the newly federated United States of America, a country whose social, political, and economic systems were heavily dependent on race-based slavery. Although the Constitution of this new country referenced the "Blessings of Liberty," that same document failed to condemn slavery or even count every American of African descent as a whole human being.

With the fall of that mighty prison known as the Bastille on the Right Bank of Paris on July 14 of the same year and the eruption of the French Revolution, there followed in August a Declaration of the Human Rights of Man, setting forth in equally lofty language that "Men are born free and are equal before the law." As had also been true in the United States, however, the revolutionaries responsible for such rhetoric—including a call for "liberty, equality, and brotherhood"—were at the same time profiting in important ways from institutionalized racism that included the enslavement of Africans. Obviously the revolutionaries who produced such lofty rhetoric on both sides of the Atlantic were focused more on the political and social elites than on the abused and oppressed masses as they simultaneously called for freedom for the former while largely ignoring their own exploitation and abuse of the latter.

History would demand a more honest reckoning, however, although more immediately and most explosively as a result of the French Revolution and those it inspired. Even in Ireland, where selfish English landlords owned virtually all of the land thereby condemning the disenfranchised and landless Catholic masses to suffer from periodic famines, the French Revolution raised hopes that it might be possible for the oppressed masses of Ireland to more forcefully demand basic rights. Unlike in the United States where the American Revolution brought few immediate changes in the system of institutionalized racism and slavery, to so-called free people of color in various French colonies who were treated as inferior and less deserving of full rights of citizenship than "white" settlers the French Revolution gave more hope and inspiration. In the French colonies of the Caribbean, the destinies of Europeans and Africans, with the former being a numerical minority, had become too entwined to allow the new freedoms offered by the revolution to be parceled out according to some simplistic scheme based mostly on color, caste, or class.

During the French Revolution, a battalion made up of "blacks" from Nantes participated in combat even as France continued to vacillate concerning the rights of people of African descent. Moreover in Saint-Domingue, by far the most important French colony in the Caribbean, free people of color were about equally divided between so-called blacks and so-called mulattoes. As a consequence, various racio-ethnic groups and classes in Saint-Domingue could not be any more politically, culturally, and ideologically disentangled than they could be biologically disentangled.

To put this situation in a global and temporal context, there existed unequivocal opposition to slavery in no country on Earth as of 1789. Also, no country dominated by people of European ancestry was unequivocally opposed either to racism or to the system of European colonialism that was increasingly encircling the globe. With a so-called democratic revolution having taken place in North America and another one about to take place in France, however, the genie was out of the bottle. Contradictions with the democratic spirits underlying the spirit of revolution was already manifest in North America and was about to become manifest in France, where they would be especially explosive. Until the French Revolution erupted in 1789, French people shared no common status except as subjects of the king, and civil law was but an incoherent composition of customary law, royal decrees, Roman (written) law, and case law of the different *parlements* and sovereign courts of the kingdom (Sahlins 2004: 1, 3-9).

Even in September of 1789 when French revolutionaries abolished the monarchy under King Louis XVI and replaced it by the First Republic, this change in governance could not mask the obvious contradiction between the spirit of the French Revolution, on the one hand, and racism and slavery, on the other. During an early stage of the Revolution, French planters scored a temporary victory by getting a group of their delegates accepted as members of the National Assembly, leaving free "mulattoes" who were resident in Paris somewhat isolated to protest this development in the capital without much success. Similarly, chambers of commerce in various French ports put pressure on the Admiralty to control the movement of people of color between the colonies and metropolitan France in an effort to keep news of the revolution in Europe from spreading to the colonies where they feared it might contribute to insurrection by oppressed French subjects in ways that could threaten the advantages of exploitation that most Europeans had come to expect.

Reacting to these contradictions, a large number of free people of color from Saint-Domingue who were resident in France, including especially well-to-do "mulattoes" like Julien Raimond, began working cooperatively with the recently established *Société des Amis des Noirs* to achieve additional freedoms at least for free people of color from the French colonies even if not immediately for the masses of "black" slaves (McCloy 1961: 67-68, 73-78). On the one hand, colonial planters and chambers of commerce located in various French ports pressured the Admiralty to control the movement of people of color between the colonies and metropolitan France in an effort to keep news of the revolution in Europe from spreading to the colonies. On the other hand, a number of free people of color from Saint-Domingue in Paris, including especially well-to-do "mulattoes" like Julien Raimond, worked to counter this.

While at times this latter contingent worked cooperatively with members of *Les Amis des Noirs* in an effort to assist their cause, some of them also produced pamphlets that emphasized contradictions between the revolution in France and continuing racist oppression in the colonies. At a time that many of its aristocratic members were already under great suspicion from revolutionaries, *La Société des Amis des Noirs* was faced with a major problem: how to work for freedom in mainland France for people of appreciable African descent while not doing the same for people of appreciable African descent in the colonies whose exploitation and abuse were still acceptable to most people in France (McCloy 1961: 67-68, 73-78).

As some slaves from French colonies continued to accompany their owners to France despite the desperate efforts of colonists to prevent this, officials in France in 1790 eventually established special jails called *dépôts des noirs* (i.e., jails for blacks) in which to at least detain such slaves in the hope of keeping them in isolation from metropolitan society, including its revolutionary thinking. France's Committee of Reports, meanwhile, ruled that all French citizens should be able to travel as they wished, including citizens of color. This made it possible for Vincent Ogé the Younger from Saint-Domingue, who had been educated in France and who was considered a "mulatto" although he was much more of European than of African ancestry, to clandestinely send a shipment of munitions to Saint-Domingue by way of England and the United States (McCloy 1961: 67-69, 79).

Reacting to the new challenges to their profits earned on the backs of "blacks," France's pro-slavery lobby in the Assembly was sufficiently powerful that it was able in March of 1790 to secure passage of a decree specifying that "Whoever works to excite rising against the [white] colonists will be declared an enemy of the people" (Thomas 1997: 522). In the same spirit, most French planters from the colonies worked cooperatively with major slave traders located in such ports as Bordeaux, Nantes, and Le Havre to oppose the abolitionist agenda of *La Société des Amis des Noirs*. As in 1790 France was again facing economic insolvency in large part because of assistance that it had recently given to American revolutionaries in North America during their war to become independent of Britain, the Assembly in Paris developed a novel approach to dealing with many of the contradictions involving racism, slavery, and the revolution. It voted to allow "whites" in various French colonies to determine who should have political rights abroad and under what conditions.

As this decision was made at a time when the number of free people of color in Saint-Domingue was almost equal to the number of "whites," it was incendiary and resulted in some three hundred "mulattoes" led by against Vincent Ogé (a "mulatto" predominantly of European descent who had been born in France and educated in Paris) rising up against "white" planters in open rebellion. When this rebellion by "mulattoes" was put down with many being tortured and killed by their own relatives who were considered "white," including Vincent Ogé, the Constituent Assembly in Paris on May 15, 1791 stepped into the void it had created by declaring by means of a motion set forth by Abbé Grégoire that all free men of color with two free parents were accorded full citizenship rights.

Although the Assembly hoped by this hurriedly promulgated decree to win the loyalty of free people of color in Saint-Domingue, its action did not achieve that end (McCloy 1961: 63; Mazauric 2006). One reason that this decree did not accomplish the intent of the Assembly was that it produced more technical change than real change in the lives of free people of color in the colony. Another was that it was impractical as well as immoral to grant enhanced rights to free people of color while ignoring the much greater oppression of the enslaved masses. A third reason that it did not work was that "whites" in a number of French colonies began scheming as to how they could break away from metropolitan France. It was against this background that in August 1791 a major slave revolt erupted in Saint-Domingue. Reacting to this general insurrection of slaves in the northern part of the island by August, the members of *La Société des Amis des Noirs* were so surprised that from September 1791 the organization ceased to function (although it would be briefly resurrected during a two-year period beginning in November 1797).

In September 1791, the Assembly in Paris (hoping to pacify the "whites" in the colonies) revoked its decree of May 15 of the same year whereby it had accorded full rights of French citizenship to all free men of color with two free parents. It dispatched a three-person civil commission to Saint-Domingue to restore order. With regard to metropolitan France in August 1791, the Assembly declared any French subject who landed there free on arrival but it was operating under the close scrutiny of the fraternal Jacobin Club, which arrogated to itself the right to discuss in advance questions to be decided by the National Assembly.

The members of the Jacobin Club in Paris in 1791, of which Maximilien Robespierre was the leader, were self-righteously willing to use any means of pressure or violence they could summon to protect republicanism in France. Although Robespierre was virulently opposed to emancipation of the slaves in the colonies, two "mulatto" women were members (McCloy 1961: 84). It is interesting to note by contrast that the participation of people of appreciable African ancestry in such positions of influence in governance during and after the French Revolution had no parallel in North America during or immediately after the American Revolution.

In March, the right wing of the Jacobin Club known as the Girondins came to power in France. The following month, the Paris Assembly reversed itself by again issuing a decree that enfranchised free "blacks" and free "mulattoes" but without emancipating the slaves. As the situation in Saint-Domingue remained tense during the middle of 1972, a second civil three-person civil commission was dispatched there along with some 600 soldiers to relieve the first commission. Consisting of Léger-Félicité Sonthonax, Étienne Polverel, and Jean-Antoine Aihaud, this second commission was only authorized to maintain control of the colony by enforcing citizenship rights for free people of color such as had been approved by the National Convention and to induce slaves to return to the plantations. By the time it arrived in the Caribbean, however, events on the ground made this an impossible course to follow. Nonetheless, Sonthonax attempted to control the north, Polverel the west, and Ailhaud the south of the colony. When however Ailhaud abandoned his post, Polverel attempted to gain control of the south as well.

Around this time, France was facing challenges both in Europe and in the Caribbean. While in Europe, one major concern of Prussia under Frederick William II was to annex additional Polish territory, another was to contain what he considered threats to Europe's social order that he viewed as emanating from the French Revolution. During a conference convened in 1791 by Frederick William II of Prussia and Leopold II (emperor of the Holy Roman Emperor and brother of France's Queen Marie-Antoinette) that had as its *raison d'être* to deal with the so-called Polish Question and Austria's conflict with Ottoman Turkey, they also used the occasion to appeal to French revolutionaries for the restoration of King Louis XVI and threatened war should he be harmed by means of the so-called Declaration of Pillnitz that they issued. This declaration included a statement to the effect that the return to order and of monarchy in France was an object of "common interest to all sovereigns of Europe."

Complicating the situation for France in the Caribbean around this same time, King George III of Great Britain was longing lustfully over France's colonial possessions and was quite willing to promise French planters the reimposition of race-based slavery to gain their cooperation as "a fifth column." In part, this was because he was still bitter over his loss of his North American colonies south of Canada during the American Revolution due in no small part to the help that they had received from France. Saint-Domingue produced more sugar than all the British colonies in the Caribbean combined. The British remained heavily dependent on slavery in their own nearby colonies and did not wish that situation to change. Also, they were annoyed that French revolutionaries had begun hinting that they might aid attempts by other Europeans to overthrow their monarchies as had happened in France. Despite prior claims to be opposed to the slave trade, British Prime Minister William Pitt the Younger even promised anti-abolitionist planters in Saint-Domingue that his country would be willing to declare slavery reimposed if they would ally themselves with Britain.

Saint-Domingue was complexly stratified along racist caste lines as well as class divisions that separated planters, wealthy "whites," *petits blancs*, "mulattoes" (some of whom were wealthy and free and some of whom were not), and masses of "blacks," most of whom were enslaved. Adding to this complexity, after the "whites" in the colony were not successful in convincing the "mulattoes" there to join them in seeking independence from France, they conspired to hand the colony to Britain rather than tolerate interference with the prevailing system of race-based slavery. Meanwhile offshore in nearby Jamaica, the British could hardly wait to enter into the fray in hopes of gaining possession of this very rich French colony.

The Assembly in Paris reacted to British interference by adopting still a new position, albeit a half-hearted and indecisive one. It officially granted freedom to already freed slaves rather than to those who remained enslaved. Faced with this situation of tremendous confusion on the ground among numerous factions by the time he arrived in Saint-Domingue, Sonthonax on August 29, 1793, granted limited freedom to slaves who were rebelling in the northern province on condition that they remain loyal to France. Hoping to bring additional calm to this situation, he and/or Polverel further extended this order between September and December 1793 to apply throughout the colony although slaves were still required to work on their former plantations. Despite this, considerable opposition continued from slaveholding planters, including some of whom were well-to-do "mulattoes."

Following the beheading of Louis XVI in January 1793 and France's declaration of war on Great Britain for interfering with Saint-Domingue around the same time, Britain (with William Pitt the Younger as its prime minister) retaliated by taking part in the First Coalition against France, an alliance that also included Austria, Prussia, Sardinia, Spain, and the Dutch United Provinces. One consequence of this was that revolutionary forces from France invaded the United Provinces. However, the First Coalition came apart in 1795 thereby leaving the nationalities that we now know as the Dutch, Belgians, and Luxembourgians under France control until between 1813 and the Battle of Waterloo in 1815.

Of more immediate relevance to the issue of race-based slavery and imperialist rivalries in the Caribbean, however, Britain in September 1793 sent an expedition to Saint-Domingue under the command of Colonel John Whitelocke that was welcomed by the "white" colonialists as it began to capture town after town, especially in the south and west of that French colony. Not wishing to be left out of the spoils, even forces of the Spanish Bourbons operating in league with Toussaint Louverture, a former slave at the head of 4,000 "black" troops, also invaded the French colony from the east. Only as a strategic expedient that he hoped would maintain Saint-Domingue under French control at a time that France wished desperately to maintain control of it, Léger-Félicité Sonthonax declared all slaves in Saint-Domingue freed in 1793.

Though not united in a single faction, virtually all people of appreciable African ancestry in France and in the French colonies were fervent supporters of the French Revolution. By the time Sonthonax issued his decree freeing all slaves, the despotic rule of metropolitan France (under Maximilien Robespierre as head of the Jacobin Club with a Committee of Public Safety at its core) had morphed into a Reign of Terror that would continue into 1794. Adding to the prevailing sense of confusion in France, Charles Étienne Thevenau, a naturalist and journalist born on the Caribbean island of Saint Lucia, who had arrived in France a couple of years before the revolution, was one of the most fierce opponents of *La Société des Amis des Noirs* and became so provocative with his opposition to the abolitionist cause that he was imprisoned. As the Reign of Terror ebbed and flowed, sometimes consuming its various supporters, many suffered much more severely than mere imprisonment.

One victim of the guillotine during the Reign of Terror was a "mulatto" named Delorme, despite the fact that he had been an enthusiastic Jacobin. Another man of color named Carstaing was elected to the National Convention from a constituency in metropolitan France in December 1793 to replace another deputy who had been executed. Of note, Carstaing was married to the comtesse Françoise de Beauharnais, the daughter of Claude de Beauharnais, comte des Roches-Baritaud and Anne-Marie Mouchard. Through the first marriage of Carstaing's wife to comte François de Beauharnais, she was the sister-in-law of Alexandre François Marie, vicomte de Beauharnais, who had fought both during the American and French Revolutions as well as the first husband of Joséphine de Beauharnais, who later married Napoleon Bonaparte and, as a consequence, became the Empress of the French in 1804. Hortense de Beauharnais, who was the half-sister of Carstaing's wife, was also the mother of France's Louis-Napoleon Bonaparte, who after becoming the President of the first President of the French Republic in 1848 became Emperor Napoleon III of the French in 1852.

Well before this time in February of 1794, however, when a National Convention assembled in Paris that would among other things consider whether the actions taken by Léger-Félicité Sonthonax and Étienne Polverel in Saint-Domingue to emancipate the slaves amounted to treason, the three deputies from Saint-Domingue in the National Convention included a "mulatto" and a "black." When the issue of abolition of slavery in Saint-Domingue was put to a vote at the National Convention, it declared slavery abolished immediately without the matter even first being referred to a committee for study as was customary. Although this action made France one of the first countries in Europe to at least temporarily abolish slavery, that it in no way outlawed continued French participation in slavetrading was apparently lost on many people of African descent amid the celebrations that followed.

The most elaborate celebration was held at Bordeaux, with 200 "black" people being present at the Cathedral of Saint-André and with Tallien, a representative of the Convention, giving an enthusiastic speech. At a smaller celebration in Nantes, a "black" officer also eloquently gave thanks to the republic. That around this same time in Martinique, the most important French colony apart from Saint-Domingue, a "mulatto" was elected a deputy to the National Convention in Paris contributes to a picture of France as likely having the government with the most racio-ethnic diversity existing anywhere in Europe at this time. This is not to suggest, however, that France was by any means a completely willing "melting pot," nor a country untouched by the pseudo-scientific racism that was diffusing widely throughout Europe by this time.

Despite the technical liberation of French slaves in February of 1794, including those being held in the *dépôts des noirs* (i.e., jails for blacks), and their obtaining the rights of citizenship, the effects in the colonies were varied. Martinique fell to the British in March 1794, and its British conquerors refused to recognize the decree freeing slaves. In the colonies of Ile-de-France and Ile Bourbon (now Réunion) off the coast of eastern Africa, the decree was not enforced. The decree of February 4 did take effect in Guadeloupe and in French Guyana, however. While eventually bringing at least a temporary and tentative end to slavery in France and in some of its colonies, the French Revolution greatly slowed the immigration of people of African descent into France (McCloy 1961: 53, 82-83).

Although the French National Assembly in 1794 had at a moment filled with desperation more than moral resolve made France one of the first countries in Europe to at least temporarily declare slavery abolished, France's flirtation with abolition was little more than tactical window-dressing by which it aimed to ensure the prolongation of racist exploitation in its colonies. Most other European countries were much more concerned with the restoration of social order that included race-based slavery than with the continuation of French-inspired democracy. In fact, many dismissed France's democratic rhetoric rather derisively as Jacobinism.

Under France's Reign of Terror as the revolution ran its course, thousands were guillotined merely as "suspects." Antoine-Auguste Journu, a merchant of Bordeaux heavily invested in the slave trade, was guillotined on March 5, 1794, for vaunting his nobility and for impeding freedom for slaves. In Paris's *Place de la Révolution* (before 1792, *Place Louis XV* and now *Place de la Concorde*), Madame du Barry, a courtesan who had been the mistress of King Louis XV as well as other aristocrats, was accused of treason and killed. Rather than for her commission of a crime, this was because of her royal connections based in part on the testimony of her "black" retainer named Zamoré. It was in such ways that most of the foes of the National Convention were eliminated during the Reign of Terror. Among these were Queen Marie-Antoinette and Jacques Pierre Brissot, who had been an inspirational figure in the founding of *La Société des Amis des Noirs*.

Also done away with in this way were Pierre Vergniaud, a spokesman for the moderate Grondin faction, George Jacques Danton, a lawyer, great orator, and member of the Cordeliers who were concerned with keeping an eye on the government as well as Camille Desmoulins, a journalist closely associated with Danton. The life of Louis de Saint-Just, a close ally on the Committee of Public Safety of Maximillien Robespierre, the architect of the Reign of Terror, came to an end in this way. On the same day, even the life of Robespierre was ended by the guillotine during the terror that he and such colleagues as Saint-Just had played a major role in unleashing.

Until France dispatched Victor Hugues to Guadeloupe to rally the slaves and *gens de couleur* there, Guadeloupe remained under the British, who had been invited to interfere by its French planters. From 1794 to 1798, while Hugues remained the colonial administrator of Guadeloupe, he devoted much effort to emancipating the slaves under orders from the National Convention. With an army composed of "white," "mulatto," and "black" soldiers, he also worked to export the revolution to neighboring islands, including Dominica, Saint-Martin, Grenada (or *la Grenade*), Saint-Vincent, and Saint Lucia (or *Sainte-Lucie*). Underscoring the importance of "blacks" and "mulattoes" in French affairs internationally as well as domestically during this revolutionary period, even when between Britain and France large numbers of prisoners were exchanged as in 1795 and again in 1797, many of the prisoners returned to France were of African descent (Debrunner 1979: 98-99, 128).

Although during most of the years from 1793 to 1801 when France and Britain were at war in the Caribbean, a British blockade complicated normal travel by sea between France and its Caribbean colonies, no similar blockade impeded a flow of Africans across the Mediterranean into Europe. Despite the fact that Marseille was officially closed to Muslim and Jewish immigration after the French Revolution, France's African population continued to increase as Jews and Muslims entered the country clandestinely from south of the Mediterranean (Blanchard and Boëtsch 2005: 9). Farther east, moreover, the slave trade northward across the Mediterranean into Europe thrived as hired ships that were sometimes French, sometimes Venetian, and sometimes British carried Africans of varied ethnicities, religions, and complexions to such places as Chios and Smyrna, to Izmir and Istanbul, as well as to Athens, Salonika, and Morea (Thomas 1997: 511).

In 1795, French revolutionaries compromised some of their commitment to pure democracy by approving a new constitution that provided for government under five so-called Directors that constituted the legislature and executive. Between 1795 and 1799, the Directory was unwieldy, weak, and ill-equipped to restore the colonial empire, solve financial problems, or protect itself against the ambitions of a charismatic national hero and warrior such as Napoleon Bonaparte. It was under this Directory that Napoleon invaded the Italian Peninsula in 1796, thereby beginning the so-called Napoleonic Wars. It was during this same year that Napoleon seized Mantua in northern Italy from the Hapsburgs of Austria despite Austrian and Russian attempts to prevent this.

In addition to bringing about the extinction of Venice as a republic in 1797, Napoleon Bonaparte was concerned that a destabilized and no-longer neutral Order of St. John might lead Malta into the fold of Great Britain or Russia at a time that he wished to extend French hegemony across the length of the Mediterranean Sea. With these concerns in mind, he suggested in a letter to Talleyrand (foreign minister in the Directory) that he hoped to make the French "the masters of the Mediterranean." On September 13, 1797, Napoleon led a French expedition to capture Egypt via Malta (Lloyd 1973: 10).

Although Napoleon personally remained in Malta but a few days, this was long enough for him to demand that the Order of Saint John give up its slaves consisting mostly of some 700 convicts from the Kingdom of the Two Sicilies for the huge sum of 548,680 *scudi* in ransom money. That included among these slaves were some approximately 500 who were described as Turks and Moors who served as galley slaves (Wettinger 2002: 26, 584-588) indicates the contemporary presence of Africans in southern Italy. As there exists not a shred of evidence to suggest that Napoleon was offended by slavery on moral grounds and much to indicate that he was not, it would appear that his decision to demand that the Knights of Malta release their slaves, many of whom were Muslim, was either a mere display of his authority or perhaps more likely a tactic he wished to employ to lessen the opposition he anticipated he would face especially from the Muslim masses in Egypt by invading their country.

Using Malta largely as a stepping stone, Napoleon crossed south of the eastern Mediterranean basin into Egypt, where he rationalized France's intrusion in large part on claims of Mamluk and Turkish incompetence in governing. During the period of the French Revolution, France had relied heavily on soldiers of African descent, including several who were generals. In a continuation of this pattern, Napoleon invaded Egypt in 1798 with considerable assistance from soldiers of African descent. Among the generals who accompanied Napoleon to Egypt was General Thomas-Alexandre Dumas, who had been born in Saint-Domingue and who was the "mulatto" father and grandfather of the famous French writers Alexandre Dumas the Elder and Alexandre Dumas the Younger, respectively. In the same way as Napoleon drafted a number of Maltese into his army (Goodwin 2002: 47), no doubt because Maltese spoke an Afro-Asiatic language that was closely related to Arabic, he calculated that his soldiers of African descent would facilitate his acceptance by the Egyptians.

At the Louvre is a painting by Antoine-Jean Gros that shows Napoleon at Jaffa (now on the edge of Tel Aviv), which Napoleon visited in 1798 shortly after his invasion of Egypt. This work stands as but one important graphic testimony to an intense French involvement with a wide variety of people of African descent during this period. Quite in addition to the geopolitical motivations of Napoleon in undertaking his invasion of Egypt, it occurred at a time of increasing European interest in Africa, in Orientalism, and in Masonic symbolism.

Reflective of this trend, it was in the same year of the death of Wolfgang Amadeus Mozart in 1791 that his opera *Die Zauberflöte* (or the Magic Flute) was first performed at the Theater auf der Wieden in Vienna. Although this opera combined simple German folk tunes and classic operatic writing with brilliant musical effect, its libretto was based on an oriental story by Liebeskind set in Egypt. *Die Zauberflöte* contains numerous references to symbols of African derivation such as the gods Isis and Osiris as well as to symbolism that counterpoises white against black as good and evil respectively. Perhaps reflecting some larger disquiet in the consciousness of some Europeans around this time concerning richly pigmented skin, this work also portrayed Sarastro, a "black" Moor, as an evil sorcerer continually trying to seduce the fair Pamina, daughter of the Queen of the Night. *Die Zauberflöte* was a product of an era during which the largest scale slave empires in the world were under the domination of Europeans and Turks, although also operated in many other parts of the world, including in Africa. Against this background, the fact that the Papageno character in the opera was initially frightened by Sarastro's dark complexion and that Sarastro, depicted as Moor, was portrayed as a slave-driver, are highly suggestive that certain themes incorporated into the libretto of this work plausibly mirrored some broader thinking concerning Africa, the Orient, slavery, color, and guilt that was taking root in Europe.

In any case, as is reflected in *Napoleon in Egypt: Al-Jabaritis Chronicle* (Al-Jabarti 1993), based on the description of the occupation from the point of view of Shaikh Abd al-Rahman al-Jabarti, an astronomer at Al-Azhar University who Napoleon appointed to the Diwan, Egyptians became more acquainted with Western culture and approaches to scholarship during their country's Napoleonic occupation. Perhaps of even greater importance was Egypt's influence on France and the larger world in large measure due to the discovery of the Rosetta Stone that made it possible to translate ancient Egyptian hieroglyphs into other languages. The 28-volume work based on research compiled by French scholars during the occupation entitled *Description de l'Egypt* became fundamental to the discipline later known as Egyptology (Goodwin 2006: 397-398).

Napoleon's intrusion into Egypt stirred up great resentment in Britain at a time that Britain was hoping to extend its network of imperial communications to India through the Mediterranean and across Egypt. Faced with Napoleon's conquest of Egypt, Britain turned its attention from rivalry with France in the Caribbean to the Old World. In fact, it joined Austria, Russia, Turkey, the Vatican, Portugal, and Naples in the so-called Second Coalition against France. Although this coalition did not last long, an ongoing alliance continued between Britain and Turkey that was focused on hurriedly expelling the French from Egypt. Among the early Ottoman forces to enter Egypt was a contingent from Turkish-controlled Albania in which Muhammad Ali, sometimes called "the father of modern Egypt," was a junior commander.

By the end of the Anglo-French war in the Caribbean in 1802 when even Britain's promise to planters in most French Caribbean colonies to restore slavery had not been sufficient to accomplish British imperialistic ends in the region and the confrontation with France in Egypt, Britain's national debt was so large and its gold reserves so depleted that the government prohibited the Bank of England from any longer paying out gold, in lieu of which it began issuing banknotes for the first time. In addition to taking a heavy toll on the British trea-sury, the war in the Caribbean alone, according to Sir John Fortescue in his 20-volume *A History of the British Army*, cost the lives of some 100,000 men. In-cluded within this number were 13,000 slaves from Africa and from the Carib-bean who were acquired by William Pitt the Younger before he left office as prime minister in 1801 to make up for a shortage of men in his West Indian re-giments.

When the 1802 Peace of Amiens was signed and Britain officially declared the control of Saint-Domingue (now Haiti) returned to France, both countries remained without any commitment to the abolition of slavery. Also, neither had any commitment to eliminate racism where it might interfere with imperial am-bitions to control a large empire. With Britain no longer a threat to France in Saint-Domingue, Napoleon dispatched General Charles Leclerc, the husband of his sister Josephine, to the Caribbean with his secret mission being to capture Toussaint Louverture in order that slavery could be reimposed there. When General Leclerc arrived at Le Cap on February 2 and addressed the people of the colony in a proclamation from his headquarters in the north of Saint-Domingue, he neither mentioned the true aim of his mission nor hinted that Napoleon was about to reverse a major accomplishment of the French Revolution by decreeing slavery reestablished in its colonies.

Napoleon hoped that, after capturing Toussaint Louverture and restoring sla-very in Saint-Domingue, General Leclerc might be able to continue on and re-capture Louisiana, which Spain had returned to France some two years before. The United States had long accused France of having such designs on Louisiana, however, as developments in Saint-Domingue did not go as planned and as Lec-lerc died of yellow fever in November 1802, the race-based system of slavery that continued to operate in Louisiana remained under American rather than Napoleonic control. Despite Napoleon's failure to retake Louisiana, as part of a grand scheme for strengthening the French Empire in the New World, he still managed to send forces to French Guyana to capture that colony from a Victor Hugues who was in rebellion in that he was engaged in piracy from his strong-hold in Guadeloupe and this caused considerable conflict between the United States and France although it brought considerable wealth to that colony.

When in 1799, Hugues was assigned as a government envoy to French Guyana, however, he had no difficulty in actively supporting legislation that provided for slavery. This was a period during which many Europeans as well as European governments not infrequently pursued changing policies that were propped up by duplicitous rhetoric with respect to slavery and its abolition in order to pursue the goals of holding on to, or extending, their colonial empires. Such duplicity meant that the lives of people of African descent living under their control, and most especially in colonial settings, were characterized by much uncertainty, with a sense that peril might not be distant.

For people of color under the control of Europeans, it was a period during which to some extent it was even sometimes difficult for them to feel secure in their social alliances with Europeans even on the continent of Europe. The pos-sibility of a racist collusion among Europeans that might turn against them was always present. The fact that William Pitt the Younger as the prime minister of Britain both claimed to be in favor of abolition and showed himself quite willing to assure French colonists in the Caribbean of his willingness to reestablish slavery when he calculated that it would assist him to expanding the British Empire at the expense of the French Empire was but one illustration of such duplicity.

By 1802, the oppressed "mulattoes" and "blacks" of Saint-Domingue had launched a major anti-colonial revolt that helped to precipitate a major course change by Napoleon with respect to some of the most basic principles of the French Revolution. That, only three weeks after Louverture signed an agreement with Leclerc in which Leclerc promised that France would not restore slavery, Leclerc had Toussaint Louverture and some of his closest family members seized for shipping as prisoners to France was another illustration. Reaching France aboard a military ship on July 2, 1802, Louverture was separated from his family, badly treated, and repeatedly interrogated. From August 25, his humiliating and brutal treatment continued within the cold confines of France's Fort-de-Joux, located in the Alps Mountains, until he finally died of pneumonia in April 1803 (Patrick 2002; James 1989; Kennedy 1989; Parkinson 1978).

When General Charles Leclerc died attempting to subdue Saint-Domingue by any means possible in late 1802, Napoleon selected as his successor to whom he similarly gave *carte blanche* General Rochambeau. This General Rochambeau was Donatien-Marie-Joseph de Vimeur, vicomte de Rochambeau, a son of Jean-Baptiste Donatien de Vimeur, comte de Rochambeau, the French lieutenant-general who a few decades earlier led several thousand French soldiers fighting against the British during the American War of Independence. Unknown to Louverture, the former enslaved freedom fighter at the time of his passing, his army back in Saint-Domingue under his former general Jean-Jacques Dessalines was by that time resisting the 60,000 French troops dispatched there by Napoleon to steal freedom from the masses. Also unknown to him, General Rochambeau the Younger, in France's desperate attempt to reinstitute race-based slavery, had gone so far in his use of terrorism as to import from Cuba man-eating dogs to assist in massacre.

After the death of Toussaint Louverture, his family members in France were exiled to Bayonne and later to Agen. Despite the terror tactics to which Napoleon Bonaparte had given his approval, France would never again be able to effectively establish control in Saint-Domingue (now Haiti), although it maintained its control of Martinique, Guadeloupe, and French Guyana as major sugar-producing colonies in the Caribbean area.

The American and French Revolutions, as well as the beginning of the Industrial Revolution at least in Britain, all occurred in the late 18th century and were destined to alter in rather dramatic ways Europe's interaction with Africa as well as with peoples of African descent in general. In addition to pushing to new heights European peripheral explorations in Africa, the Industrial Revolution accelerated new international interdependence as Britain, and eventually other nations closest to industrial takeoff, began to interact with a larger unindustrialized world that they used largely as a storehouse for new resources and as a marketplace for their manufactured products. As Africa became increasingly important in this context, a number of European powers devoted much more attention to learning as much as possible about the continent in order to better tap its riches and exploit its peoples.

In contrast with the United States, which was not seeking to establish colonies in Africa or Asia around this time as it was fully occupied colonizing westward in North America, numerous European explorers and scholars acting as agents for their countries were very active in African reconnaissance in the late 18th century. In 1790, for example, James Bruce published his *Travels in the Highlands of Ethiopia*, and François Le Vaillant published his *Voyage dans l'Interieur de l'Afrique dans les années 1780-1785* (Freeman-Grenville 1973: 137). Already in 1790, the African Association commissioned Major Daniel Francis Houghton to find Timbuktu by traveling through Senegambia in western Africa. Though Houghton never returned, the Association later dispatched the Scotsman Mungo Park to the interior of western Africa in hopes of learning more about the river Niger and gathering information about the riches of this area, first in 1795 and again in 1805. In 1798, between Park's two expeditions, Germany sent Friedrich Konrad Homemann toward the Sudan from Tripoli even as Britain's interest in tapping riches from Africa was fed both by its direct reconnaissance near the coasts and by reports that it began receiving from its representatives located in Malta and Tripoli about commerce that regularly reached the Mediterranean across the Sahara from western Africa.

Meanwhile, the failed siege of Vienna by Turkey in 1683 was the last important Turkish threat to European power apart from the Balkans and Cyprus. Under the Treaty of Karlowitz of 1699, the Hapsburgs (who were allied with Poland, Russia, and Venice) had taken control of Hungary (including Croatia) while Russia wrestled control of the Ukraine. From this time, the Ottomans were essentially on the defensive vis-à-vis most of Europe as a European focus on Orientalism became more intense. One indication of this was the Austro-Turkish War that took place between 1788 and 1791. Further evidence of the tension came in 1774 when Russia defeated Turkey again and the two powers signed the Treaty of Kuchuk Kainarji. By this treaty, Russia gained access to the Black Sea coast and the right to enter the Black Sea, the Bosphorus, and the Dardanelles, and it became protector of the Orthodox Christians of Turkey, with special rights in Wallachia and Moldavia. As a result of this treaty, a major competition among the great powers (including Russia, Britain, France, Austria-Hungary, Italy, and Germany) for influence in Turkey began so as not to allow Russia or any other single power to dominate the vast Ottoman holdings.

A third reflection of Turkey's being on the defense in the face of a more aggressive Europe would come in 1797 when Napoleon, after defeating the Austrians in Italy, began seizing territory in the Balkans, an area widely considered until that time as within Turkey's sphere of influence. France seized and then annexed the Ionian Islands, the chain of islands lying at the mouth of the Adriatic between Italy and the west coast of what is now modern-day Greece. At certain points, the British replaced the French as occupiers. Nearby Dalmatia also became part of the French Empire known as the "Illyrian Provinces." A further provocation to Turkey came when Napoleon in 1798 led an invasion force, by way of Malta, to Egypt, which was technically a Turkish province. The decision by Britain to support Turkish and Egyptian resistance at this time had little to do with any charitable British attitudes toward them and much to do with Britain's vested interest in ensuring its continued access to the Isthmus of Suez for the sake of maintaining the integrity of its global empire, including especially its link with the sub-continent of India through the Mediterranean.

The disastrous French defeat in Egypt between 1798 and 1801and the major uprising in Haiti coupled with the personal, national, and international ambitions of Napoleon who had crowned himself emperor of France with essentially no checks on his power, were at variance with French rhetoric about *liberté, égalité, fraternité*. While in Haiti the people involved in chasing out the French had been predominantly of African descent, those involved in Egypt (although assisted by the British) were also of African and so-called Oriental descent. Adding to these other humiliations for the French, France had even been chased out of tiny Malta, whose people spoke a Semitic language, hence, one of Afro-Asiatic derivation. In some respects, therefore, motives for Napoleon's restoration of slavery in French colonies were both geopolitical and retaliatory because of recent humiliations suffered in Egypt, Haiti, and Malta. In addition to being perceived as humiliations against France, they were perceived as a challenge to racist prerogatives increasingly being exercised by people of European descent against "others."

Contrasts between the French and British governments with respect to a commitment to outlaw the slave trade were hardly so stark as much Anglophile scholarly literature focusing largely on the behaviors of certain individual abolitionists would suggest (e.g., Curtin 1964; Bolt 1971; Drescher 1992). Throughout the period being discussed in this chapter, British concern with the abolition of slavery at the governmental level was at most a concern that was secondary in comparison with the British focus on acquiring and maintaining a vast colonial empire. The situation in France was very similar.

A resolution in the British Parliament declaring that slavery was contrary to the law of God failed to win a majority in 1776, suggesting a definite lack of empathy with enslaved "blacks" on the part of most of the ruling elite in Britain at the time. On the other hand, when in 1783 the crew aboard a British ship operating from Liverpool known as the *Zong*, in an act of extreme cruelty, engaged in throwing live Africans into the sea, this action at least for a while turned much opinion in Britain against slavery. This was not, however, the first or last time that such a thing occurred. Still, in the same year, a bill that was introduced into the House of Commons forbidding officials of the Royal African Company from selling slaves failed as the home secretary said that slavery was "necessary to every country in Europe" (Thomas 1997: 490-491). In April 1792, with reference to the slave trade, William Pitt the Younger, while still prime minister, stated in the House of Commons, "No nation in Europe . . . has . . . plunged so deeply into this guilt as Great Britain" (Thomas 1997: 235).

It is important not to confuse attitudes of the British government and those of certain individual abolitionists and religious organizations in Britain during this period. The predominantly Quaker Society for the Abolition of the Slave Trade was founded in London in 1787 and was chaired by the abolitionist Granville Sharp. While William Pitt the Younger in his role as British prime minister during the following year supported Wilberforce's anti-slavery motion in Parliament, Pitt's commitment to abolitionism was largely tactical. In still a somewhat different category, the Association for Promoting the Discovery of the Interior Parts of Africa that was founded in London around the same time was little more than a front for people interested in advancing British imperialism at all costs. Demonstrating that the British government was interested in abolition largely as a mechanism that it could use in building its empire, an inquiry in the House of Commons into the condition of slavery in Barbados in 1788 resulted in a determination that, in practice, the law of a master over a slave was "unlimited" (Thomas 1997: 474).

What was occurring around the same time in the United States offers some useful insight into attitudes of some other "whites" toward people of African background. Although the importation of new slaves into the Unites States became a felony effective January 1, 1808, the slaves already in the United States could reproduce themselves by this time, and the institution of slavery in the South was allowed to thrive with little interference because of a broad national resolve. As had occurred in Great Britain after the American War of Independence, some European Americans were greatly concerned with how to rid America of their compatriots of African descent. Against this background, the United States produced its own Back-to-Africa Movement that was in some respects very similar to the Sierra Leone Scheme that had emerged in Britain. It was as a result of this that Liberia became established on the western coast of Africa immediately adjacent to Sierra Leone as a new home for people of African descent in the United States who could be induced to relocate there. It is telling, however, that as Britain and France competed for large empires in Africa during the 19th century, both countries periodically exhibited considerable hostility toward Liberia (Goodwin 2006: 135-136).

Unfortunately, few scholars have focused on a comparison between the long legacy of enslavement of Africans and the contemporary enslavement of Europeans and others in many of the same locations in Europe and nearby northern Africa. From 1782 to 1789, the Sultan Mohammed ibn Abdallah of Morocco, who had an ambassador in Malta, was engaged off and on in attempting to bring about the ransom of all Muslim slaves in this country. Even after some 600 of them departed from Malta in September 1789, several hundred baptized slaves—mostly of southern Italian and Sicilian origin—were left behind in Malta (Wettinger 2002: 579-583).

This in no way marked the end of the enslavement of people not usually considered "black" in Europe. Within a couple of days after Napoleon's conquest of Malta in 1798, he instructed the French consuls in Tripoli, Tunis, and Algiers to inform the *beys* of those places that as the Maltese had recently become subjects of France all Maltese slaves under their control should be liberated and returned to Malta, at which time the liberated Muslim slaves from areas of the Mediterranean under Turkish control would be transferred to Turkish authorities, regardless of whether they had originated from Greece, from Syria, from Libya, and so forth. It would take until 1801 before all such exchanges of slaves were completed (Wettinger 2002: 26, 584-588).

Even more often overlooked in analyses of slavery and the rise of pseudo-scientific racism during this period is the well-documented history of European slaves in nearby Africa. During the two and a half centuries leading up to 1780, probably at least a million Europeans were enslaved in northwestern Africa, largely as a result of having been captured by pirates or as prisoners of war (Baepler 1999; Matar 1999; Davis 2003; Vitkus 2001; Busuttil 1971; Clissold 1977; Earle 1970). Although many of them eventually were ransomed, many others were gradually assimilated into African populations in much the same way that Africans were assimilated into the populations of Europe. It was only in 1808 that thirteen Englishmen who had been enslaved by Kabyles in what is now Algeria were ransomed with funds from the estate of William Betton, a wealthy London ironmonger who had died in 1724, specifying that his fortune be used for just such a purpose (Clissold 1977: 145).

Such omissions as these to the historical dialogue have overly racialized our understanding of human intercourse among peoples in Europe, overemphasized African "otherness" in the context of Europe, and placed too much emphasis on Africans as slaves in a static way while placing too little attention on the enslavement of Europeans in Europe and nearby Africa. This has also diverted attention away from the assimilation of Africans into European societies, which has a long and uninterrupted history. While such ways of looking at the past provide more than a fig leaf of comfort to people cherishing notions of European racial purity and racial superiority, they distort in serious ways our understanding of how Europeans and Africans have actually interacted with each other and how they have experienced life comparatively. It is also unfortunate that even serious students of slavery and racism often focus on developments of this period primarily from the perspective of present-day racist and ethnic stereotypes as though reading history in reverse as well as through lenses that produce distortion.

Oddly, we also live in a world that tends to more idealize "white" abolitionists who never were enslaved more than "black" abolitionists who were. Haiti (the original Indian name for Saint-Domingue) declared itself independent of France effective January 1, 1804, and could not any more than any other society tainted by colorism and racism immediately rid itself of those problems, including tensions between "blacks" and "mulattoes." To its credit, however, the government of Haiti, no matter how flawed, was not attempting to build an empire on foreign lands where it considered the people being colonized to be racially inferior to its own citizens, as were such countries as Britain, France, Denmark, and Spain.

At the turn of the 19th century, there emerged in Haiti a government which, despite its many flaws, was perhaps the most unequivocal on record anywhere in the world in declaring slavery to be reprehensible and immoral. However, we live in a world where most historians and those who control mass media, diverting us from this reality, prefer to pretend that it was really Britain that was the pioneer nation in committing itself to the abolition of slavery. One is left to wonder if Haiti is ignored in this context because it is a nation whose population is largely of African descent and the accomplishments of such people are not due the respect sometimes easily conceded to others. One may wonder if the leadership of the Haitians in battling against slavery is so often ignored because so many of its people live in poverty. One may even wonder if Haiti is still being used over two centuries after its masses dared bolt from slavery against the wishes of a major European power as a case study to remind us of the retribution that can ensue when a people that is predominantly of African descent seizes the leadership in rebelling against European domination, even if in flight from racism and in pursuit of liberty.

In 1795, the whole of Hispaniola, including the eastern two-thirds that had been a Spanish colony, came under the control of France. A few years later in early 1801, Toussaint Louverture managed for a while to abolish slavery throughout Hispaniola. Haitians again abolished slavery in the Spanish part of Hispaniola known as Santo Domingo (now the Dominican Republic) in 1822, although their imperialist invasion was accompanied by considerable harshness. European-instigated drives to abolish slavery since the beginning of the 18th century have quite a different history.

Even into the early 18th century, the willingness of European to tolerate slavery or campaign for its abolition was largely driven by empathies and antipathies that were associated with religion. As Europe became increasing diverse in terms of religion and as colorism became increasingly incorporated into various European cultures, the involvement of Europeans in campaigns to abolish slavery was directed especially at freeing European slaves. Only from the mid-1700s did a relatively few Europeans interested in abolition begin to expand their focus to include "others." When William Betton died in 1724 and left his fortune in trust for the purpose of ransoming English slaves from northwestern Africa (Clissold 1977: 145), there exists no evidence suggesting that he was equally concerned with the fact that Africans were at that same time being freely bought and sold in London, Liverpool, Bristol, and other British seaports. Even five years after Betton's death, the British Attorney General ruled that baptism did not automatically bestow freedom on these latter people nor automatically change their status as slaves in cases where they were transported by owners from overseas colonies into England (Padmore 1955: 24-25).

While certain powers in Europe and far beyond remained deeply involved in slavetrading, some Europeans, including especially merchants and government officials, began to use abolitionist rhetoric as a ruse or tactic to facilitate colonization and imperial greatness in large measure at the expense of peoples of African descent. At a time when European enslavement of others alongside European colonialism was flourishing and some peoples who identified as Europeans were increasingly using the rhetoric of freedom to describe an idealized system of governance that was quite at variance with what they practiced, contradictions surrounded Western attitudes concerning democracy, slavery, abolition, and imperial conquest. It is doubtful that a massive system of slavery can be established and maintained anywhere in the absence of an enduring economic rationale. Hence at the same time that certain European governments profited from

slavery systems in their colonies abroad, the same government restricted or outlawed slavery in their metropolitan homelands.

In 1803 when Denmark outlawed slavetrading, it was likely more concerned
about Danes falling victim to slavery in the Mediterranean area than about help-
less people of darker hues from Africa and elsewhere that were being denied
their freedom within systems such as slavery and colonialism. Even as the brutality of slavery was fueling abolitionist movements in Europe and the Americas
against introducing new people into slavery, the economic gains to be had from
colonialism were convincing to other factions in those same societies that people
of European descent were justified in continuing to exploit the slaves they already had. Although in 1803 the Danes carried out their agreement of 1792 to
abolish the slave trade, the number of slaves that they transported to their Caribbean colonies in their last years of participating in the trade exceeded all previous levels. Consequently, by 1802 the few small islands of the Danish West
Indies counted over 35,000 slaves in comparison with the approximately 28,000
who had been there in 1792 (Thomas 1997: 549).

When in 1804 Napoleon overthrew the First Republic and gave up his position as consul-for-life to crown himself emperor of the French, it was clear that
France had drifted away from some of the most fundamental principles of its
recent revolution. As Napoleon was by this time married to the former Josephine
Beauharnais, whose previous husband had been guillotined during the revolution, it was Josephine de Beauharnais, the wife of Napoleon, who became
France's first empress. Around two years after Napoleon defeated Austria in
1806 the Holy Roman Empire came to an end, and Napoleon was practically in
control of most of Europe except Great Britain.

Although in 1806 the House of Commons voted 35 to 13 in favor of a bill
forbidding British captains to sell slaves to foreign countries, much of its moti-
vation was that the British West Indies were in debt, as there existed a strong
surplus of sugar on the market. Not surprising under these circumstances, the
bill passed in the House of Lords, in fact, by 43 to 18 (Thomas 1997: 553).
When shortly thereafter in June, Charles James Fox, British secretary of state,
and William Wyndham Grenville, the prime minister, moved a resolution to
abolish the slave trade "with all practicable expedition," both houses urged the
government to negotiate with other countries in order to achieve a general abolition of the traffic. Most Britons as of 1806 understood that any legislation their
country approved to curtail slavetrading would not eliminate all British participation in the slave trade, nor abolish British participation in slavery itself by
means of slaveholding.

In January 1807, William Wyndham Grenville, the British prime minister
who succeeded William Pitt the Younger, moved a bill that would outlaw British participation in the slave trade by making it illegal to transport slaves on
British ships. He argued in favor of the bill not on humanitarian grounds but
rather on the claim that it was necessary to ensure the survival of the older Caribbean colonies. Despite the fact that many lords in the upper house owed their
seats to their investments in the slave trade, the bill passed there and shortly thereafter in the House of Commons, thereby becoming effective on May 1 of the

same year. Although this bill provided for fines and confiscation of cargo for violations (Thomas 1997: 554-556; Padmore 1955: 35-36), it did not make violations a felony. That would come only in 1811. Equally significant, the law did not abolish the institution of slaveholding, which would come still later.

Some individuals of European descent in various Western countries around this time remained genuinely concerned about abolitionism and the fate of people of African descent who were being oppressed by slavery, but they were quite exceptional. One such person in France, for example, was Abbé Henri Grégoire, who had an early affiliation with *la Société des Amis des Noirs*. Even in the case of Grégoire, however, he initially supported abolition mostly for "mulattoes" and at a later time he was a determined supporter of French imperialism well beyond the Caribbean. This notwithstanding, and despite the restoration of slavery by Napoleon, a book that Grégoire courageously authored was published in Paris in 1808 about the literary contributions of people of African ancestry with the title *De la litérature des Nègres* (Debrunner 1979: 187).

In the competitive rush among European nations to establish empires in Africa, even Sierra Leone eventually ceased to be conceptualized primarily as a "province of Freedom." After many of its original settlers from overseas were lost to disease shortly after the founding of Freetown, new settlers arrived in 1792 consisting of over a thousand "blacks" from Nova Scotia as well as others from Jamaica along with approximately a hundred "white "people (Padmore 1955: 30-32). Under the leadership of Lieutenant John Clarkson, a brother of Thomas Clarkson, who had been an abolitionist leader in Britain as well as an advisor to *Les Amis des Noirs* in Paris, these newcomers settled in and around Freetown. In 1808, however, the area in and around Freetown became a British colony (Thomas 1997: 498; cf. Padmore 1955: 30-32). A British Vice-Admiralty court was located there that was largely concerned with enforcing Britain's newly enacted legislation against slavetrading. When British ships carrying slaves were interdicted on the high seas, they were often brought to Freetown where this court liberated and resettled their human cargo.

Even when Britain was eventually in the vanguard of the crusade against slavery, it was also among the vanguard of European nations professing interest in abolition as a means for diverting attention from its growing interest in global imperialism, including in Africa. As of 1815 or the approximate end point discussed in this chapter, the evidence is overwhelming that neither Britain nor any other European government factored the abolition of slavetrading into its national policy purely on humanitarian or moral grounds. Rather, they gradually began to place constraints on slavetrading where it was not at variance with their larger national interests. Britain was moving more decisively toward outlawing slavetrading because the trade in slaves was no longer viewed as vital to its national interests. According to at least one scholar, a quarter of the ships in Liverpool in 1792 were probably engaged in the African trade. The city had five-eighths of the African trade of Britain and three-sevenths of the European slave trade (Thomas 1997: 515).

A similar situation existed with regard to the Dutch. During most of the 17th and 18th centuries, they were major participants in the Atlantic Ocean and Indian Ocean slave trade. Even for brief periods during the 17th century, they dominated the Atlantic slave trade. As early as 1721 some Africans even began serving in the Dutch army as kettledrummers under the Swiss mercenary from Neuchâtel named Pierre Frédéric de Meuron (Debrunner 1979: 127). The principal reason that the Dutch were prepared to outlaw slavetrading in 1814 was because it was no longer viewed as vital to their national interests (Vink 2004: 1-2). As these examples illustrate, attitudes toward slavetrading, slavery, and the abolition of these practices should not simply be viewed from a moralistic perspective. In 1815, Spain for geopolitical rather than moral reasons merely restricted its slave traders to the area south of the equator, and Portugal did the same thing a couple of years later.

During the Napoleonic Wars, the so-called War of the Third Coalition accelerated the dissolution of the Holy Roman Empire under the domination of German-speaking peoples. In July 1806, sixteen princes in what is now southern and central Germany formed the Confederation of the Rhine. On August 1, under pressure from Napoleon, they also declared their withdrawal from the Holy Roman Empire. Five days later, Emperor Franz II abdicated the German Imperial throne. This humiliation, for which many Germans blamed the French, would play a major role in awakening German nationalism at a time that a rising wave of pseudo-scientific racism across Europe was about to become a factor in some important geopolitical realignments between Europeans and those they tended to consider "others."

By 1815, the Napoleonic Wars had ended, and King Louis XVIII had succeeded Napoleon Bonaparte. It was in keeping with these changes that, at the end of the short dynasty of the three Bonapartist kings in the Kingdom of Sicily in 1815, Muslims slaves in Sicily were emancipated. As for France, by 1815 there was a reopening of sea commerce that permitted more traffic between metropolitan France and its colonies with the result that increasing numbers of planters came to France accompanied by their slaves (McCloy 1961: 62).

Chapter Three

Social Thought, Milieu, and Survival

1760s to 1815

This chapter, like the previous one, focuses on the period roughly from the end of the Seven Years War in 1763 though the Congress of Vienna in 1815 but from somewhat different perspectives. With less emphasis on geopolitics, the primary focus of the first part of this chapter is on the prevailing social thought about human diversity and the social milieu that it helped to create for people of African descent in Europe. It ends by focusing on the lives of some specific people within this category in order to illustrate through vignettes and analysis some of the challenges and complexities that surrounded their lives.

Throughout this period, racism continued morphing into several varieties. In some parts of Europe as well as the Ottoman Empire including parts of Africa under its influence, racism with a strong religious component remained important. Racism as manifested in "Orientalism" in Europe also took on great importance (Said 1994). Both of these varieties of racism were important in how Europeans reacted to what they were inclined to view as "the Eastern Question," which is to say what would happen to outlying parts of the Ottoman Empire which they viewed as in decline. Contributing also to racism, the Enlightenment (which German speakers called the *Aufklärung*, French speakers *les Lumières*, Spanish speakers *la Ilustración*, and Italian speakers *l'Illuminismo*) had left increasing numbers of Europeans believing that a hierarchy of superiority based on physical features or places of origin was somehow logical or rational. This part of the Enlightenment's legacy that is racist has much too seldom been openly acknowledged and denounced. To some extent, as a consequence, the Enlightenment sometimes worked to the detriment of people of African descent and as well as to the detriment of masses of Europeans vis-à-vis each other as well.

After all, there exists much variety among Europeans in color, head shapes, heights, facial features, places of birth, and so on, which eventually could be exploited through elaborations of physical and origin-based racism associated with Enlightenment thinking to the detriment or advantage of perceived or imagined sub-groupings.

People of African descent, wherever they were in Europe, were surrounded by a large sea of indigenous Europeans and continually being assimilated to a much greater degree than is often realized or acknowledged. This was occurring in Europe to a much greater degree than in overseas colonies under European domination. It was precisely because of greater openness and social fluidity in Europe, coupled with more humane conditions as compared to conditions in overseas European colonies, that many people of African descent wished to relocate from the colonies to what many of them came to think of as their mother continent although Europe was hardly free of racism. By contrast, it was exceedingly rare for people of African descent to voluntarily relocate in the reverse direction from the so-called metropolitan countries, which were located in Europe, to the various European-dominated colonies, which were in most cases located overseas. Because in Europe, the lives and experiences of people with ties to Africa differed considerably from one place or sociocultural setting to another, moreover, Africans in Europe were to some extent in continuous circulation across the continent. This was part of what it meant to become assimilated and to behave as did other Europeans around them.

Already in 1676 when Sir William Petty, a founder of the Royal Society in England, had written his essay "The Scale of Creatures" the African presence in Europe was quite substantial. In this essay Petty suggested a hierarchy of races that opposed Europeans and Africans to each other in terms of physical and intellectual characteristics. Shortly thereafter in 1684, François Bernier authored a book in French with a title that translates as *New Division of the Earth by the Different Species or Races That Inhabit It*. In contrast with previous writers apart from Petty, Bernier characterized all the world's people as divided into a very small number of races based on a fairly small number of surface physical features such as complexion, facial contour, cranial profiles, and certain hair characteristics. In this way, he introduced into mainstream European literature in quite a substantive way a new concept of race (Stuurman 2000: 1-21).

Although there was hardly anything that was consistent or scientific about the four-race typology presented in the book by Bernier, it was a seminal and largely original work of the Enlightenment. It has sometimes been suggested that the Enlightenment begins with the seminal works of John Locke and Sir Isaac Newton, proceeds through the incursions of idealistic philosophers, and ends in an outpouring of romanticism (Smith 1962: 21). To be sure, it did not take place throughout Europe, it did not manifest itself in exactly the same ways, and it did not last everywhere for the same amount of time. In at least some areas of Europe, however, it extended at least from around the time that Bernier was authoring his book until the late 1700s. In fact, some students of the attitudes associated with the movement see it as extending to around the beginning of the Napoleonic Wars in 1804. As a consequence, social thought about human variation as associated with the Enlightenment is of especial relevance to the period being discussed in this chapter.

Wherever the Enlightenment had a major impact, social philosophers tended to reflect the view that Europe was progressing beyond the more or less general simplicity that in the remote past had characterized the social life of all the world's peoples in general. This way of thinking was destined to impact the attitudes of many Europeans concerning how they thought of themselves within their own societal configurations as well as vis-à-vis peoples at home and abroad whom they did not consider to be of European descent. Within this development, scholarly people in numerous European countries became fascinated by schemes that seemed to rely on rationality as a means of establishing authoritative systems of aesthetics, ethics, and logic. In this context, the book by Bernier made an important impact. It was only a very short time after the publication of Bernier's book that numerous other creative observers who considered themselves to be of European descent began to produce alternative racial typologies, suggesting a variety of different races based on an array of contrasting criteria.

Much of the social thought that would characterize Europe in the second half of the 18th century and early decades of the 19th paved the way for a social climate of pseudo-scientific racism. This social climate existed alongside an unprecedented European preoccupation with colonial conquest on a global scale. In fact, racism of some kind was *de rigueur* among the vast majority of Enlightenment social philosophers. Although much social thought of the period was anti-elitist in some respects, numerous scholars believing that they were relying on logic and pure reason led multitudes of Europeans into thinking about race in new ways that, while in most cases merely figments of their imaginations, presumed the inherent perfection and superiority of Europeans vis-à-vis other peoples in the world.

In keeping with much of this thinking that lacked any factual basis through objective reliance on empiricism, Enlightenment scholars increasingly projected images of Africans and Europeans as different types of people. European social thought during the period between the end the Seven Years' War in 1763 and the Congress of Vienna in 1815 was one when many European scholars and officials were obsessed with understanding human variation, with rationalizing either slavery or its abolition, and with reconciling such rationalizations with an array of religious beliefs that lay beyond the domain of science. Toward these ends, they produced some very remarkable theories. These theories were impacted by the fact that Europeans were increasingly in contact with people they considered "others" who lived outside of Europe as Europe stood ready to extend its colonial thrust around the world, including deep into Africa.

At the same time, there was a considerable African presence in Europe. Hence the period under discussion in his chapter is the end of the so-called Enlightenment as well as that period from around 1804 to 1815 that is associated with the Napoleonic Wars. European social thought during this time was a major factor contributing to the social climate to which people deemed to be of African ancestry had to adapt their daily lives. While the first half of this chapter focuses on how social thought and social climate were developing at this time, the second half focuses on how the prevailing social climate shaped the lives of people in Europe considered to be African or of African descent as they attempted to make the adaptations requisite to their survival.

Among the theories that emerged were some about how Europeans were thinking about the world, how they were thinking of the various types of humanity they believed to inhabit it, and how they believed these various types of people were related to each other and should interact with each other. Some of these theories tended to be open, objective, and largely based on empirical inquiry within the context of what their proponents could know about the world at that time. More often, however, these theories were little more than fanciful and prejudicial attributions of self-importance to Europeans at the expense of others, and most especially of Africans. Hence they set the stage for a sweeping Western commitment to pseudo-scientific racism that would follow.

Much of this pseudo-scientific racism has never been fully confronted and repudiated in the West. Typical of this approach is Berlin's Museum of German History where, as recently as 2008, items in its collection associated with Enlightenment thought were presented under the general label "Worlds of the Mind," with no critical comment appended. Similarly in textbooks on philosophy and social theory in use in many parts of the world, many fallacious and racist theories set forth by European scholars in this period and eventually disseminated globally are simply ignored in a conspiracy of silence while their originators continue to be praised as giants of reason and logic because they contributed to so-called Enlightenment thought. Conditions of life for people of African descent in Europe in the late 1700s and early 1800s were made extremely challenging in large measure because of the various social milieus that Enlightenment social thought played a major role in shaping.

Adding to the situation in Europe that was so interesting and challenging for people of African descent was the fact that this was a period during which Europeans were beginning to consider themselves especially enlightened compared to the rest of humanity. Social thought as emanating from European political, social, and intellectual elites did not fully encapsulate the prevailing social climates in Europe. Still, it helped to mold for masses of Europeans popular beliefs and attitudes about human variation, color, imperialism, and worth.

Further complicating this situation, Europeans were interacting with a greater array of peoples than ever before, due in no small measure to expanding European exploration and imperialism beyond the continent of Europe. As a result of these increasingly frequent European and non-European interactions, offspring were not infrequently produced that intensified European obsessions with notions of racial purity. Even where Europeans found it difficult to reconcile ideas that they were superior to other peoples with contrary evidence before their eyes, social thought often provided a nexus between what seemed contradictory. Numerous social philosophers of European descent set the stage for thinking about humanity in ways that were highly speculative, sometimes ethnocentric, and often racist. Although race thinking in Europe did not produce on the continent of Europe societies characterized by rigid race-based caste divisions such as existed in many colonial societies under European control, thinking about race emanating largely from Europe was changing in ways that increasingly suggested that some kinds of people were more closely related to each other than they were to others within a racial hierarchy.

Carolus Linnaeus, a famous Swedish botanist, zoologist, and taxonomist, drew on "the scholastic naturalization of Aristotle's doctrine of the Predicables of Genus, Species, Difference, Property, and Accident" and adopted "the concepts of Class, Species, and Genus from the theologians" (Montagu 1969: 3). In using these concepts as systematic tools in the first edition of his *Systema Naturae* published in 1735, Linnaeus, a brilliant scientific observer, undertook the monumental task of classifying most of the entire organic universe as he understood it. Until the 1740 version of his work, however, Linnaeus did not incorporate humans within his taxonomic system.

It was at this time that Linnaeus classified humanity as divided into four so-called races corresponding largely with continental landmasses: *Americanus, Asiaticus, Africanus,* and *Europaeus.* In addition to associating his races with different places and with different colors, beginning with the 10th edition of his work, he also attributed to them some contrasting character or behavioral traits (e.g., alleging that Africans were relaxed and negligent while Europeans were gentle and inventive). That within the species that he labeled *Homo sapiens* (meaning, "the wise man") his most favorable view of people was reserved for people he deemed to be European was likely more ethnocentric than racist.

Unlike Linnaeus, David Hume, a philosopher, historian, and economist held in high esteem as a giant of the Scottish Enlightenment, cannot be given the benefit of doubt with regard to his racism, however. Showing an immense lack of respect for people he considered to be of African origin, Hume in a footnote to his essay "Of National Characters" that he authored in 1748 set forth his views quite explicitly. "I am apt to suspect the negroes and in general all the other species of men (for there are four or five different kinds) to be naturally inferior to the whites. There never was a civilized nation of any other complexion than white, nor even any individual eminent either in action or speculation." In the same footnote, Hume further claimed that even the most accomplished "negroe" is "admired for slender accomplishments, like a parrot who speaks a few words plainly."

An irony of social thought in Europe at this time is that even as rhetorical professions showing concern for the abolition of slavery were reaching a crescendo, a strong basis for pseudo-scientific racism was being laid. Further adding to this irony, increasing numbers of people of European descent were embracing revolutionary ideologies predicated on rhetoric about human rights, social contracts, and the inalienability of certain preordained universal rights and freedoms. This impacted in complicated and contradictory ways how Europeans interacted with people of African heritage living among them.

Contributing to this complexity at one level was a long legacy of ancient relationships of Europeans with Africans nearby in which social and political statuses were considered more central than presumed physical differences and similarities. Adding to this complexity at a second level were relationships among Europeans with Africans since the 16th century where a number of European peoples were becoming heavily involved in transporting multitudes of people from Africa to overseas European colonies in ways that factored into their subordination, abuse, and exploitation for the profit of Europeans. Contributing to this complexity in relationships of Europeans with Africans by the second half of the 18th century at still a third level was exploration that was being transformed in stages from benign inquisitiveness to thirst after resources to domination and imperialism justified through racism.

This transformation led Europeans from mere exploration of Africa to its colonization rationalized by theories predicated in loose and contradictory ways on Christian evangelization, on ethnocentrism, and on presumptions of multidimensional European superiority in some primal and global sense. As this European-driven transition from exploration to colonization progressively extended deeper into Africa, it contributed to sensational theories of physical differences that sometimes were even alleged to have a basis in religion itself. Illustrative of this was an alleged Hamitic curse that large numbers of Europeans believed rested on people of dark complexion and a Great Chain of Being that many of them believed essential to an understanding of Christian ontology and the maintenance of social order.

Some Europeans alleged that sub-Saharan Africans were allegedly descendants of Ham, one of Noah's children. They further argued, obviously without historical or scientific foundation, that as virtually no inter-breeding had taken place between "black" Africans and the rest of humanity over many millennia, their blackness was the mark of Ham. Many Europeans also relied on the notion of a Great Chain of Being to believe themselves superior to other peoples. Traceable to Plato and others in classical antiquity largely as a non-racist abstract philosophical concept, the notion of a Great Chain of Being had by the late 18th century (Pandian 1995; 103-116) become conflated with ethnocentrism and "colorism" in ways that eventually lent support to the emergence of pseudo-scientific racism (Woodard 1999: 1-29).

The evolutionism of the 1700s, with its emphasis on a "state of nature" and a belief in man's perfection through enlightenment, focused attention on the degree to which people perceived as belonging to different branches of humanity had progressed toward the utopia of reason. Against this background, numerous folk varieties of racism, including some that were scholarly, compounded each other in ways that allowed some people to account for human conditions, including that of slavery, vis-à-vis cultural and biological variation. With respect to the nurture-nature controversy, until late in the 1700s radical environmentalism, associated with the former, tended to be a more dominant perspective than blatant pseudo-scientific racism, associated with the latter (Harris 1968: 82-83).

Georges-Louis Leclerc, comte de Buffon, a French naturalist, was a pioneer in introducing race as a concept with quasi-biologic referents. He did this in his *Histoire naturelle, générale et particulière* (i.e., Natural History), the first volumes of which appeared in 1749. In the volume *The Varieties of the Human Species*, Buffon discussed humanity as divided into six major groups of people. He continued publishing various volumes of this series until 1804 and for the most part attributed the variation within humans to contrasting environmental conditions. In his *Histoire Naturelle*, Buffon even used an environmental explanation for why, in his view, French people who were poor tended to be more "ugly and ill made" than other Frenchmen. Of especial relevance to our present discussion, he stated in his fourth volume that men of Guinea (by which he meant sub-Saharan Africa) were idle and inactive, lacking any sense of imagination or innovation, and that they died young due to exhaustion caused by engaging in sex too frequently.

Europeans were hardly of a single opinion on such matters. Horace Walpole of Britain, for example, went on record from 1755 as being critical of slavery. When Walpole published his "Account of the Giants Lately Discovered" in 1766, he even mocked the slave trade (Thomas 1997: 469, 471). This was at a time when few of his contemporaries seemed moved by the abuse and racism involved in slavery's institutionalization.

Once the president of the *parlement* of Bordeaux, Charles-Louis de Secondat, baron de la Brède et de Montesquieu, published one of the most widely honored volumes of the Enlightenment in 1748, his *L'Esprit des lois* (meaning The Spirit of the Laws). In this work, he expressed his firm belief that climate was determinant of manners and that in the climates of the north people have fewer vices than in the climates of the south. Although he recognized slavery as against nature, and asserted that it was bad both for masters and slaves, he justified it for its economic value. He also set forth the view that one could not be expected to work without being afraid of punishment. Among the Scottish intellectuals who took up the matter of slavery was George Wallace, a lawyer who published his *System of the Principles of the Laws of Scotland* in 1761. Although he claimed to have been influenced by Montesquieu's *L'Esprit des lois*, Wallace reached the contrary conclusion that slavery should be abolished. More specifically, he heaped scorn on what he considered to be both African savagery and European exploitation of Africans (Haavik 2001: 134).

Voltaire (the pen name of Parisian-born François-Marie Arouet) believed in a separation of church and state and the right to fair trials, denouncing what he considered the hypocrises and injustices of France's *ancien régime*. In *Candide*, Voltaire mocked the Catholic Church for having accepted slavery. Although occasionally offering some oblique criticism of slavery, as in *Candide* in 1759 and in his *Dictionnaire philosophique* in 1764 (Haavik 2001: 130-132), Voltaire never campaigned for its abolition, however, and claimed that "Negroes are beings almost as savage and ugly as monkeys." Having grown very wealthy at a young age mostly from his investments in the enslavement of Africans no doubt helped him to rationalize this exploitation by his implication that they were subhuman and of inferior intelligence.

In "*Essai sur les moeurs*," Voltaire put it this way: "Their round eyes, their flat nose, their lips which are always thick, their differently shaped ears, the wool on their head, the measure even of their intelligence establishes between them and other species of men prodigious differences." On the same subject and in the same essay, he stated: "If their understanding is not of a different nature from ours, it is at least greatly inferior." In a collection of his personal correspondence known as *Lettres d'Annabed*, he stated, "It is a serious question among them whether [the Africans] are descended from monkeys or whether the monkeys come from them." That Voltaire was anti-Jewish is also noteworthy (Harris 1968: 27, 38, 87; Thomas 1997: 464-465).

Although Voltaire was very critical of the marriage of church and state as well as that the middle class and the masses were burdened with most of the taxes, his being critical of France's *ancien régime* was not the equivalent of empathizing broadly with all victims of social oppression who were African. Born in Geneva and a contemporary of Voltaire, Jean Jacques Rousseau insisted that the essence of slavery was its dependence on force. Both in his *Discours sur l'origine et les fondements de l'inégalité* of 1755 and in his *Du contrat social* of 1762 he condemned the institution absolutely (Thomas 1997: 466).

Rousseau was responsible for many ideas about social-contract theory and to some degree about democracy. Rousseau was not thinking primarily about Europe when he advocated direct democracy and self-reliance as a way of avoiding much societal inequality. After having raised numerous questions about absolutism, Voltaire and Rousseau by mere coincidence both died in 1778, the latter still a strong believer that human physical features as well as behavior varied in conformity with environmental experience.

In this belief, Rousseau was rather like James Burnett, Lord Monboddo, a Scottish judge, philosopher, and student of language evolution. Although a strong believer in environmental determinism, Lord Monboddo did not consider what he thought of as the various branches of humanity as equal to each other. In his *Of the Origin and Progress of Language*, which was published in 1773, he held that since the time of Tower of Babel referred to in the Bible, humanity had been divided into a number of separate species adapted to different climates. He further argued that the "black colour of negroes, thick lips, flat nose, crisped woolly hair, and rank smell" distinguished them most profoundly from all other branches of humanity (Fryer 1984: 168).

As Lord Monboddo was one of the most respected judges at Edinburgh's Court of Session, there can be little doubt that for many Europeans seeking biblical sanction for their racist beliefs his line of thinking had great appeal. While seeming to be biblically based in accepting the notion of monogenesis (i.e., a single origin for all people), it allowed for the concept of evolution while encouraging people he deemed "white" to accept themselves as representing greater perfection in their persons and in their social and cultural accomplishments than others.

In the 1760s, France for the first time began the policing of race on its territory in Europe with a special focus on Africans (Peabody 1996: 137). In 1762 France ordered the registration of all "blacks" and "mulattoes," regardless of whether they were enslaved or free. According to a circular letter dated June 30, 1763, written by the Duke of Choiseul while he was France's secretary of the navy, "a very large quantity of black slaves" resided in France. Personally disturbed by this, the duke ordered all slaves from France's Caribbean colonies out of the country. His letter also referenced the need "to put an end to the disorders that they [the slaves] have introduced in the kingdom by their communication with the whites, which has resulted [in] a mixed blood, which increases daily" (Boulle 2006: 23). When however the termination of the Seven Years' War the following year resulted in the immediate shipping of numerous people of color from mainland France to the colonies, the Duke of Choiseul rescinded his circular at around the same time that the government countermanded it (McCloy 1961: 45-46).

As reflected in France, the sensitivity that some Europeans had acquired about people living among those whose origins could even in part be traced to Africa by this time was not atypical during the latter part of the Enlightenment. Perhaps it reflected feelings of inadequacy that some Europeans felt about themselves vis-à-vis people with African associations. In any case, Africa had become an ideological construct produced through stereotyping as much as a place or a vast number of peoples associated with a particularly large landmass. Some social philosophers, government officials, and even Europeans at the bottom rungs of society needed Africa as a projection of what they considered to be the opposite of Europe. Where such mental projecting became too difficult, some conjured up Africa in the notions of a Hottentot, for example, as presented in the travelogues of William Dampier, Sir Thomas Herbert, and John Ovington (Woodard 1999: 102-103). Others used the notion of an Australian aboriginal or perhaps the notion of the Orient—in other words, whatever was convenient.

According to Said (1994: 3), "European culture gained in strength and identity by setting itself off against the Orient." Where such ideological oppositions as these were beyond reach, stereotypes of Jews, Muslims, and Roma (also known as Gypsies) were sometimes substituted to sustain Africa as a much-needed ideological construct (Mudimbe 1994) from which to distinguish themselves. In other words Africa was needed ideologically in much the same way that "blacks" were needed in certain of the graphic works of William Hogarth, a very prolific painter, engraver, satirist, and cartoonist in England who lived until 1764. By often depicting "blacks" in diminution or as servants in various attitudes of deference toward "whites," Hogarth projected the latter as superior (Woodard 1999: 113-114).

In a 1743 work by Hogarth in London's National Gallery that is called "The Toilette," one of a series of six on the theme "Marriage à la mode," this artist attacked marriages of convenience while also marginalizing people of African descent in Europe by depicting them as intrusive as well as somewhat caricatured, in this case showing the "black" servant with exaggerated lips serving a beverage to a "white" woman in the company of elegantly dressed Europeans. Adding to the impression of people of African descent as a distinct and servile minority, Hogarth also included in the lower right corner of this work a "black" page who is seated on the floor.

In 1764, the Swiss naturalist Charles Bonnet wrote of human gradations, implying that "the most perfect man" was European, whom he associated with whiteness and beauty, while the most imperfect was the African, who was dark of color with wooly hair and was most especially exemplified by "the Hottentots." It was not necessary for Bonnet to have had any direct contact with Hottentots of southern Africa for him to consider them especially filthy as compared to the Dutch (Fryer 1984: 166). That Bonnet chose these references to Hottentots was a direct result of the fact that Jan van Riebeeck in 1652, on instructions from the Dutch East India Company had established a supply station at the southern tip of Africa for Dutch ships traveling around southern Africa into the Indian Ocean basin.

Subsequently, colonists of Dutch ancestry at the southern tip of Africa became racist propagandists, and their propaganda diffused through Europe well beyond the Low Countries. By denigrating the indigenous peoples whose labor and resources they coveted, these Dutch settlers created Hottentots as mythological and stereotyped people in order to justify their mistreatment and exploitation of them. Despite the greater tendency toward facial prognathicism (i.e., forward projection of the lower face) in African than in European populations, that Bonnet described Africans as flat-faced when this is actually more likely to be characteristic of Europeans coincides with the fact that racism, though real as a social construct, exists quite apart from any careful reading of human variation that is empirical.

Immanuel Kant, a philosopher of German descent born in a part of East Prussia that is now in Russia, defined the Enlightenment in an essay ("Answering the Question: What is Enlightenment?") as an age shaped by autonomous thinking free of the dictates of external authority. Unfortunately for Kant, however, he thought of race rather rigidly as a real thing that caused people of color and Jews to be different from others. As well as being virulently anti-Jewish, Kant was a committed racist who focused on richly pigmented skin as one of the major indicators of race and assumed it to be associated with an array of behavioral characteristics that he divined as indicative of deficiency in mental capacity.

During a teaching career that spanned from 1755 to 1796, Kant lectured often on physical geography. In one of his lectures, he placed on record his belief that "humanity is at its greatest perfection in the race of the whites." Immanuel Kant wrote in 1764 that "The Negroes of Africa have received from nature no intelligence that rises above the foolish. The difference between the two [the black and white] races of man is thus a substantial one; it appears to be as great in regard to mental capacities as in color." Kant also gave expression to his racism in his *On the Different Races of Man*, published in 1775, and in his *Anthropology from a Pragmatic Point of View*, which was published in 1798.

According to Louis de Jaucourt in his 1765 article in Diderot's *Encyclopédie*, slavery was a business that violated religion, morality, natural law, and human rights. The *Encyclopédie* also stated, that in accordance with long usage that had acquired the force of law, if any slave entered France and was baptized, he was automatically supposed to be considered free (Thomas 1997: 465). In reality, France had been less than consistent in enforcing this principle. When in the late years of the regime of King Louis IX the French pirate Jean Bernard Louis Desjeans, baron de Pointis, succeeded in carrying out a major raid on Cartagena in Colombia where he was greatly assisted by slaves who surrendered their weapons in hopes of gaining their freedom, this led to a number of "black" slaves being brought to France in 1699. Despite the assistance they had rendered to Desjeans in capturing vast amounts of booty that were greatly needed in France, even after having touched French soil, the slaves were manumitted in

Europe only in those cases where their masters were paid for them (Peabody 1996: 13).

No European consensus on slavery existed at this time. In England, a pamphlet that Granville Sharp published in 1769 titled "A Representation of the Injustice and Dangerous Tendency of Tolerating Slavery in England" toward the end of the Jonathan Strong case caused certain slaves who were kidnapped or threatened with kidnapping to seek Sharp's help (Thomas 1997: 475). In the same year, Adam Ferguson, a Scottish professor of philosophy in Edinburgh, published his *Institutes of Moral Philosophy* based on his lecture notes in which he took the position that no one is born to be a slave (Thomas 1997: 465, 470; Harris 1968: 20-21, 29-30). In the same spirit, Dr. William Paley in 1785 published his *Moral Philosophy* based on lectures he had given at Cambridge, where he severely condemned the slave trade.

In contrast to such anti-slavery sentiments, Peter Camper, a surgeon, obstetrician authority on medical jurisprudence, graphic artist, and sculptor in the Dutch Republic claimed to find "a striking resemblance between the race of Monkies and of Blacks" and claimed that this conclusion on his part was based on facial and skull measurements that he had taken (Fryer 1984: 167). Although Camper did not support slavery per se, he developed within the context of physiognomy a racial hierarchy in which he claimed the superiority of the European form while implying that it was associated with superior cranial capacity and intelligence.

The fact that Camper was a very talented artist caused his racism to influence attitudes among many European artists as they took to producing caricatured renditions of "blacks" and idealized renditions of "whites." Peter Camper's *Works on the Connexion Between the Science of Anatomy and the Arts of Drawing, Painting, and Statuary* was first published in Amsterdam in 1791 and translated into English in 1794. Sometimes credited to Camper is the following assertion: "If I make the facial line lean forward, I have an antique head; if backward, the head of a Negro. If I still more incline it, I have the head of an ape; and if more still, that of a dog, and than that of an idiot."

To better appreciate how Camper contributed to an intellectual legacy and social climate in Europe and beyond that denigrated and misrepresented human connections and relationships among human beings, one need only refer to such works as Stephen Jay Gould's *The Mismeasure of Man* (1996) and David Bindman's *Ape to Apollo: Aesthetics and the Idea of Race in the Eighteenth Century* (2002). In 1792, the English merchant John Scattergood authored *An Antidote to Popular Frenzy, Particularly to the Present Rage for the Abolition of the Slave-trade*. In this work, Scattergood considered it "madness" to admit blacks to the privileges of Europeans "and treat them as our equals" (Fryer 1984: 164).

Johann Friedrich Blumenbach, a German greatly influenced by Buffon, was much interested in the comparative study of skulls. On the basis of his classification of skulls, he divided the human species into five races, one of which he classified as the Caucasian and another as the Ethiopian or "black" race. That Blumenbach coined the term *Caucasian* to refer to people he deemed to be "white" resulted from a convergence of three of his beliefs, none of which was scientific.

The first of these beliefs, based loosely on an interpretation of a major flood as presented in the Bible, was that Noah's ark, on which all life had been rescued, eventually landed near Mount Ararak near the Caucasus Mountains. The second was his belief that fair-complexioned women from this area survived as the embodiment and the essence of human beauty. The third was his belief that the skulls he studied of people living near the Caucasus Mountains were more beautiful than the skulls of peoples belonging to darker races. In this way, he chose as his label for his "white" race (i.e., those to whom he arbitrarily attributed cranial perfection) the term *Caucasian* (Harris 1968: 83-84).

Blumenbach managed ideologically to reconcile his belief in monogenesis with a belief in "white" supremacy largely through arguing that members of more richly pigmented branches of humanity had become less perfect as a consequence of devolution or degeneration (Harris 1968: 83-84). In classifying human beings into first four, and later five, varieties that he considered to be races, one irony lay in the fact that some populations living close to the Causasus Mountians are often relatively dark in complexion by European standards.

In Blumenbach's *De generis humani varietate nativa*, published in 1770 (Blumenbach 1969), he argued that among the most important factors accounting for some people's "degeneration" from superior Caucasoid stock were climate, diet, mode of life, hybridization, and disease. Rather late in the course of his life, Blumenbach began to believe that the variation that he classified as within a single race could be as great as that among his so-called races. That he eventually began to turn away from his earlier idea that members of what he called the Ethiopian race were somehow inferior to what he viewed as other races was perhaps the result of his becoming a friend by correspondence of Ignatius Sancho (see page 106), coupled with his eventual acquisition of a library of books by authors of African descent (Harris 1968: 85; Fryer 1984: 167). Also contributing to this change in Blumenbach's change of view concerning people of African descent was his acquaintance with Pauline Hippolyte Buisson, a "black" midwife resident in Yverdon, Switzerland, and originally from Saint-Domingue, whom Blumenbach met when he visited the Treytorrens brothers there in their new "residence d'Entremont," and whom Blumenbach found extraordinarily beautiful and engaging. Despite Blumenbach's fascination with Buisson, when she later gave birth to her "mulatto" out-of-wedlock son named Samuel Hippolyte Buisson, Samuel encountered some social barriers in his native Switzerland (Debrunner 1979: 142-145).

Following in the footsteps of Blumenbach, numerous other scholars began to use *Caucasian* (and in some cases *Caucasoid*, which though derivative is equally misleading from a scientific perspective) to refer rather broadly to people they deemed to be "white" (Palter 1996: 378-379, 392-394; Bernal 1987: 219-222). When in 1770 France's Abbé Raynal prepared to publish a book that argued that slavery was contrary to nature and thus wrong, his argument engendered so much hostility in France that the book had to be published outside the country in Amsterdam. Even the clergy of Bordeaux, which remained a major slave-trading port, was so opposed to its message that it demanded the book be prohibited as an outrage to religion. The *parlement* of Paris also ordered it burned by the public executioner. Despite the existence of such opposing voices in France, Abbé Raynal (and his collaborators, who included Denis Diderot) argued that slavery was contrary to nature and universally wrong in his work *Histoire philosophique et politique . . . des deux Indes.* Somewhat oddly, however, Abbé Raynal also argued for making slavery more humane (Thomas 1997: 483-484).

That Abbé Raynal's main focus was on slavery in the colonies does not alter the fact that this was a period when Frenchmen remained somewhat confused or at odds with themselves about bondage, slavery, and race even as they were developing attitudes toward peoples they conceptualized as racial "others." Although racism was thriving in the colonies of France in the late 1700s, abolition, which had been a *cause célèbre* for some of the oppressed in various French colonies for some time, began to receive support in Europe despite its importance to the shaky state of the French economy. Still, this made most of the French in Europe hesitant to alter the status quo. When King Louis XVI succeeded Louis XV in 1774, there remained a multiplicity of French attitudes concerning race.

Meanwhile in England Charles Johnstone, the novelist, declared in his book *The Pilgrim* in 1775 that if English people produced children with Jews or "blacks" their offspring would no longer "have reason to value themselves on their beauty, wit, or virtue" (Fryer 1984: 161). Greatly angered and dismayed that some people considered white and others considered black dared to marry each other, numerous other racists who were English or of English descent during the 1770s and 1780s also railed against this practice, which they believed led to miscegenation or what some simply harangued against as "race mixing." As many of these racists used their pens to denigrate the people involved and to spread malicious and unscientific falsehoods about their progeny, this contributed to the hysteria that Europeans had to be portrayed as distinct from Africans at all cost.

Numerous were the European writers from around this time who conjured up baseless ideas having to do with the human condition, including the allegation that "blacks" had an especially close kinship to apes and monkeys. This allegation was likely designed both to discourage mating between Europeans and people deemed to bare a taint from Africa and to justify their exploitation whether as slaves or in other ways. Some people of European ancestry even alleged that a single ancestor who could be traced back to Africa among a multitude of others was sufficient to transmit the taint by interfering with alleged racial purity from which emanated racial superiority. Although this whole way of thinking was without any basis in science, it was an important part of the legacy of the European Enlightenment.

While some of these people claimed such progeny were automatically tainted, others claimed an inability to imagine them as human beings in any normal sense. Among those holding such views was James Tobin, a British planter on the Caribbean island of Nevis. It is of some importance that he also happened to be opposed to the abolition of slavery. Another person with similar views was Philip Thicknesse, from the English-controlled colony of Georgia in North America. In his book *A Year's Journey through France and Part of Spain*, Thicknesse devoted an entire chapter to the denigration of people he considered black (Fryer 1984: 161-162).

Conflicting social theories espoused by people of European descent around this time contributed to variety and confusion in the thinking of scholars about evolution and human variation. As the race construct became more closely associated with human variation as perceived in terms of physical characteristics in the second half of the 18th century a division developed between evolutionists who believed in monogenesis or one human origin, on the one hand, and those who believed in polygenesis or several human origins, on the other. As pointed out by Harris (1968: 89), some of the most rabid defenders of slavery happened also to have been doctrinal polygenists, including Charles White, a Manchester physician, and Edward Long.

Edward Long, an admirer of Buffon, though born in Cornwall was a member of an English planter family that had grown rich from sugar production by means of slaveholding in Jamaica. As a young adult, he decided to live there for several years. Five years after his sojourn in Jamaica ended, Long returned to England in 1764 feeling compelled to describe not only Jamaica from his parochial and prejudiced perspective but also people of African descent in general. What he published under the title of *History of Jamaica* in 1774 was a racist diatribe against all people whom he deemed to be black. This notwithstanding, this work was for many years warmly received in Europe as a serious product of Enlightenment scholarship.

Breaking ranks with the majority of his European contemporaries who still believed that all human beings had a single origin, Long argued that "white" people of European and "black" people of African ancestry belonged to different species. Ostensibly drawing upon the notion of the great chain of being as presented in the work of the French natural historian Buffon, he further revealed his commitment to pseudo-scientific racism by claiming that people of African descent, whether in Jamaica or elsewhere, were essentially subhuman, morally depraved, lazy, mentally deficient, and lacking in any admirable qualities. He was extraordinarily hostile to sexual relations between what he considered to be blacks and whites. As he put it in his *History of Jamaica*, "the lower class of women in *England* are remarkably found of the blacks, for reasons too brutal to mention; they would connect themselves with horses and asses if the laws permitted them." Without any pretense that he had specialized training in anatomy or paleontology, the extraordinarily insecure and racist Edward Long even claimed that "black" people were in an intermediate position between humans and apes. More specifically, he claimed that they were more closely related to orangutans than to "whites" (Harris 1968: 89; Fryer 1984: 70-71, 74, 134-135, 157-160).

After Thomas Jefferson returned home from the Continental Congress to Virginia where he was elected to the new House of Delegates, he supported a bill that would have abolished slavery in that rebelling British colony on a limited basis. Though Jefferson obviously felt some guilt about profiting from slavery, such guilt never prevented him from equivocating about slavery or from personally profiting from this system. While the governor of Virginia from 1779 to 1781, the erudite and scholarly Jefferson authored his only book, *Notes on the State of Virginia*, a work largely written to refute ideas of Buffon that animals, vegetation, and even humankind degenerated on the American continent due to the climate. Primarily written in 1781 and privately published in 1784, Jefferson used his book to come to the defense of the Amerindians essentially as a "noble savage" while at the same time setting forth many of his racist beliefs with respect to people of African descent. Among these latter were that "blacks" required less sleep than "whites" and that the orangutan preferred females who were "black" to females of their own species. In this book, Jefferson also placed on record his belief that "blacks" were inferior to "whites" in reason and that "blacks" had "a very strong and disagreeable odor."

Perhaps Jefferson adopted this last-mentioned belief from Oliver Goldsmith, the Anglo-Irish literary giant who, despite having studied theology at Trinity College in Dublin, was on record some three decades earlier as describing the smell of "black" people as "insupportable." Quite apart from Goldsmith's racism, his lifestyle was sufficiently dissolute that Horace Walpole gave him the much quoted epithet of "inspired idiot." Outstanding by its omission from Jefferson's *Notes on the State of Virginia* was any allusion to his own presumed odor after a hard day's work in a field or to his own odor after his various intimacies with his enslaved concubine. Although Thomas Jefferson clearly had more nuanced views about slavery than did Bryan Edwards, he freed few of his slaves, including not even Sally Hemings, the "mulatto" half-sister of his late wife with whom he apparently fathered one or more offspring.

Obviously, Jefferson was a conflicted and paradoxical man living in an age of many complexities and contradictions as concerned racism. Thomas Jefferson and Bryan Edwards, both born in 1743, helped to fan the flames of pseudo-scientific racism in the late 18th century and in so doing contributed to a social and political milieu in which Europeans not infrequently reacted to people of African descent living among them in condescending and hostile ways. Though Edwards was English-born in Westbury, Wiltshire and Jefferson was born in the British colony of Virginia, both had connections to wealth in European colonial settings derived from the exploitation of slave labor. Both eventually began to make a name for themselves as politicians in colonial assemblies, Edwards in the assembly of Jamaica and Jefferson in the Virginian House of Burgess. While the lives of these two contemporaries born as British subjects of King George II show parallels, vis-à-vis people of African descent, they also show differences.

In 1769 while a member of the House of Burgess, Jefferson, though a slave-holder, proposed the abolition of slavery. Except between 1785 and 1789 when he was American minister to France, during which time his teen-aged enslaved sister-in-law and mistress Sally Hemings resided in Europe with him, Jefferson was resident in North America. By contrast, Edwards spent his life in England except from 1759 to around 1775 and from 1787 to 1792, when he was in Jamaica. In 1793 while Jefferson was Secretary of State of the United States some ten thousand slave-owning planters from Saint-Domingue (now Haiti) entered his country through the port of Norfolk, Virginia, after making a decision that they would rather continue their slaveholding in the United States than to continue living under French jurisdiction where slaves had begrudgingly been emancipated. Although Jefferson did not recommend that public funds be used to assist them, he left no doubt about where his sympathies lay. In a letter that he wrote on July 14 to Senator James Monroe about this development, Jefferson deplored the fate of the "white" refugees, noting in documentation in the Library of Congress Manuscript Division that "The situation of the St. Domingo fugitives (aristocrats as they are) calls aloud for pity & charity. Never was so deep a tragedy presented to the feelings of man."

After 1800, when Jefferson was elected President of the United States, he urged Congress to consider outlawing the importation of additional slaves into the country. However, he was motivated less by humanitarian concerns for the slaves than by his wish to put economic pressure on British shipping, which was already suffering from an economic slump in the West Indies. He was also motivated by his strong feelings that the United States already had too many "blacks." Already a decade before this time, the first national census in the United States, that of 1790, had classified one-fifth of all residents in the United States as of appreciable African ancestry. In contrast to President John Adams who preceded him as president, and who was more sincere in his abolitionist sentiments, Jefferson was hostile to what had been Saint-Domingue after it emerged as the independent country of Haiti under General Jean-Jacques Dessalines. It would appear that this was at least in part because of Jefferson's belief that the example of a predominantly "black" Haiti that was independent set a bad example for African-Americans in the United States, many of whom remained entrapped in slavery.

In any case, a twenty-year limitation contained in the U.S. Constitution for limiting the importation of slaves into the country was due to run its course in 1807. On the initiative of Jefferson, the United States Congress enacted legislation whereby effective from January 1 of 1808 it would be illegal to import any "negro, mulatto, or person of colour, as a slave." Although this legislation provided for a schedule of punishments for violators, it provided no machinery for serious enforcement and was breeched with considerable frequency. Also, it neither outlawed the domestic slave trade within the United States nor provided for the abolition of slavery itself.

While it is difficult to determine whether Edwards or Jefferson was more rigid in his belief that "whites" were innately superior to "blacks," Jefferson's racism was more contradictory and more nuanced. Outliving Edwards by twenty-three years, Jefferson managed to reconcile his racism with occasionally offering support to abolition, at least as a theoretical concept. Still, both men were duplicitous in that they had no problem with exploiting and denigrating the same "blacks" from whom they profited. Bryan Edwards, for example, founded a bank at Southampton and he was secretary of the Association for Promoting the Discovery of the Interior Parts of Africa. It was this bank which in 1795 first dispatched the Scotsman Mungo Park to the interior of western Africa in hopes of learning more about the River Niger and gathering information about the riches of the area. In the same year that Park returned from this trip, Edwards, after several earlier attempts that had proved fruitless, was elected to the British parliament. Until his death in 1800, Edwards spent his life as an implacable foe of abolition, even claiming in his *The History, Civil and Commercial, of The British Colonies in the West Indies* that "black" people were possessed of a "cowardly, thievish, and sullen disposition" and of a "strong and fetid odor."

Thomas Jefferson, a scholar in numerous disciplines ranging from architecture, natural history, and botany to languages, philosophy, and paleontology, was also founder of the University of Virginia. This, coupled with his prominence as a diplomat and statesman on both sides of the Atlantic, facilitated the circulation of his racist views to a much larger audience than that familiar with the views of Bryan Edwards. In 1795, for example, Charles White, an influential English physician in a lecture at the Literary and Philosophical Society of Manchester referenced the statement by Jefferson in *Notes on the State of Virginia* to the effect that he suspected that "the blacks . . . are inferior to the whites in the endowments of both body and mind." With the publication of this lecture by White in 1799 under the title of *Account of the Regular Gradation in Man*, pseudo-scientific racism became more firmly embedded into the prevailing social climate of the times (Fryer 1984: 169).

In this climate often characterized by contempt for people associated with Africa, many Europeans fantasized that lighter complexions represented racial purity and superiority in ways that made most of them distinct from Africans. Many also set about distorting history in ways that sought to camouflage or deny historic human connections with Africans. Numerous were the southern Europeans in particular who felt great pressure to prove that they were "true" Europeans by distinguishing themselves from Africans. Many attempted to do this in ways that relied heavily on myth and distortion.

In Malta (a European country that is located further south then some parts of northwestern Africa) where the national language—being Semitic—is linguistically classified as Afro-Asiatic, many Maltese rushed to find an explanation for how they had acquired their language that would seem to clearly distinguish them from nearby Arab-speakers in Africa. Arab speakers dominated the Maltese Islands for over six centuries beginning around 870. The Maltese language is grammatically and phonologically much more similar to Arabic as spoken in nearby Africa than to any other. It is only in the narrowest sense of titular feudal ownership that a claim may be made that Malta's Muslim Period of cultural development lasted but 220 years. Of greater cultural significance, the demographic and economic dominance of Muslims continued for at least another century and a half. Even after this time, forced conversions to Christianity undoubtedly permitted many former Muslims to remain permanently in Malta (Goodwin 2002: 31).

Despite these facts, a virtual guilt obsession driven by a need to avoid racial taint often attributed to Africa led many Maltese over a long period of time to deny close connections to Africa and to insist that the Maltese language evolved from Phoenician rather than Arabic (Aquilina 1970: 45). Another defensive reaction was to insist against unimpeachable historical evidence to the contrary

that when Count Roger and his son Roger II extended their authority over southern parts of the Italian peninsula, Sicily, and Malta in the 12th century all Muslims had been expelled at least from Malta. In reality, these Norman rulers neither expelled all Muslims from southern Italy nor from Malta. They did not even
restore a Catholic bishopric in Malta (Luttrell 1975: 33).

Further determined to deny any close relationships with nearby Africans,
Gian Francesco Abela, a patrician Maltese clergyman who eventually became
vice-chancellor of the Order of St. John in Malta intentionally distorted Maltese
history in an effort to portray Malta as innately European and Christian by
deemphasizing periods during which Malta had especially strong links with Islam and nearby Africa. In an 18th-century effort to strengthen the case for Abela's distortions and misinterpretations, a Maltese priest named Giuseppe Vella
even generated forged Arabic documents. Other prominent Maltese subsequently contributed to popular folklore and legends that held that Muslims of African
origin had never resided in Malta in large numbers. One person who perpetrated
such historical myths was a priest named Domenico Magri. As for southern Italy
most of whose Muslims presumably had been from nearby Africa, most of them
were never expelled from Europe. On the contrary, after Normans came to power there, many of them remained in Sicily while others eventually ended up living in and around Lucerna as well as in other parts of Italy (Luttrell 1975: 1-3, 9;
Luttrell 1977: 105; Smith 1998: 51-52; Goodwin 2002: 23-24, 86, 93, 94).

Consequences of racist theorizing in Europe also had an impact in late 18th-
century Portugal, another country of southern Europe with ancient connections
to Africa. In addition to officially banning slavery from its metropolitan territory
in 1773, Portugal during the same year banned the entry of people from its colony of Brazil whose skins were richly pigmented, undoubtedly hoping this policy
would position the country beyond racist reproach (Thomas 1997: 485).

Much social thought being disseminated among people who considered
themselves Europeans by this time conflated Africa with imperfection, and in
order to avoid the taint of such imperfection a social climate prevailed where
common heritage among Europeans and "others" increasingly denied, deempha-
sized, or distorted, often on the basis of alleged differences of race. So obsessive
did many Europeans become about the question of origin that preoccupation
with race took precedence over the fact that biology in no absolute sense was
ever the basis of any type of absolute differentiation between Europeans and
Africans. In this process, myths of racial purity were born despite known facts to
the contrary and became central in how many Europeans thought of themselves
and how they managed their interactions with people they considered "others."

Neither *African* nor *European* is a biological term. Even while many European social theorists were beginning to emphasize alleged differences between
Europeans and Africans, no pan-European identity existed with fixed boundaries
of inclusion and exclusion that was universally recognized. Rather *European*
was the conceptual antithesis of what was presumed to be not European. European had in common with all terms deemed to refer to large and multi-ethnic
groupings of people the attribute that its boundaries were situational and often
shifted. Despite the fact that people of a great range of colors and appearances

had been present in Europe since antiquity, there increasingly developed a climate of quasi-exclusion toward those with dark complexion and certain other features that were associated with the taint of presumed racial inferiority, but nowhere to the same degree as in those colonial settings where the economies relied on race-based system of exploitation. As people living in Europe hastened to avoid racial taint, however, it was not uncommon for certain Europeans to distort their personal, group, and national histories in the hope of diverting attention away from any intimate associations with people deemed to be *African*.

Such changes in attitudes and behaviors set the stage for many Europeans and others to begin incorrectly assume that Africans had the same relationship to slavery in Europe as was more characteristic of the New World. The fact that Ibn Khaldun from the area that is now Tunisia made disparaging remarks about Africans of dark coloring in the 14th century as did also Al-Abshibi, an Egyptian, a century later, demonstrated that colorism does not have its genesis solely in European culture. Still, colorism likely reached its apex under the influence of Europeans, and Europeans were especially important as agents facilitating its diffusion around the world at least from the Age of Global Exploration in which they were major pioneers. In contrast to the situation that prevailed in the New World, the majority of the people in bondage in Europe as slaves and serfs were always native Europeans.

Neither slavery nor any other type of bondage in Europe or northern Africa provided for an absolute line of demarcation between Africans and Europeans nor between different peoples based exclusively on color. In contrast to the New World, people held in various forms of bondage in Europe and in large parts of Africa were often war captives or captives held for political or other cultural reasons, including religious differences. Captives of competing religious-based empires like those controlled by Muslim Ottoman Turks and Catholic Austro-Hungarians, for example, often fell into this category. Hence, in the Old World, differences between slaves and non-slaves were until recent centuries conceptualized in political and religious ways as often as in physical ways, although some exceptions likely existed. How various people conceptualize human diversity, in any case, is not static and therefore likely undergoes change over time as we are continually interacting with others with a variety of backgrounds and attitudes in a variety of situations.

Adding to this complexity of people of African descent in Europe, during the two and a half centuries leading up to 1780, probably at least a million Europeans were enslaved in northwestern Africa, largely as a result of having been captured by pirates or as prisoners of war (Baepler 1999; Matar 1999; Davis 2003; Vitkus 2001; Busuttil 1971; Clissold 1977; Earle 1970). Though many of them were eventually ransomed and returned to Europe, this was not at all universal. Many became renegades while others simply remained permanently in Africa (Goodwin 2006: 125). The nexus between slavery and so-called race in some quasi-biological sense is often less than clear and most especially in the Old World. In addition to Europeans who were in northern Africa in bondage, many others were there of their own free will, including not only in northwestern Africa but also in northeastern Africa and occasionally elsewhere.

Loose extrapolation from conditions of slavery and race in the New World back to Europe has seldom contributed to clarity even where parallelism has seemed to exist. Human trafficking and bondage tended to operate in Europe in ways that were less race-driven than in overseas European colonies. As people in metropolitan Europe sought increasingly to separate themselves from Africans, experiential continuities constituted more of a problem to overcome in order for racism to work. Throughout the period under discussion in this chapter, however, peoples of European descent in Europe expended considerable effort on constructing and maintaining the myth of European racial purity.

Given such an investment in myth about the history of human variation and social interactions, it is quite remarkable that we know as much as we do about the African presence in Europe in the second half of the 18th century and early decades of the 19th. It is also remarkable in view of surging racism, continuing slavery, and a growing determination by European elites to build empires that would contribute to their sense of self-importance and sustain creeping industrialization by incorporating under their rule peoples they increasingly considered their inferiors. When focusing on Europe during the period under discussion, historians and other students of society often fail to take account of the fact that the looseness and overlapping of ethnic labels does not permit us even today to clearly distinguish between all Europeans and all Africans, especially as assimilation was an ongoing process both north and south of the Mediterranean Sea. Even while the Old World was the genesis for many of the racializing theories that made it possible for Europeans to rationalize exporting multitudes of African slaves across the Atlantic Ocean under horrendous conditions for inhumane labor exploitation in the New World, everyday life was quite different for Africans living in Europe than for those living in colonial settings outside of Europe.

One may reasonably infer, however, that as European consciousness of abusive slave conditions in colonial settings increased and became coupled with Enlightenment social thought that tended to denigrate people of African descent, these developments eventually added to the precariousness of life for many people with African backgrounds in Europe, including especially those who were loosely considered "black." We now turn to look at the lives of some of these people to ascertain how, in fact, they were surviving, both by bonding with each other and with European allies, across a broad spectrum.

That a number of elite Africans sent their children from Africa to Britain to be educated in the 1700s has few parallels among "black" people in the more rigidly racialized New World apart from the fact that a few prosperous "mulattoes" from the Americas and the Caribbean did occasionally study in Europe. In the mid-1700s, an African ruler from Anamabo on the Gold Coast whose name was John Corrantee entrusted a son and a friend of his son to a Liverpool ship captain who promised to transport them to England to learn European manners. Instead of keeping his promise, however, the captain transported these African nobles to Jamaica and sold them into slavery. When eventually the captain died and the ship's crew informed authorities in Jamaica what had occurred, however, Prince William Ansah Sessaracoa and his friend were freed, sent to England,

and placed in the care of the Earl of Halifax, then the very wealthy president of the Board of Trade and Plantations. While being educated in England, the two boys were introduced to King George II. According to Horace Walpole, they also became the "fashion at all the assemblies" and were even in attendance at Covent Garden at one of the many theatrical versions of Aphra Behn's "Oroonoko." Apparently in a manner befitting their high status, they were eventually returned home to the Gold Coast in 1752 (Thomas 1997: 468).

A considerable number of "black" Sierra Leoneans traveled to England to be educated. While some remained there temporarily, others remained permanently and were eventually assimilated into European society. Christopher Fryer estimates that in 1789 there were approximately 50 boys and 28 girls in Liverpool, London, Bristol, and Lancaster from the Sierra Leone region of western Africa. Other young people of African or mixed African and European ancestry also were sent to Britain to be educated by their parents or patrons from the West Indies (Gerzina 1995: 12-13). Perhaps one reason that scholars have expended relatively little effort on studying the assimilation of Africans in Europe during the period under discussion is because they too tend to be influenced by myths that suggest distinctiveness and purity for so-called white Europeans.

Certain advertisements published in English newspapers during the mid-1700s clearly document that some people of African background were being publicly traded or at least employed as servants with particular attention being given to perceived racial features. In 1756 or the year that the Seven Years' War began, the *Liverpool Advertiser* carried a request for a "Black Boy of deep black complexion . . . not above 15 nor under 12 years of age." A careful study of the wording in this advertisement suggests that some people of appreciable African descent in England at the time were not especially black in complexion. Though some Africans were bought and sold as slaves in British ports, not all the Africans in Britain at this time were perceived as "black" people, nor did all those perceived as "black" come to Europe directly from Africa. Some came from the Caribbean and the Americas while others came from elsewhere in Europe, Oceania, and from India, Arabia, and other parts of Asia.

After having been a slave for approximately fifteen years in the British colony of Jamaica, Francis Barber was transported to England by Colonel Bathurst, his owner, in 1750. After attending school briefly in Yorkshire, Barber entered the service of his master's son. In 1752, however, Barber was hired out to Dr. Samuel Johnson, following the death of Mrs. Johnson, who was 21 years her husband's senior. This was during the years that Johnson was writing *A Dictionary of the English Language*, the best-known work of this English poet, essayist, biographer, lexicographer, and critic of English who some claim is the most widely quoted writer of English apart from William Shakespeare. As this was at least a decade before Johnson was awarded a government pension and his first honorary doctorate from Trinity College, Dublin, he was still quite poor. Perhaps one reason that he was willing to reach out to a person subject to oppression was that he had been in Dublin at a time that England's infamously oppressive Penal Laws were achieving their intended effect there against the Irish Catholics by reducing them to abject poverty. This was a period when almost all

Irish Catholics remained illiterate and when over nine-tenths of all land had been seized by greedy non-Irish landowners.

Despite Johnson's considerable fame as a writer, as he was not in a particularly good financial situation he was more a tremendous intellectual influence on Francis Barber than a reliable patron in a material sense. While Johnson's tenuous financial situation perhaps helps to explain why Barber ran away to serve on the *HMS Stag* in the North Sea before returning to Johnson's service two years later in 1760, the fact that he did this illustrates both that he was not in absolute bondage and that people of African descent living in Europe during this period worked in many different capacities. So close was the friendship between Francis Barber and Samuel Johnson that after attending Bishop's Grammar School from 1767 to 1772 Barber was promoted from Johnson's butler to his secretary.

Even after Barber wed an Englishwoman with no appreciable African ancestry, the married couple resided in the home with Johnson, although racism and opposition to such marriages was widely championed. Among those who were upset by the closeness of the relationship between Johnson and Barber was Sir John Hawkins, who was Johnson's biographer. Figuring prominently in Hawkins furor, Johnson bequeathed to Barber a gold watch, guardianship over all of his literary work, and an annuity significantly greater than what Hawkins had suggested to Johnson as appropriate (Fryer 1984: 67, 69, 424-426; Woodard 1999: 73, 94).

In 1762, Ukawsaw Gronniosaw arrived at the English port of Portsmouth at age 15 in service to his master, who was a minister. Gronniosaw had been born between 1710 and 1714 into a noble Muslim family in Borno, in what is today northeastern Nigeria. Kidnapped from his homeland, Gronniosaw had been taken from the interior to the Gold Coast while still a young lad. While being transported from there to Barbados as a slave, he was converted to Christianity aboard the ship. After being transported to the area of New York City and nearby New Jersey by a Dutch captain, Ukawsaw Gronniosaw was soon thereafter shipped off to Europe. Although Gronniosaw was firm in his Christian faith long before arriving in England, so ingrained was the belief among many Europeans that all Africans were heathens that Gronniosaw was refused membership in a church until he agreed to be re-baptized, whereupon he took the name James Albert (Gronniosaw 1774: 32-38). In 1764, the year following the conclusion of the Seven Years' War, Gronniosaw was in Amsterdam relating the story of his conversion to incredulous Calvinists who insisted on writing down every word that he spoke.

Although a sea of indigenous Europeans surrounded a visible minority of African ancestry, the latter continually interacted with the former. In 1765, a modestly educated English clerk employed at the Ordnance Office at Tower Hill named Granville Sharp was on his way to visit his brother in London who was a physician when he accidentally stumbled upon a badly battered 17-year-old slave. Named Jonathan Strong, this slave, who had been imported into Britain from Barbados had been very inhumanely abused by his master and was close to death. Having been pistol-whipped and otherwise physically abused by David

Lisle, his master, Strong, who was seeking medical help, had a swollen head, was lame, and was almost blind. Lisle, moreover, had left his slave abandoned in the streets of London. After being admitted by Dr. William Sharp (the brother of Granville Sharp) into St. Bartholomew's Hospital for four months of medical treatment, Strong, though still in poor health, was sufficiently recovered such that the Sharp brothers arranged for him to obtain employment by running errands for a surgeon and apothecary as well as for him to be baptized at London's St. Leonard Shoreditch Church.

Two years later while Strong was on an errand for his employer, David Lisle happened to see him. After secretly following him to his house shortly thereafter, Lisle arranged to have Strong kidnapped by two slave-hunters. Lisle then arranged for Strong to be held in a local jail called the Poultry Compter in preparation for making a profit of £30 for Strong's resale to a planter intent on shipping him from England to Jamaica. Though a British colony, conditions for slaves were vastly more horrific in the colonies than in Britain. When Strong was already aboard the ship on which the planter intended to send him away from Europe, Granville Sharp learned of what he considered to be a great injustice about to occur and quickly began working with allies to bring a legal injunction on Strong's behalf.

This case was heard at Mansion House in September 1767 in front of Lord Mayor Sir Robert Kite, who ordered Strong released because "the lad had not stolen anything, and was not guilty of any offence, and was therefore at liberty to go away." When, despite this ruling, the planter to whom Strong had been sold attempted to seize him in the presence of the Lord Mayor, it was only through the physical intervention of the Sharp brothers that this was prevented. Still not reconciled to this turn of events, the Jamaican planter retaliated by suing the Sharps for trespass, claiming that they had deprived him of his property. In addition to the complications that this involved for the Sharps, the ruling on the original case by Sir Robert Kite had in no way emancipated slaves residing in Britain and was completely without any legal relevance to the status of slaves in overseas British colonies.

In 1765 when Granville Sharp, with like-minded allies, was focused on the case of Jonathan Strong, Olaudah Equiano (or Gustavus Vassa), despite having been many times in England, was in the West Indies laboring under very harsh conditions and hoping one day to save enough money to purchase his freedom. Against the wishes of an unhappy owner, this day finally came on July 11, 1766. Continuing to work aboard ships after obtaining his freedom, Equiano traveled widely, including to Jamaica and other islands of the Caribbean, to Central America, Turkey, Italy, Portugal, and British North America. Olaudah Equiano was even on one of the ships in the Phipps Expedition to the Arctic that in 1772 and 1773 attempted unsuccessfully to discover a passage to Asia from Europe via a new route toward the north.

When shortly after this time Equiano became an aide to a slave ship's captain, slavery remained ingrained in British culture. Even after Olaudah Equiano gained his freedom, he was several times kidnapped and forced to work as a slave while traveling in the British West Indies. Eventually making his way back to England, Equiano settled down and devoted himself almost full-time to the cause of fighting for the abolition of the slave trade.

Originally from Africa, James Somersett had been sold to a colonial customs official in Virginia named Charles Stewart. After later being relocated to Boston, Somersett arrived in London under the control of Stewart in 1769. In February 1771, James Somersett was baptized at St. Andrew Holborn with Elizabeth Cade and John Marlow as his sponsors. This was a period during which slaves in England ran away from their owners with considerable frequency as demonstrated by numerous advertisements appealing for their recovery. When without permission Somersett left the service of Charles Stewart on October 1, 1771, Stewart set about having Somersett hunted down and incarcerated in preparation for sending him to Jamaica for resale. Although occurrences such as this were not rare, given that Granville Sharp brought a court action on the part of Somersett in a case to be presided over by Lord Chief Justice William Murray, first Earl of Mansfield, the most eminent lawyer in Britain at the time, it drew considerable attention from the public at large. Among those in attendance at the trial was a large number of "black" residents of London.

Though in Mansfield's ruling in the Somersett case the justice took note of the fact that the laws of the British colony of Virginia provided for slaveholding, he stated that no law in England did. Consequently, he ruled that, in the absence of "positive law" in England in the matter of slavery, slaves could not be forcibly returned from Britain to the colonies against their will. Because he ordered James Somersett released, many people erroneously concluded that this implied the emancipation of British slaves residing in the mother country. In fact, Manfield's ruling in this case was a very limited ruling. It neither emancipated slaves living in Britain nor ameliorated in any way the harsh and abusive slaveholding practices then prevailing in colonies under British control. Also, it did not outlaw the buying and selling of slaves in Britain, a practice that continued without pretense for a long time thereafter. Even when it eventually would be outlawed, it overlapped with a long period during which slaveholding in Britain was often disguised as a system of apprenticeship with slaves not infrequently being shipped both against their wishes and against the law from Britain to various British colonies (Fryer 1984: 124-127, 132, 156, 203-206).

Shortly after Lord Mansfield's ruling in the Somersett case, African-born Joseph Knight, who had been purchased by John Wedderburn in Jamaica and brought to Scotland in 1769, demanded that his owner begin to pay him wages on the assumption that the Mansfield ruling applied to all of Britain. When Wedderburn refused, Knight ran away and was subsequently arrested on a complaint lodged by his master. When the case was heard in the Sheriff's court of Perth, the court ruled that as the laws of Britain's colony of Jamaica did not apply in Scotland, Knight was to be considered free. When Wedderburn appealed this decision to the Court of Session in Edinburgh, the matter was considered of sufficient importance to warrant a full panel of judges, including Lord Kames, to rule on it. Contributing to the public attention associated with the case, James Boswell and Samuel Johnson assisted in preparing the case for sustaining the original ruling. Although the Court of Session in 1777 delivered its verdict that slavery was against the law in Scotland without formal recourse to the Mansfield ruling, there can be little doubt that Mansfield's earlier ruling in the Somersett case was influential at least in a contextual sense.

Quite apart from his being a distinguished jurist, Lord Mansfield was the great-uncle of a "mulatto" girl named Dado who lived in his home. She was the daughter of his nephew, Rear Admiral Sir John Lindsay, with a slave mother whom he had captured from a Spanish vessel during the siege of Havana. Mansfield was also a friend and benefactor of Sir William Blackstone, a prominent English judge, whose multi-volume *Commentaries on the Laws of England* was published between 1765 and 1769. This work by Blackstone was an immediate success and was very influential in stating the case against slavery (Thomas 1997: 470-471).

Of relevance to the African presence in London in 1768, *Gentleman's Magazine* estimated that London had some 20,000 "black" people out of a total population of 676,250 at that time. This publication was of such a standing in Great Britain that beginning in 1737 Samuel Johnson began writing for it. If the periodical's population estimate was at all correct, the people so characterized were well over 3 percent of the total population of the largest metropolis of Europe around the time when it was for the first time surpassing Paris as Europe's largest city in population. In connection with the Somerset case, Lord Mansfield had estimated the total number of "blacks" in Great Britain between 14,000 and 15,000.

As illustrated by these vastly differing estimates, terms such as "African," "Euro-African," "Moor," "Negro," and "black" were not uniformly synonymous. Moreover, they were sometimes used as terms of reference for people in 18th-century Britain who were essentially Asian as well as descendants of long-time Europeans. It follows therefore that such terms must be understood as fluid constructs rather than as words with operational definitions that described people with exactness and in consistent ways. That the same thing also was true in other parts of Europe underscores both the relativity of terminology and its inability to fully reflect the complexity and overlapping of human variation in a biological sense.

An American of African descent, who though only temporarily in Europe, made a big impact there during the period under discussion was Phillis Wheatley. Captured from the Senegambia region of western Africa and enslaved in Boston, Phillis Wheatley managed even while held in bondage to study the Bible, Greek, Latin, astronomy, geography, history, and British history. When she was aged thirteen years, Wheatley created a sensation by having her first poem published in *Mercury*, a publication produced in Newport, Rhode Island. When however she wished to have additional poems published, she was forced to undergo a humiliating judicial examination that involved rigorous questioning by a panel of officials to prove that she possessed the mental capacity to produce the writings she claimed as her own. Despite winning judicial recognition that her poems were hers, no Boston publisher was willing to publish additional poems by her.

It was against this background that young Phillis Wheatley while still enslaved in 1773—that is between the Seven Years' War and the American War of
Independence—was allowed to travel to London with Nathanial Wheatley, her
master's son, in an effort to find a publisher for her work. Due in large measure
to assistance afforded them in London by Selina, Countess of Huntingdon, and
the Earl of Darmouth, Phillis Wheatley's book *Poems on Various Subjects, Religious and Moral* was published in London in the year of her arrival in Europe.

In 1776 or well after her return to America, Wheatley wrote a poem in ho-
mage to George Washington that lauded his appointment as commander of the
Continental Army. She eventually received a personal thank-you note from
Washington after he had received a copy of it. Meanwhile, still illustrating a
lack of British resolve around the issue of slavery's inhumanity as of 1776, the
very year when a majority of colonists of European descent in lower North
America made a declaration of their independence from their mother country, a
resolution in the British Parliament holding that slavery was contrary to the law
of God failed to win a majority.

Another slave who eventually reached England by way of the New World
was Ignatius Sancho. Born on board a slave ship that was carrying his parents
from Africa toward South America via the West Indies in 1729, his mother died
shortly after giving birth. Soon afterward, his father chose suicide over a life of
enslavement. It was on the arrival of this infant in Cartagena, on the coast of
what is now Colombia, that he was christened Ignatius. When Ignatius was two
years of age, his master brought him to England where Ignatius's ownership was
transferred to three maiden sisters who lived in Greenwich. As Ignatius reminded them of the squire known as Sancho from the well-known Spanish novel
by Miguel de Cervantes Saavedra, *Don Quijote de la Mancha*, they added Sancho to his name of Ignatius.

Despite the fact that Ignatius Sancho showed himself to be very intelligent
and even taught himself to read, the refusal of his three mistresses to allow him a
formal education led him to eventually escape to nearby Blackheath, where he
entered the service of the Duke and Duchess of Montagu as a butler. As his new
masters supported his intellectual development, Ignatius managed both to work
and to indulge his passion for reading and creativity. In addition to writing poetry and two stage plays, he composed a number of classical compositions for
flute, harpsichord, violin, and mandolin as well as produced a book on the
theory of music that he dedicated to the Princess Royal. Fond of theatre, Ignatius
Sancho attended plays in London with some frequency. Despite his humble origins, Ignatius won considerable acceptance among London's literary and artistic
set. With a legacy left to him by the Duchess of Montagu in the early 1770s, he
purchased a grocery business on Charles Street in Westminster, which he operated with his wife, Anne. Although he died in 1780, a compilation of his letters
was published two years later that quickly became a best seller. In the words of
one of its reviewers, "Let it no longer be said by half informed philosophers, and
superficial investigators of human nature, that Negers, as they are vulgarly
called, are inferior to any white nation in mental abilities."

In 1764, which was the year following the Seven Years' War, Captain Stair Douglas of the Royal Navy mentioned to the Duchess of Queensbury that he had in his possession a smart and intelligent "Negro" boy, aged about 10, whom he had bought in St. Kitts, and asked the duchess if she would like him as a gift. After accepting, she gave him the name of Soubise, dressed him well, and generally made him a pet as was the fashion of the day among many well-to-do Europeans. She and the Duke provided Soubise with schooling that included attending Domenico Angelo's Academy, a premier school for fencing and niceties of riding. Much taken with himself, Soubise eventually took on princely airs, accumulated large debts, and was eventually considered guilty of attempting a sexual assault on one of the duchess's maids. Unwilling to tolerate further indiscretions by him, the Duchess of Queensbury in 1777 had Soubise exiled to the British colony of India where he established a successful fencing and riding academy in Calcutta (Woodard 1999: 86-88, 91, 98).

Meanwhile in France 1763, a freedom petition case came before the senior Admiralty court. Guillaume Poncet de la Grave, the King's attorney at the Admiralty court, while reluctantly supporting the petition, sketched a situation that to him seemed horrendous as a result of exceptions granted to the edicts of 1716 and 1738 that controlled the entry of colonial slaves into metropolitan France. On the one hand, Poncet de la Grave claimed that "France, and especially the capital, had become a public market where men are sold to the highest and last bidder; not a Bourgeois or a worker is without a black slave." On the other hand, the King's attorney stated that such abuses of the earlier edicts could not be tolerated. According to him, "the introduction of too many blacks in France, whether slaves or of any other sort, has dangerous consequences. Soon, we shall see the French nation disfigured . . . ; in any case, blacks in general are dangerous men" (Boulle 2006: 23, 25).

Contributing to Poncet de la Grave's racist expression at this particular time, though not accounting for it, was the fact that the war years had interrupted travel between France and its colonies in the Caribbean to sufficiently allow many "black" subjects from the Caribbean to remain in Europe longer than provided for by law. This was a period during which the French colonies remained under the control of the navy, and the Duke of Choiseul, who was secretary of state for the navy, went on record in 1766 as being in opposition to the mixing of blood between blacks and whites (Boulle 2006: 42n20). Given the Enlightenment focus on severing as much as possible of the historic bonds between Europeans and Africans, this was not a surprising position.

A representative case in France of the late 18th century involving a "black" person's seeking legal recognition as a freedman and the back wages owed to him since his arrival in Europe came before France's senior Admiralty court in 1775. Described in considerable detail by Boulle (2006: 19-20), this case concerned a slave named Jean-Louis who in 1768 had been sent from Martinique by his master to Rochefort to his master's wife as a gift. After the death in France of his mistress, however, the slaveholder wished to retain Jean-Louis in slavery back in Martinique. Without waiting for the court's decision in the case, he had Jean-Louis seized and jailed in preparation for having him returned to Martinique, a procedure apparently followed with considerable frequency by masters in similar cases.

In this case, however, Guillaume Poncet de la Grave, the royal procurator, decided to make a legal issue of what he considered to be a master acting outside of the law. The jailer holding Jean-Louis was brought before the court on the initiative of Poncet de la Grave and was ordered to not release Jean-Louis to anyone until the court handed down its decision. Although the court soon handed down a decision that granted Jean-Louis his freedom, its ruling also created a backlash that reflected a growing prejudice within elite circles against residents in France considered nonwhite in general and against such residents who were deemed "black" in particular (Boulle 2006: 21).

In 1776, the same Guillaume Poncet de la Grave, who had argued in 1762 that because many people of African ancestry were residing in France one might "soon see the French nation disfigured" and who in 1768 had intervened forcefully to prevent the extralegal re-enslavement of Jean-Louis, complained that because Africans "multiply each day in France," they tend to marry Europeans and that as a result "the colors mix" and "the blood is altered." The blatant racism reflected in these ideas notwithstanding, to a remarkable degree they were incorporated in a royal declaration of August 9, 1777, that consisted of thirteen articles. Among other things, this royal declaration forbade entry of "blacks" into France, provided for fines of 1,000 *livres* against every ship captain transporting any "black, mulatto, or other person of color" into the country, and provided that people of color whether slave or free should carry special identity cards or risk being arrested in preparation for banishment to the colonies. Although this declaration undoubtedly made the populace of France more conscious of what by this time was considered racial "otherness," there was little attempt to enforce this declaration strictly, and it did not prevent additional people of African descent from entering France.

A "black" man named Hercule, whose status in France was murky and who had been placed under the King's protection via the Admiralty court, was arrested by the Paris police on the steps of the tribunal, and the very same day two other blacks, one named Pampy and the other named Julienne, though granted their freedom by the court heard their Jewish master publicly boast that he would arrange for their arrest. Such lack of clarity led Antoine de Sartine, who from 1767 was *conseiller d'État* and who from 1774 was secretary of state for navy, to have the law clarified. He had Lettres-Patent issued, forbidding the Admiralty court to hear further freedom cases until the royal will could be expressed in a new law (Boulle 2006: 20-21). In the legal confrontation that followed, it was Guillaume Poncet de la Grave (the King's attorney at France's senior Admiralty court) who urged Antoine de Sartine to conform with the law recognizing the freedom of former slaves in France while at the same time warning him of the dire consequences of doing so based on reasons that were tactical, opportunistic toward people of African descent, and racist in suggesting that their blood tainted that of the majority population in France (Boulle 2006: 25).

Not surprising, therefore, Poncet de la Grave wrote again to Sartine a little later proposing that a separate tribunal be created to deal with the newly estab-

lished *Police des Noirs* (meaning Police Authority for Blacks). Sartine responded by naming as the senior official in charge of the dossier Daniel Marc Antoine
Chardon, who had previous experience in the French-controlled West Indies, as
intendant of Sainte-Lucie or Staint Lucia and as a *maître des requetes*. In covering letters in which Sartine authorized this new undertaking, Sartine complained
about the "abusive" immigration of blacks to France that resulted in the mixing
of colors causing blood to become tainted. While asserting that the laws pertaining to metropolitan France did not recognize slave status, he lamented that if
slaves were returned to the colonies after living in Europe that the independent
spirit they had acquired while living in France could diffuse among more oppressed colonial slaves in ways that might cause them to rebel. In keeping with a
wide body of opinion during the late decades of the Enlightenment, Sartine also
stated that in his opinion it was part of the natural order that people who were
"black" should serve those who were "white" (Boulle 2006: 25-26).

A treatise on colonial law dated 1777 by Emilien Petit, the Saint-Domingue
deputy of commerce, stated that black skin was an indelible "stain [*tache*] of
slavery" and that it was retained even in mixed blood as the result of "an infamous prostitution" so that even so-called mixed blood people at most constituted
an "intermediary estate between the whites and the slaves." Further, Petit
praised the *Code Noir* adopted by France for Louisiana in 1724, which prohibited mixed marriages on the claim that such marriages were considered dis-
tasteful to the families of the "white" husbands as well as resulted in shameful
births. Arguing against provisions contained in the edict of 1716 that permitted
slaves to be transported to France for education in religion and training in a
craft, Petit held that such privilege would instill in them "laziness and debau-
chery, which lead to crime" (Boulle 2006: 24-25; Peabody 1996: 114).

By a royal decree in 1777 during the reign of King Louis XVI, France forbade the entry of additional "black" people into France because "they marry
Europeans, they infect brothels, and colors are mixed." Despite this obvious
French surge in the direction of racism with the sanction of law, the sometimes-
conflicting sentiments within Guillaume Poncet de la Grave about "blacks" in
some ways paralleled similar attitudinal conflicts among French people more
generally. Whether the royal decree of 1777 had any effect on the continuing
entry of people of African descent into France is doubtful considering that six
years later in 1783, a ministerial *circulaire* complained that "black" servants
were still being disembarked in France (Thomas 1997: 485). Despite such hostility as well as attitudinal and legal hurdles, so-called people of color continued to
enter France with considerable frequency.

A ten-year- old boy from western Africa by the name of Lubin, for example,
was settled in La Rochelle by French captains to be trained as an interpreter in
1777, as they wished to later use him in this role along the Guinea coast of Africa (McCloy 1961: 36). Still, the declaration enacted into French law in that same
year undoubtedly made the French more conscious of so-called racial differences as associated with color. This declaration, in fact, represented a giant step in
the direction of more intensive policing of race in metropolitan France. It was
this declaration of 1777 that for the first time in France established a number of

dôpôts des noirs or holding facilities for incarcerating "black" slaves who reached metropolitan France, including even those who arrived in the company of their owners (McCloy 1961: 64; Peabody 1996: 113-120, 137).

That elitist social thought associated with the Enlightenment was likely a factor in this development seems indicated by the fact that there exists little evidence that the strict enforcement of the declaration of 1777 was as great a concern for the French masses as for some government officials. Except that these facilities were specifically for people of African or quasi-African descent, slave prisons were hardly a new invention in Europe. In Malta, slave prisons had been in operation since the 1500s, at which time the majority of enslaved prisoners continued to be "whites." Segregation of most slaves from the general populace in Malta, however, ran a different course, as it continued to be based more on differences of religion more than on differences of color (Wettinger 2002 *passim*).

A slave trade involving French people that focused specifically on people of African ancestry had begun as early as 1672 and continued at its height through the French Revolution, in fact, at least until 1792. Because it was always more firmly established in the colonies than in Europe, however. With regard to French participation in the African slave trade via the Atlantic Ocean as of 1691, Nantes was the most important French port involved. Between 1713 and 1792, some 1,313 slave ships left Nantes for Africa. In 1716, France officially restricted French ships participating in the slave trade to the cities of Rouen, La Rochelle, Bordeaux, Nantes, and Saint-Malo. In line with these developments, there were many baptismals and marriages registered in Nantes that mentioned Africans, and after 1736 those involving newly arrived African slaves and freedmen were registered separately in Nantes. In 1741, France also permitted ships participating in the slave trade to operate out of Calais, Dieppe, Le Havre, Honfleur, Morlaix, Brest, Bayonne, Marseille, Dunkirk, and Vannes to participate. While some of the slaves acquired were distributed among various colonies, others were shipped to Europe. In 1768, for example, the Admiralty office at Nantes complained that the number of slaves being sent to France was too great (Debrunner 1979: 88-89, 91).

On February 23, 1778, a new French ordinance directed ship officials afresh to refrain from bringing "blacks" and "mulattoes" into France without special authorization. That this measure was difficult to enforce is indicated by the fact that two "blacks" who entered Nantes in March 1778 were reported to be members of a ship's crew, both of whom had made several transoceanic crossings. A subsequent decree of the same Council on April 5, 1778 forbade "blacks" from marrying "whites" on penalty of their being expelled to the colonies and provided fines for notaries who issued marriage licenses in such cases (McCloy 1961: 46-49; Peabody 1996: 139). By this time, however, numerous people of appreciable African descent living in France were already married to their fellow Frenchmen without regard to color.

Irrespective of what laws the French brought into existence, some people of color with allies or patrons highly placed in French society or government managed not only to survive but to thrive in mainland France (McCloy 1961: 53,

55, 57-58). Despite the fact that racism was thriving in the colonies of France in the late 1700s, abolition, which had been a *cause célèbre* for some of the oppressed in various French colonies for some time, also was receiving support in Europe despite the fact that the shaky state of the French economy made most of the French on the continent hesitant to campaign for changes in the colonies.

In a report of 1782, France's Committee on Legislation estimated the number of "black" slaves in the country to be between four- and five thousand (McCloy 1961: 52), but France was by this time also home to many other people of African descent. Although the Act of 1777 resulted in the establishment of holding facilities in the port cities of Dunkerque, Le Havre, Saint-Malo, Brest, Nantes, La Rochelle, Bordeaux, and Marseille, judging by complaints in a ministerial *circulaire* of 1783, overall enforcement of the 1777 declaration as approved by King Louis XVI remained somewhat lax, and so-called people of color continued to enter France, especially through Nantes and Bordeaux. In January 1778 an Order of the Council of State that consisted of nine articles directed all so-called people of color in France who had not already registered with an Admiralty to do so immediately or run the risk of being arrested, imprisoned, and deported to the colonies (McCloy 1961: 49).

Meanwhile further north in Europe, due to the assistance that Granville Sharp in London rendered to Jonathan Strong beginning in 1765, Sharp was certainly the best-known "white" abolitionist in Great Britain by this time. However, there were also important London-based abolitionists of African descent, with Olaudah Equiano, likely of Igbo heritage and originally from what is nowadays southeastern Nigeria, being one of the most prominent among them by 1789. Sold to an officer in the Royal Navy named Michael Pascal when he was around ten years old, Olaudah Equiano knew firsthand the abuse and indignity of slavery. Somewhat against Equiano's wishes, Pascal had renamed his slave Gustavus Vassa, in remembrance of a 16th-century Swedish nobleman who had been involved in leading the Swedes out of a sort of slavery from the Danes.

After being sold to slavers along the Gulf of Guinea, Equiano was eventually transported to Barbados. First arriving in England as a slave when he was about twelve years old in the spring of 1757, Olaudah Equiano passed much of his youth on board a battleship during which time he traveled widely in Canada, Europe, and the Mediterranean. The experience of Olaudah Equiano reminds us that some people of African descent were very well traveled in the 18th century. In addition to obtaining some schooling aboard the vessel, Equiano also received some education during periods when the ship on which he usually traveled was in various ports in England. Despite his early exposure to literacy, Christianity, and intimate associations with free people that eventually led him to consider that he was no longer a slave, Equiano remained technically in bondage. In fact, this was painfully brought home to him, when at the end of 1762 Captain Doran, his owner, suddenly sold him to another master who transported him as a slave back to the Caribbean (Equiano 1988: 57-59).

After enduring several years of hard labor and harsh treatment in the Caribbean, Equiano eventually managed to purchase his freedom and make his way back to London. There he worked cooperatively with Granville Sharp and in

1789 published his best-selling abolitionist autobiography, *Interesting Narrative of the Life of Olaudah Equiano or Gustavus Vass, The African, Written by Himself.* That this autobiography had a major impact especially in Great Britain cannot be doubted. The Irish abolitionist Thomas Digges, who lived during the period that the book was produced, observed that it was "a principal instrument of bringing about a motion for the repeal of the Slave-act" (Edwards 1988: vii).

It was Olaudah Equiano, in fact, who became the first abolitionist in England to assert as a principle that slaves had not only a moral right but a moral duty to resist enslavement. Unequivocal in his opposition to the slave trade even by prevailing abolitionist standards, Olaudah Equiano authored a work titled *Thoughts* and sent copies to King George III, the Prince of Wales, and the politician Edmund Burke, all of whom were apologists for privileges that sometimes permitted Europeans to enslave people of African ancestry (Equiano 1988; Edwards 1988: vii-xxxviii; Woodard 1999: 31-56).

Another liberation work by a man of African ancestry that appeared in Britain during this period was by Ukawsaw Gronniosaw. Born in what is now northeastern Nigeria, Gronniosaw arrived in England in 1762 from New York at age 15 at which time he took the name of James Albert. After arriving in England, he apparently remained enslaved until his master was dying. On his deathbed, Gronniosaw's master freed him and gave him 10 pounds. Gronniosaw, however remained in service to other members of his master's family for a number of additional years. He then enlisted in the British Army, where he served in Cuba and in Martinique. His autobiography, *A Narrative of the Most remarkable Particulars in the Life of James Albert Ukawsaw Gronniosaw, an African Prince*, was published in 1772.

That we know so much about the life of Gronniosaw is because this narrative about his life was apparently written by Countess of Huntingdon, an English patron, and then edited by Olaudah Equiano. Though in Europe Gronniosaw married an English weaver and fathered a child, fellow Christians discriminated against him and his family, even when it was necessary to bury his infant daughter who had died from fever. Needing to find some way to reconcile his strong belief in Christianity with his victimization through racism, Gronniosaw continued throughout much of his life to blame his unfortunate enslavement to some extent on his own personal sins as well as on his origin as a non-Christian.

London-based Quobna Ottobah Cugoano lived during the same period as Olaudah Equiano. Born in Ajumako on the coast of what is today Ghana, Cugoano had been captured at around age thirteen and was carried to the Caribbean island of Grenada. Arriving in England in 1772, he was given the surname of Stuart by a "Master John Stuart" and given instruction in Christian doctrine by a Dr. Skinner who advised him to get himself baptized in order not to be enslaved again. With the name John Steuart, he entered the service of Richard Cosway, who was a principal painter working for the Prince of Wales. Through Cosway, John Stuart also became well acquainted with the poet William Blake. In 1786, Steuart worked cooperatively with the "white" abolitionist Granville Sharp and others in managing to rescue Henry Demane, a "black" man scheduled to be shipped from England into slavery in the British West Indies against his will.

Steuart, under his earlier name of Quobna Ottobah Cugoano, published *Thoughts and Sentiments on the Evil of Slavery and Commerce of the Human* Species in 1787, which was a powerful abolitionist work on which Olaudah Equiano is thought to have collaborated.

Records of cases from the Court of Session in Edinburgh whereby runaway baptized slaves of African descent in Scotland attempted to regain their freedom on a permanent basis without threat of their owners being able to ship them from Scotland to overseas colonies as slaves survive from the period between 1756 to 1778 in the National Archives of Scotland. Three documented cases in this category are Montgomery v Sheddan (1756), Spens v Dairymple (1769) and Knight v Wedderburn (1778). That these cases qualified for adjudication suggests that the issue of whether one could be a slave in abeyance in Scotland was not settled as of this period. The first two of these cases never reached a conclusion because of the deaths of one of the parties involved.

In the third case involving Joseph Knight, however, the Justices of the Peace had found in favor of Wedderburn, his master. When Knight appealed his case to the Sheriff of Perth, he received a ruling in his favor. It was when this case involving Knight was appealed by Wedderburn to Edinburgh's Court of Session that a final decision on this matter was reached in Scotland. This ruling held that as Scots law, as of that time, recognized neither the status of slavery nor perpetual servitude, that Joseph Knight was free to continue living in Scotland with the woman of servant background he had married there. To what extent the fact that Knight was a Christian as well as married to a woman who was then pregnant might have factored into the ruling handed down is not clear.

In addition to the tremendous work on behalf of abolitionism that was unfolding due to continuous struggle, protest, and resistance by people of African descent who were residing in Britain in the late 1780s, a number of "white" Britons were also committed to the abolitionist cause. Dr. William Paley, for example, published his *Moral Philosophy*, based on lectures he had given at Cambridge and which severely condemned the slave trade (Thomas 1997: 492). Thomas Clarkson and certain of his Quaker friends took the lead in founding in London a Committee for Effecting the Abolition of the Slave Trade. This committee was important in helping the European abolitionist movement attract national and international participation (Thomas 1997: 492-493; Freeman-Grenville 1973: 137). By the end of the 1780s, William Wilberforce had succeeded Granville Sharp as the best-known "white" abolitionist in Britain, and Olaudah Equiano was undoubtedly the best known of numerous London-based abolitionists of African descent.

As the American War of Independence from Britain was winding down, one of the "black" men from the former American colonies who turned up in Britain was William "Bill" Richmond, born on Staten Island, New York as the son of former slaves from Georgia, who had started life as a slave or servant to British General Earl Percy. Percy was the commanding general of British forces in New York during the war and Richmond was a loyalist. According to some accounts, Richmond had likely been the hangman of Nathan Hale, an American spy on the British during the war. In 1777, General Percy, who would later become the

Duke of Northumberland, sent 14-year-old Richmond to Britain and arranged for him to be schooled in Yorkshire. Then apprenticed by Percy to a cabinet maker in York, Richmond also continued to develop his skills as a bare-knuckle boxer or pugilist, for which he had already shown considerable talent before leaving America.

Another "black" boxer from America who arrived in Britain shortly after this time at around the turn of the 19th century was Tom Molineux. Molineux, who had been born in Georgetown, West Virginia, in 1784, eventually won his freedom by winning fights against other slaves in bouts on which plantation owners laid bets. He eventually moved to England as he believed he could make more money fighting in Europe than in the United States. Shortly after Tom Molineux's arrival in Europe, "Bill" Richmond became one of his friends as well as his trainer.

On January 23, 1804, William "Bill" Richmond was defeated by George Maddox in a fight with George Maddox at Wimbledon Commons. The following year, however, Richmond had two victories, one against a Jewish boxer named Yossoup at Blackheath and another against a coachman named Jack Holmes, who was known as "Tom Tough," at Kilburn. Although these successes helped earn "Bill" Richmond the nickname of the "Black Terror," at the end of a 90-minute bout later in October of the same year he lost to Tom Cribb, future English heavyweight champion.

Among the largely poor people of dark complexion living in Britain in the late 1700s was a considerable number who were of Indian as well as of African or African-American descent. In 1786, a "Committee of Gentlemen" that consisted of bankers, merchants, and MPs was established to organize relief for distressed laid-off Asian seamen called Lascars. This committee soon extended its activities to helping "black" people of African descent as well, of whom there were at least 1,144 living in London around that time (Fryer 1984: 194). It was against this background that the Sierra Leone plan discussed in the previous chapter was launched in 1787, more as a scheme to rid Britain of poor "black" people living in London than as a philanthropic undertaking. No doubt contributing to Britain's concern with this segment of the population, the country was rife with anxiety over solidarity and rebelliousness among working-class people existed quite apart from color. In fact, working-class masses that the upper-classes sometimes referred to as "the mob" not infrequently came to the aid of "black" neighbors. Around this same time, the government enacted legislation to prevent the immigration of so-called radicals and subversives in an effort to try to prevent the "mob" from being influenced by ideas emanating from the French Revolution (Paul 1997: 65).

This period was one of imperial expansion by Britain, and Britain was anxious to increase the number of people subject to its control in Africa. Between 1779 and 1781 in what is now South Africa, for example, the first of the so-called Frontier Wars was fought in the Zuurveld between the British and Boers along with servile African auxiliaries, on one side, and the Xhosa, on the other. In connection with seizing control of the Cape Colony in 1795 from the United Provinces of the Seven Netherlands while they were under Napoleonic occupation, Great Britain wished to strengthen its claim on the area (Goodwin 2006: 231-232), and a pioneering demographic work by Thomas Robert Malthus that appeared at this time played a role in how the British were thinking about Africa, Africans in Britain, Africans abroad, and imperialism.

In his *An Essay on the Principle of Population* that was first published in 1798, Malthus predicted that, if left unchecked, population growth would overwhelm the available food supply. He also proposed that the burden for exercising restraint in ways that might avoid this problem rested disproportionately on the shoulders of the working and poor classes in keeping with British class attitudes at the time. Thomas Malthus, also a minister, additionally favored the gradual abolition of British poor laws at a time when certain residents of African descent were among the most destitute of England. While furnishing ammunition to certain people in Great Britain who were unsympathetic to the poor at home, this position by Malthus also fed the British appetite for controlling a vast empire through which it might relieve the domestic overcrowding predicted by Malthus.

This emergence of Malthusianism provided Britain with an additional justification for sending more British settlers to Africa, including not only "blacks" to Sierra Leone but also "whites" to southern Africa. The latter was rationalized as a way of protecting the eastern frontier of the recently seized Cape Colony from the Xhosa. As part of a simultaneous terror campaign that amounted to ethnic cleansing against the Xhosa of southern Africa's Zuurveld where some 700 Xhosa were killed, the British government (suddenly oblivious to its professed commitment to the abolition of slavery) did nothing to change the slave basis of the economy in the Cape Colony that it was acquiring. This general period for the British government was one of concentration on imperial expansion more than one of providing new freedoms for people deemed "others." Further underscoring this point, instead of granting the franchise to the long-suffering Irish that it dominated, Britain further formalized Ireland's suppression in 1801 through its incorporation of Ireland into the newly established United Kingdom of Great Britain and Ireland.

Although these developments were occurring in Great Britain around the same time that France was still experiencing the after shocks of its Revolution, France's new constitution of 1795 compromised much of its commitment to democracy with checks and balances by placing the country under the control of five so-called Directors, who held both legislative and executive powers. It was under France's Directory in 1796 that Napoleon Bonaparte, accompanied by an army that included numerous soldiers of African descent, launched his Italian campaign that resulted in an astounding number of victories for France. Among the accomplishments of the French military with Napoleon as its commander-in-chief within the first year alone was the recovery of Corsica from Britain, the defeat of the Austrian Empire as well as the Kingdom of Sardinia, the annexation of Savoy and Nice, and the capture of many works of art from Italy.

Although the Directory continued to operate rather inefficiently until 1799, it was during this period that Napoleon undertook to turn the Mediterranean largely into a French Sea by capturing the Maltese Islands on his way to occupying

Egypt. Although Napoleon Bonaparte personally remained in Malta only a few days, he lost little time while there in 1798 in impacting slavery. Napoleon, although by no means a true abolitionist, instructed the French consuls in Tripoli, Tunis, and Algiers to inform the *beys* of those places that, as the Maltese had recently become subjects of France, all Maltese slaves under their control should be liberated and returned to Malta, at which time the liberated Muslim slaves from various areas of the Mediterranean under Turkish control would be transferred to Turkish authorities, regardless of whether they had originated from Greece, Syria, Libya or elsewhere in Africa (Wettinger 2002: 26, 584-588). A particularly interesting aspect of Napoleon's instructions on slavery is that their wording offer additional evidence that even as late as the turn of the 19th century, and quite irrespective of color, some Europeans and Africans (both from north and south of the Sahara) remained entrapped in slavery in Europe alongside each other.

Moreover, Napoleon's instructions on slavery did not mean that all Muslim slaves immediately left Malta as many Maltese like to claim. A close reading of the most comprehensive work on the subject suggests something quite different from this. In some places, Wettinger (2002: 26, 584-588) states that it would take until 1801 before all such exchanges of slaves were completed while in other places the he concedes that even after the British had effectively taken over control of the islands from the French a couple of years later (rather than in accordance with the terms of the 1802 Treaty of Amiens according to which Malta was to be returned to the Order of Saint John) that some Maltese who were formerly slave owners petitioned Captain Ball of Britain for permission to regain possession of certain of their freed slaves (Wettinger 2002: 589, 591; Goodwin 2002: 50). One may reasonably infer therefore that at least a few former slaves, irrespective of color or place of origin, remained in Malta permanently and were likely assimilated within the majority population.

Although Thomas-Alexandre Dumas was only one of several generals of African or partial African ancestry in the armed forces of France at the time that Napoleon invaded Malta and Egypt in 1798, a vignette of his personal situation is very revealing with regard to the status of so-called people of color in France around the time of the French Revolution and shortly afterwards. Let us look first at the circumstances of his birth.

To the aristocratic Marquis Alexandre-Antoine Davy de la Pailleterie and Marie-Césette Dumas, originally his "black" slave and later his emancipated mistress in Saint-Domingue, a son was born in 1762. While the original name of this son was Thomas-Alexandre Davy de la Pailleterie, he was destined to eventually become best known Thomas-Alexandre Dumas, the father of the writer Alexandre Dumas the Elder and grandfather of Alexandre Dumas the Younger. Despite the aristocratic status of the father of Thomas-Alexandre who served in Saint-Domingue in the exalted post of *général commissaire* of the colony, his relationship with Marie-Césette and Thomas-Alexandre, their son, was apparently a good one. When Marie-Césette died in 1774, the marquis remained devoted to their young son.

In 1780 when Thomas-Alexandre was eighteen, Marquis Alexandre-Antoine Davy de la Pailleterie returned to France taking his "mulatto" son, Thomas-Alexandre, with him. In France, the marquis provided his son with an education typical for a child of noble birth. Despite this seeming acceptance of Thomas-Alexandre in privileged French society, however, it was qualified.

When, for example, Thomas-Alexandre enlisted in the French army in 1786, his father and paternal relatives prevailed on him to use Dumas, the surname of his late mother, so as to protect their aristocratic reputation from scandal. Although the fact that Thomas-Alexandre Dumas had been born to a mother who had been a "black" slave would have been sufficiently scandalous to embarrass his aristocratic paternal relatives, his superb education, outstanding talent, and privileged connections did not prevent him at the age of 31 from achieving the rank of general. It was in this rank that he served France in the civil war between French royalists and republicans in Vendée from 1793 and 1796 and that he served in France's Italian Campaign from 1776 to 1797. It was also as a general that Dumas served in Napoleon's doomed Egyptian Campaign, at least from 1798 to 1799, after which time, ill and disillusioned, Dumas departed Egypt for France.

It was a great disappointment to Napoleon that his audacious attempt to capture Egypt, and in that process to make France the super power of the Mediterranean, did not go as planned and he never forgave General Dumas for openly stating to the general staff in Egypt that Napoleon's Egyptian Campaign was foolish and its direction incompetent as disaster followed disaster. That around the same time Napoleon was busy fabricating rosy reports on the progress of the Egyptian Campaign to send to the Directory created some enmity between the two men. Whether Napoleon was unable to dominate the strong-willed Dumas or whether Dumas, because of illness by 1799, was reluctantly allowed by Napoleon to return to France is a matter of some dispute (Gallaher 1997: 146-147; Ribbe 2002).

It is not disputed, however, that Dumas was a patriotic republican who repeatedly risked his life for France. What is also clear is that, as Dumas was returning to France from Egypt, the ship on which he was traveling was inadvertently blown into the Italian port of Taranto. This misfortune enabled Ferdinand III, King of Sicily, who was at the same time Ferdinand IV of Naples and on hostile terms with France, to capture Dumas and to keep him imprisoned incommunicado for two years under very brutal conditions. In addition to being nearly starved, General Dumas was made partially blind, partially deaf, and partially paralyzed in part during repeated attempts to poison him with arsenic. What is also clear is that France, during this time while under the steadily increasing dominance of Napoleon, made no attempt to ransom him. Even after the release of the physically broken warrior, France's refusal to offer him the customary pension left him to live out the remainder of his life in poverty in his wife's French village of Villers-Cotterêts, where he succumbed to stomach cancer in early 1806, shortly before reaching forty-four years of age.

Considering that about two years of Napoleon's entry into Egypt, France's retreat was underway along with a similar retreat from tiny Malta (Goodwin

2002: 46-50), it is obvious that General Dumas had assessed France's situation in northeastern Africa accurately. It is possible that Dumas also correctly sensed that Napoleon was neither sincerely opposed to racism nor slavery. Following much lobbying by French planters in the Caribbean as well as by Joséphine de Beauharnais, his wife, who was the daughter of a wealthy plantation owner and governor in Martinique, Napoleon showed himself increasingly willing to seek greatness and prosperity for himself and France on the backs of people of African ancestry. He reintroduced slavery to French colonies in May 1802. This was only shortly before he also declared himself Consul-for-life on August 2 of the same year. When by means of the Treaty of Amiens in 1802 Napoleon was assured that a British takeover of Haiti was no longer a threat, Napoleon lost little time in sending his brother-in-law General Charles Leclerc on an 1802 mission to Saint-Domingue or Haiti with secret orders to restore race-based slavery there as well.

Given that Dumas was a genuine republican who believed in liberty and democracy, Napoleon's attempt to restore slavery even on the island where Dumas's mother had once been a slave, coupled with Napoleon's coronation of himself as emperor in January 1804, was not geared in any way to improve their relationship. The two men were still very alienated at the time of Dumas's death. Some evidence suggests that Napoleon's bitterness toward the general, whom Napoleon sometimes dismissively referred to as "that person of color," even carried over to his widow Marie-Louise Dumas and their son, eventually known as Alexandre Dumas *père* or the Elder (Gallaher 1997: 7-8, 146-147).

Britain or the United Kingdom, meanwhile, followed a somewhat different course with respect to dealing with slavery. It approved legislation in 1807 that prevented allowing slaves from its colonies to remain slaves in Britain in cases where they had accompanied their owners to the mother country. Still, some British slaveholders who arrived in the mother country with slaves after this time used diversionary tactics to get around this new British ban. More than a few former slaves in such a circumstance, however, took matters into their own hands by simply escaping from their masters and blending rather unremarkably into British urban life (Walvin 2003: 1-8). In addition, the British government abolished the slave trade to its colonies effective March 1808 (Freeman-Grenville 1973: 145)

Many people remain unaware that people of African descent have a long history of serving in European armies and on European ships. Between 1768 and 1779, for example, Captain James Cook, an Englishman, an explorer, a navigator, and a cartographer led three voyages into the Pacific Ocean, which resulted in the accurate charting of many areas until that time not known to Europeans, including eastern Australia, New Zealand, and the Hawaiian Islands. When the first of these voyages departed London on August 26, 1768, with 91 men aboard the HM Bark *Endeavour* under the sponsorship of the Royal Society, in addition to the 83 marines on the ship was Joseph Banks, a wealthy gentleman well versed in natural history, with his civilian staff of eight.

As Cook had once been a student of Carolus Linnaeus, the famous Swedish botanist, zoologist, and taxonomist, it was not odd that several members of

Banks's staff were naturalists who apparently had also been students of Linnaeus. Banks's staff of eight on this voyage also included four servants, and of these, two—Thomas Richmond and George Dorlton—were described in the logs as "Negro." While collecting botanical specimens along with Banks in Tierra del Fuego at the southern tip of South America, Richmond, Dorlton, and Banks were caught in a sudden blizzard of snow. Although Banks managed to make it back to their ship, both Richmond and Dorlton froze to death. By the time this first voyage by Cook ended in London in 1771, 38 men, or well over one-third of those who had departed London, had lost their lives. That two of the men on this historic voyage during the reign of Britain's King George III were Europeans of African descent is testimony that processes such as migration, acculturation, and assimilation were clearly at work in Europe, processes that have always been a part of the human condition in some greater or lesser degree.

In 1772 when Granville Sharp became involved in the famous legal case having to do with James Somersett, Olaudah Equiano already aboard a ship headed to the Arctic. In addition to numerous boys commonly found on British ships in the second half of the 18th century as well as in the 19th—some of whom were free and some of whom were enslaved, as had been Olaudah Equiano in his youth—there was a large number of older sailors of African, African-Caribbean, and Euro-African extraction in the British merchant marine, in the Royal Navy, and on the ships of some British privateers and pirates.

While still an enslaved adolescent aboard various ships, Olaudah Equiano fought in engagements that pitted the British against the French on numerous occasions. A number of sailors of African descent fought in the Battle of Trafalgar in 1805, where forces of the newly constituted United Kingdom of Great Britain and Ireland, under the leadership of Admiral Haratio Nelson, fought against the combined forces of First-Empire France under Napoleon in alliance with Spain under the doomed naval leadership of Pierre Charles Silvestre de Villeneuve. It was in October of that year that Admiral Nelson executed a crushing defeat on the navies of France and Spain in the Battle of Trafalgar early during the second tenure of William Pitt the Younger as British prime minister, thereby ensuring British naval supremacy for many years to come. Many of Britain's sailors of African ancestry eventually settled in London, Liverpool, and Bristol, as well as from the 1840s on in the Bute Town area of Cardiff in South Wales, where many of them found employment in the coal trade.

It can hardly be overemphasized that people of African descent residing in Britain around this time had many different types of occupations and many varied experiences. In 1810, for example, there took place at Cophall Common, south of London, a boxing match between Tom Molineux and Tom Cribb that drew great attention from throughout Europe, no doubt in large measure because they were considered to be racially different from each other. Molineux lost this match from sheer exhaustion after 32 rounds of fighting. However, a rematch between them followed the next year at Thistleton Gap, Rutland, where Molineux again lost before an excited crowd of 25,000, this time in the 19th round after his jaw was broken. As reported in the Sussex *Weekly Advertiser* in its edition of Monday, October 7, 1811, William "Bill" Richmond was in Molineux's corner during this latter fight as one of his two seconds.

Despite the two unusual defeats for Molineux that he suffered to Crib, Molineux became a celebrity in England, where he was dressed by Beau Brummell, encouraged by Lord Byron and the Prince of Wales (who later became King George IV), welcomed in Gentleman Jackson's exclusive boxing salon, and sought after by many women, including some that were very socially prominent. Molineux's friend and fellow boxer William "Bill" Richmond, meanwhile, married a rich English woman. Making use of her resources as well as his own winnings from boxing, Richmond bought a pub, the "Horse and Dolphin," that was located in Leicester Square. In addition, Richmond also operated a boxing academy. Until Richmond completely stopped fighting in 1818, he also occasionally participated in exhibition fights.

Across the Channel under French auspices, the status of numerous people of African descent in metropolitan France during the Enlightenment period was from a legal perspective frequently confused. Still, a number of them became prominent figures in the life of metropolitan France. One such person was le Chevalier de Saint-Georges, who had been born around 1739 in the French Caribbean colony of Guadeloupe with the name of Joseph de Bologne. While his father was a married aristocrat, his mother was at first his father's enslaved mistress. Joseph was brought to France at the age of three by his parents as well as his father's wife, who apparently lived at times in a kind of *ménage à trois*. Fortunately for Joseph, all three of the adults involved nurtured him affectionately.

After passing his first five years in France living a life of privilege on a plantation owned by his paternal relatives where he was tutored especially in music and fencing, his father's wife enrolled him in school in Bordeaux. Two years later, Joseph found himself residing with his father and birth-mother in the fashionable Saint-Germain quarter on the Left Bank of Paris, close to where his father held the position of Gentlemen of the King's Chamber to Louis XV. Although precluded by the circumstances of his birth, and presumably his color, from inheriting a title through his father, Joseph was at age thirteen enrolled in the academy of Nicolas Texier de la Böessiere, which catered to the sons of French aristocrats.

While achieving extraordinary fame as a fencer and duelist, Joseph, along with Böessiere, the fencing master and founder of the academy, invented the fencing mask in 1780, thereby introducing an extremely important development to the sport. While fencing was especially emphasized at this academy, the full curriculum that Joseph followed also included such subjects as mathematics, foreign languages, music, history, drawing, and dance. Although Joseph continued to study at this academy until the age of nineteen, during three months of each of the last four years while there he also held the position of officer of the King's Guard. In this highly coveted position, Joseph became widely known in Paris as Chevalier de Saint-Georges and was often seen demonstrating his superb equestrian talent in the Tuileries Gardens adjacent to the *Palais Louvre*. Somewhat later, he took to riding through Paris in a fashionable two-wheeled carriage pulled by an English horse that his father had purchased for him as a prize for having defeated a fencing champion from the French city of Rouen.

Coupled with his outstanding reputation as an almost invincible fencer, Chevalier de Saint-Georges was a superb swimmer, marksman, and dancer. In addition to mastering the harpsichord and violin, he was a composer and conductor. He composed violin concertos and a concerto for the harp and he was among the earliest French composers of string quartets, quartets concertantes, and symphonies concertantes, the last being a genre quite similar to the concerto grosso. Chevalier de Saint-Georges also composed musical comedies, at least one opera, and a children's musical that was performed in London in 1788. Involved in the founding of a musical ensemble called *Concert des amateurs* (which in French refers to "lovers" of concert music rather than "amateurs"), he was at various times its first violinist, its timekeeper, and its conductor.

Chevalier de Saint-Georges also had associations with other orchestras at various times, including one that performed under his leadership in the *Palais-Royal*, a palace originally built for Cardinal Richelieu just north of the *Palais Louvre*. Beginning in the mid-17th century, *Palais-Royal* became a Parisian seat for the House of Orleans, beginning with Phillipe de France, duc d'Orléans, the younger brother of King Louis XIV. As Phillipe and his wife Henrietta-Anne, duchesse d'Orléans (known more often at court simply as *Madame*) hosted numerous grand events there, the *Palais-Royal* was already well established as a major social venue for *la crème de la crème* of French society during the period that Saint-Georges was performing there.

Until there was uproar over the fact that Chevalier de Saint-Georges was only of European descent through one of his parents, it seemed in 1775 that he might be selected as director of the Paris Opera (then also known as the *Académie Royale de Musique*). The occasion of the uproar was that certain artists accustomed to performing at the twelve or so theaters that were a part of this state institution since the time of Louis XIV addressed a petition to the Queen Marie-Antoinette "to beg Her Majesty that their honour and the delicacy of their conscience made it impossible for them to be subjected to the order of a mulatto" (Guédé 2003: 135; Smith 2005: 63-65).

When later in 1779 on the invitation of Queen Marie-Antoinette, Chevalier de Saint-Georges began periodically performing music at the royal palace in Versailles; six men (apparently undercover police) attacked him. Enduring such ebbs and flows in discrimination inspired by racism, he became a participant in *La Société des Amis des Noirs* that was founded in 1788. After the French Revolution erupted in 1789, Saint-Georges served his country valiantly, at one point as commander of a battalion composed of some one thousand Frenchmen largely of African descent. As this course of events demonstrates, the racism prevailing in Europe during the so-called Enlightenment did not make special allowances even for Europe's most accomplished geniuses.

Chevalier de Saint-Georges had once traveled to Vienna to commission Franz Joseph Haydn to compose six symphonies before continuing on to London, where he gave concerts and even fenced in a special match arranged there at the request of the Prince of Wales. Haydn dedicated the Parisian Symphonies to him, while Antonio Lolli in 1764 and François-Joseph Gossec in 1766 also dedicated musical compositions to him. That the lives of many people of appreciable African ancestry who lived in the midst of Europeans did not conform to the prejudices and negative stereotypes suggested to Europeans by many social philosophers of the Enlightenment undoubtedly constituted dilemmas for many.

Despite the accomplishments of Chevalier de Saint-Georges and the fact that he was the son of a French aristocrat, within the increasingly racist social climate around him that oftentimes drowned out genuine reason in the name of Enlightenment, it mattered more that he be considered an "other." By this time, reason was not infrequently reduced to falsely upholding myths that Europeans were racially pure and represented the highest form of human perfection in the world. As for Chevalier de Saint-Georges, without a wife or known offspring, his life was nearing its end as the 18th century slipped away. He died quietly in a small apartment in France's capital on the Seine in 1799. Tended only by one of the old soldiers that he had once commanded in the name of France, his life ended in a societal cul-de-sac in a Europe too preoccupied with race to allow him to escape (Guédé 2003; Smith 2005).

Fearing what it considered anti-monarchist radicalism that was a part of the French Revolution, Britain lost little time in enacting legislation that it hoped would forestall the spread of influences of the French Revolution across the Channel (Paul 1997: 65). Such fears were not completely without foundation considering that this was a period in Britain when there developed a considerable amount of solidarity among working-class people, the leaders of whom the British upper classes sometimes referred to as "the mob." One person espousing social revolution in Britain in the late 1700s was Thomas Spence, a journalist who believed that all land should be nationalized. Overlapping in time with the movement inspired by Spence, Sheffield radicals organized their biggest-ever mass meeting in 1794. This meeting, attended by thousands of artisan cutlers, unanimously passed a resolution calling for the emancipation of "black" slaves as well as the ending of the slave trade.

The British government reacted with repression by effectively prohibiting public meetings in 1795 and by outlawing what it considered radical trade-union activities four years later. In so doing, it crippled both radicalism and extra-parliamentary calls for the abolition of slavery (Fryer 1984: 211-212). Although Thomas Spence died in 1814, his "forty disciples," largely of the working class, pledged that they would keep his ideas alive. In this connection, they formed the Society of Spencean Philanthropists and organized themselves into a number of small groups all over London. Their tasks were made very difficult by the fact that their movement was infiltrated with numerous government spies and that freedom of press was not recognized as an established right in Britain in the early 1800s. Two people of African ancestry—Robert Wedderburn and William Davidson—were destined to become very prominent in the leadership of the Spencean movement at a time that the government policies revolved around racism and imperialism, making in an especially attractive target for government suppression. This was a period when in Britain one could be easily imprisoned for expressing opinions that challenged religion or the privileges of the ruling class.

Jamaican-born Robert Wedderburn arrived in Britain in 1778 in his early fifties. Having seen his enslaved mother flogged while she was pregnant, his elderly grandmother flogged, as well as the brutalizing of numerous other "black" women, he arrived in Europe much embittered by British colonialism and racism. That in Britain he became a Unitarian, rejected the Trinity, and managed to meet and be influenced by Thomas Spence about nine months before Spence died did not sit well with the British establishment. In 1817, an Act of Parliament was passed with the aim of suppressing the Spenceans, and when their leader Thomas Evans and his twenty-year-old son were jailed later that year on a charge of high treason, Wedderburn came into prominence within the leadership of the Spenceans.

Also from Jamaica, William Davidson arrived in Britain of a somewhat higher socioeconomic status than Wedderburn. While his mother was "black," his father was Jamaica's attorney general. At age fourteen, he had been sent to Scotland to complete his education. After being apprenticed to a Liverpool lawyer for three years, he ran away to sea and was twice impressed into the Royal Navy. After being discharged, he studied mathematics in Aberdeen for a while but was soon apprenticed to a Lichfield cabinetmaker. Eventually settling down as a cabinetmaker in Birmingham, Davidson also was drawn to left-wing causes. As in the case of Wedderburn, this brought him to the attention of government informers.

Davidson eventually came under the influence of Arthur Thistlewood, one of London's most influential radical leaders and organizers. By the end of 1819, Thistlewood had gathered round him a group of some thirty working-class men who believed that assassination was the only way to dislodge Britain's government of "murderous tyrants." When shortly after this time Davidson became secretary of the newly formed shoemakers' trade union, a police spy by the name of George Edward entrapped Davidson into participating in a scheme directed at overthrowing the government. Eventually, Thistlewood, Davidson, and several of their companions stood trial for high treason before a series of carefully selected juries. After being convicted, they were hanged in 1820, and their bodies disposed of unceremoniously. As for Wedderburn, he was for a while incarcerated in Newgate Prison on charges of sedition and blasphemy. Although the sedition charge was later dropped, he was eventually made to serve two years under difficult conditions in Dorchester jail for "blasphemous libel" (Fryer 1984: 214-227). Almost two decades would pass before working-class Britons would again rise up to demand major social reform via the Chartism movement in the late 1830s.

One child of African descent who had been born on the island of St. Croix in the Danish Virgin Islands was brought to Europe around 1760 when he was around thirteen years of age. This very talkative lad had the nickname of Couschi. In Europe, he was given, perhaps as a present, to a Swedish civil servant named Landshövding Anders von Reiser, who rather took a liking to the fact that Couschi was very garrulous. After being presented to Queen Louisa Ulrika of Sweden the following year, Couschi was like by her so much that she attached him to her household. When the queen died shortly afterward, however, Couschi was acquired by Princess Sofia Albertina and employed as an exotic courtier. As in this household Couschi gradually began to be considered something more than an amusing toy and playful servant, however, provision was made for him to receive a strict formal education. Following his being instructed in Christianity, he was baptized in December 1768 and renamed after various members of the royal family as Adolph Ludvig Gustaf Frederick Albert Badin. After becoming a well-read, highly cultivated Swedish court secretary with the title of assessor, Adolph Badin began to exercise great influence on many policies that emanated from the court. A formal portrait of Adolph Badin executed by the artist G. Lundberg in 1775 in which Badin is seen playing chess depicts him as poised, highly animated, shrewdly calculating, and regally attired. Married to two different Scandinavian women at various times, Adolph Badin eventually died in Copenhagen in 1822 (Debrunner 1979: 104-105).

As has been shown, the period from the Seven Years' War in 1763 to around the 1815 Congress of Vienna held at the end of the Napoleonic Wars was one filled with geopolitical machinations in Europe and in European colonies abroad as well as by much racist theorizing that complicated the lives of people of appreciable African heritage living in Europe. With respect to European policies during this period having to do with so-called race, it is important to distinguish between those operative in metropolitan Europe and those that Europeans governments permitted in their colonies abroad. In 1807, Britain enacted an Abolition of the Slave Trade Act, but this was largely because its government was more interested in imperialism and/or colonialism than in persisting in a slave trade that it no longer considered to be in its national interest. Although Britain also enacted legislation in 1807 to stop participating in the slave trade the following year, it did not get around to making slavetrading a felony until 1811.

Although racism contaminated in varying degrees social milieus in Europe, racism on the continent was virtually nowhere transformed into the rigidly enforced brutalities that were commonplace in European colonies abroad. Concerning the slavery that Napoleon had reintroduced into French colonies in 1802, he never made any move to abolish it. France, hoping however to make a favorable impression on Great Britain, did at least temporarily abolish slavery again in 1818. While Europeans continued to equivocate about slavery and its abolition in their various colonies, numerous people of appreciable African descent continued to live out their lives in Europe.

To a man of African descent originally from Barbados and a woman who was likely of Austro-German ancestry two sons were born in eastern Poland in the late 1770s. The older son was named George Augustus Polgreen Bridgetower and the other Friedrich T. Bridgetower. While Friedrich developed into an accomplished cellist, George Augustus Polgreen Bridgetower was a virtuoso child prodigy who excelled at performing on the violin. In 1779 or 1780 when George was born, his polyglot father worked as a valet in the employ of Polish Prince Miklós Esterházy near where Franz Joseph Haydn resided and for whom

Haydn landed the dream position of Kapellmeister in his late twenties. It is plausible that Haydn was the early music teacher of both brothers.

In April 1789 in Paris, George Bridgetower at age 9 gave his professional debut as a violin soloist performing the *Concert Spiritual* by the fashionable Italian violinist and composer Giovanni Giornovichi. When in February the following year George's father, who supervised his son's music training in the early years, introduced him on stage at the Drury Lane Theater in England, George performed on violin between parts of the *Messiah*. George's talent was so phenomenal that an invitation for him to perform for the royal family at Windsor Castle soon followed. Included among those to whose attention he came was the Prince of Wales (the future King George IV), himself a cellist. Immediately impressed by George's talents and disposition, by 1791 the Prince of Wales placed George under his own patronage and ordered the elder Bridgetower to leave the country.

While this meant that George Bridgetower was from this time deprived of a normal life with his parents and brother, his new royal patron provided him with the most distinguished tutors available, began rearing him as a gentleman, and carefully managed his professional career in ways that brought him into contact with many of the most gifted musicians in Europe. George was involved in the premieres of the Haydn's Symphonies Numbers. 93-104, also known as "the London Symphonies," which Haydn composed during his two visits to London, the first time from 1791 to 1792 and the second time from 1793 to 1795. Although during fourteen years, Bridgetower held the post of first violinist in an orchestra of which the Prince of Wales was patron, he occasionally took on other engagements. Between February 1792 and the end of March, he performed in concerts on the mainland of Europe. Two years later in a concert arranged by François Barthélémon, a French composer, violinist, and army officer in the Irish brigade, Bridgetower and Haydn performed a Viotti concerto together.

Allowed a two-year leave of absence that began in 1802, George Bridgetower visited his mother and younger brother in Dresden. The following year in Vienna, Ludwig van Beethoven, then 32 years of age, received George warmly after they had been introduced at the home of Prince Josef Johann Schwarzenberg. Beethoven wrote letters introducing Bridgetower to several people in Vienna, including Baron Alexander Wetzlar. Together, the two musicians premiered Ludwig van Beethoven's "Kreutzer Sonata," with Bridgetower on violin and Beethoven on piano. While Beethoven, who was greatly influenced by the work of Haydn, had tentatively dedicated this composition to Bridgetower, Beethoven later changed its dedication to Rodolphe Kreutzer because of their competition for the affection of the same female.

In 1805, Bridgewater's brother visited London and they performed together at a May benefit concert arranged by the Prince of Wales in the New Rooms, Hanover Square. Around the time that George Bridgetower's mother died in 1806 or 1807 in Budissen, Saxony or Dresden, where she lived with his brother, George was a founding member of the Professional Music Society. Eventually also a pianist and composer, George Bridgetower earned a Bachelor of Music degree from Cambridge University in June 1811. In fact, the exercise that he performed in this connection at Great St. Mary's Church was *By Faith Sublime Fair Passiflora Steers Her Pilgrimage along This Vale of Tears*, an anthem for orchestra and chorus that had been set to a text by F. A. Rawdon. Two years later, George Bridgetower became one of the original members of the Royal Philharmonic Society.

Married by 1819, Bridgetower eventually fathered a daughter in Italy. He was in Rome in 1825 and again in 1827, although by this time he likely had already moved his primary residence to Paris. He eventually returned to England where he lived the last part of his life. Although George Bridgetower died in 1860 in the part of South London known as Peckham at a time that, due to its improved transport services, its green areas were rapidly giving way to houses of varying qualities, he was buried in Kensal Green Cemetery, one of London's most distinguished burial grounds (Fryer 1984: 428-430; Panton 2005; Williams 2001).

Although the combined efforts of people of African descent in Europe along with those of their "white" allies were not sufficient to halt an approaching tidal wave of pseudo-scientific racism that was reaching unprecedented heights, a substantial number of people deemed African, or partially so, not only survived but thrived. Two results of Europe's embrace of pseudo-scientific racism at home were that it added to prejudiced European thought about people of color and that it also made Europeans more fanatical about claiming racial purity in ways that they hoped would put them beyond the suspicion of racial taint that they increasingly associated with African origin.

Despite these developments, numerous people of African descent in Europe continued to be assimilated into the huge sea of Europeans that surrounded them. Alexandre Dumas *père*, for example, preferred to bear the surname of his "black" Haitian-born paternal grandmother who had once been a slave rather than that of his aristocratic grandfather. In his famous novel *The Three Musketeers* he was also proud to fictionalize many of the real life exploits of General Thomas-Alexandre Dumas, his "mulatto" father who had died when he was only three and a half years old. Although the life of Alexndre Dumas *père*, especially as a child, was sometimes touched by colorism within and without his family, including by taunting from classmates that was tinged with racism, he did not consider himself "black." His life, like the lives of people in Europe and around the world, bears witness to the fluidity and complexity in human variation and social identities that it is not particularly logical to try to contain within the rigidity that we often bring to our thinking about "self" and "otherness."

Chapter Four

Constructing Pedigrees and Empires

1815 to 1914

Although in 1792, France affirmed "the civil rights of freedman" and in 1794 approved a decree providing for the emancipation of slaves in order to reduce the incidence of slave revolts in its Caribbean colonies, this was in reality a freedom in name only. After slaves on Guadeloupe had helped the French re-conquer that island in 1786, the slaves were forced to continue working on plantations in accordance with the status quo ante. Napoleon went further in 1801 by officially restoring slavery in all French colonies that his troops could control, even allowing his troops in Saint-Domingue to use sulphur dioxide gas, arms, and dogs and those in Guadeloupe to massacre resisters, who were abolitionists, including in their homes and on the beaches, to achieve this end.

As brutal, inhumane, and despicable as slavery could be wherever it raised its head, slavery in neither Europe nor Africa near the Mediterranean tended to evolve into the same types of plantation systems as were common in many parts of the New World. Slavery in Europe and close to the Mediterranean also some-times involved many more gradations of clientship and vassal relations that tran-scended color. Among the illustrations of this was the legacy of slave kings in some parts of this area and even warrior castes of slave origin that in some cases became virtual ruling dynasties that were without parallels in the New World. Neither in the New World or the Old World, however, were people who tended to profit directly from the exploitation of slaves willing to suddenly embrace abolitionism merely out of some sense of selfless morality.

When most of the Netherlands emerged from French hegemony that lasted from 1795 by means of an 1814 treaty between Britain and what was still re-ferred to as the United Provinces of the Netherlands and sometimes simply as the United Netherlands, it included a provision that outlawed Dutch participa-tion in the slave trade. That the Dutch were prepared to outlaw slave trading in 1814 was because they no longer viewed it as vital to their national interests (Vink 2004: 1-2) in comparison with being able to regain their independence from French control toward the end of the Napoleonic Wars.

Moreover, the agreement to no longer participate in the slave trade was imposed on them and did not result from some spontaneous moral conversion. For geopolitical rather than moral reasons, Spain in 1815 merely restricted its slave traders to the area south of the equator. Although treaties were concluded in 1817 by Britain with Spain and Portugal that permitted the British to search their ships at sea for slaves, Portugal merely followed the earlier precedent established by Spain a couple of years earlier by also restricting its slave trading to areas south of the equator (Freeman-Grenville 1973: 147). When King Louis XVIII succeeded Napoleon in 1814, bringing about the end of the short dynasty of three Bonapartist kings in the Kingdom of Sicily, Muslim slaves in Sicily were emancipated. Even in Sicily, however, this emancipation was more a by-product of French state policy than a main thrust of it. Between France and its Caribbean colonies, the reopening of sea commerce that came about in 1814 resulted in more planters coming to France with their slaves (McCloy 1961: 62).

Already during the Napoleonic Wars that involved France's attempt to impose its hegemony across the face of Europe, some Europeans were arguing paradoxically that the best way to end slavery in Africa was to open it up further to their control through colonialism. Although they typically rationalized the so-called need for such control as legitimate trade and investment and even sometimes as humanitarian or in keeping with religious requirements, a contributing factor lying hardly beneath the surface was racism. Although Britain had by 1807 put an end to slave trading at the Cape in southern Africa, it was no coincidence that it also began its most serious colonial penetration of that region of Africa around the same time. Well before this time, however, Turkey already maintained a colonial hold on a swath of northern Africa from Algeria to Egypt and European penetration of Africa had been mostly from the east and the west.

Shipping in and around the waterways that separated Europe and northern Africa was at the beginning of the 19th century not completely safe, neither from the threat of piracy nor that of privateering (also known as the corso), which was essentially a licensed and recognized profession of kidnapping people for enslavement or ransom. There was nothing new in this despite the fact that the United States sent war ships against Algiers and Tripoli to retaliate and a peace treaty with those Turkish regencies was signed. Still, in the following year, a Dutch fleet under Lord Exmouth attacked the port and destroyed much of the fleet of Algiers. What was new was that by this time, a number of Western countries had come into their own as major world powers and Turkey was in decline. To the major powers of Europe, the continued enslavement of Christians, by which they generally meant "white" European Christians, had become not only inconvenient, it had become an insult to their evolving feelings of racial superiority, to their claims of national grandeur, and to the Christianity over which they had fought many battles in the past.

Whereas Morocco forbade privateering or participation in the corso in 1817, France did not even temporarily make the slave trade illegal for the second time until 1818. Oddly in this same year, an Anglo-French fleet sanctimoniously forced on the Turkish regency of Tunis the acceptance of a protocol that prohibited the enslavement of Christians. Between 1818 and 1820, the Sultan of Fezzan in what is now southwestern Libya earned considerable revenue by taxing some 4,000 slaves that passed annually through his territory mostly from south to north (Freeman-Grenville 1973: 146). While some of these captives from south of the Sahara remained in northern Africa, others undoubtedly ended up north of the Mediterranean Sea in Europe. Also after the end the Napoleonic Wars, more than two million slaves would still be transported from Africa to the Americas. Although the Netherlands was no longer involved, nations who certainly were included France, Spain, and Portugal, as well as Brazil, where authorities often closed their eyes to what was happening. This enabled most of the two million slaves transported to the New World in the 19th century to be transported somewhat clandestinely (Emmer 2005: 162-165).

The Congress of Vienna that convened in 1815 was destined to be very historically significant for Africans as well as for Europeans. Representatives from France, Prussia, Great Britain, Russia, and Austria wished to restore parts of Europe that had been overrun by France during the Napoleonic Wars to their "legitimate" rulers. Although the Congress paid some pious and perfunctory lip service to the desirability of one day ending the slave trade from Africa, its signatories took no concrete action to do so. Whereas prior to the Congress the European penetration of African was concentrated largely along the eastern and western coasts of Africa, colonial penetration from the north and south began that reached even into Africa's interior took place following the Congress of Vienna in 1815. The Europeans who would be involved had names such as David Livingstone, Mungo Park, Henry Morton Stanley, Samuel Baker, Henri Duveyrier, Gerhard Rohlfs, and Thomas Somerville.

It is ironic that so many Western historians continue to romanticize these expeditions as merely explorative, scientific, or humanitarian while overlooking that they were often geopolitical, strategic, and opportunistic, and that they prepared the way for many new abuses. We still live a world where many people considered populations as "pre-contact" or "undiscovered" until the first people of European descent have arrived wherever they live to officially proclaim them in existence. Whereas in one part of Africa, Europeans might attempt to justify such penetration of the continent immediately south of Europe on the basis of a people's undeserved prosperity, in another part of Africa they might argue that intervention was necessary because a people was backward, or perhaps simply because their strategic location put them in danger of falling under the control of rival powers. Often, it was also argued that a takeover by some European power was necessary to protect that power's financial investment.

Somewhat surprisingly, the Congress of Vienna participants reinstated France in several of the colonies taken from it by the British navy during the Napoleonic Wars including the coast along the Western Bulge of Africa from Cap Blanc into Senegal without any imposition of restrictions with respect to slavery. France lost little time before it began to encroach along the southern and western flanks of what is now the country of Mauritania. In connection with France's push to establish a new colonial empire in Africa, it was no coincidence that its Compagnie du Saint-Esprit and Lazarist missionary seminaries reopened in 1816 (Freeman-Grenville 1973: 147) at essentially the same time as the French replaced the British in the borderland between southern Mauritania and northern Senegal. It was also no coincidence that the French began to build forts there to secure their trading monopolies in the area. They constructed a fort at Bakel in 1820 and another at Dagana in 1821. From the basin of the Senegal River, moreover, they resumed their earlier behavior of meddling in the affairs of the Trarza Emirate.

Although the Duc de Broglie—as prime minister of France—brought some abolitionist sympathies with him into the government, when in 1817 France published a decree curtailing the slave trade to French colonies, enterprising merchants of Nantes and Bordeaux simply switched their destinations to Cuba. Hence, in 1818 when France for the second time made French participation in the slave trade illegal, French slavers simply converted a tolerated trade into a clandestine one. Between 1818 and 1831, as a consequence, approximately 500 expeditions to buy slaves departed from various French ports (Thomas 1997: 625-626).

Accompanied by a number of Africans who were residing in France, the French sent Colonel Schmaltz to assume control of Senegal after its return to French control from the British. Schmaltz lost little time in granting Senegalese largely under the control of "mulatto" elites concentrated in Saint-Louis and on Gorée Island special second-class rights implying French citizenship. In 1823, Gabriel Pellegrin, a "mulatto" who had supported the French Revolution in 1789, succeeded Schmaltz as governor of these areas. Nearby when Trarza Emir Mohammed al- Habib only two years later married the heiress to the Oualo Kingdom south of the Senegal River over which the French had declared a protectorate, that this brought a hostile colonialist response from France clearly indicated that France was using Senegal to begin assembling a major colonial empire in Africa.

In 1822, a French nun named Mother Superior Anne-Marie Javouhey had founded two schools in Senegal, and between 1825 and 1827 she sent eighteen Senegalese students, some of whom were "mulattoes, to France for additional education. Although the predominant religion in the area that is now Mauritania and Senegal was Islam, it was the intention of Javouhey that several of the male students be trained to become Catholic priests, and some of the boys as a consequence eventually received advanced training in theology at the Paris Seminary of the Compagnie du Saint-Esprit. Among these were Arsine Fridoil, a Senegalese "mulatto" from Saint-Louis, David Boilat, and Jean-Pierre Moussa, all of whom were eventually ordained as priests in 1840 (Debrunner 1979: 184-187).

Also reflective of a long tradition where Africans have sometimes come to Europe largely for education, Muhammad Ali, the European ruling Egypt ostensibly under the authority of Ottoman Turkey between 1811 and 1848 sent some 311 Egyptians students of privilege to study in England, Austria, Italy, and France. While France, like the other countries just mentioned, were apparently welcoming to most Africans in Europe for educational poses, the contemporaneous conditions in various European colonies were often oppressive and brutal. In 1822 on the French-controlled island of Martinique, for example, there was so much racist discrimination and abuse that "blacks" and "mulattoes" joined together in an uprising.

Among those who campaigned doggedly against the mis-treatment of "mulattos" in Martinique around this time was Cyrille Charles Auguste Bissette, a well-to-do "mulatto" from that island. Bissette was also active in Paris with regard to this cause from the early 1820s into the late 1840s. It was in this connection that he authored many pamphlets and brochures. In 1847, for example, he wrote a tract addressed to the French clergy and another to French local officials (McCloy 1961: 136-139). To be certain, *African* was not the equivalent of *slave* in metropolitan France during the early 19th-century. Like the prince named Papel from Bany who was in Nantes in 1816 or 1817, even a good number of African nobles visited Paris during this period (McCloy 1961: 135; Debrunner 1979: 189-192).

After 1830, France's King Louis-Philippe again made trading in slaves a crime. In a somewhat serious effort to enforce the king's decree, slave merchants were supposed to be imprisoned for two to five years if their ships were seized in France, for ten to twenty years if they were caught on the high seas, and for ten years of hard labor if apprehended after the slaves had been bought. That freed slaves were to be given liberty in the American colony for which they had been intended suggests that the French government did not wish to receive additional residents of African background in Europe (Thomas 1997: 627). After slaves had long been denied the privilege of using surnames, a royal ordinance of 1836 made it easier for those in French colonies to acquire them. An additional ordinance of the same year stipulated that any master wishing to bring a slave into France needed to make a "declaration of enfranchisement" for him or her before setting out on the trip. Where an owner failed to do so, the slave would be considered free on arriving in France. It further stipulated that all slaves in metropolitan France from this time were free (McCloy 1961: 142-143).

Although many slaves of African descent were manumitted in the French colonies of Martinique, Guadeloupe, Dominica, and Réunion and French participation in the slave trade was no longer lawful, French slaveholding itself was not abolished (McCloy 1961: 142). From the 1840s, increasing numbers of people of African descent entered France traveling independently, including some who were "black," some whom were "mulattoes," and presumably some whom were of other ethnic derivations, such as Jews, Arabs, and Berbers. A good number of these people who arrived from the Caribbean were women who had children with them (McCloy 1961: 134).

Europeans by this time relied heavily on pseudo-scientific and popular thinking about race; what was deemed to be the mixing of Europeans with other peoples was not infrequently condemned in various efforts to maintain a particular type of social order. To facilitate the playing out of this situation as a combination of revealed truth, common sense, and science, it did not much matter if real human connections had to be denied or misrepresented in keeping with racist myths. Racial purity could be claimed where no purity existed, superiority where no superiority existed, and benevolence where no benevolence existed.

Insecurities and a variety of self-interests sometimes even led European abolitionists to contribute to a nexus between race thinking and racism.

European policy adjustments with respect to slave trading, slaveholding, and
the abolition of these practices are not best understood as indicating some grand
European moralistic conversion, to the notion that slavery should end although
there were exceptional individuals who were committed abolitionists. In Britain,
for example, William Wilberforce introduced an abolition motion in the House
of Commons every year from 1791. Thomas Clarkson, by contrast, withdrew
from the abolitionist movement for ten years beginning in 1794 out of frustra-
tion with his compatriots who were still equivocating on slavery. Similarly in
France, although the Marquis de la Fayette and Abbé Henri Grégoire forcefully
railed against the slave trade (Thomas 1997: 623), many influential Europeans,
increasingly influenced by pseudo-scientific racism, were willing use abolition
of the slave trade as but a pretext for advocating for the establishment of even
larger empires operating on the principle of "white" supremacy.

A byproduct of these attitudes was more complication associated with assimilation into metropolitan European societies for people deemed to be "others,"
a concept that by this time almost invariably included people of appreciable
African descent. To fall within this category of "others," however, one did not
need to appear "black" or foreign. For example, vitriolic and violent outbursts of
oppression periodically were directed against Jewish and Romani populations
even when the persecuted Jews and Roma involved were Europeans. As indicated by some of the so-called mulattoes of Saint-Domingue and other places
who often looked as "white" as most Europeans and sometimes had many more
close ancestors who were considered "white" than "black," virtually any physical or cultural characteristic that could be exploited as a taint was sometimes
sufficient to cause people residing in Europe to be victimized.

In keeping with this way of thinking, Europeans developed a calculus for
classifying "otherness" in a variety of inconsistent ways. With respect to so-
called people of color or *gens de couleurs*, it was not limited to "blacks" and
"mulattoes," but also factored in so-called quadroons, octoroons, and so forth.
Moreover, there existed an array of such terms as *Moor, Negro, Saracen, Oriental, bastard, heathen,* and *infidel* that were sometimes characterized by a variety
of overlapping referents. As Europeans conjured up ideas of what they thought
could definitely not be a European, some forms of "otherness" that they focused
on were very specific.

An example of this was that of Hottentot, as presented for example in the
travelogues of William Dampier, Sir Thomas Herbert, and John Ovington
(Woodard 1999: 102-103; Mosse 1985: 15) as well as in the writings of the British MP and Board of Trade official Soame Jenyns (Fryer 1984: 166; Mudimbe
1994). As pseudo-scientific racism no less than popular racism reached unprecedented levels, it was not long before a British ship doctor named William Dun-
lop persuaded a woman from the southern tip of Africa to agree to be shipped to
Piccadilly in London. While we do not know what she anticipated on boarding
the ship for Europe, his intent was clearly to put her on display as a freakish
"Hottentot Venus" for the amusement of Europeans. She was by no means a

randomly chosen African woman. Her body was characterized by a much larger than typical accumulation of fat about the buttocks and thighs and somewhat more elongated than average genitalia, an entirely non-pathological condition known as steatopygia. Still, this added to the sensationalism of putting her on display as a spectacle to be mocked.

Originally named Sartje, this woman was renamed Sarah Bartman in Europe and was exhibited for the commercial profit of her exploiters as "the ultimate savage," sometimes for as long as eleven hours a day. Even after she was baptized in Manchester, some Europeans claimed that Sarah Bartman was the missing link in a chain of being between humanity and lower animals. Still essentially a captive, Bartman eventually died from alcoholism and small pox in Paris in 1815. Even in death however she was not allowed to rest in peace or escape her exploiters. George Cuvier, a prominent lecturer and researcher in anatomy at the *Musée National d'Histoire Naturelle*, dissected her cadaver. When George Cuvier presented various casts of her body to the Royal Academy of Medicine in Paris, he did so by pronouncing "I have the honor of presenting you the genital organs of this woman." Various of these casts remained on display at the *Musée de l'Homme* located on the Place du Trocadéro in Paris as late as 1982 (Strother 1999: 1-61; Fryer 1984: 227-230). After lengthy negotiations between France and the post-apartheid government of South Africa, the remains of Bartman were finally returned to South Africa for a state burial, but this was as late as August 9, 2002, which was Woman's Day in the country of her birth.

During many of the approximately 187 years that Bartman remained in Europe, according to Bernth Lindfors, she "continued to influence the way Africans were perceived in Europe until ultimately she became reified as a biological concept, a scientifically sanctified racial cliché" (Woodard 1999: 140-142). In reality, Bartman was but one of numerous people of African and other non-European descents exhibited for the amusement of Europeans during the 19th and early 20th centuries as though they were freaks of nature. Another "black" woman, for example, was exhibited in the nude in Paris in 1829 at the ball of the Duchess du Barry. In 1853, eleven Zulu men and one woman from southern Africa were transported to Europe where they were exhibited in England, France, and Germany rather as if in a zoo. They were even transported to Buckingham Palace for a viewing by Queen Victoria (Coquery-Vidrovitch 2007: 28) around the same time that Britons were shamelessly bragging that the vastness of their global empire prevented the sun from ever setting on it.

Further illustrating that racist objectification of people deemed to have any hereditary association with Africa by Europeans was not rare, one need only recall those Africans and mixed Europeans of part African decent resident in Europe who after their deaths were stuffed and placed on exhibit as if they had been wild animals. Some even had their skins carefully removed so that they could be used as the human covering for certain wood models or plastic casts. One African in Europe whose corpse was defiled in this way was Mmadi Make, who had been baptized at Messina, Italy, in 1731 as Angelo Soliman, and who eventually died in Vienna in 1796. Another was Joseph Hammer, a gardener who died in poverty at a Vienna hospital. Another two people of African descent whose corpses were treated in this manner were a girl made available by a King of Naples and a man who had been employed in the zoo at Schönbrunn Palace for Franz I, the first emperor of Austria (Debrunner 1979: 112-114, 145). This same ruler was also Franz II of the Holy Roman Empire, at least until his defeat by Napoleon between 1792 and 1806 brought the Holy Roman Empire to an end with his being its last emperor.

Although at the beginning of the period under discussion in this chapter, it is doubtful that whatever pan-European identity existed was very rigid in seeing "otherness" in concrete forms that many Europeans considered grotesque, Europeans quickly began to embrace such concepts as African, Oriental, Indian, and American Indian as symbolizing what Europeans were not. While some of the people disrespected in these ways ended up on display in museums only after their deaths, others were featured in traveling exhibits even while they lived. Among those involved in hosting such traveling exhibitions on both sides of the Atlantic were the American circus entrepreneurs known as Barnum and Bailey. Such exhibits as these undoubtedly contributed to an exaggerated sense of the social and biological distance that many Europeans thought of as separating them and Africans, even in situations where they lived near each other and interacted on a day-to-day basis.

A part of the process of creating a mythical opposition between Europeans and people of African descent lay in distortion and denial of relatedness to each other in ways that were consistent with prevailing tenants of pseudo-scientific racism and the new imperialist reordering of the world that was emanating especially from Europe. Around the same time that Bartman was on display in Europe, a British parliamentary committee recommended that "black" beggars in London should be transported to the West Indies, which surely would have meant their being enslaved, although some of these beggars were actually British military veterans (Fryer 1984: 230-232). Such a proposal was fully consistent with the current thinking that Europeans needed to think of themselves not only as racially superior, but also as so different as to be racially pure.

When the independence of Brazil in 1823 essentially eliminated the largest market in African slaves from which Portugal had until this time derived most of its income, Portugal became much more concerned about what it considered to be the racial makeup of its population in Europe. In an effort to portray its population as less African than it was, Portugal discontinued the gathering of any racio-ethnic data in rural areas of the country. In this way, Portugal's African presence beyond Lisbon disappeared statistically although, in reality, it continued to exist. Tinhorão (1988: 364-366) has referred to this statistical whitening process in Portugal as *branquamento*.

Underlying much of a growing European discomfort with slavery by this time was the realization that slavery resulted in a growing African presence in Europe. As the Enlightenment and the subsequent scholarly focus on human variation had made Europeans very anxious to separate themselves from people they considered their inferiors, racism such as had for a long time been used to justify slavery began to be redirected to justify European imperialism. This new focus enabled some European countries with grandiose ambitions of possessing huge global empires to become committed to the abolition of slavery without abandoning attitudes that were essentially racist.

Britain did not officially declare slave trading to be the equivalent of piracy until 1824. Three years later it declared slave trading a form of piracy that became punishable by death. This did not mean, however, that Europeans were turning against racism. The fact that Britain did not emancipate the slave populations of its empire until 1834 shows the racist double standard and self-interest that were involved in even its protestations about the slave trade. A further indication that Britain's declaration was not particularly successful may be seen in the fact that slavery had to be declared abolished in India as late as in 1838. That Pope Gregory XVI did not issue his bull *In Supremo* that condemned slavery until the following year of 1839 also illustrates how long Europeans were willing to look at slavery with a double standard. Whatever the attitudes and rhetoric about slavery and its abolition, privateering was a type of "legal" piracy that remained a widely accepted part of naval warfare from the 16th into the 19th centuries and even Britain and France did not officially renounce privateering until the Conference of Paris was held in 1856 (Freeman-Grenville 1973: 165).

So long was the reach of racism and so enticing the rewards many Europeans hoped to gain through empire building around the world that even those who campaigned for the abolition of slavery sometimes knowingly or unknowingly found themselves working in common cause with imperialists whose abuses could be as exploitative and brutal as those of slave masters. As throughout the 19th century and into the 20th racism continued to evolve and take on more complexity, many Europeans rushed to fabricate pedigrees that they hoped would protect them from any hint of racial taint and to conjure up such slogans as "the white man's burden" and "*mission civilatrice*" that they hoped would absolve them of guilt for the systems of exploitation that they were increasingly employing to reorder the world to their advantage.

Europeans as well as some of their neighbors in Africa and Asia had long been involved in exploitative policies toward people they considered "others" that relied on piracy, slavery, racism, religious discrimination, and colonialism. By the 19th century when Turkey was in decline, however, Europeans were less tolerant of reliance on similar types of abuses. In keeping with a rising tide of European assertiveness against what many considered oriental decadence and corruption, some European peoples developed nationalist attitudes that were especially hostile toward the predominantly-Muslim Ottoman Empire of Turkey for reasons that had accumulated over a very long period of time.

By this time, the elements of what the West would thereafter refer to as the so-called Eastern Question had come into play as issues of racism became ever more conflated with those having to do with slavery and imperialism. The Eastern Question directly concerned how such great powers as Russia, Britain, France, Austria-Hungary, Italy, and Germany would manage competition among themselves while seeking to divide up the spoils of an Ottoman Turkish Empire whose decline was almost in free fall, European nations such as Britain and France with growing empires in such overseas places as Africa were also concerned with how to facilitate a transition from open participation in slavery to

more subtle ways of extending their control over the people they were colonizing and exploiting as their "racial inferiors."

For several centuries, Turkey had been in control of large parts of southeastern Europe, and many Europeans resented this. European resentment was compounded by the fact that Turkey was the dominant power in the eastern basin of
the Mediterranean and by the fact that it exercised some loose authority along
the southern shore of Mediterranean as well. This situation, coupled with an
upsurge in pseudo-scientific racism and a desire on the part of certain major
European powers that were mostly Christian to expand their empires, meant that
a major contest between these Europeans and Turkey was virtually inevitable,
both in Europe and in Africa. As this contest unfolded, much contradictory and
self-righteous rhetoric about slavery and abolition led major European powers to
imagine that imperialism imposed by them, no matter how abusive, was superior
and more humane than that imposed by others. Racism was of great tactical use
in attempts to rationalize such a distinction.

In the wake of the French expulsion from Egypt in 1801, the Ottoman Turks
had been hopeful of ousting their British allies and regaining control of Egypt.
Under an Albanian contingent that the Ottomans had sent to Egypt it seemed for
a while that this might be accomplished. As these Albanians joined ranks with
the Mamluks to drive the British from Egypt largely under the leadership of
Muhammad Ali, the Turks were so elated that they elevated him first to pasha
and shortly afterward to khedive of Egypt. Soon however, Muhammad Ali began exhibiting an independent streak. After eventually overthrowing the Mamluks in Upper Egypt, he waged a two-year war of conquest against the Sudan
that began in 1820. In addition to his wish to eliminate the Mamluks as rivals
there, he wished to gain direct access to their vast supplies of slaves. Already in
July of 1820, a force of 4,000 left Egypt for the southern Balkans made up of
Turks, Albanians, and people of African derivation. The following year, a
second column left Cairo under Ismail Pasha for the southern Balkans and Aegean region in April, and in June, after Funj submitted to Ismail Pasha, Ismail
Pasha dispatched slaves from Sudan for sale in the southern Balkans to help
Muhammad Ali's intervention there (Freeman-Grenville 1979: 148).

This was an area of southeastern Europe that had been under Turkish domination for almost four centuries, and one where the Greek War of Independence
would erupt in 1821 as the second of the national revolutions in the Balkans
(since that of Serbia that started in 1804). Already during the period between
1755 and 1768, a celebrity born in the Prussian city of Stendal named Johann
Joachim Winckelmann had played a major role in the idealization of a rather
narrow aesthetic that he associated with ancient Greece. A formative essay entitled *Reflections on the Painting and Sculpture of the Greeks* that Winckelmann
authored in 1755 and a work that he published in 1764 entitled *History of the Art
of Antiquity* were widely read and discussed across Europe.

Whatever else he was, Winckelmann was an Egyptophobe as well as an anti-
Semite (Bernal 1987: 212-215, 290; Palter 1996: 376). In his work of 1764, for
example, Winckelmann contrasted the allegedly hooked nose of the Jew to what
he considered Greek perfection (Mosse 1985: 11, 14, 21-25, 29). In addition to

Winckelmann, the very influential Hellenophile historian of ancient art whom Norton (1996: 407) has referred to as "the high priest of German neo-Hellenism," Peter Camper, a Dutch contemporary of Winckelmann who in addition to being an anatomist, naturalist, and graphic illustrator had racist predilections in his own right, also contributed to an association of somatic beauty as represented in Ancient Greece with latter-day aesthetic ideals in Europe. Winckelmann left numerous Europeans believing in the superiority of Greek art. Both he and Camper contributed to a belief in the superiority of the types of physical features that would a century or more later be loosely categorized as Aryan, an unfortunate linguistic term coined by Max Müller and even more of a misnomer when referring to biology.

There existed many legitimate reasons for various nationalist movements in the Balkans in the early decades of the 19th century, including that by Greeks. As Athens since 1460 had been controlled by the Ottomans many Europeans by this time viewed their empire as in decline, many Europeans dreamed of the reemergence of a Greece that would be free of Turkish domination and oppression. Even in the first phase of the Greek campaign for liberation, Turks did not hesitate to massacre Greeks where they could, for example, on the island of Chios. European racism—of which Orientalism, colorism, race-based slavery, and paternalistic global imperialism were manifestations—both inspired the Greek rebels and complicated the meaning of the Greek Revolution for people deemed not to belong to the European fraternity.

Although himself an abolitionist, even Abbé Henri Grégoire of France apparently failed to appreciate the great degree to which unbridled racism still demarcated the world between people who claimed special privileges for themselves because of their connections with Europe and those they considered inferior as racial "others." Either through naiveté or cruel calculation, Abbé Grégoire, on record as an abolitionist, opened a lengthy correspondence with Haitian freedom fighters for the purpose of attempting to draw them into offering military support for the Greek liberation cause against Turkey (Debrunner 1979: 187-188). As he initiated this correspondence at a time when the situation surrounding Haiti's continued independence and freedom from slavery remained unsettled, it is somewhat curious. Neither France nor the United States had officially recognized Haitian independence for reasons that were essentially racist. Race-based slavery still existed nearby in the United States and in colonies controlled by France. Haiti was also experiencing considerable instability in domestic clashes between its "black" masses and its "mulatto" minority, both of which wished to exercise supreme power. Hence, Haiti was hardly in a position to ship troops from the Caribbean to southeastern Europe in order to help Europeans claiming to be Greek liberate themselves from Turks unless it wished to sacrifice its own freedom in so doing.

Although a stalemate in the Greek War of Independence set in until 1825, most people of European descent remained very sympathetic to the Greek cause, in part because while they resented seeing Europeans (many of whom were Christians) abused. Their own increasing embrace of racism however left them with no similar feelings of empathy for peoples they wished to exploit. Contri-

with no similar feelings of empathy for peoples they wished to exploit. Contributing to European indignation over witnessing people deemed to be Europeans abused by racial "others," many Britons (and by extension even Americans) were very sentimental about philhellenism. Playing a role in these feelings was British excitement about the acquisition between 1801 and 1805 of many Parthenon Marbles by Thomas Bruce, 7th Earl of Elgin while he was serving as British ambassador to the Ottoman court of Sultan Selim III in Istanbul from 1799 to 1803.

In addition to costing Elgin a personal fortune, the expensive relocation of these works of art contributed to an aesthetic cult around whiteness as presumed to be associated with race. Robert Knox was but one admirer of the Elgin Marbles who helped to promote the idea that the ancient Greeks had been an ideal race of northern European descent characterized by whiteness and blue eyes. Thanks to such figures as Carl Gustave Carus and Robert Knox, by the time the Greek War of Independence began in 1821, concepts of the Aryan with blond hair and blue eyes as well as physiques like the Greek statues so admired by Winckelmann were already in existence. With this stereotypic aesthetic symbol of Europe that was a mixture of romance, myth, and idealization, Europeans stood ready to do battle with the larger world (Mosse 1985: 34).

The vast collection of so-called Elgin Marbles already had been purchased from Lord Elgin by the British Parliament in 1816 and presented by Parliament to the British Museum in London. Britain, which had one of the largest global empires of any European power was especially reliant on racism to justify its imperialism. While it supported Greek independence, it did not wish to see Turkey become so weakened by Russia that Russia might gain access to the Mediterranean Sea. Britain greatly feared that if Russia gained access to the Mediterranean through the Turkish Straits that this would threaten British trade routes through the Mediterranean to places such as British-controlled India. Despite these geopolitical complications, European powers increasingly supported policies based on the notions that Europeans were "white," that they were Christian, and that they were innately superior to peoples with no legitimate claim to being of European descent. Such policies were adjusted as needed to make them compatible with the idealization of Greeks and the idealization of physical features that they loosely associated with many relatively lightly pigmented and often Germanic-speaking Europeans.

Faced with a nationalist rebellion by people claiming Greek ethnicity who were widely scattered in the Balkan Peninsula but most especially in the south, Turkish Sultan Mahmud II transferred control of the provincial governorships of Crete and the Peloponnesus to Mohammed Ali (its quasi-independent governor of Egypt and much of Sudan) on the condition that he take the lead in suppressing the rebellion. In 1822, Muhammad Ali of Egypt accepted control of the *pashalik* or province of Crete and began trying to quell the Greek liberation struggle. Although Greek rebels largely succeeded in keeping Egyptian forces out of the southern Balkans until 1825, at which time the Greek fleet mutinied over a lack of pay, Turkey and its Egyptian allies then won the battle at Missolonghi. With this setback for Greek rebels, which was deeply resented across Europe, a

Europe inspired as much by sense of racial solidarity as by religion and geopolitics found a *cause célèbre* it deemed worthy of pan-European support.

Between 1825 and 1827 as a consequence, there occurred much interference by Europeans generally in the Greek War of Independence. For virtually all people who considered themselves to be of European descent by this time, the cause of Greek liberation had become transformed into a conflict between youthful European vigor, on the one hand, and Asian and African decadence and inferiority, on the other (Bernal 1987: 291). Not long after the Scottish poet George Gordon Lord Byron from his home of exile in Geneva satirized in his "Don Juan" the custom of "dwarfs and blacks and such like things that gained their bread as ministers and favourites" through what he referred to as degradation, he prepared to channel his romanticism of Ancient Greece as well as a good amount of his fortune into refurbishing the fleet fighting for Greek independence. Also, some 300 Germans fought as volunteers in the Greek War of Independence, and Germans early developed scholarly interests in Greece as well as in what used to be called Orientalia (Adams 1997: 25-26).

As the major powers of Europe were not prepared to accept a powerful Sultan Mehmet Ali of Turkey in control of Egypt as well as Greece, Britain, France, and Russia pushed for a mediated peace in 1827 even as they began sinking as many Egyptian ships as possible in Navarino Bay. Turkey lacked any armed force that could reclaim Morea or resist the combined forces of these European countries. During the Russo-Turkish War of 1828-1830, which was really a final phase of the Greek War of Independence, Russia invaded Turkey and almost reached Istanbul in 1829. Despite Orientalism, this was a development that greatly concerned Britain and France. When at the end of this war Russia emerged as the victor, British and French were greatly relieved when Russia agreed to accept their participation in the peace settlement that produced a London Protocol providing for a small Greek kingdom independent of Turkey. Although not a reincarnation of Ancient Greece, what this protocol provided was a tiny area in the southern Balkans from what had long been a part of the Ottoman Empire. It also established a ruling dynasty with Prince Otto of Bavaria sitting on the throne as King Otto I of Greece. As this arrangement was acceptable to Russia, Britain, and France, Otto began his rule of modern-day Greece by importing with him into the newly established country a German cabinet and a German army. Despite agreeing to this arrangement, France, Britain, and Russia continued to intervene in Greek politics.

The War of Greek Independence was about much more than Greece. It contributed considerable rigidity to the development of a pan-European identity. It also was an important milestone in how Europeans were seeking to coordinate certain racist, nationalist and imperialist agendas in a manner that would allow a major reordering of the interactions of people who considered themselves Europeans with "others." Despite the fact that the Greece that emerged in 1830 was exceedingly multi-ethnic, it did not take long before Greek intellectuals and nationalists in collaboration with numerous other Europeans (including even some Americans of European descent) began manufacturing a "northern European" pedigree for the newly independent country in the southern Balkans. Incorporated within this pedigree as King Otto I was enthroned in 1832 were a number of carefully crafted myths. What all these myths had in common was that they were in consonance with Romantic neo-Hellenism, a very selective reading of history, and pseudo-scientific racism.

According to one of these myths, a homogeneous people who alone were the direct descendants of Ancient Greece, including Ancient Macedonia, populated newly emergent Greece. Another held that as the fountainhead and crown jewel of Western philosophy, science, and democracy Greece probably more than any other society was the very embodiment of civilization itself. A third myth held that Greeks were essentially a people characterized by racial purity. In support of this last-mentioned myth, some German writers argued that the ancient Dorians in the area had been pure-blooded Aryans exclusively from the north, possibly even from Germany. A corollary of this claim was the denial that any speakers of languages belonging to the Afro-Asiatic phylum (e.g., ancient Phoenicians, Egyptians, and Jews) could have made any major contributions to the civilization of Ancient Greece (Bernal 1987: 209, 281-399). This reasoning was very flawed, however, as no people on Earth represents biological, cultural, or linguistic purity, and racial thinking provided a convenient means by which all these fallacious arguments could be conflated and compounded.

In contrast with such myths, the Balkans (including the part that became Greece) had long been characterized by multi-ethnicity and diversity with various language groups, religious groups, and groups with vastly contrasting physical features living intersperse among each other. After Haci I Gray declared his independence from the Golden Horde and established the Crimean Khanate in 1441, this Crimean Khanate maintained a massive slave trade with the Ottoman Empire that imported Europeans into Egypt as Mamluks. This Crimean Khanate and/or its Ottoman suzerains also at times were important in importing Africans into the Balkans as well as beyond into parts of Russia such as where certain Abkhazians of African descent were settled. Reflecting on the general area of eastern Europe and nearby Asia in a broad historical context, an African presence is well documented in the Crimea, the Ukraine, and in northern Iran, Montenegro, and in the Caucasus of Russia, including a minority group of Abkhazians (Blakely 1986: 82; Fikes and Lemon 2002: 501-502, 505-506; English 1959: 49-53; Khanga 1992; Schneider 1942: 24-26; Holte 1985: 274-275). People of African descent were at times also present in southern Balkans, where Greece is located. Considering that we humans eventually colonized our entire earth by initially moving beyond Africa, the complete absence of Africans in the Balkans located immediately north of the Mediterranean Sea would have been an anomaly beyond belief.

Alongside much voluntary traffic back and forth across the Mediterranean Sea since ancient times, servile labor also moved north and south across the Mediterranean in the 15th century quite without regard to what people sometimes think of as continental or racial frontiers. It was only in the 15th century that slavery was abolished in Poland and even there, it was then replaced by a second enserfment. Bondage labor was obviously a common feature of life in eastern Europe in the 15th century. Although Pope Pius II declared slavery to be a *mag-*

num scelus or "great crime" in 1462, this was only ten years after Pope Nicholas V had authorized the hereditary enslavement of non-Christians in his *Dum Diversas*. The Kingdom of Cyprus (which had previously been a crusader state controlled by the Franks) was in February of 1489 annexed to Venice. Resenting this annexation, the Turks retaliated by attacking the Karpasia Peninsular of Cyprus and taking many of its residents to be sold into slavery.

In the previous year of 1488, Pope Innocent VIII had accepted the gift of 100 slaves from Ferdinand II of Aragon and distributed them to his cardinals and to certain Roman nobles. Moreover, Slavonic slaves were traded very extensively in Europe and beyond in the 15th century. In 1521, the combined forces of Crimean Khan Mehmed Giray and his Kazan allies even attacked Moscow taking numerous captives who were sold into slavery, with some likely being settled both north and south of the Mediterranean Sea. Although the Turkish system of devşirme that thrived on the capture of rural Christians from the Balkans was used infrequently after around 1568, it was only in 1588 that slavery was abolished in Lithuania. While in 1639 Pope Urban VIII declared himself to be in opposition to the enslavement of Native Americans living in the New World, in the same year he purchased for himself non-Indian slaves from the Knights of Malta, probably all of whom were Turks or Africans. Given such well-documented movements of people over long distances as these, anyone who believes in the existence of non-overlapping or "pure races" presumed to have been for all time associated with particular countries, regions, or continents is simply not in touch with reality.

While Slavs, Turks, Vlachs, and Greeks have a long history of being especially numerous in the southern Balkans, numerous Albanians were also present in this area long before the Greek War of Independence erupted in 1821. Even the population of Athens was likely one-quarter Albanian, one-third Turkish, and hence well less than half Greek at the time of independence. As recently as the 1790s, when the southern Balkans remained a part of the empire of Ottoman Turkey, a lively slave trade northward across the eastern Mediterranean basin was carrying Africans into some of the most heavily populated areas bordering on the Aegean Sea. Involving ships that were French, Venetian, and British, this movement of people included among its destinations Izmir and Istanbul (currently the two largest population centers in Turkey) as well as the Peloponnese Peninsula, Athens, and Thessaloniki, the last two cities being the largest in latter-day Greece (Thomas 1997: 511).

The fact that latter-day Greece consists of numerous islands as well as an especially large peninsula that juts southward into the Mediterranean Sea means that in addition to its accessibility by land, it is easily accessible by sea. People of African descent have long frequented European ports. An Ethiopian sailor in Hamburg at the end the 17th century was supposedly made fun of by other sailors there (Debrunner 1979: 91). Shipping records from the United States document that of the 132 ships bound for Vladivostok in Russia between 1798 and 1880, there was rarely one that did not have at least one "black" seaman on board. On the 12-man *Chasca of Boston* that sailed from Boston to Cronstadt, Russia, in 1869, nine of the crewmen were African American. Given that there

were numerous "black" seamen in the Russian ports of Archangel, Saint Petersburg, Nicohaiev, Kronstadet, and Vladivostok in the late 1800s as well as in
Hamburg, Germany (MacMaster 2001: 70), the proverbial ethnic diversity of the
Balkans in general and the fact that newly independent Greece was located
much closer to Africa than Russia, negates any serious argument about any pedigree revolving around racial purity or ethnic homogeneity for modern Greece.

Among people of African descent who were in Russia, and therefore well
north of modern-day Greece by the time of the Greek War of Independence,
were at least a few of whom we known even by name. One of these was an African-American named Nero Prince. It was after making two trips from New England to Russia in 1810 and 1812 that Nero Prince began to work in Russia as a
courtier at the royal court in Saint Petersburg. This was a period during which at
least twenty other men of color also worked at the same court as courtiers. From
1824 to 1833, Nancy Prince, the African-American wife of Prince and the author
of a book about her experiences abroad, also lived in Russia (Prince 1990). Africans were present even in Ancient Greece. This, along with the fact that newly
established modern Greece mounted vigorous campaigns to suppress linguistic,
cultural, and religious diversity within its borders, further undermine any claims
by latter-day Greece for racial purity or ethnic homogeneity.

The advance of military forces dispatched from Egypt toward newly-
established Greece by Muhammad Ali, Egypt's European-born ruler, was perceived as threatening both because he was a Muslim and because his forces included many men who were of African descent. Numerous African soldiers in
places such as Crete and Syria were viewed as threatening in a world that was
increasingly thinking in racial ways. According to Rogers (1952: 114), in the
classic work entitled *History of the Greek Revolution, and of the Wars and
Campaigns Arising from the Struggles of the Greek Patriots in Emancipating
Their Country from the Turkish Yoke* by Thomas Gordon that was published in
1844 in London (Volume II, p. 51), 30,000 of the Egyptians troops sent to
southern Greece in 1840 were "Negro."

At the same time that Ottoman Turkey was seen by many Europeans as
threatening their monopoly on imperialism, an expansionist Egypt under Muhammad Ali was even perceived by Turkey as threatening the European-Turkish
monopoly on imperialism. As Egyptian troops were within sight of Turkey's
capital of Istanbul, therefore, the Ottoman Turks joined forces with France, Austria, Russia, Prussia, and Britain (shortly after the ascent to the throne of Queen
Victoria) in opposing this Egyptian expansion toward Europe. According to a
treaty of 1841 imposed on Egypt, Muhammad Ali was stripped of all Egypt's
recently conquered territory except in Sudan, an area where an ongoing slave
trade was of little concern to those same European powers (Goodwin 2006:
401).

That Muhammad Ali would remain heavily invested in the Sudanese slave
trade throughout the rest of his life, even holding an Egyptian state monopoly on
it until 1843 was of little concern to European governments as of that time, including even in countries were some exceptional individual abolitionists were
active. When, in fact, Muhammad Ali's slavery monopoly in Sudan eventually

ended, Italian and Greek slave traders moved quickly into Sudan to compete for slaves there alongside Arabs and others. It is likely that a good number of the Sudanese slaves acquired by Europeans in northeastern Africa during this time eventually ended up in Europe, including in the Balkans. A woman from Abyssinia (now Ethiopia and Eritrea) whose name was Machbuba, was sold in the late 1830s to Prince Bukler on a slave market in northeastern Africa. The Prussian prince brought her to his castle of Bad Muskau near Cottbus in Germany where she died shortly thereafter. One cannot be certain whether or not she was his mistress. It is documented, however, that the prince became greatly depressed after her passing (Sephocle 1996: 24).

Quite apart from what was happening in the Balkans and in northeastern Africa, Ira Aldridge, an aspiring "black" actor from New York, arrived in Britain in the 1820s while still in his late teens after having worked his way across the Atlantic as a ship's steward. He hoped to find Britain a more receptive place than his native United States in which to pursue an acting career. Shortly after reaching England, Aldridge married an English woman named Margaret Gill, who was several years his senior. Following his first major appearance on a British stage in 1825 at the Royal Coburg (afterward the Old Vic), his reviews were as mixed as was his reception.

While the *Globe* identified his enunciation as "distinct and sonorous," the *Times* claimed that it was impossible for him to pronounce English properly "owing to the shape of his lips" (Fryer 1984: 253-254). As British racists and snobs continued to target him, most London theaters became reluctant to hire him. Despite such a mixed early reception in London, Aldridge toured continually with great success elsewhere among the major theaters of Ireland and the British Isles. He became especially well known as a gifted actor drawn to Shakespearean roles.

Around the same time, John Wood and his family arrived in England from the British colony of Antigua in 1828 in order to enroll his son in school in the mother country. Accompanying the Wood family was Mary Prince, their much-abused slave. Although essentially still a captive of the Wood family, as slavery by that name was no longer officially permitted in Britain, she became their servant. The experiences of Mary Prince reveal a great deal about the condition of some people of African descent in Britain and in certain British colonial settings in the early 19th century.

Unlike Ira Aldridge who had been born free in the United States and who had attended New York's African Free School before departing his country, Mary Price and been born in the British colony of Bermuda to enslaved parents. Enslaved from birth, she had suffered horrendous physical and psychological abuse under at least four owners prior to being sold to John Wood in 1818. While a domestic slave to Wood on the island of Antigua in 1826, her decision to marry Daniel James, a former slave who had bought his freedom, enraged John Wood, and he severely beat her for this decision. With no regard for the fact that Prince was married and her husband remained in the Caribbean, Mr. and Mrs. Wood considered it their right to transport Prince to England to be completely at their service in Britain. In fact, the Wood family experienced no difficulty in continuing their harsh treatment of Price before eventually throwing her into the streets of London with no means of support.

Facing certain re-enslavement if she had returned to her husband in the Caribbean, Prince took shelter with the Moravian church in Hatton Garden and managed soon to find employment in the household of Thomas Pringle, an abolitionist writer affiliated with London's Anti-Slavery Society. Despite a lifetime of ill treatment and abuse, Prince harbored a belief that the masses of English people were humane and would likely disappprove if they knew of her suffering as a slave. Based on this belief, she made it known to Pringle that she would be willing to have her story publicized. Shortly thereafter, Susanna Strickland, a visitor to the Pringle home as well as an abolitionist, transcribed the life story of Price. Upon the completion of this narrative in 1831, Pringle published it as *The History of Mary Prince, A West Indian Slave, Related by Herself.*

Incensed and angered by this book, Mr. and Mrs. Wood brought charges against the Anti-Slavery Society, Pringle, and Prince for libel and defamation of character. When the Woods did not prevail in court, they sought to defame the character of Mary Price, in which undertaking they had strong support from British interests who favored the continuation of color-based slavery in the colonies. In response, Price and Pringle sued for libel and were successful, suggesting at least three conclusions: that Price's character was beyond reproach, that the book was accurate, and that a segment of the British public was uncomfortable with some of the most extreme abuses of slavery. Mary Prince was still in England around 1833, and it is usually assumed that she died there around that time.

In the 1830s, working-class activism was beginning to re-emerge in England, this time in the form of a movement known as Chartism. This was around the time when Parliament after many refusals enacted the Representation of the People Act, also known as the Reform Act of 1832. Although this act provided for more proportional representation of urban areas and provided greater access than previously for male participation in voting, it specifically disenfranchised women. When in 1839 a delegation presented to the House of Commons a "People's Charter" demanding parliamentary reform to do away with inequities remaining from the Act of 1832, most members of the establishment considered this action exceedingly radical. The six major demands of the Charter were universal suffrage for all men, equal electoral districts, abolition of property requirements as a prerequisite to stand for election to Parliament, annual general elections, the secret ballot, and payment of MPs. In addition to opposition to Chartism that was occasioned by class prejudices were recollections of the earlier movement founded by Thomas Spence advocating for the nationalization of land, women's rights, and access to divorce for working-class Britons. The British establishment was likely also somewhat outraged that several people in the leadership of the Chartist movement were of African ancestry.

Of especial prominence as a Chartist leader was William Cuffay, whose African grandfather had been enslaved on the Caribbean island of St. Kitts. While his father had also been born into slavery, by the time that William Cuffay was born in Chatham, Kent, in 1788 his father was apparently free and worked as a naval cook. A tailor by occupation, Cuffay was until 1833 so conservative that he refused to support union rights for workers. He eventually changed his view however and became the last member of his lodge to join the newly established tailor's union. When he later joined other union members on a strike, he lost his job and had difficulty finding work. This experience radicalized him and, in 1842, he was chosen as president of the Chartist movement in London. Based on the testimony of a government spy, William Cuffay was brought to trial and charged and convicted of making war on Queen Victoria. At the age of 61, he was banished to Van Diemen's Land (now Tasmania) in Australia. By 1853, his English wife, who worked as a charwoman, had saved enough money to join him there. Although all the London Chartists, like Cuffay who had been sentenced to transportation, were pardoned in 1856, Cuffay chose to live out the rest of his life in Australia rather than return to his native Europe (Fryer 1984: 237-238; Gammage 1969).

Not unrelated is what Europeans would eventually refer to as "the Eastern Question," how various outlying parts Ottoman Empire would be apportioned once its decline would be complete. When shortly after capturing Malta in 1798, Napoleon invaded Egypt, he was acting both within a geopolitical framework as well as within one where genuine fascination with Egypt was mixed with paternalistic "Orientalism," As Britain was also infected with this last-mentioned type of racism, it felt no particular sympathy for Turkey that Egypt (at least in theory a Turkish province or *pashalik*) had been invaded by a fellow European country. That it moved quickly to support Turkey and the Egyptians in chasing away the French was a decision made, however, in British self interest of keeping France, its single most important imperial rival, away from its life-line through the Mediterranean. While this decision had little to do with any charitable British attitudes toward Turks or Egyptians, it had much to do with Britain's vested interest in insuring easy passage by sea to India, the crown jewel of its empire.

At around the same time as France suffered the humiliation of being chased out of Egypt, the oppressed "mulattoes" and "blacks" of its colony of Saint-Domingue by 1802 launched a major anti-colonialist revolt that led to another French defeat and helped to precipitate a major course change by Napoleon with respect to some of the most basic principles of the French Revolution. Adding to these humiliations, French forces were chased even from Malta, a tiny European island outpost hardly north of Africa whose people conversed in a Semitic language—hence, one of Afro-Asiatic derivation (Goodwin 2002: 2, 46-50; Goodwin 2006: 397-398).

While in Saint-Domingue or Haiti (which had been the most wealthy of all French colonies in the Caribbean) the people who forced a French withdrawal had been predominantly of African descent, those involved in French defeat in Egypt (although assisted by the British) were also of African and so-called Oriental descent. Although it was not always clear exactly who was to be considered European in the 19th century, a concept of Europeanism was emerging in opposition to what was deemed to be African and/or Oriental. In this spirit,

France began to focus on its deteriorating relations with the Turkish regency in nearby Algiers. Given that Algiers was at this time at war with Spain, the Netherlands, Prussia, Denmark, Russia, and Naples and that hostilities also were threatening between Algiers and the United States, France in the 1820s saw this as an opportune time to also have a showdown with Algiers.

By means of such an undertaking, France no doubt hoped in part to assuage of some of its recent humiliation having to do with having been chased out of Egypt, Haiti, and Malta followed around twelve years later by its further humiliation in the Battle of Waterloo, which had ended the Napoleonic Wars. The embrace of Orientalism by many Europeans and the declining fortunes of Turkey, which was the theoretical overlord of Algiers added to the enticement of the moment for France to move into a nearby place in Africa that theoretically remained in Turkey's sphere of control. In any case, it was not uncommon for European powers to further extend their reach into Africa in an effort to compensate for losses to each other as well as to fortify their feelings of racial superiority.

Overlooking their own involvement in the large-scale enslavement and other oppression of peoples of Africa descent, or perhaps considering it justified in view of their feeling that they were superior to Africans, the French (much like many other people of European descent in the wake of the Greek War of Independence) were less willing to see their own citizens as periodic captives of pirates operating from Algiers under the suzerainty of Turks. While Britain and Turkey remained fixated on the eastern Mediterranean, France saw this time as ideal to make a bold move against Turkish interests in and around Algiers in the western Mediterranean.

French action was initially rationalized by France as its attempt to control piracy in a backward country that permitted slavery. Casting doubt on this rationalization, however, when France began its three-year blockage of the Algerian coast in 1827, France then had slaves in its own colonies. France's lengthy blockade was followed in 1830 by a full-scale invasion of Algiers. It was at this time that France sent an expeditionary force to the area and, after a three-week campaign, captured the regency of Algiers. France's critique of this situation may have been correct when viewed against the background of some of Turkey's behavior toward its subjects, including its underlings in Algiers. Overall however, this behavior was no more inhumane than that which Europeans often imposed on their underlings, including especially the "black" slaves in their overseas colonies.

Implicit in France's attitude was a perceived need to liberate Algeria from what France considered to be feudal backwardness that not infrequently resulted in the brutal suppression of certain subjects in the Ottoman Empire. While at times the objects of such brutality had been people of African descent, at other times the victims had been Christian Europeans resident in the Balkans. In addition, there were other factors at play. Although France initially did not intend to remain in Algiers, it subsequently decided to remain there because it was in competition with Great Britain and Turkey in the Mediterranean and did not wish to leave a vacuum that might be filled by either of these rivals. It did not

take long before Algeria came to provide French writers and artists "with a con-
veniently near destination where they could pursue or construct their Oriental
fantasies" (Koos 2003: 19).

> Theses of Oriental backwardness, degeneracy, and inequality with the
> West most easily associated themselves early in the nineteenth cen-
> tury with ideas about the biological basis of racial inequality. . . . To
> these ideas was added second-order Darwinism, which seemed to ac-
> centuate the "scientific" validity of the division of races into ad-
> vanced and backward, or European-Aryan and Oriental-African.
> (Said 1994: 206)

As European racism and imperialism continued evolving in tandem with
each other, Turkey responded to the French takeover of Algiers (and eventually
Algeria as a whole) by pushing more deeply from the Mediterranean into what is
now Libya. These actions marked a turning point in relations between residents
of the western Sahara with France as well as with Turkey. Both France and Turkey were anxious to control and tax trans-Saharan trade and to make certain that
no rival colonizers would annex the African interior area beyond the coastal
areas that they controlled bordering on the western Mediterranean. As for Ottoman Turkey, in taking direct control of most of the Libyan interior from the
semi-autonomous Karamanli dynasty, it also wished to create a barrier that
would limit French influence in Egypt (Beier 1989: 518-519).

Although a "scramble for Africa" directed especially from Europe was unfolding only gradually at this time, the French seizure of Algiers marked a crucial new stage in this process. As soon as France proclaimed the annexation of
Algeria in 1834, Bertrand Clauzel, who was the French governor-general there,
begin making private land investments. He also encouraged army officers and
bureaucrats in his administration to do likewise. Quickly occupying much of the
best land around the coastal cities, European settlers drove indigenous Africans
inland toward less fertile areas. France's 1834 annexation of Algeria sent shock
waves into neighboring Tunis, which had been virtually independent since 1812,
and even into Tripoli. In Tunis, as in the neighboring regency of Tripoli, foreign
elites made up largely of Turkish jannisaries and Turko-Circassian Mamluks
monopolized political power to the virtual total exclusion of indigenous populations.

In France in 1834, four young men who were at least in part of African descent graduated with degrees in medicine from the University of Paris (McCloy
1961: 135). Among various artists from French-controlled New Orleans in
North America who traveled to France around this same time to study were at
least three Creole artists, all of whom were the products of French fathers and
mothers of African ancestry. This group included Florville Foy, Jules Lion, and
Eugène Warburg. In the case of Warburg, his mother had been a Cuban "mulatto" slave who was freed in the 1830s. Although Jules Lion had been born in
France, he immigrated to New Orleans around 1837. A fourth artist who likely
belongs to this group is Julien Hudson. Hudson traveled to Paris twice, first
around 1831 and again six years later. While Eugène Warburg was a sculptor,

the others were painters (Leininger-Miller 2001: 1-4, 252n). There were also in Paris a number of "mulatto" writers from New Orleans in the 1830s and soon after. Among those in Paris to study were B. Valcour and presumably Armand Lanusse. Others who lived most of their lives in this capital on the Seine included Victor Sejour, Pierre Dalcour, and Louis and Camille Thierry (Fabre 1991: 10-20).

In Britain in 1833, Parliament had considered an act to gradually abolish slavery throughout the British Empire. The proposed legislation, however, had much more to do with the government desire to clear the decks for British imperialism than with turning away in some very radical way from the pursuit of policies based on racism. While, for example, this legislation would provide financial compensation to slaveholders, it would provide no reparations for the enslaved. Even in 1833, Britain only provided for the gradual abolition of slaveholding alongside an ongoing system of "apprenticeship" that would in many cases involve former slaves remaining under the control of their former masters over several years (McCloy 1961: 112, 142). This last-mentioned British legislation, though effective from 1834, required in the Cape of southern Africa, for example, that former slaves would have to remain with their former master as "apprentices" for at least four years after 1834 (Goodwin 2006: 234).

Also there were other complications. In the same spirit of indifference toward the oppressed victims of racism, a new Poor Law of 1834 abolished "outdoor relief" of the poor while establishing a system of workhouses where conditions were deliberately made as harsh as possible to discourage any behavior that could be construed as malingering. According to the Irish abolitionist Thomas Digges, as quoted in the "Introduction" (p. xii) of the first edition of Olaudah Equiano's *Narrative* that was first published in 1789, as originally authored by Equiano was "a principal instrument of bringing about a motion for the repeal of the Slave-act." Although a number of exceptional individuals in Britain were active abolitions in the second half of the 18th century, it was almost a century later or from around the mid-1830s before the British government tended to pursue policies in its national interest while remaining committed to the principle that slavery should be abolished. Even after this time, moreover, there occurred a few notable exceptions from time to time in Britain's growing commitment to the abolition of slavery (Goodwin 2006: 317-320, 406-407).

On the death of Britain's King William IV in 1837, Princess Victoria of Kent, the only surviving legitimate grandchild of King George III, ascended the throne as Queen Victoria of the United Kingdom of Great Britain and Ireland. Her reign was destined to be so long that it would bestow her name on an entire era. The Victorian Era would bear witness to the height of the British Industrial Revolution as well as witness the British Empire at its apex. The Victorian Age in many parts of Europe was characterized by a social climate where statesmen and scholars tended to be beguiled by imperial greatness and obsessed with explaining human variation from an array of racist perspectives. Many of them saw no conflict between this and claims to be increasingly opposed to slavery, at least by that name.

In 1843, a lawyer in Paris argued on behalf of a person from India that the Indian should be considered free rather than enslaved as the result of his having reached the soil of metropolitan France (Peabody 1996: 138). Although by this time, public opinion in a number of European countries seemed to be turning against slavery, this did not necessarily indicate that it was similarly turning against racism. Sweden ended slaveholding in 1846 and Denmark two years later. The situation with respect to France was considerably more complicated. In fact, racism was still surging in certain French colonies. Two ordinances from Paris in the mid-1840s, for example, placed new limitations on the abuse of slaves in French colonies with reference to who could be flogged and how many lashes they could be given (McCloy 1961: 143). Arrogance associated with so-called race and culture had caused French colonialism in Algeria, which had been nominally under the control of Turkey, to be especially exploitative. In Algeria by 1836, over 14,000 Europeans had settled in the vicinity of its occupied cities or staked out claims in the fertile Mitijda Plain. Their numbers in Algeria had grown to roughly 110,000 by 1847 (Beier 1989: 519), a time when France was experiencing much instability

As of early 1845, neither France's government headed by its Soult-Guizot Cabinet nor the *Société française pour l'abolition de l'escalavage*, which was its most important abolitionist organization, was committed to the immediate abolition of slavery in the colonies. Although this abolitionist organization suddenly changed its position in mid-1845 by supporting the idea of immediate abolition, it was an organization without much public support. Contributing to the government's opposition to immediate abolition was pressure from colonial planters, on the one hand, and the fact that it was deeply in debt because of the fortification of Paris and the recent subsidization of French railroads, on the other. Quite apart from the issue of slavery in the colonies, numerous groups had grievances against the government. These ranged from disputes over who should be the legitimate king, the lack of democratic reforms under King Louis-Philippe, graft associated with the Soult-Guizot Cabinet to poor living conditions of the working classes, the humiliation that some felt about the lack of assertiveness that many perceived in Louis-Philippe's foreign policy especially after he dismissed his Foreign Minister, Adolphe Thiers, rather than risk war with Britain. As censorship retaliation against critics who were journalists forced much of the criticism underground, it was only a matter of time before insurrection would ensure.

Following a week of riots in Paris, Louis-Philippe, the *Roi-Citoyen* or Citizen-King, abdicated on February 24, 1848, and a provisional government was constituted in France. This Constituent Assembly was under France's Second Republic, and it named Victor Schoeleher, a genuine abolitionist, as the Secretary of State for colonies and as the president of a seven-member commission to examine the matter of slavery. Among its members was a "mulatto" originally from Martinique named François Auguste Perrinon who had been educated in Rouen, in Paris, and in Metz. Although the members of the committee agreed on the first day that it met that France should no longer countenance slavery, it remained for them to recommend the legal process by which France's Second

Republic would cease equivocating on the abolition of slavery. Considering that France after having twice before abolished slavery and later restored it, the cessation of equivocation was a serious matter. With France's monarchy ended and King Louis-Philippe having escaped to England, its provisional government issued a decree on April 27 that provided for the abolition of slavery throughout the French Empire, although on a series of staggered dates two months after notice of the decree was to reach various colonies.

At the first session of the National Assembly on May 4, a republican form of government was proclaimed, and an Executive Commission of five members, along with General Eugène Cavaignac as Minister of War, replaced the provisional government. Exasperated with waiting for the abolition of slavery by legal means, violence erupted among slaves demanding freedom and colonial authorities wishing to maintain the status quo a bit longer in late May, 1848. As it became clear when deaths occurred between the slaves and European settlers that this policy was not tenable, the government declared slavery on Martinique abolished immediately. Fearing a similar uprising, the governor of Guadeloupe agreed to the emancipation of slaves in that colony four days later.

When street riots erupted in Paris in June, the Assembly proclaimed a state of siege and gave full powers to General Cavaignac, a republican, and dissolved the Executive Committee. Two days later on June 26, the riots were stopped by means of violent repression, and General Cavaignac was asked by the Assembly to constitute a new government with moderate Republicans. Around the same time, new decrees restricted the rights of assembly, and in August, a new law placed new restrictions on the press in the form of the financial securities that were required. Around the same time, in fact, on August 10, slavery was abolished in Guyana.

On November 4, 1848, the French Constitution that the Assembly had been working on for months was finally adopted, incorporating many of the kinds of parliamentary reforms and democratic rights that working-class Chartists had been advocating in Britain since around 1838 although largely without success. In addition to providing for a President of the French Republic and for universal suffrage for male citizens at least 21 years of age with no special educational or economic qualification, the French Constitution of 1848 abolished both nobility and slavery.

When an election was held under the new Constitution on December 10, 1848, Prince Louis-Napoleon Bonaparte had just returned from exile in England. In addition to being a nephew of Napoleon Bonaparte, the prince was also a nephew of the comtesse Françoise de Beauharnais, whose second husband, a man of African descent named Carstaing, had been elected to represent a metropolitan French constituency in the National Convention in 1793. Unexpectedly, Prince Louis-Napoleon trounced his rivals, of whom the most important was General Cavaignac.

Although Louis-Napoleon as newly elected president, took the oath to protect the Constitution of 1848 in the National Assembly ten days after his electoral triumph, he apparently was insincere. Unable to control his dictatorial tendencies, he initiated challenges to the Constitution almost immediately and continued along this course. Meanwhile as of 1848, numerous people of African descent resident in Paris and other cities in France were being treated rather like everyone else (McCloy 1961: 144-146). Under the new Constitution of 1848 that established France's Second Republic, a number of people of African descent even from France's Caribbean colonies ran for seats in the National Assembly and some of them were elected to the 750-member single-chamber body. As the so-called emancipation of the slaves in the colonies spread from one area to another, it was on December 20 that emancipation finally came to Ile de Bourbon, which under the Second Republic was now renamed Réunion in the spirit of republicanism that was again in the ascendency in France.

Contrary to the spirit of the new constituion, however, European domination was expanding overseas alongside racism with or without outright slavery, As a consequence, France's Revolution of 1848 was not destined to dramatically change the status quo for people of color in the colonies. Even as France moved more decisively than previously away from slavery in the late 1840s, it did not necessarily move away from racist exclusions in its overseas colonies. The Constitution of 1848, for example, did not grant French citizenship on an equal footing with those deemed to be of European descent who were resident in France's African colonies. As in a number of other European nations, France's abolition of slavery overlapped with an aggressive policy of empire-building that sometimes resulted in odd statuses for people residing in its colonies.

France ended Algeria's status as a colony and declared the occupied territory to be an integral part of the *métropole* or French homeland. Although in this connection, the "civil territories" of Algiers, Oran, and Constantine were established as French *départements*, indigenous Algerians were given only an ambiguous status as French nationals rather than as French citizens. Somewhat similar to the situation in Algeria, France in Senegal declared Saint-Louis and Gorée Island (both with "mulatto" elites) to be *communes* of France. Although this meant that the residents of these communes had limited rights of citizenship, France did not provide citizenship as an option for the masses of Senegalese.

In the spirit of the Revolution of 1848, France did give more attention to rescuing small numbers of African slaves on the open seas, liberating them, and resettling them at Libreville (meaning "Freetown"), the present capital of the African country of Gabon. This activity however did not divert France from its more important objective of attempting to gain control of as huge an empire in Africa as possible. When after 1850 France conquered the Senegalese Kingdom of Saloum, Saloum's inhabitants were offered neither French citizenship nor communal status as had been offered to the populations of nearby Saint-Louis and Gorée Island with their important Euro-African "mulatto" elites. It is hard to imagine that considerations considered racial played no role in this omission.

That slavery did not immediately vanish from all French colonies under the Second Republic is indicated by the fact that Victor Schoeleher, Under Secretary of State of the Navy and Colonies, estimated that about 20,000 Frenchmen living in the colonies still possessed slaves in 1851, although according to the Constitution of 1848, all slaves were supposed to have been freed within three years. Eventually, France passed a ten-year abolition extension, reckoned from 1848 rather than from 1851 (McCloy 1961: 157). Although France's Constitution of 1848 claimed that France respected the independence of other nations, its continuing empire building in Africa did not reflect this.

Louis-Napoleon and others continued to make challenges to the new constitution and this continued until mid-1851. Meanwhile, there emerged new restrictions on freedom of assembly, new restrictions on freedom of the press, prohibitions against workers withholding their labor to demand higher wages, while education was placed under the supervision of clergy. Voting rights were eventually taken away from a majority of French citizens, and, at the end of July 1850, even some dramas began to be censored. By the following July when the Assembly rejected a constitutional revision that would have made it legal for the president to serve an additional term, the Second Republic was in great jeopardy as was France's commitment to thoroughly abolish slavery in its colonies. With the Parliament increasingly irrelevant and power concentrated in the hands of President Louis-Napoleon Bonaparte, there took place a violent *coup d'état* in France on December 2, 1851. President Louis-Napoleon declared the National Assembly dissolved and abolished the Constitution of 1848. In this way, the Second Republic ended and Louis-Napoleon Bonaparte, who had always considered himself a prince-president at minimum, was crowned Emperor Napoleon III.

Despite such equivocal results of the France's Revolution of 1848, it had a considerable influence elsewhere. As news of it spread into Germany, the middle classes instigated uprisings occurred in numerous cities. In addition, there were popular outcries in most German states for a strong German federation, representative government under a constitutional monarch, a free press, an end to serfdom, and a strong German federation. France's Revolution of 1848 also helped to prompt the abolition of serfdom in Austria-Hungary, where the Austrian Revolution of 1848-1849 brought about the collapse of the Hungarian Republic while maintaining the dominions of the Hapsburgs.

The Frankfurt Assembly of 1848, which extended into the following year, agreed to a constitution that would provide for a limited monarchy and a confederation of all the German states under Frederick William IV, who had already been the King of Prussia since 1840. The commitment of Frederick William IV to liberalism, however, was shaky at best. Prussian conservatives supported a policy that would exclude Austria under Emperor Franz Joseph as well as isolate France under Emperor Napoleon III, as King Frederick William IV of Prussia considered both of them to be his rivals.

A revolutionary movement also began in Milan. Coinciding with the revolutionary fervor of the period, Karl Marx, with assistance from Friedrich Engels, published the *Communist Manifesto* in London in February 1848. That Europe was astir with revolutionary fervor in 1848 had to do with recession, abuse of political power, and nationalist agendas. Although revolutions eventually drew in the Sardinians, Poles, Danes, Germans, Italians, Prussians, Czechs, Slovaks, Hungarians, Croats, and Romanians, human rights and the abolition of slavery outside Europe were not the driving forces behind them.

Even in Europe, Britain's Chartist movement essentially came to an end at this time. Far from having an immediate impact on racism, European racism continued to exist in several varieties, including as revolving around colorism, around Orientalism, around religion, around slavery, and in association with imperialism that was increasingly global. As of 1848, France was less preoccupied with civil rights and liberties than with nationalism and its Constitution of that year contained numerous contradictory objectives. In the view of Karl Marx in an article that he authored about France's Constitution of 1848 that was published on June 14, 1851 in *Notes to the People*, virtually all of the guarantees of liberty that the Constitution provided for, moreover, were provisional in that exceptions could be made.

Meanwhile in 1853, rivalry among Britain, France, and Russia over influence in the Balkans, including who should be the guarantors of protection for resident Christians and whether or not Russia would be allowed to gain a victory over Turkey that would transform Russia into a Mediterranean power, turned into a conflict known as the Crimean Warn. Initially a contest between France and Russia as to which of these powers Turkey would recognize as the protector of Christian sites in the Holy Land and of the Christian subjects resident within the Ottoman Empire, the Crimean War later took the form of a punitive action against Russia to neutralize the Black Sea and impose a joint European protectorate over Christians residing in the Ottoman Empire to replace one by Russia alone. Although neither Britain nor France wished to get involved, they joined with Turkey in 1854, and eventually also with the Kingdom of Sardinia, in attacking Sevastopol, the chief Russian port on the Black Sea, in an effort to keep Russia away from the Mediterranean Sea.

Numerous people of African descent, including many of whom were "black," served between 1854 and 1856 in the Crimean War that took place in the north of the Black Sea at Sevastopol (McCloy 1961: 188-189). Among numerous people of African descent in Europe around this time was a woman named Mary Seacole. The daughter of a Jamaican mother and a Scottish father, Seacole was a largely self-taught nurse whose extensive travels extended from the Caribbean, Central America, and North America, to Great Britain and eventually as far as Russia.

When during the Crimean War British government officials refused the assistance of Mary Seacole although its army's nursing system was under heavy stress, Seacole traveled to the battle zone at her own expense, providing British soldiers with provisions, and nursed many of them back to health. Not until the end of the war in 1856 did she make her way back to England, where she lived out the remainder of her life. For her good works she was awarded a Crimean Medal and Prince Victor of Hohenlohe-Langenburg, a sculptor and nephew of Queen Victoria, was commissioned to create a bust of her. Despite frequent obstacles placed in her way by racist discrimination in England, Mary Seacole refused to become discouraged and in 1857 wrote her autobiography. Although in various parts of the world much of her life involved selfless dedication to healing wounded British troops, the British establishment never lionized her in the manner as it did Florence Nightingale, her contemporary (Paravisini-Gebert 2003: 71-87; Fryer 1984: 246-252).

Although in 1846 the slave market in Istanbul was closed, this did not stop slave sales there which continued to be held in private homes. In 1855, the Ottomans imposed a ban on the trade in slaves for their entire empire, although it was soon pressured to exempt the Hijaz in western Arabia. Turkey, in fact, continued to function as a country through which Africans passed with some frequency from south of the Mediterranean Sea into parts of southeastern Europe still under its rule. Included among these lands were Montenegro, Bosnia, Bulgaria, Wallachia, and Moldova, which would not declare their independence from Turkey until 1875, and Serbia a few years later (Segal 2001: 116). Additionally in some areas of Africa such as Turkish-dominated Sudan, the Ottoman slavery ban was essentially without any effect. Even while Russia played an important role in employing pan-Slavanism to encourage Christians in the Balkans to rebel again Ottoman Turkey and to demand their independence (in part because of the harshness of their treatment and in part because Russia wished to have allies located on the Mediterranean), its Tsar Alexander II did not get around to issuing a decree officially abolishing Russia's own serfdom until 1861. Of course, this was apart from some of that country's Baltic provinces, where serfdom had been abolished in the early 1800s.

That Portugal ended slaveholding, at least in Europe, in 1856 and that the Netherlands followed four years later had less to do with humanitarianism than with geopolitics, economics, and the fact that Portugal by this time wished to portray itself as having as small an African presence as possible. Outside of Europe during the second half of the 19th century Portuguese participation in the slave trade was actually increasing. In the Cape Verde archipelago off the coast of western Africa, for example, all Cape Verdeans—including those who were "mulattoes"—lost the special status that exempted them from forced labor without pay under new *Indigenato* (indigenous) labor laws in 1863 (Fikes 2000: 18). From various parts of Africa that it controlled, Portugal was sending Africans as slaves to India, to the New World, and to its colony of Mozambique in southeastern Africa. With respect to Mozambique, it sometimes sent as many as 1,000 to a single slave owner in Sena or Tete (Pearson 1998: 161). Should one mistake these developments for a decisive turning away by Europeans from the abuse of Africans, one needs only reflect on European attitudes toward Liberia and King Leopold II of Belgium's impending involvement in central Africa to reconnect with reality.

Among the Westerners who as of 1860 were sincerely devoted to ending the slave trade as well as halting the drive by Europeans to take possession of Africa for their own colonial exploitation were two "black" men born in the New World, one a Harvard-trained African-American physician named Martin Robinson Delany and the other a Jamaican-born science teacher named Robert Campbell, both of whom were also explorers. Having been in western Africa exploring for locations that might be suitable places for freed slaves from the New World to settle, both Delany and Campbell were in the United Kingdom at this time. Dr. Delany had come to Britain as a delegate to the fourth International Statistical Congress, and during the last eight months of 1860 he addressed several crowded anti-slavery meetings in England and Scotland. In Britain, he also was invited to deliver a paper about his recent African expedition along with Campbell to the Royal Geographical Society (Fryer 1984: 275). It was during this period that there emerged in Britain an African Aid Society, which published a journal called *African Times*.

Even after Delany departed Britain to return to the United States, Robert Campbell remained in Britain and continued to be active there in working for the improvement of conditions for people of African descent in Africa and in Europe. It is quite likely that he was the same "R. Campbell" who in 1861 met with eleven other people as members of the "Native African Association and their Friends" at the home of Dr. Thomas Hodgkin in Britain. Others at this meeting included the Haitian chargé d'affaires and a number of British abolitionists (Fryer 1984: 275). Even while this was occurring, many European countries continued to equivocate about the need to abolish slavery or at a minimum to relegate the question to a low priority as they continued to pursue their conflicting nationalist agendas, which were often in conflict with each other.

Otto von Bismarck already by 1858 had become convinced that Prussia needed to ally itself with other German states in order to further exercise dominance over its rivals of Austria and France. Apart from a repudiation of serfdom, however, Otto von Bismarck of Prussia succeeded at diverting attention of Germans away from the liberal goals that had dominated the Frankfurt Assembly as the price of achieving unification with Prussia under his forceful leadership as Prime Minister and Foreign Minister by 1862. This Prussian policy contributed to rising nationalism in France and especially raised alarm in France after Prussia's crushing defeat of Denmark in 1864 and its defeat of Austria in 1866. When in 1867, Prussia and several other northern German states joined the North German Confederation with King Wilhelm I as its president and Bismarck as its chancellor; this raised new alarm in France. It remained, however, for Bismarck to achieve the long-standing Prussian goal of isolating France and imposing new restrictions on the papacy that France was protecting by inciting a conflict with France that Bismarck anticipated would also further the cause of German unification.

The means chosen by Bismarck to achieve this goal was provocation of France so as to prompt Emperor Napoleon III to declare war, and this occurred with the emperor's declaration of the Franco-Prussian War (also known as the Franco-German War) of 1870-1871. The Franco-Prussian War happened to have been one in which large numbers of Africans served among the French forces, including a good number of whom were officers. Of the numerous Africans serving, approximately one-third had been described as "black" (McCloy 1961: 188-189; Debrunner 1979: 343). In addition to this and the fact that France's Louis Léon César Faidherbe, who had been a French colonial administrator in Senegal and who later lived in Algeria, was in command of the Army of the North, this war had other implications for Africa

The major victory of the Germans in this war further secured their unification through the inclusion of the southern German states as well as the annexation from France of most of Alsace-Lorraine. The humiliating military defeat for France, the abdication of Napoleon III, the fall of the French Second Republic, and the establishment of the French Third Empire were only some of the loss for France. Contributing to a humiliating loss of face for France, the unification of an enlarged Germany was even celebrated with Germany's King Wilhelm being crowned "German Emperor" on January 18, 1871 in the Hall of Mirrors in the Château de Versailles. France shamelessly chose to use Africa to assuage its humiliation for having been defeated in the Franco-Prussian War. Many people in France attempted to mask their defeat by claiming that it was due to a loss in France of the ideals of freedom and backwardness in the pursuit of science that could only be repaired through greater investment by France in a *mission civilatrice*, thereby arrogantly implying that Africa was in need of a French civilizing mission.

Underlying this patronizing and racist rhetoric about Africa and Africans, France attempted to recoup from Africa the tremendous financial costs of the Franco-Prussian War, including indemnities that it had been forced to pay to Germany. It was against this background that naval officer Pierre Savorgnan de Brazza, a Frenchmen of Italian heritage, was in lower central Africa seeking to make new claims in the basin of the Congo River in the 1870s, not far frm the Gabon coast where slaves were still being exported from Africa as late as into the early 1880s (Goodwin 2006: 194, 207).

Reflecting French preoccupation with nationalism and imperialism around this time was a flowering of much new art that focused on Africa—for example, by the painter Eugène Delacroix, who died in 1863, and somewhat later by the sculptor Charles Henri Joseph Cordier, whose life extended until 1905. While such art is present in numerous museums around the world, Delacroix is especially well represented at the Louvre and Cordier at the Musée d'Orsay. During the same period, the sculptor J. B. Carpeaux executed his "Four Regions of the World" holding up a spherical representation of the Earth that is part of a fountain in the Jardin du Lusembourg that surrounds the Luxembourg Palace (originally called the Palais Médecis when its design was commissioned by Marie de' Médicis to Salomon de Brosse in 1615), where the French Senate now convenes.

This lovely garden sculpture by Carpeaux located along the grand vista between the Observatory and the palace that is the seat of the French Senate depicts as African one of four female figures supporting the Earth. In 1870 at Tangier, the French painter Henri Regnault completed his "Summary Execution under the Moorish King of Granada" now at the Musée d'Orsay, which depicts Africans in a sensationalist way as blood-thirsty and unjust. Shortly thereafter on a commission for the Universal Exposition of 1877, Eugène Delaplanche executed for the first palace of the Trocadero in Paris a giant figure in iron representing Africa. Although now devoid of its original gold covering, this monumental figure, at least as of 2008, sits on the out-of-doors entrance terrace of the Musée d'Orsay beside several companion works that also recall European conquests of peoples deemed to be "others."

In a move calculated in part not to alarm Britain and to keep it at odds with France through the continuation of their colonial rivalry, Bismarck until the

1877s declined to seek a colonial empire abroad or an expansion of his navy. In Britain from around 1870, however, a dockside community in South Shields in County Durham known as the "Arab Quarter" was made up mostly of Somalies and Yemenis. In the late 1800s, Henry Sylvester-Williams, originally from Trinidad, left for New York when he was 22 years of age in order to earn a better living. After two years in the United States, he spent two years in Canada, where he studied law at Dalhousie University in Nova Scotia. Three years later he arrived in London, where he enrolled in King's College. He and three other Trinidadian lawyers read for the bar at Gray's Inn and eventually became barristers who practiced at the English Bar.

Henry Sylvester-Williams fell in love with Agnes Powell, daughter of a Royal Marines officer who fiercely opposed their marriage, apparently on racial grounds. Still, they married in 1898 and had a son named Henry Francis a year later. Sylvester-Williams established intimate relations with numerous people in Britain from western Africa and eventually acted as legal adviser to several Africa chiefs and other dignitaries who visited the British Colonial Office in London (Padmore 1955: 117).

Also in the late 1800s, Yambo and Dixie Davis were one of several black-and-white song-and-dance acts from the United States that performed in Europe. Though Europe was hardly free of racism, its prevailing social climate was sufficiently better than what existed in the New World, such that a number of "black" entertainers after crossing the Atlantic to Europe settled there permanently. Another type of entertainment in Europe associated with people of African descent by the late 19th century was the field of athletics.

One "black" athlete of great prominence in Britain and sometimes in the United States from 1888 to 1892 was Peter Jackson. Although born on the island of St. Croix in 1861 when the Virgin Islands were still a colony of Denmark, Jackson went to sea and eventually spent five years in Australia, during which time he became the Australian heavyweight boxing champion. He departed Australia in 1886 to spend time in Britain and in the United States. Because of many boxing successes in these two countries between 1888 and 1892 Jackson became known as "Peter the Great," and sometimes as "The Black Prince." Although Peter Jackson was during this period one of the few boxes of any background allowed to move freely in the National Sporting Club rooms in London, he gradually fell on hard times after 1892. Around the turn of the century, his situation was so dire that a subscription was taken up for him in Britain so that he could be sent back to Australia where he was expected to tour with Fitzgerald's Circus while participating in exhibition fights. By the time Jackson reached Australia, however, he was too sick from tuberculosis to box anymore and he died in Queensland in 1901.

This happened also to have been the year that an African-American bicyclist named Marshall-Walker "Major" Taylor arrived in France on his first European tour. Indianapolis-born, Taylor had already proved himself to probably be the fastest bicyclist in North America since 1897 despite having been a frequent victim of racist discrimination in his native United States. Although Taylor did not triumph over the great French cyclist Edmond Jacquelin in two races and

victim of racist discrimination in his native United States. Although Taylor did not triumph over the great French cyclist Edmond Jacquelin in two races and Thorwald Ellegaard of Denmark in Germany in one race, Taylor won first place in all his eight other European contests in 1901. When Marshall "Major" Taylor returned to Paris the following year, he established himself as the world champion of cycling and was give the nickname of "Le Nègre Volant," meaning "The Flying Negro." After later racing in Australia, Taylor went on to win new races and establish new records in Europe in the period between 1907 and 1909 (Jobert 2006: 35-49; Debrunner 1979: 346-349).

Despite the considerable African presence in Europe in the late 1800s, major European imperial powers at this time remained more committed to the acquisition of large empires in Africa than to the freedom of people of African descent in their colonies. Although Liberia in western Africa had been established largely by freed slaves from the United States who had returned to Africa in the hope of escaping racist abuses under people of European descent, France proposed declaring a protectorate over Liberia in 1879 that threatened to end Liberia's independence. British and French threats to Liberia's independence were sufficiently strong around this time that even the United States eventually felt compelled to react, at least in symbolic concern. In this regards, it made an official inquiry of France as to its intentions toward Liberia through the American ambassador in Paris and followed this up in 1880 and again in 1884 by having its Secretary of State mildly notify Britain of its interest in the welfare and security of Liberia (Anderson 1952: 88-89).

France's Constitution of 1848 that outlawed slavery and under which Louis-Napoleon Bonaparte came into office as President notwithstanding, it would not be until between the 1860s and the 1880s that the French slave trade would truly be brought to its conclusion. Further testifying to the obsession of some European powers with possessing huge empires largely consisting of "others" at this time, it was in 1877 that Queen Victoria added to her other titles that of Empress of India. It was almost three decades after Victoria became a queen that Prince Leopold II (her first cousin through her mother's brother) in 1865 succeeded his father as King Leopold II of Belgium. King Leopold II of Belgium was destined to abuse Africans on a scale that perhaps no other single European ruler ever managed.

Under the pretense that he was engaged in philanthropy of a paternalistic type, Leopold II craftily began laying the diplomatic, military, and economic groundwork for the acquisition of a huge personal fief in central Africa beginning in 1877. It was the prevailing climate of racism coupled with the cooperation of certain European explorers and the support of numerous Western governments that enabled him to acquire the Congo Free State as his personal possession without any checks and balances. Although the requisite diplomatic sanction was provided first by the United States of America, the countries of Austria-Hungary, France, Germany, Britain, Italy, the Netherlands, Portugal, Russia, Spain, and Sweden quickly thereafter also gave official recognition to his personal acquisition of virtually the entire Congo basin, not to be confused with the much smaller French Congo, which was adjacent.

next pretended that the International African Association for the promotion of African exploration and colonization, he had founded, had philanthropic and humanitarian objectives. Soon afterward, he installed a genocidal regime of terror in the heart of Africa under which between three- and thirty million Africans were massacred and multitudes of others maimed by having their hands, ears, and genital organs mutilated or removed. In addition to adding tremendously to his already considerable personal wealth, some profits from Leopold's so-called Congo Free State were eventually used to beautify his European capital of Brussels. If ever proof was needed that slavery, forced labor, abolitionism, imperialism, colonization, racism, and genocide could be parts of overlapping agendas, the Congo Free State readily provides it (Goodwin 2006: 201-207, 444-449; Hochschild 1998: 225-233 *et passim*; Pakenham 2003: 243-246).

Reminiscent of the Basque country's connections with human trafficking of Africans, Julián de Zulueta, of Basque descent, was the last great slave trader in Cuba. Even today, a small town on the southern outskirts of the French Basque town of Biarritz and quite close to urban area of Donostia-San Sebastián in Spain bears the name of Biarritz la Négresse. This name recalls that many wealthy Europeans of this area once grew rich from the African slave trade. Nestled in the Basque country where France and Spain come together, Biarritz and nearby Biarritz la Négresse became established as important resorts for European royalty, including quite notably King Louis Philippe, and later for Emperor Napoleon III, and his wife, the Empress Eugénie. It was in 1869 in Egypt that Khedive Ismail Pasha, in pursuit of his goal of winning acclaim from the pampered elite that was European royalty, invited Empress Eugénie to preside over the opening of the Suez Canal ceremonies, and it was in July of the following year that her husband declared her the regent in France.

With France and Britain in the colonial vanguard by this time, Europeans hastily began claiming ownership of virtually the entire continent of Africa, moving gradually from coastal areas toward the interior. Meanwhile, spoils in Africa continued providing the means for accommodating European powers who suffered losses in various conflicts and rivalries with each other in Europe. When the Franco-Prussian War of 1870-1871 ended in a humiliating defeat for France and resulted in the unification of a greater Germany, for example, Africa suffered.

It was at this time that France's Jules Ferry, while prefect of the Seine *département* and a member of its Chamber of Deputies, began championing the idea that France should acquire as huge a colonial empire as possible. As Ferry put it in the Chamber of Deputies on July 28, 1885, shortly after the end of his second term as Prime Minister, "superior races have a right and a duty to civilize inferior races." As Germany grew rapidly both industrially and in population with strong-willed Count Otto von Bismarck as its chancellor and with Prussia as its dominant state, Britain and France sought to fortify themselves against the threat increasingly posed by Germany by enlarging their colonial empires, including in Africa, as well.

From 1871, France allowed Dakar and Rufisque join Gorée and Saint-Louis as Senegalese *communes* where African residents were given second-class rights

threat increasingly posed by Germany by enlarging their colonial empires, including in Africa, as well.

From 1871, France allowed Dakar and Rufisque join Gorée and Saint-Louis as Senegalese *communes* where African residents were given second-class rights of French citizenship in the very limited sense that collectively they could elect a single representative to the French legislature in Paris (Arvel 1989: 32). Until 1914 when France needed African troops to fight on its behalf in World War I, however, even this single representative of the Senegalese *communes* was European rather than African. Most residents of Senegal never enjoyed even the limited political rights of Senegalese in the four *communes*, for the quasi-assimilationist policy of France had little to do with French attitudes about Africans and much to do with France's decision to employ Senegal as its major base from which to establish as huge a colonial empire in Africa as possible for the good of France.

While open conquest was a favorite tactic by which European countries acquired colonies and so-called protectorates in Africa, another involved encouraging African officials to incur debts from Europeans well beyond what they had any means to repay. This tactic could be fully as coercive and brutal in forcing a state to mortgage its independence as could be outright military compulsion. Such underhandedness would be used at various times against numerous Africans states, including Egypt, Liberia, Ethiopia, Morocco, and Tunisia. The French used this tactic in Tunisia until eventually France was in a position to pressure Tunisia (while still officially a Turkish regency) to assert its independence from the Ottoman Empire. Considering that already in 1874 Turkey was so broke that it could not even pay the interest due on its loans and had gone into formal bankruptcy, Tunis was hardly in a position to resist the demands on it from France. Shortly thereafter, France then pressured the Turkish governor of Tunis, who was known as the *bey*, to sign a treaty that gave it cover to establish a so-called protectorate over Tunisia.

Although a newly-united Italy, which was Germany's ally, wished also to control Tunisia (much as the ancient Roman Empire had once been able eventually to control Carthage there), Germany strategically sided with the establishment of a French protectorate over Tunisia in order to direct France's attention away from its own takeover of Alsace-Lorraine in what had been northeastern France (Pakenham 2003: 181, 203). Belatedly, however, Bismarck let the other shoe drop by also entering Germany into the highly competitive European "scramble for Africa." In 1882, for example, Egypt became a protectorate of Great Britain. By the time of the Conference of Berlin in 1884-1885, the European scramble for Africa was on its way to reaching its conclusion in the sense that various European powers—exclusive of any participation by Africans—had made deals among themselves about how to divide as spoils almost the entire continent to their south.

Although the extent of his rape of Africa places Leopold II in a category of his own, the racism that was surging through Europe in the late 19th century did not require that slavery in some technical sense manifest itself. Eventually turning away from Malthusian concerns about overcrowding, but not away from institutionalized racism, Great Britain took steps to augment its population with skilled workers that were needed to sustain its industrial revolution. In this connection, it simplified the process by which immigrants deemed to be "white" might become British subjects. Affording officials the maximum latitude to be arbitrary, a successful application depended upon whether the Home Office believed the immigrant's presence in Britain was likely to be "conducive to the public good" (Paul 1997: 65-66).

Similarly, a new French code of nationality was adopted in 1889. While according to this code children born in France of foreign parents were foreigners, they were allowed to request citizenship on reaching the age of majority. Many such children did not claim citizenship in order to not be drafted into the military, and this eventually began to cause some French citizens to protest what seemed to them to be preferential treatment for young men living in France who were not citizens, including especially many born in France of Belgian and Italian fathers. Both in response to this problem and to tighten its grip on Maghreb (as of this time effectively Algeria and Tunisia) by enlarging the French colonial elite there, France reversed itself by rather liberally extending citizenship both in France and in Algeria to Europeans on the basis of *jus soli*. Not until the Constitution of 1891 were the rules determining French citizenship made definitive, extended to those born in France of a French father, born in France of a foreign father and residing in France, or those born abroad of a French father and then establishing themselves in France and swearing allegiance to France (Weil 2004: 418-421, 423).

In keeping with these changes of 1891, France automatically extended French citizenship to children of non-French Europeans resident in Algeria unless they specifically rejected it. This decision had little to do with what the French thought of such Europeans colonists but a great deal to do with France's willingness to alter their status to strengthen is colonial hold on Algeria (Smith 1998: 31). As this was during the height of the European colonialist scramble for Africa, while French citizenship was being extended quite liberally to Europeans in its colonies, many of whom made no claim to even being French, that citizenship was being withheld from the masses of Africans whom France was seeking to subject to its colonial control. Put in a slightly different way, this was a period during which French citizenship was evolving along lines that viewed Europeans in opposition to Africans, and most especially Africans who were falling increasingly under the control of European imperialism.

Offering justification for such colonial policies as these, numerous European scholars began espousing theories that suggested that the European subordination of Africans was in the interest of Africans. Much flawed scholarship by Europeans became increasingly conflated with pseudo-scientific racism. It would be virtually impossible to appreciate the social climate for people loosely considered Africans in Europe between 1815 and the outbreak of the First World War without at least a brief summation of some contemporary social thought generated by this racist scholarship. In addition to introducing high levels of racialization into the social climate, this theorizing introduced much racialization into the domain of public policy.

racist, one need only refer to some of his opinions of people of African descent
as set forth on pages 137 to 140 of the 1949 edition of his *Vorlesungen über die
Philosophie der Geschichte* (Lectures on the Philosophy of History) published in
Stuttgart and that have been quoted in Debrunner (1979: 301).

> The Negro . . . represents natural man in all his wild and untamed na-
> ture. If you want to treat and understand him rightly, you must ab-
> stract all elements of respect and morality and sensitivity—there is
> nothing remotely humanized in the Negro's character . . . cannibalism
> belonging to the essence of Africa. . . . To be a slave in America is a
> better status than for the Negro than that of freedom on his own con-
> tinent. . . . The moral senses of the African are completely weakened,
> or, to be more correct, they do not exist at all.

Auguste Comte, born in Montpellier, France, in 1798 or almost three decades after Hegel, was another scholar whose pioneering theorizing impacted the
racialization of public policies. Wishing to found a new "science of man" in the
context of which one could study social problems while being as objective and
empirically based as when working on a physics problem, Comte collaborated
between 1817 and 1823 with his mentor Count Henri de Saint-Simon on a manuscript under the title *Plan of the Scientific Operations Necessary for the Reor-
ganization of Society*. It was in this work that they suggested that their new approach to studying the social world would be called "social physics," although
we now commonly refer to it as sociology.

Despite the brilliance of Auguste Comte and Georg Hegel, according to Harris (1968: 101), they both included racial factors in their analyses of world history and were contemptuous of non-European peoples. In keeping with the spirit
of the times, moreover, when the *Société d'ethnologie de Paris* was founded
1839, it had among its principal aims to establish differences between so-called
human races (Heine-Geldern 1964: 407). Following the example of the established *Société d'ethnologie de Paris*, Adolf Bastian soon afterwards established
Berliner Gesellschaft für Anthropogie, Ethnologie und Urgeschichte or the Berlin Society for Anthropology, Ethnology, and Prehistory (Diallo 2001).

In 1843, the English anthropologist James Cowles Prichard published his
Natural History of Man in which he reiterated his belief that all so-called races
possessed the same inward and mental nature. James Cowles Prichard (despite
his professed opposition to slavery) asserted in multiple editions of *Researches
into the Physical History of Man* the novel idea that the biblical Adam had been
a "black" man. Reflective of British racism, however, his writing clearly showed
him also to believe that people belonging to races that were dark in complexion
were inferior to others. In fact, he argued that under the influence of civilization,
man had gradually turned increasingly white. At the time of Prichard's death in
1848 when he was president of the Ethnological Society and a fellow of the
Royal Society, he still believed in the inferiority of people belonging to so-
called races that were darker in complexion though he remained opposed to slavery and believed that mixed races were superior to pure races (Harris 1968: 94-
95; Mosse 1985: 70).

More extreme than Prichard because of his subscription to Blumenbach's degeneration theory was Sir William Lawrence. Also a British anthropologist, Lawrence believed in the degeneration of so-called people of color. In fact, most European social philosophers and scholars in the 19th century, including those who were opposed to slavery, were racists in that they believed in the superiority of Europeans vis-à-vis other peoples. Although anthropologists were especially prominent among those theorizing about race and the incorporation of such theories as those just mentioned into a broad base of Western scholarship, they were not exceptional in their racist beliefs. In fact, similar racism became infused into disciplines from biology, geography, and sociology to economics, psychology, and history (Harris 1968: 94-97).

In 1843 in Germany, the thrust of Gustav Klemm's ten-volume work on the culture-history of mankind was to divide humanity into "active" and "passive" races. This racial dichotomy set forth by Klemm was destined to be a major influence on Edward Burnett Tylor, the dean of British anthropology during the second half of the 19th century as well during most of the first two decades of the next. In Tylor's *Primitive Culture*, originally published in 1871 to great acclaim, he concluded his chapter "Races of Mankind" with an attempt to explain why the "white" race was the best endowed for leading a civilized existence. This was in the same year that he was elected as a Fellow of the Royal Society and only four years before he was awarded an honorary degree by Oxford University (Harris 1968: 101, 140).

Herbert Spencer, an English social philosopher and exponent of evolutionism around the same time, coined the expression "the survival of the fittest." He also advocated the abolition of poor laws in Britain. In adopting this position, Spencer was following in the footsteps of Thomas Malthus, sometimes called "the father of demography," who was also in favor of the abolition of poor laws in Britain. This position by Malthus, coupled with his emphasis on overcrowding, helped to create an atmosphere in Britain where poor people were seen as a drain on society. Even in southern Africa, a Malthusian approach to reducing overcrowding influenced the ethnic-cleansing campaigns that the British sanctioned against the Xhosa of Zuurveld as well as the relocation of some 4,000 British "whites" into the Albany district largely to replace the African victims in 1818 (Reader 1997: 465-466).

Herbert Spencer claimed to be opposed to British imperialism, at least in connection with the Boer War in southern Africa. Still, he remained a Victorian elitist who believed with respect to Britain itself that people who invested less in reproduction and more in education without national support would be better off as "the fittest" in society. These were among the ideas included in his 1852 publication, *Development Hypothesis*.

Both Spencer and Malthus had a major influence on Charles Darwin, who during, approximately the same period as Alfred Wallace, independently discovered the adaptive mechanism we know as natural selection. Long before Darwin's monumental *On the Origin of Species* was published in 1859, he had quit his medical studies at Scotland's University of Edinburgh in the 1820s because he was made uncomfortable by the sight of blood. Shortly after he returned home, it was a freed "black" former slave named John Edmonstone who taught Darwin taxidermy and excited him about South America by telling him tales of its Amazon rainforest.

As this was well before Charles Darwin began his five-year journey to South America aboard the *H.M.S. Beagle* between 1831 and 1836, it is plausible that his experience with John Edmonstone contributed at least tangentially to his belief, as expressed in *Descent of Man* (published in 1871), that "Negroes and Europeans" were biologically very similar despite differences that often seemed very significant superficially (Harris 1968: 119). Within anthropological circles in the 1800s, there existed much argument and debate among scholars who believed in polygenesis versus monogenesis—that is to say, whether human beings had a common origin or several.

When Robert Knox's *Races of Men*, which was published in 1850, was revised in 1866, Knox claimed that races were different species. As he viewed sub-racial divisions corresponding with national origin types, he considered English Anglo-Saxons as superior to all others. He also adopted Camper's ideal of facial angle and the idea of physical perfection as represented by the ancient Greeks. Knox, a doctor, natural scientist, and traveler, had early in his career been so involved in grave robbery or body snatching to obtain bodies for dissection at his private school of anatomy to prove his racist theories that he was pressured to resign in 1831 as its curator. Although he was somewhat anti-Jewish, his racism especially targeted people he considered black (Mosse 1985: 67-68, 71; Fryer 1984: 174-175). While James Hunt, president of the Anthropological Society of London, opposed slavery in a theoretical sense, he praised the American Confederacy and was an admirer of the very racist Robert Knox (Mosse 1985: 70-71; Harris 1968: 93). Both Hunt and Knox believed that a "black" person was incapable of advancing in intelligence beyond a European boy fourteen years of age.

Joseph-Arthur, comte de Gobineau, a widely traveled French diplomat from 1849 to 1877, was to be a major influence on race thinking in the late 19th century. Gobineau even adjusted his pedigree so as to focus on his father rather than his mother, who had once been a lady in waiting to the scandalous Josephine Bonaparte. His best-known work was his *Essay on the Inequality of Human Races*, originally published in the 1850s. According to this work, Gobineau believed in the existence of three primal races, "white," "yellow," and "black," arranged in a hierarchy from the most superior to the most inferior. Gobineau believed that all "white" people shared an ancient Indo-European culture. He believed moreover that "white" people were responsible for establishing all the great civilizations of the world, regardless of whether located in Asia, Africa, Europe, or the Americas.

Gobineau further believed through a confusion of linguistics and biology that within the "white" Indo-European branch of humanity there existed a master race, which he referred to as "Aryan." Although Gobineau viewed many Europeans as degenerative products of race mixing rather than as racially pure, he held Nordic types in high regard. In later life, as reflected in his *The Renaissance*, he adopted the view that Germanic people incorporated enough Aryan stock to barely revive the white race from its contamination by others. Gobineau was more of an inspiration to German composer Richard Wagner, of whom he was a friend, than to right-wing racists in his native France. Although Gobineau condemned slavery and was not anti-Jewish per se, his work was racist, to be certain (Mosse 1985: 51-59). Gobineau was on record as writing that Africans were members of the lowest of all races "driven by the greed of their senses!" Particularly hostile toward and disrespectful of Haiti, where his mother had once lived, Gobineau argued that because its people were "barbaric," Haiti could never become a civilized nation, although some of its "mulattoes" were "more intelligent and capable" than its masses (Debrunner 1979: 352).

Already in the 1850s, German scholars had established themselves as among the leading European specialists in Egyptology, and they began to expand their focus more generally into Africa in the mid-1860s when ethnographic courses began to be taught in Hamburg. In connection with this development, *Völkerkunde* emerged as an autonomous field of university study with a special focus on peoples who from a European perspective were considered primitive. It was during this period that there began to be much focus on the study of crania as a means of distinguishing so-called races and establishing a hierarchy based on the shapes of heads. Since this was a period when Jews in Germany tended to feel themselves well assimilated as European storm clouds of racism were targeting colonized peoples during the European "scramble for Africa," Jewish reactions did not stand out as particularly different from those of other Germans.

It is likely that some German Jews were less likely to question racism targeting Africans for fear that it might be diverted in their own direction. It was in 1867 that Adolf Bastian, previously a specialist in marine life, emerged as the father of *Völkerkunde* by obtaining a post as a lecturer in this new field of study in Berlin. This movement into *Völkerkunde* by Bastian and Rudolf Virchow established them among pioneer German-speaking anthropologists, and they insisted on the hybrid character of races and cultures (e.g., Mosse 1985: 92-93).

Whereas the theories of Adolf Bastian emphasized environmentalism and the psychic unity of all peoples, Friedrich Ratzel, a contemporary scholar who was a pioneer of historical and cultural studies in German ethnology, set forth theories that relied heavily on biological feedback. Following in the Ratzel tradition, Karl Weule, one of Ratzel's students, eventually published a book that in English was called *The Culture of Barbarians*, as well as some others that focused largely on Africa. One thing that these writings by Weule had in common was their underlying assumption that Europeans were superior to people with origins from other parts of the world. As pseudo-scientific racism continued its diffusion through European scholarly circles, it was Karl Weule who in the first decade of the 20th century replaced Fritz Graebner as perhaps the most prominent leader of the historico-cultural school of anthropology.

Along with Rudolf Virchow, Adolf Bastian launched a journal called *Zeitschrift für Ethnologie* in 1869. The following year, Rudolf Virchow participated in the founding of an anthropology society in Vienna. After traveling around the world, including for the first time to western Africa to collect numerous objects of material culture, Adolf Bastian established the Museum of Ethnography in

Berlin, and in 1873 he was nominated the head of *Afrikanische Gesellschaft in Deutschland*, a society for learned Africanists in Germany. A scholarly focus on Africa did not necessarily correspond with a non-racist perspective. Karl Peters, for example, a founding member of the Society for German Colonization in 1884 and of the German East African Society in 1885 stated his view of African peoples as follows: "The Negro is a born slave who needs his despot as the opium smoker needs his pipe" (Blackshire-Belaly 1996: 98). In 1890, Germany under Kaiser Wilhelm II established a government ministry totally devoted to its colonial ambitions abroad.

In the late 19th century, there was taking place a convergence of scholarship in the social and biological sciences in many European societies, on the one hand, and in the United States of America, on the other, and time and again on both sides of the Atlantic Ocean, these disciplines were used to justify racist public policies. Whereas American racism was largely reflected in domestic public policies, European racism tended quite often to influence imperialist policies designed to exploit colonized peoples most of whom lived far beyond the borders of Europe. In comparison to racism in the United States during around this time, racism in Europe and in the Ottoman Empire likely retained a more important religious component and less rigidity as associated with people's physical features. Although it was considered illegal in certain Southern states of the United States to teach a person considered black to read and write until the outbreak of the American Civil War in the 1860s, for example, Aquasi Boachi, the son of an African king of Ashanti ethnicity from what is now the country of Ghana, was in Germany studying at the Academy of Mines in Frieiber in 1847 and 1848 (Coquery-Vidrovitch 2007: 17, 74).

That in the wake of slavery British imperial policies toward people of African descent could be equally as abusive as before is well illustrated by a situation concerning Edward John Eyre that arose in Jamaica, the largest of Britain's Caribbean colonies. The son of a Yorkshire vicar and an appointee of the Colonial Office who had previously been posted to New Zealand, St. Vincent, and Antigua, Edward John Eyre was sent by Britain to Jamaica as its deputy governor in 1862. Shortly after his arrival there, he became convinced that the maintenance of social order in British-controlled Jamaica where "whites" were greatly outnumbered by so-called blacks and coloreds should revolve around a strict enforcement of a racist oligarchy. By 1865, he had risen to the position of governor of Jamaica and, when in that year a riot or small-scale rebellion erupted in the town of Morant Bay, Eyre imposed martial law with inhumane brutality.

Although those involved used no organized resistance, Eyre used British troops to execute 439 people, including a member of the Jamaican House of Assembly who was of mixed African and European ancestry who was hanged. In addition, Eyre ordered 600 men and women flogged and had more than 1,000 houses of others he suspected of having rebellious attitudes destroyed by fire. How the European-based British elite responded to the abuses and excesses ordered by Eyre in Jamaica is extremely revealing of the general social climate that likely prevailed in Britain for people of appreciable African descent resident there in the Victorian Era.

houses of others he suspected of having rebellious attitudes destroyed by fire. How the European-based British elite responded to the abuses and excesses ordered by Eyre in Jamaica is extremely revealing of the general social climate that likely prevailed in Britain for people of appreciable African descent resident there in the Victorian Era.

Some leading scholars and public figures in Britain (e.g., John Stuart Mill, Charles Darwin, Charles Lyell, Herbert Spencer, Thomas Huxley) believed that Edward Eyre had misused martial law in Jamaica. An equally prominent cast of Britons (including Thomas Carlyle, Charles Dickens, John Ruskin, Charles Kingsley, and Alfred Lord Tennyson) lined up in defense of him and his collaborators, indicating how deeply embedded racism remained in the culture of the Great Britain despite its abolitionist professions (Hall 2002: 20-65 *et passim*). By the time of the final attempt to prosecute Eyre in 1868, British public opinion had moved overwhelmingly to supporting Eyre and it was clear that the defense of rights for masses of Jamaicans of color against the "whites" who abused them was no longer even considered an issue worthy of further legal pursuit in the view of the British public (Hall 2002: 23-25).

Benjamin Disraeli, a British Anglican of Jewish descent, began a career as one of the most influential politicians in Great Britain, with a professional life spread over three and a half decades from 1852 to 1888. While serving three times as Chancellor of the Exchequer and twice as Prime Minister during the reign Queen Victoria, he largely created the modern Conservative Party in Britain. Overlapping with this period, approximately 120,000 Jews fleeing westward from Russian persecution between 1875 and 1915 settled in Great Britain (Paul 1997: 66). Although Disraeli was himself sometimes the target of racist slurs, he remained a staunch supporter of the expansion of the British Empire, which in large measure was predicated on racist assumptions about the world. He was rigid in supporting the British policy of using Turkey to keep Russia away from the Mediterranean where it might threaten Britain's life line to India that ran through the Mediterranean and across Egypt.

As a consequence, even when in May 1876 Serbian nationalists rose up in an effort to liberate themselves from Ottoman oppression, Disraeli responded by sending the British fleet to Besika Bay to defend Turkish imperialism to the detriment of the oppressed Serbs. Despite Disreaeli's support of such policies, his assistance to many Jews in Britain enabled many of them to feel grateful to him and Queen Victoria for their survival by not questioning the upsurges in racism that were directed against others in the second half of the 19th century, including some people who were "black" and some Europeans of Slavic or Slavonic heritage in the Balkans. When Britain's Colonial Secretary Joseph Chamberlain wrote privately in 1896 that "black" people in the West Indies were "totally unfit for representative institutions" (Fryer 1984: 285), his views likely reflected those of many of his British contemporaries, including many Jews.

Despite European willingness to widely tolerate racism, especially when it was perceived as needed to justify imperialism abroad, racism often had a subtlety and fluidity in Europe that it often lacked in the United States. This undoubtedly helps to explain why Ida B. Wells, a "black" woman born to enslaved

ing to her native United States to continue her uncompromising crusade for justice. Despite the racism that was inherent in the British obsession with ruling a vast global empire, this was still a period when some segments of British society were sympathetic to the victims of racist violence in the United States (King 2003: 88-109).

Such was the climate of racism in the West when *l'Action Française* first emerged in 1899 as the most powerful right-wing movement in France with a racist and anti-Semitic agenda (Mosse 1985: 57). Also in France, an anthropologist named Georges Vacher de Lapouge authored *l'Aryen et son rôle social* (*The Aryan and His Social Role*), which was published in 1899. While associated with the University of Monpellier and the University of Poitier, De Lapouge earned a reputation for himself constructing a number of racial and racist hierarchies of humanity. One pseudo-scientific hierarchy for which he was well known distinguished people living north of the Mediterranean into three major groups based on a diversified mix of traits that he attributed to them, ranging from skull shape to complexion and religion. According to this scheme, Nordic, blond, Protestants were most favorably endowed and constituted his *Homo europaeus*. His *Homo alpinus* was a lower-ranking group, while his *Homo mediterraneus* was alleged to be the most inferior, with Jews as its worst examples.

Racism conflated with nationalism had become so intermixed within the public policies of nations in Europe as well as in Turkey by the last decade of the 19th century that hardly any of these nations was truly an innocent. Tragically, it was in this decade that Ottoman Turkey began the systematic killing of masses of its Armenian citizens, most of whom were Christians. This took place largely in retaliation for Turkish feelings of insecurity associated with the country's declining fortunes as a great power and its suspicion that nationalistic organization among its Armenian minority might be facilitating this process. It was against this background of national insecurity and paranoia that, beginning in 1894, Sultan Abdul-Hamid II targeted Armenians for massive retaliation. In a frenzy of mass killing that followed, a people who had occupied much of the highland between the Black Sea, the Caspian Sea, and the Mediterranean Sea for almost 3,000 years was slaughtered in numbers that ranged between 600,000 and perhaps one and a half million while the Great Powers of the West did little to address the problem except to sometimes protest.

It would not be possible to evaluate in any meaningful way how people of African descent were being treated in Europe as the global reordering of empires was taking place in the period between the 1815 Congress of Vienna and the outbreak of World War I in 1914 except relatively and in respect to how racism or marginalization sometimes complicated the lives of other people also living Europe, in or in the shadow of Europe, around the same time. Despite the fact that the Western world during the late 19th century was greatly under the influence of pseudo-scientific racism, numerous people of appreciable African ancestry were present in Europe, with some even playing crucial roles in the configuring of history and civilization and others occasionally raising eyebrows with their self-deprecating clowning and buffoonery.

ence of pseudo-scientific racism, numerous people of appreciable African ancestry were present in Europe, with some even playing crucial roles in the configuring of history and civilization and others occasionally raising eyebrows with their self-deprecating clowning and buffoonery.

Already in 1852, or the year before the outbreak of the Crimean War, Ira Aldridge, who had arrived in Britain from the United States as an aspiring actor in the 1820s, departed Britain with his family for mainland Europe. In addition to being tired of his endless rounds of provincial tours due to special hurdles in London, he wished to undertake new challenges before a broader range of audiences. On stages across Europe, Ira Aldridge became a spectacular success, including in Hamburg, Basel, Danzig, Saint Petersburg, Moscow, Munich, Budapest, Prague, Vienna, Brussels, Paris, Belgrade, Dresden, Potsdam, Bonn, Cologne, Leipzig, and Berlin. In Belgium, King Leopold I, an uncle of Queen Victoria, even became his patron. In Prussia, Frederick IV gave him the Prussian Gold Medal of the First Class for Art and Science. He performed before Maria Alexandrovana, who was a Russian grand duchess by birth, a British royal duchess by marriage to the second son of Queen Victoria, and still later the consort and widow of a German duke. While in Russia, Aldridge became one of the highest-paid actors in the world. While there, he became well acquainted with Leo Tolstoy. In connection with an engagement in Paris, Alexandre Dumas *père*, famous writer and the son of General Thomas-Alexandre Dumas, feted Aldridge lavishly at "Reservoirs" in Versailles.

As Aldridge was lionized across Europe, the hurdles that he had once faced in London tumbled and he was welcomed to perform on the best stages of the British capital. Eventually taking Amanda von Brandt, a Swedish opera singer who claimed to be a countess, as his second wife and becoming naturalized as a British citizen, he never returned to his native United States. Aldridge died in the city of Lodz while on a tour of Poland in 1867, leaving behind his Swedish-born widow and their three young children. Among the thirty-three actors of the English stage honored with bronze plaques at the Shakespeare Memorial Theater at Stratford-upon-Avon, only his represents an actor known to be of African descent.

One American of mixed African and European descent who was three times in Europe during the 19th century had been born as the child of an enslaved "black" mother and a "white" father he never really knew on a plantation near the town of Easton, Maryland. After several failed attempts to escape from slavery, he eventually reached the area north of the Mason-Dixon Line and changed his name from Frederick Baily to Frederick Douglass hoping to avoid capture even as he campaigned relentlessly against slavery. Following the publication of an autobiography entitled *Narrative of the Life of Frederick Douglass, An American Slave* that was an instant best seller when it was published in 1845, friends advised Douglass to leave the United States to avoid possible recapture. In accordance with this advice, Douglass fled to Europe where he spent two years lecturing in Ireland and England largely on the injustices and abuses of slavery. By the end of this time, his friends and supporters in Europe had raised the $710 he needed to purchase his freedom from Auld Hugh, his last owner, as well as an additional amount to establish a newspaper in his native United States. Originally called *North Star*, this newspaper was later renamed *Frederick Douglass's Paper*.

As Douglass was relentless in campaigning for the abolition of slavery, he often found himself in the company of fellow abolitionists. After John Brown, who had several times been in his company, attacked the United States Arsenal at Harpers Ferry in an effort to start a slave insurrection, Douglass fled to Canada out of fear of being considered a collaborator of Brown. From Quebec, he then sailed for Europe in September 1859, where he remained for six months in England and Scotland. By the third time Frederick Douglass was again in Europe in 1886 and 1887, it was two decades after the end of America's Civil War. He had published two additional autobiographies and he had added women's rights to the issues with which he was concerned. By this time, one of the most famous spokesmen for civil rights on either side of the Atlantic Ocean, Douglass visited France, Italy, Greece, and Egypt in addition to Britain before returning home.

In the 1870s, an African-Cuban composer and violinist named Claudio J. B. Brindis de Sala achieved a spectacular success in newly united Germany and was even made a German citizen by Emperor William I, raised to the rank of a baron, and was allowed to marry a German noblewoman (Debrunner 1979: 352). From the United States, classically trained musician Marion Cook, who had written the music for a popular show called "All Coons Look Like Me," visited Europe for a second time during this period with another troupe called the Tennessee Students and toured for six months. Among the places they appeared were the Palace Theatre in London, the Olympia in Paris, and the Schumann Circus in Berlin. When eventually the orchestra split up, several of the musicians, including Sidney Bechet and Benny Peyton, remained in Europe (Shack 2001: 28). During the 1890s, new forms of "black" American music and dance (e.g., ragtime, the cake walk) diffused widely in Europe and even inspired French composer Claude Debussy (MacMaster 2001: 135).

Alongside negative and ambiguous images that contributed to racism and ethnocentrism, Europeans had access to numerous contrary contemporaneous images of peoples of African descent. Further illustration of the diversity of people of African descent that could be found in England around this time were John Ocansey and Sally Bonetta Forbes. John Ocansey traveled from the Gold Coast to Victorian Liverpool in 1881 with the hope of recovering money misappropriated from him by an unscrupulous English trader. African-born Sally Bonetta Forbes, by contrast, was reared and provided for in Europe largely by Queen Victoria as a patron and foster mother before eventually returning to live in Africa (Gerzina 2003: 3; Anim-Addo 2003: 11-19).

Illustrating that people of African descent influenced concert as well as popular music during this period was the African Choir (Erlmann 1999: 107-134). In 1890, moreover, an English-born Anglo-African named Samuel Coleridge-Taylor entered the Royal College of Music as a violin student. The son of a father from Sierra Leone who had come to England and earned a medical degree and of an English mother, Samuel Coleridge-Taylor's talents as a musical genius began to be revealed at a young age. Although he made a considerable contribution to British concert music, he was forced to battle against racism all his short life (Fryer 1984: 256-262).

In 1873 the choir from Nashville, Tennessee organized in 1867 by George L. White as the Colored Christian Singers and later known as the Fisk Jubilee Singers was performing in Europe under the direction of Frederick J. Loudin. This group from what is now Fisk University (not to be confused with the Tennessee Students) introduced African American spirituals to audiences in several European countries, including to royalty. In 1877 nine Fisk Jubilee Singers, of whom seven were former slaves, were in Germany attempting to raise money for their Tennessee institution (Coquery-Vidrovitch.2007: 23; Fryer 1984: 258). Another important influence from the United States on the life of Coleridge-Taylor in 1896 was the African-American poet Paul Lawrence Dunbar, son of a former slave, who was visiting London to give public readings of his works. Coleridge-Taylor set some of Dunbar's poems to music. Also in 1897, the two gave some joint public performances in London (Fryer 1984: 258).

Coleridge-Taylor was on good terms with Edward Edgar—Britain's leading composer of international stature since Henry Purcell who lived in the second half of the 17th century—and it known that one of his meetings with Loudin took place in 1896. In contrast to Edgar, who never formally studied composition, Samuel Coleridge-Taylor was at times a professor of composition at Trinity College of Music in London. At other times, he was also conductor of the Handel Society, the conductor of the Rochester Choral Society, and the conductor of the Stock Exchange Orchestral and Choral Society. Coleridge-Taylor in 1899 married a woman named Jessie, who had once been associated with the Royal College of Music over the objections of her "white" British parents. Despite the genius and fame of Coleridge-Taylor and the fact that his *Hiawatha's Wedding Feast* was the most popular English choral-orchestral work during his lifetime, it was not rare for Samuel Coleridge-Taylor to be insulted with racist taunts from street urchins while simply walking in the streets of his native London (Fryer 1984: 258-259).

Around this same time in the last decade of the 19th century, Germany began signing agreements with African leaders in its African colonies—Togoland, Cameroon, South-West Africa, and Tanganyika—whereby colonial leaders agreed to send some of their subjects to Germany to be educated. It was Germany's hope that they could be used with optimal efficiency within its colonial system upon their return to Africa. Instead of returning to Africa however, some of these Africans remained in Germany, married, and reared children (Sephocle 1996: 24). Three Cameroonians who arrived to study medicine in Hamburg under this arrangement in 1891 included 21-year-old N'Gambi ul Kuo and two companions. As they were repulsed by the sight of blood, however, they became merchants instead. As for N'Gambi ul Kuo, for the price of five marks he acquired German citizenship in 1896 and married. As a result of his one or two marriages there, he had three daughters, with the youngest two being Doris Reiprich and Erika N'Gambi.

Other students from Germany's African colonies who arrived in Europe included Rudolf Douala Manga Bell, Theophilus Wonja Michael, and the daughter of a coffee farmer in Cameroom who had converted to Protestantism. Some of the Africans who came to Germany during this period eventually taught courses on African languages and culture there, including Hassan Taufik, Muhamad Beschir, and Amur bin Nasur bin Amur Ilomeiri, the last of whom was from Zanzibar (Coquery-Vidrovitch 2007: 22, 24).

In addition to Africans in Germany during this period, more than one hundred African Americans were in Germany in 1896 alone. One fascinating African Ameircan in Europe in the late 19th century was William E. Burghardt Du Bois. Du Bois was a graduate student at the University of Berlin from 1892 to 1894 attempting to obtain a doctorate degree. The semester before he was to complete his courses, however, his fellowship was discontinued. This was at a time when in the United States northern foundations such as the George Peabody and John F. Slater Funds were powerful arbiters of what type of education their handful of wealthy "white" board members considered appropriate for African-Americans, and these arbiters were invariably wedded to a race-specific industrial model. This model had as its goal to ensure the continuation of a race-based social hierarchy in America (Robbins 2002: 81-89).

While in Europe, Du Bois had been receiving financial assistance from the Slater Fund and Daniel Gilman (the president of the segregated Johns Hopkins University in Baltimore, where no "black" was allowed to study, as well as a board member of the Slater Fund) did not view "blacks" with doctorates from prestigious German universities as a priority for the United States. Gilman convinced the other members of the Fund—Rutherford B. Hayes and Atticus Haygood—that "Negro education should be more practical." Although Du Bois was forced for these financial reasons that were motivated by racism to return to the United States as a consequence, he had already by this time traveled rather widely in Europe. Returning to Cambridge, Massachusetts, Du Bois completed his dissertation two years later in 1896, thereby becoming the first African American to earn a Ph.D. degree from Harvard University.

W. E. B. Du Bois was hardly the only person of African descent who traveled across the Atlantic to Europe to achieve greater intellectual or artistic development in the late 1800s. Another was Henry Ossawa Tanner, son of an African-American bishop. Although Tanner's destination was Paris, he traveled there via Rome in 1891, with the objective of further developing his talent as a painter. Similarly, Annie E. Anderson Walker went to Paris to study art in 1896, probably the first African-American woman to do so (Leininger-Miller 2001: 1-15).

In 1900, Henry Sylvester-Williams organized the first Pan-African Conference held in London with some financial support by ex-MP Dadabhai Naoroji of Indian descent. The conference had as one of its aims to "promote and protect the interests of all subjects claiming African descent, wholly or in part, in British colonies and other places especially Africa." A petition was sent to Queen Victoria regarding the situation of black people in South Africa and Rhodesia, drawing attention to forced labor, the indenture system where, black men, women, and children were placed in legalized bondage to white colonists, the pass system, and various kinds of segregation (Fryer 1984: 282-286). This was only one year before the end of Victorian Era, and among the strong supporters of this conference was Samuel Coleridge-Taylor, who also was in charge of the music performed at Westminster Town Hall (Fryer 1984: 261).

In Scotland in 1902 Edinburgh University was certainly an early hotbed of activity for students from western Africa. It was at this time that African medical students persuaded the dean of the medical faculty to write a complaint to the Colonial Office against the openly discriminatory policies of the West African Medical Service, which barred from appointment those of non-European ancestry (Adi 1998: 10). A Sierra Leonean medical student named H. R. Bankole-Bright was one of the founders of the National Congress of British West Africa and the West African Students' Union (Adi 1998: 10).

A contralto born in Philadelphia in 1879, Arabella Field, was likely the first "black" American to record commercially in Europe. She had already settled in Germany by 1907. A number of African-American artists pursuing operatic careers moved from Germany to settle in Russia in 1913. Hoping to find greater opportunities and likely wishing to avoid some of the racist ferment that was stirring in Germany shortly before the eruption of the first World War, one of these persons was Mexican-born Coretta Arli-Titz, who had been reared in New York. Married to Professor Boris Titz, also an accomplished musician, Arli-Titz was well received in Russia both by the public and in artistic circles. While continuing to study opera, she performed in concert to critical acclaim from a repertoire that included African-American, Russian, and Indian works (Blakely 1986: 144-145). African-Canadian William A. Harper, eventually a landscape painter residing in the United States, went to Paris in 1903 and left in 1908. William Edouard Scott, an African American, studied art in Paris beginning in 1909-1910. He returned to Europe in late 1911 and spent time in France and perhaps England. Scott only finally returned to the United States from Europe in April 1914 as war was beginning to erupt (Leininger-Miller 2001: 1-15).

Stereotypes and presumptions without any factual basis have led many Europeans and others to assume falsely that, except perhaps for a few people of color who were in bondage or had servile statuses, people with African associations only recently arrived in Europe. As Europe was never without an African presence, it hardly conformed to such stereotypes. Between the 1884-1885 Conference of Berlin and 1910, a number of European powers attempted with some success to bring almost all people living on the African continent under their control, and the means they used in this undertaking were often brutal and driven by racism.

As we approach the end of this discussion of the African presence in Europe between the 1815 Congress of Vienna and the run-up to World War I, the following points deserve clear statement. There was great variety in the circumstances that characterized the lives of people of African descent in Europe. They had arrived along numerous routes. Some were from European colonies and some were not. Some had become European citizens and some had not. Some were artists and intellectuals and some were not. Hence, they in no way constituted a single group. Feelings of European superiority were wide-spread during this period as pseudo-scientific racism reached a high point and many Europeans embraced notions that they should dominate the rest of humanity.

Although mocking, name-calling, and exhibition in virtual zoos characterized the lives of some victims of racism, still, some people of African descent in Europe made stellar contributions across a broad range of European civilization and life. Into the early years of the 20th century, people in Europe with ties to Africa and the Europeans masses around them continued to have intimate relationships, to participate together in joint ventures, and to influence each other socially and culturally. Confused distortions of social history must not draw our attention away from the fact that wherever the masses of Europeans left the doors open in genuine ways to people of appreciable African ancestry who lived scattered among them, events usually unfolded along the lines of almost uneventful acculturation and assimilation.

Competing nationalist and imperialist agendas of Europeans eventually brought them into conflict among themselves. By the middle of the new century's second decade, such conflict made war on a scale such as the world had never witnessed unavoidable. Even in the face of conflagration that would follow, however, the destinies of Europeans would become more, not less, intermixed and entangled with the destinies of people globally.

Chapter Five

The World at War

Early 1900s to 1920s

Around the turn of the 20th century, an African-American musician and comedian named Will Garland toured Europe, eventually settling in England. In 1903, Louis Douglas (also African-American) arrived in Europe to perform with Belle Davis's Georgia Picaninnies as one of the last acts that some refer to as "cooning," a genre closely related to self-demeaning minstrel performances (Shack 2001: 9-10, 25). In the same year, a vaudeville show called *In Dahomey* that had been the first all-"black" musical to play in a major Broadway theatre opened at the Shaftsbury Theater in London. A special presentation of this show at Buckingham Palace was attended by, among others, King Edward VIII. Later in the same year, it was presented on stage at the Olympia in Paris. It was likely this same company of dancers that Coquery-Vidrovitch (2007: 22) has noted appeared in Germany also in 1903.

During the following year, the Four Black Spades, the Four Black Diamonds, and Bonnie Goodwin's Picaninies played the Folies-Bergère in Paris. Advertisements for these performances were illustrated with grotesque and eccentric figures shown singing, dancing, shaking tambourines, plucking banjos, and snapping castanets. The descriptive texts that advertised these performances by African-Americans, moreover, were liberally sprinkled with terms such as *niggers*, *coons*, and *pickaninnies* (Shack 2001: 9). In 1906, Holman's American Serenaders performed in Paris, and some members of the group stayed to settle. Such was the situation in Europe for African-Americans when in 1904 at the age of ten, a "black" lad named Eugene Jacques Bullard crossed the Atlantic as a stowaway aboard a German ship called the *Matherus* that was en route to Hamburg from Newport News, Virginia. After leaving the ship in Aberdeen, Scotland, he went to Glasgow where he survived for a while by singing and dancing for organ grinders. After five months, however, Bullard made his way to Paris.

Another "black" youth who crossed the Atlantic Ocean in order to reach Europe in 1904 was Harold Moody. From the British-controlled colony of Jamaica,

Moody was somewhat older than Bullard and much better educated. Arriving in London to study medicine at King's College, Moody was unprepared for the color bar that awaited him in Edwardian London. So rigid was that color bar that he found it hard even to obtain lodging. Other students of color from various British colonies were already in London, and a number of them were involved in Ethiopianism, which in the early 1900s was another name for early Pan-Africanism. In 1904, there even existed an Ethiopian Association in Edinburgh and in Liverpool. Prince Bandele Omoniyi, a Nigerian student in Edinburgh was one of the students involved in this movement, and he authored a book about early Pan-Africanism in 1908 called *A Defence of the Ethiopian Movement* (Adi 1998: 11).

As European racial insecurities reached new heights, Great Britain in 1905 enacted the most wide-ranging intervention in the field of immigration up to that time. Its Aliens Act of that year empowered landing officers to prohibit the immigration of certain aliens traveling on ships, provided for the registration of all aliens in Britain, and imposed restrictions on the freedom of movement of aliens in the country (Paul 1997: 66). Despite such restrictions motivated by racist insecurities, Henry Sylvester-Williams, a Trinidadian, became one of the first two people of African descent to be elected to public office in Britain when he won a seat on the Marylebone borough council as a "Progressive" candidate in November 1906. The Britain government lost little time in harassing him, however, and this increased greatly after he visited Liberia the following year. Believing him insufficiently committed to the government's imperialist goals in Africa, the British Council denounced him in secret dispatches sent to London. As this harassment became insupportable, Sylvester-Williams returned to Trinidad shortly afterward (Fryer 1989: 287).

This was a period when Europeans tended to interpret the efforts of people of color who battled against racism and colonial oppression as anti-European. As France was Britain's principal imperialist rival attempting to establish a huge empire in Africa, this also impacted the French presence in Africa. In 1871, so successful was the French suppression of an uprising by the Berber-speaking Kabyle of northeastern Algeria, for example, that France began allowing some Kabyles to migrate to France shortly afterward. When in Marseille in 1906 France sponsored its first grand colonial exposition, Marseille located on the opposite shore of the Mediterranean from Algeria in a sense became "the capital of the French Empire." Although Paris also hosted a colonial exposition in the *Grand Palais* along the Champs-Elysées that opened in the same year, it was modest by comparison to that in Marseille.

France's colonial committee in Marseille was transformed into an important colonial institute. Around the same time, the local chamber of commerce sponsored a major expedition to Dahomey (now the country of Benin). Marseille was becoming increasingly enthusiastic about the prospects of colonialism also in sub-Saharan Africa (Blanchard and Boëtsch 2005: 9). Contributing to this enthusiasm, Marseille was experiencing anti-Italian xenophobia (Liauzu 1996: 183). As a consequence, the number of Africans in Marseille from Kabyle increased significantly during the years between 1905 and 1907 when they began to be used there in the place of Italian immigrants who were on strike in soap factories and in the sugar industry. Immigrants from Kabyle were also used for loading and unloading ships. It was from this tiny African presence in the huge southern port city of Marseille that Africans would eventually begin growing into the majority of immigrants in France that they are at present (Blanchard and Boëtsch 2005: 9, 14; Direche-Slimani 1997: 1).

It was in part because of this that in Germany after 1890 and into the early 20th century the African presence was also growing. So-called *Misch Ehen* or mixed marriages began to be considered objectionable. They were, in fact, considered so objectionable that they were outlawed, and marriage bureaus refused to legalize marriage vows between "whites" and "blacks" (Blackshire-Belay 1996: 109). This was not just directed at people of African descent however. When the Pan-Germanic League was founded in 1894, it expressed its opposition to marriages between so-called Aryans and others. In the same spirit, the 1898 edition of *Brockhaus*, the leading encyclopedia at that time in the German language, referenced *Mischling* as a product of a mixed union and indicated that in most cases they inherited the handicaps of their "colored" parentage (Coquery-Vidrovitch 2007: 62-63).

In this atmosphere of finger-pointing and racist accusations leveled by various European peoples toward each other to prove who was superior as opposed to who was inferior because of being more racially tainted, even Portugal enacted anti-"miscegenation" laws as though somehow such laws could undo a history of centuries during which numerous Africans were incorporated into its population. By means of a number of its declarations throughout the early 1900s, as noted by Tinhorão (1988: 376), the Portuguese government denied that the Portuguese people were in any way mixed with so-called blacks. Instead of denouncing racism and so-called race science for the mockery of science that they were, Portugal continued contributing to a romantic nationalist myth of the Portuguese as racially pure and homogeneous Europeans. Many people resident in metropolitan Portuguese become so paranoid of taint that they even began to make discriminatory distinctions between themselves and "white" Portuguese colonists associated with Africa on the theory that, irrespective of phenotypic appearances, the latter may not be racially pure because of their overseas experiences (Fike 2000: 11, 61).

Meanwhile in 1905, the German physician Alfred Ploetz played a central role in the founding of the *Deutsche Gesellschaft für Rassenhygiene* (The German Society of Racial Hygiene), which began with thirty-two members. It had as one of its major goals to return the so-called Nordic race to its "purity" through selective reproduction and sterilization. As this society received general financial backing from the German government, Alfred Ploetz soon founded the *Journal of Racial and Social Biology* as its official organ (Coquery-Vidrovitch 2007: 63). As he advocated ideas of social Darwinism, eugenics, and the protection of Germany from so-called racial diseases, new chapters of the society sprang up in a number of German cities, soon attracting into membership such biologists and human geneticists as Edwin Baur, Fritz Lenz, Eugen Fischer, and Wilhelm Welnberg.

Reflective of this great concern with eugenics in Germany, Eugen Fischer, around this same time, developed an injection that allegedly was capable of rendering people sterile. Also in 1905 the governor of German-controlled South-West Africa promulgated a decree banning both marriages and sexual relations between "whites" and "blacks." As sex drives often have a way of circumventing irrational laws, however, this decree did not prevent new offspring from being born there that were of mixed European and African descent (Blackshire-Belay 1996: 106). Even where the parents of such contrasting heritages were married, Germans often retaliated by *a priori* referring to their offspring as bastards. Meanwhile, it was in 1910 that the first non-German-speaking chapter of the Germany Society of Racial Hygiene was founded in Sweden with the name *Sallskap för Rashygien* (Coquery-Vidrovitch 2007: 63). As other foreign chapters soon emerged in Britain, the United States, and the Netherlands, the society at least for a while even changed its name to the International Society of Racial Hygiene. Racism was hardly new in the world. It had been a handmaiden of European imperialism abroad almost from as early as the Age of Global Exploration, and racism had been extensively used to keep people of color oppressed in many parts of the Americas.

While a student at the University of Berlin in the early 1890s, W. E. B. Du Bois of the United States, who was himself a product of ancestors from Europe as well as from Africa, was appalled as one of his professors at the University of Berlin delivered a lecture on the so-called racial inferiority of so-called mulattoes. Already by this time Du Bois was also aware of anti-Semitism. In fact, he had been victimized by it in Poland when occasionally mistaken for a Jew there. As racism from both sides of the Atlantic Ocean began in some respects to converge, numerous European and American scholars came to believe that it was their patriotic duty to generate racist theories that could justify the racist agendas of their various countries.

While at times such theories were meant to facilitate discrimination among various peoples long resident in Europe and America, at other times they seemed to focus more on peoples living in overseas colonial settings under European control. Throughout the Victorian Age in Britain, racism directed at non-Europeans was used to justify imperialistic colonialism, not infrequently under the adage of the "white man's burden" or some similar racist notion (Armitage 2000; Hall 2002; Lorimer 2003: 187-207). Even Benjamin Disraeli, Britain's first prime minister of Jewish ethnicity, had been an unapologetic proponent of a large and mighty British Empire despite the fact that racist slurs had sometime complicated his life in Britain while a more profound and punishing racism had complicated the lives of peoples of color in Her Majesty's overseas colonies.

With the possible exception of W. E. B. Du Bois and perhaps a few others, it is doubtful that the artists, performers, and intellectuals of African-American descent in Europe around this time had any great awareness, whatever the conditions of their daily lives, that a good number of European scholars were occupied generating theories that posed a creeping threat to people deemed to be "others." Even if not in all cases explicitly racist, this theorizing was based on a premise that some people were superior to others and for that reason alone more "fit" to survive. In 1903 when the Victorian Age was at an end and a new century had just begun, W. E. B. Du Bois prophesized in his book *The Souls of Black Folk* that "the problem of the twentieth century" would be that of "the color-line."

History proves that there was much more right than wrong in his prediction. Especially is this true if we accept color as but a metaphor for numerous missteps involving racism and ethnic cleansing coupled with human exploitation and conflict over territory and resources that would reduce Africans and most other non-Europeans to mere instruments of exploitation and manipulation by "great powers." Although the century to which Du Bois referred is no more, we still inhabit a world where Europeans and people who consider themselves of European descent struggle with treating other members of humanity as their equals. Hence, the problem of the color-line, in Europe and in its various daughter societies that we think of as Western, remains important (Bonilla-Silva 2000: 188-214).

In a world dominated by peoples of European descent that was accustomed to thinking of peoples of color as subordinates, auxiliaries or less, peoples of African descent faced new challenges as they sought to liberate themselves from racism and colonial oppression. Peoples of European background tended to be insistent that their own priorities, even when they involved conflict with each other or were exploitative of others, should take precedence over human rights for peoples of color. Francis Galton, a first cousin of Charles Darwin, in addition to being an evolutionist, began shortly after the death of Darwin in 1883 to refer to his own social philosophy as eugenics. Galton took to disparaging "black" Australians and Spaniards and went on record as saying that "the average intellectual standard of the negro race is some two grades below our own" (Fryer 1984: 160). In 1904, Galton became the founder of the Francis Galton Laboratory for National Eugenics. There, he worked closely with Karl Pearson on methods that he deemed would improve the population of Britain. The work of this laboratory was followed closely in Germany as reflected in *Archiv für Rassen und Gesellschaftsbiologie* or *The Journal for Racial and Social Biology* (Mosse 1985: 75).

One reason that eugenic theories diffused widely among peoples of European descent in the early decades of the 20th century was because these theories were widely advertized as "progressive" and "scientific." Few who were not truly prophetic foresaw the magnitude of the threat that this train of thought posed to human life in general. As a consequence, these theories were widely embraced by numerous Catholics, Protestants, and Jews alike (Rosen 2004). By the time Galton died in Britain in 1911, journals dedicated to the cause of eugenics had been founded in a number of European countries as well as in the United States.

Still largely ignored by the world at large, during the same period that the South African War was being fought, a full-scale holocaust was being carried out by the Germans in their overseas colony of South-West Africa (now the country of Namibia). This especially took a turn for the worse after the infamous expulsion or extermination order against indigenous peoples was issued by General Lothar von Trotha in 1904 under authority granted him by the German emperor or kaiser. This general also demonstrated his ruthlessness toward peoples of color in the ways in which he helped to suppress the Boxer Rebellion in China and in squashing resistance to German colonialism in eastern Africa (Goodwin 2006: 335-337, 342-344).

It was beginning in 1904 after some Africans of Herero ethnicity in the town of Okahandja offered some resistance to abominable racist practices by settlers from Germany that Germans began forcing masses of the Hereros into the wretchedly arid Kalahari Desert and poisoned many of their wells. Germans simply eliminated many others with machine guns or allowed them to end their own lives in forced labor camps. This mass murdering that victimized Africans especially of Herero ethnicity between 1904 and 1907 was likely the first genocidal holocaust of the 20th century (Coquery-Vidrovitch 2007: 29-37). As long as this treatment did not victimize people deemed to be mostly of European descent, the Western world largely dismissed it as benign racist paternalism toward peoples who, being of color, were likely "savage." Europeans as well as "white" Americans with any international awareness tended to assume that however colonized Africans were treated was simply part of the justified cost of taming and civilizing them.

By around 1907 when this holocaust in German-controlled South-West Africa had run its course, Germans, with some assistance from resident Boers, had exterminated possibly as many as 80 percent of the colony's Herero people, though a few managed to escape across the desert into Bechuanaland (now Botswana). In addition, about half of the Nama and so-called "mixed race" Oorlams who had been concentrated largely to the south of the Hereros had been eliminated. As for General van Trotha who was in charge of this savagery, Germany awarded him the Order of Merit (Reader 1997: 595-597). Though some Germans protested, this mass extermination of over three quarters of all Hereros and multitudes of Nama and Oorlams by Germans is still largely ignored by the world or responded to with silence (Hochschild 1998: 282).

In 1908, Germany established a Colonial Institute in Hamburg that continued to build upon this legacy of European colonial racism. In that same year, it also decreed that in its African colonies all German colonists who would marry indigenous Africans would lose their right to vote (Blackshire-Bellay 1996: 109). By 1911 in the German *Reichstag* or parliament, Wilhelm Solf, who was the government secretary for colonial affairs, harangued against *Misch Ehen* or "mixed marriages," saying: "Do you wish that your own sons would welcome a black daughter-in-law into your home? Do you wish that they bring you nappy-headed grandchildren in the cradle? No, gentlemen, this entire nation does not wish this" (Blackshire-Bellay 1996: 109). Because racism—however covert—was ingrained in the cultures and social climate of Europe, it was never destined to be more than somewhat dormant during the 20th century. As the threat of war made Europeans very sensitive about their limitations in terms of manpower to operate their war machines, they became more tolerant of having people they deemed "others" in their midst. In other words, Europeans were not unaware of the utility to which such colonial subjects could be put as tools in various struggles among themselves.

While this was a general pattern, obviously there were variations on this theme that unfolded in particular ways from one setting to another. Beginning in 1911, the Kaiser Wilhelm Society for the Advancement of Science was founded in Germany as an umbrella organization under which numerous research institutes as well as some other units operated. While most of these were established in and around Berlin, a few of them would eventually be established in Europe even beyond the borders of Germany. In addition to being financially supported by individuals, industries, and from the public purse in Germany, this society received major financial support from America's Rockefeller Foundation. The Rockefeller Foundation had been established by the American oil monopolist John D. Rockefeller and his family in 1909 as a tax-exempt organization that was intended to operate in the public interest.

Meanwhile in 1913, a new German citizenship law provided for national membership through the idiom of descent, as expressed by the Latin term *jus sanguinis*. This meant that while people born in Germany could not automatically acquire German citizenship, some others who had never lived in Germany acquired almost an automatic right to citizenship because of their descent, coupled of course with language or other ethnic factors as well as the assumption that they were "white." That this was rigidly enshrined in law in 1913 was intended to deny Germany colonial subjects not deemed to be "white" any right to German inheritance or right to participate in voting.

Symbolically, this construction of citizenship also emerged from a notion of blood in association with concepts of violence and contagion as well as a perceived threat of Germans being feminized (Linke 1999: 122-123, 132). This German legislation severed citizenship from territorial residence and redefined the nation as a community of descent rather than a community of residence. Numerous social historians have documented this legislation's colonial origins and have shown how German citizenship as a consequence became linked to a particular type of racial aesthetic. Citizenship became centered on Germany's preoccupation with so-called race, to whiteness, and even most especially to people loosely and confusingly considered Aryan and Nordic (Linke 1999: 45).

As by the 19th century Europeans were increasingly obsessed with distinguishing themselves from Africans and some other peoples to whom they felt superior, they began to establish human zoos for displaying specimens of the peoples to whom they felt superior. Sarah Bartman followed by other human specimens from Africa had been exhibited throughout the course of the century. Largely in the same spirit as a successful dog exhibition in Paris in 1874, zoos exploiting captive human beings from Africa for the entertainment of Europeans continued to be popular. In Berlin in 1879, six Zulus said to be "warriors" were displayed, and between 1877 and 1893 Africans said to belong to a number of "tribes" were also exhibited in the Jardin d'Acclimatation in Paris (Orlando 2001: 188n; Nordin 2005: 17; MacMaster 2001: 77). A group of Egyptians that were advertized as being Nubians were brought to Europe in 1877 and 1878, where they were viewed by approximately 60,000 Germans more or less as if in a human zoo. In 1905, a Briton bought six Pigmies in the Congo for exhibition in Europe, and they were put on display in Germany in 1906 (Coquery-Vidrovitch 2007: 28).

Helping Europeans feel superior to the rest of humanity was the periodic exhibition in Europe of live Africans, as often as not in cages or in stereotypical naturalistic settings where it was implied that they were "savages." In this vein, there was the first Great Exhibition at the Crystal Palace in 1851, shows in Paris in 1867, 1878, 1887, 1889, 1891, and 1900, and in London in 1886, 1892, 1897, 1899, 1903, 1908, and 1924. An international exhibition of this type was held in Moscow in 1872, in Vienna in 1873, in Italy in 1888, in Germany in 1891, in Antwerp in 1894, in Brussels in 1897 and 1910, in Glasgow in 1901, in Cork in 1902, in Wolverhampton in 1902, and in Bradford, Liège, Marseille, and so forth in 1907 (MacMaster 2001: 74-75). Europeans sometimes traveled to such exhibitions on special chartered trains to see their fellow human beings exhibited as sub-humans in veritable zoos, where those on display were not infrequently from Africa. Among scholars who have written perceptively and at length about this phenomenon in *Africans on Stage*, edited by Bernth Lindfors (1999), are Z. S. Strother, Shane Peacock, Robert W. Rydell, Jeffrey P. Green, Harvey Blume, Neil Parsons, Robert J. Gordon, David Killingray, and Willie Henderson.

Contributing to this atmosphere of racism in Europe was much theorizing about what was often euphemistically referred to as race science. This area was one where researchers often claimed to be innocently focusing on securing so-called strong bloodlines of races. In reality, inheritance takes place by means of genes and not through blood. Far from being innocent, in any case, they were really interested largely in maintaining the nonexistent purity of peoples that they already assumed to be superior to all others in the world through the use of methods that they advertised as consistent with eugenics. Hardly confined to Europe, an extension of the Brooklyn Institute of Arts and Sciences established the Station for Experimental Evolution in the Village of Laurel Hollow in the Town of Oyster Bay in Nassau County in New York in 1904.

In 1910, this laboratory (from 1921 reorganized as the Carnegie Institution of Washington Department of Genetics and now world-renown as the Cold Spring Harbor Laboratory) passed under the direction of Charles B. Davenport. The son of a very religious abolitionist in Brooklyn, Davenport was a prominent biologist who after teaching at Harvard University joined the faculty of the University of Chicago. Hardly an objective scientist free of racist elitism, both he and his brother William were very involved in the American eugenics movement at a time that it was especially tolerant of race-based segregation, sterilization, immigration policies, and marriage restrictions. Although the laboratory under Davenport in the Town of Oyster Bay was involved in eugenics, it also was involved in mainstream research in genetics, medicine, and eventually molecular biology.

In 1911, Davenport authored a work *Heredity in Relation to Eugenics* that was assumed to be scientific despite being tinged with racism and that was widely adopted for use as a textbook in colleges and universities. In the following year, he was elected to America's National Academy of Sciences. This was the same year that at the First International Congress of Eugenics an American Consultative Committee was appointed and given responsibility for organizing a Second International Congress in three years. Although this Second Congress would not be held until 1921 because of the eruption of World War I, the eugenics movement continued to achieve major victories on both sides of the Atlantic. In 1907, for example, the state of Indiana passed legislation that legalized sterilization for people considered to be mental defectives. By 1913, approximately one-half of all the states in the United States provided for sterilization of such classes of people as epileptics, the feeble-minded, the mentally ill, the poor, alcoholics, and certain convicted criminals (Coquery-Vidrovitch 2007: 74).

Similarly on the other side of the Atlantic where many Europeans were undergoing a race-based identity crisis, considerable research was focused on eugenics and so-called race science. In the early 1900s, the German sociologist Max Nordau had already resurrected much of the thinking set forth a half-century earlier by the Austrian-French psychiatrist Benedict Morel in 1857 regarding his theory of degeneration. Morel viewed hereditary taint as the cause of much illness, both mental and physical, and believing, that it was incurable in families and in so-called races, Morel expressed a zeal for preventing people he deemed to be degenerates from reproducing. Although this theory by Morel was not very influential in Britain and the United States, it was very influential in France and many other parts of mainland Europe.

Consistent with this way of thinking, some Europeans as well as "whites" on the other side of the Atlantic saw achievement in sports as a way of alleviating the social malady of degeneration. This eventually became significant in sports in a way that symbolized for many people competition among peoples assumed to differ from each other with regard to inferiority and superiority (Jobert 2006: 19, 20, 22). In France, the African-American cyclist Marshall-Walker "Major" Taylor had been well received when he first arrived there to participate in a cycling competition in 1901. He was periodically involved in European competitions in France and elsewhere until 1909. Although Taylor won the respect of numerous French people at that time, his triumphs were also upsetting to some who had been socialized to believe deeply that people who were "white" should excel in all domains indicative of talent and domination over those who were not. In this regard, a situation that arose in the sport of boxing is also illuminating.

Born John Arthur Johnson and nicknamed the "Galveston Giant," Jack Johnson was born in Texas of parents who had been former slaves. When on December 26, 1908, he won the World Heavyweight Title in boxing by defeating a Tommy Burns in Sydney, Australia, who happened to have been "white," many people of European descent in scattered parts of the world, feeling that this victory undermined their claim to racial superiority, reacted angrily. In Sidney, even the cameras were stopped shortly before the fight ended in order to not record the final moments of Johnson's victory over Burns. Instead of leading to a reexamination of prevailing attitudes of racism, numerous people who deemed themselves to be of European descent, including many mass media moguls, responded by caricaturing Johnson as though he were a sub-human ape and by calling for a "Great White Hope" to avenge their so-called race.

Against this background in 1910, former undefeated heavyweight boxing champion James J. Jeffries came out of retirement, saying "I am going into this fight for the sole purpose of proving that a white man is better than a Negro." This so-called fight of the century took place on July 4, 1910, in front of an all-"white" crowd of 22,000 people in Reno, Nevada. At ringside, a band played a musical selection called "All Coons Look Alike to Me" and promoters urged those in attendance to frequently chant "Kill the Nigger!" So humiliated did masses of "white" Americans feel when Johnson was victorious that race riots erupted across the United States in more than half of all the states as well as in some fifty cities. In some areas, gangs of "whites" entered "black" neighborhoods and attempted to burn down apartment buildings, while in other areas humiliated "whites" searched for "black" compatriots to lynch. Before calm had been restored, at least 23 "blacks" and two "whites" lay dead, with hundreds of other people injured. Hoping to maintain the myth of "white" racial superiority, a number of states even responded by banning the filming of any of Johnson's victories over "white" opponents.

In an effort to avoid racist prosecution through the American legal system that was aimed at Johnson because of his victories, his haughtiness, and his intimate involvements with "white" women, Johnson spent much of the period from 1911 to 1919 in Europe or elsewhere abroad rather than in his native United States. Shortly after his return to the United States, merely because Jack Johnson had sent a railroad ticket to Belle Schreiber, a "white" girlfriend, to travel from Pittsburgh to Chicago, he was forced to spend a year in an American prison on a trumped-up Federal charge that his purchase of this ticket amounted to the transporting a person across state lines for the purpose of "prostitution." Clearly, even what passed for justice in the American system of crime control did not escape from being sullied by its use in enforcing racism.

Around much of the world, in fact, this was a period when athletic competitions between people deemed "white" and others took on symbolic meanings that masses of people of European descent wished to see as confirming their beliefs in white superiority and masses of other people wished to view as contradicting such beliefs. In keeping with this latter way of thinking and the fact that European imperialism had reduced Africa to a pawn of Europe, a considerable segment of the French population greatly longed for a "Great White Hope" in sports that would extricate them from what some deemed "a racial Waterloo." This sentiment was especially strong with respect to boxing, and it gave real salience to the words of Du Bois that the problem of the 20th century would be that of the color-line.

As the approach of war in Europe at least temporarily caused such concerns to abate in France, as the country was not particularly well equipped in terms of manpower (Jobert 2006: 57-102). In 1911, General Charles Mangin published a work titled *La Force Noire* in which he argued that sub-Saharan Africa contained an almost inexhaustible supply of manpower that could easily be put in the service of France. On not a shred of scientific evidence, he also advanced the racist argument that since "black" Africans had a nervous system that was less highly developed than that of Europeans, "blacks" would be less sensitive to pain. Around the same time, significant numbers of the Algerians already in France began moving beyond Marseille to find work in other coastal or industrial cities of the country. By 1912 Algerians in France, most of whom had ties to Kabyle, numbered between 4- and 5,000 residents. By two years later, their numbers reached between 13- and 30,000 (Simon 2000: 39-40).

Amadu M'barick Fall, a ten-year-old Senegalese boy, had been brought to Marseille by a German actress in 1907 because she planned to use him in one of her shows. Soon abandoned by her in Marseille, however, Amadu M'barick Fall changed his name to Louis M'barick Fall and spent the next five or so years washing dishes in taverns in southern France and training to become a boxer. In 1910 at age thirteen, he became a professional boxer in France. As World War I was about to erupt, Louis Fall suspended his boxing in order to join the French army. The government assigned him to the Eighth French Colonial regiment, which was composed entirely of Africans.

Another boxer of color who interrupted his professional boxing career to serve in the French military during World War I was the African-America stowaway named Eugene Jacques Bullard, who had boxed professionally in Paris when he was only nineteen years old. After winning the match, Bullard joined a troupe known as Freedman's Picaninnies on a tour in Europe that included Russia, the Winter Garden in Berlin, and the Bal Tabarin in Paris. In 1914, however, Eugene Jacques Bullard joined the French Foreign Legion (Shack 2001: 22-23). Even as the African presence was growing in France, the African presence in the United Kingdom was also beginning to mushroom.

Between the 1860s and the outbreak of World War I, Arab and Somali seamen settled in South Shields. Some seamen from western Africa and from the West Indies also settled nearby. The war would increase the "black" population in this area fourfold (Fryer 1984: 299), a development that many Britons did not welcome. One gets some impression of how intense color discrimination was from the experience of Harold Moody, who in 1910 was denied a hospital house appointment because the matron refused to have a doctor she deemed to be colored working at the hospital despite his having won many academic prizes during the course of his medical studies, indicating that he was exceptionally well qualified. Similarly, he was rejected for the post of medical officer to the Camberwell Board of Guardians with the explanation that even "the poor people would not have a nigger attend them" (Fryer 1984: 326). In an effort to detour British racism, Dr. Harold Arundel Moody in 1913 started his own medical practice in Peckham. It was around this time, in fact, that he married an English nurse whom he had known from medical school (Fryer 1984: 326).

Some students from British colonies who were planning to hold a conference in 1913 in connection with the Aborigines' Rights Protection Society decided as an afterthought to consult with the Colonial Office to make certain that they were operating within regulations (Adi 1998: 14). Even as this conference for peoples of African descent met in April, the British government was making plans for new legislation called the Britain's Aliens Restriction Act of 1914, which would dramatically enlarge the authority of Home Secretary to prohibit entry and enforce registration and deportations of aliens. The act was significant less for the actual numbers controlled than for its breach of the principle of freedom of entry for law-abiding citizens of the British Empire (Paul 1997: 66). Although the government claimed that the primary purpose of this law was to standardize confusing naturalization procedures throughout the British Empire, it confirmed the *jus soli* principle of nationality whereby all individuals born within "His Majesty's dominions and allegiance" automatically acquired British nationality at birth although the reality seemed otherwise. That the act would be annually renewed from 1919 to 1971 also suggests that it masked some hidden governmental agenda with respect to the entry of people of color into Britain (Paul 1997: 66).

The act affirmed the existence of a common status—British subjecthood—and established a common code as the means by which all members of the British Empire acquired their primary nationality and became British subjects. This was at least technically consistent with the principle that all those born or naturalized within the empire possessed only one nationality. This principle of theoretical equality was a formal nationality policy that enabled United Kingdom policymakers to claim that the British Empire/Commonwealth was a universal, united institution centered upon the United Kingdom (Paul 1997: 10-11).

Britain was able to use this claim to its advantage during World War I when it was greatly in need of manpower from its colonies. To its assistance in wartime came 15,000 West Indian volunteers who were enlisted in the British West Indies Regiment as well as battalions that served in France, Palestine, Egypt, and Italy. The British-controlled islands in the Caribbean also raised £2 million for Britain's war effort. Although primarily tasked as ammunition carriers because of Britain's racist concerns, many West Indians still lost their lives. One of the persons who served in the 4th Battalion of the British West Indian Regiment was Eugent Clarke. When Bermudians enlisted for wartime service, they were divided largely on the basis of color, with "blacks" serving in the Bermuda Militia Artillery that was attached to the Royal Garrison Artillery. The first Bermudian to die during this war was William Edmund Smith, a "black" man who drowned when a German submarine torpedoed the *HMS Aboukir* on which he was serving.

Walter Tull was a Briton born in Folkestone in 1888 of a father who had arrived in Britain after having been a slave in British-ruled Barbados and mother from Kent. Before the war, Walter Tull had reluctantly been invited to join Tottenham Hotsppur in 1909. In this connection, he went on a football tour with this club to Argentina and Uruguay. Despite his achievements in football, when back home in Britain he was sometimes on the football field the target of racist taunts by hooligans who deemed him insufficiently "white."

At the outbreak of World War I, Walter Tull readily abandoned his football career and offered his services to the British army by joining the 1st Football Battalion of the Middlesex Regiment. He fought bravely in France and showed so much leadership that he was sent to officer-training school in Gailes, Scotland despite military regulations that forbade "any negro or person of colour" from being an officer. In May 1917, Tull became the first person of appreciable African descent to become a British combat officer. He fought gallantly for his country in Italy and then in Germany. In fact, he eventually was killed fighting as a British sergeant in Germany while leading his men into battle. Because of his bravery and patriotism, Walter Tull was later recommended for a Military Cross. In addition to people of African and partially African descent who served Britain during the war, some 1.5 million Indian troops also fought for Britain during the war.

The willingness of people of color to lay down their lives for Europeans during wartime failed to stop the London University Graduates' Club in 1914 from announcing that it would operate a color bar and that Africans would be ineligible for membership. In Britain throughout World War I there was a considerable number of "black" university students from a number of British colonies. The first African students' union in Britain was formed in 1915 or 1917 with E. S. Beoku Betts of Sierra Leone, a Fellow of the Royal Anthropological Institute, as its first president. He had arrived in London in 1914, joined the Middle Temple, and was called to the bar in June 1917.

Initially called the African Students' Union of Great Britain and Ireland, its name was changed to the Union for Students of African Descent when a number of West Indian students decided to join. Around the same time, some other students of color in Britain founded the African Races Association at Scotland's Glasgow University. The expressed aim of this association was promoting "closer union of Africans and African descendants in the British Isles" and the "discussion of subjects pertaining to, or affecting, the general welfare of the African race" (Fryer 1984: 324; Adi 1998: 15-16, 23).

Although Europe had an African presence since antiquity, the military faceoff in World War I largely between Allies of the Entente such as the United Kingdom, France, and Russia, on the one hand, and the Central Powers such as Germany, Austro-Hungary, and Turkey, on the other, contributed to a significant growth in this presence. By the time of France's direct involvement in the war, between 13- and 30,000 Algerians (mostly of Kabyle ethnicity) already were living in France. As French guilt about France's heavy reliance on Africans grew, there even emerged in France a racist myth that the Kabyles of Africa were actually of European ancestry (Chapman and Frader 2004: 9).

With the German invasion of northern France from Belgium, 2,500 civilian Kabyle workers were evacuated to Paris, and 6,000 eventually returned to Algeria (Simon 2000: 17-33, 39-40, 45: Direche-Slimani 1997: 14-37). Although the war caused some sons and daughters of Africa to have serious doubts about whether they should be involved in this war resulting from unresolved differences among Europeans, this was not a dilemma for the Kabyles, who since 1871 had generally been strong supporters of France. From French-controlled Morocco, Algeria, and Tunisia in northwestern Africa, to which early Muslim settlers long ago had given the collective name of Maghreb, World War I brought 293,756 Africans from France's colonies into Europe and many of these were Kabyles. Another 183,300 were recruited to work in French industries and in the countryside that were largely empty because of massive wartime mobilizations (Liauzu 1996: 119; Simon 2000: 48-49).

Ironically, the first Muslim to serve as a member of the French Chamber of Deputies or lower house in the French National Assembly was Dr. Philippe Grenie, a European rather than an African. He began a two-year term of office in 1896. A French physician who had converted from Christianity to Islam two years previously, Grenier traveled frequently to Algeria in an attempt to gather information for improving the lot of Muslims there. Although Grenier was perceived as an anomaly, he continued to be thought of as the European that he was.

By contrast, Senegalese-born Blaise Diagne, from the island of Gorée, was the first deputy "of color" to serve in the French Chamber of Deputies, in fact, as the representative of the four *communes* in Senegal, beginning in 1914. The first African in history to be seated as a legislator in the Bourbon Palace in Paris, Blaise Diagne convinced his fellow legislators in 1916 to approve a law granting full citizenship to all residents of the four so-called *communes* of Senegal: Dakar, Gorée, Saint-Louis, and Rufisque. A close friend of Georges Clemenceau, who became French Prime Minister in 1917, Clemenceau appointed him *commissaire-général* for western Africa with the understanding that his major responsibility would be to recruit troops from sub-Saharan parts of western Africa to fight on behalf of France at a time that France feared an imminent attack from Germany in World War I. Due to Diagne's patriotism, coupled with his extraordinary effectiveness as a military recruiter, thousands of "black" Africans eventually fought on the Western Front for France during World War I.

It was especially through the southern port city of Marseille that many people from France's African colonies came into Europe in this time of great need. They arrived in Marseille from French colonies and dependencies located in nearby Maghreb, from sub-Saharan Africa including Madagascar, and from Indochina in southeastern Asia. The so-called *tirailleurs sénégalais* not infrequently arrived with their wives and children who came through Marseille's Old Port and settled at Vielle Charité (Blanchard and Boëtsch 2005: 9, 15).

Thanks to the effectiveness of Blaise Diagne as a recruiter in this connection, between 140 and 189,000 troops arrived in France from sub-Saharan Africa alone during World War I. Quite apart from the Africans recruited to help in France by Diagne, several thousand "black" South Africans were brought to France as volunteers to work in a labor brigade. Of these laborers from South Africa, over 600 died when the *SAS Mendi*, the ship on which the last of four contingents was traveling from Cape Town for offloading in Le Havre, was rammed by another vessel. Paying the supreme sacrifice with their lives, some 30,000 "black" Africans never returned home from the service that they rendered to France (Thomas 2007: 29-30; Padmore 1955: 120-123; Bertoncello and Bredeloup 2004: 28).

With well over two million Africans participating directly in World War I, even though it was not a war of their own making, Africa and peoples of African descent were greatly affected. Largely not to offend racist sensibilities of certain "whites," the British (unlike the French) did not make use of "black" Africans on European battlefields during World War I. Due largely to objections from "white" South Africans, the British were also more constrained than the French in arming "blacks" even in Africa. Across the Atlantic in the United States, President Woodrow Wilson, an ardent segregationist, had won re-election in 1915 with the campaign slogan: "He kept us out of war."

With the war having been raging for over two years by 1917, however, Wilson was becoming increasingly sympathetic to the cause of the Entente Powers. Also, public support for U.S. involvement in the war increased after the sinking of the British ocean liner, the *RMS Lusitania*. Contributing to anti-German sentiment in the U.S. as well was the release of an intercepted "Zimmerman Telegram," in which the German Foreign Secretary Arthur Zimmerman promised Mexico financial aid to reclaim "the lost territory of New Mexico, Texas, and Arizona" if the United States entered the war. American neutrality finally came to an end on April 2, 1917, when Wilson appealed to Congress to make a declaration of war against Germany, claiming "the world must be made safe for democracy."

An example of an African-American publication that did not support Wilson's new policy was *The Messenger*. One article in this paper announced, "We would rather make Georgia safe for the Negro than make the world safe for democracy." In contrast, *The Chicago Defender* (under the leadership of Robert S. Abbott) and *The Crisis* (under the control of W. E. B. Du Bois) immediately and enthusiastically advocated African-American participation in the war. Within one week of the declaration of war on Germany by the U.S., its War Department stopped accepting additional "black" volunteers claiming that the quotas established for them were filled. As of this time, the United States had only four army regiments that admitted African-Americans and all of which were segregated: the 9th and 10th Cavalry and the 24th and 25th Infantry.

As the standard volunteer system proved inadequate in raising the needed troops, the U.S. Congress on May 18, 1917, passed the Selective Service Act requiring all male citizens between the ages of 21 and 31 to register for the draft. Almost all boards constituted to administer the draft at this time were composed entirely of "white" men. Especially in the South, draft board members used discriminatory practices to exempt "whites" in far larger numbers than "blacks" and in some cases conspired with Southern postal workers to have the registration cards of "blacks" arrive late so that the addressees could be seized and placed in the military as draft dodgers.

To some degree as a consequence, although African-Americans constituted only about 10 percent of the U.S. national population as of that time, they represented approximately thirteen percent of Army inductees. Since for racist reasons most "white" Americans did not consider it appropriate for these "black" inductees to fight in combat against people of European descent, African-Americans were largely restricted to serving in labor battalions. Also for racist reasons the Marines refused to admit "blacks" at all, while the Navy and Coast Guard only allowed them to serve in a very limited way in a few menial types of positions.

In response to a loud outcry by African-American citizens in the United States against such limited military opportunities for "black" servicemen, the War Department in 1917 finally decided that it would create two primarily "black" combat units. Then deciding that "black" officers would probably be needed if the members of these divisions were to be highly motivated, it made arrangements for some 1,200 African-American men to receive officer training at a military base in Des Moines, Iowa. The racism then prevailing in the United States was so great that, although Germany was considered the enemy, when many Americans learned that their country planned to use African-Americans in combat among troops going to Europe, many of them rose in opposition. Even within the highest ranks of the American military, there was greater empathy for the so-called enemy than for their own compatriots. Such duplicity and twisted logic are often endemic to racist thinking.

In the rush to save Europe, African-Americans were expected to allay seeking redress for their own oppression in order to pursue democracy for Europeans. Although Booker T. Washington, a conservative in matters such as protesting the lynching of fellow African-Americans had died in 1915, Emmett J. Scott (who for 18 years had been Washington's private secretary) was appointed a Special Assistant to Secretary of War Newton Baker in order to oversee the recruitment, training, and morale of African-American servicemen. Robert S. Abbott used his *Chicago Defender* newspaper to continue his support of African-American participation in the war through advertisements, announcements, and featured articles of various types while reframing from making any reference to President Wilson's segregationist policies during the war (Hicks 2007: 63).

Meanwhile on August 23, 1917, a dispute between a few "black" soldiers that had begun as a skirmish when "white" guards on a Houston, Texas military base attacked two "black" members of the 24th Infantry turned into a full-scale riot. As these guards (who consisted mostly of armed police and local citizens hired to patrol the base) eventually fired on the so-called colored infantrymen, the conflict so escalated that seventeen people lost their lives. That only the "black" soldiers were charged was in keeping with unwritten rules that the priorities of "whites" should take precedence over those of "others," including especially in the area of human rights. Forty-one men—all "black"—were sent to prison, and after President Wilson reviewed their cases, eighteen of these were eventually hanged. Included among these were five soldiers whose hangings Wilson temporarily suspended until early 1918. As much intimidated and perhaps perplexed as disappointed by this turn of events, *The Chicago Defender* did not report on Wilson's fateful decision with the same outrage as it had initially reported on the racist assault that began this affair in Houston.

Already believing before this time that certain important African-American journals or newspapers could not be trusted to maintain their support of the war, Wilson had such government organizations as the Post Office Department and the Bureau of Investigation of the Justice Department investigating them for possible acts of treason. Treason was so loosely defined as to cover any newspaper or other publication "containing any matter advocating or urging reason, insurrection, or forcible resistance to any law of the United States." As the Bureau of Investigation used the vague Espionage Act of 1917 to closely monitor "black" publications for their support or lack of support of the war, the government also held periodic conferences for "black" editors to make certain that they towed the line. These tactics undoubtedly succeeded in convincing many African-Americans in leadership positions to subordinate concerns with their own oppression to the prevailing urgency for the United States to help save its Allies in Europe.

Compounding such developments as these, when the United States eventually entered into World War I, it sought to encourage Europeans to openly discriminated against its own American citizens of color. That American and European textbooks tend to be silent about these issues is nothing short of a distortion of the world's history of racism and the global involvement of the world's major Western powers so that these power holders could continue to be thought of as morally superior champions of democracy and opportunity.

Among Americans who at least temporarily fell in line by placing blind patriotism before human rights for peoples of African descent during World War I was W. E. B. Du Bois. In an accommodationist "Close Ranks" editorial in the NAACP's monthly *Crisis* journal, he argued in July 1918 that African-Americans should "forget [their] special grievances and close ranks" with other Americans and the Allies for the duration of the war. Adding to the curiosity of this editorial, it was published at a time when Du Bois had applied for a commission as a captain in the Military Intelligence Branch at the suggestion of his Jewish friend Joel E. Spingarn, a professor of comparative literature at Columbia University who for almost a quarter of a century was Chairman of the Board of the Directors as well as President of the NAACP and who during World War I also was serving as a U.S.A. intelligence officer. Although Du Bois later insisted that his "Close Ranks" editorial and the military commission that he was seeking were unconnected, many of his fellow campaigners for equal rights for African-Americans suspected otherwise (Ellis 1992: 96-124; Hicks 2007: 65).

More typical of Du Bois was the outrage he expressed on discovering that the U.S. military was attempting to have Europeans discriminate against its own "black" American citizens. More precisely, the American government produced a circular titled *Secret Information Concerning Black American Troops* that was circulated among the French. This circular advised the French that it was not possible to praise "blacks" very highly without deeply wounding Americans who were "white" and that the French should not eat with African-Americans or fraternize with them under any circumstances. The circular was adamant that under no circumstances were African-American soldiers ever to converse with French women. It may be inferred that African-Americans were simply tools to be used and manipulated in service to a brotherhood of "whites," a brotherhood bound by alliances that many Americans considered more important than their shared citizenship with Americans they deemed to be "black."

That many "white" Americans were, in fact, very insecure about any praise being shown to their compatriots of color is illustrated by a situation that involved Julius Rosenwald, the Jewish president of the Sears, Roebuck Company during World War I. On behalf of Newton D. Baker, the U.S. Secretary of War, Rosenwald spent two months traveling among American forces in Europe so as to give them encouragement. On several occasions, Rosenwald mentioning to African-American troops in the presence of their "white" compatriots that in gratitude for their brave service, African-American service personnel could expect better treatment on returning home to the United States. Simply for mentioning this in passing, as reported in the New York *Times* of January 26, 1922, some "white" soldiers became so enraged with Julius Rosenwald that they considered hanging hm.

When the U.S. Military Mission distributed its circular entitled *Secret Information Concerning Black American Troops* among French *préfets*, the French government found it so offensive that France ordered the document collected and burned. Even worse than the conditions for African-Americans who were soldiers in France were those for the 150,000 "black" Americans who served in France as stevedores and maintenance personnel. After observing some of these latter African-Americans in Britanny's port at Brest, Du Bois noted with outrage that they "worked like slaves, twelve or fourteen hours a day, were ill-fed, poorly-clad, indifferently housed, [and were] often beaten" (Padmore 1955: 122; Fabre 1991: 48-51).

In France, the 92nd Division not infrequently found itself slandered by high-ranking U.S. army officials no matter how well it performed. By contrast, the French eventually decorated members of the 365th Infantry and 350th Machine Gun Battalion within the 92nd Division. Still more highly decorated, however, was the African-American 93rd Division. Although this division was never up to full strength and had a peculiar composition, the achievements of its 369th Infantry were spectacular. It was so successful during the war that France awarded the entire unit the *Croix de Guerre* as well as presented 171 awards to individual members.

World War I was also a period when African-Americans left a musical legacy in Europe. It was rather common for African-American regiments in France to be accompanied by bands playing syncopated music. Between February and the end of March in 1918, the American military dispatched a "black" musical group led by James Reese Europe, a "black" Alabama-born ragtime and early jazz bandleader, arranger and composer, which was a part of the 369th Infantry Regiment (also known as the "Harlem Hellfighters") of the 93rd Division, on a tour of some 2,000 miles. During this tour in February and March of 1918, Europe's group gave performances for civilians in 25 French cities in order to raise morale while doing the same thing for troops from the United States, Britain, and France (Shack 2001: 12, 18-19).

On August 18, Europe's band was sent from the front to perform a single concert at an Allied conference in Paris. The audience's reaction to this concert was such that American and French official requested that his band continue playing in Paris for eight weeks. It was not only African-Americans in the military who contributed to the American legacy of popular music in Europe during the war. Will Garland's Negro Opera Troupe performing in *A Trip to Coontown* also toured France as well as some other European countries in 1918, in all likeli-hood to the chagrin of some of African-Americans service personnel then in Europe who were battling for self-respect as well as for the democracy of Europeans.

In France, African-Americans saw duty mostly in segregated units at the insistence of their own compatriots who wished to ever remind them of their subordinate status. By contrast, three regiments of the 93rd Division served alongside French soldiers without negative reactions from their European colleagues. The 92nd Division suffered 1,647 battle casualties while the 93rd Division suffered 3,534. It follows therefore that multitudes of them paid the supreme sacrifice in a conflagration in no way of their own making (Thomas 2007: 29-30). There is a certain irony in the fact that while Eugene Jacques Bullard, the African-American stowaway who had arrived in Paris before the war, became the first "black" combat aviator in the French military, his compatriots serving under "the Stars and the Stripes" were at the same time precluded from becoming military pilots (Shack 2001: 22-23; Hicks 2007: 70).

Hundreds of thousands of African-Americans who served in the armed forces during World War I eventually returned home expecting at least a modicum of gratitude for their wartime military service. Instead of gratitude, they returned to a country caught up in frenzied violence directed at keeping American citizens of African descent "in their place." Suspicious of any display of assertiveness by returning veterans, mobs of Americans were quite prepared to remind them of how racism operated at home. As reported by W. E. B. Du Bois, 1919 was a year when 76 or 77 African-Americans were lynched, of whom one was a woman and ten or eleven of whom were soldiers. Eleven of these lynching victims were even burned alive. In some cases, recently returned soldiers were even attacked by mobs determined to lynch them while they were still in their uniforms (Padmore 1955: 125-126). Fearing that such a situation might occur, at least a few "black" Americans soldiers who served in France managed to be demobilized in Europe.

Faced with such harsh and inhumane discrimination in their homeland, a number of recently returned African-American veterans lost little time in returning to Europe. One such veteran was First Lieutenant Rayford Logan who settled in Paris, and another was Leon Brooks. Although Logan subsequently returned to America after a few years in exile and earned an advanced degree at Harvard University, Brooks was still in Paris when Nazis invaded that City of Lights two decades later in late 1941 and interned him at Compiegne, some forty miles north of the capital (Shack 2001: 22).

Although World War I ostensibly had been fought to make the world safe for democracy, by the time the League of Nations in 1919 rejected Japan's proposal for equality among nations it was clear that such rhetoric about democracy was not intended to apply to so-called peoples of color. Racist convulsions in the United States following World War I even caused some African-American veterans of that war to wonder aloud if perhaps they had been fighting on the wrong battlefields for democracy.

Similarly, the war had not been fought among Europeans having democracy for colonized Africans in mind. Still, there had been many African casualties during the war, including on battlefields and from accidents, exhaustion, disease, and epidemics. By the end of the war in 1919, at least 200,000 Africans had lost their lives as participants (Goodwin 2006: 147). The war, in fact, largely provided people of European descent with a respite from fighting among themselves, offering new opportunities for demonstrating European arrogance, racism, and imperialism vis-à-vis peoples they considered "others." Hardly had the armistice ended this war when racism began to manifest itself in especially virulent ways that would add new complications to the lives of people of African descent present in Europe as well as in various European colonies.

In London, the Socialist Club attracted a wide audience of people who felt marginalized in the wake of the war, including some of African descent, some of Irish descent, and some of Jewish descent. The war had left them disillusioned in part because of a rapid upsurge in racism that in Britain included frequent clashes between English, American, and Australian soldiers, who considered themselves "white," on the one hand, and people they often considered inferior interlopers, on the other hand. That many Socialists and Communists saw in this obvious and institutionalized racism a chance to recruit new members from among its victims exacerbated the tensions. One coordinated response to this upsurge in racism and the dire situation for colonized people of African descent was to begin planning for the convening of a number of Pan-African Congresses. Largely under the leadership of W. E. B. Du Bois, it was decided that the ideal place to convene the first of these congresses in the wake of World War I would be in Paris, in order to petition the Versailles Peace Conference that was meeting in the area.

Given his successful recruitment of eighty thousand African soldiers to fight on behalf of France during World War I, Blaise Diagne would have had no difficulty being inducted into France's prestigious Legion of Honor. This highest honor in France had been established by Napoleon Bonaparte in 1802 when in the spirit of equality that prevailed after the French Revolution all orders of chivalry had been eliminated (Bessière 2002: 15-18). When offered this award immediately after the war by Clemenceau and French President Poincaré, however, he declined (Padmore 1955: 120-121). Despite this display of modesty and his being called a traitor to Africa by some for his unwavering devotion to France, on the urging of W. E. B. Du Bois, Blaise Diagne succeeded diplomatically in obtaining permission from Clemenceau for the first post-World War I Pan-African Congress to be held in Paris.

This was a matter of great concern to U.S. President Woodrow Wilson, however, as he feared the Congress might discuss the discriminatory treatment of African-American soldiers during the war and the brutalities unleashed upon those who were veterans after their return home. Although Wilson was not known for trying to get any anti-lynching legislation approved by the U.S. Congress, he was sensitive about any international attention that might be drawn to lynching in the United States that was being used as one of many brutal means to keep African-Americans fearfully in their place in American society.

Even after Du Bois assured the French government via Blaise c that those matters would not be the focus of the Congress, Wilson still refused to allow his government to issue passports to African-Americans not already in Europe who wished to attend. With a warning from Clemenceau to congress organizers that the meeting should not be advertised in any manner that might offend the American government, it convened quietly in Paris in 1919, issuing a strong appeal to the victorious League of Nations on behalf of Africans and peoples of African descent (Padmore 1955: 120-125). Likely the most important among the congress demands were that the Allies administer the former German colonies in Africa under international supervision for the good of the indigenous populations and that Africans should eventually be allowed to take part in the governing of their own countries "as fast as their development permits."

Despite such modest demands, major powers in Europe with overseas empires found these demands more objectionable than that racist European domination of people of color should continue indefinitely and essentially without restrictions. Rather than objecting openly to racism, however, the Europeans found it more seemly to object to any changes in the status quo on the basis that those who advocated change were by definition suspect of being revolutionary Socialist or Communist sympathizers or that people of color were too innately undeveloped to govern themselves and their resources without "white" supervision.

Despite such challenges, hardly had the First Pan-African Congress terminated when again largely under the leadership of Du Bois, plans began to be made for a Second Pan-African Congress. It was decided that this Second Pan-African Congress would meet in several sessions in London, in Brussels, and in Paris in 1921. The aura of possible retaliation by European governments with overseas empires by this time was sufficient that although several members of the Union of Students of African Descent in Britain attended the London sessions of the second Pan-African Congress at Central Hall in August, they were careful to do so as individuals rather than as representatives of the Union. As the British government at this time was headed by the Labor Party, it was tolerant although not particularly sympathetic.

W. E. B. Du Bois delivered the presidential address and the delegates endorsed a *Declaration To The* World, which he had drafted Among the many prominent attendees at some of the London sessions were a number of British government colonial experts of Socialist persuasion. Indian-born barrister Shapurji Saklatvala, who was a British MP with ties to both the British Socialist and Communist Parties, and W. F. Hutchingson, a journalist from the Gold Coast, attended. Jessie Coleridge-Taylor, widow of the famous African-British composer Samuel Coleridge-Taylor was present at some of the London sessions as was also the African-American concert singer, Roland Hayes (Fryer 1984: 322).

Born on a plantation in Curryville, Georgia to parents who had once been slaves, Roland Hayes had only a sixth-grade education until the age of twenty but he was a quick learner and a great talent. It had been in 1920 that he first arrived in London for one of his many tours in Europe. It was on that first tour that Haynes received a personal message from King George V and Queen Mary of England requesting that he perform for them. By the late 1920s, Haynes was reputed to be highest paid tenor in the world with an extensive repertoire that consisted largely of classical music, which he sang in at least seven languages, in addition to what he referred to as "Aframerican religious folk music," much of which he carefully conserved and personally arranged for orchestral accompaniment.

When the 1921 Pan-African Congress convened for several sessions in Brussels, it ran into interference from the Belgian government, no doubt because Belgium feared having its methods of colonial exploitation in the Belgian Congo publicized. Among the active Congress participants in Brussels was Dr. Dantès Bellegarde, a distinguished Haitian hisitorian who was at that time his country's ambassador to France and its representative to the League of Nations. At the time of the Congress, all ten members of Mandate Committee charged with overseeing the former colonies of Germany and Turkey since their defeat in the war were "white" Europeans although not one of these colonies was located in Europe . Much of the discussion in Brussels focused on racial equality and the need to have at least one person of color serve on that ten-person Mandate Committee as soon as there would be a vacancy. As the hostility from the Belgian government to such non-racist thinking continued to be evident, shortly after endorsing the *Declaration* that had been approved in London, the Congress moved on to Paris (Padmore 1955: 129-135).

Brussels, throughout the 1920s, had a number of jazz clubs that hosted African-Americans musicians from Montmartre as well as jazzmen from other places with considerable frequency (Shack 2001: 27, 29-31). Despite this however, postwar Belgium regularly prevented Congolese from obtaining higher education in Europe, or for that matter anywhere. In Brussels of the 1920s as also in nearby Amsterdam to its north, where a number of Surinamese worked largely in entertainment and professional sports in the 1920s, peoples of color were more likely to be from the New World than from Africa or Asia.

By the congress reconvened in Paris, however, France had apparently been pulling its own strings behind the scene to help undermine it. This became obvious when Blaise Diagne let it be known that he considered the tone of the documents that emerged from the Brussels sessions radical in that they raised questions about the legitimacy of European colonial empires. Apparently believing that his serving as a French legislator did not permit him to question even the racism implicit in European imperialism, Blaise Diagne soon abandoned Pan-Africanism. He obviously meant this as an open demonstration of his greater allegiance to France, including its prevailing system of overseas imperialism, than to notions of racial equality and eventual African participation in home rule that would be meaningful (Fryer 1984: 323).

In 1923, Du Bois convened the Third Pan-African Congress, this time in London and in Lisbon. In addition to being less well planned and less well attended than the previous two, this congress met in the face of opposition from many quarters as investments in imperialism in Europe and in the larger Western World, sometimes only through allied support, yielded privileges and profits without which racists were not willing to live. In London, the congress still elicited enough sympathy among British Socialists that its sessions there were attended by the famous actor Lord Laurence Kerr Olivier, Professor Harold Laski, and the writer H. G. Wells, all of whom gave addresses. Among the resolutions adopted at the London sessions, a number stand out. This included an appeal that Africa be developed for the benefit of Africans as well as Europeans, that there be home rule in British West Africa and the British West Indies, that white minority government be abolished in Kenya, South Africa, and Rhodesia (now Zambia and Zimbabwe), that the ongoing trade in slaves be abolished, and that there be free universal access to elementary education for colonized people. That this congress also called for an end to the lynching of African-Americans in the United States was of importance.

The Lisbon sessions, attended by representatives of eleven countries, had been organized in close cooperation with a federation of indigenous organizations that coordinated their efforts under the so-called *Liga Africana*. Of more significance than the fact that two former colonial ministers of Portugal addressed the Congress in Lisbon was their frank acknowledgement that Portugal as of that time was still sometimes using conscript or forced labor in its African colonies (Padmore 1955: 139-142). Discussions held and resolutions approved at the Third Pan-African Congress in 1923 clearly demonstrate that under the guise of European imperialism and the so-called "civilizing" of people of African descent, colonized people were sometimes being exploited, brutalized, and killed by Europeans in ways that where in every respect as harsh as conditions that existed during the worst periods of race-based slavery.

That W. E. B. Du Bois was a central figure in the the Pan-African movement after World War I is beyond question. In sharp contrast, most of his American compatriots—including those who were African-Americans—being caught up in everyday survival issues, knew virtually nothing substantive about Africa. In the highly racialized context of the 1920s, relatively few people apart from the victims and perpetrators or forced labor and ongoing slavery likely knew or cared a great deal about what was occurring so far removed from the world of their everyday experiences. Encouraged by Europeans to believe that Africa was an inscrutable continent with little claim on world attention, even many people of African descent living in the West had acquired worldviews about Africa as well as Europe that were largely Eurocentric.

In general, African-Americans from the United States during the period following World War I were much more focused on the harsh racism that restricted their own life conditions than in manifestations of racism in the colonies of Europeans. Far less informed about the realities unfolding in Africa than a well-educated, widely-traveled, intellectual Pan-Africanist like W. E. B. Du Bois, they were more likely to focus on how to relocate from the American South to the slightly less racist American North. In some cases, to be sure, they idealized Egypt and Ethiopia and hoped that their churches might dispatch missionaries and teachers to Africa. African-Americans also became increasingly involved in homegrown civil rights movements, with some seeking solutions that ranged from separation to integration.

Only a relatively small minority of African-Americans sought solutions to the problems they faced beyond the shores of the United States although those who did were extremely influential. Some within this internationalist minority became enamored with Socialism or Communism and eventually sought support especially from the Soviet Union. Others within this internationalist minority who were less inclined to think of themselves as political change agents fled to western Europe mostly hoping to breathe more freely as whole people and in some cases wishing to further develop their talents as writers, as entertainers, and as artists. For numerous Americans, irrespective of color, the lyrics of a popular song that had been penned after their country's entry into World War I by Joe Young and Sam M. Lewis and set to music by Walter Donaldson reflected aspects of their yearnings: "How ya gonna keep 'em down on the farm after they've seen Paree'."

Contributing to the fact that so many writers, entertainers, and artists ended up in France was the reputation of Paris as a city at the pinnacle of Western civilization. An additional factor for many African-Americans was the idealization of France as a Mecca largely free of racism, at least by American standards. In addition to the roles played by World War I veterans in this type of idealized way thinking of Europe, and France in particular, many other people also contributed. One of these was Mary Church Terrell, a relatively well-to-do African-American woman who attended Oberlin College and later taught at Wilberforce University. Terrell, sojourned repeatedly in France between 1888 and 1921 during which time she also visited a number of other countries in western Europe. As the founding president of the National Association of Colored Women, Terrell helped to popularize the idea in the United States of France as a country where people of African descent were received with considerably more respect than in the United States (Fabre 1991: 37-41).

Although racism toward people of African descent in France was considerably more subtle than in the United States, thinking of France in the early decades of the 20th century as a non-racist "promised land," as many Americans believed it to be, was extremely naïve. Already by World War I in and around Paris, for example, French people intent of keeping themselves separated from "others" were already causing Algerians to become concentrated in three major areas. One of these was the 5th, 12th, 13th, 15th, 17th, 18th, 19th, and 20th zones or *arrondissements*. A second area of concentration was the near suburbs of Billancourt, Levallois, Puteaux, Clichy, and Aubervilliers. A third such concentration was in the distant suburbs of Courbevoie, Colombes, Gennevilliers, and Saint Denis (Simon 2000: 71-72).

As for the multitudes of colonial soldiers and workers who had been so helpful to France during the World War I, some 250,000 of them were repatriated at the end of the war. With respect to Algerians, for example, only a few thousands remained in the country as of 1919. World War I had left France with 1.3 million dead, 388,000 wounded, and more than a million invalids. The war also left a large number of widows and orphans. Although France had in compensation gained an additional 1,900,000 Europeans to its population through its acquisition of Alsace-Lorraine from Germany, it was already clear by 1920 that France also needed immigrants. From this time through 1930, France reached out to colonized Algerians and many of them returned with quasi-French approval to take jobs that were vital to the French economy.

On relocating to Europe especially during this period, Algerians began to become important as a segment of the resident population in metropolitan France (Simon 2000: 55, 58). In general, their housing however was terrible, and hardly any was available for other than single men. In some cases, Algerian men even had to share the same beds as several of their compatriots by sleeping in shifts. Instead of recognizing the situation as a shortcoming then prevailing in French society, Georges Mauco (see pages 218, 221, 222, 244, 271) described this horrible housing situation as natural to the Algerians who were suffering from it.

Well beyond Paris in other areas where workers from Maghreb were concentrated, the situation was similar. Included among these areas were Lyon (where many of Algerians were concentrated in the most poorly constructed areas such as the suburb of Villeurbane), in Nord-Pas-de-Calais, and at Marseille in the center and the north of the city on what were in effect islands of misery with horrible housing (Lewis 2004: 77-107). Here, the neighborhoods where many *maghrébins* settled became increasingly segregated at the same time as their inhabitants became increasingly marginalized socially and economically (Blanchard and Boëtsch 2005: 16).

Based on French racist stereotypes that were commonly associated with *maghrébins* around this time, French people commonly believed Islam was backward and that Africans from the Maghreb were infantile, oversexed, primitive, and given to thievery and delinquency (Simon 2000: 74-75, 77). Contributing to these negative attitudes about *maghrébins*, most of whom in France were from Algeria, some people in France were offended when Messali al-Hajj founded an organization called *Étoile Nord-Africaine* in Algeria in 1919 that opposed all forms of union between Algeria and France. During World War I and the years immediately following, the situation with regard to racism was much more complex, contradictory, and nuanced in France than most Americans in France thought it to be.

Arthur Briggs, though born in Canada, had been reared in the state of South Carolina. Although he had returned to the United States after serving in New York's 15th Infantry Regiment, he led his band called the Syncopates to London on a tour 1921. While there, his band even performed before King George V. A number of African-American veterans had returned to Paris immediately after being discharged and settled on its Right Bank in the Bohemian quarter known as Montmartre. In 1922, Arthur Briggs departed Britain on his way to Montmartre, at least a corner of which was already by this time becoming a "home away from home" to a small expatriate community of people of color from several parts of the world, including especially a group that was interested in popular entertainment, night clubs, and the arts.

Meanwhile in 1921, René Maran, a "black" writer who had been born aboard a boat carrying his parents from French Guyana to Martinique, won the prestigious French literary award known as *le prix Goncourt* for his second novel, *Batouala*, in 1921. Dealing at least in its preface with excesses of French colonialism in equatorial Africa based largely on what he had witnessed there in Gabon and later in Oubangui-Chari (now Bangui, Central African Republic), the book caught many in France off guard who were not as of that time ready to admit such realities. By this time Marseille's growing population from Maghreb was becoming increasingly segregated into ethnic enclaves (Blanchard and Boëtsch 2005: 16). Still, in 1923 France honored the African-American painter Henry Ossawa Tanner with the prestigious Legion of Honor and in that same year banned the racist American-made film *Birth of a Nation* that had been made by D. W. Griffith in 1915 (MacMaster 2001: 138).

While certain African-American expatriates were often to be found in Montmartre, these people were obviously but one of the many faces of Africa in Paris and other parts of France by the early 1920s, this community in Montmartre thrived on ingenuousness, creativity, and *joie de vivre* and was not segregated or pretentious. Its members arrived and settled for greatly varying amounts of time, and they interacted with other parts of France and Europe. One indication that those in Montmartre were cosmopolitan is suggested by the fact that the new jazz band that Arthur Briggs founded there in 1922 included members from the United States, Canada, Italy, Belgium, and several Caribbean islands. Thanks largely to this network of mostly-Western expatriates of color, Montmartre was home to several night clubs in which jazz was a standard feature by 1924.

Florence Embry Jones was the first African-American *chanteuse* to entertain in these Montmartre nightclubs. The second arrived only slightly later—West Virginia-born Ada Beatrice Queen Victoria Louise Virginia Smith. Because of her red hair and freckled face, however, it did not take long for her to become popularly known as Bricktop. Already by this time Langston Hughes, an African-American writer who was spending six months in Paris, was on the scene in Montmartre. Around the same time, Joel Augustus Rogers (an American citizen since 1917 though originally from Jamaica) arrived in Europe on the first of several trips in 1925 to conduct investigations in various libraries and museums on the history of Europe's African presence. It did not take Rogers long to make contact with fellow "blacks" living in Montmartre. Also often in the same neighborhood by 1926 was Panama Al Brown. Born in Panama, he had relocated to New York's Harlem before coming to Paris. In France, he also earned considerable fame for himself as a boxer (Shack 2001: 38-39).

"Battling Siki," a boxer from Senegal, was transformed into a celebrity who could often been seen around Paris, including in Montmartre. Although racism in France during this period was much more subterranean and nuanced than in the United States and Britain, as indicated by certain particulars surrounding "Battling Siki" it was by no means nonexistent. For his bravery during the war fighting for France in the trenches of France, Turkey, and Romania, Louis Fall was decorated four times, including with the *Croix de Guerre* and the *Médaille Militaire*. After the armistice ending the war, Louis Fall was released from the French military and returned to professional boxing with his manager A. M. Hellers advertising him as "Battling Siki." That France had suffered a military defeat in World War I seemed compounded for many people in France when in October 1919 Paul Hams, born in Guadeloupe, won the heavy-weight boxing championship of France. For some people in France it mattered less that Hams was a French citizen who, because of fighting for France during the war, had been decorated with the *Croix de Guerre* than the fact that he was of African descent; to certain French, Hams was part of their national and racial humiliation (Jobert 2006: 123n).

Now that people of African descent had dutifully fulfilled their expected roles as auxiliaries of their "white" overlords during the war, it was time for racism to surge forth with full vigor. Against this background, a boxing match between Louis "Siki" Fall of Senegal and Georges Carpentier was arranged to take place in September 1922. As Carpentier was a handsome French war hero known as the "Orchid Man" who had been knocked out by Jack Dempsey the previous year, the fight took on great significance for masses of French people. As the bout was scheduled to take place before 40,000 Paris fans at the brand new Stade Buffalo at Montrouge near the Porte des Ternes virtually on the eve of the opening in France of an imperial exhibition, French pride was at stake. For nationalistic as well as for racist reasons, a number of French industrialists, wishing Carpentier to win at all cost bribed Louis "Siki" Fall to lose the fight on purpose. When during the fight "Siki" began to be badly injured, however, he decided to fight in earnest. Even after "Siki" vastly outperformed Carpentier, Henri Bernstein, the referee, ruled that because "Siki" had tripped Carpentier the latter was consequently the victor. So loudly did the fans in attendance protest this ploy however that the judges were compelled to intervene and declare "Siki" the world light-heavyweight champion as well as the European heavyweight champion.

So bitter was the backlash that followed in France that there took place an organized media campaign heavily colored with racism to publically denigrate "Siki." He was referred to as a "child of the jungle," "feeble-minded," and an uncivilized interloper who was unable to properly comprehend and adjust to his existence in a "civilized" environment, and it was claimed that he had only beat Carpentier in a freak explosion of primitive inspired fury (Jobert 2006: 115-156; Benson 2002). Adding to the racist furor against "Siki," even A. M. Hetters, his manager, told reporters that he resembled a highly trained gorilla, that he had something in him that was not human, and that he was a little crazy by human standards. This was even conveyed via a special trans-Atlantic cable to the *New York Times*, with the result that Edwin L. James wrote an insulting article about "Siki" that appeared in the paper on September 26, 1922, the day immediately following his victory over Carpentier.

It is likely that some "whites" involved in the racist conspiracy against "Battling Siki" may even have been upset by the fact that he had twice married "white" women. Three months following the victory of this African fighter over Georges Carpentier in September 1922, the still-disgruntled French Federation of Boxing deprived him of his titles, thereby making it virtually impossible for him to continue boxing in most parts of Europe. This caused such a scandal in France that it threatened to rival the anti-Semitic Dreyfus Affair (Jobert 2006: 12) of the late 1800s. Even Blaise Diagne, the very conservative Senegalese representative in the French Chamber of Deputies, charged that the Federation was discriminating against colonials to assuage the pride of Parisians. One would have to be almost blind not to see similarities in the way that "Battling

Siki" was treated largely in Europe and the even the worst way that the "black" boxer Jack Johnson had been treated in the United States shortly before.

In post-World War I-Britain, due in no small measure to racism, the boom for "black" labor fizzled out as quickly as it had begun, and shipping companies lost little time in showing a preference to sign up "white" seamen rather than those whom they considered "black." In adopting these policies, this industry had the full backing of the government and of the two forerunners of the National Union of Seamen. In this upsurge in racism at the end of the war, so-called race mattered much more than subjecthood, nationality, and even citizenship to such an extent that even foreign "white" seamen were preferred over those from the colonials who were British subjects if they were deemed non-"white." Among those in this latter category were many Arabs, Malays, Chinese, Africans, Indians, and West Indians, more than a few of whom had lost limbs and eyesight fighting for Britain during the war. Additionally, post-war racist discrimination impacted some Europeans of color.

In addition to the discrimination against seamen that followed wartime demobilization, many British subjects resident in the United Kingdom also lost other jobs to "white" competitors based solely on racism. Among numerous people of color who even were physically attacked in Britain were some who had recently been veterans engaged in fighting as members of the British armed forces. Sensational and racist reporting by various mass media added to the mass hysteria and frequent failure by the police to protect minority populations. Some people of color were even attacked in the places where they lived, including quite a large number of men who were married to European women. Some of the rioters, in fact, seemed greatly annoyed by what they considered interracial coupling and attacked many people of color with insults such as "Nigger, go home! This is our country and not yours!"

Against this background, the African Progress Union and the Society of Peoples of African Origin were founded in the United Kingdom and temporarily merged. The problem of surging racism in Britain became a main concern of these organizations, as attacks on African, Arab, and Caribbean seamen and others not deemed sufficiently European intensified. In 1919, numerous British cities experienced race riots, including Cardiff, Liverpool, Manchester, South Shields, Glasgow, Hull, and London (Adi 1998: 16-18; Fryer 1984: 298-313). The riots were hardly limited to discrimination and property damage, for as they continued to erupt, a "black" resident named Charles Wooten was murdered by a "white" mob in Liverpool.

Some Greek and Portuguese establishments also came under attack in racist outbursts that occurred in Britain in the wake of World War I. Among those who were active as leaders among many of the lynch mobs were colonial soldiers from Australia. Although some 600 terrified Arabs, Somalis, and Egyptians were evacuated from the United Kingdom to their homelands in 1919, most British residents of African descent remained. Even in the wake of the riots, the United Kingdom dealt to its residents of African descent an added racist insult when it decided not to allow any "black" troops to take part in London's victory celebrations in the much-triumphed Peace March on July 19, 1919 (Fryer 1984: 298-315).

One civil rights and pan-African activist in Britain during most of this time was Dusé Mohamed Ali, who claimed to be the son of an Egyptian officer and a Sudanese mother. Sent to Britain for education, he lived there mainly as a poorly paid journalist and touring actor. By 1912, he had already launched a magazine called *African Times and Orient Review* in partnership with the Sierra Leonean businessman and journalist John Eldred Taylor. Despite occasional lapses in the publication of this periodical, Dusé Mohamed Ali managed to keep this first political journal by and for people of African descent ever published in Britain alive until 1920 (Fryer 1984: 287-288; Padmore 1955: 88). Meanwhile against the wishes of many Egyptian nationalists who were pushing Britain for independence in the wake of World War I, Britain formally annexed Egypt to the British Empire. When Egyptian nationalist agitation in favor of independence continued, Britain merely agreed to renounce its protectorate in favor of a largely sham independence there in 1922. Along with this action, Britain changed the title of Ahmad Fuad, Egypt's non-Egyptian figure-head ruler, from sultan to king as a sign of Egypt's supposed sovereignty (Goodwin 2006: 422).

In contrast to hardly more than twenty university students of African descent from various colonies in Paris in 1922, London had an estimated 300. During the early 1920s, many British students from Africa in league with others from the West Indies and even a few associates who were English and Indian organized themselves into the Union of Students of African Descent. Although initially concerned largely with the need for student housing in a society where discrimination was widely practiced, the Union also functioned as a literary and social club. Its first president was the Trinidadian Percy Acham Chen and A. M. Fanimokun, a female student from Nigeria, was one of its most active members. After C. F. Hayfron-Benjamin from the Gold Coast (now Ghana) became its president in 1923, the African students who were members grew considerably, including a number who were matriculating at Cambridge and Edinburgh universities (Adi 1998: 19; Thomas 2007: 30).

Despite the racism that continued to surge in Britain, some British subjects of color from a number of the colonies chose to remain there in accordance with British laws, though in defiance of contradictory Colonial Office directives. Largely as a consequence, their numbers were somewhat significant, especially in such port cities as Cardiff in Wales and in Liverpool. In an effort to curtail this in 1925, the government enacted the Coloured Alien Seamen Order, which ostensibly was intended to prevent alien seamen from falsely claiming British nationality, and thus rights of residence, in the United Kingdom.

In practice, this order was used by the government to harass "coloured seamen" regardless of whether or not they were British subjects or aliens and to prevent as many as possible from settling in the United Kingdom. At a time that the Home Office knew that the majority of "black" British seamen did not have "proper" documentation, as a consequence of the Coloured Alien Seamen Order of 1925 many of them lost all privileges of citizenship and became subject to deportation. During the same approximate period and continuing into the 1930s, the government in collaboration with employers worked to segregate the labor market to prevent further migration to the United Kingdom by so-called blacks at a time when racism was surging (Paul 1997: 113).

This was a time when the United Kingdom was characterized by widespread racial segregation in public accommodations that was often referred to as a color bar. One case from 1932 that received much attention occurred when New Mansion Hotels, Lancaster Gate, London were sued for having refused to accommodate O. A. Alakija, the son of the Chairman of the Nigerian Printing and Publishing Company, and a nephew of the Alake of Abeokuta, one of the most important traditional rulers from western Nigeria. Although Alakija succeeded in suing the establishment and won some damages, a color bar continued to operate in Britain (Adi 1998: 54).

The racism fallout from World War I would be especially complex in what had been the Hapsburg Empire. In this largely German-speaking empire, which extended well into the Balkans and which was under the rule of Emperor Karl I from the end of 1916, it was clear by the autumn of 1918 that Austro-Hungary was on the losing side in war. The Hapsburg Empire had already lost control of German South West Africa (now Namibia) in 1915, and its holdings were also beginning to crumble in Europe as various subject European peoples began declaring themselves autonomous or independent. In an effort to preserve the monarchy and maintain its multi-ethnic cohesion, Emperor Karl began granting various nationalities under Austro-Hungarian domination in Europe more autonomy and accepted the formation of a state where smaller entities were federated. This action however was too little too late.

Beginning in Bavaria, various German sovereigns were forced to abdicate their thrones. On November 9, 1918, while Emperor Wilhelm II was in the Belgian town of Spa, refusing to step down, Chancellor Max von Baden on his own authority declared the abdication of the emperor. On November 11, 1918, Ferdinand Foch (Commander in Chief of the Allied forces) and Matthias in a railway car in the woods outside of Compiegne signed a ceasefire agreement under which Germany ceased to be a major military and political power. The following day on November 12, 1918, the German-Austria Republic was established with its capital in Vienna. In this newly established republic, the citizens generally considered the conditions that the ceasefire imposed unduly severe. They began to demand more democratic rights for themselves domestically, with Christmas riots soon erupting in Berlin. Soon afterwards on January 19, a German National Assembly was elected and began to operate in Weimar, although the Weimar Republic did not actually come into being until July 31, 1919. The approval of a new liberal constitution followed—in fact, the first democratic constitution of the German Reich.

During the early stages of the war, Germany seemed little inclined to use graphic racism directed at colonized Africans in its conflict with France. In the summer of 1916, for example, several prisoners held by Germany from French-controlled northern Africa were used as models by the renowned Berlin painter Hans Louschen with no hint at racist caricature. As most Germans were not prepared for the magnitude of their defeat by the war's end and felt very humiliated by it, Germans became more willing to use racism in expressing their extreme bitterness over the fate with which they were faced. They schemed against the status quo, including against France and its African subjects in particular, and this even began to be reflected in much of the postwar propaganda art that Germans produced.

A particularly racist poster that caricatures France and its military auxiliaries of African descent from the early postwar period was prominently displayed in the Berlin's Germany History Museum as recently as 2008. On this poster is a depiction of a "black" soldier with abnormally large bright red lips and a buffoon-like appearance. As the French words meaning liberty, fraternity, and equality were blazoned prominently across the poster, the flag that the soldier held obviously represented that of France. As this poster on display lacked any interpretive labeling pointing out that it was a racist graphic produced only a little more than a decade before Adolf Hitler came to power, it continued to perpetuate the same type of racism as it did originally. Without a doubt, the sense of humiliation from which Germans suffered at the end of World War I not only contributed to the exponential growth of German nationalism, it at the same time contributed to a growth in German racism that was in part a reaction to Germany's defeat in World War I and its subsequent supervisory occupation in part by soldiers that its populace had been encouraged to think of as racially inferior.

Contributing to the rise of racism in Germany after World War I was the unhappiness of many Germans with the conditions in which the war ended and a sense of humiliation that they had about losing their African colonies as well as about having Africans among occupation troops on German soil. It was not only Germans who were unhappy about this latter situation, but also many "white" people in general, including even some who had been content to make use of Africans as their allies and auxiliaries during the war. To the extent that World War I emphasized contradictions in the thinking of many people of European descent about the importance they accorded to political alliances, on the one hand, and alliances deemed, racial, on the other, it left a legacy of inconsistency with respect to racism.

Edmund Dene Morel, a shipping clerk and journalist of English and French background, had prior to World War I on his own initiative played a crucial role in uncovering the genocidal rape of the Congo Free State by Belgium's King Leopold II especially between 1890 and 1910 (MacMaster 2001: 131; Pakenham 2003: 589-594; Hochschild 1998: 209-224). In the wake of World War I however, Morel showed himself to be a ranting racist when he learned that Africans were among the troops left in Germany to help insure German compliance with the terms of the Treaty of Versailles that had ended the war, which he opposed in any case. In addition to opposing the Treaty of Versailles, Morel considered it inappropriate on racial grounds that Africans should have even temporary control over people he deemed superior to them by virtue of being European. Not hesitating to attract others to his view through the use of derogatory rants, he authored a blatantly racist article entitled "Black Scourge in Europe: Sexual Horror Let Loose by France on the Rhine" for the front page of the *Daily Herald*, a Socialist newspaper. Along with a pamphlet in which he further elaborated his thinking, Morel claimed that the objects of his furor were "primitive African barbarians," "black savages," and oversexed "spreaders of syphilis" (Fryer 1984: 316-320; Fabre 1991: 93).

The immediate targets of Morel's attacks were soldiers from Maghreb, from Madagascar, and from Senegal loosely referred to as *tirailleurs sénégalais* (Blackshire-Bellay 1996: 110), who were assigned duties in Rhenish areas of Germany as well as Mainz and Frankfurt. Without a shred of evidence, Morel referred to those whom he attacked as rapists and claimed that sex between "blacks" and "whites" in general not infrequently resulted in injury for the latter, sometimes with fatal results. Continuing to vent his racism, he wondered if perhaps tomorrow such "African mercenaries" would be let loose on "white workers" elsewhere. Many Germans who were still feeling humiliated both by the war and by the fact that soldiers they considered their racial inferiors were in parts of their country undoubtedly welcomed the specious support that Morel offered them.

People of African descent in particular did not welcome this highly offensive and racist broadside against Africans. Besides, multitudes of so-called blacks in many parts of the world were as Westernized as Morel and much better informed about science and human geography. As a large proportion of them moreover had "whites" among their ancestors, they were less traumatized than Morel about so-called miscegenation. As it became obvious that Morel's ignorance about human variation could not go unanswered, it fell to Claude McKay to rise to the challenge. A Jamaican-born writer who had settled in the United States before moving on to London in 1919, McKay requested from the *Daily Herald* space to respond. When the *Daily Herald* refused him this opportunity, the *Workers' Dreadnought*, another Socialist paper in the United Kingdom, albeit with a much smaller circulation, provided him the opportunity for a public rebuttal.

As "white" racists on both sides of the Atlantic rose up to demand that Germany be spared the shame of "black" soldiers being stationed anywhere on its soil in the wake of World War I, 59,000 Swedish women signed a petition demanding that "black" soldiers depart. The government of Germany solicited and found much sympathetic support in the United States as a result of a series of articles that appeared in the *Daily Herald* that openly called for maintaining the so-called purity of the white race. As such protests unfolded, 12,000 Americans mostly of Irish and Germany descent protested at New York's City's Madison Square Garden in February of 1921, demanding that all African-American troops be removed from the German Rhein. Rather than acting as a moral conscience against the racism that was surging among peoples of European descent, even Pope Benedict XV added his voice to the chorus of those asking for the removal of "black" soldiers from Europe. Such leftist French journalists and writers as Romain Rolland, Henri Barbusse, and Jean Longuet, who was the son-in-law of Karl Marx, joined in the racist outcry against soldiers of African descent—whether from sub-Saharan Africa, Madagascar off the eastern cost of Africa, or northern Africa or African-Americans from the United States and the Caribbean (Coquery-Vidrovitch 2007: 50-51).

Having been used by peoples of European descent in the interest of settling rivalries among themselves, the general feeling among masses of "whites" was that soldiers of African descent had dutifully served their purpose in Europe and could now be banished. Ironically, at the same time, many Germans, unhappy about the loss of their African colonies as the result of World War I, were preoccupied with regaining control of Tanganyika, Togoland, Cameroon, and South-West Africa. Hence, Germany shrewdly distinguished between Africans it planned to use as the vanguard in recapturing its former colonies, on the one hand, and the much-despised African soldiers known as the *tirailleurs sénégalais*, on the other. With respect to the former group, which had favored status, some members were used as actors in propagandistic undertakings such as traveling shows and films. In fact, some members of this group were well educated, were married to "white" Germans, and had put down roots in Germany well before World War I. Even where their German-born offspring were held in low regard, they were not targeted for sterilization in the manner of the so-called Rhineland Bastards (MacMaster 2001: 73, 133-134).

As for Russia during and after World War I, its experience led it to interact with people of African descent in a way that in many respects was quite different from what occurred in western and even central Europe. This had less to do with geography, however, than with revolutionary changes that were about to unfold. Tsar Nicholas II and his subjects had entered the war with enthusiasm along with Russia's fellow Orthodox Slavs. As events turned out, however, he was forced to abdicate in 1917. Shortly thereafter, Vladimir Lenin returned to Russia from exile in Switzerland with the help of Germany. From 1917 to 1921, Russia was embroiled in civil war as well as periodic resistance to foreign intervention (Wren 1958: 559-569).

Among at least a few people of African descent who were resident in Russia prior to the October Revolution, as reported by Blakely (1986: 95), was a "black" woman from the Southern United States of America named Emma Harris, who had been the mistress of a Russian duke and who had six servants and a footman. Two others were Michael Egypteos, who attained high rank in the Russian navy, and an African-American named George Thomas, who amassed a fortune as owner of a vast amusement complex in Moscow that included restaurants and hotels (Blakely 1986: 351-361).

In addition, Abkhazians, some of whom were of African descent, fought for their Russian homeland during the Russian Civil War. Even a few servicemen of African ancestry from North America and from other scattered places fought in this war. Some sources suggest that an entire regiment of Senegalese also eventually became involved. Amid the instability with which Russia was seized during this bloody civil war, one person engaged to help raise the spirits of the Red Army as part of a troupe of artists who performed on the southwestern front was the Mexican-born African-American soprano Coretta Arli-Titz. Arli-Titz eventually graduated from the Tchaikovsky studio of composer Michael Ippolitov-Ivanov that was located in Moscow in 1923 (Blakely 1986: 82, 144-145).

By the time Russia's monarchy was overthrown by Communist Revolutionaries, some people of African descent half-way around the world had become so disillusioned with Western racism in the wake of World War I that they began looking toward Socialism and Communism for solutions to their oppression. One such person was Claude McKay. A gifted poet, McKay, already in response to the Russian Revolution, had written in "Exhortation Summer 1919" the following:

> In the East the clouds grow crimson with the new dawn that
>   is breaking,
> And its golden glory fills the Western skies.
> O my brothers, dreaming for long centuries,
> Wake from sleeping; To the East turn, turn your eyes!

Lenin had raised the so-called Negro question in reference to conditions for African-Americans in the United States at the Second Comintern Congress in 1920. Around the time that Russia's civil war was ending in 1921, the country founded as part of Comintern's training program the Communist University for the Toilers of the East (sometimes referred to also as the Far East University) that was attached to the Comissariat of Nationalities. Although it was intended mostly for students from Asiatic parts of the Russian Empire and from colonies in various parts of the world, among its earliest students were four African-Americans and an African (Blakely 1986: 82).

During a part of 1922, Claude McKay worked in London with a Communist group that supplied a number of groups that it deemed to be especially oppressed with revolutionary literature and this included a segregated club for soldiers and veterans of African descent that was located in Drury Lane. Later in 1922, he arrived in the Soviet Union from Britain, intending to offer his support to forces that were ideologically disdainful of racism as well as the exploitation of the working classes. Another African-American who arrived in the Soviet Union that same year was Otto Huiswood. Originally from Dutch Guiana, Huiswood was one of the original 94 founders of the American Communist Party. Arriving in Moscow just in time for the fourth Comintern or Communist International Congress as well as for the fifth anniversary of the Bolshevik Revolution, McKay and Huiswood were welcomed as celebrities and comrades even by top government leaders. Both were made honorary members of the Moscow Soviet or city council. McKay, whose visit lasted until 1923, also met numerous Russian artists, was paid handsomely to write articles, and managed to complete work on a new book.

Meanwhile on the territory of the Russian Empire, a Union of Soviet Socialist Republics or Soviet Union was established in 1922 that initially involved four associated republics: Russia, Transcaucasia, Byelorussia, and Ukraine. Over time, the growing USSR came to contain peoples who were Indo-European, Slavic, Turkic, Uralic and Altaic, Caucasian, Paleo-Siberian, Jewish, and Romani as well as others. Abandoning the tsarist policy of openly discriminating against the more than 200 national minorities in the country, the new regime preferred incorporating them into Soviet life. Toward this end, the Soviet Union initiated a policy of indigenization in the 1920s that was called *korenizatsiya* and that had as its main objective to recruit non-Russians citizens into various Soviet political institutions for the purpose of reducing conflict between Russian and other elements within the country. Also recognizing the great revolutionary potential of cultivating allies within the international working class among oppressed peoples and nations very broadly in their revolutionary struggle against capitalism, the Bolsheviks proclaimed their support for all oppressed "people without equal rights."

The Soviet Union supported the ideological proposition that Communism and racism could not coexist, and this ideology sometimes made Communist sympathizers out of multitudes of people concerned with racial and economic justice. Despite outstanding support that the Soviet Union offered to peoples oppressed by racism on numerous occasions, it was impossible for such ideology to always reflect reality. In addition to certain of its own policies that were dictatorial and paternalistic toward oppressed peoples, the Soviet Union sometimes chose to overlook racism in furtherance of alliances that it perceived as in its state interest.

In the wake of World War I, racism continued its surge both in Europe and in the wider world. While some targeted individuals and populations put their confidence in assimilation and silence hoping that this situation would rectify itself, such was not to be for the roots of racism were too deeply embedded in the soils of the West. In any case, invisibility was not in most cases an option for many people of African descent. Many forces on the right wished to condemn any opposition to the racist status quo as inspired by despicable revolutionary forces on the left. Similarly, many leftists also sought to discredit any forces that they could not control as misguided, reactionary "petit-bourgeois" irrespective of their stance on racism and imperialism (Padmore 1955: 139-141).

Positioned between extremes of left and right were other opponents of the status quo who preferred to use solidarity brought about around issues of race, color, ethnicity, and/or religion to oppose racism and imperialism in somewhat targeted ways (e.g, Black Nationalism, Pan-Arab Nationalism, and Jewish Nationalism). These rather targeted approaches sometimes overlapped and sometimes were quite divergent from, or even at odds with, each other as well as associated with distrust of more secular or universalist approaches. This distrust existed at times regardless of whether the proponents in a particular situation seemed to be more to the left or to the right. As neither Europe nor the world had ever broadly enough confronted the fallacies within racial thinking, racism was free to search out new channels and new victims.

Chapter Six

Aryan Fascination and Hallucination

1920s to 1940s

The 1920s and 1930s was a period characterized by a great increase in the number of African-American visitors to Europe and many of these were attracted to Paris. Some were wealthy, some were civil rights or so-called race leaders, and some were intellectuals, some artists, and some musicians. In France, many of these African-Americans came into contact with a great diversity of people, including Europeans, Americans, and Asians as well as other people of African descent from widely scattered places with a variety of agendas. Through many of these contacts that took place in France, people who would eventually be important in the Harlem Renaissance or the "New" Negro movement, the pan-African movement, the *Négritude* movement, and even the Back-to-Africa (or Black Zionism) movement spearheaded by Marcus Garvey would eventually get to know and influence each other.

Among the older of the African-Americans who were in France with some regularity during this period were W. E. B. Du Bois, James Weldon Johnson, Jean Toomer, John F. Matheus, Walter White, and Eric Walrond. Slightly younger was Alain Locke, who had become the first African-American Rhodes Scholar after he graduated from Harvard College in 1907. Upon his arrival in Britain as a Rhodes Scholar, Locke had been denied admission to several Oxford colleges for racist reasons before finally being admitted to Hertford College, where he studied from 1907 to 1910. After departing from Oxford, Locke continued his study of philosophy at the University of Berlin. Still later, Locke attended the College of France in Paris.

A scholar of philosophy, Greek, and Latin who was proficient in French and German, Locke was employed as a professor at Howard University even before he earned his Ph.D. in philosophy at Harvard University in 1918. Locke traveled widely in Europe almost every summer during the 1920s and 1930s. It was in the summer of 1924 that he met the African-American poet Langston Hughes in Paris, after which they became close friends. This was the same summer that

Hughes also became a friend of an Anglo-African student named Anne Coussey from London who was in Paris studying at the Raymond Duncan school. In comparison to Locke, Hughes was part of a somewhat younger generation of African Americans attracted to France, a generation that included such figures as the Jamaican-born poet and novelist Claude McKay, Anna Julia Cooper, Jessie Fauset, Gwendolyn Bennett, and Countee Cullen (Fabre 1991: 67-71, 129).

In addition to the rather long periods of time that Claude McKay spent in Paris and in the south of France, he also traveled in Spain and in Morocco. Eventually leaving France in 1934, McKay never returned again (Fabre 1991: 92-112). The daughter of a former slave in the United States, Anna Julia Cooper earned a doctorate in history from the University of Paris in 1925. Jessie Redmon Fauset, the first "black" woman to study at Cornell University, majored in classical languages and graduated Phi Beta Kappa before later earning an M.A. degree in French from the University of Pennsylvania. Countee Cullen, for a short time the son-in-law of W. E. B. Du Bois, was a Francophile poet and educator who after graduating Phi Beta Kappa from New York University earned an M.A. in French from Harvard University. He continually traveled back and forth between the United States and France from 1928 to 1934 in order to perfect his French and engross himself in French literature and culture (Fabre 1991: 114-127).

In addition to the considerable number of African American veterans of World War I who found their way back to Europe, and especially to Paris, so did numerous entertainers, male and female, who arrived in Europe for the first time. In the New York City borough of Manhattan in the mid-1920s, Spencer Williams and Caroline Dudley Reagan happened to walk into the Plantation Club one night when Josephine Baker was performing for Ethel Waters, the star, on a night that Waters happened to be ill. This was at a time that Williams had just been engaged to compose the music for a show involving "black" performers that was to open in Paris. Reagan was the wealthy impresario who was to finance the venture. Regan and Williams were so struck by the performance of Baker that evening that they shortly afterwards offered her an opportunity to star in the show. Although Baker did not accept immediately, she eventually did, and what followed would eventually become nothing less than a *coup de théâtre*.

In September of 1925, Josephine Baker, who had been hired by Reagan to star in the show, along with the other members of the troupe arrived in France after crossing the Atlantic on board the *Berengaria*. After their arrival in Europe, the French artistic directors of the show shifted the background of the show from a minstrel/plantation setting to one in Africa that emphasized eroticism in the setting of a tropical rain forest. In keeping with expectations, Baker performed a somewhat ambiguous role dressed mostly in scant feathers below her waist.

Although *La Revue Nègre* opened at the Théâtre des Champs-Élysées on October 2, 1925, to mostly to rave reviews, there were rare exceptions. For example, Robert de Flers, who was a member of the French Academy as well as a critique writing for *Le Figaro*, described Josephine Baker's famous erotic dance act in *La Revue Nègre* as "lamentable transatlantic exhibitionism which makes us revert to the ape in less time than it took to descend from it" (MacMaster 2001: 136-137; Onana 2006: 13). This critique, however, did nothing overall to dampen the sensational demand for Baker nor that for jazz.

The run for *La Revue Nègre* was extended twice before it moved on November 19 to the smaller Théâtre de l'Étoile, also on the Champs-Élysées, where it ran until late December. It opened in Berlin in time for New Year's Eve festivities at the Nelson Theater before continuing on to the Alhambara in Brussels (Sephocle 1996: 25). Baker quit the troupe of *La Revue Nègre* before the Brussels opening as a superstar, however, in order to open in *La Folie du Jour* at the Folies-Bergère, where she would wear the shockingly erotic banana skirt for which she would forever after be known.

It was still at the end of 1926 when Josephine opened her own nightclub on rue Pigalle in Montmartre, which shortly thereafter relocated nearby to rue Fontaine. Before 1927 had run its course, "La Baker" was a sensation throughout France and well beyond and had appeared in her first film, *La sirène des tropiques*. French women copied the style of her hair, the poet Jean Cocteau dedicated verses to her, and the American writer Gertrude Stein enjoyed a new banana pudding that Alice B. Toklas, her lesbian lover, concocted and called the "Josephine Baker." On tour in 1928 and 1929, Baker performed in Vienna, Prague, Oslo, Copenhagen, Bucharest, Belgrade, Berlin, Munich, Dresden, and Leipzig among other places and during the next year she was in Argentina and Chile (Hammond and O'Connor 1988; Sephocle 1996: 25; Shack 2001: 35-37; MacMaster 2001: 136; Onana 2006: 17-20).

Among those who were a part of the African presence in Europe for at least a short period in the late 1920s was Jomo Kenyatta. Born Kamau wa Ngengi in the British colony of Kenya around 1894, Kenyatta had traveled to Britain in 1928 to testify against a proposed merger of the British colonies of Kenya and Uganda with the neighboring British-controlled former Germany colony Tanganyika. Also reflective of the great diversity that characterized people of African descent during this period as well as their contrasting worldview was Philadelphia-born Marian Anderson. A classically trained contralto, Anderson made her first trip to Europe in the fall of 1927. Over the next three years, she made several other trips to Europe, spending most of her time in Germany and Scandinavia, where she focused on the study of German and song interpretation and where Kosti Vehanen, a Finnish pianist, became her accompanist. After Anderson met the great Finnish composer Jean Sibelius when he was 70 years old, the two became friends. He even dedicated his song "Solitude" to her saying, "The roof of my house is too low for you." Although Sibelius was already a musical giant, as over subsequent years Anderson added a number of his compositions for voice to her repertoire, she further contributed to bringing his music to the world.

Thanks to a fellowship made available to Marian Anderson in 1931 by the Julius Rosenwald Fund, a philanthropy founded by the son of Jewish immigrants from Germany that in the first half of the 20th century donated millions of dollars especially to Jewish and African-American causes, Anderson left the U.S. again for Europe in October 1932, coincidentally the same year that Julius Rosenwald died. After going first to Sweden, she lived for a while in Germany with a German family while continuing her language study and broadening her repertoire with a special focus on German *Lieder*. During these two years that she remained abroad, she also performed across Europe, including 142 concerts in Scandinavia alone. Anderson performed a bit in Asia as well.

Tragically by the time of Anderson's Paris debut on May 2, 1934, however, Germany under the Nazis had become so hostile toward peoples of Jewish, African, and some other backgrounds that her engagements in Berlin were cancelled. In addition to the fact that Anderson was "black," one of her grandfathers was a Jew. She moved on to Salzburg, Austria, where she performed in an international festival called the *Mozarteum*. There, the well-known Italian conductor Arturo Toscanini who heard her perform told her, "Yours is a voice such as one hears only once in a hundred years."

When this great African American vocal artist was again in Europe in 1935, the Soviet Union was one of the places she had been invited to perform. As the invitation that the Soviet government extended to her stipulated that her performance should not include any music of a religious nature, she had to have a translator slightly alter the names of certain songs on her program to disguise that they had religious content. Enthusiastically received in the Soviet Union, even Joseph Stalin reportedly attended one of her performance. While in the Soviet Union, Anderson was approached by the legendary theater director Konstantin Stanislavski who proposed that she appear in an opera he wished to produce. Leaving Russia without committing to this proposal, Anderson toured the Ukraine, Georgia, and Azerbaijan before returning to western Europe. With rave reviews following her across Europe, it was still in 1935 that Marian Anderson was featured in a concert at the Opera of Paris.

Other African Americans were drawn to Europe, and most especially to the City of Lights, during the interwar period, to study as artists at various studios, academies, and institutes of fine arts. In a volume that is fascinating and brilliant, Leininger-Miller (2001) has documented the lives and work of twelve African-American artists who lived and studied in Paris during the period between 1922 and 1934, including four women, two of whom were sculptors. Most of these artists however were painters. The women included Gwendolyn Bennett, Nancy Elizabeth Prophet (whose paternal grandmother was a Native American), Laura Wheeler Waring, and Augusta Savage. The male artists were Aaron Douglas, William Thompson Goss, William Emmett Grant, Palmer Hayden, William Henry Johnson, Archibald J. Motley, Jr., Albert Alexander Smith, and Hale Woodruff. Although most of these artists eventually returned to the United States, Prophet remained in Paris for twelve years and Smith eventually died in France in 1940.

Although this was not a period when a great many colonials of appreciable African descent were being educated at the highest levels in France, there were some. Already in the 1920s, some of these students were involved in debates and writings that led to the founding of a number of short-lived journals. In common with students in Paris from French colonies in Maghreb and Indochina or southeastern Asia, many of them were concerned about whether or not continued French colonization in their various homelands had any justification. While on the one hand some were assimilationists who favored a greater integration of their peoples with those of France, others were anti-colonialists. Among this latter group were some who were Communists, some who were Garveyites or "back-to-Africa" nationalists, some who supported trade unions, some who were pan-Arab nationalists, and some who were pan-Africanists. Blaise Diagne, who although a member of the French Chamber of Deputies representing four *communes* in Senegal alienated many political activists of African descent in Paris as well as in the colonies when in 1923, Diagne abandoned his earlier demands for the Africanization of the European-dominated economy in Senegal in exchange for support of French and "mulatto" elite merchants who dominated the economy of this colony.

Infuriated by what many considered a betrayal, African students from Dahomey (now Benin), Senegal, and Soudan (now Mali) in the following year helped Tovalou Houénou, a Togolese intellectual, to found *La Ligue pour la Défense de la Race Noire* or LDRN, which for a short time published a monthly journal called *Les Continents*. This was a publication that regularly included reports on the conditions in various colonies, on precolonial African history, on Gandhism, and on the plight of African-Americans in the United States. Because of this liberation agenda as well as the frequent attacks of members of LDRN on Blaise Diagne, the government of France soon forced it underground. In 1926, however, LDRN was succeeded in Paris by a group that was even more suspicious of French assimilationism that was called the *Comité de la Défense de la Race Nègre* or CDRN as well as another in 1927 called the *Ligue de la Défense de la Race Nègre* or LDRN. While CDRN was headed by Lamine Senghor, a Senegalese student, LDRN was headed by Timého Garan Kouyaté of the French colony of Soudan. Lamine Senghor, while still head of CDRN, was in February 1927 also elected to the executive committee of the *Ligue Française contre l'Oppression Coloniale et l'Impérialisme* (Langley 1969: 69-94; Harney 2004: 252n47).

As assimilationists became more influential in CDRN than those who were in favor of decolonization, Lamine Senghor cut his ties with this association that he had founded, thereby leaving the way open for the assimilationists who dominated it to change its name from the *Comité de la Défense de la Race Nègre* to the the *Comité de la Défense des Intérêts la Race Noire* or CDIRN. As Lamine Senghor continued to raise questions about the sincerity of those advocating for French assimilationism and founded a new organization called the *Ligue de la Défense de la Race Nègre* or LDRN, he continued to be harassed by French authorities and for a short while was even incarcerated on highly suspect charges that he had misappropriated some funds. By the time that an international campaign helped to secure his release, his health was so compromised that he died shortly thereafter in November 1927 (Midiohowan 1998: 72-73).

Another young person of appreciable African descent who was in France during this period was Gaston Monnerville. Born in French Guyana the grandson of an African slave but also partially of European ancestry through some members of his mother's family, Monnerville earned his doctorate of law degree in 1927 after a sensationally brilliant academic career in Toulouse that began in 1912. After completing his studies in the southern French city of Toulouse, he left for Paris in order to begin preparing for a practice in law in the capital. In 1931, Monnerville became famous as one of the lawyers involved in defending fourteen Guianese implicated in France's sensational Galmot affair.

Jean Galmot was a wealthy rumrunner and eventually a politician from Guyana who was poisoned in 1928 while much of his cache in jewels was spirited away. He had prior to this time been surrounded by a cast of shady characters and shadowed by a rival named Alexandre Stavisky. Racism was casting a long shadow across Europe generally by this time, and contributing to the sensationalism of the Galmot affair was the fact that Alexandre Stavisky, a Jew, was a politically connected financier, swindler, and embezzler who had managed repeatedly from 1927 until his mysterious death in early 1934 to obtain judicial immunity on several occasions as well as delays in his prosecution.

The French public's suspicion surrounding Alexandre Stavisky, stoked in part by anti-Semitism, so infuriated many that it undermined their confidence in France's parliamentary democracy. Contributing to the sensationalism that surrounded Galmont, Stavisky, and others with whom they had been involved were murder, missing jewels, bribery, suicides, and electoral fraud. Undertaking direct action to reform French politics the month after Stavisky's death, the council of the French Confederation of War Veterans boasting 3,500,000 members along with major right-wing forces united in a major demonstration in Paris that quickly turned into riots. The involvement of Gaston Monnerville as a brilliant attorney in the legal defense of suspects associated with the Galmont affair greatly facilitated his astronomical ascendancy in the center of French public life in a manner that had not previously been achieved by any other person of African descent in France.

Quite apart from Monnerville, one of the reasons that French assimilationsm was viewed with such distrust around this time was because of conservative Blasé Diagne, who had been a deputy in the French National Assembly from 1914. A collaborator of French colonialism, he was accused of allowing the French government to rig his reelection in 1928 in exchange for supporting the continued domination of Senegal's economy by an elite group of Europeans and "mulattoes" or so-called *métis*. Two years later, moreover, he even defended France's policy of forced labor before the League of Nations (Thomas 2007: 29). For this shameless testimony, Diagne was repaid with an appointment as France's undersecretary of state for colonies. Considering that Blaise Diagne would remain a deputy representing four Senegalese *communes* in the French National Assembly from 1914 to 1934, his advocacy of French pursuit of a policy of colonial assimilationism brought the policy very much in question. Such was the situation in France when in 1931 France held a major colonial exposition and Vincent Scotto composed for Josephine Baker her signature song, "*J'ai deux amours, mon pays et Paris.*" Although a beautiful composition, it also reflected the spirit of French assimilationism that prevailed.

Some people of African descent who were living in France around this time had worldviews that were decidedly more skeptical about assimilationism.

Thanks largely to *salons* that were arranged by two sisters from Martinique named Paulette and Jane Nardal beginning in 1931, for example, a small Paris-based French-speaking group began assembling together with some frequency as well as with some "black" North American scholars and writers who were also resident or visiting in Paris. One of the common interests that brought these young intellectuals together was a shared identification with blackness while another was concern about the status of "black" people in the larger world, including especially those then under French colonial and the cultural domination. Among those periodically at these gatherings were Langston Hughes and Mercer Cook of the United States, Léon Gontran Damas of French Guyana, René Maran, and Louis Thomas Achille of Martinique.

An early concrete result of these interactions, in part literary and in part political, was the new journal *La Revue du monde noir* (meaning The Journal of the Black World), which was founded by Paulette Nardal and Dr. Leo Sajou of Haiti in 1931. Although only six issues of *La Revue du monde noir* ever appeared, it included some contributions in English as well as French. The mere appearance of this journal in France, a country that shied away from blatant affirmations of divisions deemed racial, was perhaps its greatest historic importance (Fabre 1991: 71).

La Légitime Défense, another journal largely in the spirit of *La Revue du monde noir*, appeared in 1932 but had an even a shorter lifespan. Among those involved in this project were Étienne Léro, Maurice Sabat-Quitman, Jules Moonnerot, and René Menil, all students from Martinique. After the issuing of a single number of this Marxist, surrealist journal, the French government moved to suppress it. Other literary magazines and journals that began to be published by Paris-based "blacks" around this time were *Le paria*, *La voix des nègres*, and *La race nègre* (Thomas 2007: 29). Building on such undertakings as these, *L'Étudiant noir* (The Black Student) appeared in 1934 on the initiatives of Aimé Césaire of Guadeloupe, Léopold Sédar Senghor of Senegal, and Léon Damas along with Paulette Nardal, Gilbert Gratiant, and Leonard Sainville.

These were in fact the founders of the new literary and political movement that would eventually become known as *Négritude* or "blackness," although they did not attribute a single meaning to this term. Likely, however, there was some consensus that it had literary and political dimensions that incorporated Marxism, assertiveness of "black" identity, and multiculturalism as alternatives to French colonialism as predicated on an ideology of assimilationism. As this group tended to be more associated with the Left Bank than the Right Bank, it did not have strong ties to the community made up of people of color in Montmartre. To the degree that they took their "blackness" as a unifying bond, they also tended to operate largely apart from Africans whose ties were especially with the northernmost part of Africa.

Still, Muslim attacks on Jews in the Algerian city of Constantine in 1934 were followed the next year by more widespread nationalist stirrings in Algeria. These events contributed to further alienation and distrust between French colonials in Algeria and the masses of colonized Algerians, who were Africans. Racism was of sufficiently important concern for the French public by 1935 such that French parties of the left and center came together at that time and formed the Popular Front. As a result of a major victory by these parties in the election of 1936, Léon Blum was to become the first ever Socialist and the first ever Jewish prime minister in the country, perhaps leading some who were viewing developments in Europe superficially to see this primarily as a demonstration of a low level of racism.

Shortly after ascending to his position, Blum was dragged from a car and almost beaten to death by a group of anti-Semites with royalist sympathies. Although he recovered, he also remained a favorite target of Catholics belonging to the extreme right. Additionally, a number of right-wing newspapers in France were extremely hostile to the Popular Front and helped to whip up anti-Semitism that frequently targeted Blum's government. Despite the lofty rhetoric of leftist parties in France about immigration during this period, even in the cabinet of the Socialist Léon Blum during his first term, which extended from June 1936 to June 1937, there was no minister with an immigration portfolio. In lieu of this, Georges Mauco was a member of a committee for French population in Blum's cabinet, and Mauco, unfortunately, brought along much racist baggage as he assumed his new position.

It is ironic that many Americans often romanticize Europe during the interwar years as a continent virtually free of racism. Such assessments have no basis in fact apart from the fact that in most of mainland Europe, and sometimes in Britain, racism directed openly against residents of African descent was manifested in more subtle ways than in the United States. Europeans tended to refrain from violent physical assaults such as lynching, tended to provide more access to public accommodations, and were often more accepting of marriages and sexual intimacies involving people deemed to be of different races than were most Americans. Still, the contemporary assessments of American artists and entertainers about racism in Europe, although first-hand, were often impressionistic and not probative in ways that required broad social and historical analysis. Also, romantic assessments of Europe as largely non-racist seldom took account of the fact that ongoing European colonization and the growing European idealization of people deemed to be Aryan at the expense of others had rationalizations that were deeply racist.

Germany was increasingly concerned with "cleansing" its population in ways deemed racial by the 1920s. Despite the African presence in Germany, Adolf Hitler had published his thoroughly racist *Mein Kampf* in 1925 in which he left little doubt that he considered people he deemed non-Aryan as inferior. Ironically, the Roma, whom he included, claimed heritage to an Aryan language that was Indo-European. Racism, however, seldom allows facts and technicalities to get in the way of a demagoguery that is intended to claim for some branches of the human race a general superiority and apartness that is lacking in reality. In addition to Jews, another small group against which Hitler harangued in his blatantly racist *Mein Kampf* were the so-called Rhineland Bastards. He claimed that history offered irrefutable evidence that whenever Aryans mixed their blood with the blood of inferior people, the resulting offspring led to the ruin of civilization.

In 1926, the Kaiser Wilhelm Society's Institute of Anthropology, Human Heredity, and Eugenics was established in Berlin-Dahlem as one of the first eugenics research institutes to exist. It began to operate the following year with Eugen Fischer as its founding director and the Rockefeller Foundation founded by John D. Rockefeller as its chief financier. This institute's emphasis on genetics placed it in a pivotal position to use its findings for biomedical crimes. Eugen Fischer, in fact, had performed his first biomedical crimes as experiments on so-called race, genetics, and eugenics in the former German colony of South-West Africa where he had used as his guinea pigs both Africans of Herero ethnicity and those of mixed Herero-German ancestry. Under his supervision, moreover, the preserved bodies and severed heads of a number of Herero who had been hanged in this part of southern Africa had been sent to Germany for dissection (Gewald 1999: 145).

In addition to monopolizing American medicine in the 1920s, the Rockefellers along with I. G. Farben, Germany's leading industrial organization, which was led by the Warburg family, held the monopoly on the world's chemical and pharmaceutical industries. The racism that periodically erupted in mass atrocities during the 20th century from many helped to set the stage for the genocidal outrages perpetrated largely at the hands of German Nazis beginning in the 1930s. As many of these racist atrocities were directed against Africans, however, few people in the world who considered themselves to be of European descent showed much concern. In the wake of World War I, where people of African descent were targeted by racists, such racist attacks received much support among people who considered themselves of European heritage in numerous countries.

Germans along with many non-German supporters took to denigrating the offspring of *tirailleurs sénégalais* and German women as "Rhineland bastards" immediately in the wake of World War I. Beginning in 1918 or 1919, Germany, in an effort to free itself from what many Germans considered its "black shame," permitted the German Society for Racial Hygiene to begin a program of secretly sterilizing the much despised German-born children of mixed African and European heritage. Racist attitudes widely accepted by Germans left many feeling that these children were a humiliation (Blackshire-Belay 1996: 111). Adding to this feeling was a textbook that Eugen Fischer, appointed by Hitler in 1933 as rector of the University of Berlin, co-authored with Edwin Baur and Fritz Lenz in 1921 called *Menschliche Erblichkeitslehre und Rassenhygiene* (or *The Principles of Human Heredity and Race Hygiene*). While according to *Sterilization of the Rhineland Bastards: The Fate of a Colored German Minority, 1918-1937* (Pommerin 1982) an estimated 500 German children were involved, other estimates place the number between 600 and 800.

Ironically by the 1930s when these German children were still being sterilized, the majority of anthropologists in Germany were in favor of German colonial expansion in Africa. In fact, they were quite willing to generate racist theories as well as to set forth racist findings and interpretations that the *Nationalsozialismus* Party or Nazis could use in justification of their goals, whether in Europe or abroad. In anticipation of a major German colonization push into the continent of Africa in the 1930s, new ethnographic courses were organized within the German Colonial Society. Within a short time, *Rassenkunde* or the so-called science of race in Germany, had been largely co-opted by Nazis, but it also had its advocates elsewhere.

As early as 1930 in the Free State of Thuringia in central Germany, laws also were passed forbidding the playing of jazz, dance, and even works of theatre deemed to be associated with "black" people. Even later during 1930 while Joseph Goebbels was Germany's minister of culture, he some time made an effort to categorize together so-called black and Jewish music while outlawing all such artistic expressions as non-Aryan and, hence, degenerate (MacMaster 2001: 136; Coquery-Vidrovitch 2007: 118-131). In September 1930, that is, some three years before Hitler became chancellor of Germany, Wihelm Frick, the Thuringian Minister of the Interior, issued a decree "Against Negro Culture—For German Nationhood." This decree had as its aim to suppress jazz because Frick reasoned that it threatened to "undermine the moral strength of the German nation." These developments were indicative that in the Western world mankind had been sliding down a slippery slope toward a racist disaster at least since early in the 20th century when eugenists and so-called race scientists were bestowing scientific respectability on multiple forms of racist thinking (Larson 1995: 138).

According to Miller (1998: 54), the question of African immigration was first posed as a problem in France in the 1920s, when France was much more concerned about the small size and low density of its population than was Germany. This latter concern caused the French government to pass its law of 1927 (Chapman and Frader 2004: 9; Camiscioli 2004: 54-76), which liberalized access to citizenship through naturalization. Such naturalization could be requested as early as age 18 after a stay of only three years in the country. This was a liberalization of the previous requirement that one be resident on French soil for ten years. Its objective was to bring about 100,000 naturalizations annually, and it began to yield results immediately.

Largely to accommodate Muslims in France, most of whom were Africans, the Grand Mosque of Paris was constructed in a composite Moorish style on land donated by the municipality of Paris in its 5th zone or *arrondissement* long home to Paris's Sorbonne and more recently of its main botanical garden called the *Jardin des Plantes*. Constructed in honor of Muslim soldiers who died fighting in the French Army in World War I, the Grand Mosque was partially financed by the French state and inaugurated by President of France and Sultan Mohammed V of Morocco in 1926 during the period that Morocco was a French protectorate. This, by the way, was the same Mohammed V who twenty-seven years later would be deposed by France and exiled to Madagascar when Moroccans were clamoring for independence so that he could be replaced by a French puppet.

Because of race-based demographic concerns with regard to its population, France placed restrictions on the exercise of some rights by its recently naturalized citizens around this time. In the 1930s, racist ideas set forth by Gobineau during an earlier period were rediscovered and disseminated in France. This was partly through the efforts of his grandson Clement Serpaille and partly through the efforts of a radical right-wing journal *Je suis partout*. In that journal in 1933, Pierre-Antoine Costeau presented Gobineau as the forerunner of Fascist thought. The next year, moreover, the *Nouvelle Revue Française* published a special edition devoted largely to Gobineau. Some of Gobineau's thinking influenced the Swiss botanist Alphonse de Condole, one of whose disciples was Comte George Vacher de Lapouge, a librarian and lawyer. Even more than Gobineau, George de Lapouge was the most influential thinker for the right in France. Lapouge authored *The Aryan and His Social Role (L'Aryen, Son rôle social)* in 1899 in which he, like Gobineau, was concerned about so-called race degeneration (Mosse 1985: 58-62).

In 1932, Georges Mauco published an academic thesis under the title *Les étrangers en France: Leur rôle dans la vie économique* (which is to say, *Foreigners in France: Their Role in Its Economic Life*). In this work on the geography of foreigners in France, Mauco argued that Asians, Africans, and Levantines with ties to the eastern Mediterranean could not be assimilated in France. Although Mauco was a Socialist, like the right wingers who would a few years later support France's Vichy government that would collaborate with the Nazis, he popularized the concept of a hierarchy of ethnic groups. This hierarchy was based on what he presumed to be the physical and moral compatibility of various peoples within France. Mauco was particularly opposed to what he considered to be mixed marriages (Liauzu 1996: 185; Chapman and Frader 2004: 6; Dewitte 2003: 50-62).

Among organizations on the right that were very much involved were *l'Action française* and *la Solidarité française*. Although the Vatican condemned the first of these organizations for its espousal of xenophobia and anti-Semitism in 1926, *l'Action française* continued along the same path. Founded in 1933, *la Solidarité française* had a similar outlook, including Fascist sympathies. The 1934 Fascist riots in Paris marked a crucial moment in the history of contemporary France, for it opened a period of confrontation between the extreme right and the extreme left. In large measure over questions of immigration, racism became a major issue of public debate in French society. In part, this also had to do with unhappiness about refugees at a time that the country was undergoing economic difficulties. Against the background of this situation, it is highly significant that a Federation of Students from French sub-Saharan Africa or FEANF was founded in France in 1935.

That a Franco-Muslim hospital opened in the northeastern Parisian suburb of Bobigny in 1935 with a Muslim cemetery next to it was an indication that French assimilationism sometimes worked better as an abstract concept than in reality. While a separate burial ground for Muslims was a religious necessity, the establishment of a separate hospital for *Maghrébins* was an indication that segregation of Muslims from Maghreb was ongoing. In terms of overall national statistics on foreigners domiciled in France before 1921, those from Africa constituted a relatively small proportion. According to censuses in 1921, 1926, 1931, and 1936, Africans in metropolitan France constituted 2.6 percent, 3.0 percent, 3.9 percent, and 4.0 percent in those years respectively (Weil 2004:

533). The figures however included neither people of appreciable African descent in France who were citizens nor those of appreciable African descent who were not Africans. Between 1926 and 1930, 315,066 foreigners acquired French citizenship in contrast to the 95,215 who obtained it during the five preceding years. This fast rate of naturalization was not welcomed by some segments of French society who were unnerved by certain racial and/or ethnic implications of this development.

France's restrictive attitudes regarding immigration reached a new plateau in 1936. It was at this time that Darquier de Pellepoix (who would become *commissaire général* of Jewish questions under the France's Vichy regime that would govern as a puppet of Nazi Germany beginning in 1940) proposed the cancellation of all naturalizations that had been approved since the end of World War I (Weil 2004: 424-425). Although Mauco in 1937 authored a paper in which he recommended that Jews in France be exiled to the countryside, Blum rejected this proposal without inquiring further into the racial thought of Mauco so as to determine if he should be repudiated and removed from his position of influence. As long as one did not feel that he or his ethnic group constituted a bull's-eye for racists, Europeans tended more often than not to avoid confronting the larger issue of racism per se, and Léon Blum was no exception.

Algerian demands on the Popular Front government of Léon Blum in France in the late 1930s had among their objectives universal male suffrage in Algeria, the complete administrative absorption of Algeria into France, and permission for Muslims in matters concerning personal status to live by Muslim law. While these were not positions that Blum was prepared to support, he did agree to sponsor a Blum-Viollette Bill in the Chamber of Deputies that would confer full French citizenship on Algerians who had been former officers in the French army as well as on Algerians who were university graduates. Even this modest proposal to provide French citizenship on but a handful of Algerians infuriated France's extreme right as well as European colonists resident in Algeria. So intense was their opposition, in fact, that legislators in Paris could never even debate the bill.

A certain irony resides in the fact that, apart from Paris, Berlin was in the mid-1920s one of the major European cities attracting African-American artists, including Louis Armstrong, Sidney Bechet, and even Sam Wooding's "Nigger Jazz Band." Well after World War I, people of African descent in Europe were occasionally referred to publicly as "niggers" in some parts of Europe. As late as the late 1920s, for example, British Prime Minister Baldwin did this at least once on the BBC (Fryer 1984: 331). Even in the early 1930s in Britain, racism and the color bar remained one of the most important issues affecting students of African descent as well as other people of appreciable African descent resident in the country (Adi 1998: 77, 90-91). In addition to the sensational involvement of New Orleans-born Sidney Bechet as a musician in *La Revue Nègre*, he resided and performed in France, England, Russia, and Germany during various periods from 1925 to 1929. Into the early 1930s entertainers of African descent could be heard in Germany performing especially at the Scala Casino, the Mercedes Palast, or the Heinroth Palast. At times, they performed with Germans considered "white" and at other times with Germans of mixed African and German ancestry.

Meanwhile in the United States in 1929 the prominent eugenist Charles Davenport published a work under the title of *Race Crossing in Jamaica*, purporting to be an objective study relying on statistical data, Davenport argued that evidence for biological and cultural degradation followed interbreeding between people who were "white" and "black." Further illustrating American and European collusion in such racist thinking, Thurman B. Rice, a professor at the Indiana University School of Medicine in the same year as Davenport published a work titled *Racial Hygiene* in which he argued that colored races were a threat to the white race and that over time this threat was destined to become greater. In this work, Rice further suggested castration as appropriate treatment, and a preventative measure, for anyone with proclivities toward or associations with sexual criminality (Byrd 2002: 74; Coquery-Vidrovitch 2007: 74).

While such racism was surging, Switzerland, beginning in 1926, allowed an organization known as the *Oeuvre d'entraide pour les enfants de la grand-route* (roughly, the Association for Assistance to Nomadic Romani Children) that had been founded by Alfred Siegfried to forcibly remove many Swiss children of Yenish Roma (i.e., of Gypsy ethnicity) from their families with help from the Swiss police for institutionalization under conditions Siegfried controlled. It was only in 1972 when Siegfried died that the Swiss weekly *Der Schweizerischer Beobachter* succeeded in bringing this affair to the attention of the public. While the Swiss police were assisting Siegfried in carrying out his racist policies, Ernst Rüdin, a psychiatrist from German-speaking Switzerland, was director of the Psychiatric Clinic at Basel University.

It is difficult to miss the parallels in the thinking that targeted these children and that which targeted Jews, Slavs, and others. Despite numerous open manifestations of racism in Germany as of 1926, the fact that Adolf Hitler was the leader of its National Socialist or Nazi Party, and the wide-spread German uneasiness with abiding by the armistice that had ended World War I, Germany was accepted as a "peace-loving country" into membership of the League of Nations, of which Britain and France were the most powerful members. The same Eugen Fischer of Germany who ostensibly developed an injection that would render people sterile and who had founded the first German society for racial hygiene before World War I, reemerged after the war to take up the cause of protecting Germany from so-called racial diseases.

In preparation for this, Fischer gave his support to the fad whereby Germans used physiognomic documentary photography to exalt certain facial characteristics over others for explicitly racial-ideological ends. Eugen Fischer and the racial anthropologist Hans F. K. Günther also became coeditors of a volume published in 1930 under the title *Deutsche Köpfe nordischer Rasse* about German faces said to represent the Nordic race. Produced by the publishing house owned by Julius Friedrich Lehmann, which had a reputation for printing much literature tinged with racism, this volume resulted from a contest sponsored by that publisher in which numerous photographs had been submitted with Fischer and Günther acting as the judges. The volume was a compilation of what they selected as the best photographs typical of the so-called Nordic race in seven categories (Gray 2004: 354-355).

By no means was growing racist intolerance limited to Germany at this time. "Even though eugenics was born in Britain," according to Larson (1995: 21), "the principal legal methods of negative eugenics developed primarily in the United States." Also in Sweden, as fascination with eugenics increased in the wake of World War I, attitudes toward immigration became more rigid and more influenced by racist thinking. It was during this period that at Stockholm's Karolinska Institute phrenologic experiments were undertaken with the objective of confirming Teutonic racial superiority. With a similar objective, the Swedish government funded Herman Lundberg in setting up Uppsala University's State Institute for Racial Biology in 1921, where a compulsory sterilization policy would be pursued from 1924 until 1975. Between 1923 and 1927, Hermann Wilhelm Göring, a disciple of Adolf Hitler, lived in exile in Sweden, and it was in 1924 that the brothers Birger, Sigurd, and Gunnar Furugård chartered the first of a series of national socialist political parties. As European obsession with protecting "the race" through purification spread, even Switzerland's canton of Vaud in 1928 passed a law providing for the sterilization of the mentally ill.

Racism was not nonexistent in the Russia during the interwar years. In fact, that the 1917 Bolshevik Revolution in Russia took place during World War I at a time when a major European identity crisis revolving around so-called race was underway impacted the newly established Soviet Union in important ways as well as how the USSR was perceived in the West. As Communism began diffusing into other areas of Europe from its new base in Russia, a number of world leaders in the West began to view Communist Russia, and then the Soviet Union, as a far greater threat to social order than the racism with which many of them were quite comfortable.

Communism, at least in theory if not in fact, was very hostile to racism as well as to imperialism. As there existed in the Soviet Union a social history and social organization that gave a context to racism and domestic colonization that in some ways was different from what existed in most parts of the West, even Russian Communists were not necessarily always aware of these contradictions. In addition to the fact that Slavs reduced to slavery were distributed at various times very widely across Europe and beyond, there existed in the Russian empire a long history of domestic serfdom, anti-Jewish pogroms, discrimination against Roma, and hostility toward Muslims. History also reflected a longstanding desire by Russians to be accepted as European and "white" even as they progressively expanded eastward, meaning that much of the territory of their empire lay well east of Europe and the people of the Soviet Union were very ethnically diverse and in no sense uniformly European.

From around 1923 into the 1930s, there was much political and economic turbulence in the Soviet Union. This turbulence, along with revolutionary rhetoric emanating from the country, led many anti-Communist leaders in Europe and in the United States to overlook even the racism being espoused by German Nazis, as they viewed Germany as a power obstructing the diffusion of Communism. Despite such anti-Soviet attitudes by many leaders in the West, a good number of people of African descent who were desperate to extricate themselves from the oppressions of Western racism and colonialism found in Communist ideology a source of inspiration despite some contradictions between Communist theory and Soviet practice.

The Communist Party Worker's School that William L. Patterson had been attending in the United States, for example, sent him to the Soviet Union in 1927 at a time when racist discrimination was wide-spread in American society. In Moscow, Patterson enrolled in the Far East University. Other African-Americans attending the same university while Patterson was there included the brothers Haywood Hall and Otto Hall, James Ford, Maude White, and Denmark Vesey. Both Patterson and Haywood Hall married Russian women and were in the Soviet Union in 1926 when W. E. B. Du Bois—well-known African-American civil rights activist, pan-Africanist, sociologist, and writer—made his first trip there in 1926. Du Bois returned to the Soviet Union in 1936 and would also visit three other times after World War II.

All people are to some degree ethnocentric. Where ethnocentrism among Europeans was coupled with racism and certain extreme forms of nationalism, however, it sometimes became an especially powerful form of institutionalized arrogance. While Meierhold was adapting a novel by Ilya Ehrenburg for the Russian stage complete with jazz band in 1922, for example, he implied that jazz functioned as part of a sinister plot by American capitalists with anti-Semitic undertones. This theatre piece was staged at the height of the Rhine crisis in Germany when many middle-class Europeans already fantasized that Western civilization was being swamped by "blacks," contributing to a social atmosphere of anti-African racism and ethnocentrism. In a similar vein, Maxim Gorky, one of the most influential ideologues in the Soviet Union around this time, depicted jazz as part of a capitalist conspiracy to brainwash and control "black" Americans. Gorky also displayed an extreme ethnocentric paranoia in imagining that African-American music posed a subversive danger to Soviet society. As Gorky put it in 1928, "one involuntarily imagines an orchestra of sexually driven madmen, conducted by a man-stallion brandishing a huge genital member" (MacMaster 2001: 137-138).

Despite such Russian ethnocentrism tinged with racism, Haywood Hall transferred to the new Lenin School in the Soviet Union as its first student of African descent in 1927. While he was there, a number of other "blacks" enrolled, including Otto Huiswood, H. V. Phillips, Leonard Patterson, and Albert Nzula, the Zulu national secretary of the South African Communist Party. Haywood Hall became vice chairman of the Negro sub-committee of the Eastern (i.e., colonial) Secretariat of the Comintern Congress of 1928, the same year in which he completed his studies at Lenin University.

This was also the year that Josef Stalin launched the First Five-Year Plan under which the Soviet government set about collectivizing agriculture in ways that caused many to perish and multitudes to migrate to rapidly growing cities, which fueled industrialization and rapidly increased Russia's urban population. The following year, Malcolm Ivan Meredith Nurse, a Trinidad-born student of law from Howard University who would change his name to George Padmore, arrived in the Soviet Union. Padmore had been invited to travel there by William Z. Foster, a Communist, in whose campaign for President of the United States the previous year he had worked (Blakely 1986: 88, 90-92; Fryer 1984: 334).

Taking what he thought would be a short break from his law school studies at Howard University, Padmore was warmly received with great respect on arrival in the Soviet Union. In fact, he soon became a prominent figure in Profintern, a trade union component of Comintern that was also known as the Red International of Labor Unions. Expected to remain abroad by the Communist leadership because of his considerable talent as a writer, organizer, and recruiter, Padmore also was elected to the Moscow Soviet in the presence of party dignitaries that included Josef Stalin. He was immediately put to work writing, lecturing at Far East University, and attempting to recruit people of African descent internationally into the Communist Party.

After Haywood Hall completed his studies at Lenin University in 1930, he remained in Moscow to attend the Red International Labor Union there. In addition to Hall and Padmore who were in attendance, five other "black" delegates with connections to the United States were present, including three who were newly arrived. Padmore, being both a Communist and non-U.S.American citizen, was never allowed to return to the United States. By contrast, while both Patterson and Haywood Hall eventually returned home, where they continued their Party work, they returned to the Soviet Union on a number of occasions (Blakely 1986: 88, 90-92). In 1930, Issac Theophilus Akuna Wallace-Johnson from Freetown, Sierra Leone, represented Sierra Leonean railwaymen at the first International Conference of Negro Workers in Hamburg, Germany. The following year, with likely encouragement from George Padmore, he also visited Moscow (Fryer 1984: 341).

This was during a time that millions in the Soviet Union were unemployed and famine was widespread. Still, the population worked desperately to revolutionize the Soviet economic structure. Reminiscent of the feudal internal passport system by which Russia under its tsars bound serfs to various fiefs, a bureaucratic *propiska* system (which had been abolished by the Bolsheviks as a result of the Russian Revolution in 1917) was re-established by Stalin in the 1932. This *propiska* system incorporated both a residence permit and the residential registration of a person and a *propiska* was required to apply for jobs, to get married, to receive medical treatment, and in many other situations. This system helped to force the concentration of Soviet labor in particular ways, and it made it very difficult for a person to obtain a local *propiska* in a major city without having relatives already living there. As a consequence, ethnicity and familial background operated as factors in how the *propiska* system operated. Soviet citizens belonging to certain "risk groups," and those who did not look Slavic found it especially difficult to obtain a *propiska* that permitted them to live in many large cities of Russia.

Despite such contradictions, Communist ideologues claimed that racism officially "did not exist" in the Soviet Union and its satellites; and many Communists, with apparent earnestness, continued to champion the cause of the downtrodden and oppressed around the world in ways that attracted many people of

African descent to Communism. At a time that African-Americans not infrequently faced all matter of racist discrimination as well as the constant threat of violent attack in their homeland, many were favorably impressed that American Communists, despite the fact the most were not "black," seemed to openly advocate on their behalf. Fellow Americans who were Communists often campaigned on their behalf at various relief offices, helped them to find housing after evictions, and supported them when they were demanding inclusion in an American labor union movement that wished to exclude them.

At the same time that American "blacks" were fighting on their own behalf, it mattered a great deal to some of them that Communist compatriots were part of the vocal opposition to the Scottsboro Case. This resulted from a situation where in 1931 nine African-American youths were indicted in Scottsboro, Alabama, of raping two "white" women and sentenced to death on evidence that seemed very contrived. Similarly, it mattered that when in Atlanta, Georgia, in 1932 Angelo Herndon, an African-American Communist leader and organizer of protests in the American South, was sentenced to 18 to 20 years in prison supposedly for "attempting to incite an insurrection," his Communists comrades came to his defense. It also mattered that in 1932 the American Communist Party nominated James W. Ford, an African-American, as its candidate to run for the vice presidency of the United States despite the fact that many "black" Americans could not even exercise a basic right to vote without risking their lives and livelihoods.

Apart from being oppressed, another reason that members of this American minority population was targeted for recruitment by the Soviet Union was likely that some of them were well educated and possessed talents and skills that the Soviets wished to use in its development. Another reason was that their prominence as American citizens among peoples of color in the larger world meant that they could be used to attract other people of African descent to Communism internationally. While some visitors of African descent were in the Soviet Union for relatively short periods, others settled there permanently.

It was in 1932, for example, that an African-American named Wayland Rudd, who aspired to be an actor, sailed for Russia and adopted it as his new homeland. After graduating from the Theatrical Art Institute in Moscow, he pursued a successful career in Russia on stage and in film. For a while, Rudd was even the director of his own drama company. Except for a brief trip back to the land of his birth, Rudd remained in Europe. In fact, it was in Moscow that he would eventually die in 1952. Among other people of African descent who were in the Soviet Union during the 1930s and early 1940s were Ulamei Scott, a Russian-born ballerina who danced at the Bolshoi, Lloyd Patterson, an African-American actor, and Tito Romalio, a Brazilian-born actor (Blakely 1986: 145-147, 155).

A majority of the African-Americans who were in the Soviet Union in the 1920s and the decades immediately following eventually returned to their homeland despite the long legacy of ingrained racism and discrimination in the United States that caused them much suffering. Some African-Americans remained in the Soviet Union, however, became naturalized citizens, and even married and reared families. As in the case of Lovett Fort-Whiteman, some also suffered the grave consequences of eventually falling out of political favor in the Soviet Union. Racism was so common among people of European descent worldwide during the 1920s and '30s that, whether Communists or anti-Communists and whether in North America or Europe, they often were discriminatory with regard to the welfare of peoples of appreciable African descent. At least in terms of rhetoric and ideology, however, the Communists bested the West in maintaining support of the oppressed as a central plank of their propaganda.

The holocaust on European soil that eventually by the 1940s became so horrific that no reasonable person can deny its occurrence did not suddenly spring forth full-blown just in Europe. It was preceded by an earlier genocidal holocaust perpetrated by Germany in South-West Africa as well as by much indifference among many people of European descent toward oppression that they imposed on "others." In accordance with this state of affairs, major powers in the West showed little willingness to make major sacrifices for people with whom they did not identify merely on moral grounds for at least three reasons. First, pseudo-scientific racism, often in the form of eugenics, was widely supported in the United States and Europe. Second, there came to exist much distrust and hostility between the Soviet Union, on the one hand, and powers that were decidedly anti-Communist, on the other, that for many took precedence over racism. Third, although European colonialism in Africa and elsewhere was predicated on an array of racist assumptions, European powers with colonial empires were not prepared to voluntarily give up those empires. World War I had ended in a way that contributed to ongoing tensions with respect to all these situations, and the emergence of Nazism in a world that was already functioning in a very racialized way greatly intensified these tensions.

That Communists (just like non-Communists) often did not act in ways consistent with the humanism of their propaganda is well documented. One example of this may be seen in the case of Lovett Fort-Whiteman, who had founded the American Negro Labor Congress as an affiliate of the American's Communist Party in the late 1920s. By the time Fort-Whiteman immigrated to the Soviet Union in 1930, the Soviet Union, under the leadership of Josef Stalin, was undergoing massive industrialization and internal struggles that were causing great suffering for multitudes of people. This suffering was especially acute between 1929 and 1939, and people of African descent then in the Soviet Union were not exempt from this suffering. A number of African-American Communists apparently perished as prisoners in Soviet camps near Warsaw, (Blakely 1986: 100), and even Lovett Fort-Whiteman vanished into a Soviet *gulag* in 1939. In retrospect, there exists much evidence that the Soviet Union was no more committed than the so-called Western democracies to fighting for human rights for people of African descent except where it was consistent with its prevailing state interests of the moment.

A further indication of this is how the Soviet Union reacted toward Harold Arundel Moody, when he was president of the London Christian Endeavor Federation in Britain. In 1931, with considerable encouragement from Charles Wesley, an African-American history professor who was visiting Britain at the time,

Moody founded the League of Coloured Peoples at a meeting held in the Central YMCA. Moscow, through its various leftist operatives in Hamburg, Copenhagen, and London, repeatedly attempted to undermine the League and to reject Moody's leadership rather than support him. Similarly, the Soviet Union, for reasons of its own momentary self-interest in 1933, instructed George Padmore through a series of directives to stop publically criticizing French and British imperialism although they remained as exploitative and racist as ever (Fryer 1984: 327-329).

It was when Jomo Kenyatta returned to Europe for a stay of fifteen years beginning in 1931 that George Padmore first made contact with him and proposed that he visit the Soviet Union. Soon afterward when Kenyatta spent two years studying at Moscow State University, however, Padmore had been relocated from his Kremlin office to another in Vienna. With Vienna as his new base of operations, Padmore traveled around Europe and occasionally in Africa, attempting to convince various contacts of African background that Communism offered them more hope for finding freedom and escaping racism and imperialism than did continued allegiance to so-called Western democracies.

Padmore was still in Britain in 1934 when Stalin, perhaps thinking that he had defected to the West, decided to further appease Hitler rather than maintain a consistent stance against racism by expelling George Padmore from Comintern (Blakely 1986: 91-93). During at least two of the years that Kenyatta was in Britain he studied anthropology at the London School of Economic and wrote a thesis that eventually was published in 1938 under the title *Facing Mount Kenya*. In addition to again crossing paths with George Padmore in Britain, Kenyatta interacted with numerous African students and dignitaries in Britain. This was also a period when Kenyatta traveled extensively in Europe and to took note of how easily democracy could be manipulated and undermined by racism.

For people who believe as a matter of principle that democracy is an automatic check on racism and the concentration of power in the hands of a self-perpetuating elite, a sobering corrective to this belief may be seen in the fact that it was through democratic elections that Germans established Nazis as the second largest political party in government in 1930. This was at a time when Ernst Rüdin was director of the Kaiser Wilhelm Society's Institute of Anthropology, Human Heredity, and Eugenics. In 1932, Rüdin also became president of the worldwide Eugenics Federation. By 1933, Eugen Fischer and another German named Alfred Ploetz were focusing their racism on Jews and others they considered non-Aryans in particular (Sephocle 1996: 25; Blackshire-Belay 1996: 111; Mosse 1985: 76).

Such was the situation when in 1933 Adolf Hitler became the chancellor of Germany, largely through means that were technically democratic. In the same year, German Nazis began to establish concentration camps as places of detention to hold their opponents in what they called "protective custody." By autumn, the Nazis began detaining in their camps certain so-called asocial elements such as beggars, homeless people, and chronic criminals. Although during the period from 1933 to 1936 the mostly German people in these camps were not limited to members of any particular ethnic group, the Nazis by means of their racist propaganda left little doubt that they wished to target so-called non-Aryans in particular. Hilarius (Lari) Gilges, a German professional dancer, was killed in 1933 by the *Schutzstaffel* or SS, which operated under Heinrich Himmler (who since 1929 had been its *Reichsführer*), apparently merely for being deemed black (Onana 2006: 42-43). Captured in Germany during the same time, George Padmore was briefly jailed on suspicion of opposing Nazism and was then expelled to Britain.

This was the same year that Hans Macco published a pamphlet entitled "Racial Problems of the Third Reich," which focused particular attention on African-German "mulattoes" who were made to seem less than human by being referred to as "bastards." Around the same time, Hermann Göring, Prussian Minister of the Interior, after reviewing dossiers on these same children of mixed African and German heritage, demanded that a study be undertaken in four large German cities to gather statistics of this population. The results of this study undertaken in Dusseldorf, Cologne, Koblenz, and Aachen were forwarded to the Kaiser Wilhelm Society's Institute of Anthropology, Human Heredity, and Eugenics (Onana 2006: 27-28). Hitler had already moved to confirm Ernst Rüdin as head of Germany's Racial Hygiene Society. In this capacity, Rüdin and members of his staff at the Kaiser Wilhelm Society's Institute of Anthropology, Human Heredity, and Eugenics such as Otmar Verschuer and Franz J. Kallmann (whose Christian father was descended from Jews) functioned as part of the Task Force of Heredity Experts who assisted the new Nazi regime in drawing up its new sterilization law based in large measure on American models.

During the 1930s, the number of sterilizations in the United States exceeded 2,500 annually and in one of these years nearly reached 4,000 (Larson 1995: 119). Further demonstrating that the great concentration on sterilization during this period was not a uniquely German phenomenon, the American journal entitled *Eugenical News* celebrated both American laws and German laws providing for sterilization in 1933 and found them to be compatible with laws in both countries that forbade so-called interracial marriages (Coquery-Vidrovitch 2007: 74). In September of 1933, American journal *Eugenical News* even published the new law over Hitler's signature without offering a hint of criticism. To put this in a broader contemporary context, it was only in the 1930s that Europeans began to discontinue the displaying of people they considered exotic and/or inferior in human zoos, a significant proportion of whom were of African backgrounds (Garrigues and Lévy 2003).

Meanwhile in Germany, chairing the Task Force of Hereditary Experts established by Hitler was Heinrich Himmler (*Reichsführer* of the SS). Rüdin supported passage of Germany's Law for the Prevention of Hereditarily Diseased Progeny, which anticipated the extermination of any individual or group of people that might be considered mentally, physically, or racially "unfit." Almost as soon as Göring established the *Geheime Staats Polizei* or Gestapo (really, a secret police force) on April 26, 1933, it began sometimes forcing the mothers of children with African-German backgrounds to sign papers allowing the sterilization of their offspring. In reality, such sterilizations already had been taking place discretely since the end of World War I. The mothers of a few such children however managed to hide them in convents in an effort to avoid this inhumane assault on their personhood. Greatly involved in the undertaking was Dr. Wilhelm Abel, the same Dr. Abel who was eventually one of the so-called anthropological evaluators in charge of establishing race membership in the Special Commission Three (Sephocle 1996: 25; Campt 1996: 74).

Moving far beyond eugenic and racist laws existing in the United States by 1934, German Nazis enacted laws and decrees that were aimed at sharply curtailing the rights of the so-called non-Aryans. It was during this period that discrimination directed primarily at Jews and Roma began to include other categories such as homosexuals, Jehovah Witnesses, Communists, and people of African descent. In addition to the sterilizations that were carried out on many children of African-German heritage, some of these children were also sent to work camps. One such person was Theodor Michael Wonja, the German son of a father originally from the former German colony of Cameroon and a German mother. In the name of *Fremdengesetz*, or the Law for Foreigners, the passports of people of known African or even partial African descent as well as those of their German spouses were withdrawn by the government, causing them to become stateless. This made it impossible for them to legally leave Germany. Many Germans of African descent also lost their jobs, hence, and an ability to earn a decent living (Onana 2006: 27-29).

While most of Europe as well as the United States and Canada adopted a wait-and-see attitude toward a racist and militaristic Germany under the leadership of the Nazis, Germany's first concentration camp began operating at the location of Oranienburb, outside of Berlin, in March of 1933. Shortly thereafter in June, Germany authorized the opening of a concentration camp at Dachau. Although racism had been building among peoples of European backgrounds over a long period, it became inseparable from official state policy in Germany when Hitler became the dictatorial Fuhrer there in August of 1934 following the death of German President Paul von Hindenburg.

In 1934, Ernst Rüdin prepared the official commentary on the "Law for the Prevention of Genetically Diseased Offspring" and drafted racial purity laws against cohabitation of so-called Aryans and non-Aryans. When this was done, Otmar Verschuer, with Josef Mengele as his assistant, wrote reports regarding how special courts should enforce those laws. Quite apart from the German "mulattoes" who were the so-called Rhineland Bastards, the 1930s came to be an especially difficult period for children of African or mixed African and German descent who were left to grow up in Germany under the rule of the Nazis. Most of these people were destined to become victims of discrimination and were not infrequently openly abused by many Germans, even including some pupils of color by their school teachers. Almost without exception, they were eventually deprived of an opportunity to pursue advanced studies and to compete in sports. Not infrequently, they were barred from using such public facilities as swimming pools, playgrounds, and parks, and their parents often were forced to give up their employment and their housing in the stead of inferior employment or housing (Coquery-Vidrovitch 2007: 28, 69, 102-112). In addition to such deprivation, humiliation, violence, and worse, they experienced the

psychological damage of constant fear of growing up in a society that considered them inferior almost to the point of being subhuman.

Despite this development, Europeans as well as Americans remained largely
passive. Given such passivity, it is not surprising that Hitler felt free in March of
1935 to openly violate the Treaty of Versailles that had ended World War I by
introducing military conscription. The month after a conference of German ministers was held in late August, an annual Nazi Party congress convened at Nuremberg on September 14 and 15. This congress was especially infamous for
two new German "race laws" that were approved, the first being announced
immediately and the other in November. These so-called Nuremberg Laws
were: (1) The Law for the Protection of German Blood and German Honor and
(2) The Reich Citizenship Law. The first law forbade mixed marriages between
Jews and so-called Aryans. Its preamble also stipulated that purity of blood was
essential for the future existence of the German people. In November of 1935,
the second of the so-called Nuremberg Laws was enunciated, withdrawing from
German Jews their citizenship and any remaining political rights. While making
explicit reference to Jews and to Roma, as these laws also were aimed at "individuals with foreign blood," they could also be applied against people of appreciable African ancestry. This happened also to have been the same year that the
Swastika was approved as the major symbol on the official flag of Germany.

With so much of Europe afflicted with racism and more interested in appeasing Nazis and Fascists than in challenging them on their concentration of power
and racist brutalities, Benito Mussolini sent General Pietro Badoglio with
400,000 troops to invade Abyssinia (now Ethiopia) in 1936. In a world where
Europeans were long accustomed to believing that they had a right to exploit
and rule peoples they considered their inferiors, the League of Nations responded rather half-heartedly in condemning this unprovoked aggression. Complicating the situation, this was around the same time that Germany occupied the Rhineland and that the proclamation of a Rome-Berlin Axis by Mussolini sent shivers throughout Europe and well beyond.

That neither the so-called Western democracies nor the Communists insisted
on immediate and effective punitive action against Fascist Italy for its aggression in northeastern Africa was clear proof that, while Africans were expected to
fight in conflicts in which European interests were at stake, Europeans did not
consider people of African descent worth risking their lives or expending their
resources. At a time when Britain and France ruled over the largest colonial empires in the world, both countries were more interested in appeasing Fascist Italy
and Nazi Germany than in providing genuine assistance to newly colonized Abyssinians.

So ineffective were the sanctions against Italy that the League of Nations
imposed while Italy pursued a course of using mustard gas and flamethrowers
against the Abyssinians that Italy succeeded in capturing the Abyssinian capital
of Addis Ababa in May 1936, forcing its Emperor Haile Selassie to flee to London, where he and other members of the royal family would spend several years.
Even as Italy continued reinforcing its occupation of Ethiopia, the League lifted
its ineffective sanctions against the Italian aggressors on July 4, 1936. In doing

this, the League—which was dominated by Britain and France—signaled that racism and the self-interests of European nations was more central to the League's *modus operandi* than color-blind global justice. In this way, so-called Western democracies were also able to avoid self-examination with respect to the institutionalized racism and class oppression that they sometimes tolerated, and oftentimes supported, both domestically and internationally.

As Europe's ambivalent response to Italy's aggression against Abyssinia seemed to undermine whatever semblance of legitimacy had ever been claimed for European imperialism in Africa, it infuriated colonized peoples quite broadly. It also contributed to an intensification of political activism among many-peoples of African descent around the world (Adi 1998: 67; Padmore 1955: 144-146, 330). That a new treaty between Britain and Egypt the following year gave Egypt an increased degree of independence was less due to a British interest in liberating Africans than a British realization that Italy's presence in Ethiopia as well as Eritrea posed an invasion threat to its interests in Egypt from three directions: from north of the Mediterranean, from Libya located to the west of Egypt, and also from the Eastern Horn of Africa. With the Suez Canal located in Egypt, an Italian invasion there could have imperiled Britain's control of much of its colonial empire.

Meanwhile in 1937, Italy banned conjugal relationships between Italians and Africans in its colonies. That a five-year penalty was to be levied only against Italians involved in transgressions but not against the Africans involved was based on the racist premise that Europeans, being "morally superior," should be held to a higher standard. Despite such distorted thinking, these prohibitions never stopped Italians and Africans from procreating together. Under pressure from Germany, Italy's Fascist government on September 12, 1938, issued its notorious racial purity laws. Implemented across the country, these laws glorified ideas of racial purity, homogeneity, and national unity. They also stipulated among other things that Italians could not marry any non-Aryan people and that even many classes of government officials and employees could not marry Aryans of foreign nationality. In November of the same year, Italy promulgated its "Laws for the Defense of the Race."

Jews were denied civic status, barred from military service, excluded from all levels of public administration, and forbidden from entering mixed marriages because their supposedly bad blood threatened to contaminate lines of Aryan pedigree. While these laws were anti-Jewish, to be certain, they were also anti-African. Oddly, also in 1938, Mussolini declared Libya, although located south of the Mediterranean in Africa, annexed to Italy. In addition, he forbade Italian men from passing on their last name and their Italian citizenship to their African-Italian children, thereby breaking with a tradition that had existed at least since 1912. Despite this desperate attempt by Italian Fascists to redirect the historic course of reproductive biology, Italy's King Victor Emanuel III maintained an eerie silence, no doubt because he opted not to risk his regal status by being a voice of reason.

As Britain and France abandoned the concept of collective security in favor of appeasing Germany, Britain's Lord Rothermere began arguing as early as

1934 that Germany's African colonies (which since the end of World War I were being administered as Mandates by various European Allies under the authority of the League of Nations) should be returned to the control Germany. Of particular importance, this argument was being advanced at a time that Germany was under the racist and dictatorial rule of Adolf Hitler and his Nazi Party (Adi 1998: 71). When faced with increasing racism and militarism on the part of German Nazis and Italian Fascists, Europe's major so-called democracies showed themselves willing to offer Africans to the Nazis and Fascists as sacrificial lambs in order to save themselves. Around the same time, they also were willing to sacrifice masses of long-oppressed Spaniards whom they likely thought of as quasi-"others" in much the same way not surprisingly.

With the 1931 collapse of a thirteen-year dictatorship in Spain under General Primo de Rivera, its poverty-stricken masses overwhelmingly elected a Popular Front Republican government causing Spain's figurehead monarch, King Alfonso XIII, to go into exile. As Spain's somewhat fractured and unstable new Republican government that he left behind was in the process of distributing land to the peasants and improving conditions for workers in the mines and factories, right-wing forces of reaction began scheming against it. Despite having a Republican president, the leftist Republicans lost to the conservative Nationalists in the elections of 1933. Because Spain, unlike Abyssinia, was widely recognized as a European country, the stage was set for a Spanish Civil War where both sides would soon garner considerable international support. When the Spanish Republicans then won a narrow election victory over their opponents and General Francisco Franco began executing plans to overthrow Spain's Republic in 1936, open warfare really erupted. This was a war where Republican forces, made up of Communists, Socialists, anarchists, trade unionists, Basque separatists, Catalonia separatists, and anti-racists, on one side, were opposed by so-called Spanish Nationalists, many of whom identified as Fascists, Nazis, the wealthy elite, and conservative Catholics, on the other. Franco requested and secured military assistance from Hitler's Germany and Mussolini's Italy.

As well as numerous African-Americans who were in Europe in the interwar period, so were many of their "white" compatriots, especially in Paris. Some of these, in fact, were literary notables who belonged loosely to the group that the American writer and patron of the arts Gertrude Stein famously labeled "the lost generation." In addition to Stein, this network included such figures as Ernest Hemingway, F. Scott Fitzgerald, Ezra Pound, Sherwood Anderson, Waldo Peirce, T. S. Eliot, and Sylvia Beach. Many of these Americans could frequently be found on Saturday nights at a *salon* in the apartment of Stein and at other times in the Parisian bookshop called Shakespeare and Company, which had been founded by Sylvia Beach with her friend Adrienne Monnier. Paul Robeson and some other African-Americans were occasionally among them as were also a number of European confederates such as George Orwell, André Gide, and James Joyce. The members of this lost generation network in addition to being in frequent communication about art—including jazz, painting, sculpture, and literature, also conversed about politics. In the late 1930s, many of them were paying especially close attention to Nazism in Germany, Fascism in Italy, Communism in the Soviet Union, and civil war in Spain.

Already in 1936, the Gestapo had been placed above the law, and all of Germany's regular police forces absorbed into the *Schutzstaffel* of which Heinrich Himmler remained the *Reichsführer* (Coquery-Vidrovitch 2007: 64). Meanwhile, as Georges Vacher de Lapouge survived until 1936, he was able to see the Nazis embrace many of his theories (Mosse 1985: 58-62). Even as German Nazis were openly targeting people of color, Jews, Roma, and others for incarceration as well as for murder, anti-Communist leaders in Britain and France exhibited a great unwillingness to confront Nazi Germany. Many Europeans felt that since they were not targeted that the appeasement of Germany would be a more self-serving policy than one involving a broadsided confrontation with European racism within and beyond the borders of their various countries.

While in the United States the government was also watching these same developments, it was especially fixated on Russian-based Communism, apparently considering it a greater threat to social order than Fascism, Nazism, or even racism. While the United States government took no concrete steps to oppose the Nazis and Fascists in Spain, for example, it was quite hostile toward the Spanish Republicans, as it considered them leftist. Some American citizens, including many living in Europe, however, saw this situation quite differently and were quite willing to put their lives in jeopardy to stand in opposition to reactionary forces in Spain. While the Spanish Civil War was continuing, Nazi Germany was involved in the construction of a number of newer and larger camps to incarcerate mostly Jewish prisoners and under worse living conditions than previously (e.g., Sachsenhausen, Buchenwald, Mauthausen, Flossenburg, Ravensbrück, Auschwitz, Majdanek, Natzweiler, Neuengamme, and Stutthof). From 1937 onward, moreover, a number of companies used certain prisoners from throughout Nazi territory for forced labor.

As Hitler and Mussolini aided General Franco's Nationalist insurrectionists and the Soviet Union aided the Spanish loyalists, the League of Nations refused to intervene to help the Popular Front government in Spain. The League, moreover, attempted to ban even the support offered to the struggling Spanish Republicans by volunteers, no doubt in large measure because of pressure from the government of the United States, which was not even a League member. As it became apparent that the Republicans were likely to be overrun and defeated without receiving outside assistance, they began to receive support from Stalin's Russia as well as from numerous volunteers internationally who poured into the country.

Organizing themselves into so-called International Brigades, these volunteers struggled during the three years that the Spanish Civil War continued. Numbering approximately 18,000 people from over fifty countries, they transcended all boundaries of color, language, and ethnicity. While some of the Republican volunteers were Ethiopians seeking redress against the Fascists because Mussolini had invaded their country, others were Finnish, Cuban, Russian, French, Japanese, Canadian, British, American, and so forth. Of the between

2,800 and 3,000 American volunteers who participated, perhaps 30 percent were American Jews. Among the others from the United States, almost a hundred were African-American. Oliver Law, who died in battle in July 1937 while commander of the Abraham Lincoln Battalion made up of "white" and "black" troops from the United States, for example, was an African-American. Another of the African-Americans who risked their lives supporting the Republicans in Spain as a volunteer was a female nurse named Salaria Kea.

Although forbidden by the U.S. State Department to travel to Spain, the African-American writer Langston Hughes traveled there anyway and remained for six months as a correspondent for the Baltimore *Afro-American* (Fabre 1991: 72-73). Although a Jew and a feminist as well as a close friend of Hemingway, Gertrude Stein was partial to the same Nationalist cause as was the United States and Nazi Germany. However, Stein had a more negative attitude toward the Nazis a few year later after their occupation of much of France sent her and Alice B. Toklas fleeing to Culoz in the south. By contrast, Earnest Hemingway, who harbored pro-Republican sentiments during the civil war, volunteered to work with the Red Cross in Spain. Also, the British writer George Orwell was wounded while fighting for Republican forces there.

With the example of no decisive Western action against Mussolini's aggression in the Eastern Horn of Africa and no decisive Western action against Nazi and Fascist meddling in the Spanish Civil War, the same Dr. W. Abel of the Kaiser Wilhelm Institute for Anthropology, Human Genetics and Eugenics in Germany, who in 1933 carried out research on 27 children of color in Wiesbaden, claiming to demonstrate numerous "half-caste" flaws, including early psychoses and low intelligence, recognized that he had a green light to act as a race evaluator of the "Special Commission 3." With this recognition, Abel felt free of constraints to continue discreetly sterilizing German-born children of mixed European and African heritage (MacMaster 2001: 134).

The West continued to maintain its silence even as Hitler remilitarized the Rhineland, occupied the German-speaking part of western Czechoslovakia known as Sudetenland, and masterminded an *Anschluss* or union with Austria in March of 1938, all of which was forbidden by the Treaty of Versailles that had ended World War I. The Nazis, around the same time, began to more freely arrest and imprison people merely for being deemed to belong to certain inferior races, with particular focus on Jews and Roma. Despite this, British Prime Minister Chamberlain showed himself willing to appease Hitler at Munich at the end of September of '38. As by this time Stalin realized that the Republicans in Spain could not win, he ended his support of them, and the Spanish Civil War ended the next year in March of 1939 with the badly outnumbered and ill-equipped Republican forces resoundingly defeated.

As multitudes of defeated Republicans from Spain known as *la Retirada* fled across the Pyrenees into southern France, many French people resented their presence because of xenophobia, tinged with racism. Long after this time, there remained an abiding faith in the hearts of many who were not afraid of being targeted with the label of "left of center" that the fight against Fascism in Spain had been a just cause where some selflessly sacrificed much while others opted to appease the Nazis and Fascists by looking away.

In no sense were the Nazis and the Fascists the only racists of note in the world during the period leading up to World War II. People claiming European descent in many parts of the world were fascinated with issues they deemed racial, and this was reflected in numerous domains of life. One such domain was sports, where there was considerable racialization. Even under the Nazi governance in Germany, it took a few years for the ruling party to decide how it would be influenced by such racialization. Well after it had forced such Germans as the amateur boxing champion Eric Seelig, the tennis player Daniel Press, and high jumper Gretel Bergmann (who were Jewish) and the middleweight boxing champion Johann "Rukelie" Trollmann (who was Romani) out of German national sports associations, there remained some inconsistencies in is policies. The German heavyweight wrestler Louis Brody-Alcolson, who was "black" and African-born with the original name of Louis M'bele Mpessa, for example, was allowed by the Nazis to remain on the country's national wrestling team alongside other members who were "white" Nazis until at least 1936 (Lusane 2003: 217).

Also reflective of global racialization in sports was the Nazi reaction when the German-born boxer Max Schmeling defeated the African-American boxer Joe Louis in the United States a few weeks before the opening of the Olympic Games in Berlin in 1936. Similar to many other racist propagandists on both sides of the Atlantic, the Nazis were quick to hail the victory of Schmeling over Louis as a demonstration of "white" superiority. Germany even produced the propaganda film *Max Schmeling's Sieg—Ein Deutcher Sieg*, that implied that this victory demonstrated by means of sports the validity of Nazi racist theories. The tremendous need that was felt by masses of people of European descent to view achievements in sports as proof of their superiority over so-called races that they assumed were inferior was reminiscent of American longing for a "Great White Hope" to defeat the boxer Jack Johnson between around 1908 and 1910 as well as the French longing for their own "Great White Hope" to defeat "Battling Siki" in the early 1920s for the same racist reasons.

Outstanding achievements at the 1936 Olympic Games in Berlin by the African-American athletes Jesse Owens on the track and Cornelius Johnson in the high jump, in any case, challenged claims of "white" racial superiority in sports and led to the generation of alternative racist theories. Where people of color were victorious over "whites," some "white" racists then opined that it was because people of color were physically more subhuman. A boxing rematch between Joe Louis and Max Schmeling in 1938 in which Schmeling was soundly defeated created a new situation for Nazi racists to try to explain away. There was sufficient hostility between Nazi Germany and the many ordinary citizens in the United States by this time that even masses of "white" Americans wished for the victory of Louis over Schmeling.

In addition to the racialization of sports in the first half of the 20th century, there was a parallel racialization in some branches of what was peddled as "objective" science, especially as it related to human diversity and variation. Often overlooked is the fact that even a number of Jewish scholars specializing in the areas of eugenics and so-called race science, including some early Zionists, contributed to the racialization of science. Included within this last-mentioned group, for example, were Elias Auerbach of Berlin, Aron Sandler, Felix Theilhaber, and Ignaz Zollschan, all of whom were opposed to Jewish intermarriage and argued that this opposition was necessary to preserve Jewish "racial purity." Their worldview failed to take account of the fact that neither Jews nor any other group of human beings was racially pure and that this notion lacked any sound basis in science (Efron 1994: 126).

Those Jews who had been reared in the West surrounded by Western doctrines of racism were no more exempt from being seduced into sometimes supporting pseudo-scientific racism when it was perceived as working to their advantage than were other contemporary Westerners who thought of themselves as fundamentally "white" and of European derivation. When Judge Julian Mack of the American Jewish Committee testified before the Dillingham Commission on immigration in 1909 that Jews did not constitute a race, for example, many Zionists living in the United States protested vigorously against this non-racial pronouncement on Jewish ethnicity (Cohen 1972: 47).

Similarly in 1936 Franz Josef Kallmann, who had specialized in the study of so-called hereditary degeneracy under Ernst Rüdin, felt sufficiently threatened as the son of a father of Jewish background who had converted to Christianity that he fled Germany for the United States. As Rüdin had been instrumental in assisting this escape and had subsequently arranged for some of Kallmann's massive body of research data to be delivered to him in New York, Kallmann for several years continued to work cooperatively with the German Research Foundation for Psychiatry in Munich that was under the leadership of Ernst Rüdin, although Rüdin had become a Nazi. Moreover, when Kallmann's *The Genetics of Schizophrenia* was published in 1938, Kallmann expressed thanks to Rüdin, his former patron and mentor, in print. Tragically, it is plausible that this work by Kallmann provided Nazi Germany with some of the rationalization that its T4 unit began using shortly afterwards to kill 250,000 people with gas and lethal injections because it considered them "defective."

Even at end of 1930s, most Western psychiatrists and geneticists had not gotten around to strongly denouncing eugenic abuses despite the pseudo-scientific racism on the basis of which they were often rationalized. At least in the United States, however, some of the practitioners and theoreticians of eugenics began to belatedly receive more critical scrutiny in the late 1930s. Ironically, this additional scrutiny was directed more at how eugenics was victimizing certain "whites" than people of color. Although the Carnegie Institution withdrew its funding from the Eugenics Record Office at Cold Spring Harbor Laboratory at this time, Charles Davenport and Harry Hamilton Laughlin, his chief assistant there, had already done considerable damage. Both believed that so-called Nordic Europeans were superior to other "white" people, and well before the Carnegie Institution withdrew its support their purportedly scientific testimony on this matter had greatly influenced the U.S. Congress when it was enacting the federal Immigration Act of 1924. As a result, in addition to reflecting a definite preference for "white" immigrants to the United States, this act also reflected a preference for those who were deemed to be Nordic over those from southern and eastern Europe, because of the presumed inferiority of the latter (Larson 1995: 100-101).

It was not only in terms of biology that many people of European descent felt threatened by people they deemed to belong to so-called inferior races; they were also threatened culturally. Germany's 1938 Exhibition of Degenerate Music at Düsseldorf, for example, was meant to be critical of the influence of jazz and other so-called degenerate music associated with "blacks" and Jews on music that it considered traditional to Germany. This exhibition convened at a time that Joseph Goebbels was German minister of culture and, for the occasion, Hans Severus Ziegler, director of the German National Theater located in the city of Weimar, published a book titled *Degenerate Music: An Accounting*. On the front cover of this book was a caricatured illustration of a "black" person with white lips that were much exaggerated in size playing a saxophone. Prominent on the lapel of his jacket was a Star of David (Mosse 1985: 34; Coquery-Vidrovitch 2007: 121-122). While the city of Weimar was home to such cultural luminaries as Bach, Goethe, Schiller, and Herder, it also was located quite close to where the World War II concentration camp of Buchenwald was established in 1937.

Despite the disordered attempt by the exhibition at Düsseldorf to discredit jazz, "blacks," and Jews simultaneously through a combination of ethnocentrism and racism, it was not destined in any lasting way to prevent the diffusion of jazz. An indication of this in Germany was the fact the Goebbels was still trying to enforce laws that prevented the recording of what he considered jazz and other types of non-Aryan music well into the early 1940s. Faced with the realization that the Nazis could not eradicate jazz and swing music from German culture, Goebbels, under the influence of a *Luftwaffe* pilot named Werner Molders, who very much liked these types of music, eventually resolved to try to create forms of them that the Nazis could consider acceptable (Coquery-Vidrovitch 2007: 123-124).

Although some conservative and Eurocentric African-American intellectuals at times during the interwar period were shamed into also feeling threatened by these genres of music, this shame had to do with how they wished to be perceived by "whites" rather than any feelings that music created by African-Americans like themselves was instinctively inferior. This notwithstanding, these genres of music eventually were to evolve into idioms that belonged to people around the planet with the creative roles of African Americans remaining central as they evolved. While volumes by Bergmeier and Lotz (1997), Lotz (1997), Kater (1992), and Budds (2002) specifically focus on the influence of African-Americans and jazz on German musical culture, numerous other works document jazz as a part of an African-American influence on European cultures that in ebbs and flows has been continuing at least since World War I (Goddard 1979; Feigin 1985; Godbolt 1986; Godbolt 1989; Raphael-Hernandez 2004; Heffley 2005).

Even as World War II became almost inevitable, neither the Western democracies nor the Soviet Union found the outrages of racism per se a sufficient cause for going to war. Mounting a firm opposition to racism, Nazism, and Fascism after Italy's rape of Abyssinia likely could have circumvented an especially large-scale holocaust as well as World War II, but peoples of European descent were much too mired in racism generally to pursue this path. To be certain, the Spanish Civil War was another missed opportunity. Although the sympathies of Prime Minister Léon Blum of France lay with Spain's Republican Popular Front, he was already on shaky ground as a Jew at a time when anti-Semitic racism was surging in Europe. For fear of spitting his governing alliance and possibly instigating a civil war in France, he was not able to support Spain's democratically elected Republicans. Hence, while Léon Blum was in too weak a position to intervene during the Spanish Civil War, such Western powers as Britain and the United States chose covert hostility masked as official neutrality when Spanish democracy was in jeopardy merely to deprive forces they considered left-wing a victory there. The war in Spain ended even as race-based oppression continued to characterize the lives of people of African descent in the United States and in European colonies scattered widely around the world and even as across increasingly large parts of Europe unprovoked imprisonments, enslavements, and mass killings justified solely by racism under the Nazis and others were taking place.

Despite the fact that racism seemed to be present almost everywhere in Europe by the 1930s, Britain during a five-year period beginning in 1933 opened its borders to allow in some 11,000 Jewish refugees who were attempting to flee the growth of Fascism and Nazism in central Europe. Due to a combination of domestic anti-Semitism and unemployment, this policy largely came to an end in 1938. Meanwhile, even after Italy withdrew from the League of Nations in 1937 in order to not submit to the League's judgments, Britain and France continued in their attempt to appease Italy and Germany. During a nine-month period beginning in 1938 Britain admitted an additional 44,000 Jewish refugees under pressure from Anglo-Jewish groups. Many of these refugees were subsequently interned during a panic in the spring 1940 when it was perceived that the country was being invaded by too many "others," reflecting British racism as well as government reluctance to antagonize racists at home and abroad. These refugees were later released, though only because the anti-Jewish atmosphere in Britain became less hostile and industry demanded more labor in order for the country to more effectively prepared to wage war. This situation clearly illustrates that Britain was primarily sympathetic to victims of racism when the government assumed that they could be useful to it (Paul 1997: 66-67).

In this same spirit, a number of "blacks" from British colonies, including especially from the West Indies, would serve as soldiers and seamen in Europe during World War II. Both the British government and the Merchant Navy recruited and accepted several thousand colonial subjects as volunteers for military labor battalions, munitions factories, and naval service. Though theoretically equal to "white" British subjects, in practice these colonials tended to be segregated from others and treated as inferior. The Colonial Office also kept them under close observation. Such conditions of service were predicated on the racist notion that "black" British subjects were free to come to "the mother country" only so long as they accepted their relocation to Europe as temporary and submitted to controls that were discriminatory and strict (Paul 1997: 112-113).

World War II was destined to reveal numerous contradictions between supposed commitments to opposing imperial inclusiveness and colonial assimilationism, on the one hand, and racist public policies of European governments, on the other. With a definite focus on French-controlled Tunisia and a driving desire to reconstitute the ancient Roman Empire on a perversely racist foundation, Italy demanded additional colonies in northern Africa around the same time that it seized Albania in 1939. On June 29, 1939, a new Italian law banned Jews from all skilled professions. Affected by this law were approximately 1,600 Jewish doctors, lawyers, architects, journalists, dentists, and engineers. Other laws prohibited Jews from frequenting popular vacation spots, placing advertisements and death notices in newspapers, owning a radio, publishing books, giving public lectures, listing their names in telephone books, and entering certain public buildings. During the same year, "penal sanctions for the defense of racial prestige against the natives of Italian Africa" were enacted, which provided a comprehensive legal framework for racist segregation in Italy's African colonies in Eritrea, Italian Somaliland, and parts of Libya.

By the time the Nazis captured Czechoslovakia and invaded Poland in March of 1939, Stalin was fully aware of the West's opposition to his large-scale brutalities as well as to Communism in general. As willing as leaders in Western democracies were to equivocate on racism when they deemed it to their advantage, Stalin agreed in August to a Soviet-Nazi pact of mutual non-aggression. As violent attacks on Jews and others people considered racially inferior became widespread in Germany in 1939, many Europeans continued on the course of appeasing militant racists. Only after Adolf Hitler seized Czechoslovakia, Madrid surrendered to General Franco, Mussolini seized Albania, and Hitler invaded Poland did Britain and France finally contemplate declaring war on Germany.

Shortly before the entry of France into the war, in fact, some French people were claiming that Marseille was in decline and becoming too populated with "blacks." Only after the Germans bombarded Marseille did such racist anxiety abate. It was against this background that tens of thousands of new soldiers and workers arrived from France's colonies, including especially from Africa, to patriotically assist the "mother country" at a time of great need (Blanchard and Boëtsch 2005: 16). Even after Great Britain along with France, New Zealand, and Canada declared war on the racist Nazi regime in Germany in August of 1939, Britain was so unwilling to take a firm stand against racism per se that it limited its recruitment of soldiers from Northern Rhodesia (now Zambia) to "whites" only. That racism in general was but a tangential concern of Allied major powers in World War II emphasizes the hypocrisy of much of their wartime propaganda.

In Britain, some "white" people working as stretcher-bearers quit, for example, because they objected to other people who were of African and Indian descent doing the same kind of work as themselves. Many who were the targets of discrimination, on the other hand, demanded of the government that there be an end to discrimination and equal admission for all to the armed forces and the colonial civil service. Even some church officials made similar demands, including William Cosmo Gordon Lang, the Archbishop of Canterbury. The West African Student Union was especially active as a pressure group during this period (Adi 1998: 89-90, 91).

The United States—still viewing Nazi Germany, despite the inhumane and racist policies it was pursuing, as an effective check on the diffusion of Communism from Russia—continued to proclaim its neutrality. This was around the same time that the Nazis established labor, hard labor, and "re-education" camps. At the end of September of 1939, the Nazis and Soviets were dividing up Poland. The Nazis began euthanizing on sick and disabled people in Germany by November as the Soviets were invading Finland. Nearby, Scandinavian countries were not immune to the racism and indifference to racism that was widespread in Europe during this period.

Although Sweden until the world depression in 1930 lost more people through emigration than it gained from immigration, for example, Swedish fascination with eugenics made many Swedes especially susceptible to much of the perverse thinking about race and ethnicity that prevailed. Sweden's *Riksdag* in 1931 prohibited peoples deemed "colored" from visiting or settling in the country. Because of support from social planners like Gunar and Alva Myrdal no less than that from certain committed racists, according to Nordin (2005: 17-19), a program of secret sterilization of thousands of women without their authorization was undertaken in Sweden during the interwar years. In 1935, Denmark and Finland also passed eugenic laws allowing for compulsory sterilization under certain conditions. Norway, shortly afterward, did likewise. At Sweden's Uppsala University's State Institute for Racial Biology, in fact, the compulsory sterilization policy undertaken there for purported social and racial hygiene continued from 1934 until 1975.

Although from the beginning of the Third Reich to *Kristallnacht* near the end of 1938 in Germany about 3,000 Jews received permits either to settle in Sweden or to travel through the country, in the late 1930s when German Jews were under direct assault Sweden's borders remained largely closed to them. Sweden was greatly unnerved when in April of 1940 the Nazis invaded nearby Denmark and Norway. By officially remaining neutral, however, Sweden was able to provide refuge to half the Jews from Norway and almost all of those from Demark. In addition, the Swedish diplomat Raoul Wallenberg much later during the war would be able to save the lives of thousands of Jews largely by furnishing them with false papers. Unfortunately, he would never be seen again after being summoned for a meeting with Soviet authorities on January 17, 1945.

Well before this time, in August of 1940, Italy invaded British Somaliland and further intruded into Africa by invading Egypt a few months later. By attacking Greece at around the same time, Italy was almost attempting to recreate the Ancient Roman Empire in the mid-20th century, albeit one that would be held together by racism emanating from a Fascist dictatorship headquartered in Rome. In its effort to bring this to fruition, Italy was already fighting against considerable African-based opposition to control Libya. Around this same time, Germany began constructing in southern Poland Auschwitz-Birkenau, which would be the largest of all the Nazi concentration camps. In defiance of the non-aggression pact that Germany had reached with Stalin, Germany moved against the Soviet Union via Ukraine by June 1941. After murdering nearly 34,000 Jews in Kiev in Ukraine, German troops set about invading the Soviet Union following a two-year period during which the Soviet Union, on the one hand, and Germany under the Nazis, on the other, had been aggressively attacking other countries in Europe but not each other. In addition to the purely political significance of Germany's invasion of the Soviet Union, it also had racist significance. Some Germans were unhappy about long-standing migratory patterns whereby enclaves of peoples of Germanic and Slavic backgrounds had come to live in close proximity to each other, with some even falling under the governance of Slavs. In the clash between pan-Slavism and pan-Germanism that was unfolding, the Nazis believed that the Germans, as representatives of an "Aryan" master race, were superior to the Slavs. Germany made several attacks on the Soviet Union in mid-1941.

In late 1941 and early 1942, extermination camps were set up at Chelmno, Treblinka, Sobibor, and Belzec. Majdanek and Auschwitz, originally built as concentration camps, were enlarged to take on extermination functions. While Auschwitz and various of its sub-camps continued to function as a center for forced labor, Birkenau (sometimes referred to as Auschwitz II) primarily existed to murder masses of its inmates. The battle at Stalingrad (now Volgograd) that began in August of 1942 caused destruction and resulted in the loss of so many lives that it moved the war toward a turning point. From this time, large numbers of Soviet prisoners of war were sent to Nazi concentration camps.

Around this same time, the Nazis started deportations from the Warsaw Ghetto to existing concentration camps and established the new Treblinka camp. Working essentially as slaves both for government-owned and private concerns, numerous prisoners in Nazi camps provided much forced labor that was vital in manufacturing armaments and other goods that supported Germany's war machine. At the same time, the atrocities and mass murder continued. In addition to invading Romania in the same year, the Nazis also invaded France, Belgium, Luxembourg, and the Netherlands. Although the invasion of the Netherlands in May of 1940 came as a surprise to the Dutch, racism had diffused so widely in Europe before this time that people of color working at Amsterdam's Negro Kit Cat Club as entertainers already had been fired in 1937.

Already by 1940 the distinction between Nazi concentration camps and labor camps was becoming blurred, as hard labor was also performed in the concentration camps. These developments helped to bring Winston Churchill to power as prime minister in Britain, who was less given to appeasing Germany than Chamberlain, his predecessor. In France, however, these developments also helped to bring to power Prime Minister Marshal Pétain, who was sympathetic to the Nazis. With the fall of Paris to Germany in 1940, France was decidedly less ambivalent than Great Britain about the use of African troops. Although Germany installed in parts of France a puppet Vichy regime, so-called Free France recruited 130,000 troops from *AOF* or French West Africa alone.

As for Gaston Monnerville, the brilliant attorney originally from French Guyana who had achieved prominence in *l'affaire Galmot* in 1931, he had already surprised many people of European as well as of African descent when he agreed to serve as French Secretary of State for colonies in the third and fourth cabinets of Camille Chautemps in 1937 and 1938. A real French patriot, Monnerville also served in the French Chamber of Deputies from 1932 to 1946, during five years of which he also remained the mayor of Cayenne, the Guyanese capital. Although Monnerville at age 40 was too old to be mobilized when World War II erupted, he managed with the assistance of a few other deputies to have a special law passed by which he was able to serve in the French navy, at least for a year until the formation of the Pétain regime that was sympathetic to the Nazis. Even when Gaston Monnerville could no longer serve in the navy, he openly protested at Vichy against its early discriminatory measures directed against Jews, Arabs, and peoples of color, at considerable risk to his well being.

Reflecting the racism that penetrated rather deeply in France by 1940, the regime of Henri-Philippe Pétain agreed to the removal of a statue of "mulatto" General Thomas-Alexandre Dumas that had stood in Paris. This was done despite the fact that Dumas between 1786 and 1799 was one of the most important leaders in the French military as well as a strong Republican during and after the French Revolution (Gallaher 1997; Ribbe 2002). Hence, the Vichy regime signed an armistice with the Nazis on June 22, 1940, and when Adolf Hitler toured Paris the following day the statue was nowhere to be seen. Only as of 2008, in fact, did Paris in the face of an active campaign requesting the erection of a replica, commit to do so.

Alexis Carrel, surgeon and biologist who in 1912 had won the Nobel Prize for medicine, was an exponent of eugenics under France's Vichy regime. Carrel was actively involved in a program for establishing a "hereditary biological aristocracy" in 1941. In his view, a race was duty bound to reproduce its best elements, and he established the *Fondation française pour l'étude des problèmes humains*, which was intended to move the French population in this direction. Further complicating the situation for people of African heritage once Nazi Germany had invaded France, Germans still carried a great grudge against French colonials as a result of the "black shame" Germans felt in the wake of World War I. This grudge was stoked by perverted racist doctrines of the Nazis.

When in November 1942 the Nazis occupied southern France, France's Vichy regime promulgated racist laws for Algeria. Already in 1940 Georges Montandon, a well-known French anti-Semite, had founded the journal *L'Ethnie française* (or French Ethnicity) in collaboration with Georges Mauco. That Mauco had been involved in this project shows how problematic had been the association of French Prime Minister Léon Blum with him in the mid-1930s. Even while many people of African descent were shedding their blood on behalf of the liberation of Europe from Nazis and Fascists, Georges Mauco returned to the racist themes that had long occupied him. In a March 1942 article in

L'Ethnie française, Mauco argued that the most desirable immigrants for France were those of Europe's north, followed by Spaniards and Italians from the north of their respective countries, and then the Slavs. Moreover, he expressed selective hostility against open immigration or what he referred to as "*l'immigration imposée*." The four years of rule in France by the Vichy regime that began in 1940, coupled with racist thought such as found in *L'Ethnie française*, left many people of African descent with ties to France distrustful of continued French colonization.

Despite such displays of racism by some people in France, many French citizens and French subjects of African descent still worked hard to aid the liberation of France during World War II. Frantz Fanon, while only eighteen years of age, for example, left his native Martinique in 1943 and traveled to nearby British-controlled Dominica in order to join the Free French Forces loyal to General de Gaulle. After enlisting in the French army, Fanon eventually saw service in the Alsace region of eastern France. After being wounded in Colmar east of the Vosges Mountains in 1944, he would be decorated with a *Croix de Guerre*. Even after no longer being able to serve in the French Navy, Gaston Monnerville (*see* pages 213-214, 242) worked for the military arm of the Resistance or *Forces Françaises de l'Intérieur* (FFI), in which connection he operated under the alias of Saint-Just, in honor of a maternal uncle who had helped finance his education. Within the FFI, Monnerville eventually obtained the rank of commander.

Still another person of color in France who was very active in the French resistance at considerable risk to her life was Josephine Baker. In 1937, three years before Paris fell to the Nazis, Baker had renounced her American citizenship to become naturalized as French, by which time she also had converted to Judaism and was married to Jean Lyon, a Jewish industrialist. From 1939 when World War II erupted, Josephine Baker was active near the front lines, both working as an entertainer to motivate troops and working with the Red Cross in Belgium. In Belgium, she attended to the needs of numerous refugees, also helping many to escape as the Nazis were advancing. With the fall of Paris to the Nazis, she refused on principle to sing—unlike many other renown French singers of the period—in the occupied north of the country until its liberation came in 1944. During this period, she abandoned the area of France under the rule of the Vichy regime and for a while took up residence in *les Milandes*, a chateau in the unoccupied Dordogne area further south. Allowing herself to be recruited into the counter-intelligence arm of the French Resistance by Captain Jacques Abtey, Baker agreed to be associated with a nursing section of the French Red Cross as a cover for her new role as an undercover intelligence agent for those working secretly for the liberation of France.

On one occasion the Germans, suspicious of Baker, even searched her chateau for hidden arms. While she was not hoarding arms there and the Germans found nothing incriminating, in her chateau were hidden documents intended for General Charles de Gaulle. Shortly afterward this close call, she abandoned the comfort of this chateau and broke a contract to appear at the Opera of Marseille in order to leave France for northern Africa to continue her work in the cause of

French Liberation. This was done at considerable risk to her personal safety, with Captain Jacques Abtey traveling on a forged passport as Jacques Hebert, a member of her entourage. On the sheet music carried with her, information intended to assist the French resistance had been transcribed in invisible ink by Abtey (Onana 2006: 55, 57, 62-63, 66).

Baker's presence in northern Africa at this particular time was especially fortuitous for the forces of Free France because, as of 1941, Hitler had launched with marginal success a campaign to win the Arabs to his cause in large measure through the cooperation of Mohamed Amin al-Husseini, who was the Mufti of Palestine. Helping to attract al-Husseini to the Nazi cause at this time were at least three factors. First, al-Husseini distrusted the British who were the colonial overlords of Egypt as well as of Palestine as a result of a League of Nations Mandate. Second, the mufti was suspicious of the long-term intentions of new Jewish settlers who were increasingly seeking refuge in Palestine. Third, anti-Nazi Bolsheviks flaunted an ideological commitment to atheism. From the time of Baker's arrival in the African Maghreb early in 1941 until a peritonitis left her hospitalized for more than a year beginning in June of that year, she pursued a busy schedule of entertaining troops across the north of Africa and giving performances in such countries as Lebanon, Iraq, Iran, Switzerland, Portugal, and Spain at the request of the Resistance while continuing her secret espionage work, which with some frequency required her to travel behind enemy lines gathering and carrying intelligence information pinned on the inside of her brassiere or written in invisible ink on the pages her sheet music. Despite receiving no income during this time, Baker even used some of her own shrinking resources as well as funds raised from her performances to assist the Resistance (Onana 2006: 69, 74-76, 98, 108).

Still weak and recovering when forces of the American military first arrived in northern Africa in 1944, Josephine Baker arose from her bed to entertain them against the advice of her physicians. Many "whites" from the United States saw no contradiction between the racist and segregationist practices in the American military and the fact that those American forces had traveled overseas at least in part to oppose the racism of the Nazis. Baker, on the other hand, perceived this contradiction clearly, and with great pain. Baker remained firm in her campaigning that her performances for Allied troops be open to Arabs, "whites," "blacks," and so forth without regard to any so-called racial distinctions.

Even among the Allies, racism was seldom far beneath the surface during World War II. Although Britain had in 1942 established a so-called Advisory Committee on the Welfare of Colored People in the United Kingdom and a Colonial Labor Advisory Committee, the fact that Africa House of West African Students' Union (WASU) was still one of the few hostels in London open to "black" people suggests that the government's supposed concern about the welfare of people of color was shallow or disingenuous. So rigidly was the color bar still enforced in Britain that even the Colonial Office sometimes was forced to use WASU's Africa House as an accommodation for peoples of color who were munitions workers as well as others who were temporarily resident in Britain during the war (Adi 1998: 105; Freeman-Grenville 1973: 223). Even when the mass murder of Jews by gassing began at Auschwitz in 1942, the American forces committed to fight in Europe were limited mostly to Great Britain. By the time the United States began its air attacks in Europe in August of 1942, deportations from the Warsaw Ghetto to concentration camps were underway and the Treblinka extermination camp had opened.

Otmar Frieherr von Verschuer, the last director of the Kaiser Wilhelm Institute of Anthropology, Human Heredity, and Eugenics, beginning in 1942 also supervised some of the work of the notorious Josef Mengele, the "Angel of Death" of Auschwitz, when Mengele was still a doctoral candidate. While a candidate for a second doctorate degree under the supervision of Otmar Frieherr von Verschhuer, Megele regularly sent body parts from victims who had perished at the Auschwitz-Birkenau complex to the Kaiser Wilhelm Institute of Anthropology, Human Heredity, and Eugenics. During the same period, Mengele also drew on methods developed at the institute to justify Nazi racist ideology and mass murder, including his own biomedical criminality. The Nazis greatly increased their mass murder of people belonging to so-called inferior races in 1942 with a particular focus on the gassing of Jews at Auschwitz.

Somewhat in contrast, when Gdańsk was again incorporated into Germany in 1939, N'Gambi ul Kuo, who was originally from Cameroon and whose wife was Prussian, continued to live without great difficulty in Gdańsk. Even under the Nazi rule in Germany, N'Gambi ul Kuo continued to serve as a member of the local Citizen's Army there. By 1943, the same year that Himmler ordered the liquidation of all Jewish Ghettos in Poland, however, the situation for the elderly father of African-Prussian "mulattoes" Doris Reiprich and Erika N'Gambi had deteriorated so drastically that he requested from German authorities the return of his German passport so that he could return to his native Cameroon. They responded that this would only be possible if he would promise to serve there as a foreign agent for Germany's Nazi government. N'Gambi ul Kuo asked government officials how they could expect such service of him when they despised his color. Faced with this dilemma, he suffered a heart attack on a Berlin street shortly afterwards and died a few days later. Even at this time, the Nazis were scheming to regain control of the African colonies that Germany had lost in 1919 so that the Nuremberg laws used in Europe could be adapted to colonial conditions in Africa (Coquery-Vidrovitch 2007: 66, 69-70; Reiprich and N'Gambi 1992: 56-76).

Berlin-born Theodor Michael Wonja, the "mulatto" son of circus performers in Germany who was orphaned as a young child, was at age 18 sent to a Nazi work camp near the city of his birth and made to work 72 hours a week in a factory where armaments were manufactured. It was not until well after the war in June 1946 that Soviet forces liberated him. After marrying a German woman in 1947, Wonja eventually became well known as a Shakesperian actor (Onana 2006: 27-28; Coquery-Vidrovitch 2007: 162-163). Fasia Jansen, of mixed Liberian and German heritage, was forced to leave her dance school in Germany in 1942 when she was only 14 years of age. After this time, she was pressed into hard labor as a kitchen helper at Neuengamme concentration camp, which the SS had established as a subcamp of Sachsenhausen in 1938. Although not interned in the camp herself, she often worked next to camp internees from Ukraine. Forced along with others in the kitchens where she worked to serve buckets of meager food to Jews and others who were incarcerated in the suburb of Hamburg where this camp was located, she was traumatized by numerous atrocities that she witnessed. Only through a mix-up that confused Libya with Liberia did she manage to escape being sterilized. Although people of appreciable African descent were not systematically sent to extermination camps by the Nazis, some were, including certain inmates at the Ravensbrück camp for females.

One such person was Erika N'Gando, a woman originally from the former Germany colony of Cameroon who was hardly 35 years of age at the time of her incarceration. Forced to perform hard labor, N'Gando complained almost constantly about the frigid conditions to which she was habitually exposed. Among other women of appreciable African descent who were also at Ravensbrück were Bolau J., Johanna Peters, and at least another who was a Jehovah's Witness (Lusane 2003: 157; Coquery-Vidrovitch 2007: 163-165).

After being arrested at Brno, Czechoslovakia in 1939, the jazz trumpeter Eric Vogel was made to organize a jazz school in the Jewish ghetto of that city. At Saint-Denis in France was an internment camp of some two thousands prisoners of whom about fifty were "black," including the African-American jazz trumpeter Arthur Briggs. From the time of Briggs's arrest in Paris in 1940, he was at this camp until it was liberated in 1944. The jazz pianists John Welch, Charlie Lewis, and Freddy Johnson, also African-Americans, were arrested and interned by the Germans during the war as was the female jazz pianist and trumpet player Valaida Snow. One African-American musician who was arrested in Paris and subsequently interned became the conductor of a symphony orchestra of some fifty "white" internees in the subcamp of the Dachau concentration camp at Kassel. Inmates there were forced to work in 12-hour shifts for the company of Henschel and Son after it turned from its major work of making transportation equipment to manufacturing Nazi tanks and other armaments (Lusane 2003: 165-168; Coquery-Vidrovitch 2007: 125-127).

Carlos Grevkey, originally from the Spanish colony of Fernão do Pó (now Equatorial Guinea) off the coast of western Africa lived with his family in Barcelona. As his family had Republican sympathies during the Spanish Civil War, they moved from Barcelona to France as did many other Spaniards around the time that the Spanish Republicans were defeated in 1939. When the Nazis invaded France the following year, Grevkey was arrested and sent to Mauthausen, where for a while he was made to work as a groom for the SS commander of the camp who dressed him up ridiculously as a footman (Akpo 1997). Tito Romalio, a Brazilian-born actor, was liberated by the Soviets from a Nazi camp in Lithuania in July of 1940 (Blakely 1986: 155).

A Haitian citizen named Jean Nicolas was incarcerated in Buchenwald and later in the Dora-Mittelbau camp. Before arriving in Europe, Nicolas had worked as a nurse in a hospital located in Fort-de-France on the French-controlled island of Martinique. When he was captured by the Nazis, he first pretended to be an African-American aviator named John Nicolas. When this ploy no longer worked, he used his ability to learn languages fast along with his medical knowledge and claimed for a while to be a physician. Working as a nurse as well as a translator of several languages while incarcerated, he saved many lives. By the time he was liberated from Nazi detention in 1945, he was so terribly ill with tuberculosis that he died soon afterward, in fact, on September 4 in Saint-Antoine Hospital in Paris (Akpo 1927).

Josef Johan Cosmo Nassy, a "mulatto" artist born in Dutch Guiana (now Surinam), was descended from Jewish stock on his father's side. While the holder of an American passport, he had moved from Brooklyn, New York, to live in Europe in 1929, first spending several years working as an electrical engineer in England, France, and Belgium before beginning in 1934 to study painting at an art academy in Brussels. Marrying a Belgian woman soon after beginning his studies at this academy, he was still living in Belgium when the Nazis occupied the country in May 1940. Eventually arrested by the Germans in 1942, Nassy was detained for seven months in Belgium's Beverloo transit camp before being transferred to Germany. He was made to spend the rest of the war imprisoned between the Laufen internment camp and in the subcamp of Tittmoning, both located in Upper Bavaria along Germany's border with Austria (Lusane 2003: 161-164; Onana 2006: 43; Coquery-Vidrovitch 2007: 154-155).

Timého Garan Kouyaté, of what is now the country of Mali, had in 1927 founded in Paris the *Ligue de la Défense de la Race Nègre* in the hope of effecting "the political, economic, moral, and intellectual emancipation" of what he referred to as "la race nègre," or the Negro race. The Nazis captured and executed him in 1942. Jean Johny Voste, a Belgian citizen partially of Congolese heritage, had lived in the Netherlands as well as Belgium before the war. Eventually captured by the Nazis after his attempt to sabotage a railway near Antwerp in 1942, he was imprisoned in Dachau. Here, unlike the nearby prisons where Nassy was interned, the Germans made no attempt to follow the Geneva Conventions and Dachau prisoners suffered much worse treatment. Although very emaciated by the time Dachau was liberated by Americans on April 29, 1945, Voste survived (Lusane 2003: 160-161; Coquery-Vidrovitch 2007: 165).

Bayume Mohamed Hussein, originally from Tanganyika (now Tanzania) which until the end of World War I had been a German colony, was arrested by the Nazis in August 1941 on the charge of racial defilement, perhaps because his wife was Czech or perhaps because he also had fathered by his German mistress a child whose birth he considered his duty to declare. Despite the fact that his father had fought for Germany in World War I, that Hussein had taught Swahili at the University of Berlin before Hitler became Germany's chancellor, and that he had later acted in some propaganda films for the Nazis, he was considered a trouble-maker and sent to the Sachsenhausen concentration camp near Berlin. At the hand of his captors, Hussein's life ended there in November 1944 (Lusane 2003: 159-160).

Among some ten or so other "blacks" documented as interned in the Sachsenhausen concentration camp was an African-American named Robert Demys. Another was Anton de Kom, a militant anticolonialist originally from the Dutch colony of Surinam in South America, who was arrested in August 1944. After being first deported to the Vugt concentration camp in the Netherlands, he was next sent sent to Oranienburg-Sachsenhausen. Finally deported to the Neuengamme camp on the outskirts of Hamburg, Anton de Kom died there in April of 1945.

Racist brutalities and atrocities had been allowed to traumatize and dehumanize most of Europe and much of the larger world well before military forces of the United States made their D-Day landings into France on June 6, 1944. As by the end of the year it had become increasingly likely that Germany faced imminent defeat, the Nazis closed down most of the camps they operated outside of Germany and Austria, compelling many of the inmates from those camps to undertake death marches to camps located in the Reich, marches that for many Jews and Poles began on January 19, 1945. As Soviet forces advanced deeply into Germany, the camps of Belsen, Dachau, Buchenwald and Mauthausen, Sachsenhausen, and Ravenbruck became new destinations for thousands of prisoners evacuated from other camps.

Dominique Mendy, who in 1909 had been born in Senegal, was a photojournalist for the French periodicals *Sud-Ouest* and *France-Soir* when the Nazis invaded France in 1940. Shortly thereafter, he began to work for the Resistance. Among his responsibilities were guiding aviators and parachutists to Bordeaux and helping to transport war material across the Channel between England and France. Arrested on April 21, 1944, Mendy was carried to the Draney transit camp where he was badly tortured, which included being burned by cigarettes and other items all over various parts of his body and having his left hand so badly crushed that he could never use it again. He was eventually deported to the Neuengamme camp in Germany. Remaining at Neuengamme for a year and a half, Mendy was separated from other prisoners taken from France while the Nazi torture of him continued.

Dominique Mendy was hardly the sole person of color being held at Neuengamme because of his patriotic service for the cause of French Liberation. Among others there around the same time were John William, Isidore Alpha, Paul Pintard, Ambroise Bilan, and Sidi Camara. While John Williams had been born in western Africa with the name of Ernest Armand Huss to an Ivorian mother and a French father from Alsace, Alpha, Pintard, and Bilan had been born in French colonies located in the Caribbean (Lusane 2003: 164-165). Like Dominique Mendy, Sidi Camara was originally from Senegal. Just like the other inmates incarcerated in Neuengamme, all these inmates of color were also stamped with identification numbers. Only a few days before Neuengamme was liberated, Sidi Camara suffered the misfortune of being transferred to the Bergen-Belsen concentration camp and it was there that he died and was hurriedly buried in ditch alongside heaps of others (Herzberger-Fofana 2005). Although Dominique Mendy had been condemned to death at Neuengamme, he was saved by the Danish Red Cross before the sentence was carried out. Taken by boat to Copenhagen, he eventually made his way back to Senegal by way of Paris.

More than a few African-American soldiers fell into the hands of the Nazis, some being summarily murdered after capture and more than a few being very badly mistreated. Apparently a "black" Tuskeegee Airman, one such person was

Lieutenant Darwin Nichols, a pilot incarcerated in a Nazi prison at Butzbach in 1944. In December of the same year, eleven African-American servicemen were executed near the city of Wereth, Belgium after having been first badly mutilated. In still another case, an *SS* physician working out of the municipal hospital in Salzburg, Austria instead of rendering assistance to six African-American servicemen from an airplane that had crashed, decided to execute them instead.

In the spring of 1945, at least two "blacks" (one a South African and one an African-American) were murdered by the SS in the German prison camp known as Moosburg. In May and in December, other executions of "black" servicemen took place in Hungary, sometimes by firearms and sometimes by hanging. Twenty or so other captured African-American servicemen were executed by Nazis near Merzig in September of 1944 and some others three months later in December at the Muehlberg camp. A Pole deported from the Gross-Rosen camp testified having witnessed the murder of a number of "blacks" there (Coquery-Vidrovitch 2007: 151). Lionel Romney, an African-American sailor captured by Italians in June 1940 after his ship the *SS Makis* sank, was turned over to German Nazis who imprisoned him at Mauthausen, mostly a slave labor camp, near the Austrian city of Lintz (Lusane 2003: 158).

Numerous captured "black" soldiers fighting for Britain, and especially for France, were also captured by the Nazis. After working long shifts as virtual slaves or forced laborers, they were sometimes made to dance for the entertainment of their captors. Large numbers of service personnel from France's African colonies were even massacred without even being imprisoned. One such contingent consisted of men captured by the Nazis near the French city of Lyon in June 1940 (Onana 2006: 43-44). That the world knows so little about World War II racist atrocities aimed especially at people of African descent in Europe perhaps reflects a continuing lesser degree of general concern with the suffering of people of color than typically is countenanced. Germans sometimes committed horrendous abuses that were specifically aimed at soldiers of African descent within French military forces in an effort to retaliate for the humiliating "black shame" many Germans felt because of the presence on German soil of *tirailleurs sénégalais* following World War I.

Massacres of colonial troops captured by the Nazis in France included, for example, around 100 or so lined up and shot at Erquinvillers in June of 1940 and another 500 near Chartres during the same month. Approximately two hundred others were massacred at close range by machine gun in the little village of Chasselay-Montluzin around the same time and afterward their bodies were crushed under tanks. When captured, some "black" victims of the racist madness were beaten mercilessly, seemingly at random, with some even having their eyes gorged out and their ears cut off. In August of 1944 about a hundred Senegalese captives near the French city of Tours were made to dig their own graves before being executed by the SS. Apart from soldiers of African descent massacred or interned in France in prison camps that the Germans called *Frontstalags*, several thousand "black" prisoners of war were also sent from France to Germany, where they were mistreated, humiliated, badly fed, and often used as forced laborers.

According to Lusane (2003: 158), the Swedish ship *SS Gripsholm* arrived in the port of New York in March 1944 with thirteen African-Americans aboard who had been released from either internment or concentration camps, including one of whom was female. One of the twelve males on this ship was George Welch, who had left the United States in 1901 "to see the world" and had remained abroad for over four decades. After being arrested in Brussels, he had been imprisoned in the Tittmoning concentration camp.

Although a number of excellent works have focused particular attention on the treatment of at least some three thousand or so soldiers of African descent captured by the Germans in France in 1940 (e.g., Scheck 2005, Scheck 2006, Friedman 1990, Kesting 1998a, Kesting 1998b, Coquery-Vidrovitch 2007, and Lusane 2003), the following extract from an account of one "black" officer whose unit was captured is not atypical. After many of his comrades were massacred at close range and disarmed, he and the other survivors were made to march in segregated order as follows: English, French, Arabs, and blacks. Averaging 60 to 70 kilometers a day despite being kept largely hungry and thirsty, they were forced to keep up with cyclists who continually harassed and threatened them as they marched northward out of France, across parts of Belgium and Holland, toward Germany.

Although the people through whose villages and towns they passed were warned against offering them any food or drink, some villagers placed water along the route at great risk to themselves. On occasion, these captives were also tortured by being placed close to a fountain where those who attempted to assuage their thirst would be shot to death in the spirit of amusement for their guards. Also in the spirit of amusement, the guards on one day chose a certain captive of color named Mamadou N'Diaye for the purpose of bleaching him with soap and scalding water, which naturally left him so badly injured that he could not continue. Although many died or were simply murdered along the way, some survived to reach to the Dalume camp in Germany, where Nazis continued to segregate them, with those deemed to be Arab or "black" incarcerated on one side and those deemed to be "white" on the other (Onana 2006: 30-37).

When the liberation of France finally began in 1944, no provision was made to honorably receive France's colonial soldiers of color who had suffered so much under the Nazis. Often, they had been segregated from other prisoners by the Nazis and especially badly treated. While an estimated 55- to 65,000 soldiers from Africa alone died fighting for France during the war or subsequently lost their lives at the hands of the Nazis (Lusane 2003: 150), many of those who survived received no official acknowledgement of France's gratitude. In some cases, they were even shipped off to Africa without receiving pay of any kind. When after the war some 35 Senegalese veterans treated in this way protested at the Thiaroye camp on the outskirts of Dakar in the French colony of Senegal, some of them were simply gunned down (Coquery-Vidrovitch 2007: 144-145, 147). That racist brutalities, including sterilizations, forced labor, malnutrition, exposures to cold, torture, medical experimentations, humiliations, and murder took place in Europe in the 1930s and 1940s victimized many people of African descent is beyond question. Even Léopold Sedar Senghor (one of the founders of the *Négritude* movement in the mid-1930s while a student in Paris and the future first president of Senegal from 1960), was captured during the war in June 1940 while he was a colonial soldier defending a bridge in La Charité-sur-Loire, France, and subsequently incarcerated in seven different Nazi camps (Lusane 2003: 172-174).

In some ways, the conflagration that was to become World War II was much more than a global conflict among numerous peoples with conflicting nationalist and geopolitical agendas, it was also the result of racism, which that had been running amok in the world for a long time, undermining the very basis of what passed for civilization. Between the beginning of the Enlightenment and the end of the 19th century, numerous people claiming European descent had gradually come to believe that humanity was (or should be) divided into non-overlapping races some of which they thought of as innately superior to others. By the turn of the 20th century in many Western countries, *Rassenkunde*—or so-called race science, based in reality on a combination of pseudo-scientific racism and racist mysticism, had emerged with its emphasis on the importance of good blood lines so-called racial purity and the embracing of eugenics. Under the influence of race science, many people identifying as Europeans came to believe that some branches of humanity were simply more "fit" to survive than others.

With the global success of European imperialism as well as so-called race science, many people of European heritage came to believe that they were endowed with superior abilities to rule over others. Additionally, race science played a role in the eventual romanticizing of certain constellations of physical and cultural traits as ideal superior for people in general. Along with these other scientifically flawed ways of thinking about human variation and diversity, many Europeans came to believe that in order to protect themselves from bogus phenomena such as racial disease, racial degeneracy, racial taint, and racial defilement, they were duty-bound to separate themselves from people whom they imagined to be threats to their superior racial standing (Mosse 1985: 94-112; MacMaster 2001: 1, 31).

World War I had ended without confronting any of the fundamental flaws inherent such race fantasies, the 1920s and '30s witnessed a dramatic increase in racist intolerance in some quarters of the Western world that was often coupled with a belief in the existence of an imagined Aryan, Germanic, or Nordic super race whose purity was especially in need of protection. Although such racial fantasies had no basis in real science, they functioned well as "folk" myths capable of contributing to extreme expressions of nationalistic romanticism that could be extremely lethal when craftily manipulated.

There existed considerable ambivalence in most European countries toward racism during the period from the 1920s into the '40s regardless of whether they were governed by Communists or not. Even a decidedly racist Nazi Germany still allowed Africans to participate in German propaganda films. During this period, it was not unusual for "white" film-makers to make propaganda films in an attempt to influence people of African descent into thinking of particular countries as their allies or protectors irrespective of the degree to which the countries so portrayed genuinely cared about the oppressed masses targeted. In one such Soviet film titled "Circus" that was produced in the 1930s a "white" female acrobat from the United States falls in love with a handsome Russian male while performing in Moscow. Objecting to this affair, her manager threatens to reveal to her Russian lover the secret that she has mothered a baby who is in part of African-American descent. Eventually the manager moves beyond threat, and in a vindictive, punitive, and racist spirit produces the child in front of a circus audience in a calculated move intended definitively to end the love affair to which he objects. To his great disappointment and surprise, however, the Soviet audience depicted as especially humane, in total acceptance of the situation, responds by tenderly passing the toddler among themselves while singing him a Russian lullaby. While a fictional contrast between Communism and Capitalism in association with racism was central in "Circus," a nonfictional or real life contrast was to become apparent during the Spanish Civil War of the same period.

Another propaganda undertaking in the Soviet Union that was intended to attract partisans to its side was sponsored by Comintern in 1932. It involved recruiting twenty essentially middle-class non-Communist African-American college graduates and one working-class "white" American (who was a Communist) to perform as actors in a film extolling the urgency of union organizing in the Southern United States. Although the rather unrealistic script for this proposed propaganda film had already been written. Still, engaged as a writing consultant of this project was the same Langston Hughes who had sometimes worked as a dishwasher in the Montmartre area of Paris to sustain himself in 1925 was by this time quite famous as a poet with some left-of-center sympathies. While waiting for filming to begin in Odessa, this group of Americans was settled in one of the finest hotels in Moscow. As most members of this group were simply seeking a paid adventure including summer travel and an undemanding schedule, they had ample time to do some sightseeing and to practice singing various traditional African-American songs that they were told would be used in the film.

For reasons that remain unclear, the filming on this project never began. Three African-American members of the group opted to remain in Moscow, and the others accepted fares provided by the Soviet Union to return home. While not a great deal is known about those who remained or about the group that returned home through western Europe, those who opted to travel back to the United States via Soviet Asia had a chance encounter in Tashkent, Uzbekistan with Bernard Powers, an engineering graduate of Howard University. Powers told them of a group of more than a dozen other African-American agricultural experts from Alabama's Tuskegee Institute who were working on a nearby experimental farm, which underscores that the value the Soviet Union cultivated in its relationships with people of African ancestry often had as much to do with needed development assistance as with political and propaganda matters (Blakely 1986: 92-101).

A number of propaganda films produced in the West in the 1930s and 1940s portrayed "saintly" European physicians working selflessly in opposition to forces portrayed as negative to save the lives of people of African descent. One such film made in France in 1934 *Itto*, was likely inspired by missionary doctors such as Albert Schweitzer, who spent many years between 1913 and the 1960s working from a clinic in Lambaréné, Gabon—except when he was interned in France during World War I because he was a German. Germany also had a practice of allowing people of African descent to appear in films that reinforced whatever happened to be the current policy objectives of the government in power toward Africa and peoples of African descent. Interestingly, this German practice was continued under the Nazis. Some of the people employed in this way during World War II even included African-American prisoners of war. Of some 4,000 such prisoners sent to Luckenwalde in 1940, 300 of them were forced to act as extras in *Germanin – Die Geschichte einer kolonialen Tat* in 1943, an Axis co-production that was directed by Max W. Kimmich, the brother-in-law of Joseph Goebbels, who from 1933 through 1945 was the Reich Minister of Public Enlightenment and Propaganda under the Nazis. Other such African-American prisoners also appeared in *Quax in Afrika*, another film made in the same year. Among German "mulattoes" occasionally employed in this way were the African-Prussian sisters Doris Reiprich and Erika N'Gambi.

In 1942 and '43 when Kmmich directed *Germanin*, Germany still hoped to regain control of the colonies in Africa that it had lost as a result of its defeat in World War I. In keeping with this hope, the film was about a heroic doctor working in former German East Africa to find a cure for sleeping sickness when British officers destroy his medical station (MacMaster 2001: 138-139). Such undertakings of the past awaken our suspicions to the possibility that even some reports on genuine crises involving health, food, and welfare in Africa and elsewhere nowadays may be products of mass media and governments working collaboratively on propaganda as much as objective reports of selfless humanitarianism.

Ultra-nationalism coupled with racism and policies of aggression were destined to eventually bring Europe almost to its knees as social orders crumbled, as obsessions associated with race replaced reason, and as multitudes of innocents found mere survival first challenging and eventually impossible. Perhaps it was in part to maintain their sanity in the midst of this hellish reality that Aimé Césaire, also a founder of the *Négritude* movement, along with his wife Suzanne Césaire, launched a new journal in France in 1941 called *Tropiques*. It included contributions that ranged from poetry and politics to essays on history and anthropology—whatever the Césaires considered relevant to "black" people of African ancestry, irrespective of their citizenship. Perhaps by mere coincidence, the last issue of *Tropique* was published in 1945, the same year that the Allied forces in World War II proclaimed themselves victorious.

By the time World War II ended, unfortunately there existed no evidence that the world was any less racist, any less stratified, or any less tolerant of imperial exploitation than before it began. In some ways the war had changed the world a great deal by bringing a much belated halt to an especially large-scale spasm in genocide. Also, some of the boundaries between various powers were redrawn and there was greater contact among the world's peoples and even more rhetoric about democracy, social justice, and self-determination. In other respects, however, the world remained much the same, with Eurocentric racism still a suffocating given to which all the world's peoples were expected to adapt.

Although Europeans had made lavish use of manpower and resources from Asia, Africa, and the Caribbean during the war in order to settle scores among themselves, the world seemed no more prepared to turn away from racism after the guns fell silent than it had been during the heat of battle. As had happened before, Europeans during wartime had tended to somewhat warmly receive large numbers of "others" in their midst and to utilize their services but later receive them with more reserve, or even with hostility, when their services were no longer required. World War II had hardly ended when wartime alliances and interdependencies gave way to many realignments and much racist thinking reminiscent of the past.

As Allied troops began occupying Hamburg, Hans-Jürgen Massaquoi, the son of a Liberian father and German mother who had been reared in Germany mostly during its rule by Nazis, searched for some way to survive and to support Bertha Baetz, his German mother. In this regard, he used his complexion, which was darker than usual in Germany, to frequent certain clubs that were open to the Allied forces but closed to his compatriots. Beginning around 1944, this enabled him to use talents that he had developed largely in private as a culturally rebellious "swingboy" during the Nazi era to perform as a jazz musician in these clubs frequented by foreign soldiers and sailors during Hamburg's postwar occupation. In order to supplement this club work, Massaquoi also gained money by smuggling cigarettes. This became his way of life until 1948, when he was able to leave Germany for Liberia in hopes of establishing a relationship with his father, though his father had made no effort to provide any support for Massaquoi and his mother after leaving Germany in 1929.

During the war, Josephine Baker had given up earning a livelihood and undertook numerous risks as a part of the French Resistance for which she earned not a franc. Between 1943 and 1946, she had been honored with the medals in the form of a Medal of Free France with a rosette and a *Croix de Lorraine*, symbol of the Resistance. She also received a medal of the War of 1939–45. France's liberation thrilled few more than Baker, who sang her way across her adopted country and beyond until she reached the infamous camp at Buchenwald. Still, the way she was treated after the war when nominated for the Legion of Honor, the highest distinction that France could offer her, was odd.

A commission unanimously rejected the nomination for this French heroine in 1947, claiming that she was unworthy. When Baker was nominated for this honor a second time in January 1949, members of the same military in which she had served even opened a criminal investigation as well as an investigation of her morality and honor in an effort to justify a second rejection. Despite the fact that the forces of Free France had no such concerns when beginning in 1944 Baker was promoted to the rank of sub-lieutenant in the Air Force, a second rejection was issued on March 8, 1949 by the French Secretary of State of the Air Force. After new appeals for a review of this odd situation and the submission of further extensive documentation and testimony from additional military officials who had served alongside Baker, Jacques Chaban-Delmas, in his role as Minister of National Defense and of the Armed Forces only then, in 1957, finally give his approval to the nomination of Baker as a Chevalier of the Legion of Honor (Onana 2006: 95-110).

On August 18, 1961, slightly less than fourteen years before her death and State funeral at La Madelaine in Paris, Josephine Baker actually received from the hands of General Vain the insignia of the Legion of Honor along with a Croix de Guerre complete with a bronze palm. He did this with the traditional phrase, "In the name of the President of the Republic and by virtue of the powers conferred upon me, I pronounce you Chevalier of the Legion of Honor" (Baker and Bouillon 1988: 233). Although Dominique Mendy, originally from Senegal, had also been decorated as a Chevalier in the Legion of Honor for his outstanding service in the Resistance in 1982, the length of time that it took for Baker's service to France during wartime to be recognized in this way suggests that elitism, perhaps tinged with racism and sexism, were in play. Considering that France was badly in need of American reconstruction assistance after the war, it is even possible that there was influence from the United States not to grant Baker this honor. J. Edgar Hoover of the F.B.I. and certain other highly-placed Americans were very hostile toward Baker, in part because she had renounced her American citizenship and in part because of her uncompromising stance in opposing racism (Onana 2006: 117-126, 151-155).

World War II had left European governments that were in possession of large empires as well as many people from their overseas colonies wondering what challenges colonialism would, or should, face in the wake of the war. As Jomo Kenyatta of Kenya had remained in Europe from 1931 through World War II, he had an opportunity to witness first-hand European racism at its worst. Virtually at the end of his fifteen-year European stay, Kenyatta assisted W. E. B. Du Bois in organizing a Fifth Pan-African Congress. Convened in Manchester in 1945, in addition to Du Bois and Kenyatta, prominent attendees at this congress included among others Awolowo of western Nigeria, Nkrumah of Gold Coast (now Ghana), Garba-Jahumpa of Gambia, Hastings Banda of Nyasaland (now Malawi), Wallace Johnson of Sierra Leone, George Padmore, and Amy Ashwood Garvey, the first wife of Marcus Garvey (Ali 1998: 127).

In the aftermath of World War II, Kenyatta as well as others could easily observe that many Europeans longed once again for a world that would be fundamentally divided according to what Du Bois at the dawn of the 20th century referred to as "the color-line." Contributing to this "problem," many peoples of European backgrounds longed to see Europeans retain control of their widely scattered colonies where governance was based in large measure on assumptions of European superiority and *noblesse oblige*. In some cases, imperial powers argued that it was necessary to maintain the colonial systems in order to prevent "natives" from becoming the innocent prey of Communists. After Kenyatta's departure from Britain 1946, he did not return to Europe until 1962, at which time he was involved in negotiating the terms of Kenya's independence from Britain.

Increasingly arrayed in opposition to colonial continuity and restoration were multitudes of colonized people, living mostly outside of Europe, who in some greater or lesser degree perceived themselves to be in bondage and hoped for a new order. World War II had left the world divided between a Communist bloc and an opposing anti-Communist bloc that shrewdly described itself as "democratic" although certain of its members (e.g., the dictatorships in Portugal and Spain and the apartheid regime ruling over South Africa and South-West Africa) obviously were not.

As after the war the United States and the Soviet Union each gathered a bloc of allies (or satellite nations) about itself, Bernard Baruch, a close adviser to U.S. President Harry Truman, coined the term "Cold War" in 1947. In this same year, U.S. Secretary of State George C. Marshall, while speaking at Harvard University, outlined what would come to be known as the Marshall Plan. Neither the Marshall Plan, which provided American funds to rebuild certain European nations—including Turkey—that the United States government deemed friendly or wished to court as allies, nor COMECON (the Soviet rebuttal to it) was meant to change the global stratification system that had prevailed before the war. Both blocs showed themselves ready to use propaganda, manipulation, economic leverage, and force to attract new allies and mercilessly punish perceived enemies. This geopolitical dichotomization of the world by two super powers both of whom were ruled by people most of whom identified themselves as of European descent greatly complicated struggles by people of African descent battling against racism and imperialism in the wake of World War II. Both Washington and Moscow were inclined to be suspicious of any large-scale campaign for political and social change that they could not control and to demonize its leadership.

In concluding this chapter, some words enunciated by Frantz Fanon in *Black Skin, White Masks*, his first major publication, which originally appeared in French in 1952, remind us how much the period under discussion was about something more transcendent than its particulars. "Every time a man has contributed to the victory of the dignity of the spirit, every time a man has said no to an attempt to subjugate his fellows, I have felt solidarity with his act" (Fanon 1967: 226). Despite the fact that in April of 1945 Mussolini was hanged and Hitler committed suicide, the racism with which they came to be associated as well as the eugenic notion that some peoples are more "fit" to survive than others continue to thrive in many people's worldview. As so-called race science came eventually to be conflated with Aryan and Nordic idealization, it victimized people living in Europe as well as people living elsewhere. We still live with the fallout of these developments, fallout that has diffused quite widely in the world.

A battle against allowing science to be hijacked by either racists or subverted by politicians as earlier occurred with so-called race science must continually be waged. Eugenics reached frenzied heights in Nazi Germany, to be certain, but the pseudo-scientific racism underlying it neither began nor ended with the Nazis. Although in Europe itself the results of the holocaust of the late 1930s and early 1940s had been particularly horrific, hardly had World War II ended before neo-Nazism sprang forth alongside numerous other equally vile manifestations of racism. It is a given of such hate that particular victims may change from one situation to another. Wherever such notions find harbor that some people are innately superior to others, that some people are racially pure, that some people are born to rule over others, that some people are due special rights because they are "chosen," that some people are members of a master race or are more "fit" to survive than others, a danger lurks. It would be especially tragic should we allow such thinking to become the basis of new perversity and rampage because we fail to confront our deeply flawed and unscientific perspectives regarding human diversity and variation.

Chapter Seven

Africa Inside, Africa Outside

Mid-1940s to Mid-1970s

The ways that people of African descent were received in Europe during the first three decades following World War II varied considerably from country to country and area to area. Variables included the need for their labor at various times, their exact places of origin, the complexions of their skin, and their social statuses. Additional factors included the environment of colonial entanglements, prevailing attitudes toward citizenship and nationality, and the recent histories of the various countries in connection with racism and racio-ethnic discrimination. Global politics would also play a major role.

A background global conflict between supporters and opponents of Communism also was in play and resurfaced with a vengeance in the wake of World War II. World War II had at most provided a brief diversion from this larger conflict, whose legacy went back at least to the 1920s. In 1922, for example, Josef Dzhugashvili, who took to calling himself Josef Stalin, became General Secretary of the Communist Party of the Soviet Union's Central Committee. Soon after, his relationship with Leon Bronstein, commonly known as Leon Trotsky, commander of the Red Army and heir apparent to Vladimir Lenin, deteriorated. In large measure this had to do with Stalin's heavy-handed and chauvinistic management of his merging Soviet republics into one federal state, the Union of Soviet Socialist Republics (USSR). Following the death of Vladimir Lenin two years later, a power struggle ensued between Stalin and Leon Trotsky. In 1927, Trotsky was expelled from the Communist Party as well as from the Soviet Union. This cleared the way for Stalin to emerge as *de facto* party leader and ruler of the Soviet Union.

Already in the 1930s Stalin had clearly demonstrated his willingness to use political repression and brutal persecution to purge the Soviet Union's Communist Party of undesirables and to persecute unaffiliated persons as well. In fact, his Great Purge involved the use of uncontrolled police surveillance to imprison and extinguish masses of people on the mere suspicion of disloyalty to any aspect of his dictatorial rule. After failing to conclude a Soviet and Franco-British mutual defense pact, Stalin in 1939 agreed to a German-Soviet Non-aggression Pact with Hitler that contained a secret annex providing for the division of Poland and the incorporation of some other neighboring parts of Europe under Stalin's control.

Four months after Germany's invasion of Poland on September 1, 1939, sparked the beginning of World War II, Stalin approved an order of execution for more than 25,700 Polish "nationalist educators and counterrevolutionary" activists in parts of the Ukraine and Belarus Republics, annexed from Poland. Although he eventually was forced during the course of the war to ally with France, the United Kingdom, and the United States against Germany and the other Axis powers, Stalin distrusted these Allies. Although World War II involved horrific killing not infrequently for purely racist reasons, still at the war's conclusion European and American governmental concerns with racism rather rapidly receded into the background as preexistent distrusts relating to Communism reemerged. Although the United States had suffered little damage during the war, it had a strong industrialized economy, and had earned superpower status through its unprecedented use of atomic bombs in Japan, the nation came away from the war more determined than ever to contain Communism. Stalin, on the other hand, was equally determined to build the Soviet Union into a superpower in its own right.

When postwar United States and the Soviet Union began competing for world dominance, both sides were often willing to overlook the ingrained racism of people of European descent toward peoples of African derivation except where it fit into their larger overarching objectives. While each side considered it more important for peoples of African descent to be mobilized and manipulated in the fight for and against Communism than for their own liberation from racism, the Soviet Union remained at least in Communist theory more concerned with the need to oppose racism and imperialism. As countries in western Europe and North America focused most of their attention on containing Communism, Belgium, the Netherlands, Luxembourg, France, and the United Kingdom on March 17, 1948, became signatories to the Treaty of Brussels. This action was a precursor to the 1949 North Atlantic Treaty Organization, or NATO, under the leadership of the United States.

In keeping with NATO's *raison d'être* to contain Communism, every person, organization, and movement was defined first and foremost on a scale that separated Communists and Communist sympathizers, from those committed to a struggle against Communism. On May 14, 1955, in response to the emergence of NATO, the Treaty of Friendship Co-operation and Mutual Assistance (more commonly known as the Warsaw Pact) came into being as the military nemesis to NATO. The pact eventually included as signatories all the states of central and eastern Europe with leaderships supportive of Communism except for Yugoslavia. Playing a major role in bringing the Warsaw pact into being was the integration of a "re-militarized" West Germany into NATO on May 9, 1955. This rigid division of the world made any fight against racism at most a side issue for many Europeans.

Many Europeans (and by extension many people claiming European ancestry scattered about the world) remained largely uncommitted to eradicating racism against non-Europeans, impacting victims of racist oppression broadly. Included among such victims were people belonging to a number of minority groups in Europe. The period from the winding down of World War II until 1973 was destined to be one when Europe would struggle with its Africa inside and its Africa outside, both in a state of flux. European concern with Africa-related issues attracted relatively little attention apart from any bearing these issues had on the grand confrontation between proponents and opponents of Communism.

The recent war in large measure had been a conflagration begun with competing nationalisms at its core and racism as its fuel, but in the post-war period many took to memorializing the conflict largely as a fight against anti-Semitism. Although Raphael Lemkin only coined the word "genocide" in 1944, there can be no doubt that the systematic and planned mass murder and extermination of Bosnian Orthodox Serbs and Bosnian Roma as well as Bosnian Jews between 1941 and 1945 amounted to genocide. Although, in terms of sheer numbers, Jews resident in Europe suffered the worst in the racist holocaust that unfolded in genocidal proportions during the World War II, racism has always been opportunistic and, despite the millions of innocent victims who died in World War II, including almost six million Jews, the numbers to some extent are secondary to the fact that racism continued to thrive almost unchecked.

This new and simplified interpretation of underlying racism during World War II sometimes enables us to overlook that its assaults on the human condition sometimes targeted Slavs, homosexuals, Roma, Africans, "blacks," the handicapped, and others as well as Jews. This myopic way of viewing the war has enabled racists to gain the upper hand through that ancient technique of divide and conquer, while those wishing to fight racism are preoccupied with the details of a battle even as a war to defeat racism remains to be won. Viewing World War II as anything other than a battle has permitted European racism, later filtered through new concerns associated with the Cold War, to continue diffusing largely unimpeded, despite numerous European governments banning negative racist stereotypic depictions of Jews as thick-lipped, hooked-nose people grasping for money as politically incorrect (MacMaster 2001: 173). To be certain, other manifestations of racism—including anti-Semitism—remain a daily occurrence.

Developments in some Nordic countries, the United Kingdom, France, the Netherlands, Germany, the Soviet Union, and Greece illustrate a larger and more complex reality that continued unfolding after the Allies declared victory and the battlefields were silent. It has been said that until we know our history, we shall be destined to relive it. That would include our most deadly flirtations with racism in peace and in war. Both Iceland and Norway had particularly long legacies of anti-Semitism that remained largely unchecked between the World Wars (Bergsson 2007) as well as European racism, whether overt or covert, against people of African descent.

In the late 1940s, Anne Brown from Baltimore, who had created the role of Bess in George Gershwin's *Porgy and Bess* over ten years before, married Norwegian Olympic ski-jumper Thorleif Schjelderuf and settled in Oslo, Norway. Although African-American, the fact that Anne Brown was largely "white" in appearance, a classically trained musician of some fame, and married to a Norwegian facilitated her assimilation into her adopted homeland. By a regional agreement signed in 1954, citizenship in one Nordic country guaranteed the right of free movement in the others. As a result, most immigrants in these countries through the 1970s tended to come from within northwestern Europe.

Until 1967 Norway did not experience any significant immigration from so-called non-Nordic countries and this continued into the 1970s. Most of its non-Nordic immigrants in the 1970s, however, were Pakistanis, Vietnamese, Turks, Yugoslavs, Iranians, and Moroccans. In reaction to this situation, Norway introduced restrictions on the immigration of people with non-Nordic backgrounds in the mid-1970s. These restrictions were considerably more exclusionist than those in nearby Denmark and Sweden. Norway also made it difficult for persons from non-Western countries to apply for asylum or even obtain tourist visas to visit the country (Hagelund 2003: 47-65). Although a law enacted in Norway in 1972 prohibited discrimination based on race, ethnic background, or religion in most areas, it did not apply to private real estate rentals.

Iceland, still without a defense force, required the United States, Canada, and western European countries to provide it with a military defense. Despite this dependence and the fact that Iceland was a recipient of America's Marshall Plan thanks to the generosity of American taxpayers, the American-Icelandic Defense Pacts that were in force from 1941 to 1949 barred African-American servicemen from serving in Iceland. When Iceland agreed to the establishment of a NATO base in Kelavik during the 1950s, it secretly insisted that the United States refrain from sending African-American servicemen there. Although the United States did not consistently respect this racist request, that it was made and accepted suggests that racism continued to thrive in both of the countries involved. Although the population of Iceland was almost totally Nordic with hardly any Jews it had some neo-Nazi sympathizers at that time (Atlason 2007; Bergsson 2007).

When Swedish actress May Britt married the African-American entertainer Sammy Davis, Jr. in 1960, they received a number of death threats, largely in Hollywood. Sweden during the 1960s and first half of the 1970s granted asylum to many Americans refusing to serve in the Vietnam War, including a considerable number who were largely of African descent. Beginning in 1969 and continuing into the 1970s, Sweden also granted refugee status to some 11,000 people from the Eastern Horn of Africa (about half of whom were Muslims and half Christians) who were fleeing hostilities associated with the war against Ethiopia for Eritrean Independence. Sweden also absorbed numerous Muslim refugees from Turkey, Lebanon, and Iran in the 1970s (Nordin 2005: 26). Although Europeans of Nordic background did not remain completely separate from those of African descent during the first decades after World War II, interactions between Scandinavians and people of African descent tended to be much less frequent than in many other parts of Europe.

At the end of World War II Britain remained the world's largest colonial power, controlling numerous colonies including many in Africa and in the Caribbean. As of 1945, Britain confronted a major labor shortage in certain industries deemed essential for postwar reconstruction and recovery, including agriculture, coal mining, textiles, construction, foundry work, brick making, health services, and institutional domestic service. By early 1946, the number of United Nations Relief and Rehabilitation Administration camps for displaced Europeans increased to 762. Hoping to attract many of these Europeans in camps to settle in Britain, the government appointed the Foreign Labor Committee (FLC) to examine the possibility of introducing foreign labor to address the problem and instituted a *de facto* resettlement scheme for refugees and other "displaced persons" that focused on Europeans deemed to be "white." Although the FLC was wary of aliens, Britain's Ministry of Labor consistently worked to facilitate the aliens' immigration to the United Kingdom (Paul 1997: 69-72).

Between 120,000 and 125,500 former members of the Polish armed forces and their dependents were already living in the United Kingdom and expected to remain permanently. Others were resident in camps elsewhere in Europe who were the financial responsibility of the British government. Prime Minister Churchill promised that none of them or their dependents would be forced to return home under Communist rule against their will. Although Britain wished to have many of these refugees work in its essential industries, the Ministry of Labor took the view that it could not compel them to work mostly in these areas (Paul 1997: 68-69).

By April 1947, British Ministry of Labor officials enthusiastically prophesied that 4,000 foreigners per week would soon be entering Britain and by May the Ministry had a special foreign-labor branch in Germany and Austria and soon extended its recruitment area to include the American zones in Germany and Austria. Britain also relaxed age and dependency qualifications to attract more women and was ready to provide English lessons in the camps (Paul 1997: 72-73).

Britain's population of so-called colored people in 1945 was close to 30,000, depending of course on definition, source, and perspective of who was to be considered "coloured" (Paul 1997: 113, 229n). A number of law suits having to do with the "colour bar" in public accommodations led some in Britain to call for new anti-discrimination legislation to penalize racist discrimination, but no bills passed in Parliament.

Hoping for additional settlers in late 1948, Britain's FLC broadened its recruitment area to include non-refugee but unemployed labor in Austria, Germany, and Italy (Paul 1997: 75). Although Britain had discriminated against workers of color from its colonies during wartime, its post-war recruitment of manpower revealed even a greater degree of racism. Largely unnoticed by British racists, late in 1947 108 passengers of color entered the country on board the *Ormonde* (Paul 1997: 113-114). However, similar lack of notice was hardly the case when the British government learned the following year that the *Empire*

Windrush was on its way to the "mother country" and that among its many passengers were 492 British subjects of Jamaican origin, many of whom had served in the British army during World War II and were returning there in response to news of its labor shortage.

Shortly before the ship's arrival at Tilbury Docks near London on June 21, 1948, British government leaders reacted as though a major crisis was underway. The impending arrival of these colonials of color threw Britain into a panic at a time when government officials felt themselves under extreme obligation to keep the country "white." Although British citizens living in the British colonies of the West Indies possessed the right to migrate to the "mother country," they were not expected to make use of this right except as visitors unless summoned by the British to fulfill some temporary need that it might have, such as risking their lives fighting for the country during wartime.

The colonial subjects aboard the *Empire Windrush* had not been recruited by the British government and were not seamen. Rather, they were traveling as independent British subjects at their own expense and were thus beyond the public control of the Colonial Office. Colonials with richly pigmented complexions were perceived by the Britain governing elite as ineligible for assimilation within British society. When it became apparent that it would not be possible to bar the Jamaican immigrants without provoking a crisis without the empire, the government began to stereotype the Jamaicans as a problem and a threat to the social order. Instead of being referred to in government documents as volunteers or British subjects, as were the Irish and other Europeans where appropriate, they were referred to as "Jamaican unemployed," thereby implying that they were somehow parasites. Even before the ship on which they were traveling reached harbor the government demanded that they be presorted for temporary housing together in an air raid shelter in the Clapham tube station together with an assigned warden, presumably to keep them under surveillance (Paul 1997: 111-119).

In addition to the workers of color who immigrated to Britain after the war, increasingly large numbers of students of color also entered the country. This was partly due to the Africanization of local government in some British colonies in Africa, which created a need for trained personnel. Their presence added to the strength of student organizations already in existence. As over 1,000 students from western Africa alone arrived in Great Britain by 1948, the Colonial Office Welfare Department found it necessary to open new student hostels in London, Cambridge, Edinburgh, and Newcastle. The Colonial Office considered trying to limit the numbers entering the country, in part because it feared these students might be influenced by left-wing or nationalist ideologies (Adi 1998: 120-121). At the same time, there was an increase in physical racist attacks and even murders of "black" people in Britain.

A report from the Royal Commission on Population in 1949 recommended that immigration into Britain should be welcomed "without reserve" provided that the migrants were "of good stock and were not prevented by their race or religion from intermarrying with the host population and becoming merged into it" (Holmes 1988: 116). The problem of housing discrimination in Britain was so serious in 1949 that Creech Jones, the Secretary of State for the Colonies, officially opened a new West African Students' Union hostel (Adi 1998: 151, 159-160).

By contrast, between May 1946 and the end of December 1950 close to 93,000 work permits were issued to European settlers coming into Britain for domestic service alone, and by April 1950 aliens with permits were arriving at an annual rate of 35,000. This generous distribution of work permits continued through the Churchill administration with 265,230 permits issued between 1947 and 1954. Two-thirds of recipients entered domestic service (Paul 1997: 74-75). While Britain continued to clamor for European settlers whom it deemed "white," the late 1940s and early 1950s witnessed an increase in racist attacks and even murders of "black" people resident there. Despite such an obvious problem of racism in society, Sir Winston Churchill in February of 1954 argued that existing British laws pertaining to discrimination, though based more on reconciliation than punishment, were adequate (Mullard 1973: 53).

In the early 1950s, the press continued to report many cases of racist discrimination throughout the country, ranging from "black" mothers barred from buying children's clothes and hairdressers refusing to cut that children's hair to problems of accommodation and employment. In a protest against such conditions, fourteen students in Britain from western Africa, most of whom were from Nigeria, participated in a stay-in strike in 1951. Among the demands of these strikers was that the Secretary of State give a written undertaking that additional accommodations would be provided for them (Adi 1998: 155). An average of two thousand people from the West Indies alone migrated to the United Kingdom during each year between 1948 and 1955 to the consternation of British officials (Paul 1997: 119).

In 1951, the Africa League in Manchester with a membership of some 200 students and workers sent a letter of protest to the Colonial Secretary demanding the appointment of a committee to study the general conditions of Colonial workers in all parts of the United Kingdom and to make recommendations. Although two WASU hostels existed in London by 1952, there were over 1,000 students from western Africa alone just in London. As a color bar and blatant discrimination remained, workers and students of color had no trouble finding causes against which to protest and shortcomings to address, including that more hotels be established (Adi 1998: 154-157). That so many workers of color were immigrating to the United Kingdom during this period did not indicate that Britain was becoming less racist; rather, it indicated that the country was encountering greater difficulties in attracting much-needed labor that it deemed to be "white" (Paul 1997: 76).

It was against this background that in 1953 a British gang attacked Nigerians living in north London, thereby bringing about what would be known as the Baynes Street Riot. Similar attacks on people of color took place in East London two years later (Adi 1998: 159-160). In 1950, Sir Cyril Osborne began an incendiary campaign that centered on what he referred to as "the race problem." Although he insisted that color never entered his argument, there was little mistaking that his campaign was tinged with racism, and it was one of at least two influences that caused some Tory politicians in the mid-1950s to begin lobbying for immigration-control legislation to bring an end to the entry into Britain of additional "blacks" (Mullard 1973: 47).

Another influence lay in the fact that several of Britain's African colonies were moving toward independence. Sudan won its independence in 1956 and the Gold Coast (now Ghana) its independence in 1957. Implicit in these developments, Great Britain was changing from a great imperial power at the helm of an empire so scattered that over it the sun never set into a rather small island country. Given this passing imperial glory along with that of its Royal Navy that was long the dominant power on the world's oceans, many Britons were resentful that this transition was being forced on their country in large measure by peoples of color in Africa and elsewhere. Complicating this transition in national identity for some Britons, the country had by this time become one that was more multi-ethnic and multi-colored than ever although Europeans remained obsessed with thinking of themselves in somewhat arrogant ways as superior to other peoples by virtue of being "white."

This combination of occurrences along with an economic downturn that came to Britain in 1958 after a decade of prosperity and full employment proved to be sufficient cause for some of the most violent conflict centered on racism that the country had ever seen. Although the mild recession impacted West Indian migrants in Britain four times harder than the general population, that many in the general population lashed out at this minority group of color suggests that the underlying cause of the violence was racism per se.

As mobs of "white" Britons determined to punish other British residents they deemed to be colored, major rioting took place from late August through early September 1958. Beginning in Nottingham in the East Midlands of England, a mere chat between a "white" woman and a "black" man proved sufficient to cause a bar brawl between British "whites" and West Indian "blacks" that later escalated into major riots. A week later in the Notting Hill section of West London, a crowd of "white" men violently attacked a Swedish resident over resentment that she was married to a "black" man of West Indian origin in the area. Although the police eventually arrived and escorted the injured woman to her home, her attackers could not be pacified. West London exploded in daily rioting while hundreds of "whites" roamed the streets in order to attack West Indians and other "blacks." Although most "blacks" in the area remained indoors in hopes of avoiding confrontations, a few of them fought back violently. "White" mobs, intent on punishing "blacks," even broke the windows of shops that sold to "blacks," fought the police, and ignored appeals from George Rogers (the Labor Party MP who represented the area) to cease rioting. The areas of West London that suffered the most were Notting Hill and nearby Notting Dale.

Instead of confronting the underlying racism in British society, government leaders set about planning to curtail the immigration of additional people of color into the country. Lord Home, Secretary of State for Home Affairs, told a Canadian audience that "curbs will have to be put on the unrestricted flow of immigration to the United Kingdom from the West Indies" (Mullard 1973: 48). During the period from 1948 to 1961, Prime Ministers Clement Attlee, Winston

Churchill, Anthony Eden, Harold Macmillan, Alec Douglas-Home, and Harold Wilson as well as Enoch Powell (who though not a Prime Minister was a government leader) tried to protect the domestic community of Britishness from the presumed social impurities carried by British subjects of color (Paul 1997: 178).

In contrast to what occurred in Nordic Europe and in the United Kingdom, France ended World War II and began coming to terms with xenophobia, racism, Africa, and Africans in a somewhat different manner. This may have been because France, occupied during the war, was dependent on many of its colonists, including especially those from nearby Africa where the forces of Free France had a major base of operations, to help in its liberation struggle. Very grateful to the numerous colonists of color, including Africans, who had rallied to France's side during the war, the forces of Free France under the leadership of Charles de Gaulle convened a conference at Brazzaville in the heart of French Equatorial Africa to establish certain parameters for post-war relationships between France and its colonies in 1944 even before the war ended.

At Brazzaville, de Gaulle stated that he intended to support more autonomy for French colonies at the end of the war. Revealing a certain paternalistic condescension toward the Africans in attendance, however, he also enunciated the principle that it belonged to France alone to decide what structural imperial reforms would be made concerning France's sovereignty and the future of its colonies at the end of the war. But by the time the conference ended on February 8, certain points included in its Declaration were much more conciliatory. The French Empire would remain united. Semi-autonomous assemblies would be established in each colony. Residents of France's colonies would share equal rights with French citizens in having the right to vote for the French legislature in Paris. Economic reforms would be made to diminish the exploitative nature of the relationship between France and its colonies. Later on August 25, 1945, at Brazzaville, the Provisional Government of France further agreed that elections in the French Empire would take place by means of a double electoral system with citizens of metropolitan France and the four *communes* in Senegal in one college and with the other subjects of the French Empire voting in the other college.

In this way, the French Assembly reached a compromise between the idea of total assimilation, which the promoters of the Brazzaville Conference favored, and that of association. For any other imperial European power except France would have reached such a fraternal agreement with colonized Africans in the mid-1940s would have been unthinkable. De Gaulle was much more respectful of, and grateful to, Africans for their support during the war than Britain was. This was clearly reflected in the Declaration of Brazzaville. De Gaulle was genuinely grateful to men such as the late Fèlix Éboué, originally from French Guyana and "black," who had faithfully served France as an administrator in several of its colonies. Éboué, having recruited some 40,000 Africans to fight on behalf of Free France, had made it known to de Gaulle that after the war the various territories in the French Empire, including metropolitan France, would have to operate together on the basis of equality.

One of the members of France's Provisional Consultative Assembly that would meet from 1944 to 1946 was Gaston Monnerville, originally of French Guyana and an important participant in the French Resistance. During this same period, he was a member of the first and second Constituent National Assemblies and president of the national commission charged with preparing the political statute for the French colonies. Meanwhile in 1945 General de Gaulle approved two decrees that were to have a major impact on France's future population growth, one on October 19 and the other on November 2.

Though showing favoritism toward those from European countries and territories broadly considered to be neighboring France, these decrees were rather liberal in providing that foreigners would be able to remain in France, providing that they had already been present there for at least three months although people such as foreign tourists and diplomats were excluded. These decrees also had the effect of providing for a rather liberal policy toward refugees and asylum-seekers without regard to their ethnic backgrounds. With the establishment of a national office of immigration soon afterward, however, it did not take certain French people long to reveal that they had a hierarchy of preferences for immigrants from some areas over others that was in part racist (Weil 2004: 79-81).

Taken together, these decrees were intended to regulate access to French nationality and the conditions by which people outside of France would be allowed to enter and remain in the country. France found itself in a delicate predicament because many French people were concerned about not radically changing the European character of the country. Still, the country found itself face to face with a number of challenges about from where it would obtain workers and what it would mean in the future to be a French citizen as opposed to a French colonial subject. Soldiers from Algeria and Morocco played a major role in librating Marseille from the Germans. An influx from Maghreb to Marseille continued after the war, and increasingly the immigrants involved began to see it as much as a city of refuge as one of passage (Blanchard and Boëtsch 2005: 9).

Despite the eventual victory in Europe of the Western Democracies and their colonial auxiliaries in alliance with the United States and the Soviet Union over the killing machines of Mussolini and Hitler, it cannot be claimed in honesty that the end of the war in any way put a lid on European racism. As the Provisional Government of the French Republic, for example, rushed to salvage its empire, a new French Ordinance in 1944 approved by its National Assembly provided both for Algerian Muslims and Africans south of the Sahara to have substantial increases in legislative representation even before forces of the Free French under General Charles de Gaulle entered Paris.

Still, all was not well in the French Empire; France quickly became embroiled in a war intended to maintain its colonial domination in Indo-China. Hardly had a month passed since the deaths of Mussolini and Hitler moreover when French police suppressed nationalist demonstrations in Algeria so harshly that this action left 10,000 people dead. Although in November of the same year France allowed colonized Africans in French West Africa to elect six representatives to the French Constituent Assembly, it is likely that this was only a way of buying time in one part of its colonial empire while using blunt force in two others.

On the one hand, Lamine Guèye (Senegal), Léopold Senghor (Senegal), Félix Houphouët-Boigny (Côte d'Ivoire or Ivory Coast), Apithy Sounou Migan (Dahomey, now Benin), Fily Dabo Cissoko (Soudan, now Mali), and Yacine Diallo (Guinea) were elected to represent *AOF* in France's Constituent Assembly. Although a deputy in the Fourth Republic that followed World War II, Guèye later became a Senator and eventually the Under-secretary of State to the presidency of the Council of the Republic as well as Minister of State under the Fifth Republic established by Charles de Gaulle. Houphouët-Boigny, after serving as a Deputy in the National Assembly from 1945 to 1959, became French Minister of State during 1958 and 1959.

On the other hand, from 1945 to 1970, it would be Mauco who would be chosen as France's secretary of its High Commission on Population, a position that would provide him much opportunity to influence public policy in line with his well-known racist and ethnic prejudices (Liauzu 1996: 185: Chapman and Frader 2004: 6). Even in Georges Mauco's last book, *les étrangers en France et le problème du racisme* (Foreigners in France and the Problem of Racism), which would be published much later in 1977, his racism was still apparent. Turning logic on its head, Mauco asserted in this work that racism was the unconscious responsibility of victims of racism.

France suffered from an acute housing shortage, and much of the housing that it did have was therefore overcrowded despite being dilapidated. A significant part of the housing, in fact, was located in so-called *bidonvilles* or shantytowns near large cities. As France sought new immigrants, it was not operating in a vacuum, as other European countries were also seeking new workers. Thanks in large measure to Africans who settled in France from nearby Maghreb and from south of the Sahara, including especially from Algeria, the period from 1945 up to a time marked by the petroleum crisis that began in 1973 would turn into one widely known in France as *les trente glorieuses*, meaning "the thirty glorious years." The period was so named by the demographer Jean Fourastié because he recognized it as one during which the government grew at high rates, constructed a good highway system, and in 1948 began benefiting from America's Marshall Plan in the amount of around 2.5 billion dollars thanks to a number of French promises, including that by Léon Blum in 1946 that France would open its movie market to American cinema.

Already by the time de Gaulle entered Paris at the head of Free France forces in August 1944, Algerian Muslims had fifteen deputies in the National Assembly and seven senators. Still, an uprising in the Algerian town of Sétif that began on May 8, 1945, in which 90 European settlers died brought forth such a reaction by French forces that 40,000 Algerians lost their lives. In the wake of this massacre, it mattered much less that by 1946, *AOF* or French West Africa had sixteen legislative representatives in Paris.

On April 25, 1946, France approved the Lamine Guèye Law, which was named after a Senegalese deputy of that same name. All people living in the French colonies were to have the same citizenship as those in metropolitan

France. This law thus bestowed French citizenship on all the subjects of the preexistent French Empire, which was accompanied by a considerable extension of suffrage. At the same time, on a proposal put forward by Félix Houphouët-Boigny, a deputy of Côte d'Ivoire, France voted for the suppression of forced labor in the colonized parts of the French Empire. That such a law outlawing forced labor was enacted in the wake of World War II underscores how difficult it is to apply a date certain to when vestiges of European slavery really ended.

Similarly, a Portuguese Law of 1899 called Regulations for Native Labor greatly facilitated forced labor into the 20th century in Portugal's African colony of Cape Verde under the guise that Portugal was only making Africans who were lazy work as contract laborers. Many Cape Verdeans, including "mulattoes," were made to work on Portuguese plantations in São Tomé and in Angola as a consequence. Portugal justified this on the theory that it was turning "non-assimilable" *vadios* or vagrants into productive workers of the Portuguese Empire (Fikes 2000: 19-21). Substantial research by scholars such as Todd Cleveland, Douglas Wheeler, Jeremy Ball, and Augusto Nascimento, moreover, that forced labor was a fact of life in some of Portugal's African colonies as late as the second half of the 20th century. From the time of the founding of the *Companhia de Diamantes de Angola* or Diamang in 1917 following the discovery of diamonds in Angola, for example, coercive recruitment and forced labor were used extensively by Diamang in ways that impacted over 20,000 Angolans and Congolese. Even nowadays, organized crime is a large contributor to ongoing human-trafficking into Portugal through which as late as 2000 an estimated 75,000 women from Brazil, many of whom were of appreciable African ancestry, had been recently smuggled into European countries by way of Portugal in a huge operation involving up to 100 organized crime gangs who then moved many of them into multiple European countries covered by the Schengen Agreement as well as beyond, including into the United Kingdom.

To return to France in the wake of World War II, the French Constitution established its so-called Fourth Republic on October 27, 1946, and at the same time established a French Union to replace the French Empire, which was modeled after the British Commonwealth. In the French Union, *colonies* were transformed into overseas *départements* or DOM and overseas *térritoires* or TOM (often known collectively as the *DOM-TOM*). Under the Fourth Republic, French citizenship was extended to all former colonial subjects although with limited franchise. Still, there was a great swelling in the number of legislators of African descent serving both in the lower and upper houses of France as deputies and senators. Overseas representatives played such important roles in the French National Assembly that some indigenous French wondered aloud if France risked being colonized by its colonies.

Despite this considerable political evolution in France, the number of African students in metropolitan France prior to 1946 remained negligible (Thomas 2007: 31) in contrast to the considerable presence of students from British colonies in various cities of the United Kingdom before and during World War II. This situation was only beginning to change in 1947 when Alioune Diop of Senegal—with assistance from Léopold Senghor, Aimé Césaire, André Gide, Jean-

Paul Sartre, Albert Camus, and others—founded a new journal in Paris. Called *Présence africaine*, it was largely devoted to the dissemination of ideas about peoples of African descent from an Africanist perspective.

Among those attracted to this new journal were intellectuals and university students from throughout the French-speaking world, including especially those in Paris. Around the same time as *Présence africaine* was founded, growing numbers of students from the French colonies began to study in Paris as well as in other French cities with universities. With only a few exceptions, French colonies did not have good systems of higher education. South of the Sahara, for example, only Madagascar and Senegal among French colonies had substantial higher education systems even as late as 1958 (Thomas 2007: 31).

In the late 1940s many Jews and Muslims left Marseille, the former more often than not for Israel and the latter to work in various industries close to Paris or elsewhere in the north of France (Blanchard and Boëtsch 2005: 11). A reduction in the numbers of European immigrants coming to France was compensated for by a large influx of immigrants from the nearby colony of Algeria between 1949 and 1955 (Weil 2004: 84). Algerian families began to be united in France in large numbers from 1954 (Liauzu 1996: 165).

Sudan, Morocco, and Tunisia gained their independence in 1956, no doubt in part encouraged by the fact that nearby Libya had become independent five years earlier. More ominous for the survival of the French Union, Algeria's War of Independence against France began to be waged with intensity in 1956. An Algerian union movement had organized as *Union Générale des Travailleurs Algériens* on February 24 of that year. During that same year, France and Britain joined Israel in an attack on the Suez Canal Zone in Egypt, which failed to win the backing of either of the world's two super powers—the United States and the Soviet Union. Egyptians controlled their entire country for the first time since the era of the ancient pharaohs. These developments greatly strengthened the cause of those seeking African independence as an alternative to colonial bondage.

With such a phenomenal movement toward independence in northern Africa, there was little certainty that the French Union could last. Indo-China as well as Tunisia and Morocco withdrew from it by 1956. Hoping to induce Africans south of the Sahara to remain closely associated with France, the French Assembly on June 23, 1956, approved a *Loi-Cadre* that had been proposed by Gaston Deferre. This law altered the status of French-controlled African colonies south of the Sahara by providing for universal suffrage, by reinforcing the powers of the overseas assemblies established in 1946, and by providing for more administrative decentralization. Against this background of considerable stress and uncertainty within the French Union and raging war in Algeria, the First Colloquium of Black Arts convened in Paris in 1956.

After France's Fourth Republic had been established at the end of World War II, General Charles de Gaulle had withdrawn from public life and gone into retirement at Colombey les Deux Eglises with the hope that others would be able to guide France through its postwar development while maintaining its vast empire. Although parts of this vision succeeded in terms of France's internal economic development during *les trente glorieuses*, France was not succeeding as an imperial power of great importance. Not only had it been forced to withdraw from Indo-China in defeat in 1956, Tunisia and Morocco won their independence around the same time. Muslim riots erupted in Algiers in December 1956 and settler terrorist organizations such as *Comité pour le Renaissancae de France* and *Organisation de la Résistance de l'Algérie Française* continued to operate clandestinely. As this was occurring Algerian nationalists leaders met in Cairo to form *Front de la Libération Nationale* or FLN, which soon ordered a general strike by students in Algeria.

While France placed more emphasis on strengthening its relations with Tunisia and Morocco and struggled to keep a lid on nationalism in Algeria, the Gold Coast (now Ghana) won its independence from Great Britain effective March of 1957, thereby adding to grave misgivings in some French circles concerning whether or not European imperialism, by whatever name, could any longer serve as the basis of relationships between Africans and Europeans. Already the so-called Battle of Algiers had began on January 7, 1957. Also in 1957, many colonists in Algeria who considered themselves to be of European descent (popularly known as *Pieds-Noirs*) founded *l'Association nationale des Français d'Afrique du Nord de l'outre-mer et de leurs amis or Anfanoma*. With France desperate for new leadership and a new vision that might inspire national confidence, de Gaulle emerged from retirement.

Hoping to reverse the tide toward independence in Algeria and to find a framework whereby most of France's other African colonies could have an association with France that would be something less than complete independence, General de Gaulle used his considerable prestige to bring about the founding of France's Fifth Republic in 1958. The new Constitution abolished the French Union, replacing it by what was called a Franco-African Community. It was within this new framework that France in 1958 held a referendum in all its colonies located in western and equatorial Africa expecting that the voters in all the colonies involved would vote "*non*" to immediate independence in order to maintain their ties with the "mother country."

With only the exception of Guinea under the leadership of Sékou Touré, France's colonies voted as De Gaulle had hoped. Amid great bitterness and disappointment on the part of France, however, Guinea voted to accede to independence from France immediately. This development left many in France feeling uncertain about the long-term prospects of French colonialism in Africa; it also complicated the situation of Africans in France, and most especially for Algerians, the masses in Algeria had been engaged in an active revolt against French colonialism for at least two years.

It was during this period that De Gaulle brought into his government a number of pro-French Algeria politicians, the most important of whom was Algerian-born Nafissa Sid-Cara. The first woman to ever serve in a ministerial capacity in the Fifth Republic as well as the first Muslim woman to ever serve as a minister, Nafissa Sid-Cara was appointed Secretary of State responsible to the Prime Minister and charged with social questions in Algeria and with the evolution of the personal statute for Muslim rights. She served in this capacity from

1959 to 1962. In addition to her brother Chérif Sid-Cara, who was a pro-French Algerian minister in France shortly before this time, another French minister of Algerian origin was Abdelkader Barakrok.

Meanwhile, French forces, supplemented by Algerian auxiliaries known as Harkis whom the majority of Algerians considered traitors to the cause of their independence, used brutality, torture, and terror in a desperate attempt to suppress Algerian nationalism (Fanon 1965; Cole 2005: 125-141; Durmelat 2005: 142-159). As these events unfolded just south of the Mediterranean, Algerians resident in France—often in squalid living conditions and not infrequently in outlying areas around large cities called *banlieues*—eventually responded by using *bombes plastiques* to spread insecurity even in Paris and elsewhere in *le métropole*. Frenchmen became increasingly suspicious and resentful of the many Africans living among them, including most especially those from northwestern Africa whom they called *les maghébins*, a majority of whom had ties to Algeria (Stora 1997: 18-19).

By the time the Second Colloquium of Black Arts convened in Rome in 1959, the continuing war in Algeria made some people of African descent begin to question the applicability of the *Négritude* movement to all things African in view of the fact that human variation in Africa had never conformed with racial homogeneity. Although the other territories controlled by France in western and equatorial Africa, unlike Guinea, had voted for new alignments within a French-African community rather than for immediate independence, they too opted for their independence in 1960. This was the same year that independence also was granted to British-ruled Nigeria, the most populous country in all of Africa, and to Belgian-ruled Congo, and the evolution toward independence in the nearby French colonies could no longer be resisted. In "the hexagon" —which is to say metropolitan France—these developments both complicated French reactions to African immigration and led to an intensification of France's efforts to resist independence for Algeria.

Eventually bowing to the inevitable, the Évian Accords signed between France and the Algerian FLN at Évian-les-Bains on March 18, 1962 formally ended the War for Algerian Independence. In France, this agreement was so disliked by most Pieds-Noirs and many others that the right-wing *Organisation armée secrète* set off several bombs in protest and even attempted to assassinate President Charles de Gaulle. While during the Algerian War of Independence there was a major reduction in the vast number of Algerians entering France as immigrants (Weil 2004: 85), there was an increase in Africans coming to France from within the French-African community, virtually all of whom were "black."

In the 1950s and 1960s, Africans originally from south of the Sahara could often be seen in various public establishments in Marseille, such as cafes, restaurants, game parlors, and music clubs. Also by the 1960s, some who formerly were sailors could be seen there as well as peddlers of the Mouride religious brotherhood from Senegal (Bertoncello and Bredeloup 2004: 43-64; Dewitte 2003: 63-75). A bit later, numerous African women appeared in Marseille, including some widows and some divorcees. While many of these women earned money in the center of the city as independent entrepreneurs dealing in traditional foods for their compatriots, others sold similar foods in restaurants or worked as peddlers (Barou 1997: 31-47).

As a large number of people of mixed ethnic backgrounds relocated to France from Algeria at the end of this bitter war, certain contradictions in French immigration policy became manifest (Weil 2004: 85). In addition to the so-called Pied-Noirs of several nationalities, who considered themselves Europeans, France was also obliged to permit the entry of many Harkis, Algerians soldiers who, as French loyalists during the course of the war, would likely have been slaughtered if left behind. Between June 11 and 24 in 1962, each day saw 3,500 Pieds-Noirs and French Muslims alone arrive in the port of Marseille. In 1962, more than one million left Algeria and more than 650,000 settled in France. When they arrived, each had to fill out a form, in pink, blue, or white: pink for those who had nowhere to go, blue for those who needed some assistance, and white for those who possessed their own means (Blanchard and Boëtsch 2005: 155).

Already due to the very limited construction of housing in France between the two World Wars and loss of housing during wartime, France found itself very short of sufficient modern housing after World War II. As postwar France sought to provide housing for its growing working-class population in the Paris area, its most moderately priced housing in the suburbs had already in 1945 passed from the health officials' authority to that of the social service officials and took on the name of HLM (*habitations de logement modéré* or *habitations de loyer modéré*) built on large estates known as *grands ensembles*. These years when they were being built are also known as *années de béton* (*béton* being a kind of concrete), for bulldozers and concrete mixers were busy at work during long hours clearing France's overcrowded inner-city slums and *bidonvilles* and replacing them with other housing, much of which was hastily built in high-rise estates in the *banlieues*. In some areas close to Paris such as La Courneuve, the manner in which industrial estates and cheap housing began to emerge in the midst of bean plantations later would contribute to urban social problems that were not anticipated and that eventually would impact immigrants in France disproportionately.

During the 1950s and 1960s, French public opinion was divided as to what extent France should heavily invest in urban renewal around the *bidonvilles* or shantytowns that were by this time a fixture on the outskirts of a number of large French cities, and the housing problems had been exacerbated by the "baby boom" that followed the World War II. Massive flows of people into France from Algeria in 1962 caused a serious housing problem. Amid the competition for housing and lingering bitterness over France's loss of Algeria, racism—though never absent from France—surged to new levels.

The government tried to limit press contact with the 90,000 Harkis and their families who entered the country as well as the Harkis' contact with the general French population (Blanchard and Boëtsch 2005: 159). Although the Harkis risked their lives, it did not take long for graffiti to appear on some walls with messages such as *Halt the Arab invasion*. Whatever the French expected of the Harkis, many of these latter intended to stay in France. Late in 1962, there were still as many as 70,000 persons per week entering France from its former colony. To the dismay of many and the glee of others, France chose this time to install controls at its border to limit or prevent the entry of Algerian immigrants whom it considered ill or handicapped (Weil 2004: 86).

The Évian Accords provided for the free circulation of people between Algeria and France in order to work though without rights of citizenship, however, the circulation was strictly south to north from Africa into Europe to the resentment of many French people, and some of this resentment continues to exist. Another important *Pied-Noir* organization called *l'Union syndicale de défense des intérêts des Français repliés d'Algérie* or Usdifra was founded in 1965 (Blanchard and Boëtsch 2005: 176).

In addition to Pieds-Noirs from Algeria, significant numbers of other settlers formerly living in Morocco and Tunisia also relocated to France and these settlers are also sometimes referred to as Pied-Noirs, especially if they are not Muslims. As the Pieds-Noirs make up about 3 percent of France's population, without counting also their sympathizers and the Harkis, it is apparent that they constitute an important segment of French society as well as one that tends to be right-wing. In Marseille, which is the second-largest city in France, for example, Pieds-Noirs played a major role in helping its population to increase from 660,000 in 1954 to 882,000 in 1968. They also impacted the demographic and political composition in such other southeastern cities as Toulon, Nice, Perpignan, and Montpellier as well as in such small nearby towns as Antibes, Cannes, Menton, Marignanne, Fréjus, and Saint Raphaël. Of course, many other Pieds-Noirs settled in Paris, including many working-class Jews in the neighborhood known as Belleville (Simon and Tapia 1998). Included among the Pieds-Noirs is Tunisian-born Bertrand Delanoë, a Socialist, who in 2001 became the mayor of Paris.

Meanwhile barely north of Paris in 1964, the old *département* of the Seine was divided into eight new *departments*: Hauts-de-Seine, Seine-Saint Denis, Val-de-Marne, Val-d'Oise, Yvelines, Essonne, and Seine-et-Marne. It was at this same time that Paris was designated a *Ville-Département*. The following year, President de Gaulle gave his approval to the urban development scheme for the area down river of Paris known as SDAU where Paul Delouvrier conceptualized perhaps 14 million people would live in modern housing by 2000. Unfortunately, however, the suburban aspect of this vision did not turn out well.

As has been mentioned, La Courneuve, like most of the other working-class suburbs of Paris, was urbanized quickly by means of the construction of large tower blocks and various inexpensive types of subsidized housing known as HLMs after World War II. Between 1962 and 1968, the population of La Courneuve almost doubled. During this period, it emerged as part of the Red Belt of Paris in the sense that its location placed it in an area that traditionally had been a stronghold of the Communist Party or more generally of the left-wing coalition known as Le Front Populaire. It did not take long for the word *banlieue*, which earlier had meant merely a *suburb*, to take on the new meaning of any working-class area containing a large density of public housing (or projects known as *cités*) with many social problems and much crime, physical dilapidation, economic deprivation, and immigration. Voting habits also changed in Red Belt in that a significant percentage of the French people living in the *banlieues* who used to vote for the left-wing Front Populaire began voting for France's ultra right-wing Front National.

The *cités*, projects, or public-housing estates of the French urban periphery suffer from a negative public image that instantly associates them with rampant delinquency, immigration, and insecurity. To dwell in a low-income estate means to be confined to a branded space; to a blemished setting experienced as a "trap" (Pialoux 1979: 19-20; Bachman and Basier 1989). Residential discrimination hampers job search and contributes to entrenched local unemployment, as inhabitants of the Quartre Mille encounter additional distrust and rejection among employers as soon as they mention their place of residence. There is typically a change of attitude of policemen when they notice their address during identity checks (Dubet 1987: 75), for to be from a *cité* almost triggers reflexive suspicion of deviance if not outright guilt. It suffices for inhabitants of the Quatre Mille or any other *cité* to hide their address in order to "pass" in broader society.

As for the poor *banlieues* on the outskirts of Paris that many French people stigmatize as dangerous, decrepit, having large immigrant populations, and euphemistically as "sensitive," La Courneuve is especially infamous for its so-called Quatre Mille section. Some 4,000 units without good facilities that were constructed by 1963 characterize this part of La Courneuve. Quatre mille is often referred to by many of its residents as well as other Parisians as the "dumpster," "the garbage can," or "the reservation" of Paris. When many of its residents who work in central Paris are asked where they reside, they are likely to reply "vaguely that they live in the northern suburbs" rather than reveal that they live in La Courneuve (Avery 1987: 13, 22).

Most residents of La Courneuve are working-class French *de souche*, a distinguishing term used in some right-wing circles to distinguish French people they view as native to metropolitan France from others (Wacquant 1997: 332-333). Of the residents of La Courneuve who are immigrants or the children of immigrants, most have Algerian connections. Many others there come from other parts of Africa, Asia, the Pacific, and the French Antilles. This suburb was not even connected to the rest of Paris by metro until the first station opened there in 1987 as La Courneuve in Aubervilliers.

Not all suburbs around Paris have evolved in this way, however. Saint-Germain-en-Laye, Saint-Cloud, Versailles, and Sceaux, for example, have a long history as Parisian suburbs of high standing for the well-to-do. Other successful suburbs at the extreme west of Paris include Nanterre, Courbevoie, and Puteaux where La Défense, the largest district in Europe that has been specifically reconstructed for business, is located with its numerous futuristic skyscrapers, Grande Arche, and esplanade known as *le Parvis*. Such exceptions as these notwithstanding, when most Frenchmen think of *les banlieues* nowadays, they generally think of suburban failure and also poor people of recent immigrant background and consider the way that France has not been willing or able to integrate certain segments of its population into the mainstream of French life, including many of whom happen to be of African descent.

Meanwhile on May 25, 1963, the Charter of the Organization of African Unity was signed by thirty-two independent African states. These included members of the Casablanca Group that had been formed in 1961 by Egypt, Ghana, Guinea, Mali, Libya, and at least for a short time Morocco. Reacting to such independence in Africa, and without a great deal of sophistication about various challenges in many African societies, some French people have difficulty understanding why there is such a large African presence in France that continues to grow. Perhaps some of them are not even aware or prefer to forget that incorporated into France or under French rule are still a number of islands in the Caribbean and near Africa, where most people are of African descent. The wave of Comorians from a chain of islands off the coast of eastern African began settling in Marseille in the 1970s (Blanchard and Boëtsch 2005: 11) is a direct result of this.

Colporteurs in Marseille marked the beginning of a major presence of Muslims in France belonging to the Mouride Muslim brotherhood from Senegal. They began to arrive in 1967 as the first wave of peddlers and hawkers specializing in Islamic devotional literature from that country. Most of these people lived more or less in areas in Marseille where they were largely segregated from the masses of French people (i.e., between the Rue des Dominicains, the Rue des Bagnoires, and the Rue de Petites Maries) in the heart of Balsunces, an area that was largely peopled by immigrants from Maghreb. As a result, Marseille stood out in France as a city known for having a large population of *Maghrébins*, people from western Africa, and third-generation Armenians (Bertoncello and Bredeloup 2004: 33-64).

Gaston Monnerville, originally from French Guyana, was perhaps the most prominent person predominantly of African descent in French public life between in the 1950s and 1970s. While a number of French citizens such as Léopold Senghor and Houphouët-Boigny became important in France as politicians representing various French-controlled lands overseas, Monnerville was likely the first to also achieve great prominence as a politician representing metropolitan France. Already the French delegate to the United Nations in London in 1946, his prominence enabled him between 1951 and 1970 to become an important elected official in metropolitan France. It was during this period that he was president of the *Conseil Général* of Lot, located in the Midi-Pyrenees region of southwestern France and one of the original 83 *départements* created in 1790 during the French Revolution.

From 1964 to 1971, moreover, Monnerville was mayor of the town of Saint-Céré in Lot. From 1947 to 1968 as president of the upper house of the French national legislature, first called the Council of the Republic and from 1958 the Senate, Monnerville achieved a prominence as a French politician that was unique for a man of color. From 1959 until 1960 under the Fifth Republic that emerged under Charles de Gaulle, Gaston Monnerville was president of the Senate for the French Community. Further reflecting his prominence in France, he was from 1959 to 1968 a member of the Council of the University of Paris, a recipient of the Croix de Guerre, a recipient of the Medaille of la Resistance avec Rosette, made a knight of the Legion of Honor with a military title in 1947 and eventually made an officer of the same in 1983.

The acquisition in 1971 of the Marseille newspaper called *Le Méridional* by Gaston Defferre, a long-time Socialist politician and former mayor of Marseille, corresponded with incitement of the local population by much anti-Arab discussion in that newspaper. There even began to appear in *Le Méridional* some racist editorials by Gabriel Dononech, who advocated using municipal powers against Algerians (Liauzu 1996: 205). Around this same time, France both renegotiated an accord with Algeria to reduce the number of Algerians entering the country and at the same time began adopting policies showing favoritism to immigrants who where not from nearby northern Africa, including from Yugoslavia, Turkey, and Portugal, suggesting that even non-French-speaking Europeans were being favored over people living in parts of Africa with long historical ties to France (Weil 2004: 89).

On July 23, 1971, France announced in an official statement that it would fulfill current arms contracts with Portugal, Rhodesia (now Zimbabwe), and South Africa although all those countries were abusing their "black" majority populations in Africa. Still, statistics show that there was a new wave of migrants especially from northwestern Africa who arrived in Marseille in the late 1960s and early 1970s, including especially Algerians and Moroccans, many of whom were increasingly housed in slums, ghettos, and high-rise estates that surrounded the city. The murder of Djilali Ben Ali in Paris by a concierge in this same year reflected the sensitivity of this kind of situation.

The following year in Versailles, Mohamed Diab was killed in a burst of machine gun fire while in the custody of the police (Blanchard and Boëtsch 2005: 167). When on August 25, 1973, a mentally unstable person of Algerian origin who lived in Nice killed a Frenchman, the reaction by many of the latter's compatriots was immediate and enormous. The victim's colleagues at work went on strike for two days, and some several thousand people attended his funeral. Although many people made this murder a *cause célèbre* against Algerian immigration, probably no less than twenty-three murders of immigrant workers had taken place in and around Marseille that same month.

On September 1, 1973, many Maghrébins accompanied the body of an Algerian immigrant through the streets of a suburb to the north of Marseille who in late August was the victim of a racist crime. In situations such as this, seldom was anyone ever arrested and convicted. Just before his departure for Algeria, Khali Hamoud, a young physician of Algerian origin and director of the MTA or *Mouvement des travailleurs arabes*, appealed to those of Maghrebian origin to launch a massive general strike and to participate in a day of mourning in order to call attention to the problem of racism in and around Marseille. In response to this appeal, a large demonstration took place two days later in Marseille and several other cities of southeastern France. Some leftists and trade unionists were unhappy about this, however, claiming rather insensitively that this action could divide the labor movement. Although this was a big turning point in Marseille, it was not long before several other immigrants were killed and, on the other side, some local people organized themselves into vigilante groups to seek vengeance for a bus driver who was murdered (Blanchard and Boëtsch 2005: 17).

On September 19, Algeria reacted to French restrictions on Algerian immigration by completely stopping it, citing officially that the reason was due to racism in France. What could not be ignored by this time was that xenophobia and racism had played a role in numerous attacks on immigrants in France, including disproportionately against Africans, and that a right-wing anti-immigration faction was increasingly campaigning against what it sometimes referred to as "savage" immigration (Weil 2004: 101-103). As the anti-Arab violence exploded, Houari Boumediene, the president of Algeria, decided to suspend the departure of additional Algerian migrants for France beginning on September 20, 1973. He added that if France did not want Algerian immigrants that Algeria was willing to take them back (Blanchard and Boëtsch 2005: 179). It was also in Marseille in 1973 that a bomb exploded at the Algerian Consulate, killing four people and injuring about twenty others. Around the same time, a right-wing group associated with Charles Martel issued a tract saying that "occupation of France" by people of northwestern African descent involved contagion and was catastrophic.

According to statistics of the French Ministry of Interior, more than 1,200,000 people from northwestern Africa (probably an underestimate), in other words, one out of six, were living in the southeast of France. Already by 1973, there were tendencies for many of these people to live in *bidonvilles,* shantytowns or slums largely segregated from the mainstream of society. Some who expected to be there for a short time remained on a long-term basis under deteriorating circumstances amid rats and sewers that did not work efficiently. There also began to be an influx of mostly single or unattached sub-Saharan Africans into Marseille, including first immigrants from Mali, Mauritania, and Senegal, then later Ivoirians, Beninians, and Cameroonians.

The French code of nationality adopted in 1889 in its version as revised in 1973 anticipated two main paths to naturalization: (1) its attribution by birth and (2) its acquisition subsequently. According to that code, a person could become French by the rule of *jus sanguinis* when one parent was French, and since 1927 that parent could be the mother as well as the father. By the rule of *jus soli,* a child born is France is considered French if at least one parent was also born in Algeria before 1962—in other words, on French territory before Algerian independence. That provision with regard to Algeria, however, would be changed in 1993 (Liauzu 1996: 241-242).

Meanwhile causing a scandal in France in 1974, news spread of the existence in the port of Marseille of a secret prison in a hanger called the Prison of Arenc that had been in existence for ten years, most of whose inmates were presumably African. Of its five compartments, one was specifically for African men, one for persons considered to pose special risks being secretly expelled from France by ministerial order, one for women and children, and another for undocumented immigrants. In 1974 alone, 3,000 foreigners were detained there (Blanchard and Boëtsch 2005: 167).

The Netherlands provides an additional vantage point from which to view Europe's African presence in the early decades after World War II. Nola Hatterman, a Dutch artist of Amsterdam, founded a painting school in Suriname (formerly Dutch Guiana) in 1953 and painted Jimmy Lucky, a "black" tapdancer resident in Amsterdam, perhaps in the 1950s. This portrait now hangs in the Amsterdam Historical Museum. In 1954, a charter came into effect governing relations between the Netherlands, Suriname, and the Netherlands Antilles. It provided Suriname and the Antilles with more autonomy but also created one nationality for the entire Kingdom of the Netherlands, thereby in principle granting all citizens free access to the European "mother country." Initially, those who came were mostly middle class, and there were few problems (Vermeulen and Penninx 200a: 7).

Immigration to the Netherlands from the Dutch Antilles was minimal and consisted largely of students (Vermeulen and Penninx 2000a: 7). Beginning in 1964, however, the stream of immigration from the Dutch Antilles broadened to include large numbers of immigrants from the working class lured there under contract by Dutch businesses. Large-scale migration to Europe was still relatively new as it did not gain full momentum until the late 1960s. A surge in immigration from Suriname to the Netherlands preceded Suriname's independence in 1975 (Vermeulen and Penninx 200a: 7).

In 1974, coinciding with what in western Europe began to perceived as an immigration crisis (Liauzu 1996: 147), the Dutch Ministry of Development Co-operation initiated and funded a project widely known as REMPLOD in order to explore ways in which international labor migration could contribute to development abroad, thereby combating the causes of emigration from sending countries such as Morocco, Tunisia, and Turkey. At that time, it was generally expected that labor migration from Mediterranean countries to the Netherlands would be temporary and that most migrants from Morocco, Tunisia, and Turkey would eventually return home. Research on immigration undertaken by REMPLOD led to two policy measures in the Netherlands. Even before the research was finished, the Dutch government developed a policy of assisting migrants to return from the Netherlands to their home countries and to establish small businesses there. Secondly, the Dutch government concluded bilateral agreements with sending countries (with a special focus on Morocco, Tunisia, Yugoslavia, and Turkey) to implement projects in which returning migrants would have attractive opportunities to participate (Haas 2006: 33-34).

Following a long period of skepticism about REMPLOD, some other European countries, also began to adopt a policy of return migration coupled with remittances that was being used in the Netherlands (Haas 2006: 54). Meanwhile as growing numbers of workers migrated from Suriname and the Antilles to the Netherlands who were unskilled, they were less well received than those who had come beginning in the mid-1950s (Vermeulen and Penninx 200a: 7). Although in 1969 the Netherlands concluded an agreement to recruit workers from Morocco, at least through the early 1970s the number of new Moroccan immigrants in the Netherlands remained rather small.

As for Germany, World War II left it divided with a large western portion, initially under the occupation of the western Allies (Britain, France, and the United States), and a smaller eastern sector, under the occupation of the Soviet Union. Although the government in the western section officially denounced its Nazi past early on and even agreed to pay certain reparations to Jews, it did not always act in a manner consistent with renouncing racism per se. This becomes apparent, for example, when we reflect on certain actions vis-à-vis people of appreciable African ancestry present on its territory. At various times between 1947 and 1952, the fate of the so-called Rhineland Bastards who had been involuntarily sterilized for racist reasons was debated in the West German *Bundestag* or Parliament. Rather than admitting to the shameful behavior of Germany toward these German-born people of European and African heritage however, German MPs preferred to label them "a special problem" while diverting attention from any German blame. Also, it refused to pay any reparations to them, or for that matter to offer even a public apology (Sephocle 1996: 25).

Following World War II, a number of offspring were born to German women and African-American soldiers. Commonly called "brown babies" in the United States, they were referred to as *Besatzungskinder* or illegitimate colored occupation children in Germany (Blackshire-Belay 1996: 112). Although Germany economically needed foreign workers and immigrants, as it set about regulating relationships between Germans and racial "others," it depended on notions of racial "otherness" as an ideological and structural phenomenon that it simultaneously sought to exploit and to destroy (Linke 1999: 133).

Against all scientific knowledge to the contrary and the fact that people of African ancestry lived in virtually all parts of the world, even a government report of 1952 would claim that climatic conditions in Germany were ill-suited for Germans of mixed European and African ancestry. The implication was that Germans with fathers of African descent might be better off living in the home countries of their fathers. In the same vein a 1952 study by Walter Kirchner titled "An Anthropological Study of Mulatto Children in Berlin" avoided looking at the sociocultural conditions of Afro-Germans in the context of their European homeland (Sephocle 1996: 25).

In West Germany (really the Federal Republic of Germany) a 1952 film called *Toxi* dealt with the five-year-old daughter of a "black" American soldier and a light-complexioned German mother. This film led to a period of much discussion of so-called *Rassenfragen* or race questions. In the film, the German-born protagonist eventually found her father and happily traveled "home," except it was not her home, in the United States (Jobatey 1996: 29). Germans had a long history of thinking that it was more natural for the United States to be a multicultural and multi-colored society than for Germany. Hermann Baumann, the well-known culture-historian who had associations with the ethnographic museum of Berlin until his death in 1972, like many other culture-historians, was never able to grasp that there could be discordance between phenotypic variety and sociocultural variety (Goodwin 1999: 12-16).

Through biological reductionism as applied to Bushmen and the Hottentots, for example, Baumann concluded that the cultural, racial, and linguistic boundaries separating them were coterminous—that is, were part of the same set of social facts. In keeping with this perspective, Baumann posited a neat fit among race, culture, and physical habitat that was sufficiently idealized to suggest a type of geographical predestination (Baumann and Westermann 1948: 21, 22, 24).

Despite considerable post-war German reserve concerning people of African descent, Trinidadian-born Peter Mico Joachim, who had studied singing and trumpet at the London College of Music, relocated to Hamburg in 1956. He also made jazz recordings under the name of Billy Mo, played in clubs, and acted in a number of German musical films as well as in a German television series about Mark Twain. After marrying a German woman named Sylvia Hartjenstein, Joachim eventually settled in Wünstorf, Lower Saxony, while remaining active as a musician in many parts of his adopted country. The African-American Ron Williams took up residence in West Germany in the 1950s after having served there earlier in the U.S. military. His career sometimes included co-anchoring for Deutsche Welle TV International. Over time, Williams assumed a German identity and became known as a rock musician and an entertainment personality on television (Jobatey 1996: 32-33).

Beginning in the late 1960s, a number of industries in West Germany attempted to address labor shortages by importing foreigner workers from southern Europe and in some cases a bit beyond. Though initially called *Fremdarbeiter* or foreign workers, that they were later called *Gasarbeiter* or guest workers emphasized German expectations that they would even eventually return to their homelands outside of Germany.

The first major exposure of a "black" German outside the traditional entertainment sector occurred when in 1972 Erwin Kostner played with the German national team in its opening game in Mexico for the world football or soccer cup. Although his play was not outstanding, Kostner was a well-accepted member of the team (Jobatey 1996: 30-31). This was the same year that an organization called IAF or *Interessengemeinschaft der mit Ausländern verheirateten Frauen* (meaning the community of interests of women who are married to foreigners) was founded in West Germany. This was at a time when German law only recognized the children of German men as German citizens but not those born of German mothers. This organization was intended therefore to provide German women a way of keeping their children, and it was also both feminist and anti-racist. Largely as the result of this organization, as of January 1, 1975, children born of a German mother and a foreign father are also recognized as German (Sephocle 1996: 17).

The German career of the Cuban Roberto Blanco became a classic show-business story. In the early 1970s, the producers of a German television show needed a black Samba dancer. They hired Blanco, who subsequently was discovered by the German pop music *Schlagermusik*, producer Jack White. Blanco's first and best-selling record was *"Ein bißchen Spaß muß sein"* (You need to have a little fun). Later in the 1970s, Blanco had his own popular show on Germany television, albeit with many sketches that focused on skin color and race in an amusing way (Jobatey 1996: 31-32).

A book authored by historian Reiner Pommerin titled *Sterilization of the Rhineland Bastards: The Fate of a Colored German Minority, 1918-1937*, which was based on secret documents found in the archives of the German Department of State from the time of the Nazi regime, was published in Düsseldorf in 1979. Despite this written proof of the sterilizations of 385 victims because of racism that was written in German and based on primary documentation, that the government of the Federal Republic of Germany made no arrangement to compensate any of the victims is worrying.

Such western European countries as the United Kingdom, France, the Netherlands, West Germany, and Belgium sometimes have been compared to each other as attributing either a more pluralistic or more assimilationist meaning to integration, a central concept introduced in immigrant policies of some western European countries in the 1960s and 1970s (Kruyt and Niessen 1997). From a different perspective having to do with contrasting ways of dealing with immigrants, France has often been seen as a model of assimilation, Germany as a model of partial exclusion, and Sweden as a model of multiculturalism. Although the term *integration* has been used in all three of these last-mentioned countries to indicate a greater degree of tolerance and respect for ethno-cultural differences, its use had tended to be avoided after the early 1970s. More recently, the term *incorporation* has been used as an alternative that implies "a process through which a social unit is included in a larger unit as an integral part of it" (Vermeulen and Penninx 2000a: 2-3).

Perhaps nowhere is it clearer that World War II had accomplished no lasting victories against racism than when one focus on how conflict between the Communist and non-Communist worlds unfolded during the late stages of the war and in the early decades that followed. Although neither Africa nor people of African descent played a major role in the unfolding of this conflict, they were at times present as witnesses and at other times caught up in it as instruments that were being manipulated. One such witness, for example, was Tito Romalio, a Brazilian variety actor imprisoned by the Nazis in Lithuania. After his liberation by Soviet forces, he eventually became a Soviet citizen and acted in a number of films in his new adopted home (Blakely 1986: 155).

Already before World War II had concluded, the United Kingdom was so intent on containing Communism in the Balkans that it allied itself with neo-Fascist forces in Greece rather than against a powerful Communist-controlled resistance movement known as EAM (the Greek acronym for National Liberation Front). When in 1941 a joint German, Italian, and Bulgarian occupation of Greece following that country's defeat in 1941, it had been the EAM that emerged to defeat this Nazi-inspired occupation of Greece, complete with the usual Nazi racist agenda. Well before this occupation, Greek laws had required Greeks to carry identity cards that indicated their religion in keeping with a nationalist ideology that to be authentically Greek means to be a part of a quasi-theocratic "Hellenic-Orthodox Christian civilization." When the Nazis invaded, these identity cards carrying religious identity proved fatal for many Greek Jews.

Despite the fact that it was the EAM that had finally been successful in defeating the Nazi occupation of Greece in October 1944, Britain remain an implacable enemy of the EAM, in part because the EAM was Communist-controlled and in part because Britain was sheltering a Greek government-in-exile that it wished to see reinstalled. By 1945, the British were promoting a bloody conflict between the ELAS (EAM's partisan army, the National Popular Liberation Army), on the one side, and neo-Fascist Security Battalions devoted to a restoration of the monarchy, on the other. Despite the racist sympathies of the Security Battalions, Britain under the leadership of Winston Churchill, urged right-wing irregular bands of Greeks to enter into fierce combat with Greek leftists, although most of the casualties from this conflict were Greek civilians. Even when Clement Attlee succeeded Churchill as head of a labor government in 1945, Britain continued its support to royalists who were neo-Fascist in their confrontation with Greek leftists. Even apart from Cold War, this policy by Britain was consistent with its long-stranding efforts to keep Russia or the Soviet Union, as well as any of its potential allies, as far from the Mediterranean Sea as possible.

Although Marshall Tito, himself a Communist in control of neighboring Yugoslavia, offered some support to the Greek leftists, the Soviet Union refused to become involved. Under pressure from the government of British Labor Prime Minister Clement Attlee, U.S. President Harry S. Truman of the United States also eventually became involved in this Greek civil war. In 1947, Truman requested and received Congressional authorization for a program to offer economic and military aid to Turkey and Greece from a "Communist threat." On the basis of the authorization he received, Truman then sent 74,000 tons of military equipment to the right-wing government in Athens in the last five months of 1947 alone.

During the Cold War, mere strong opposition by a person, an organization, or a country to racism or the Truman Doctrine was sometimes sufficient to invite punishment and repudiation as being either Communist or sympathetic to Communism. Among people who were obsessed with Cold War matters were many who were only tangentially interested in mounting any serious opposition to racial discrimination or imperial exploitation. Truman's Executive Order #9835 issued on March 25, 1947, providing for a domestic search for any "infiltration of disloyal persons" paved the way for a subsequent witch hunt in the United States that targeted Communists and Communist-sympathizers, both real and imagined.

It was against the background of this Cold War that Winston Churchill in 1946 warned that an "iron curtain" was descending through the middle of Europe, thus implying that this should send shudders around the globe. Less often pointed out to those who tend to lionize Winston Churchill as a great statesman is the fact that Churchill favored neither British decolonization in Africa nor strong anti-racism legislation in Britain. When during World War II Deputy Prime Minister Attlee gave public assurances to a group of West African students that "we fight this war . . . for all peoples" and that "I look for an every-increasing measure of self-government in Africa," he was promptly contradicted by Churchill (Fryer 1984: 333).

Following World War II when two super powers led by people mostly of European descent competed fiercely to win the allegiance of as many people as possible worldwide, it was not uncommon for both of those super powers—the United States and the Soviet Union—presume that whether one was Communist or non-Communist was of much greater importance than anything having to do with one's attitude toward racism or imperialism. So intense was this new type of competition between the world's two super powers, each surrounded by a number of allies or satellite countries, that in 1947 the Americans Bernard Baruch and Walter Lippmann using the term "Cold War" to describe the situation. Whatever the Cold War was in reality, it was hardly simply a conflict involving a face-off between "saints" on one side and "sinners" on the other. There were more than a few self-serving vested interests and corrupted parties involved on both sides to suggest that many contradictions were in play.

The Cold War provided for no coordinated assault on racism, as the opposing blocs were too distrustful of each other to support any coordinated policy or either did not view an assault on racism a major priority. In the West, for example, numerous activists campaigning against racism fell under suspicion as Communist sympathizers, regardless of whether they were or not. They were not infrequently stigmatized, harassed, discredited, or forced to retire from positions of influence. Using Cold War logic, it became acceptable in the West to pretend that any system of government that was anti-Communist—no matter how dictatorial, how repressive, or how racist—was a worthy ally in the cause of democracy. Suspicions and presumptions that defied logic were equally prevalent within the Communist sphere of influence.

It was against this background in 1948 that the European Recovery Act of the United States (more commonly known as the Marshall Plan) began to operate. In Germany, without prior notification to the Soviet Union, Western powers revoked the worthless German currency and replaced it with the deutschemark. The USSR quickly retaliated by blockading Berlin, which forced the Western occupation forces to undertake an airlift to keep West Berlin supplied with essential food and supplies. The Cold War also impacted the stability of Greece. By 1949, the Joint U.S. Military Advisory Group was virtually directing the war effort for the Greek neo-Fascists royalists against the Greek leftists, including the EAM, which, only five years earlier had forced Nazi forces to quit the country. By the time the nationalist forces backed by Britain and the United States triumphed later that year, at least 150,000 Greeks had been killed and between 700,000 and 800,000 caused to flee as refugees from a total population of around 7,000,000.

With this so-called civil war now at an end, the Communist Party (KKE) was banned in Greece. Around the same time, a quasi-police state committed to an ideology of cultural and religious purity ostensibly based on "Hellenic-Orthodox Christian" civilization was established in Greece. In lieu of finding serenity in this unexpected prolongation of World War II by proxy, however, the world was about to be jolted again as a result of the Cold War. This came later in 1949 as the result of two quite different developments. First, Communist forces seized definitive control of mainland China despite great U.S. financial support that had been given to the defeated Kuomintang. Second, the Soviet Union successfully tested an atomic bomb on which it had been working in secret, thereby ending the monopoly of the United States on atomic power. Given that Communist governments everywhere were rigidly controlled dictatorships, these developments further intensified the constant rift between the two Cold War blocs.

From the mid-1940s to the mid-1950s, United States officials conducted a paranoid witch hunt for Communists and their sympathizers at home and abroad that was characterized by intolerance, aggressive surveillance, loyalty oaths, "black lists," public denunciations, and the compilation of dossiers on almost anyone advocating an type of social change. As what eventually became known as McCarthyism diffused throughout American society, even the slightest suspicion that an American might believe that Communism was anything but absolutely evil sometimes caused him to be branded a spy or a traitor. While one of the most activist American officials who specialized in stigmatizing and punishing various Americans as suspects during this period was Senator Joseph McCarthy of Wisconsin, who functioned more as the leader of one of several packs of wolves than as a lone agent.

There eventually existed numerous anti-Communist committees, panels, and "loyalty review boards" at all levels of government as well as in many private agencies. America's Federal Bureau of Investigation (FBI) under J. Edgar Hoover was a major player. The most important Congressional bodies involved in the cause were the House Un-American Activities Committee, the Senate Internal Security Subcommittee, and the Senate Permanent Subcommittee on Investigations. Wire tapping, mail opening, police surveillance, imprisonment, aggressive investigation, "blacklisting," and selective leaks of incriminating information, both true and false, were among the many tactics used to root out and punish people suspected of being Communists or Communist sympathizers. People were fired from their jobs, evicted from their homes, deprived of their livelihoods, and made to turn on their relatives, neighbors, colleagues, and friends in order to survive. Even many books were burned or "suspect" authors deprived of an opportunity to be published, and people were forced to surrender their passports though guilty of no crime.

Those favoring liberal social reforms ranging from child labor laws, women's suffrage, and New Deal Programs for the poor to non-discrimination laws were especially targeted. Outlandish claims were eventually even launched against employees of the U.S. State Department, against employees of Voice of America, and against employees of the U.S. Army as well as against numerous actors, filmmakers, musicians and others in the entertainment industry. Even the National Association for the Advancement of Colored People or NAACP—the oldest and largest civil rights organization in the United States—was pressured into at least passively joining the Cold War witch hunt at home and abroad by avoiding any connection with Americans, including African-Americans, who were deemed ideologically "suspect" (NAACP 1993). It was in this connection that the long-standing and cooperative relationship between W. E. B. Du Bois, one of the founders of the NAACP, and Walter White, its long-serving Executive Secretary, experienced a rupture.

Trinidad-born and New York-reared Hazel Scott after studying music at the Juilliard School of Music became in 1950 the first women of color in the United States to host her own television program. Even this spouse of a U.S. Congressman (the Reverend Adam Clayton Powell, Jr.), however, felt compelled to continue her career in Europe for five years after her public opposition to McCarthyism and to racism led to accusations that she was a Communist sympathizer, causing the prompt cancellation of her program. Mississippi-born African-American writer Richard Wright also longed to live where there could be some respite from American racism, and he had heard that France might be such a place. He faced the difficulty, however, in getting there.

Under surveillance by the CIA and FBI beginning in 1943, Wright managed during the summers of 1944 and 1945 to go to Quebec as the next best place to France. Finally in 1946 through the intervention of the American writer Gertrude Stein and French anthropologist Claude Lévi-Strauss, Wright, the most renowned of all "black" writers in the United States, received an invitation to travel to France as a guest of the French government, where he was well received by French intellectuals, including Jean-Paul Sartre and Albert Camus. Ironically, 1946 was also the year that Wright's anti-Communist anthology *The God That Failed* was published in the *Atlantic Monthly*. In France, such "black" writers as René Maran, Léopold Senghor, and Aimé Cesaire also embraced Richard Wright.

In 1949, the year following writer James Baldwin's initial arrival in France, the U.S.'s Congress for Cultural Freedom invited Richard Wright to join, but he refused, correctly suspecting that it had connections with the CIA. Due to the failed attempts of the CIA to manipulate Richard Wright and his pre-World War II history as a Communist, Hollywood movie studio bosses blacklisted the works of Wright's throughout the era of McCarthyism. Wright married in Europe, traveled widely there and in Africa. Wright's writing was an influence on that of Frantz Fanon, essayist, psychoanalyst, and philosopher originally from Martinique, Fanon rejected the concept of *Négritude* as relevant to his worldview. Wrote Fanon about his encounter with the larger world, "I am endlessly creating myself." Without ever feeling free to return to the land of his birth, it was in 1960 that Richard Wright died in France. Fanon died the following year. During some four decades, Fanon was perhaps the 20th century's most brilliant contributor to social thought on anti-colonial liberation (Fabre 1991: 175-193; Fanon 1967).

Paul Robeson was likely one of the most brilliant intellectuals and gifted artists that the United States ever produced. Passionate in his support of the working classes, Paul Robeson was well traveled in Europe, including in the Soviet Union. Like Ernest Hemingway, George Orwell, and Pablo Picasso, Robeson had sympathized with the Republican cause in the Spanish Civil War. Robeson had also supported Welsh coal miners in their struggles and he had been unequivocal in opposing racism in all its forms. His own father had been a slave in the

American South until he eventually escaped to the state of New Jersey, where he became a Presbyterian minister. Robeson was an excellent athlete in college, a Phi Beta Kappa scholar, valedictorian of his graduating class at Rutgers University, and later the recipient of a law degree at Columbia University. He sang superbly in over twenty languages and acted in eleven films.

Robeson was aware that between 1900 and 1914 alone there had been more than eleven lynchings of "blacks" in his native country. He was also aware that in the summer of 1919, the streets of America were virtually flushed with the blood of slaughtered "black" Americans. Some Americans were resentful that between 1922 and 1924, Robeson worked with the playwright Eugene O'Neill, whom they considered a leftist, in *All God's Chillun Got Wings* and *The Emperor Jones*. While speaking out against racism, Robeson went on record praising the 123rd Article of the Constitution of the Soviet Union for declaring equality of all Soviet citizens "irrespective of their nationality or race, in all fields of economical, state, cultural, social, and political life" (Duberman 1995: 211). Such a pro-human rights acknowledgement by Paul Robeson with regard to the Soviet Union was tolerated in the United States during the 1930s and early 1940s as it in no way exceeded recognized boundaries of so-called free speech.

Even more importantly, Paul Robeson's declaration was momentarily convenient, as the Soviet Union was considered sufficiently anti-Nazi and anti-Fascist for occasional flattery. In the wake of World War II when Cold War reasoning became an obsession, especially with respect to civil rights, however, it was almost inevitable that an American Establishment permissive of McCarthyism would eventually target Robeson for his belief that universality of music could bring people of diverse cultural backgrounds together and his devotion to the cause of social justice quite apart from Cold War considerations. After singing in Paris at the World Peace Conference in 1949, Robeson was interviewed by an American journalist who subsequently quoted him incorrectly in a dispatch that was widely circulated in the United States. Whereas he was quoted as saying "Negroes won't fight for U.S.," what he had really said was "It is unthinkable that American Negroes will go to war on behalf of those who have oppressed us for generations . . . against a country [the Soviet Union] which in one generation has raised our people to the full dignity of mankind."

Robeson was excoriated in many newspaper articles across the United States for merely exercising his freedom of speech during an era dominated by Cold War propaganda and counter-propaganda. The FBI induced a number of well-known African-Americans to denounce him, jailed a number of people who came to his defense, and confiscated Robeson's passport, thereby preventing him from further foreign travel for nine years. Also, the Council on African Affairs, which Robeson himself had helped to found, and the Civil Rights Congress, where he held the office of vice president, were both labeled subversive. When he attempted to perform in a concert in Peekskill, New York, mob violence ensued. Robeson, who was honored as a recipient of the Stalin Peace Prize in the 1950s had to accept his prize from the United States as his passport had not yet been returned. Around this same time, Wayland Rudd, an African-

American actor of some renown, died in the Soviet Union as a Soviet citizen after having moved there from the United States in the early 1930s.

After having ruled over his country for twenty-five years, Stalin was replaced as General Secretary or First Secretary of the Central Committee of the Communist Party of the Soviet Union by Nikita Khrushchev in 1953. Considering that under Stalin between 15- and 20 million people likely died from unnatural causes, his rule had been a particularly brutal one. Likely some 800,000 were executed for political or criminal offenses, 1.7 million likely died from privation or other causes in the gulags, some 390,000 likely perished from ethnic deportations or resettlement under inhumane conditions, 4 million through suppression, and perhaps another 6 million from famine.

The same year that Nikita Khrushchev came to power in the Soviet Union, Dwight Eisenhower was elected president of the United States, and Eisenhower lost little time in strengthening and extending Truman's loyalty review program while decreasing the avenues of appeal that were available to "suspect" American citizens dismissed as employees from their jobs. In 1954 Dwight D.Eisenhower formed an historic alliance with Francisco Franco of Spain, a dictator in his own right, who had taken office by means of the Spanish Civil War as the result of support from Hitler and Mussolini. At the time of his alliance with Eisenhower, Franco was still suppressing Africans in at least two colonies in western Africa as well as in a small part of Morocco.

Such happenings as these were part of the context in which Europe was dealing with an identity crisis involving its Africa inside and its Africa outside in the wake of World War II. As for people of African descent who had been so long suffering under the yoke of European racism, the Cold War greatly complicated their ability to protest their ongoing oppression without either being targeted as an enemy "suspect" or worse, if not by the Communist bloc largely, under the hegemony of the Soviet Union, then by the anti-Communist bloc, largely under the hegemony of the United States. Although pseudo-scientific racism pretending to be based on biology had been largely discredited, at least in academic circles, the Cold War that followed World War II was in some respects little more than another way by which rivalries largely among peoples of European decent would continue to dominate the agendas of the entire world, even to such an extent that to be non-aligned could sometimes to extremely risky and fraught with danger.

Under Khrushchev, the Soviet Union continued to recruit masses of students from developing countries to study there, including from Africa, providing most of them with financial aid. Some 285 boarding schools opened in the USSR in 1956, with some of them accommodating Africans. After 1956, the number of Egyptian students in the Soviet Union and its satellites rose very sharply, reaching about 1,500 in 1959. Overall however, 1956 was not a banner year for human rights in the Soviet bloc for it was on the first day of September in this year that Soviet tanks began rolling into Budapest to crush the Hungarian uprising.

Despite efforts by the Soviet Union and the United States to keep the world sharply divided into opposing ideological blocs, the launching by the Soviets in 1957 of Sputnik as the first man-made satellite to orbit the Earth showed irrefutably that the destinies of people on the entire planet were becoming more intertwined. As the United States in a technological panic set about investing heavily in space research and science education, Paul Robeson's passport was restored to him. When in 1958, he again visited the Soviet Union, he was warmly received, in fact lionized, as the great artist and humanitarian that he was. In 1959, W. E. B. Du Bois and Ethiopia's Emperor Haile Selassie also visited the Soviet Union.

Until the 1960s, masses of British immigrants who were not considered "white," despite being full citizens, were relegated to jobs that others did not want such as street cleaning and night-shift assembly production lines, and were often paid less than "whites" performing the same types of work. As happened during World War II, Britain did not hesitate to recruit workers of color when they could perform some vital service that no one else was available to do. In order to compensate for understaffing in its National Health Service in the 1960s, for example, Britain was quite willing to recruit large numbers of immigrant workers without regard to color.

Near the end of the tenure of Prime Minister Harold Macmillan of the Conservative Party, his Commonwealth Immigration Committee debated the benefits of a new act designed to limit Britain's "net coloured intake." A concrete result of these deliberations coupled with concern about the recent rioting resulted in the the Commonwealth Immigration Act of 1962. This legislation had as its primary purpose to control unwanted colonial migration by British subjects of color to Great Britain. When during the year following its adoption, Home Secretary Henry Brooke declared the Act "inadequate for the intended purpose," and British ministers began actively considering additional means to "keep the rate of coloured immigration within acceptable bounds" (Paul 1997: 171; Mullard 1973: 48-49). Rather than confront domestic racism, they were seeking to appease the racists.

A fringe organization called The Newcastle Democratic Movement formed in the early 1960s with a six-point manifesto that included the following three: (1) the deportation of all Jews to Israel, (2) the compulsory repatriation of *all* colored Commonwealth immigrants, and (3) harsh penalties for scroungers and people who live off the state. Even more ominous, a subculture of youth with shaved heads, working-class values, and certain distinctive modes of dress began to emerge in the 1960s. Known as skinheads, the members of this subculture were much influenced by American soul groups, British R and B bands, rocksteady music, Rastafarianism, punk groups, and Carnaby Street clothing merchants and they were not homogeneous with respect to ethnicity or values. An important element among them began gradually to became politicized around a combination of racism and violence.

Not all early skinheads identified with right-wing organizations like the National Front and the British Movement, but by the end of the 1960s many British skinheads were "white" and were focused on the idea of protecting the interests of working-class "white" people and "white" culture through violent attacks on people deemed to be non-European. As skinhead subculture spread beyond Great Britain especially to other parts of Europe, moreover, skinheads increasingly specialized in random acts of unprovoked racist violence and became for many people almost indistinguishable from neo-Nazi and neo-Fascist groups that often targeted people deemed to be of Asian, African, and Jewish descent. Skinheads sometimes lashed out at some people they deemed "white" merely for fraternizing with people belonging to the minority groups that skinheads despised.

Quite apart from the skinheads, Britain was losing its historic status as a great imperial power as many colonies in Africa were becoming independent, contributing to feelings of resentment by many Britons toward people of African descent. In terms of territory, newly independent Sudan was the largest colony in Africa. In terms of population, newly independent Nigeria was the largest African colony in population. Both in territory and population, the former Belgian Congo, which had become independent in 1960, had been by far the largest colony in central Africa. So embittered were some Western countries about the independence of the former Belgian Congo that they conspired in the overthrow and murder of Patrice Lumumba, its first president (De Witte 2001; Hochschild 1998: 3; Braeckman 2002). In large measure because the southeastern Congo was especially rich in minerals that many of them coveted, because Patrice Lumumba resented the racism of its colonial past, and because he anticipated opening diplomatic relations with the Soviet Union, certain Western countries conspired to bring about his murder. In fact, both the Catholic Church and Belgium's King Baudouin detested Lumumba, and he was assassinated in the presence of a senior Belgian police officer and three other Belgian officers after which even the United Nations was used to divert attention from the affair and a puppet beholden to the West was installed in Lumumba's place.

The Soviet Union founded the Peoples' Friendship University in 1960 with a primary goal to help provide higher education in engineering, agriculture, and other disciplines as well as to recruit young Communists in developing countries at the height of the Cold War. In the first year, it enrolled 57 Soviet students plus 539 foreign students from 59 countries including many of appreciable African ancestry from Africa, Latin America, and Asia. The following year, Moscow's Friendship University was renamed Patrice Lumumba Peoples' Friendship University in honor of the recently murdered president of Congo whose death had been arranged by Western governments infuriated that he wished to established diplomatic relations with the Soviet Union, who had been their implacable enemy.

In fact, the Cold War was heating up in 1961, for this was the year that a botched Bay of Pigs invasion from the United States attempted to overthrow the Fidel Castro regime in Cuba. It was also the year the Berlin Wall was constructed to keep East Berliners contained in East Berlin. Much farther east, the first United States advisors arrived in Vietnam hoping to reverse gains that the Communist North Vietnamese had achieved when the French, after being defeated at Dien Bien Phu, withdrew from Indo-China in 1954. The Cold War mentality that so dominated the period did not allow the American Establishment to realize that more than being a war between Communists and non-Communists, the Vietnam War was a war of independence against colonial rule.

In Vietnam, as elsewhere, the West often mistook any anti-racist struggle or struggle for self-determination as Communist-inspired and, hence, as evil. In a world where thinking was so simplistically dichotomized, one reason that anti-racist and liberation campaigns often adopted the language of Communism was because if Western democracy was the status quo and the status quo was unjust, Western democracy could not ideologically embrace its opposite.

Moves toward self-determination in Africa merely gave greater exposure to deeply ingrained racism in Europe as, for example, the discriminatory 1962 Commonwealth Immigrants Act, which had as its main purpose to reduce the number of people deemed "coloured" entering Britain. Clearly by this time, some Europeans, both at the government level and at the street level, were not adjusting well to the end of colonialism in Africa. As resentments against African demands for self-determination in Africa grew, they sometimes contributed to backlash for people of African descent in Europe. When Kenya became independent from Britain in December 1963, a rather wealthy community of Indian background whose members held British passports was living in the country. As members of this community had great economic influence in Kenya that was quite disproportionate to their numbers and were viewed by many in independent Kenya as a privileged relic class from the era of British colonialism, newly independent Kenya lost little time implementing an Africanization program aimed at forcing them out of positions of great influence through policies that favored their own citizens rather than these British citizens of Indian heritage.

Because the vast majority of these British citizens of Indian ethnicity resident in Kenya held passports issued prior to Kenyan independence by the Britain's High Commission, Britain's discriminatory 1962 Commonwealth Immigrants Act did not exclude them from entering the United Kingdom. This created a racist crisis in London. As many Britons remained opposed to the immigration of people of color, the government passed a Nationality Act (1964) that facilitated the immigration into Britain of colonists that were deemed "white" (Paul 1997: 179).

Race so dominated the British election of 1964 that in Smethwick (now Warley East), located in the West Midlands of England and which had long been a focus of immigration, it was rumored that Conservative candidate Peter Griffiths was able to narrowly defeat Gordon Walker (Shadow Foreign Secretary of the opposition Labor Party) because Griffiths's supporters had circulated the slogan, "If you want a nigger for a neighbour, vote Liberal or Labour." Despite this particular loss for the Labor Party, Labor was still able to win enough seats overall to enable its Harold Wilson to emerge as the new prime minister.

Even with the new Wilson government at the helm, the new cabinet was concerned that the "net intake of coloured Commonwealth immigrants in 1964 was 9 percent higher than it had been in 1960." After much discussion the Wilson government opted to rely more on the approach of reconciliation than on compulsion to deal with problems of blatant racial discrimination in British society. Intent on making Britain face up more honestly to its racism even at the highest levels of government, Malcolm X, an African-American Muslim activist with racism in his own background accepted an invitation from a BBC journalist who wished to arrange a debate between him and Peter Griffiths.

Although the debate never took place due to a late refusal by Griffiths to participate, Malcolm X publicly chided the voters of Smethwick before the press as Fascists and Nazis. Malcolm X was assassinated in Harlem only nine days later, and his flap with Giffiths had occurred during the short period after he had left the so-called Nation of Islam, become a Sunni Muslim, turned away from referring to all people he deemed to be "white" as *devils*, and emerged as a prominent mainstream spokesman for civil rights in the United States and for Pan-Africanism in the larger world.

Shortly afterward, a notorious White Paper from Wilson's government called on the House to recognize the issue revolved around "the question of colour." The Home Secretary was now empowered to deport without a court recommendation individuals who had entered Britain by evading the 1962 act. Shortly thereafter the number of work vouchers were cut to a mere 8,500 per year, reserving 1,000 of them for immigrants from the tiny Maltese Islands, as they were at least deemed to be located on the right side of Europe's divide with the non-European world. This came as a major disappointment to "black" Britons who had campaigned very hard to put the Labor Party into power (Paul 1997: 174-175; Mullard 1973: 51-52).

That on the other side of the Atlantic by this time, African-Americans mobs, ostensibly in reaction to racism, had torched certain neighborhoods in a number of the largest cities of the United States doubtlessly contributed to a feeling of urgency in Britain regarding the need for new legislation. It was against this background that Britain enacted its first Race Relations Act in April 1965. The first Race Relations Bill focused much less on penalizing discrimination than on the maintenance of public order. It did however provide for the establishment of the first Race Relations Board. Even some Labor MP's did not support its passage until all criminal sanctions had given way to mere recommendations for conciliation. Some hotels and all private clubs, moreover, were excluded from coverage. This Race Relations Act, was extremely narrow and lacked provisions for strong enforcement. While it outlawed "incitement to racial hatred" and forbade discrimination in "places of public resort," it did not criminalize discrimination in such other areas as employment and housing. Although virtually without any enforcement power, this was the strongest anti-discrimination act ever approved in Britain as of 1965 (Mullard 1973: 55-56).

In 1968, Harold Wilson's Labor government enacted an additional Race Relations Act that had as its purpose to extend the Race Relations Act of 1965 by providing some coverage relating to employment and housing. It was while this legislation was under discussion that Enoch Powell made his infamous "Rivers of Blood speech." In this infamous speech, Powell attempted to justify racism by going on the public record while still in Heath's Shadow Cabinet (i.e., a cabinet of the party not in power) as claiming the proposed legislation to be offensive and immoral. Although Heath sacked him the day after the speech, Powell's speech became a rallying crying for many racists throughout Britain, including many trade unionists. In reality, this was but one of several speeches that Powell delivered that year in which he implied that "black" minorities could never be assimilated into British society and that they represented a cultural difference that would always be an alien danger to British identity (MacMaster 2001: 182).

These developments in Britain anticipated that many of the approximately 345,000 Asians resident in the African countries of Kenya, Tanzania, Zambia, Malawi, and Uganda, mostly of Indian derivation, might eventually wish to im-migrate to Britain, where they held citizenship. With respect to their passports and citizenship, they were unlike approximately 800,000 Asians in South Africa, most of whom were of Indian origin although about 100,000 of these were orig-inally from China. Although most of these Afro-Asians in in eastern and south-ern Africa had been encouraged to settled by Britain in order to help it sustain its colonial empire, Britain was poised to turn its back on even those Asians stranded in Kenya with British citizenship. In a mere three days, the government headed by Harold Wilson rushed through Parliament new legislation in 1968 that had has its main purpose the prevention of their entering Britain.

In 1971, Britain's Heath government passed an additional Immigration Act that for the first time formally divided British subjects into partials (i.e., family British) and nonpatrials (i.e., political British), implicitly on a basis considered racial. Partials were defined as British subjects and UKC citizens (meaning, citi-zens of the United Kingdom and Colonies) who themselves or whose parent or grandparent had been born, adopted, naturalized, or registered in the United Kingdom, or UKC citizens who had lived for five years in the United Kingdom. Nonpatrials not living in the United Kingdom could settle there only with work permits. While this Act allowed "white" subjects such as those fleeing the tran-sition to majority rule in Rhodesia to migrate into Britain at will, it placed non-patrials on virtually the same footing as aliens (Paul 1997: 180-182).

Other indications that British racism was thriving included the fact that Brit-ain continued to make weapons available to the *apartheid* government of South Africa, support that it justified as combating African Communists although South Africa was conducting a campaign of brutality and racist terror to sup-press the majority of its population. In the autumn of 1971, President Kenneth Kaunda of Zambia and President Julius Nyerere of Tanzania visited London to strongly protest the further supplying by Britain of arms to *apartheid* South Africa. In December of the same year, the UN General Assembly adopted six resolutions condemning *apartheid*.

Whereas independent Kenya and Tanzania sought to break the hold that res-ident Asians had on their economies without expelling them outright, when in 1971 President Idi Amin of Uganda ordered all Asians to leave his country without their assets. Britain—by this time under the leadership of Edward Heath as Prime Minister—once again found itself in the eye of a storm that revolved around its deeply engrained racism, on the one hand, and its imperial legacy and grants of citizenship, on the other. Although the dictator Idi Amin was hardly a poster child for any type of civil rights, the Western media colluded with Britain to deflect attention away from British racism by negatively portraying only Idi Amin as a racist. In reality, Britain was discriminating against its own citizens and Idi Amin was by contrast mostly showing favoritism toward his own citizens. This was just one incident in a long pattern of Western media failing to be objective in their reporting about Africa vis-à-vis Europe.

Meanwhile, Edward Heath announced in 1972 that his government was duty-bound to supply maritime helicopters and other naval spare parts to South Africa. This was the same year that the UN International Court at The Hague ruled that South Africa was under obligation to withdraw from South-West Africa (now Namibia), where it had also implanted *apartheid*. Only with the greatest reluctance did the government of Edward Heath in 1972 finally admit 30,000 "Ugandan Asians" holding British passports into the country in order to protect its reputation when it became evident that these citizens had nowhere else to go. Even then, Britain did this without recognizing the immigrants as having any rights to settle permanently in this country where they were citizens.

In the 1960s and early 1970s, Portugal and *apartheid* South Africa continued to wage anti-liberation battles driven by racism and greed—and justified by Cold War rhetoric implying that people of African descent who campaigned for self-determination and basic human rights were indistinguishable from Communists. Claiming only to be acting in opposition to Communism, they continued disallowing any meaningful participation in governance by the indigenous masses in the areas of Africa that they dominated. In lieu of fighting in colonial wars in Africa, however, many Portuguese males by this time preferred seeking economic opportunities by relocated north of the Iberian Peninsula in countries of western Europe with booming economies. As a result of emigration of many workers out of Portugal to other parts of western Europe, new employment opportunities began to be created for Africans wishing to relocate to Portugal. Led initially by Cape Verdeans from the island Santiago, there began to take place in the mid-1960 the first large-scale movement of African immigrants in modern times from Portuguese colonies into metropolitan Portugal. As this flow of people from Africa into anti-Communist Portugal illustrates, what many oppressed Africans wanted more than Communism was enhanced opportunity to succeed wherever they could find it.

When on December 18, 1963, African students in Moscow demonstrated against the death there of a Ghanaian student, they were obviously aware that Communism per se did not offer any guarantee of a utopia. This was, by coincidence, the same year that José Eduardo dos Santos of the Portuguese colony of Angola, who two years earlier at age nineteen had joined the Popular Movement for the Liberation of Angola or MPLA, had to flee his homeland for education and safety. Studying in Moscow on a scholarship at Patrice Lumumba University between 1963 and 1969, he received a degree in petroleum engineering. He remained there an additional year in order to take a military course in telecommunications and radar.

In 1974, a *coup d'état* overthrew Portugal's neo-Fascist regime under Antotonio de Oliveira Salazar that so-called Western democracies had seldom denounced although it had been entrenched since 1926 and was closely tied to imperialism, forced labor, and racism. When Angola became independent of Portugal in 1975, it was José Eduardo dos Santos, who had completed his higher education in the Soviet Union, who became Angola's first minister of foreign affairs. Although during his student days in the Soviet Union, Eduardo dos San-tos had been married to a Russian woman, by the time he succeeded Agostinho Neto as the second president of Angola in 1979, he was married to Ana Paula Dos Santos, an Angolan. As president, José Eduardo dos Santos lost little time in guiding Angola from the path of Marxism to that of democratic socialism.

Despite this transition under difficult circumstances, the United States re-fused to recognize Angola's independence for several years while giving covert assistance to opponents of the government as they engaged the government in a bloody civil war. The United States attempted to justify its position because Cu-ba, to which it was very hostile largely because it was ruled by a Communist dictatorship, had dispatched troops there to help during Angola's War of Inde-pendence to help protect it from aggressions and threats of the nearby South Africa government, which was governed by a racist and system of *apartheid*. Although under *apartheid*, South Africa was a rogue terrorist police state where the majority of its indigenous residents had no right to even vote, compete for jobs in an open employment market, or even live where they wished, still mired in its Cold War logic, the United States maintained diplomatic relations with South Africa while refusing for several years to recognize the independence of Angola because it deemed Angola's leadership leftist, and therefore not suffi-ciently opposed to Communism.

In the post-World War II period being discussed here, issues of self-determination, immigration and how the world should deal with racism were largely overshadowed by the Cold War. Still as of the mid-1970s, the African presence in Europe was more substantial than ever. By the time the United States hastily pulled its last troops from Vietnam in 1974, the Cold War was entering a period of temporary détente. The ban on the Communist Party in Greece was expiring. Globalization was accelerating.

In a bizarre twist of logic and expectations, it was the determination of so many people of African descent to circumvent the racism and limited opportuni-ties that continued to frame their lives well after World War II that led many of them to Europe. Among numerous students of African descent who entered Eu-rope shortly after the end of World War II in large numbers to avail themselves of higher education was one now widely known as Cheikh Anta Diop of Seneg-al. He had completed his baccalaureate in Dakar, Senegal's capital, with special concentrations in philosophy and mathematics in 1945.

It was the following year at age 23 that Diop traveled to Paris to continue his educataion. While studying physics, he also devoted considerable time to the study of anthropology, sociology, economics, linguistics, and ancient history with a particularly keen focus on the meaning of Ancient Egypt within the larger context of African civilizations. Politically active during the fifteen years that he remained in Paris, Diop beginning in 1950 served for three years as Secretary-General of the *Rassemblement Democratique Africain* or RDA and helped to organize the first Pan-African Student Congress that convened in Paris in 1951. This was the same year that he presented a doctoral dissertation on Ancient Egypt as an African civilization that was rejected. Continuing to rework his the-sis during nine additional years, Diop successfully completed his *doctorat d'etat en lettres* in 1960. Returning to Senegal after this time, Cheikh Anta Diop operated a carbon-14 laboratory, devoted himself to university teaching, and continued research and writing focusing mostly on Egyptology, human variation, and African civilization.

Only three years after Diop arrived in Paris, Dean Dixon, a brilliant African-American musician who had been born in New York and educated at the Julliard School of Music and Columbia University, departed the United States for Europe in 1949. In search of more promising prospects as a symphony conductor than were available to him at home, Dixon began his career as an expatriate conducting the Radio Symphony Orchestra of the French National Radio. Although he conducted the Israel Philharmonic during 1950 and 1951, he also accepted invitations that took him to Italy, Denmark, and Sweden. After holding the post of artistic and musical director of Sweden's Gothenburg Symphony from 1953 to 1960, Dixon acted as musical director at the Frankfurt Radio Symphony (then called the *Hessische Rundfunk*) for the next thirteen years. Dixon's recordings with the Vienna State Opera Orchestra and the London Philharmonic Symphony Orchestra are among his best. Though Dean Dixon also conducted in Africa, in South America, and from 1964 to 1974 was conductor of the Sydney Symphony in Australia. Among the earliest of Americans to conduct major orchestras across Europe and well beyond, it was in Zurich that Dean Dixon died in 1976—a son of Africa, a son of Europe, and a citizen of the world.

Chapter Eight

Color, Identity, and European Union

Mid-1970s to Early 2000s

The first three decades after World War II in much of Europe were characterized by unprecedented economic growth and low unemployment as well as much sympathy for welfare states and/or for Socialism. The period was one when a disavowal of blatant anti-Semitism corresponded with minimal popularity of right-wing extremist politics. Although extreme right-wing politics tinged with racism did not disappear, parties such as the German National Democratic Party (NPD), the Italian Social Movement (MSI), the British National Front (NF), and the French Front National or FN seldom received more than 5 percent of the vote in elections (MacMaster 2001: 190). This was the period that in France was called *les trente glorieuses*. Welfare states have not historically been able to adjust easily to massive waves of immigration without the eventual rise of hostility either toward immigrants in general or immigrants on some type of selective basis. In reality, European racism that seemed to be somewhat dormant and constrained during the first three decades after World War II was only awaiting an opportunity to spring forth with new vigor.

One of the conditions that allowed this resurgence to take place was European bitterness toward what was called the Third or Developing World over the end of European domination and exploitation in the form of colonialism. This condition impacted Germany especially early when in the wake of its defeat in World War I it was forced to renounce control of its overseas colonies. A second condition that contributed to the resurgence of racism well beyond Germany however, or what Barker (1981) has called the "new racism," was that declines in population growth in Europe after World War II had become very pronounced by the 1970s, creating needs at an unprecedented level for peoples who considered themselves Europeans to depend on "others" to supplement their aging populations in ways that would sustain and grow their economies at home.

Although consistent with traditional forms of European racism in terms of institutionalized social domination and exclusion, "new racism" tended to code the presumed superiority of peoples of European derivation to others as much in terms of culture and ethnicity as in terms of pseudo-scientific ways of viewing human biology. With a focus on Germany, France, and the Netherlands among others, Bonilla-Silva (2000: 188-214) has similarly written about the convergence of "new racism" of Western nations within the world system in recent decades.

As waves of Europeans during the decades of the late 20th century were moving from some less-industrialized parts of the world to some highly industrialized countries in Europe and beyond, so also did non-European refugees, asylum seekers, and people attempting to better their own circumstances long-term. Many of these non-European newcomers were not prepared to serve as temporary laborers who could be cycled in and cycled out for the convenience of Europeans. Also, these "others" arriving in Europe were not prepared to settle long term or relegated to the fringes of European societies in the ways that Europeans assumed would be possible, as Europeans invested great energy in the ideal of European unification.

The *Europe* and *Europeans* had never been other than loosely defined constructs with fuzzy boundaries. By the early 1970s, the fact that Europe needed "others"—that it had so long denigrated—in order to survive was made more complex by the fact that the still-evolving and experimental construct of the European Union was ill equipped to suppress strong feeling of European xenophobia, nationalist populism, and dormant racism. This dormant racism, by this time sometimes called "new racism," was about to surge at a time that increasingly large numbers of people from many parts of the world, including from Africa, were laying claim to a right to be, or to become, European—and to some extent on their own terms. The last chapter of *Racism in Europe* by MacMaster (2001) and a collection of essays edited by Pierre-André Taguieff (1991) under the title of *Face au racisme: Analyses, hypotheses, perspectives* have been particularly pointed in describing some aspects of this ideological and societal metamorphosis in Europe.

During the 1960s, oil had replaced coal as the major source of energy in Europe, and, as an important series of oil crises began to occur in 1973, Europe experienced a massive economic downturn, industrial restructuring, and increasing unemployment. Under these circumstances, many Europeans became more likely to criticize and even discriminate against those they considered to be outsiders regardless of their technical citizenship status. Dramatic changes occurred in long-established patterns of south-to-north trans-Mediterranean migration from Africa into Europe even as many European countries began to close their borders to African immigrants, including especially those wishing to enter for economic reasons. Immigration from Arabic-speaking countries into western Europe was perceived by many Europeans as problematic, including possibly as a threat to internal security (Haas 2006: 10; Pastore 2002: 107). While nowhere in Europe was there an objection to the utilization of African natural resources, the ready acceptance and integration of Africans into European societies quite often caused Europeans consternation.

Although numerous European countries faced a future characterized by labor shortages, virtually all had misgivings about augmenting their population with additional people of African descent on a long-term basis. Justice and home-affairs ministers of the European Union increasingly favored bloc-wide "circular migration" of Africans through the granting of so-called "temporary visas." In the German Federal Republic (West Germany) between 1955 and 1973, many non-German workers who were intended to be temporary eventually put down roots and remained after their contracts expired. As a consequence, West Germany's SPD-FDP coalition government in 1977 appointed a commission to define a framework for *Ausländerpolitik* or foreigner policy (Triadafilopoulos and Zaslove 2006: 181-182).

As West Germany became less welcoming of foreign guest workers, it was one of the countries that closed its borders to them and initiated elaborate and costly programs of repatriation while tightening its laws concerning refugee and immigration rights (Blaschke 1998: 60). Hostility toward people of appreciable African ancestry in West Germany became so blatant from around 1976 that they were sometimes confronted by Germans physically attacking them or shouting such obscenities as "Nigger, out! Nigger, go home!," "Germany must be clean!," or "Germany for the Germans!" Even some German citizens who were partially of African descent were targeted in this way. Ironically, such victimized German citizens sometimes found themselves with less protection than foreigners.

When African Germans complained to the police, they were often directed to the *Auslanderbeauftragte* or office of foreigner affairs. When the office of foreigner affairs learned that they were German citizens, however, they were typically sent back to the police, usually with no action being taken. Hoping for an enhanced sense of security and belonging, many Germans of appreciable African ancestry settled in West Berlin. Still under occupation by the Allied forces of the United States, France, and Britain, this largest of all German metropolises maintained a very international and cosmopolitan atmosphere. Contributing to its openness toward people with some African heritage in the 1970s was its popular culture, influenced by African-American artists especially in the domain of music (Sephocle 1996: 14, 21, 26).

Shortly after Heinz Kühn became West Germany's first Federal Commissioner for the Integration of Foreign Workers and Their Families in 1978 while the country was being governed by the SPD-FDP coalition, he recommended radical new reforms whereby the country would for the first time recognize itself as a country of immigration and begin earnestly attempting to develop policies that would integrate its foreign residents, provide them with improved access to education, and allow them to vote in local elections. These proposals were not well received by large segments of the electorate, however, and a new CDU-CSU coalition came to power in 1982 that was headed by conservative Helmut Kohl, whose priorities were more focused on immigration restriction and repatriation.

The decade of the 1980s was an especially interesting one for people of African descent or European-African descent in West Germany. Unlike France,

Germany had no history of assimilationism where people not claiming to be "white" per se were concerned. As Helmut Kohl was chancellor of West Germany from 1982 to 1998 and of a reunited Germany until 2000, his tenure as German chancellor was the longest since that of Otto von Bismarck, the first chancellor of the German Empire in the late 19th century. In 1983, the Kohl government passed legislation that provided payment for foreigners to return to their countries of origin. It also proposed policies intended to sharply limit family reunification by drastically lowering the age of entitlement.

Germany intensified its policies of repatriation in the early 1980s as Germans became increasingly disconcerted by an increase in refugees from Asia and Africa in their midst, many of whom were seeking asylum there as victims of political persecution. Some German politicians reacted by openly referring to such refugees in terms of an invasive "flood" of foreign bodies, a dangerous "rising tide" that threatened to inundate the country, a stream, a deluge, a river, and a torrent (Linke 1999: 133-135).

As of the 1980s, most Germans remained in denial about the concept that that one could even be both African as well as German in any meaningful sense. Although some Germans had met a few Afro-Germans here and there and seen them as entertainers, a stereotype that they did not exist remained prevalent. Such widespread denial was still taking place when Christian Democratic Party Chairman Heinrich Geißler formulated the concept of a multicultural society as a goal for the major political parties in the mid-1980s (Jobatey 1996: 29).

Audre Lourde, a "black" poet originally from Saint Croix in the Virgin Islands, taught a course on African-American women poets in the spring of 1984 at the Free University of Berlin. Around the same time, the representation of Germans of appreciable African ancestry in film and television increased dramatically. From about this time, the German pop singer Ramona Kraft (now Ramona Wulf), born in Bavaria in 1964 and reared by her mother's family, began to become famous. Commonly known simply as Ramona since she secured a record contract with Phillips, this singer was the daughter of a "black" American GI and a "white" German mother. In part to counter certain sexual stereotypes about "black" women, the German youth magazine *Bravo* took to emphasizing her strict Catholic upbringing and beliefs. Also in the mid-1980s, the actor Charlie Muhammed Huber played a detective in the popular mystery series *Der Alte* on Germany's ZDF channel, where his ancestry was discussed only in the beginning parts of the show (Jobatey 1996: 31, 33).

Carol Campbell, the Munich-born daughter of an African-American jazz musician and a "white" German mother, began her career in the performing arts and set design at the German Opera of Berlin in 1985 before later working in Paris and the United States as well as in German film and on television. A number of African Germans earned a reputation in popular music and dance; one of them named Rob Pilatus worked from 1987 through 1993 with a "black" Frenchman named Fab Morvan under the name "Milli Vanilli."

In 1986, a group of thirty African Germans founded the *Initiative Schwarze Deutsche* (ISD) or Initiative of Black Germans and began holding meetings in Berlin. ISD provided a variety of cultural, political, and social activities. Affiliate groups later emerged in more than ten cities stretching from Hamburg in the north to Munich in the south. The German journals *Afro Look* and *Invisible* began to be published, and a organization of African German Woman known as ADEFRA also began publishing *Afrekete* (Blackshire-Belay 1996: 112-113). In the late 1980s, the Austrian television presenter Arabella Kiesbauer, daughter of a Ghanaian-born father and an Austrian mother, began a successful career on German television. Among other African Germans on television who appeared with regularity in the late 1980s and early 1990s was Cherno Jobatey, a news reporter rather than an entertainer (Jobatey 1996: 33).

Meanwhile from the mid-1980s in the German Democratic Republic (also known as East Germany), foreign workers and students were recruited from so-called fraternal socialist countries. While West Germany turned to recruiting more diaspora Germans from eastern European countries, East Germany was involved in recruiting workers especially from Vietnam, Mozambique, Cuba, Poland, and Angola to the resentment of many in both of the Germanies. Of the 190,000 such foreigners from fraternal socialist countries who were living in the East Germany as of early 1990, 106,500 were employed, 28,900 were in vocational training, and another 10,200 were enrolled in various universities and colleges (Blaschke 1998: 61-62).

The Western world collaborated in a massive public-relations campaign about freedom after the fall of the Berlin Wall in 1989 that had been made possible after many decades of sacrifice and investment by peoples of numerous countries and ethnic backgrounds. At the societal level far beyond the claims of Cold War propagandists, Germany would soon after unification be faced with the need to reconstruct the economy in former East Germany at a time and in a way that would place it under intense strain and make life less secure for its ethnic minorities. Shortly after unification on October 3, 1990, the unemployment rate in former West Germany rose to 8.2 percent and that in former East Germany to 15.2 percent.

Under these difficult economic circumstances, a debate became more intense among Germans concerning who should and should not be considered German. Unification contributed to ethnonationalism that could be traced back at least as far as Germany's Nationality Act of 1913 when for the first time Germans became citizens or subjects not primarily through their being recognized as citizens of various federal states but rather by being directly linked to the *Kaiserreich* at the center of the empire. In addition, unification gave new support to ethnonationalism in Germany and contributed to an upsurge in aggressive racism that manifested itself in rising hostility toward people deemed to be foreigners, including especially those deemed to be non-Germanic.

Under the German law of 1913, citizenship was distinct from concepts of residency or territory in that only ethnic Germans—sometimes known as *Volksdeutsche*—could become citizens almost automatically, even if they were born outside the country to non-citizen parents and if they had never lived inside Germany. By contrast, non-ethnic Germans born inside Germany typically could not claim citizenship for themselves or their children or else could claim it only with great difficulty. Germany's traditional citizenship policy had produced and perpetuated a class of resident "non-Germans," and this continued to be the case after unification although non-Germans obviously were not expatriated, put into concentration camps, or killed *en masse* as happened under the Nazis (De Soto and Plett 1995: 107-108, 110-111; Linke 1999: 122-123, 132).

The Ronald Regan and George Herbert Walker Bush Administrations that governed the United States from 1981 through 1993, along with like-minded administrations in Europe and cooperating media moguls, celebrated these events in self-congratulatory ways almost as if singing from a single sheet of lyrics. Using the rhetoric of Cold War success, they also celebrated enthusiastically that a united Berlin within a united Germany would greatly improve the prospects for European unity. While this was undoubtedly true, they took virtually no note of the upsurge in xenophobia and racism that found more open expression in Germany after this time.

The eight largest foreign groups in the Federal Republic of Germany's population in 1988 shortly before it began discussions with the German Democratic Republic (East Germany) about reunification were Turks, Yugoslavs, Italians, Greeks, Spaniards, Portuguese, Moroccans, and Tunisians, in that order (Liauzu 1996: 189-190). As by this time Germans in the west were much more enthusiastic about the prospects of reunification with other people sharing the same language and culture than non-Germans, there began to be evoked numerous negative images of foreigners in Germany, including especially those deemed to be non-European or Muslim. Images set forth included those of a country being threatened by a "flood" of foreigners.

After reunification in 1990, these types of images reemerged and politicians often proclaimed a wish to stop the flood or dam up the stream. Chancellor Helmut Schmidt, for example, wished to change the right of political asylum (Linke 1999: 135-136). In what had been East Germany, individual factories terminated a large number of contracts with foreign workers or put them on an individual footing with the result that many foreign immigrants left that part of Germany (Blaschke 1998: 62). Also contributing to such departures or relocations westward was an outpouring of hostility and violence against foreigners there, and most especially against those with dark complexions.

Skinhead groups with racist agendas emerged in East Germany by the early 1980s. Because they tended to be very anti-Communist, the West to some extent looked at them as part of the drive to win the Cold War rather than as the threat to human rights that they were. Established in several major cities of East Germany, they followed Western skinhead fashions, and upon unification their violent tendencies turned into naked brutality.

Feeling angry and somewhat marginalized because in the former German Democratic Republic living standards were much lower than in the West Germany, skinhead feelings of resentment translated easily into violent attacks on the minority populations that they most despised. Although the former German Democratic Republic contained only about one-fifth as many people as West Germany had, the eastern population was responsible for about one-third of all the acts of racist violence after unification.

Already Germany was increasingly obsessed with a perceived threat of *Uberfemdung* (foreign inundation or over-foreignization). Daniel Cohn-Bendit, a prominent member of the leftist Green Party, received hate mail accusing him of being an "enemy of the German people" for his failure to join in a chorus of xenophobic and racist alarmism requiring drastic measures. The "drastic measures" advocated included a call of some for internment camps for foreign refugees perceived as of problematic racial or ethnic origins. German media tended to project images of refugees as having a voracious appetite for wealth, money, status, power, and social-welfare payments. The writings of political analyst Rudolf Wassermann equated refugees (not infrequently referred to as *Scheinasylanten* or pretend-refugees) with economic opportunists or unproductive parasites in ways that seemed to legitimate the use of race-based violence against them.

Along with such notions as these, some Germans even spoke of a *Harrenrasse*, implying that there was a master race in Germany. These images revived earlier Aryan or Fascist racial aesthetics that were deeply rooted in German cultural memory. Although the people so targeted were living in Germany and often crammed into impossibly small places, their foreign bodies evoked for many Germans images of dirt, filth, and improper hygiene that endangered the clean and proper bodies of Germans. Instead of evoking pity, this situation for many evoked repugnance toward "otherness" that was deemed a racial threat. Whether these immigrants from Africa, the Indian sub-continent, or other places deemed to have no organic tie to Europe, German politicians began to perceive them as a foreign flood or as an indistinguishable tangle of brown flesh (Linke 1999: 137-147).

Germany passed a new *Ausländergesetz* or Foreigners Law in 1990, but Chancellor Helmut Kohn avoided any dramatic personal expression of sorrow as attacks on foreigners in Germany increased. He even turned down an invitation to go on television to condemn the murder of five Turkish women in Solingen. As such attacks multiplied, Kohl (a close ally of France's François Mitterrand, Britain's Margaret Thatcher, and America's Ronald Reagan) took the position that, as chancellor of Germany, he should not signal public penance for racist attacks on people in Germany deemed insufficiently European in ways that might shame Germans as exaggerated as had once done Willy Brandt, one of his predecessors, when he kneeled at the Warsaw Ghetto Memorial.

By this time, Andy Strassmeir (son of Guenter Strassmeir who had been Kohl's chief of staff) was involved with white supremists and neo-Nazis both in Germany and in the United States, including even Timothy McVeigh, who eventually was convicted of being involved in the bombing of the U.S. Federal Building in Oklahoma City. Neo-Nazis were so active and well organized in some parts of former East Germany or the German Democratic Republic that they established virtual "no-go areas" there for people of dubious European ancestry wishing to survive. When in 1992, five German Neo-Nazis or Neo-Fascists beat an Angolan named Antonio Amadeu Kiowa in Eberswalde to death, the local court in Frankfurt-Oder awarded sentences that ranged between two years on probation and four years imprisonment for those convicted. Two

years later, the regional court in Frankfurt-Oder even threw out the prosecution
of the two policemen who had apparently watched the murder without taking
any action.

With the oil crises that began in 1973, liberal French immigration policies
that had recently allowed some three and a half million new people into France
were also discontinued. Most numerous among these immigrants into France
were some 750,000 Portuguese, approximately the same number of Algerians, a
half million Spaniards, 460,000 Italians, and 260,000 Moroccans (Weil 2004:
79-81; Loisy 2005: 125; Assouline and Lallaoui 1997: 9-11; Schor 1996: 330).
Along with Germany and France, the Netherlands began to experiment with
specific measures to discourage family reunification and to encourage migrants
to return to their countries of origin. The measures employed included departure
bonuses, training programs before return, and investment programs for return
migrants.

Overall, such policies intended to facilitate return failed, probably in large
part because of the lack of investment and employment opportunities for those
to be repatriated to have opportunities for investments and employment in their
countries of origin (Haas 2006: 11, 32). As France was shutting off many types
of legal immigration in 1974, its immigrants from Maghreb or northwestern
Africa continued to become more heavily concentrated in various *banlieues* on
the outskirts of Paris as well as in increasingly stigmatized working-class en-
slaves in or along the fringes of certain other cities. One such area that was
emerging around this time was Belsunce in Marseille, a major business area that
many French people resented. This area largely catered to merchants and buyers
with connections to Africa (Blanchard and Boëtsch 2005: 17). This tendency for
many immigrants to be segregated from the mainstream of French society was in
no way altered by the fact that a change in French law in 1974 gave workers
from northwestern Africa permission to bring spouses and children into France
(Nordin 2005: 7).

In fact, racist attacks on *Maghrébins* or Maghrebians increased in the mid-
1970s to such an extent that many of them, along with some fellow Africans
resident in France, attempted to organize a genuine civil rights movement
against racism in France. The killing of Laïd Moussa in 1975 led to a large protest demonstration the same year there were several attacks on interests in southeastern France that were associated with Algeria. At times in the mid-1970s,
Africans from south of the Sahara and Africans from Maghreb in Marseille, in
sharp competition for jobs, were overtly hostile to one another. By the 1980s
however, local Algerians and Moroccans were facilitating the settlement of fellow Africans in the section of Marseille known as Noailles (Bertoncello and
Bredeloup 2004: 136-141; Gaspard and Servan-Schreiber 1985: 16-179; Dewitte
2003: 76-100).

France showed itself increasingly willing to experiment with multiculturalism, which amounted to a virtual about-face in a country with a very long tradition of assimilationism. Between 1973 and 1982, for example, France implemented its ELCO program. This involved the teaching of some ancestral languages as second languages, along with special cultural courses, to immigrant

children and French children of immigrant backgrounds, including some children of Portuguese, Tunisian, Moroccan, and Algerian backgrounds. In large measure this was a response to the fact that many children in France with immigrant backgrounds were unable to communicate with their parents in the mother languages of the parents. Multiculturalism in France also was supported by a program known as CEFISEM, established in the late 1970s to help educate some very young children of immigrants and nomads using special methodologies (Liauzu 1996: 213). Still another opening toward multi-culturalism in this country with a strong tradition of assimilationism was the establishment of a facility in Marseille in 1976 called *Maison de l'étranger* or House of the Foreigner that celebrated foreign culture in France.

Despite these unprecedented experiments with multiculturalism in France, a disaster was unfolding. As René Backmann, a journalist for the *Nouvel Observateur* noted, seventy murders of Algerians between December 1971 and December 1977 took place in France for virtually none of which anyone ever was punished. As increasingly politically conscious French youth of *Maghrébin* heritage were forced to deal with serious problems relating to identity, immigration, and racism in French society, many began to accept the newly coined slang term of *beur* to refer to themselves. In the same spirit, a new station called Radio Beur began broadcasting in 1981. Reflective of this change in society, *beur* first appeared in the French dictionary known as *Robert* in 1985 and in the *Larousse* in 1986 (Liauzu 1996: 207-208, 214).

What could not be denied is that French society was becoming more tense as attacks on Africans continued. Even as many marginalized French youth from the northwest of Africa became *beurs* instead of just *Maghrébins* or Maghrebians, many of those with connections to Africa south of the Sahara began to identify themselves by the English label of "black" instead of *noirs*, which was the traditional word in French. Intent to keep a firm grip on this societal tension, France in 1982 launched an operation to regularize 132,000 of its undocumented immigrants (Loisy 2005: 125).

In a suburb of the French city of Lyon where many poor people of minority ethnicities lived in 1983, the police shot a 28-year-old *Maghrébin* named Toumi Djaïdja when he tried to free a friend from the grip of a police dog. Although Toumi Djaïdja was not expected to survive, by some miracle he recovered. His shooting nonetheless increased the tension building in French society around the issues of immigration and racism. It also pushed a number of French youth of African background, including especially beurs, toward open protest. Over time, there began to diffuse across France this feeling that there had to be protests against the injustices being visited on many marginalized people of African backgrounds, and it was only a matter of time before some discrete coordinated actions would be taken.

When, also during 1983, a beur named Habib Grimzi was thrown to his death from a train traveling between Bordeaux and Vintimille, additional public attention was trained on the marginalization and discrimination that frequently victimized even French citizens perceived to be "others," especially including many who were of African origin and not well integrated within the mainstream.

Somewhat spontaneously, forty concerned persons, most of whom were beurs, began marching from Marseille toward Paris, much in the spirit of Mohandas Karamchand Ghandi in India or the first historic march to the National Mall in Washington, D.C. in 1963, where Dr. Martin Luther King, Jr., delivered his famous "I have a dream" speech. By the time the marchers and their sympathizers headed into Paris one month later, their numbers had grown to 100,000. Many new slogans in exaltation of freedom, liberty, and equality appeared on the signs and banners that they carried, including one that proclaimed "Let us live equally with our commonalities, whatever our differences" (Liauzu 1996: 212-213; Stora and Messaoudi 1997: 111-135). In the capital, François Mitterrand, then president of the Republic, greeted the leaders of the march.

On this and other occasions, collegial alliances brought together *beurs* with "blacks," Jews, students, and leftist progressive elements in French society who shared a common interest in fighting for equality and against racism and anti-Semitism. Especially notable among these allies were Black-Blanc-Beur and SOS-Racisme. While SOS-Racisme was founded in 1985, France-Plus was born on the Villetaneuse campus of the University of Paris 13, located in a northern suburb of Paris, around the same time. It was around this time in 1986 that France made the African-American writer James Baldwin, who had returned to the United States from Europe for brief periods during the first half of the 1960 to participate in America's civil rights struggles alongside Dr. Martin Luther King, Jr. and multitudes of others, a Commander of the Legion of Honor. This was the year before Baldwin's death in France from stomach cancer.

Meanwhile, despite what at first seemed like the auspicious beginning of a new multi-ethnic civil rights movement in France that joined together French people from northwestern Africa and from sub-Saharan Africa, French Jews, and others, it did not take long for its original beur leaders to be overwhelmed by despair associated with an array of personal and social problems. Also contributing to the demise of this proto-movement were conflicts inherent in its heterogeneity and conflicting agendas and associated distrust and conflict. While, for example, some Jewish elements associated with SOS-Racisme were Zionists, some Muslim elements were anti-Zionists. Moreover, the activists involved had contrasting views concerning the Gulf War as well as the subsequent United States domination of air space over Iraq that culminated in an eventual Iraq invasion and occupation (Rouadjia 2004: 17-98; Liauzu 1996: 215, 217).

Even during the 1970s when France was publicizing its experiments with multiculturalism, it was also pursuing an immigration policy that was strongly associated with the return of non-European migrants to their countries of origin. From 1977 to 1986, France attempted to diminish its migrant population through stimulating return migration mainly under the *aide au retour* (1977-1980) and *aide à la réinsertion* (beginning in 1983) programs. A main instrument of this policy included return bonuses to help migrants establish a new livelihood, and, in the case of Algerian and Senegalese migrants, another sometimes involved professional training before their return. As part of these so-called new co-development policies by France, four African countries were chosen for pilot projects (Morocco, Mali, Senegal, and Comoros). These projects built on the long experience France had accumulated with regard to return migration and co-development through earlier projects that involved Mali and Senegal (Haas 2006: 71). In general, only a few migrants availed themselves of participation in these schemes however and the majority who did were Europeans from Spain and Portugal.

Overall, the number of African immigrants in France who used France's reinsertion program during the first seven years that it operated was small, and most of those who did were emigrants returning to northwestern Africa or to Turkey (Liauzu 1996: 147-148). France's extreme right-wing *Front National* (FN) founded by Jean-Marie Le Pen in 1972, which during the first decade of its existence drew much of its support from neo-Fascist sympathizers and Pieds-Noirs (i.e., former colonists resident in Maghreb), strongly supported the rein-sertion program. That support, tinged with racism, helped to discredit the pro-gram in the eyes of many immigrants (Haas 2006: 67: Gaspard and Servan-Schreiber 1985: 180-213).).

Although the *Front National* would remain almost irrelevant in terms of its ability to gain votes in elections until 1983, from its very beginning it was suc-cessful in spewing out hate and racism contributing to a climate of tension in French society. The *Front National* under Le Pen's leadership, for example, was hostile to the continued immigration of Africans into France, what it considered miscegenation, reproductive choice of French women through abortion, and a "permissive society" allegedly encouraged by Left-wingers, homosexuals, and feminists. Although opposed also to anti-racist legislation introduced in France in 1972 as *liberticides* that destroyed freedom of speech while proposing the repatriation of three million non-European immigrants and the reduction of so-cial benefits and access to housing for those remaining, the FN managed in 1983 for the first time to win a significant part of the electoral vote, sending shock waves through France. In the small city of Dreux located about 65 miles west of Paris, the FN and some other extremist parties running on a single list in a local by-election won almost 17 percent of the total votes cast.

Already by this time, Le Pen of France's FN was on public record as propos-ing to restrict the number of asylum seekers in France, the isolation of all in France who were infected by the virus responsible for AIDS or SIDA in a *sida-torium* apart from the rest of society, creating a special National Guard to pre-vent any civic unrest or subversion by immigrants, strengthening police powers, and reintroducing capital punishment for some crimes. Although French law does not permit the gathering of census data by any variable deemed racial, the FN had by this time discovered a way in which to exploit a serious identity crisis in France whereby some French people were disturbed and anxious over the large African presence in the country, including most especially in the regions of Île de France, Rhône-Alpes, and Provence-Côte d'Azur.

North of the Channel in 1975, Britain's Labor government under Prime Mi-nister Harold Wilson recommended the appointment of David Pitt, a prominent "black" Briton born in Grenada, to the House of Lords. Pitt had served on the London Council, was associated with a number of anti-discrimination organiza-tions including the League of Coloured Peoples and the Campaign Against Racial Discrimination, and served as president of the British Medical Association. This was the same year that Bernard Alexander Montgomery Grant, known commonly as Bernie Grant, originally from Guyana, began his service as one of three "black" MPs then sitting in the British House of Commons. Still, all was not well with respect to immigration and racism in Britain. In the 1970s and 1980s, "black" community-based groups were set up across the United Kingdom to campaign against racist street attacks on peoples of color. Also in 1976, "black" youths fought the British police at the end of the Notting Hill Carnival. In 1981, a number of riots erupted in various inner cities of the country as Britons living in "black" communities protested against what they considered to be ill treatment by the police.

The government of British Prime Minister Margaret Thatcher reacted by introducing a bill for a new nationality law prompted by the public's alleged fear "that this country might be rather swamped by people with a different culture." In fact, the Britons most upset about the prevailing situation were likely more concerned about people of a different color than about people of a different culture. Already in 1971, the Heath government had passed an Immigration Act that for the first time formally divided British subjects into partials (i.e., family British) and nonpartials (i.e., political British). This legislation supported by the Thatcher government took this division further by placing more emphasis on parentage than on residential geography.

Home Secretary William Whitelaw defended the proposed 1981 British Nationality Act as necessary because some "holders of the present citizenship may not unnaturally be encouraged to believe, despite the immigration laws to the contrary, that they have a right of entry to the United Kingdom." Intended to remove any such misconceptions, the act of 1981 for the first time divided British nationality into three tiers in ways that favored people deemed to be "white." More specifically, it differentiated among (1) British citizenship, (2) British Dependent Territories citizenship, and (3) British Overseas citizenship, and confined the right of abode in the United Kingdom only to the first tier although all three theoretically could seek British consular protection.

Similarly, it provided for certain exceptions, all of which had racist implications. Former partial British subjects resident in the "old dominions" who did not qualify for British citizenship retained the lifetime right to migrate to Britain and to register as British citizens. Also, children born abroad within five years of the act's commencement to British citizens by descent retained the right to be registered as British citizens if their grandparental connections would have ensured partial status but for the passing of the act of 1981. Further illustrating that Thatcher was not so much anti-immigration as anti-immigration into Britain by people her government deemed to be "black," it supported an additional exception in 1982 within the British Nationality (Falkland Islands) Act. According to this last-mentioned exception, British subjects in the Falkland Islands off the coast of Argentina were recognized as British citizens (Paul 1997: 182-185). Still believing themselves to be ill-treated by the British police, residents of many inner cities again protested in 1985.

Although Portugal, Spain, and Italy remained countries of emigration through the 1960s in that they sent significant parts of their populations to settle abroad, they later began to attract numerous immigrants, including from Africa. The waves of African immigrants that began arriving in Portugal from parts of Africa where Portuguese remains an official language began with males who mostly entered with work visas obtained as part of their contracts to work for state recognized construction companies. By contrast, the females from the same countries who began arriving in Portugal later were usually unemployed upon arrival. Despite this, however, Portuguese authorities, likely anxious to restrict so called miscegenation, also eventually began allowing African females to immigrate in the hope that they would provide companions for most of the African males who were Portugal.

As the African females in Portugal felt as obliged as the males to send remittances to their family members back in Africa as well as to obtain the means to survive in Europe, they also sought employment. Due to the low skill levels of many of the females as well as racial stereotyping, the major type of work open to these females of color is low-waged household and janitorial work in homes as well as businesses and other institutions that is known as *limpeza*. Against great odds and much police harassment, however, some African women in Lisbon and the nearby city of Setúbal also work as unlicensed fish vendors who are known as *peixeiras*.

Although Lisbon has numerous *bairros de lata* or shanty communities that provide very substandard housing for a large proportion of the working poor living in the area of the Portuguese capital, including native Portuguese, Roma, Indians, Timorese, and Africans. Although there are more than sixty shanty communities in the suburbs of Lisbon whose residents are mostly "black," by no means are all the immigrants and Portuguese citizens of African descent living in the area of Lisbon concentrated in such *bairros de lata* (Fike 2000: 12, 33, 53-56, 134, 137, 140-146, 156).

After Spain joined the European Union (EU) in 1986, it became a new destination for migrants, in particular from Morocco and Latin America. In addition to the sharp increase in migration to Madrid, the Basque country, and Andalusia, Catalonia, attracted immigrants at the highest rate. This new pattern of immigration in Italy and Spain focused attention on discrimination, employment, and the place of Islam in public (Haas 2006: 89). From 1983 onward, first with the French-led "Mediterranean Forum" and then with the 5+4 summits (which became 5+5 with the entry of Malta), France, Italy, Portugal, and Spain initiated a broad dialogue with Tunisia, Algeria, Morocco, and Mauritania in which migration was discussed. Because the countries of emigration and countries of immigration had different vested interests however, it became clear by 1992 that this African-European dialogue across the western Mediterranean basin was not succeeding in a meaningful way (Pastore 2002: 109).

In the late 1980s when the Soviet Union was breaking up, many Western governments and cooperating media moguls with narrow and parochial ideological agendas also hailed the rupture as merely a great victory for democracy in the Cold War. From quite a different perspective however, this corresponded to

an upsurge in xenophobia and racism in the Soviet Union as well as in some
nearby Communist countries formerly under its domination. In Russia, members
of the *Pamyat* group, for example, dressed in black and began to openly parade
their anti-Semitism. Russian women married to members of resented ethnic or
national groups dealt with slurs as they walked through the city streets (being
called prostitute), while their husbands and children became targets of insults
and violent attacks.

The breakup or collapse of the USSR, hailed in the West as a Cold War triumph for democracy, corresponded with a nationalistic turning inward in Russia
that marked a major upsurge in racism that the West has not wished to acknowledge. Many young Russians came to resent foreigners who could more easily
travel back and forth to western Europe than they could and who sometimes had
access to such luxuries as jeans, chewing gum, and musical records that many of
them still found it very difficult to obtain.

There was great economic resentment that targeted people deemed to be non-
Slavic in particular, and most especially those with swarthy or dark complexions
or who were assumed to be Muslims, regardless of whether they were Russian
citizens or foreigners. People of Caucasian, central Asian, Turkic, Jewish, Armenian, and Romani ethnicities among Russians citizens as well as citizens of
the former USSR, Africa, Asia, and Latin America became frequent targets of
racist and/or political attacks. Along with various values that surged to the forefront in Russia especially since 1991 have been many that are racist and hyper-
nationalistic. In some respects this situation parallels that of former Communist
East Germany.

Around the same time the Cold War was ending, the Swedish government
invited many foreign workers to relocate there due to labor shortages. While a
majority of these immigrant workers were Europeans from Finland and from the
former Yugoslavia (Nordin 2005: 26-27), many were of other nationalities. The
presence of so many new foreigners in the country was sufficient to contribute
to a backlash that was nationalistic, xenophobic, and racist. As part of a campaign directed against the increasing ethnic diversity in Swedish society, many
Swedes began to idealize King Charles XII who during the late 17th and early
18th centuries had brought the Swedish Empire both to the pinnacle of its power
as well as to its downfall as a Great Power.

Beginning in the late 1980s, Swedish skinheads were particularly active on
November 30, the date that Charles XII died in battle, in inflicting numerous
violent attacks on foreigners. Athletes deemed to be of non-European backgrounds often found themselves the targets of racists taunts in Sweden, and a
number of Swedish bars and restaurants refused service to people deemed not to
be "white." The press has often played a role in stirring up animosity against
foreigners by often describing negative behaviors attributed to them collectively
or in ethnic terms rather than individually.

By the 1990s, *invandrare* (originally meaning "immigrants" in Swedish) became a derisive term roughly the equivalent of *svartskallar* (literally meaning
"black heads"), but also implying dark complexioned and inferior. Although the
Swedish public was becoming more critical of immigrants, that it was most ac-

cepting of those with Nordic, Baltic, and Germanic backgrounds and least accepting of those from Bulgaria (including especially those of Turkish and Kurdish backgrounds), Turkey, Iran, Vietnam, Chile, Ethiopia, and Eritrea suggests
that variation perceived as racial and ethnic—and often religious—influenced
such attitudes (Pred 2000: 73; Nordin 2005: 32, 43, 71).

When Swedish skinheads in 1995 participated in the murder of Gerard
Gbeyo, an African refugee originally from Côte d'Ivoire, his killer, aged seventeen years, received a sentence of only a four-year prison term. The compensation that the government paid to Gbeyo's family was very moderate by Swedish
standards. Among people who are sometimes targeted by Swedish skinheads for
being insufficiently European and Nordic are Jews (Nordin 2005: 143-153).
Since the early 1980s, Sweden has been home to a strong Anti-Racist Movement, which grew stronger in the wake of Gbeyo's murder. This movement
helped prepare the way for a small number of Africans to rise to prominence as
politicians. In October 2002 when Sweden's King Karl Gustave inducted the
country's new *Riksdag* or parliament, for example, for the first time two African-born Swedes were among the parliamentarians, Joe Frans from Ghana and
Nyamko Sabuni born in Burundi of Congolese parents. Though they were only
two out of 349, their presence was highly significant of a Europe becoming
more reconciled with its inner Africa.

After arriving in Sweden as an exchange student in 1980, Joe Frans decided
to settle there. It was as a member of the Social Democrats that he was elected to
the *Riksdag*. Nyamko Sabuni arrived in Sweden a year later at age twelve along
with her mother and three of her brothers to join her father, already granted asylum there. After eventually studying law at Uppsala University, migration policy
at Mälardalen University, and information and media communications at Berghs
Schools of Communication in Stockholm, Sabuni married a Swede. Unlike Joe
Frans who belonged to the Social Democrats Party, Sabuni first stood for election to the *Riksdag* in 1998 as a member of the conservative Liberal People's
Party. Both Frans and Sabuni were successful in winning election to the *Riksdag*
in 2002. After serving four years in this post, Nyamko Sabuni however was appointed Minister for Integration and Gender Equality, thereby becoming the first
person of known African descent to ever serve as a government minister in
Sweden.

Although Carl I. Hagen, the leader of Norway's Forward Right Party (*Frem-
skrittspartier* or FRP) is on record denying that he is ethnocentric and chauvinistic, he is known for demagoguery that on occasion has stirred up popular hostility against residents of his country deemed to be non-Nordic. In neighboring
Denmark, Mogens Glistrup, also a party leader, has been especially hostile toward Muslim residents. In 1999, he even suggested that they should be ordered
to leave the country within three months and that those who failed to comply
should then be detained for sale to the highest bidder. Only two months later
when a Danish-born Turkish citizen was deported, a riot erupted in Copenhagen's Nörrebro neighborhood. Pia Kjaersgaard, leader of the far-right People's
Party (DPP) that was formed in 1996, is similarly hostile to Muslims resident in
Denmark (Nordin 2005: 12-13).

Pia Kjaersgaard only became a significant player in national politics after the Conservatives and Liberals formed a coalition government in Denmark in 2001 that had to rely on DPP for the parliamentary majority that enabled it to oust the Social Democrats. Helping Pia Kjaersgaard to earn 12 percent of the vote for his recently established party was his campaign poster that showed a Danish girl next to a demagogic slogan saying, "When she retires, Denmark will have a Muslim majority." Although in reality only one about out of every 27 people residing in Demark was Muslim at that time, Kjaersgaard's appeal to the ethnic fears of Danes was largely successful. The following year, Denmark introduced what then were plausibly Europe's strictest immigration laws. As a result of this legislation, of the asylum applications to Denmark, Sweden, and Norway collectively, Denmark's proportion fell from 31 percent in 2000 to 9 percent in 2003. In contrast, Sweden's proportion rose from 41 percent to 60 percent and Norway's from 28 percent to 31 percent. These developments meant that Denmark, legendary as a liberal country, with a long tradition of jazz going back to the 1920s as well as the first country in the world to legalize same-sex marriage in modern times, had taken a sharp turn to the right.

Located even more on the northern fringe of Europe, Finland has traditionally been more a country of emigration than one of immigration. Finland instituted a quota system in 1985 that provided for the acceptance of only 100 refugees per year. Finland had only 18,000 immigrants as recently as 1987. After much international criticism, however, Finland agreed to admit 300 refugees in 1988 (Solsten and Meditz 1990: 287). Still by 2000, between 1.6 and 2.5 percent of Finland's population consisted of immigrants, largely from Russia, Estonia, Sweden, Somalia, the former Yugoslavia, Iraq, the United Kingdom, and Germany.

Thousands of Somalis were settled in Vainkkala as refugees during a short period in the early 1990s when the Finnish economy was about to experience a downturn. It was during this period when about a hundred Somalis along with a few other refugees from Pakistan and Afghanistan also were dispatched to the small town of Joensuu. Soon, a local group of skinheads emerged and began to attack these refugees with considerable frequency. Though Finland had no well-established political party with a right-wing anti-immigrant agenda as of 2006, surveys show that Finns tend to be least negative about immigration from Anglo-Saxon and Nordic countries, Estonia, and Germany, at least when these immigrants are deemed to be "white."

Significant numbers of Finns, especially in rural areas, have developed negative attitudes toward immigrants who are Russians, who are Muslims, who are Roma, and who are deemed to be of Africa background. Finns often openly use insulting terms to refer to such people—for example, *neekeri* for a "black" person, *ryssä* for a Russian, and *mustalainen* for a Rom or Gypsy. That intense employment discrimination, hostility at bars and discotheques, verbal abuse, and social exclusion especially target certain immigrant groups in Finland is well documented (Hyttinen 2005). Still, some recent evidence points in the direction of greater acceptance: a few mixed-marriages, the election of some immigrants to local councils, and Somali representation on the Labor Ministry's Ethnic Relations Commission.

In October 1989 in Creil, a suburb just north of Paris, three female students of Moroccan origin attempted to enter Gabiel Havez Middle School wearing a scarf headcovering (i.e., a *khimar* or *hijab*) as is worn by some female Muslims, including many who do not consider it a religious requirement. Deemed as an act of proselytization and one not in keeping with the traditions of French assimilationism or with the Law of 1905 providing for the separation of church and state, the principal of their school prevented them from entering. As pointed out by Ghazli (2006: 145-146), there did not actually exist in 1905 a separation of church and state in colonized Algeria, which was a part of France. The students involved did not intend initially to challenge this school prohibition. As many other people became involved, this so-called *l'affaire du voile* or *l'affaire du foulard* became a national issue and drew much international attention (Leveau and Hunter 2002: 21-22; Liauzu 1996: 208). Some supporters of the girls challenged the government to change its attitude and practices ostensibly in conformity with the rules of the EU. Although this affair was unfolding in France as an issue at a time that French society was already tense, France still enacted new anti-racist legislation in 1990 that was opposed by its FN or *Front National*. Because Islam was the second largest religion in Europe, it raised issues for all Europeans having to do with immigration, discrimination, racism, assimilation, and secularism.

Although French citizens in metropolitan France in contrast to those living in overseas parts of the country tend to show reluctance to electing compatriots who are Muslim or people of color to represent them in the National Assembly and Senate, *l'affaire du voile* or *l'affaire du foulard* at least temporarily influenced this pattern. As Ernest Chénière, a Frenchman of color originally from Martinique and principal of the college in Creil where the controversy began, came so much into public favor that he was elected as the Deputy to represent Oise in the National Assembly from 1993 to 1997, a definite departure from the usual voting patterns in metropolitan France. More than a genuine new willingness by the French to overlook ethnic status in casting their votes, the election of Chénière at this time and place was likely meant as a rejection of what many voters viewed as Islamic extremism.

Contributing to tension in French society in 1995, an Islamist bombing campaign was underway in Algeria apparently under the sponsorship of the *Groupe Islamique Armé* or GIA, a group widely believed to have at least some collateral interest in punishing France. Given that mass media earn much of their profits from sensationalism, such developments as these received much more media coverage than the facts that as of 1990, an estimated two million people in France were living in families where one or both of the parents were of Maghrebian heritage and that France's Maghrebian immigrant population represented 40 percent of all its immigrants. Also adding to the atmosphere of alarm surrounding Islam and immigration issues in France around this time, Dominique Schnapper, French sociologist and director of the *École des Hautes Études en Sciences Sociales*, expressed concern as to whether or not the new immigrants had an aptitude for democracy and whether they had the ability to assimilate in present-day Europe (Liauzu 1996: 169-170, 179).

Italy was another part of Europe where there existed a large and growing African presence at this time. In Italy, Africans were only 9 percent of documented immigrants in 1981 yet were more than 26 percent in 1991. In the same year, Moroccans constituted more than 4 percent of the documented immigrants in Spain (Liauzu 1996: 170). Due to the fact that Maghreb had once been under French control, immigrants from northwestern Africa tended to favor countries where at least one of the official languages was French: France, Belgium, and Switzerland. For other reasons, large numbers of Moroccans also settled in the Netherlands, Italy, and Germany in that respective order. Whereas Algerians greatly outnumbered settlers of African descent from Morocco and Tunisia in France, immigrants from the three countries of Maghreb were more or less equally represented in Switzerland as of 1991. In Spain, however, Moroccans were much better represented than Algerians and Tunisians. Of all the undocumented immigrants from Mediterranean countries in Italy as of late, more that half are thought to come from Maghreb, with the largest number being Moroccans followed by Tunisians (Liauzu 1996: 171, 173-174). More Africans of Moroccan background reside in Europe than from any other single country.

Besides African immigrants who come to Europe from Maghreb, many others come from Egypt and from most countries south of the Sahara. The archipelago country of Cape Verde in western Africa is interesting in this regard. More Cape Verdeans live abroad than live in Cape Verde. Most important among the destination countries for these Africans in addition to Senegal and the United States are France, Portugal, and Italy.

In some respects, European citizenship came into being on February 7, 1992, at least for Europeans living in those countries that signed the European Union Treaty in Maastricht, The Netherlands. Article 8 of this treaty distinguished between citizenship and nationality by stipulating, "any person having the nationality of a member State is a citizen of the Union." It therefore recognizes that the nation, as a community, defines itself in several ways: largely politically (as in the French case, based on the social contract, the foundation of national consensus symbolized by the Constitution), largely culturally (as in the German case), and largely territorially (as with the United Kingdom).

Consequently, from the perspective of the Treaty of Maastricht, the definition of *European* varies with the way *nationality* is defined in different countries, with their diverse historical consciousness, in some cases colored by a colonial past. Citizenship based on reciprocity of rights rather than a common language or shared history was in some respects a new frontier. By this time from a legal perspective, there were both community Europeans and non-community Europeans. From cultural, psychological, and physical perspectives however, while some people outside of Europe were recognized as honorary Europeans, others who were fully community Europeans were not consistently recognized and treated as Europeans. Certain Europeans who are perceived to be Muslim or non-white are not infrequently excluded, treated as criminals, seen as different and dangerous, and, above all, seen as racialized "others."

The original Maastricht Treaty of 1992 did not contain any specific provision granting the European Community (now the European Union) legal authori-

ty to combat racism. Also, this community of countries has been somewhat ti-
mid in handling some refugee and immigration matters in a comprehensive
manner. These shortcomings often left the community unprepared to deal effectively with the dramatic upsurge in racist intolerance and violence and the rise of
openly right-wing parties oriented toward the marginalization of immigrants, of
Roma or Gypsies, and of certain religious minorities.

They also inhibited the crafting of good integration policies. The European
Parliament had a limited legislative role compared to the Commission and
Council. Although Parliament had been in the forefront of the drive to amend
the Maastricht Treaty with respect to racism, the European Commission repeatedly refused to propose legislation against racism to the Council, opting instead
to adopt mere non-binding resolutions and declarations against racism. Without
specific legal authority, the EU institutions showed reluctance to enact any
Community-wide legislation in the area of criminalizing racism (Due 1996;
Nordin 2005: 14).

Such shortcoming would be especially serious for people of African backgrounds living in EU countries. As of 1994, there were between 150,00 and
340,000 people of physically appreciable African ancestry estimated to be living
in Germany (Sephocle 1996: 26; Jobatey 1996: 34). The murder of a "black"
Londoner named Stephen Lawrence by racists in the same year was followed by
police racism that involved poor collection of evidence that resulted in the care-
less release rather than the conviction of five suspects. During that time an estimated 30 percent of Metropolitan Londoners belonged to ethnic minorities, but
only 3.9 percent of the 26,000 people working in the crime-control system were
of non-Anglo-Saxon backgrounds (Nordin 2005: 8).

Some European countries do not officially gather census statistics based on
so-called races, for example, Portugal and France. Such policies are difficult to
interpret, however, as they may be driven by at least four different ways of
thinking. First, it could be thought, that such statistics would have a deleterious
impact on national unity in various countries and, in fact, contribute to racial
thinking. Second, a counter argument could be made that the gathering of racio-
ethnic statistics is an effective tool in identifying and opposing racism. A third
argument, based largely on racist thinking, could be that undermining myths that
Europe is overwhelmingly "white" and "Christian" would be a shameful thing
raising old fears of racist taint and the lack of racial purity. Fourth, not gathering
census data reflecting so-called races could also be based on the recognition that
no such unambiguous and non-overlapping groups among human beings as races actually exist. While this fourth approach to policy would be post- or anti-
racial and fully in concert with science, this writer does not mean to suggest that
only this approach would be pragmatic. Only an in-depth study examining numerous aspects of public policy, social identity, social problems, and the collection of particular types of demographic data will help to determine optimal policy options as Europe deals with its greater-than-ever complexity in terms of
human diversity.

What one calls *mixed marriages* in France, moreover, refers primarily to a
difference of religion rather than a so-called racial difference. From 1918 to

around 1995, at least a million marriages between spouses of different religion took place in France, largely between Muslims and Christians with a large portion of the former being of African origin and a large portion of the latter being indigenous Europeans. From the 1970s, the annual number of such marriages has been around 30,000. As this impacts the young even more than the elderly, there is the probability in the future of a growing but youthful French minority that is less integrated into the mainstream and more or less aggressive about their marginalization. Whereas in 1964, 4.8 percent of marriages registered in France were mixed, they were 6.7 percent of marriages in 1982, and 11.5 percent of all marriages in 1992. According to changes that France made in its Code of Nationality in 1993, every foreigner born in France would acquire French citizenship between 16 and 21 years of age if he or she wanted it, and providing that he or she had not been convicted of certain serious crimes such as trafficking in drugs, thieving, or homicide (Liauzu 1996: 234-241; Calvès 2004: 219-226).

It is estimated that some ten million people born in France as of the mid-1990s had an origin that was at least partially foreign from the perspective of their parentage. In the 1920s, the Belgian and the Swiss had the greatest tendency in western Europe to undertake mixed marriages followed by the Italians and the Spaniards. Although in Germany nowadays, such mixed marriages are ten times less common than in France, these marriages especially involving Europeans with people from northwestern Africa who are usually men are common in Italy and in several western European countries although not in Portugal (Liauzu 1996: 234-235, 237-238, 241).

In 1992, Germany moved to ban various neo-Fascists groups that had shown themselves to be very violent, but the resurgence of racism or "new racism" there by this time was very strong (Blaschke 1998: 79). Chancellor Helmut Kohl of Germany and Present François Mitterand of France at the June 1994 Summit of the EU Council spearheaded a joint initiative on racism and xenophobia that resulted in the establishment of a consultative committee. Despite the Commission's unwillingness to initiate legislation in this area without prior treaty amendment, the establishment of this committee chaired by Jean Kahn of the European Section of the World Jewish Congress indicated some willingness by the Commission to utilize already existing provisions in the Maastricht Treaty to combat racism.

When in 1995 in response to recommendations of the committee headed by Kahn the European Council president proposed a Draft Joint Action against racism and xenophobia with criminal penalties based on Article K of the Maastricht Treaty rather than waiting for the treaty to be amended, Britain blocked the Council's Joint Action preferring instead another non-binding resolution. Although Stephen Lawrence had been murdered in south London by British racists only two years before, Britain claimed in this connection that it did not need lectures from beyond its borders as it had "a longer history of laws affecting race relations than almost any other country in the EC, more comprehensive legislation and better race relations" (Due 1996). This claim however rested in large measure on nationalist arrogance, a distorted reading of history, and Britain's refusal to recognize the need of European countries to combat racism across as well as within their borders.

Also in 1995 the Schengen Convention came into effect thereby superseding the Schengen Accords that had been reached a decade earlier in Schengen, Luxembourg, among France, Germany, Belgium, Luxembourg, and the Netherlands. In addition to the original signatories, by the time the Schengen Convention came into effect in 1995, Portugal and Spain had also agreed to implement it. Although Italy, Greece, and Austria signed the Convention by this time, they did not implement it until later (Lallaoui 1997: 93, 106).

The purpose of the Schengen Convention was to remove all controls at internal land, sea, and airport frontiers within the signing members of the European Union in order to allow Europeans nationals and holders of visas within those countries to circulate freely in an unrestricted manner as well as goods. They also were intended to strengthen the external borders around the signatories of the accords. Upon implementation of the Schengen Convention came freedom of movement within the Schengen space after one initially entered any of the countries who were parties to the convention. Since the Schengen Convention has not operated to contain racism and xenophobia in Europe, however, some people who are visible minorities have still not found the convention's promise a complete reality.

In 1996 when a devastating fire gutted a house for asylum seekers in Lübeck, Germany, ten residents of the house lost their lives as they slept. Among these were refugees from Lebanon, Syria, Togo, Poland, and Zaire (presently the Democratic Republic of the Congo). German authorities initially suggested that a Lebanese resident had set the fire while ignoring that skinheads shouting Fascist slogans as well as other Germans wearing Nazi armbands had on numerous occasions threatened to murder the refugees. Despite having knowledge of this, the government did not supply security guards for the refugees.

In 2000, in the main park of Dessau, located in eastern Germany, three neo-Fascists or neo-Nazis assaulted Mozamabican-born Alberto Adriano by repeatedly kicking him in the head after shouting "Blacks out" and "What do you want here, nigger?" He died a few days later. It did not matter to his assailants that he had lived in Germany for twenty years, that he was married to a German woman and was the father of three German children, and that he was merely on his way home after visiting friends. After this murder, the mayor of Dessau seemed especially focused on making it clear for public relations reasons that the murderers had come from neighboring Wolfen and Brandenburg rather than from Dessau.

Quite apart from refugees who do not have the same freedom of movement in the Schengen space as citizens, there remain many places in the so-called Schengen space where it is not safe even for certain EU citizens to travel, work, or settle for reasons having to do with their perceived ethnicity, religion, or so-called race despite their possessing legal rights under the Schengen Convention to be present. It is also difficult for some people to exercise their rights under the Schengen Convention because of national laws having to do with under what conditions outsiders are permitted to work in certain countries that despite being in the Schengen space are not EU members such as Iceland, Norway, and Switzerland. That predominantly Islamic entities lying completely or partly in Europe such as Albania, Bosnia, and Turkey are not included in the Schengen space reflects at least in part some lingering ambivalence among many Europeans toward conceptualizing Muslims as true Europeans. Similarly, that certain overseas regions of France such as Réunion, Guadeloupe, and Martinique, as well as certain overseas regions of the Netherlands such as Aruba and the Netherlands Antilles—where many of the residents are of appreciable African descent—are not included plausibly has some ethno-racial implications.

Although Sweden was included within the Schengen space by 1996, from 1994 through 1997 it deported 25,829 people of the 50,229 asylum seekers processed there. This means fewer than 50 percent of arrivals received residence there. In addition to Africans, some of these people were South Americans, some Poles, and many European Muslims. Included among this last-mentioned group were immigrants from Croatia, Bosnia, Kosovo, Albania, and Bulgarians of Turkish backgrounds, some transported out of the country with financial incentives but others in straitjackets and in handcuffs as well as under the influence of tranquilizers and sedatives (Nordin 2005: 70-78).

When ten new countries—Cyprus, Estonia, Hungary, Latvia, Lithuania, Malta, Poland, Czech Republic, Slovakia, and Slovenia—joined the EU in 2004, even this did not involve the automatic or immediate lifting of the frontier checks between these countries and others in the so-called Schengen space. Because Great Britain remains reluctant to surrender its own border control and work-permit systems and share in a Common Travel Area with the Republic of Ireland, these two countries complied with parts of the Schengen agreements relating to police co-operation but not to those relating to asylum, visas, and border controls.

When in January 1997 Michael Menson, a musician originally from Ghana who had become famous as member of the group Double Trouble and was already resident in Britain, was doused with flammable liquid and set on fire in north London, police initially moved prematurely without good investigation to suggest that it had been a suicide attempt. After Menson's death a few days later, police conceded that Menson's protestations, that he had been attacked by a gang of "white" youths, had not been acted upon and that they had not even sealed off the scene to conduct a forensic analysis. Considering that youths of Asian descent in the United Kingdom also took to the streets in Oldham, Burnley, Bradford, and Stoke to protest racist harassment, police indifference and the lack of opportunities as late as 2001 suggests that the protests of the 1980s by "blacks," coupled with what occurred in the handling of the Michael Menson case, were reflective of some real problems with respect to racism in British society.

A so-called Barcelona Process involving a European-Mediterranean Partnership that involved twelve Mediterranean countries on three continents held a number of meetings in the late 1990s. As a result of these meetings, little was accomplished other than reiterating a commitment to strengthen European-Mediterranean cooperation on migration issues. As a result of an agreement between the EU with Tunisia and Morocco outside the framework of the European-Mediterranean Partnership, however, both Tunisia and Morocco received immigration visa quotas based on the assumption that this move would help to stem illegal immigration from their territories into EU countries (Pastore 2002: 111-113, 119n).

During the period from the mid-1970s through the late 1990s, many countries in western Europe gradually came to realize the permanent, non-temporary character of immigration into Europe, and they began to focus more on the integration of immigrants and less on the developmental consequences of migration for the sending countries (Haas 2006: 10). In legislation passed in 1986 and in 1998, Italy attempted to strike a balance between regularizing immigration and granting immigrants rights while at the same time improving its control over its borders. Such a position in Italy was hardly arrived at with ease. In various contexts, concepts of race have had many shifting meanings over time. *Race* has been used at times to differentiate among Europeans as well as between Europeans and "others."

It is not uncommon for some Italians, for example, to generalize among Italians of the north and those of the south in terms of an alleged racial inferiority of the latter. Adding to long-standing intra-Italian racism, mass media frequently intermix discourse emanating from alarmist demographers about a greatly declining fertility rate in Italy with fears about the demise of an Italian people and culture. *L'Espresso* in July 1990 reported an interview with a former labor minister who responded to such alarmist discourse by urging Italians to produce more babies "to keep away armadas of immigrants from the southern shores of the Mediterranean" (Krause 2001: 594-596). In 1992 as well as in 1994, Gianfranco Fini, while president of the National Alliance Party, publicly praised Benito Mussolini as "the greatest statesman of the twentieth century." Although he later claimed to have changed his mind about Mussolini while on a trip to Israel, Fini's conversion was suspect. The Northern League had its first brush with power in 1994, although not long afterward its disagreements with Forza Italia and Allenanza Nazionale or AN led it to leave the coalition (Triadafilopoulos and Zaslove 2006: 179).

Silvio Berlusconi, who served as Italian prime minister longer than any other since World War II, was a media mogul and also the richest man in Italy. First becoming prime minister in 1994 and again in 2001, Berlusconi's Forza Italia Party governed both times in coalition with two extremely right-wing parties: National Alliance and the Northern League. Whereas the National Alliance had strong ties with neo-Fascism, the Northern League under the leadership of Umberto Bossi consistently pursued anti-immigrant policies and for a time in the 1990s even favored establishing northern Italy as an independent country with the name of Padania. One city of northern Italy where the Northern League thrives is Brescia, a provincial capital east of Milan, where there exists a street called Via San Faustino that is lined with shops catering to residents of Asian and African descent and where Europe's second-largest mosque is being constructed. This is not pleasing to many Italians, including many of those who tend to support the Northern League. The right-wing coalition that so long supported

Berlusconi as prime minister sharply limited legal immigration into Italy, and most especially for people who were Muslims or deemed to be non-Europeans.

Beginning informally in February of 1993 under the name of the Erythros Association or Young Eritreans Group, a network developed in Rome that had as its major focus to provide services that ran the gamut of social problems plaguing residents there of Eritrean descent. It became increasingly multi-ethnic though still with a focus on migrants from the Eastern Horn of Africa. Its activities include providing assistance to human-trafficking victims and the homeless and operating shelters from 1996 in collaboration and with support from a number of organizations and agencies including the municipality of Rome. Important legislation was passed in 1998 and subsequently amended by Italy's Bossi-Fini Law in 2002 that included the linkage of employment and work visas, stronger control of illegal immigration, tougher provisions with regard to family reunification, and the granting of financial incentives to neighboring countries to help fight illegal immigration into the European Union.

Pursuant to the Treaty of Amsterdam (signed in 1997 and which made substantial changes to the Treaty on European Union that had been signed at Maastricht in 1992 and came into force on May 1, 1999), the European Council held a special October meeting in Tampere, Finland. One particularly important focus of this meeting was to develop common policies on asylum and immigration while taking into account the need for a consistent control of external borders to stop illegal migration. The European Parliament and the Council subsequently put several components of such a comprehensive EU policy into force, although significant incompatibility among the legal systems of member states has remained a challenge. Another challenge has been achieving the coordination and acquiring the technology and manpower to provide strong external action against organized crime and illegal immigration.

In June of the following year, the EU's Common Strategy on the Mediterranean was approved at the Feira Council in June 2000 and focused some particular attention on the need for cooperation on migration issues, perceived in Europe as more complex because many of the non-European countries involved also were becoming transit areas for irregular and illegal migration flows from sub-Saharan Africa and Asia (Pastore 2002: 114, 117). As of 2002, the European Council meeting in Seville concluded that by supporting development in migrant-sending countries, EU countries might be able to help control migration.

Consistent with the European Council Meeting in Seville, the Netherlands in the following year began to adopt a policy that involved both migration and development in place of an earlier policy that had focused mostly on curbing migration in accordance with the absorptive capacity of Dutch society with a view to preventing the abuse of the system and illegal migration, while offering protection to all those who genuinely needed it. Somewhat confusingly in 2004, however, the Netherlands *Development and Migration* policy memorandum proclaimed that circular migration was an optimum strategy to reconcile the interests of the migrant and of the sending and destination countries (Haas 2006: 26, 34-35).

Illustrating the obvious complexity of distinguishing what is European from what is not, the Azores, Madeira, and Canary Islands as well as Ceuta and Melilla are Schengen areas. That some areas within the Schengen space and European Union such as Malta, a small part of Sicily, and the entire Italian island of Lampedusa lie further south than parts of northernmost Algeria and Tunisia remind us that the popularly accepted boundaries dividing Africa and Europe are somewhat arbitrary. Moreover, they have always allowed for much fluidity in terms of human intercourse. Although the periphery of the Schengen space is ostensibly protected by a frontier agency known as Frontex, this agency frequently finds itself outmaneuvered on one frontier after another.

An electronic coastal surveillance system was installed at the Strait of Gibraltar in 2002, causing the south-to-north crossing by illegal migrants to decline in this area while diverting them to other areas such as to the Canary Islands, to the Spanish enclaves of Ceuta and Melilla on the mainland of northern Africa, to Italy, to Malta, to Greece, and to Cyprus. In 2003, Italy regularized 700,000 undocumented aliens, and in August 2004 Spain launched its sixth campaign that involved a million such persons. Spain more than any other country in the EU did this. Also in 2003, Spain accounted for 35 percent of the total number of undocumented aliens in the European Union (Loisy 2005: 125). Although tiny Malta has traditionally been a country of emigration rather than one of immigration (Goodwin 2002: 80-86), the approximately 1,800 new illegal migrants who reached its shores in 2005, mostly from Africa, were equal to about 0.5 percent of its entire population. As soon as Romano Prodi replaced Berlusconi as Italy's prime minister in a narrow electoral victory in 2006, the Italian government, as reported by the Munich-based *Süddeutsche Zeitung* on May 26, announced its intention to regularize residency for almost 500,000 illegal immigrants living within its borders.

To evade the electronic coast surveillance system installed at the Strait of Gibraltar in 2002, undocumented immigrants from Africa devised new ways of reaching Spain. Although in May of 2006 the EU decided to deploy planes, boats, and so-called rapid-reaction aid teams from eight member states in an effort to stop the influx of undocumented Africans anxious to reach the European Union from landing in the Canary Islands, the borders between Africa and Europe remained almost as porous as ever.

Nearly 30,000 African immigrants managed to reach the Spanish-ruled Canary Islands in 2006 alone. As these migrants typically discarded all their identification papers before boarding rickety fishing boats called *pirogues* from various places along the coast of western Africa on treacherous voyages to the nearby Spanish-controlled Canary Islands, officials were often unable to deport them to their places of origin. Under Spanish law illegal immigrants on Spanish soil can only be held for a maximum of forty days in a reception center. Anxious that these immigrants not compromise the tourist industry in the Canary Islands, Spain eventually shipped many of them to mainland Spain before forty days had passed. While some of them remained in Spain, many eventually made their way into France and other parts of Europe.

Meanwhile, new waves of people from tropical Africa arrived in Marseille in the 1990s, including some who worked preparing and selling food, some who attended to the hair needs of "black" Africans, and some who sold specialized cosmetic products to them. Although more than a few of these Africans entered Marseille clandestinely or with forged documents, once in Europe some of them traveled with considerable frequency between Marseille and such other major European cities as Lyons, Paris, Rouen, Le Havre, Naples, Rome, and Barcelona (Bertoncello and Bredeloup 2004: 13-15). During 1997 and 1998, France launched an operation to regularize many of the undocumented immigrants within its territory. This involved 90,000 of the 130,000 undocumented persons who requested it (Loisy 2005: 125). Also in 1998, France changed its official way of working with Africa by abandoning the model provided by the Ministry of Cooperation and incorporated African matters into the Ministry of Foreign Affairs (Thomas 2007: 30).

Of the ten countries whose citizens in the largest numbers were offered asylum in France in 2002, six were African or had populations predominantly of African descent, namely the Democratic Republic of Congo, Mauritania, Algeria, Mali, Congo, and Haiti, in that respective order (Weil 2004: 538). The notion of Africa in Europe has become conflated with increasing globalization. When in 2003 France deported 120 Senegalese back to their homeland, for example, Senegal reciprocated by deporting to France around thirty French citizens to Europe that it claimed were in Senegal under irregular circumstances. Even some human traffickers operating from China now send Chinese clients into France via Africa and Latin America (Loisy 2005: 26, 123-124).

As pointed out by Felouzis, Liot, and Perroton (2005) with respect to France, more than nationality, cultural origin, and complexion of skin are associated with the scholarly *apartheid* that currently exists in numerous colleges in France. They point out that it weighs most heavily on Africans and Turks and is especially pronounced along a geographical axis that extends from Lille through Paris to Lyons and on to Marseille. Of those typically presumed to be recent immigrants in France, Turks and peoples of African ancestry tend to be especially disadvantaged academically. It is not uncommon in France for French citizens or subjects from overseas *départements* and *territoires* (i.e., *Domiens et Tomiens*), many of whom are of appreciable African ancestry, to be victimized by academic discrimination in metropolitan France though to a lesser degree than masses of the more marginalized foreign Africans (Felouzis et al. 2005).

Northern Paris suburbs appear to be falling apart as symbolized in large measure by their under-schooled and marginalized youth—as pointed out in the film *La Haine* or "Hate," written and directed by Mathieu Kassovitz and released in 1995, which won numerous awards including at the Cannes Film Festival. Although the three main youth characters in the film were a Jew, a "black" boxer, and an Arab, they symbolized both troublemakers and victims of despair and discrimination in confrontation with the police. In contrast to the fictional characters in *La Haine*, 2005 would be a year in which real residents of *les banlieues* would find themselves in confrontation with Nicolas Sarkozy while he was Minister of the Interior as well as the police in a way that would impact the course of political and social history in France.

Adolescents from poor Parisian *banlieues* regularly go "hang out" in the upscale districts of the capital to escape their neighborhoods and gain a sense of excitement. Though foreigners and especially families of northern African descent became concentrated in peripheral Red Belt *cités* since the shutting off of legal immigration in 1974, the French *banlieue* remain a highly heterogenous universe in which racial or ethnic categories have little social potency. In La Courneuve, youths are both the cause and the victims of violence in the *cité*. "They bust the light bulbs so we can't see what they do." "They shoot drugs in broad daylight." "They sit there and smoke reefer all night long." "They piss in the stairwells." "We don't like to encounter them at night." A pervasive pattern of anti-youth discrimination prevailed both inside and outside their estate. "They treat us like rats" (Lapeyronnie 1992: 11).

Although a significant percentage of people in La Courneuve vote for the Front National, there is not blatant racial intolerance. In an isolated working-class project in the western suburbs of Paris, Calogirou turned up slightly more "ethnicized" forms of perception of space; separate sections of the estate and specific buildings tend to be identified and referred to by the assumed racial or ethnonational membership of its most visible tenants. The concentration of immigrant families in the most degraded housing projects of the urban periphery, including in La Courneuve, doubled between 1968 and 1982 to reach 22 percent (Wacquant 1997: 331-355).

Nicolas Sarkozy, born in Paris of a Hungarian father with some noble connections and a mother who was of French and Sephardic Jewish descent, was well known for his conservative law-and-order attitudes. While France's minister of the interior in June 2005, Sarkozy further stigmatized *les banlieues* when he vowed rather unsympathetically to clean out the northern Parisian suburb of La Courneuve with a high water-pressure hose known as a Kärcher. On October 27, Sarkozy declared a "war without mercy" on violence in those marginalized suburbs. On the occasion of a visit to the Paris suburb of Argenteuil only two days later, he was pelted with stones and bottles. He responded to this pelting by referring to the rebellious youths of such *banlieues* as "*racaille*" (meaning rabble, riff-raff, or scum).

The day after this insult and counter-insult in the Parisian suburb of Clichy-sous-Bois located in the Seine-Saint Denis area, three teenagers of *Maghrébin* descent (15-year-old Bouna Traoré and 17-year-old Zyed Benna along with a friend named Altun), though apparently not guilty of any crime, decided to flee from police who were chasing them. As a result of climbing a wall of an electrical relay station to hide, Bouna and Zyed were electrocuted and Altun severely burned. Angry about the deaths of the two local teenagers, some 500 people marched in silence through Clichy-sous-Bois in their memory the following evening under the watchful surveillance of police, who undoubtedly had the support of Nicolas Sarkozy in his role as interior minister.

Adding to their anger was an attack on a local mosque the same evening. Without minarets, the Bilal Mosque was located in a converted warehouse behind a local market. In a complex that it shared with a pastry and meat shops as well as a *hammam* or public bath, its plastered cinderblock walls bore faded lettering in Arabic. Inside were some 700 worshippers celebrating the end of the month-long Ramadan fast who fled into the night in terror when someone lobbed into this house of worship a tear-gas canister identical to the kind issued to the police in the area. Some 400 local youths clashed with police in Clichy-sous-Bois on October 29, throwing stones, bottles, and Molotov cocktails. Twenty-three officers were hurt, and their colleagues fired rubber bullets to push back the rioters.

Alienation, marginalization, and racist discrimination that locked numerous residents of the French suburbs out of the social mainstream coupled with the accidental deaths of Zyed Benna and Bouna Traoré and the gassing of the Bilal Mosque provided a fuse and fuel for riots that exposed major weaknesses in the prevailing social order. Expressed largely through property damage that targeted automobiles and buildings, although a few people were injured or killed, these riots gradually spread to all regions of France. Except for Lyon, this civil unrest was confined largely to the outskirts of various cities and towns. Still, the disorder resulted in numerous arrests, the invocation of an emergency curfew law on the books from 1955, and threats from Sarkozy to expel from the country any convicted foreigners participating in the riots before quiet calm finally returned to France some three weeks after the rioting began.

Nicolas Sarkozy in 2006, while still the French interior minister, stated that his immediate goal was to deport 25,000 persons. Coupled with the fact that France had a high unemployment rate, this strategy on the part of Sarkozy doubtlessly was meant to send a message to the French electorate that he was prepared to retaliate against foreigners he deemed to be potential troublemakers. Tension in French society associated with racism and immigration even before riots lit up the night skies with burning vehicles and buildings corresponded with an upsurge in attacks on immigrants and in support for right-wing policies in Europe rather generally.

According to Germany's constitutional protection authorities, violent acts motivated by right-wing extremists in 2005 increased by nearly a quarter over those of the previous year to nearly 4,000 incidents. Although Brandenburg and Saxon-Anhalt were among the worst areas, as reported in the *Tages-Anzeige*'s "Das Magazine" section (June 19-25, 2006: 22, 33), attacks were widely scattered, including in Potsdam, in Dresden, and even in Berlin's Lichtenberg district. Among victims in 2006 were an Indian, an Ethiopian, a German politician of Kurdish background, a Cuban, and a man originally from Mozambique. In the same year, Uwe-Karsten Heye, a former government spokesman, warned dark-skinned tourists attending the World Cup matches against visiting eastern German regions because they "might not leave the area alive." Still, more or less in line with recent developments in Italy and Spain and in contrast with France (which was accelerating its deportment of illegal immigrants, with special emphasis on those who were single and without children), Germany announced mass amnesties for illegal immigrants.

Although Germany remained in need of foreign workers, officials such as Wolfgang Schäuble, the interior minister as of 2007, was careful to avoid referring to the needed workers by the earlier terminology of *Fremdarbeiter* (meaning, foreign workers) or *Gasarbeiter* (meaning, guest workers), as this would risk reminding the populace of a recent immigration legacy that many Germans preferred to forget. In fact, Germany, Hungary, Italy and Latvia were experiencing labor shortages amid demographic transformations that increasingly produced more elderly populations and shrinking workforces. Most other countries of the European Union, moreover, were rapidly moving in the same direction.

Although Switzerland was not a member of the European Union at this time, more than one fifth of its resident population consisted of foreigners in comparison to France were only an estimated eight percent of the population consisted of immigrants. Despite these facts, Philippe De Bruycker, founder of the Odysseus Network, an academic consortium on immigration and asylum in Europe, observed in the World Edition of the *Christian Science Monitor* (May 7-June 2, 2006: 4): "In Europe, we are still unable to accept that we are a continent of immigration." According to Mouloud Aounit, a representative of the Movement against Racism and for Friendship between People, "France is afraid of itself because it is a country of immigration, but has never accepted itself as such" (Nordin 2005: 6; Dewitte 2003: 104-106).

Belgium houses the headquarters of the European Commission, the Council and many institutions linked to the European Union, yet it is a deeply fractured country. In addition to the deep linguistic differences that divide the Flemish north from the French-speaking Walloon south of this country, right-wing resentment of immigration tends to be much stronger in the former. Antwerp, the largest Flemish city in Belgium, has become the stronghold of the right-wing Vlaams Belang (formerly the Vlaams Blok or Flemish bloc in Belgium's parliament), a racist party that campaigns for Flemish independence from the Walloon south. With slogans such as "Our own people first," its members frequently agitate against being "overwhelmed by foreigners."

In Belgium, the federal bicameral legislature consists of a 150-member Chamber of Representatives and a 71-member Senate, not including three seats reserved for the royal family. The first federal Representative of non-European heritage to be elected in Belgium was Chokri Mahassine, a Flemish Socialist of Moroccan and Palestinian origin who was seated in February 1999. The Chamber was dissolved only two months later but a small number of other Representatives of non-European heritage soon followed Mahassine. While more of these were of Moroccan than any other single heritage, others were Algerian-Flemish, Turkish, Indian, and Columbian mixed with Hungarian. Also in 1999, the Belgium Senate received its first members of appreciable non-European ethnicity beginning with Fauzaya Talhaoui of Moroccan background and Dalila Douifi of mixed Algerian-Flemish background. Most Belgian Senators of non-European backgrounds are descended from Africans from Morocco but the heritage of Senator Joälle Kapompole is Congo-Rwandanese. Although Belgium is acutely divided by linguistic nationalism, discrimination and violence are sometimes directed against residents and citizens deemed insufficiently European.

On May 11, 2006, 18-year-old Hans van Themsche (whose family is affiliated with Vlaams Belang and whose paternal grandfather was a Nazi collaborator during World War II) purchased a hunting rifle and began a shooting spree in Antwerp in broad daylight that was apparently motivated by racist intolerance. By the time he stopped, three people lay dead, a woman from Turkey, a woman from Mali, and a blond infant who had been in the care of the latter. Already before this tragedy, Belgium had adopted policies emphasizing long-term migration prevention through supporting development projects in the countries of origin from which immigrants come, not much different from those adopted to prevent long-term migration in France, Germany, and the Netherlands (Haas 2006: 85).

In Switzerland, also a much-fractured country with a federal system of government, voters between 1968 and 2000 voted on seven anti-immigrant measures that had been presented to them as the result of popular initiatives (Pignet 2006: 71-78). In each case, the voters rejected these initiatives, with almost two-thirds of the Swiss electorate voting, for example, against establishing a ceiling of 18 percent on foreigners in 2000. However, the federal government followed the defeat of this initiative with a proposal to make immigrating into Switzerland more difficult for non-European Union nationals.

Contrasting views on immigration were clearly evident in the voting in September 2006 on a proposed law to tighten asylum requirements. While the French-speaking cities of Geneva, Neuchâtel, and Lausanne followed the advice of the Socialist and Green Parties in voting against the asylum law, apart from Berne, even the major German-speaking cities often thought of as leftist (including Zurich, Basel, and Biel-Bienne) voted in favor of it. As analyzed by Andrea Fisher in the left-leaning *Tages-Anzeiger*, a Zurich-based daily newspaper (September 28, 2006: 3), this difference in voting behavior was more than linguistically based. Many of the leftist unions, wishing to protect their members from competition from immigrant workers, urged their members to vote in favor of the proposed law and voters in large German-speaking cities followed this advice more often than those in large French-speaking cities of Switzerland. The proposed Swiss law, as a result, prevailed by a wide margin.

Europe is continually being tested by its ability to operate as a humane part of our increasingly globalized world and this is complicated by the fact that for many Europeans Africa conjures up images of peoples deemed *a priori* to be non-Europeans or "others." So great is this emphasis on otherness that in some cases the kinds of targeting that is often directed at peoples of African descent are also directed at other minority groups in Europe who have neither direct nor indirect ties to Africa, such as Roma. According to 1999 estimates, the Czech Republic is the European country with the highest percentage of Roma after Macedonia, Romania, Slovakia, Bulgaria, Hungary, and Serbia-Montenegro (Ringold 2000: 1). When in 2004 Hungary, Slovakia, the Czech Republic, and Slovenia joined the European Union, this added approximately 1.2 million Roma to the population of the EU. The number of Roma in the EU roughly tripled again when Bulgaria and Romania joined in 2007.

Between 1926 and 1972, Switzerland allowed an organization known as the *Oeuvre d'entraide pour les enfants de la grand-route* (roughly, the Association for Assistance to Nomadic Romani Children) that had been founded by Alfred Siegfried to forcibly remove many Swiss children of Yenish Romani or Gypsy ethnicity from their families for institutionalization under conditions Siegfried controlled. Although the *Oeuvre* received assistance from Swiss police, it was only in 1972 when Siegfried died that the Swiss weekly *Der Schweizerischer Beobachter* succeeded in bringing this scandalous affair to the attention of the public. Even in 1987 when all files concerning *Oeuvre d'entraide pour les enfants de la grand-route* were transferred from cantonal authorities to the federal archives in Berne, they were made subject to a 100-year ban on publication. In March 1998, after a six-month investigation, an official committee of inquiry proposed to the Swedish government that it pay a compensation of up to 175,000 Swedish *kronor* to the victims of its compulsory sterilization program (*The Guardian*, London, March 6, 1999).

Forcible sterilizations of Romani women still occurs in parts of Europe where people remain especially afraid of accepting as European those who do not conform to certain behavioral, cultural, and aesthetic ideas. Even in such countries as Greece, France, and Italy, the provision of basic services such as health and education is frequently reported to involve discrimination in the case of resident Roma. Considering that relocations from eastern Europe by Europeans to such countries as Britain and Sweden sometimes excite hostility by skinheads and others who wish to hurriedly erect special barriers suggests that the issue of Africa in Europe cannot be totally divorced from those of Europe in Europe, Jews in Europe, Muslims in Europe, Turks in Europe, West Indians in Europe, Latin Americans in Europe, Indians in Europe, and so forth. The situation that looms before us stands as a stark reminder of what sometimes occurs when we focus more on "otherness" than on our fundamental connectedness and interdependence.

The frontiers between what we nowadays refer to as Africa and Europe have also been fluid, flexible, and porous ones. Europe and Africa are places with much human diversity and this has been true of each of them at least since it has been populated by large numbers of people. As peoples of Africa and Europe have a common genesis and have interacted with each other since antiquity, they have never been non-overlapping or mutually exclusive of each other. In addition to the direct biological and cultural linkages that connect peoples considered Africans and those considered European, there also exist indirect linkages through connections that they have with peoples on other continents.

In this sense, Europeans on the one hand, and Africans on the other, refer to rather arbitrary ways of thinking about humanity that have global implications. The same kinds of stereotyping and launching of insults that have sometimes targeted Africans has never targeted them exclusively. During a rebellion in India against British rule in 1857, for example, British officers wishing to express contempt and loathing for the rebels took to repeatedly referring to the Indians involved as "niggers" (MacMaster 2001: 59). Although most Irish, Cypriots, Jews, and many people of African descent or partially of African descent have complexions much like those of most Europeans, they have sometimes been targeted in racist ways (Anthias 1998: 179). Anti-Semitism and Islamaphobia, in fact, can potentially target a person of almost any appearance, including Europeans, Africans, and others.

As human beings are mobile and move about with considerable frequency among various continents, concepts such as African, European, Asian, and African American, Arab, Indo-European, South African, and Afro-European can take on many contrasting meanings. It is simplistic to assume that any such terms can encapsulate everything about a person or group of people throughout history from biology through places of residence and from culture through nationality and citizenship. The longing of some Europeans for a continental homeland that is unequivocally "white" and Christian amounts to desiring something that never existed in the past and that is not realistically obtainable in an age of globalization.

It has oftentimes been noted that human beings have a need to create myths to legitimize their existence and to maintain cohesion within groups. While some myths are perhaps harmless, others can be very dysfunctional for the people who believe in them as well as for the common good. Races as discrete and non-overlapping segments of our species do not exist other than as myth. When applied to human beings therefore racial thinking has no scientific basis, nor do the related concepts of racial purity, racial distinctiveness, racial superiority, racial inferiority, and racial destinies. To essentialize any large group of people simply by a color label is to deny much of their vast biological and cultural diversity as well as the overlapping ways in which they are related to other peoples. Similarly, to essentialize any large group of people simply by a religious label is to deny much of their vast biological and cultural diversity as well as the overlapping ways in which they are related to other peoples.

The earliest diffusion of Christianity into Europe was via Jews who ventured there from Asia, and in some cases from Africa. Well before large populations of Europeans had been converted to Christianity, Islam was an established religion in parts of Europe and there have been Muslims in some parts of Europe ever since. Among the reasons that a major influx of peoples largely of African descent into Europe nowadays is viewed by some Europeans as novel rather than a continuation of ancient patterns of migration is that for a long time many myths about race have confused the ways in which we tend to view Africans and Europeans and the many types of human connections among them.

The fact that race lacks a scientific basis in human biology does not mean that racism is nonexistent. A mere belief in the existence of race—especially when coupled with a belief in racial purity, racial distinctiveness, racial superiority, racial inferiority, or racial destinies—is sufficient to cause racism to exist. Racism is essentially a faith-based way of thinking that operates outside the parameters of science. It intrinsically incorporates distorted logic about human variation and how peoples are related to each other. Stereotyping, unfounded generalization, and the overlooking of inconsistencies figure prominently in thinking that is racist. Insecurities involving economics, social status, identity, sex, and competition sometimes contribute to racism (see e.g., MacMaster 2001: 1, 58-59).

Human beings are habitually discriminatory in their interactions with each other, but not all discrimination is racist. Racism contributes to many types of discrimination that threaten human co-existence and world stability. Racism can be manifested through omission as well as commission. Through the selective presentation of information as well as through the selective omission of information, such as mass media and public institutions sometimes contribute to racism and provide justifications for racist discrimination. Remaining silent while hearing racist speech or witnessing discrimination sometimes implicitly provides such behaviors with an aura of sanction. While some racists act out their racism noisily as demagogues and hooligans, others with great sophistication as intellectuals, statesmen, and prominent citizens watch it acted out from the sidelines, pretending to have little knowledge or control over what the demagogues and hooligans are doing.

Discrimination based on racism is not infrequently used to carry out or justify assaults on other human beings. Included among such assaults are murder, enslavement, injury, exploitation, deprivation of resources, deprivation of territory, deprivation of liberty, segregation, negative labeling, unprovoked insult, withholding of privileges, and profiling for the differential allocation of rights and opportunity. Discrimination based on racism also is sometimes manifested through sexual slander, provocation, and assault. Fear of terrorism is a justification for enhanced caution and the tightening of some social controls and some surveillance systems. It is not however an adequate justification for discrimination based on racism. Information can now be transmitted throughout the world much faster than ever before and it can be manipulated more easily than ever before. Hence, control over information is power, for information controls our perceptions of terror, of human variation, of territorialism, of what should be considered infallible, and also of our perceptions of what should be considered so inviolable as to be sufficient for war.

Already at the turn of the 21st century, an estimated one out of every 35 people living in the world was an international migrant of some kind. While all diaspora concepts suggest various scatterings of people beyond their traditional homelands, we now live in a world where there exist diasporas based on language, on religion, on places of origin, on physical appearance, on shared experiences, as well as diasporas that are political. Almost everywhere we look in the world, a long series of relocations has left such a diversity of people superimposed on each other that the concept of diaspora is fast becoming in some ways as much one of confusion as an analytic term of clarification. We now inhabit a world when one can legitimately wonder where and when the diasporas begin or how many overlapping diasporas really exist. Many of us can never go home again because the places where we once established our homes may not be our homelands, or our homelands have been continually changing as we have continued to colonize and re-colonize the same planet. Now that we have all become global, we are faced with making new accommodations with each other and thinking of each other in less rigid ways for the common good.

In a number of cases that received wide and sensational coverage in the Swiss press, Africans and Asians entered Switzerland with valid visitors' visas that authorized them to participate in cultural, educational, and athletic events but vanished clandestinely in Europe prior to their scheduled departures to return home. A few recent examples include the Dzinpa Dance Ensemble from Ghana, which disappeared in Zurich, a Moroccan folk-music group in Basel, the national handball team of Sri Lanka in Bavaria, and a soccer or football team from Cameroon in Meiner in Canton Geneva. A number of European countries including Great Britain and Germany reacted by exercising greater reluctance in granting visitor's visas to Africans and Asians and exercising greater reluctance in accepting Africans as refugees, or as they are increasingly described "asylum seekers." Such cases notwithstanding, not all people with richly pigmented skins in Europe are there out of desperation or wish to remain permanently and become citizens.

While some such people are Europeans in every sense of the word, "others" are diplomats, students, tourists, businesspeople, or just people who happen to be in transit. Too often, mass media are profiting from sensationalism and stereotypes in ways that further racism and even expose people with certain appearances to random discrimination and physical attack. Mass media in many Western countries regularly refuse to publish images and stories about people deemed to be of different races interacting normally and frequently with each other across the full range of human activities. Through such omission or self-censorship, perhaps media moguls hope to lend credence to the unscientific notion of discrete and non-overlapping races. It is also possible that they simply wish to garner great earnings in parts of the world where people are greatly invested in racial thinking. Such arbitrary ways of attempting to impose social order on human beings is not just benign; such decisions have consequences that are sometimes extremely lethal.

That in the Western world many people consider it more or less normal for a man stereotyped as European to be portrayed in a sexual relationship with a women of any ethnic background but as incendiary when a male of non-European ancestry is portrayed in a relationship of similar intimacy with a European woman is reflective of institutionalized racism that still thrives. In some parts of Europe, racists first spread falsehoods alleging that people of African descent are capable of extraordinary sexual feats while others, out of resentment or feelings of insecurity, then target them for having been so stereotyped in the first place.

Reflecting back on the riots of 1958 that swept through Nottingham in England's East Midlands and through Notting Hill in West London only a week later, there is great relevance here. In the former case, a crowd was angered merely because a man classified as "black" was conversing with a woman classified as "white." In the latter, a Swedish woman considered "white" was married to a "black" man from the West Indies. The real story here is not so much what the racist attackers did but what the media moguls and those in charge of the education system had failed to do to lead so many enraged attackers to believe that they were protecting European racial purity, which is nonexistent in any case.

European mass media give most of their sensational coverage about illegal immigrants to Africans reaching the European Union largely from the south and southwest. As reported by Stephan Israel in the Zurich weekly *NZZ am Sonntag* (October 22, 2006: 8)—the Sunday edition of the financial daily *Neue Zürcher Zeitung* and more moderate than its more conservative parent—most of the illegal immigrants entering the European Union actually arrive in an unspectacular manner over the borders of eastern Europe. These include Turks, Albanians, and those who come from and through such countries of the former Yugoslavia as Serbia, Montenegro, Bosnia-Herzegovina, and Croatia.

Most of the news about African immigrants in Europe as presented through European mass media is exceedingly negative. In October of 2005, the Swiss tabloid *20 Minutes* let it be known that a particular police raid against 28 suspected drug dealers involved "black Africans." Soon afterward another Swiss paper, *Freiburger Nachrichten*, reported that the person involved in a felony case was a "black African." The complexions of the suspects were so irrelevant to the reporting of these stories that CRAN, an antiracist organization headquartered in western Switzerland, complained to these publications that they were contributing to latent racism. Both papers, however, rejected the charge as without merit.

It is doubtful that such coverage, though contributing to European xenophobia and intolerance as well as racism, bothers the disseminators of this type of news. Rather, stories about conflict and fear help to increase sales by making their products more attractive to advertisers. The appetite for such coverage is also fed by public attitudes about "others," often presumed to have little right to be in Europe and few connections with Europeans. In contrast to NGO spokesmen who typically discuss immigration trends in Europe in long-winded and scholarly ways, many journalists choose simplistic *"j'accuse"*-style one-liners whose "hard-hitting" sensationalism directed at the public jugular vein is calculated to get their stories major coverage in newspapers, magazines, and on television.

Christoph Blocher, a multimillionaire from Zurich who became Switzerland's head of its Department of Justice and Police, so successfully used such tactics in unsettling many Swiss that by the early 2000s he transformed his Swiss People's Party (SVP) into the country's largest political party. While occupying one of the seven seats on Switzerland's Federal Council, Blocher was liberal in allowing the publication of statistics showing that almost one quarter of Switzerland's population consisted of foreigners and that foreigners constituted almost half of all people charged with felonies. Unlike Switzerland's Federal Office of Migration (FOM), however, Blocher did not similarly emphasize that Switzerland had a "substantial integration deficit among certain groups of foreigners" and that foreigners resident in Switzerland were three times more likely than others to be unemployed.

Although the vast majority of foreigners resident in Switzerland are Europeans, Zurich's left-leaning *Sonntags-Zeitung* (January 19, 2003: 21-23) suggests that Swiss police are thought to be especially focused on checking the papers of people "with dark skins." During four decades Switzerland has been involved in a program providing for development cooperation and humanitarian aid in Africa. Christoph Blocher is on record to Lausannes's *Le Matin Dimanche*, however, as arguing that Africa should be left to itself and as being critical of Swiss financial aid to Africans, whom he implied were lazy.

In Europe, as elsewhere, most printing presses and electronic mass media operate well outside the control of people who are socially marginalized and suffer most from economic, political, and cultural insecurity. What Europe is and who is to be considered European is often as convoluted and difficult to understand as what Africa is and who ought to be considered African. In part, this is reflected by the fact that we are reluctant to recognize some people who are European citizens as European while for reasons deemed racial, ethnic, or cultural we are willing to reach out to include others whose ancestors have not lived there for many generations. In Germany, nationhood is embodied and expressed in a definition of citizenship that is remarkably open to ethnic German immigrants from eastern Europe but remarkably closed to immigrants not claiming Germanic ancestry, and most especially if they are not perceived by the masses of Germans as of European ancestry (Giugni and Passy 2006a: 6-7).

Sensationalized reporting in certain Russian newspapers that loosely use collective ethnic, racial, and national constructs to label in critical ways people in Russia who were law-abiding as well as those who were not has exacerbated the atmosphere of racism. Such reporting, for example, did not distinguish the vast majority of people of Chinese background in Russia from those who illegally immigrated into the country after 1991 nor from the vast majority of people of African descent from those who sometimes are claimed to be doing something that is not in accordance with the law.

Although the Netherlands has been a country of immigration since the 1960s, it took the Dutch some time to recognize this. With regard to immigrants of appreciable African descent, this especially involved so-called guest workers from Morocco, immigration from the Caribbean—including the surge from Suriname after Suriname's independence in 1975 (Vermeulen and Penninx 2000a: 7)—and some refugees and asylum seekers. A large increase in the number of Moroccan immigrants between 1973 and 1980 was largely due to family reunification, sometimes referred to as marriage immigration (Vermeulen and Penninx 2000a: 5, 7). Hans Janmaat, leader of a group of right-wingers in the Tweede Kamer (the Dutch lower house of parliament), largely in reaction to this growing African presence in the country, began advocating the forced removal of all foreigners from the Netherlands.

Beginning in 1985 as immigration from the Dutch Antilles involving the lower classes as well as others greatly increased, the Dutch enacted regulations intended to encourage return migration. Again from 1984 to 1991, in fact, there was another large increase in the number of Moroccan immigrants in the Netherlands largely due to family reunification (Vermeulen and Penninx 2000a: 7). In 2002, an amended version of the remigration regulation that the Dutch government had adopted in 1985 mainly targeted former guest workers from Mediterranean countries, but also included migrants form Suriname, the Indonesian Moluccas, and Cape Verde as well as acknowledged refugees. This Reimigration Act offered those who wished to re-migrate to their country of origin the facilities with which to realize this desire (Haas 2006: 37).

The Dutch politician Pim Fortuyn, conservative, anti-immigrant and anti-Islamist, was likely assassinated in early May 2002 in part for having suggested that the Netherlands was "full." For many Dutch people, his assassination raised new questions about how much immigration was enough. The subsequent November 2004 assassination of Theo van Gogh, a descendant of the brother of the painter Vincent van Gogh by Mohammed Bouyeri, a Dutch-born Muslim of Moroccan descent, further impacted in a negative way Dutch receptivity toward immigration of Moroccans. Complicating this situation was the fact that Theo van Gogh from the late 1990s expressed much hostility toward Islam and Muslims. Adding to the fury of some Muslims, he also produced a film about what he considered the objectionable treatment of females in Islam for television from a script written by a Somalian-born immigrant into the Netherlands named Ayaan Hirsi Ali.

While the short film was perhaps within the boundaries of what was allowed by the free speech traditions of a liberal European democracy, titled *Submission* (a synonym for Islam), it was perceived by many Muslims in the Netherlands as a direct attack by Theo van Gogh on their religion. The number of asylum seekers in the Netherlands fell by more than 80% between 2004 and 2006 under right-wing Immigration Minister Rita Verdonk of the conservative VVD Party. Verdonk made no secret of her intention to deport some 26,000 asylum seekers, including many who had resided in the Netherlands for years. Well before this time, Somalian-born Ayaan Hirsi Ali had won election to the Dutch parliament, largely through the support of Theo van Gogh.

When in May 2006, Verdonk informed Ali, also a member of the VVD party, who had been granted Dutch citizenship in 1997 and a Dutch MP for three years that she might lose her Dutch citizenship because of inconsistencies in Ali's original application for asylum in 1992, including whether she had arrived in the Netherlands directly from Somalia or Germany and whether her real name was Hirsi Magan. Ali resigned from parliament and announced her intention to depart the country. Only when this created a crisis in the Parliament did Verdonk reverse herself and inform Ali that she would not lose her Dutch citizenship. Meanwhile, well beyond the best-known tourist areas of Amsterdam, two neighborhoods particularly associated with underprivileged immigrants were Amsterdam West and the Bylmer section of Amsterdam Southeast. In some of the worst housing in these areas, there was no central heat and only a single stove on each floor. Sometimes, the main entrance on the ground floor had to be opened with a rope that extended up to the various floors for use of the tenants who lived at the higher levels.

Few of the widely circulated media of the Western world that reported on the killing in the Netherlands of columnist and filmmaker Theo van Gogh considered it relevant to also report that Theo van Gogh was on record as frequently referring to Muslim men as people who habitually engaged in sex with goats and on occasion to Jews as "fornicating yellow stars in a gas chamber." While even such selectively biased reporting obviously does not excuse murder, it certainly suggests that extreme provocation and racism were prominent on van Gogh's "free speech" agenda. Far from being a marginalized court jester in Dutch society, Gerrit Zalm, a deputy prime minister and finance minister, had appeared in one of his films.

Some forces not associated with the West began contesting its control of information, including its view of what constituted free speech or how free speech should be. A lecturer at the Niebuhr Institute at the University of Copenhagen was in October 2004 assaulted by five Muslims who opposed his reading of the Qur'an to non-Muslims during a lecture. The daily Danish newspaper *Jyllands-Posten* (meaning, Jutland Post) at the end of September 2005 published an article entitled "*Muhammeds ansigt.*" Twelve cartoons, some of which pretended to depict the Prophet Muhammad, accompanying it. This caused consternation among many Muslims residing in Europe and elsewhere. Although the masses of Europeans likely recognized that this was insensitive, they probably viewed it largely as expression in conformity with established rights of free speech. Without doubt, battles over the control of information, especially in connection with faith-based ideologies, were complicating globalization and at times making it difficult for us to know to what extent we are moving forwards and backwards.

By the time soldiers quit the battlefields at the end of World War II, Nazism had suffered only a momentary defeat, for its underlying racism was still thriving in the world. That even today in some European countries April 20, the birthday of Adolf Hitler, has become one of the most dangerous for Jews, Roma, and peoples of African descent to venture out on the streets is but one indication of this. In general, the nations who after great reluctance decided to wage a war against Hitler and Mussolini were unwilling to recognize the parallels between their own internal racism and that espoused by Nazis and Fascists. World War II was not really a war against racism and it is not surprising therefore that hardly any European country nowadays is without its skinheads, neo-Nazis, neo-Fascists, or their ideological equivalents as well as underground sympathizers. In Hungary, such groups have taken to drawing swastikas and SS symbols on the houses of some Jews as well as to holding anti-Semitic demonstrations opposite the parliament and in the metro system in Budapest. Racists have become so threatening toward people belonging to some despised minority groups in Hungary on holidays that leaders of the Hungarian Jewish community called on Jews to leave the country on the eve of a national holiday in 2006.

While an estimated 12,000 Africans lived in Russia as of 1998, Russia also had numerous other people with appreciable African ancestry from Latin America and various parts of Asia. A good many of these were married to Russians and some had offspring of mixed heritage. In addition to these people who resided in Russia in terms of years or decades, other people of Africa descent lived in Russia, most especially in the Abkhazia sub-region of Transcaucasia, for centuries (Williams 1998: 12; Fikes and Lemon 2002: 500-503; Blakely 1986: 6-12, 76-77, 165-167). It is ironic that Hitler murdered multitudes of Slavs largely because he considered them inferior to Germans and now Russian Slavs sometimes dress up as neo-Nazis and attack other people whom they consider to be their inferiors. Swarthy-complexioned Russian merchants at Moscow's Yasenevo market came under attack in 2001, including especially Russians from the Caucasus area such as Chechnyans and others presumed to be Muslims.

In 1993, Vladimir Zhirinovsky, the populist leader of the Liberal Democratic Party of Russia or LDPR, achieved unexpectedly good results in elections for the Russian Duma on the back of nationalist rhetoric interlaced with racism. In fact, his party came in first by capturing 23 percent of all the votes cast across Russia. Until 2001, this ultra-nationalist anti-Semitic denied that his father was Jewish. Even afterwards, he continued his tirades against Jews, blaming them for wrongs as varied as selling to Western countries Russian women as prostitutes, body parts, and children. He even blamed them for the holocaust of the 1930s and early 1940s that almost brought them to extinction in Europe. As of 2002, there were some 200 nationalist publications in Russia many of which printed articles tinged with racism. In that same year racist attacks escalated to such a level that ambassadors from 37 African nations appealed to the Foreign Ministry of Russia for protection of their citizens. In December 2003, a dozen political parties in Russia campaigned on extremist nationalist agendas, most with considerable success. Some of these ran as members of Vladimir Zhirinovsky's LDPR. As of 2007, Zhirinovsky was vice-chairman of Russia's Duma and a member of the Parliamentary Assembly of the Council of Europe.

In post-Soviet Russia, while certain peoples were disproportionately the victims of violent attacks by skinheads, they were also often the victims of police indifference and abuse as well as ethnic profiling. Not infrequently they were insulted on public streets, in subway or metro stations (e.g., the Green Line which it has been alleged that a member of an ethnic minority takes around 6 o'clock only if he wishes to die), and increasingly were injured and murdered. Hooligans with racist, nationalist, and other agendas also harassed and attacked Europeans they assumed supported policies at variance with those favored by the government of Russia, for example, Chechnyans, Georgians, Estonians, irrespective of whether they were Russians, citizens of countries that were formerly a part of the Soviet Union, or others. Even where one did not have an extremely dark complexion, the mere assumption that a person was Romani, Jewish or Muslim could increase the likelihood that the person was viewed as belonging to a "suspect" or "enemy" nationality or ethnic group.

In addition to sometimes being targeted for racist insults on the streets by the general public, people falling into this category were often singled out by police for document checks, bribery, and even robbery. Following a strictly scientific methodology, the Open Society Justice Initiative in partnership with JURIX conducted a study to determine the extent of disproportionate ethnic profiling of people with non-Slavic versus Slavic appearances by police on the Moscow metro system. Although people with non-Slavic appearances made up only 4.6 percent of riders, they were 50.9 percent of all persons stopped at metro exits. At one station, according to this study, the former were more than 85 times more likely than people with Slavic appearances to be stopped by the police (Adjami

It is not only in Moscow that this happened; similar patterns of ethnic profiling were reported from places scattered across Europe.

That some Swiss officials often have a disproportionate concern with treating so-called asylum seekers from Africa different from others is reflected in attempts by Switzerland in 2003 to conclude agreements with Nigeria and Senegal whereby asylum seekers of uncertain national origin whose applications it had rejected would be expelled to holding stations in those two countries. To the degree that concern in Europe with inhibiting illegal immigration has a special focus on Africa, it sometimes finds expression in discrimination against people of dark complexion even where there exists no likelihood that they intend to become asylum seekers. Among those potentially vulnerable to such treatment are a great many law-abiding African, Asian, European, Caribbean, Pacific Island, South American, and North American citizens.

Using posters that depicted a white sheep kicking a black sheep off the Swiss flag and that were widely considered racist, Switzerland's Christoph Blocher managed in parliamentary elections held on October 21, 2007 not only to secure the position of his far-right Swiss People's Party as the largest single party in his country's Parliament but to slightly increase its strength to occupy more seats than any one party in Switzerland's history. Ironically in the same election, the Swiss for the first time also elected a "black" compatriot to serve in Parliament. The new member was Angolan-born Ricardo Lumengo, a Social Democrat, who first arrived in Switzerland as an asylum seeker in 1982 after which he first worked as a dishwasher in a restaurant. He eventually became a lawyer and became involved in Swiss politics. Although he received much hate mail along the way, both he and his fellow Swiss are contributing to the ongoing story of Africa in Europe.

Despite such problems as ethnic profiling and physical assaults on people targeted for not looking sufficiently European, "white," Aryan, Nordic, Slavic, Germanic, or Christian, as the case might be, many European countries—including those in the European Union—lacked anti-discrimination laws or showed little resolve in enforcing the laws that were on the books. This was noted as a problem in the *2000 Report on the State of Human Rights in the Czech Republic* that was produced by the Human Rights Commissioner and Chairman of the Council of the Government of the Czech Republic for Human Rights. As stated in the report, "the belittlement of the importance of racially motivated criminal activities of the skinheads appears to be a rule rather than an exception" and "even if the attackers were sentenced, they received, as a rule, a sentence at the bottom of the sentence range for very violent crimes against the Roma or foreigners" (Czech Helsinki Committee 2001: 56-57).

The number of racially motivated incidents that were criminally prosecuted overall in Europe remained small. Although a European Union Monitoring Center on Racism and Xenophobia was based in Vienna, member governments seemed unable to agree on appropriate penalties, at least according to Karin Gastinger, the Austrian justice minister. Until 1990, the right-wing Freedom Party (FPÖ) was a marginal part of the country's political life. Since that time however Jörg Haider, the controversial leader of that party known for dubious statements about Jews, hostility toward immigrants, and praise of Nazism during the Third Reich where he claimed "they had an orderly employment policy," realized great success in a number of elections. Among these were the national election of 1994, the 1997 elections to the European Parliament, and his 1999 landslide re-election as governor of the state of Carinthia in southern Austria.

Contributing to the formulation of the ÖVP-FPÖ right-wing coalition in Austria in early 2002 was a heated controversy over immigration there. Jörg Haider, the party leader of the FPÖ, in addition to arguing for tougher asylum laws eventually insisted that applications for asylum in Austria should be made outside the country and that only Europeans should be eligible to apply. On the other hand, the Austrian Social Democratic (SPÖ) and Green parties as well as some Austrian human rights organizations have objected to what they considered to be objectionable attitudes toward non-Austrian and non-European Union citizens (Triadafilopoulos and Zaslove 2006: 178-179). Although Austria's ÖVP-FPÖ right-wing coalition seemed so conservative and racist in 2002 that the European Union imposed sanctions on Austria after the FPÖ was invited to form the government, in 2006, Austrian right-wing parties fared well in elections based on promises to increase the pace of deporting immigrants.

During the same period that the EU was trying to isolate Austria, similar problems of xenophobia and racism were widespread elsewhere in Europe, including well beyond the EU. As of 2003, Peoples' Friendship University of Russia in Moscow enrolled approximately 13,000 graduate and undergraduate students from more than 100 countries, most of whom were Russian but about a third of whom were from developing countries. On November 24 that same year, a mysterious fire in a university dormitory left over 40 foreign students dead. Among the countries and territories that the dead and injured of appreciable African ancestry came from were Ethiopia, Angola, Ivory Coast, Morocco, Dominican Republic, Nigeria, Palestine, and Tanzania. In the summer of the same year, a 19-year-old medical student from Malaysia was attacked in a McDonald's restaurant in Moscow apparently because she was identifiable as a Muslim because of her head scarf. In 2006, one group of Russian racists murdered a nine-year-old Tajik girl in St. Petersburg and another group murdered a street vender of Chinese ethnicity in Vladivostok.

In November 2005, over 1,000 students and local residents of Voronezh, Russia participated in a march against racism and hatred after the murder there of Enrique Arturo Urtado, a Peruvian first-year student at the Voronezh State Architecture and Civil Engineering University. He died as the result of an attack with metal clubs and wood objects that were used by 15 to 20 young men. Around the same time in Voronezh, an African student from Guinea-Bissau was also killed. In Volzhsky, a city in central Russia, skinheads attacked a Romani camp with steel rods, killing a man and a woman in 2006. Even in small Russian towns, one can encounter with considerable frequency nationalist graffiti, swastikas and slogans such as "Russia for the Russians" and "Death to Jews."

If we target one group in order to give ourselves a feeling of security, or in some cases a feeling of superiority, that is little more than a figment of our imagination today, we can easily juxtapose another group as victims to be targeted tomorrow to fulfill a similar need. The world's diversity provides us with many choices and there has never existed any firm dividing line between Europeans and others. Those deemed insufficiently "white" to qualify as Europeans today can be Jews, Africans, "blacks," Armenians, Turks, Slavs, Arabs, Muslims, or people stereotyped as having narrow skulls and tomorrow they can just as well be Caucasians, southern Italians, Irish or Roma.

Even as the European Union grows larger and more inclusive, Europe struggles with an identity crisis that can be traced back at least as far as the Enlightenment concerning what it means to be European. In 1996, Dominican Republic-born Denny Méndez, whose mother was a naturalized Italian and whose stepfather was from Italy, was elected as Miss Italia and competed in that role in the Miss Universe Contest of 1997. Because she was of appreciable African descent, a controversy ensued over who could be Italian. Two judges were eventually suspended for protesting that a "black" woman could not represent Italian beauty. This crisis is not merely confined to beauty contests.

Jean-Marie Le Pen, head of France's extreme right-wing Front National Party, repeatedly complained over several years that his country's national football team had too many "black" players. When in late 2006, however, Georges Freche, a prominent member of France's Socialist Party, said essentially the same thing and added that it made him feel ashamed, Pandora's box was truly open. Embarrassed by his remarks only months before an upcoming presidential election, his party expelled him for having made statements incompatible with Socialist values. Across Europe, the question of what it means to be European remains a very controversial one and can have consequences that go well beyond mere words.

In numerous Western countries said to be democracies, many people pay lip service to the notion that open competition is a central principle of their political, social, and economic organization. Many of these people also claim to see in the Olympiads of ancient Greece an athletic manifestation of open competition in athletics. MacMaster (2001: 47-48) has pointed out that the tremendous expansion of the revived Olympic movement was accompanied by "a growing feeling that success or failure in competition was a mark of the biological fitness of the race-nations." Eventually, a connection between "ideal white bodies and sport" received idealization in the film of the 1936 Olympic Games by Leni Riefenstahl in which great emphasis was placed on parallelism between the Greek aesthetic and the German Aryan as the perfect body type. Although Adolf Hitler did not snub the star African-American track athlete James "Jesse" Owens at the 1936 Games in Germany, as has often been alleged, Hitler did appear to shun the "black" American Cornelius Johnson who won the first gold medal for the United States on day one of the event by leaving the stadium precipitously.

Although athletes of African ancestry were found even in ancient Greece, many Europeans with no sense of the diversity of their past fill in voids handed down to them with racist myths and stereotypes. What most of the world knows as football, and North Americans call soccer, is a sport about which some are passionate to the point of almost becoming manic. It is doubtful that many Europeans realize that Andrew Watson, a "black" man originally from British

Guiana (now Guyana) came to Scotland to study at Glasgow University in 1876 and ended up playing football for Queens Park, the leading team of Scotland. It is doubtful that many Europeans realize that Arthur Wharton, whose father was half-Grenadian and half Scottish and whose mother was from Ghanaian royalty, played British football professionally as early as 1889 when he became a goal keeper for Preston North End. Similarly, it is doubtful that many Europeans realize that in 1938 when "black" Ben M'Barek arrived from Morocco to play the game in Marseille, France, he was such a superstar without equal that he was dubbed "*Le Perle noire de Casablanca*" or The Black Pearl of Casablanca (Blanchard and Boëtsch 2005: 108-109).

Many European football clubs have hired players of African heritage, a number of whom so distinguished themselves by outstanding performances that they earned princely wages and became sports superstars. One of the many "black" footballers in Europe whose fame seems to be rising is André Stéphane Bikey Amugu originally from Cameroon. After starting his professional career at Espanyol in Spain, he moved to Shinnik Yaroslavl in Russia in 2005. Not long after arriving in Russia, however, Bikey encountered intense racist harassment and learned that Russian police were reluctant to protect people with dark complexions. As a consequence, he departed from Russia for Reading in 2006 where he signed a four-year contract in excess of £1 million.

Clearly, all is not well in European football, for such players are frequently the targets of unprovoked racist taunts from fans and outlandish attributions by commentators. Racist lashing out at people of African descent is hardly restricted to football. Finns usually are favorably disposed to having North Americans deemed to be "white" immigrate and work among them. When during the early 1990s an African-American basketball player named Darryl Parker arrived in Joensuu, Finland to play on the town's team, his reception was different. He was attacked and so intimidated by local skinheads that he soon had to return to the United States out of fear for his safety. Racism in Europe has not only victimized non-Europeans; as was true during the holocaust of World War II, it has also victimized Europeans.

According to 1999 estimates, the Czech Republic is the European country with the highest percentage of Roma or Gypsies after Macedonia, Romania, Slovakia, Bulgaria, Hungary, and Serbia-Montenegro (Ringold 2000: 1). As recently as 2003, three underage Roma girls were sterilized without any parental consent in a hospital and without any notification to competent state authority empowered to make medical decisions on behalf of minors. When a complaint was initially brought, the Slovakian state prosecution service dismissed it.

Hungary, Slovakia, the Czech Republic, and Slovenia joined the European Union in 2004, thereby adding about 1.2 million Roma to the population of the EU. The number of Roma in the EU roughly tripled again when Bulgaria and Romania joined the EU in 2007. In March of this same year, the UN Committee on the Elimination of Racial Discrimination formally expressed concern over the "lack of sufficient and prompt action" by the authorities in the Czech Republic "to impede the illegal performance of coercive sterilization" of Romani women. In many respects, these developments are reenactments of old scripts that have not changed and will never change unless we commit ourselves to think and act in dramatically different ways concerning what we have done and are doing to each other.

Shortly after winning a third term as Italy's prime minister in April 2008, Silvio Berlusconi ingratiated himself with his right-wing base of supporters by urging the government to declare a national state of emergency after which he dispatched thousands of troops to Italian streets largely away from tourist areas to harass and profile people seeming to belong visible minorities. Especially controversial among Berlusconi's policies were his plans to fingerprint people living on the outskirts of Italy's large cities, the vast majority of whom were Roma. Undertaken some eight centuries after Roma first entered Europe and began to make their own contribution to European history and civilization in the 1300s, Berlusconi claimed these discriminatory measures were merely to prevent crime and control immigration. One could hardly imagine European dance and music from Russia and Hungary to the Flamenco of Spain or the opera *Carmen*, set in Seville, without the presence in Europe of Roma.

It is not sufficient just to tolerate diversity; we need to embrace it. This would be an important way of being genuinely both pro-human and humane. When we can understand and embrace the concept of Africa in Europe as easily and as honestly as we understood that Europe's impact on Africa has been relentless and indelible, we shall truly be moving in the direction of greater self acceptance as a species as well as in the direction of mutual respect and coexistence. Although war has always involved tradeoffs among life, death, and so-called principles or rights, for people increasingly inhabiting the same globalized village, recent reminders that some of our fellows have values more important than survival have proved terrifying. The destruction of the twin World Trade Towers in lower New York City on September 11, 2001 sent shivers throughout the world while demonstrating that technology per se cannot protect us from ourselves.

Similarly, the ten bombs detonated by men on four trains in three stations in and around Madrid during the busy morning rush hour on March 11, 2004, in ways that killed at least 180 commuters and wounded many others further terrorized us. On July 7, 2005, men with selfish and self-righteous agendas coordinated a series of terrorist bomb blasts that hit London's public transport system during the morning rush hour. The bombings killed 52 commuters and four suicide bombers. They also injured some 700 other people. As horrific as these killings were, terror more recently produced even higher totals in Iraq and some people would have us believe that the innocent lives extinguished there are an acceptable price to pay for protecting those of Westerners and has nothing to do with the long legacies of racism and faith-based fanaticism that still confront us on all sides.

Similarly, it is unfortunate for ethical reasons as well as for world stability when any group, large or small, sanctions killing some people because of whom they wish to marry. This includes, but is not limited to some Muslims who sanction so-called honor killings of females by their family members. Periodic descents into barbarism are not uniformly associated with any one segment of humanity. Moreover, it is not only among some Muslims that one sometimes encounters people who would rather see others dead than married to those whom they love. Any temptation to view history with arrogance and self-righteousness merely to divert attention from our own distorted habits of viewing human variation in unscientific ways must be resisted. While there can be no justification for barbarism, it is not likely that the recycling of racism will provide any lasting protection against it.

It is no coincidence that in virtually all prisons under the management of peoples claiming to be primarily of European descent, we are much more likely to find prisons disproportionately filled with people of dark hue and brown eyes than with blue-eyed blonds. Conversely in the same societies where females are concerned, we are likely to see people belonging to the latter category rather than the former held up as the ideal of beauty and as symbols of unadulterated purity. Those who perceive such thinking as based on self-evident rationality perhaps have more in common with some Nazi ideologues than they ever realized. In comparison to all the people who openly threaten the safety of public places as skinheads and neo-Nazis, covert racists are perhaps more dangerous, for their numbers are likely much larger and many of them occupy positions of great prominence in the world.

We live in a world where we pretend that there is much less inequality in the distribution of resources and wealth than there really is by frequently blaming the victims of poverty for their own despair and by pretending that they have more opportunity than they really do. In a world such as ours that is sharply dichotomized between societies of wealth and privilege, on the one hand, and societies of poverty and despair, on the other hand, many people resident in the former are naturally upset to find their relatively high standards of living are vulnerable to outsourcing, to attack by terrorists, and by immigration often perceived as out-of-control. Multitudes living in societies of privilege and wealth feel insecure behind boundaries that are ill-equipped to protect them from peoples, languages, cultures, and ideologies that they consider threatening. Multitudes of other people living amid poverty and despair expend considerable time and ingenuity in finding ways to penetrate those boundaries. Many of them, in fact, are fleeing terror. This is a drama that is being played out worldwide.

There is nothing novel either about an African presence in Europe or about a European presence in Africa. Western historians have long accepted as more natural that Europeans should expand into other parts of the world than that people not deemed of European heritage should settle in Europe. Western historians have been somewhat thorough in documenting the presence of Greeks and Romans in Africa in ancient times as well as the later presence of Franks, Venetians, and others from Europe in Asia and Africa during the Crusades. They have tended to accept as natural that as an extension of the so-called Renaissance Europeans eventually initiated an age of discovery that not infrequently abused and exploited non-Europeans on a global scale.

Western historians have been much less thorough and balanced in documenting the historic presence of Africans in Europe. In those situations where they have documented such a presence—for example, in the Iberian Peninsula—more often than not they have so conflated their accounts with religious parochialism, biased and incomplete accounts of slavery, and racism that they have left Europeans largely in denial about the large African presence in their past and in terror about the prospect of a large African presence in their future.

The current waves of Africans wishing to settle in Europe in hopes of improving their lives follow on the heels of multitudes of Europeans who earlier did the same thing during a long period of imperialism and colonization beyond the confines of Europe. European powers still quite frequently seek natural resources from south of the Mediterranean Sea, for example, petroleum products from Libya, Algeria, Nigeria, and Angola. They also seek inexpensive labor from Africa to maintain the economies of their aging societies in times of prosperity and set about trying to discard many of these same people in times of economic downturn.

Although our borders have always been porous, they nowadays offer many of us a diminished sense of security. Even as Europeans struggle to become reconciled with increasing numbers of peoples most Europeans think of as foreigners and outsiders in their midst, the rest of the world is similarly challenged. One of the major challenges of globalization lies in moving in the direction of more honest assessments of how we humans are and can be related to each other within and beyond the various territories that have traditionally been considered our homelands.

As of 1997, there were nineteen members of the British Parliament of African or Asian heritage, nine of whom were members of the House of Common and ten of whom were peers of the House of Lords. Of these Parliamentarians, the "black" MP Oona King was also Jewish. It is obviously not possible to focus on the recent impact of Africa in Europe from a political perspective in each society but France serves especially well as a good case study. While French citizens who are considered "white" and non-Muslims tend to experience no trouble in winning legislative elections in metropolitan France, including among those born in Africa, this is not equally true for French citizens of color or those who adhere to Islam. While of the 555 Deputies from metropolitan France in 2002, 20 or 21 from Maghreb held seats in the French National Assembly, none of these were Muslims from Maghreb. French citizens in metropolitan France who were both of African background and considered "black" were somewhat better represented.

Togo-born Kofi Yamgnane became a naturalized French citizen in 1975. After being elected mayor of the French town of Saint-Coulitz in 1989, he served for a while as French Secretary of State for Integration responsible to the Minister of Social Affairs. After serving as a region councilor in Brittany from 1992 to 1997, he won an election as Deputy in the French National Assembly from 1997 to 2002, representing the Finistère area of Brittany. While it is not uncommon for the sixteen French Deputies and ten Senators representing the overseas areas of France known as Guadeloupe, Matinique, Guyana, Réunion, and Mayotte to be people largely of African descent, Kofi Yamgnane was likely only the second "black" to represent a part of metropolitan France in the national legislature since the founding of the Fifth Republic in 1958. In June 2007, however, the election of George Pau-Langevin, a female attorney born in Pointe-à-Pitre in Guadeloupe as one of the Deputies representing Paris increased this number to four. Contributing further to the African presence in French governance was another person of color born in Pointe-à-Pitre who served as a French Secretary of State from 1988 to 1991, Roger Bambuck. His appointment was as a junior minister in charge of youth and sports.

So great were the bitterness and distrust toward northwestern Africa that lingered in France after the end of the Algerian War in 1962 that it took four decades before any Muslim French citizen of indigenous *Maghrébin* heritage would be chosen as a Secretary of State, a Deputy, or a Senator in France. Although Nora Zaïdi and Dijda Tazdait, both French women of Algerian heritage were elected as Eurodeputies in 1989. Tokia Saïfi, a Muslim French woman of Algerian parentage, who had been elected in 1999 to the European Parliament to represent the North-West of France resigned from that position in 2002 in order to serve the French government as Secretary of State responsible to the Minister of Ecology and Sustainable Development, thereby becoming the first Muslim citizen of northwestern African background to serve in the French government since the end of the Algerian War. That it would still be two years later before the election of Alima Boumediene-Thiery and Bariza Khiari, both of indigenous *Maghrébine* heritage, to the National Assembly suggests that perhaps French voters in metropolitan France were beginning to show their willingness to being represented by compatriots who reminded them of their loss of northwestern Africa.

Many sensitivities in how Europeans are learning to adapt to that part of themselves that is African remain. On February 4, 2005, for example, France passed a law to teach the "positive role" of France during its colonial period "in particular in North Africa." This law caused such a backlash outside as well as inside metropolitan France that Interior Minister Nicolas Sarkozy postponed a trip to the French Caribbean islands of Martinique and Guadeloupe to discuss illegal immigration and drug trafficking. Many labeled the new law "the law of shame." Some criticized the law as an attempt to impose an "official history" on educational institutions. Even Dominique de Villepin, who at that time was prime minister, stated "It's not up to politics, its not for Parliament to write history or tell the memory."

If one had any doubt that Europe is undergoing fundamental change both internally and in relationship to Africa, he or she need only observe that the major two candidates in the 2007 French presidential election were a second-generation immigrant of Jewish heritage who had made a reputation for himself largely by taking strong stances against immigrants, many of whom had African roots, and a French woman born in Dakar, Senegal. When Sarkozy won the election, many waited to see if France might explode. Meanwhile, Sarkozy quickly appointed the most diverse cabinet in French history. Ramatoulaye Yade-Zimet (also known as Rama Yade), a Frenchwoman born in Senegal, was chosen as the State Secretary in charge of foreign affairs and human rights within the Ministry of Foreign Affairs.

Only five years after the first minister of *Maghrébin* heritage since the end of the Algerian War was welcomed into a French cabinet, Sarkozy also reached out to two Muslim women of northwestern African heritage. One of these was Fadéla Amara (also known as Fatiha Amara), of Kabyle heritage. She was appointed Secretary of State for urban policies. Attracting even more attention was the position chose for Rachida Dati, a Frenchwoman of Moroccan and Algerian heritage who during Sarkozy's 2007 presidential campaign was his spokeswoman. Dati was chosen as France's Justice Minister, an appointment that made her the first person having a non-European immigrant and Muslim background to ever head a key French ministry. On the other hand, the fact that Sarkozy was on record as intending to curb immigration and that he created a new Ministry of Immigration and National Identity as a part of this policy was disquieting to many people in France, including many people of African ancestry.

To appreciate how diverse Europe really is as well as how fast it continues to change, one cannot focus solely on its public face as portrayed on cinema screens, through paintings on the walls of museums, in centers of great wealth, and in the seats of concentrated power. In these places, the Europe that one sees is often quite at variance with the equally skewed Europe that dwells in substandard housing, that studies in schools that largely serve the underprivileged, that washes dishes in restaurants, that sweeps streets and metro stations, and that populates the prisons. While some people in this latter Europe are undocumented immigrants that the French label *sans-papiers* and the Italians call *clandestini*, others are simply marginalized Europeans who have not managed to enter the mainstream.

We live in a world where we pretend that sovereign states are our major political actors although multinational corporations, the World Bank, the International Monetary Fund, communications conglomerates, and numerous criminal organizations have long brought this into question. Still, all independent states have a right to control immigration across their borders and within their borders. It is difficult to imagine that exercising this right in racist ways, however, will contribute to world peace. Physical boundaries, psychological frontiers, modes of travel, and ways of being in touch with each other are changing the world in ways that cause immigration control to take on new importance. That applies both in its function of manifesting sovereignty externally and in its function of maintaining sociocultural control internally (Brochmann 2002: 181). As immigration control has become an important part of the management of ethnic and international relations in a global context, concerns with people of African descent have figured prominently in how transnationalization of citizenship and integration have been impacting Europe quite broadly.

On October 18, 2007, Norway gained its first government minister of African descent when Manuel Myriam Henri Ramin-Osmundsen became its Minister of Children and Equality Affairs. That this was only a few months after she first became a Norwegian citizen is a reflection that growing numbers of Europeans belong to visible minorities, some of whom are at least in part of appreciable African descent. Born a French citizen on the West Indian Island of Martinique in 1963, she fell in love with a Norwegian citizen while studying law at

Pantheon-Assas Paris II University in France. As a consequence she married and moved from France to her newly adopted country of Norway to live with her husband in 1991 at age 28. Although continuing to have a French accent and a fondness both for Martinique and France, she learned to speak Norwegian. Two years after joining the Norwegian Labor Party, Manuel Myriam Henri Ramin-Osmundsen, having served as head of Norway's Center Against Ethnic Discrimination and part of a small but increasingly visible minority in Norway with connections to Africa as well as Europe, was appointed a Norwegian government minister.

We humans can never unthread the needle of our complex past, a past that transformed many of our ancestors into wanderers. Notions of being related through common "stock" or "bloodlines" are devoid of scientific meaning. Alongside numerous other complex ways in which we are tied together, thanks to sexual intercourse coupled with reproduction, an invisible mechanism known as gene flow operates continually to maintain our unity as a single species. Our destinies are, and must remain, intertwined in ways much more profound than most of us have been willing to think deeply about.

In some respects the complexity in our thinking about human variation and the sensitivity that is required in our thinking about human diversity could be seen in the conscientious efforts of two Parisian museums to deal with these subjects in 2007. With respect to France, for example, the *Cité Nationale de l'Histoire de l'Immigration* placed considerably emphasis on human interactions and diversity regardless of places of origin of various immigrants. By contrast, at least two exhibits at the *Musée de l'Homme* concerning human variation and diversity suggested more rigidity in approach. One of these tended to suggest that the ultimate focus of human evolution was largely focused on the peopling of Europe per se, for example, with its emphasis on Neanderthal and Cro-magnum types with no mention of their hominid contemporaries less associated with Europe. Another exhibit supposedly about demography in this same museum posed the alarmist and antiquated race-based question as to whether or not Europeans were disappearing. The curators involved were obviously insensitive to the fact that the mere posing of such a question could conceivably play into the hand of racists. It would have been a much more worthy point for this latter museum to have emphasized that *European* has always been a fluid concept and Europeans, like people in other parts of the world, are continuing to evolve and change.

As we near the end of this work, let us return at least briefly to certain foundations of history and also to some issues that relate to our gift of language. Perhaps on this terrain, we may be able to see where we have made some of the wrong turns that have so complicated our ability to deal with our present and our future. Ancient Greece was a part of Europe that was in contact with at least the north of Africa from a very early period. Snowden (1970: 102), pointed out that long before the time of Homer in the 8th century B.C., in fact, there existed Minoan and Pylos frescoes depicting individuals with characteristically African physical features. If Harris (1981b: 5) is correct, it is from Homer's references to Ethiopia in his *Iliad* and the *Odysey* that we encounter our earliest European documentary references to sub-Saharan Africa, including to the richly pigmented and wooly-haired Ethiopian Eurybates whom he described as the herald of Odysseus. From references of certain of Homer's Greek contemporaries to African pigmys (Snowden 1970: 101, 102), it is even possible that ancient Greeks were familiar with some of the Africans of very short stature that originate from as far south as Rwanda and Burundi. Archilochus wrote about a spendthrift Ethiopian who had participated around 743 B.C. along with others from Corinth in the founding of the Greek colony of Syracuse in Sicily (Snowden 1970: 103).

Among numerous other ancient Greeks who spoke of Ethiopians in a generic sense, in other words of "blacks," were Solon, Themistocles, Aristides, Pericles, Aeschylus, Sophocles, Euripides, Aristophanese, Thucydides, Demosthenes, Mnesicles, Ictinus, Socrates, Philostrates, Menander, Plato, and Aesclepiades. There is at least the possibility that the Greek explorer named Euthymenes from Massilia (now Marseille) may have reached western Africa as far south as the Senegal River in the early 6th century based on an account of a voyage by him into the Atlantic Ocean that we know secondhand from Plutarch. Around the same time, the Carthaginians founded the cities of Hadrumetum and Leptis Magna along the Mediterranean coast of Libya in the region known as Tripolitania. Even before the dependence of Carthage on its Phoenician mother country came to an end around 524 B.C. when Tyre and Persia entered into an alliance that recognized the hegemony of the latter, Carthage was already emerging as the dominant political and commercial force in the western Mediterranean (Goodwin 2002: 4, 5, 8, 9). Despite such particulars, history clearly informs us of numerous instances of wide-ranging cultural intermingling among diverse populations that we nowadays tend to associate with different continents, and much of this intermingling occurred close to the Mediterranean Sea apparently with little if any thought being given to any concept as race.

The strong Carthaginian presence in northwestern Africa was not in conflict with the impressive Carthaginian settlements in nearby Europe such as at Gades, the Balearic Islands, Sardinia, parts of Sicily, and Malta, where competitors such as the Greeks, and later the Romans, were for a long time prevented from trading. Similarly, long before the founding of the Republic of Rome, perhaps around 510 B.C., areas close to the Mediterranean Sea were important meeting places for peoples of many appearances and many ethnic backgrounds including from Africa and Europe. Herodotus visited Africa as far south as Elephatine in Egypt and Greeks quite apart from him such as Democritus, Simonides the Younger, and Dalion apparently visited sub-Saharan Africa. Thanks especially to Herodotus, the father of history, we know at least from his Greek perspective that much of this intermingling occurred even before Athenians were beginning to build their monumental Parthenon in the mid-5th century B.C.

Although interethnic intermingling sometimes contributed to interdependences and sometimes to conflicts, it did not require us in much later times to adopt a racialized view of history, nor of anthropology or linguistics. When Alexander the Great reached Egypt in 332 B.C., he wanted nothing more than to be accepted as its pharaoh. Shortly after his death, Ptolemaic Egypt engaged in a very active trade with Carthage as well as with a number of other African-based countries while maintaining close relationships with other parts of the Greek-speaking world. Diodorus Siculus, a Sicilian of the first century B.C., wrote forty volumes about world history. Although much of his monumental work was naturally based on uncritical compilation, taken as a whole, it still leaves no doubt that Greeks and Romans of ancient times were well acquainted with Africans, including a good number of whom were "black."

In addition to impressive documentary evidence of wide-ranging intermingling among Europeans, Asians, and Africans from very ancient times, there exists considerable graphic evidence such as is illustrated, for example, in *The Image of the Black in Western Art: From the Pharaohs to the Fall of the Roman Empire* (Vercoutter *et al.*1991). By 264 B.C. when the series of Punic Wars was beginning, people with associations to what we now refer to as Europe, Africa, and Asia were being drawn into additional intermingling. Although a Roman army landed south of the Mediterranean in Carthage in 254 B.C. and caused much destruction, when it was eventually routed it departed for Europe with 20,000 captives. Although ethnocentrism is probably as old and as ubiquitous as culture itself, evidence for an ideology of racism among ancient peoples is essentially nonexistent. A number of well-known Latin writers were born in what we now refer to as Africa and some Africans, according to Pliny and Narcissus, occupied positions of great prominence in the Roman Empire, with some of these amassing great wealth and power. Despite this long history of human intermingling over long distances in the absence of any barriers that were racial, racism eventually seeped into virtually all areas of scholarship, including in linguistics, and we are left the poorer for this.

Although classification or taxonomy is a fundamental pursuit of science, it is not easy to know exactly when language began or to trace genetic relationships that connect incipient-language to language and to particular languages in terms of genetic relationships. That language is highly symbolic, open-ended, generative, and continually changing complicates tracing connections of the past. Most of today's linguists view African languages as classified into four phyla, one of which is widely known as Afro-Asiatic but was formerly widely known as Hamito-Semitic. While it is widely recognized today that the Afro-Asiatic phylum of languages includes six linguistic superfamilies—Ancient Egyptian, Berber, Chadic, Omotic, Cushitic, and Semitic—many Western linguists for racist reasons long denied that the Chadic superfamily could conceivably belong to the same phylum as the others. This was because the Chadic superfamily included Hausa, a language spoken by more than ten percent of all Africans, most of whom are "black" and now live largely south of the Sahara desert, although at an earlier time many speakers of Hausa lived much further north (Murdock 1959: 131-132).

> Most nineteenth-century scholars (and a good many in the twentieth century as well) suffered from an ethnocentrism that often included outright racism. For scholars who fervently believed in the superiority of the 'white race,' white languages, and the like, the idea of a

black branch (Chadic) in a white family (Hamito-Semitic) was disconcerting, if not repugnant. (Ruhlen 1987: 88)

This was just one example of when many scholars claiming that their highest loyalty was to science ended up sacrificing their science on an altar of racist
myth-making that injected much confusion into history, into anthropology, and
into linguistics because of an inability to see beyond their own racism. What had
been even more disconcerting for some of them than findings that people did not
have to look similar to each other to share similar languages was growing evidence pointing to sub-Saharan Africa rather than Asia as the birth place of the
languages belonging to the Afro-Asiatic phylum. According to Blench (1995:
137), "the centre of origin of the three principal phyla of African languages
[meaning all except the smallest one] was in the same ecological zone, and
roughly adjacent to each other," namely in the southern reaches of the Sahara or
in the borderlands a bit further south sometime before the advent of agriculture.
For scholars who would like to pretend that the Sahara has functioned as some
type of impregnable barrier to human interactions, equally interesting has been
recent research on the Nilo-Saharan phylum and on the Kordofanian phylum of
African languages, which like the Afro-Asiatic languages, defy categorization as
belonging exclusively to northern or to sub-Saharan Africa (Ruhlen 1987: 76-
114; Ehret 1995).
      For many linguists incapable of seeing beyond their own racial myth-
making, however, the intercontinental Afro-Asiatic phylum of languages was
especially baffling. Despite its name, this language phylum actually extended
into slightly into Europe (e.g., Malta, Sicily, the Iberian Peninsula) as well as
into Africa and Asia and the recognition of this frayed many nerves. Even today,
historical diffusion of this phylum remains at the center of much debate that is
pertinent to ongoing scholarly reappraisals of how Africans and Europeans have
interacted over a long period of time. A recent controversy that stirred up similar discussion arose when Martin Bernal (1987: 45, 263-65, 369-73, 482-86) in
*Black Athena, The Afroasiatic Roots of Civilization II: The Archaeological and
Documentary Evidence* argued that a very significant proportion of the vocabulary of ancient Greek was derivative from languages belonging to the Afro-
Asiatic phylum. Although this is not a thesis advanced in this work, this writer
nonetheless finds revealing the explosion of discourse that this suggestion advanced by Bernal ignited.
      With great indignation, for example, Jasanoff and Nussbaum in *Black Athe-
na Revisited* (1996: 201) responded: "Certainly there are Semitic and Egyptian
borrowings in Greek, but they are, as standardly believed, relatively few in
number—and with some conspicuous exceptions on the Semitic side—late in
date." They further rejected even the mere "possibility" of a distant genetic link
between Indo-European languages and Afro-Asiatic languages as "a largely un-
substantiated conjecture."
      While this writer agrees with Jasanoff and Nussbaum that a genetic link be-
tween Indo-European and Afro-Asiatic languages has not thus far been demonstrated by proof, their rejection of even the "possibility" that such a genetic link
could exist is puzzling. While Jasanoff and Nussbaum are more correct than

wrong in noting that "in general, linguistic and racial boundaries rarely coincide" (Jasanoff and Nussbaum: 180), this is in part for reasons that they imply
(i.e., that biology is not correlated with language use) and in part for other reasons. Primary among those other reasons is that "racial boundaries," other than
as inconsistent social attributions, are mere figments of the imagination. Despite
the fact that all the world's languages are more or less equally complex from a
linguistic perspective, even religion has long been an area rife with language
prejudice and favoritism. In fact, it was only in 1893 that the Vatican finally
lifted its ban that, with only some "select" exceptions, had disallowed even the
translation of the Bible into languages indigenous to Africa (Freeman-Grenville
1973: 189).

As linguists with increasing frequency turn their backs on racist attitudes toward culture and people, including racial approaches to the classification of their
languages that was once so common, they join colleagues in other disciplines in
playing major roles in undermining notions of rigid frontiers existing among
human beings. Taken as a whole, this work should give pause to anyone wishing
to believe in the existence of discrete, mutually exclusive, and non-overlapping
races or wishing to superimpose such a groundless belief on anthropology, on
biology, on linguistics, or on history, either ancient or modern. Moreover, all
human beings are gradually coming to inhabit a single global village. Within
this village, there is nothing about immigration control or the selective distortion
of how we human beings have interacted, even if through feigned amnesia, that
will ever be able to change the fact that Africans and Europeans have been in
continuous contact since antiquity. In this sense, they are, and will always remain, a part of each other.

Bibliography

Composite for Volumes One and Two

Abbas, Tabir, and Parveen Akbtar. "The New Sociology of British Ethnic and Cultural Relations: The Experience of British South Asian Muslims in the Post-September 11 Climate." Pp. 130-146 in *Crossing Over: Comparing Recent Migration in the United States and Europe*, edited by Holger Henke. Lanham, MD: Lexington Books, Inc., 2005.

Abdul-Rauf, Muhammad. *Bilal ibn Rabah: A Leading Companion of the Prophet Muhammad*. Burr Ridge, IL: American Trust Publications, 1977.

Abu-Lughod, Janet L. *Before European Hegemony: The World System A.D. 1250-1350*. New York: Oxford University Press, 1989.

———. *The World System in the Thirteenth Century: Dead-End or Precursar?* Washington: American Historican Association, 1993.

Adams, Robert. "The Narrative of Robert Adams." Pp. 205-246 in *White Slaves, African Masters*, edited and "Introduction" by Paul Baepler. Chicago: The University of Chicago Press, 1999.

Adams, Williams Y. "Anthropology and Egyptology: Divorce and Remarriage?" Pp. 25-32 in *Anthropology and Egyptology: A Developing Dialogue*, edited by Judith Lustig. Sheffield: Sheffield Academic Press, 1997.

Adi, Hakim. *West Africans in Britain, 1900-1960: Nationalism, Pan-Africanism and Communism*. London: Lawrence & Wishart, 1998.

Adjami, Mirna. *Ethnic Profiling in the Moscow Metro*. New York: Open Society Institute, 2006.

Ahmad, Aziz. *A History of Islamic Sicily*. Edinburgh: Edinburgh University Press, 1975.

Akpo, Catherine. "Des noirs dans les camps de la mort." *Jeune Afrique* 1927 from 9-15 December, 1997. http://www.serge-bile.com/noir_mort.htm. (June 13, 2007).

Alioua, Mehdi. "La migration transnationale des Africains subsahariens au Maghreb: l'exemple de l'étape marocaine." *Maghreb-Machrek* 185 (2005): 37-57.

Al-Jabarti, Abal R. *Napoleon in Egypt: Al-Jabarti's Chronicle of the French Occupation, 1798*. Princeton, NJ: Markus Wiener Publications, 1993.

Allievi, Stefano. "Islam in Italy." Pp. 77-96 in *Islam, Europe's Second Religion: The New Social, Cultural, and Political Landscape*, edited by Shireen T. Hunter. Westport: Praeger, 2002.

Amellal, Karim. *Discriminez-moi! Enquête sur nos inégalités*. Paris: Éditions Flammarion, 2005.

Amselle, Jean-Loup. *Logiques métisses: Anthropologies de l'identité en Afrique et ailleurs*. Paris: Éditions Payot, 1990.

Anderson, R. Earle. *Liberia: America's African Friend*. Chapel Hill: The University of North Carolina Press, 1952.

Anim-Addo, Joan. "Queen Victoria's Black Daughter." Pp. 11-19 in *Black Victorians, Black Victoriana*, edited by Gretchen Holbrook Gerzina. New Brunswick: Rutgers University Press, 2003.

Anstey, Roger T. "Religion and British Slave Emancipation." Pp. 37-62 in *The Abolition of the Atlantic Slave Trade*, edited by David Eltis and James Walvin. Madison: The University of Wisconsin Press, 1981.

Anthias, Floya. "Connecting Ethnicity, 'Race,' Gender and Class in Ethnic Relations." Pp. 173-191 in *Scapegoats and Social Actors: The Exclusion and Integration of Minorities in Western and Eastern Europe*, edited by Danièle Joly. New York: St. Martin's Press, Inc., 1998.

Aquilina, Joseph. *The Structure of Maltese*. Valletta: Royal Universitiy of Malta, 1958.

———. *Papers in Maltese Linguistics*. Malta: The Royal University of Malta, 1970. [Corrected reprint of 1961 printing by Progress Press, Co., Ltd., Valletta]

Ardener, Shirley, ed. *Swedish Ventures in Cameroon 1883-1923: Trade and Travel, People and Politics. The Memoir of Knut Knutson with Supporting Material*. New York: Berghahn Books, 2002.

Armitage, David. *The Ideological Origins of the British Empire*. Cambridge: Cambridge University Press, 2000.

Arvel, Anne. *Sénégal*. Paris: Éditions Arthaud, 1989.

Asante, Molefi Kete. "African Germans and the Problems of Cultural Location." Pp. 1-12 in *The African-German Experiences: Critical Essays*, edited by Carol Aisha Blackshire-Belay. Westport, CT: Praeger, 1996.

Assouline, David, and Mehdi Lallaoui, eds. *Un siècle d'Immigrations en France: 1845 à nos jours, Du chantier à la citoyenneté?* Paris: Diffusion Syros, 1997.

Atlason, Gudjon. "Defending Immigrant Rights in Iceland." http://www.inmotionmagazine.com/iceland.html. (6 April 6, 2007).

Auslander, Leora, and Thomas C. Holt. "Sambo in Paris: Race and Racism in the Iconograhy of the Everyday." Pp. 147-184 in *The Color of Liberty, Histories of Race in France*, edited by Sue Peabody and Tyler Stovall. Durham: Duke University Press, 2003.

Austen, Ralph A. "From the Atlantic to the Indian Ocean: European Abolition, the African Slave Trade, and Asian Economic Structures." Pp. 117-140 in *The Abolition of the Atlantic Slave Trade*, edited by David Eltis and James Walvin. Madison: The University of Wisconsin Press, 1981.

Avery, Desmond. *Civilisations de La Courneuve: Images brisées d'une cité* Paris: L'Harmattan, 1987.

Ayalon, David. "The Mamluks: The Mainstay of Islam's Military Might." Pp. 89-117 in *Slavery in the Islamic Middle East*, edited by Shaun E. Marmon. Princeton: Markus Wiener Publishers, 1999.

Azurara, Gomes Eannes de. *The Chronicle of the Discovery and Conquest of Guinea*. Translated by Charles Raymond Beazley and Edgar Prestage. London: Hakluyt Society, 1896.

———. *Conquests and Discoveries of Henry the Navigator*, edited by Virginia de Castro e Almeida. Translated by Bernard Miall. London: G. Allen & Unwin. Ltd, 1936.

Bachmann, Christian. "Les cahots de la prévention." Pp. 196-207 in *Face au racisme: Analyses, hypotheses, perspectives*, edited by Pierre-André Taguieff. Paris: Éditions la Découverte, 1991.

Bachmann, Christian, and Luc Basier. *Mise en images d'une banlieue ordinaire. Stigmatisations urbaines et stratégies de communication.* Paris: Syros, 1989.

Baepler, Paul, ed. *White Slaves, African Masters: An Anthology of American Barbary Captivity Narratives,* edited and "Introduction" by Paul Baepler. Chicago: University of Chicago Press, 1999.

Baker, Jean-Claude, and Chris Chase. *Josephine Baker: The Hungry Heart.* New York: Random House, 1993.

Baker, Josephine, and Jo Bouillon. *Josephine.* Translated by Mariana Fitzpatrick. New York: Marlowe & Co, 1988.

Baker, William J. "Jesse Owens and the Germans: A Political Love Story." Pp. 167-176 in *Crosscurrents: African Americans, Africa, and Germany in the Modern World,* edited by David McBride, Leroy Hopkins, and C. Aisha Blackshire-Belay. Columbia, SC: Camden House, Inc., 1998.

Balász, György, and Károly Szelényi. *The Magyars: The Birth of a European Nation* translated by Zsuzsa Béres and Christopher Sullivan. Budapest: Corvina, 1989.

Barbosa, C. "La question des étrangers, enjeu du contrôle du territoire en Espagne." Pp. 71-108 in *L'Europe du Sud face à l'immigration: Politique de l'Étranger,* edited by Évelyne Ritaine. Paris: Presses Universitaires de France, 2005.

Barker, Martin. *The New Racism.* London, Junction Books, 1981.

———. "Het nieuwe racisme." Pp. 62-85 in *Nederlands racism,* edited by Anet Bleich and Peter Schumacher. Amsterdam: Van Gennep, 1984.

Barou, Jacques. "Les immigrations africaines." Pp. 31-47 in *Un siècle d'Immigrations en France: 1845 à nos jours, Du chantier à la citoyenneté?,* edited by David Assouline and Mehdi Lallaoui. Paris: Diffusion Syros, 1997.

Bataille, Philippe. *Le racisme au travail.* Paris: Éditions la Découverte, 1997.

Baubóck, Rainer, and Dilek Çinar. "La législation sur la nationalité et la naturalisation en Autriche." Pp. 265-280 in *Nationalité et citoyenneté en Europe,* edited by Patrick Weil and Randall Hansen. Paris: Éditions la Découverte, 1999.

Bauman, Janina. "Demons of Other People's Fear: The Plight of the Gypsies." Pp. 81-94 in *Stranger or Guest? Racism and Nationalism in Contemporary Europe,* edited by Sandro Fridlizius and Abby Peterson. Stockholm: Almqvist & Wiksell International, 1996.

Bauman, Zygmunt. "Making and Unmaking of Strangers." Pp. 59-80 in *Stranger or Guest? Racism and Nationalism in Contemporary Europe,* edited by Sandro Fridlizius and Abby Peterson. Stockholm: Almqvist & Wiksell International, 1996.

———. "The Making and Unmaking of Strangers." Pp. 46-57 in *Debating Cultural Hybriadity: Multi-Cultural Identities and the Politics of Anti-Racism,* edited by Pnina Werbner and Tariq Modood. London: Zed Books Ltd., 2000.

Baumann, Gerd. "Dominant and Demotic Discourses of Culture: Their Relevance to Multi-Ethnic Alliances." Pp. 209-225 in *Debating Cultural Hybriadity: Multi-Cultural Identities and the Politics of Anti-Racism,* edited by Pnina Werbner and Tariq Modood. London: Zed Books, 2000.

Baumann, Hermann R., and Diedrich Westermann. *Les peoples et les civilisations de l'Afrique.* Paris: Payot, 1948.

Beard, J. R. *Toussaint L'Ouverture: A Biography and Autobiography.* Boston: James Redpath, 1863.

Beardsley, Grace Hadley. *The Negro in Greek and Roman Civilization.* New York: Russell & Russell, 1967.

Beaud, Stéphanie, and Gerard Noiriel. "Penser l'intégration' des immigrés." Pp. 261-282 in *Face au racisme: Analyses, hypotheses, perspectives*, edited by Pierre-André Taguieff. Paris: Éditions la Découverte, 1991.

Beck, Hamilton H. "Censoring Your Ally: W. E. B. Du Bois in the German Democratic Republic." Pp. 197-232 in *Crosscurrents: African Americans, Africa, and Germany in the Modern World*, edited by David McBride, Leroy Hopkins, and C. Aisha Blackshire-Belay. Columbia, SC: Camden House, Inc., 1998.

Beier, S. "The Sahara in the Nineteenth Century." Pp. 515-536 in *General History of Africa. VI, African in the Nineteenth Century*, edited by J. F. Ade Ajayi. Paris: UNESCO, 1989.

Bender, Gerald. *Angola Under the Portuguese: The Myth and the Reality*. Berkely: University of California Press, 1978.

Benedict, Ruth. *Race: Science and Politics*. New York: The Viking Press, 1968.

Benigni, Umberto. "Sacred Congregation of Propaganda." *The Catholic Encyclopedia. Vol. 12*. New York: Robert Appleton Company, 1911. http://www.newadvent.org/cathen/12456a.htm (1 Aug. 2008).

Bennett, Alastair. "Constructions of Whiteness in European and American Anti-Racism." Pp. 173-192 in *Debating Cultural Hybriadity: Multi-Cultural Identities and the Politics of Anti-Racism*, edited by Pnina Werbner and Tariq Modood. London: Zed Books, 2000.

Bennett, Jr., Lerone. *Before the Mayflower: A History of Black America*. Chicago: Johnson Publication Co., 1969.

Bensaad, Ali. "Introduction: Le Sahara, vecteur de mondialisation." *Maghreb-Machrek* 185 (2005a): 7-12.

———. "Les migrations traanssahariennes, une modialisation par la marge." *Maghreb-Machrek* 185 (2005b): 13-36.

Benson, Peter. *Battling Siki: A Tale of Ring Fixes, Races, and Murder in the 1920s*. Fayetteville, AR: The University of Arkansas Press, 2006.

Ben-Tovim, Gideon. "Why 'Positive Active' is 'Politically Correct.'" Pp. 209-222 in *The Politics of Multiculturalism in the New Europe: Racism, Identity and Community*, edited by Tariq Modood and Pnina Werbner. London: Zed Books Ltd, 1997.

Bergmeier, Horst J. P., and Rainer Lotz. *Hitler's Airwaves: The Inside Story of Nazi Radio Broadcasting and Propaganda Swing*. New Haven: Yale University Press, 1997.

Bergsson, Snorri G. "Iceland and the Jewish Question until 1940." http://notendur.centrum.is/~snorrigb/jewicel.-htm. (April 4, 2007).

Berlinerblau, Jacques. *Heresy in the University: The Black Athena Controversy and the Responsibilities of American Intellectuals*. New Brunswick, NJ: Rutgers University Press, 1999.

Bernal, Martin. *Black Athena: The Afroasiatic Roots of Classical Civilization. Vol. 1*. New Brunswick: Rutgers University Press, 1987.

Bertoncello, Brigitte, and Sylvie Bredeloup. *Colporteurs africains à Marseille, Un siècle d'aventures*. Paris: Éditions Autrement, 2004.

Bertrand, Louis. *The History of Spain*. New York: D. Appleton-Century Co., 1934.

Bessière, Danièle Déon. *Les femmes et la Légion d'honneur depuis sa création*. Paris: Les éditions de l'officine, 2002.

Bichot, Jacques. "L'incidence sur les comptes sociaux." Pp. 135-158 in *Ces migrants qui changent la face de l'Europe*, edited by Jacques Dupâquier and Yves-Marie Laulan. Paris: L'Harmattan, 2004.

Bilé, Serge. *Noirs Dans les Camps Nazis*. Monaco: Le Serpent à Plumes, 2005.

Bindman, David. *Ape to Apollo: Aesthetics and the Idea of Race in the Eighteenth Century*. Ithaca, NY: Cornell University Press, 2002.

Birnbaum, Pierre. "Citoyenneté et particularisme. L'exemple des Juifs de France." Pp. 283-295 in *Face au racisme: Analyses, hypotheses, perspectives*, edited by Pierre-André Taguieff. Paris: Éditions la Découverte, 1991.

Bjørgo, Tore. "'The Invaders', 'the Traitors' and 'the Resistance Movement': The Extreme Right's Conceptualisation of Opponents and Self in Scandinavia." Pp. 54-72 in *The Politics of Multiculturalism in the New Europe: Racism, Identity and Community*, edited by Tariq Modood and Pnina Werbner. London: Zed Books Ltd, 1997.

Blackshire-Belay, Carol Aisha. "Historical Revelations: The International Scope of African Germans Today and Beyond." Pp 89-124 in *The African-German Experiences: Critical Essays*, edited by Carol Aisha Blackshire-Belay. Westport, CT: Praeger, 1996.

Blake, John William. "The First Century of Portuguese Enterprise in West Africa" Pp. 3-63 in *Europeans in West Africa, 1450-1560*, translated and edited by John William Blake. London: The Hakluyt Society, 1942a.

———. "Some Early Castilian Voyages to West Africa." Pp. 185-199 in *Europeans in West Africa, 1450-1560*, translated and edited by John William Blake. London: The Hakluyt Society, 1942b.

Blakely, Allison. "The Negro in Imperial Russia: A Preliminary Sketch." *The Journal of Negro History* 61 (1976): 351-361.

———. *Russia and the Negro: Blacks in Russian History and Thought*. Washington, D.C.: Howard University Press, 1986.

———. *Blacks in the Dutch World: The Evolution of Racial Imagery in a Modern Society*. Bloomington: Indiana University Press, 1993.

———. "African Diaspora in the Netherlands." Pp. 593-602 in *Encyclopedia of Diaspora: Immigrant and Refugee Cultures Around the World*, Vol. 2, edited by Mel Ember, Carol R. Ember, and Ian Skoggards. New York: Kluwer Academic/Plenum Publishers, 2005.

Blanchard, Pascal, and Gilles Boëtsch. *Marseille Porte Sud, un siècle d'histoire coloniale et d'immigration*. Paris: Éditions la Découverte, 2005.

Blanckaert, Claude. "Of Monstrous Métis? Hybridity, Fear of Miscegenation, and Patriotism from Buffon to Paul Broca." Pp. 42-70 in *The Color of Liberty, Histories of Race in France*, edited by Sue Peabody and Tyler Stovall. Durham: Duke University Press, 2003.

Blaschke, Jochen. "New Racism in Germany." Pp. 55-86 in *Scapegoats and Social Actors: The Exclusion and Integration of Minorities in Western and Eastern Europe*, edited by Danièle Joly. New York: St. Martin's Press, Inc. 1998.

Blaum, Paul A. *The Days of the Warlords, A History of the Byzantine Empire: A.D. 969-991*. Lanham, MD: University Press of America, 1994.

Bleich, Erik. "Anti-Racism without Races." Pp. 162-188 in *Race in France*, edited by Herrick Chapman and Laura L. Frader. New York: Berghahn Books, 2004.

Blench, Roger. "Recent Developments in African Language Classification and Their Implications for Prehistory." Pp. 126-138 in *The Archaeology of Africa: Food, Metals, and Towns*, edited by Thurstan Shaw, Paul Sinclair, Bassey Andah, and Alex Okpoko. London: Routledge, 1995.

Blier, Jean-Michel, and Solenn de Royer. *Discriminations raciales, pour en finir*. Paris: Éditions Jacob-Duvernet, 2002.

Blion, Reynald. "Les associations françaises issues de immigration, nouveaux acteurs de la solidarité internationale?" Pp. 233-244 in *Europe des migrations/ Europe de développement*, edited by Reynald Blion and Nedjma Meknache Boumaza. Paris: Institut Panos Paris-Karthala, 2004.

Blouet, Brian. *The Story of Malta.* London: Faber and Faber, 1967.

Blume, Harvey. "Ota Benga and the Barnum Perplex." Pp. 188-202 in *Africans on Stage: Studies in Ethnological Show Business,* edited by Bernth Lindfors. Bloomington: Indiana University Press, 1999.

Blumenbach, Johann Friedrich. *On the Natural Varieties of Mankind. De generis humani varietate native,* translated and edited by Thomas Bendyshe. New York: Bergman Publishers, 1969.

Blumenthal, Debra. "'La Casa des Negres': Black African Solidarity in Late Medieval Valencia." Pp. 225-246 in *Black Africans in Renaissance Europe,* edited by T. F. Earle and K. J. P. Lowe. Cambridge: Cambridge University Press, 2005.

Bolt, Christine. *Victorian Attitudes to Race.* London: Routledge and K. Paul, 1971.

Bonilla-Silva, Eduardo. "This Is a White Country": The Racial Ideology of the Western Nations of the World-System." *Sociological Inquiry* 70 (2000): 188-214.

Bonnafous, Simone. "'Immigrés', 'Immigration' De quoi parler?" Pp 144-153 in *Face au racisme: Analyses, hypotheses, perspectives,* edited by Pierre-André Taguieff. Paris: Éditions la Découverte, 1991.

Bonnett, Alastair. "Constructions of Whiteness in European and American Anti-Racism." Pp. 173-192 in *Debating Cultural Hybriadity: Multi-Cultural Identities and the Politics of Anti-Racism,* edited by Pnina Werbner and Tariq Modood. London: Zed Books Ltd., 2000.

Boswell, Christina. "Labor Migration Programs in Europe: History Repeating Itself?" Pp. 223-234 in *Crossing Over: Comparing Recent Migration in the United States and Europe,* edited by Holger Henke. Lanham, MD: Lexington Books, Inc., 2005.

Boulle, Pierre H. "François Bernier and the Origins of he Modern Concept of Race." Pp. 11-27 in *The Color of Liberty, Histories of Race in France,* edited by Sue Peabody and Tyler Stovall. Durham: Duke University Press, 2003.

———. "Racial Purity or Legal Clarity? The Status of Black Residents in Eighteenth-Century France." *The Journal of the Historical Society* 6 (March 2006): 19-46.

———. *Race et esclavage dans la France de l'Ancien Régime.* Paris: Perrin, 2007.

Bovill, E. W. *The Golden Trade of the Moors.* London: Oxford University Press, 1958.

Bowen, E. G. *Britain and the Western Seaways.* New York: Praeger Publishers, 1972.

Bowen, John R. "Does French Islam Have Borders? Dilemmas of Domestication in a Global Religious Field." *American Anthropologist* 106 (2004): 43-55.

Boyzon-Fradet, Danielle with Serge Boulot. "Le système scolaire français: aide ou obstacle à l'intégration?" Pp. 236-260 in *Face au racisme: Analyses, hypotheses, perspectives,* edited by Pierre-André Taguieff. Paris: Éditions la Découverte, 1991.

Brackett, John K. "Race and Rulership: Alessandro de' Medici, First Medici Duke of Florence, 1529-1537." Pp. 303-325 in *Black Africans in Renaissance Europe,* edited by T. F. Earle and K. J. P. Lowe. Cambridge: Cambridge University Press, 2005.

Bradford, Ernle. *The Great Siege.* London: Holder and Stoughton, 1961.

———. *Mediterranean, Portrait of a Sea.* London: Holder and Stoughton, 1971.

Bradley, Eliza. "An Authentic Narrative." Pp. 247-284 in *White Slaves, African Masters,* edited and "Introduction" by Paul Baepler. Chicago: The University of Chicago Press, 1999.

Braeckman, Colette. "Brussels Repents Its African Sins: Belgium's Murky History." *Le Monde diplomatique.* March 14, 2002. http://www.hartfordhwp.com/archives/61/-150.html. (May 2, 2002).

Brantl, Markus. "Studien zum Urkunden- und Kanzleiwesen König Manfreds von Sizilien (1250) 1258-1266" [Studies of the Documents and Chancellery Deeds of King Manfred of Sicily], Registry 263. Ph.D. diss., Ludwig-Maximilians-Universität, Munich, 1994.

Braudel, Fernand. *The Mediterranean and the Mediterranean World in the Age of Philip II.* 2 vols. London: Collins, 1972.

Brett, Michael. "Ifriqiya as a Market for Saharan Trade from the Tenth to the Twelfth Century A.D." *Journal of African History* 10 (1969): 347-364.

Brewin, Christopher. "Society as a Kind of Community: Communitarian Voting with Equal Rights for Individuals in the European Union." Pp. 223-239 in *The Politics of Multiculturalism in the New Europe: Racism, Identity and Community*, edited by Tariq Modood and Pnina Werbner. London: Zed Books Ltd, 1997.

Brochman, Grete. "Citizenship and Inclusion in European Welfare States: The EU Dimension." Pp. 179-194 in *Migration and the Externalities of European Integration*, edited by Sandra Lavenex and Emek Uçarer. Lanham, MD: Lexington Books, 2002.

Brochman, Grete, and Sandra Lavenex. "Neither In nor Out: The Impact of EU Asylum and Immigration Policies on Norway and Switzerland." Pp. 55-74 in *Migration and the Externalities of European Integration*, edited by Sandra Lavenex and Emek Uçarer. Lanham, MD: Lexington Books, 2002.

Broos, Ton J. "Travelers and Travel Liars in Eighteenth-Century Dutch Literature." Pp. 29-38 in *History in Dutch Studies*, edited by Robert Howell and Jolands Vanderwal Taylor. Lanham, MD: University Press of America, 2003.

Broughton, T. R. S. *The Romanization of Africa Proconsularis.* New York: Greenwood Press, 1968.

Brown, Jacqueline Nassy. "Black Liverpool, Black America, and the Gendering of Diasporic Space." *Cultural Anthropology* 13, no. 3 (1998): 291-325.

Brown, Leon Carl. "Color in Northern Africa." *Daedalus* 96, no. 2 (1967): 464-482.

Budds, Michael J. *Jazz and the Germans: Essays on the Influence of "Hot" American Idioms on the 20th-Century Germany Music.* Hillsdale, NY: Pendragon press, 2002.

Buonfino. Alessandra. "Beyond the Security Dilemma? The Hegemonic Political Discourse on the Europeanization of Immigration in Italy and Britain." Pp. 77-97 in *Crossing Over: Comparing Recent Migration in the United States and Europe*, edited by Holger Henke. Lanham, MD: Lexington Books, Inc., 2005.

Burstein, Stanley, ed. *Ancient African Civilizations: Kush and Axum.* Princeton: Markus Wiener Publishers, 1997.

Busuttil, Joseph. "Pirates in Malta." *Melita Historica* 5 (1971): 308-310.

Byrd, W. Michael. *American Health Dilemma: Race, Medicine, Health Care in the United States.* New York: Routledge, 2002.

Caglar, Ayse S. "Hyphenated Identities and the Limits of 'Culture.'" Pp. 169-185 in *The Politics of Multiculturalism in the New Europe: Racism, Identity and Community*, edited by Tariq Modood and Pnina Werbner. London: Zed Books Ltd, 1997.

Calvès, Gwénaële. "Color-Blindness at a Crossroads in Contemporary France." Pp. 219-226 in *Race in France*, edited by Herrick Chapman and Laura L. Frader. New York: Berghahn Books, 2004.

Cameron, Fraser. "The Islamic Factor in the European Union's Foreign Policy." Pp. 257-270 Goldberg, Andreas. "Islam in Germany." Pp. 29-50 in *Islam, Europe's Second Religion: The New Social, Cultural, and Political Landscape*, edited by Shireen T. Hunter. Westport: Praeger, 2002.

Camiscioli, Elisa. "Intermarriage, Independent Nationality, and the Individual Rights of French Women: The Law of 10 August 1927." Pp. 54-76 in *Race in France*, edited by Herrick Chapman and Laura L. Frader. New York: Berghahn Books, 2004.

Campt, Tina. "African German/African American—Dialogue or Dialectic? Reflections on the Dynamics of 'Intercultural Address.'" Pp. 71-88 in *The African-German Expe-*

riences: Critical Essays, edited by Carol Aisha Blackshire-Belay. Westport, CT: Praeger, 1996.

————. *Other Germans: Black Germans and the Politics of Race, Gender, and Memory in the Third Reich*. Ann Arbor: University of Michigan, 2004.

Capitein, Jacobus Elisa Johannes. *The Agony of Asar: A Thesis on Slavery by the Former Slave*. Translated with commentary by Grant Parker. Princeton: Markus Wiener, 2001.

Carbon, Philippe Bourcier de. "Essai de projection des populations d'origine étrangère résidents en métropole et observées au recensement général de la population du 8 mars 1999." Pp. 159-194 in *Ces migrants qui changent la face de l'Europe*, edited by Jacques Dupâquier and Yves-Marie Laulan. Paris: L'Harmattan, 2004.

Carr, Firpo W. *Germany's Black Holocaust, 1890-1945*. Kearney, NE: Morris, 2003.

Casares, Aurelia Martin. "Free and Freed Black Africans in Granada in the Time of the Spanish Renaissance." Pp. 247-260 in *Black Africans in Renaissance Europe*, edited by T. F. Earle and K. J. P. Lowe. Cambridge: Cambridge University Press, 2005.

Castle, Kathryn. "The Representation of Africa in Mid-Victorian Children's Magazines." Pp. 145-158 in *Black Victorians, Black Victoriana*, edited by Gretchen Holbrook Gerzina. New Brunswick: Rutgers University Press, 2003.

Cathcart, James Leander. "The Captives, Eleven Years in Algiers." Pp. 103-146 in *White Slaves, African Masters*, edited and "Introduction" by Paul Baepler. Chicago: The University of Chicago Press, 1999.

Cazenave, Odile. *Afrique sur Seine: A New Generation of African Writers in Paris*. Lanham, MD: Lexington Books, 2005.

Chalaye, Sylvie, ed. *Traces noires de l'Histoire en Occident*. Paris: L'Harmattan, 2005.

Chapman, Herrick, and Laura L. Frader. "Introduction." Pp. 1-19 in *Race in France*, edited by Herrick Chapman and Laura L. Frader. New York: Berghahn Books, 2004.

Charnley, Joy. "Communication, Language and Silence in *Suisse Romande*." Pp. 265-274 in *Francophone Post-Colonial Cultures*, edited by Kamal Salhi. Lanham, MD: Lexington Books, 2003.

Chavanne, Josef. *Die Sahara Oder von Oase zu Oase*. Vienna: A Hartlebens Verlag, 1879.

Clark, George P. "The Role of Haitian Volunteers at Savannah in 1779: An Attempt at an Objective View." *Phylon* 41 (1980): 356-366.

Clissold, Stephen. *The Barbary Slaves*. Totowa, NJ: Rowman and Littlefield, 1977.

Cohen, Naomi W. *Not Free to Desist: The American Jewish Committee 1906-1966*. Philadelphia: Jewish Publication Society of America, 1972.

Cohen, William B. *The French Encounter with Africans: White Response to Blacks, 1530-1880*. Bloomington: Indiana University Press, 2003.

Cole, Joshua. "Intimate Acts and Unspeakable Relations: Remembering Torture and the War for Algerian Independences." Pp. 125-141 in *Memory, Empire, and Postcolonialism: Legacies of French Colonialism*, edited by Alec G. Hargreaves. Lanham, MD: Lexington Books, 2005.

Collum, Danny Duncan, ed. *African Americans in the Spanish Civl War: This ain't Ethiopia, but it'll do*. New York: G. K. Hall, 1992.

Comaroff, Jean, and John Comaroff. "Africa Observed: Discourses of the Imperial Imagination." Pp. 689-703 in *Perspectives on Africa: A Reader in Culture, History and Representation*, edited by Roy Richard Grinker and Christopher B. Steiner. Maiden, MA: Blackwell Publications Ltd., 1997.

Conde, José Antonio. *History of the Dominion of the Arabs in Spain*. 3 vols. London: H. G. Bohn, 1854-1855.

Conklin, Alice L. "Who Speaks for Africa? The René Maran-Blase Diagne Trial in 1920s Paris." Pp. 302-337 in *The Color of Liberty, Histories of Race in France*, edited by Sue Peabody and Tyler Stovall. Durham: Duke University Press, 2003.

Connah, Graham. *African Civilizations, Precolonial Cities and State in Tropical Africa: An Archaeological Perspective*. Cambridge: Cambridge Universisty Press, 1987.

Conlin, Joseph Robert. *American Past: A Survey of American History*. New York: Harcourt Brace Jovanovich, 1984.

Cook, James J. "The Maghrib Through French Eyes: 1880-1929." Pp. 57-92 in *Through Foreign Eyes: Western Attitudes Toward North Africa*, edited by Alf Andrew Heggoy. Lanham, MD: University Press of America, 1982.

Coquery-Vidrovitch, Catherine. *Des Victimes Oubliées du Nazisme: Les Noirs and l'Allemagne dans la première moitié du XXe siècle*. Paris: Le cherche midi, 2007.

Costa-Lascoux, Jacqueline. "Les lois contre le racisme." Pp. 105-134 in *Face au racisme: Analyses, hypotheses, perspectives*, edited by Pierre-André Taguieff. Paris: Éditions la Découverte, 1991a.

———. "La délinquance des étrangers." Pp. 189-195 in *Face au racisme: Analyses, hypotheses, perspectives*, edited by Pierre-André Taguieff. Paris: Éditions la Découverte, 1991b.

Cote, Marc. "Ces itinéraires du Moyen-Âge qui font les flux d'aujourd'hui." *Maghreb-Machrek* 185 (2005): 95-99.

Cowdery, Jonathan. "American Captives in Tripoli." Pp. 159-186 in *White Slaves, African Masters*, edited and "Introduction" by Paul Baepler. Chicago: The University of Chicago Press, 1999.

Crone, G. R., trans. and ed. *The Voyages of Cadamosto and Other Documents on Western Africa in the Second Half of the Fifteenth Century*. London: The Hakluyt Society, 1937.

Curtin, Phillip D. *The Image of Africa: British Men and Action, 1780-1850*. Madison: University of Wisconsin Press, 1964.

———. *Cross-Cultural Trade in World History*. Cambridge: Cambridge University Press, 1984.

Czech Helsinki Committee. *2000 Report on the State of Human Rights in the Czech Republic*. Prague: Czech Helsinki Committee, 2001.

Dabydeen, David, ed. *The Black Presence in English Literature*. Manchester: Manchester University Press, 1985.

Daget, Serge. "France, Suppression of the Illegal Trade, and England, 1817-1850." Pp. 193-220 in *The Abolition of the Atlantic Slave Trade*, edited by David Eltis and James Walvin. Madison: The University of Wisconsin Press, 1981.

Dathorne, O. R. *In Europe's Image: The Need for American Multiculturalism*. Westport, CT: Bergin & Garvey, 1994.

Davidson, Basil. *African Civilization Revisited: From Antiquity to Modern Times*. Trenton, NJ: Africa World Press, Inc., 1991.

———. *The African Slave Trade*. Boston: Little, Brown and Company, 1980.

Davies, Norman. *Europe, A History: A Panorama of Europe, East and West, From the Ice Age to the Cold War, From the Urals to Gibraltar*. New York: HarperPerennial, 1998.

Davis, David Brion. *The Problem of Slavery in Western Culture*. Ithaca: Cornell University Press, 1966.

———. "Looking at Slavery from Broader Perspectives." *The American Historical Review* 105 (2000). http://www.historycooperative.org/journals/ahr/105.2/ah000452.-html (May 6, 2008).

Davis, Robert C. *Christian Slaves, Muslim Masters: White Slavery in the Mediterranean, the Barbary Coast, and Italy, 1500-1800.* New York: Palgrave Macmillan, 2003.

Debrunner, Hans Werner. *Presence and Prestige: Africans in Europe, A History of Africans in Europe before 1918.* Basel: Basler Afrika Bibliographien, 1979.

————. "Africa, Europe, and America: The Modern Roots from a European Perspective." Pp. 3-28 in *Crosscurrents: African Americans, Africa, and Germany in the Modern World*, edited by David McBride, Leroy Hopkins, and C. Aisha Blackshire-Belay. Columbia, SC: Camden House, Inc., 1998.

Derderian, Richard L. *North Africans in Contemporary France: Becoming Visible.* New York: Palgrave Macmillan, 2004.

Desanges, Jehan. "The Iconography of the Black in Ancient North Africa." Pp. 246-268 in *The Image of the Black in Western Art: From the Pharaohs to the Fall of the Roman Empire*, edited by Ladislas Bugner. *Vol. I.* Cambridge: Menil Foundation, Inc. and Harvard University Press, 1976.

Désiré-Vuillemin, Geneviève. *Histoire de la Mauritanie: Des origins à l'indépendence.* Paris: Éditions Karthala, 1997.

De Soto, Hermine G., and Konstanze Plett. "Citizenship and Minorities in the Process of Nation Rebuilding in Germany." *PoLAR* 18 (1995): 107-121.

De Witte, Ludo. *The Assassination of Lumumba.* London: Verso, 2001.

Dewitte, Philippe. *Les mouvements nègres en France, 1919-1939.* Paris: L'Harmattan, 1985.

————. *Deux siècles d'immigration en France.* Paris: La Documentation française, 2003.

Diallo, Mahamadou. "Literature of Empire and the African Environment." Pp. 105-126 in *Images of Africa: Stereotypes and Realities*, edited by Daniel M. Mengara. Trenton, NJ: Africa World Press, Inc., 2001.

Diallo, Youssouf. "L'africanisme en Allemagne hier et aujourd'hui." *Cahiers d'Études africaines* 161 (2001): 13-43.

Diop, A. Moustapha. "Negotiating Religious Difference: The Opinions and Attitudes of Islamic Associations in France." Pp. 111-125 in *The Politics of Multiculturalism in the New Europe: Racism, Identity and Community*, edited by Tariq Modood and Pnina Werbner. London: Zed Books Ltd, 1997.

Direche-Slimani, Karina. *Histoire de l'émigration kabyle en France au XXe siècle.* Paris: L'Harmattan, 1997.

Dodwell, Henry. *The Founder of Modern Egypt: A Study of Muhammad 'Ali.* Cambridge: Cambridge at the University Press, 1931.

Dokos, Tanos P., and Dimitris A. Antoniou. "Islam in Greece." Pp. 175-190 in *Islam, Europe's Second Religion: The New Social, Cultural, and Political Landscape*, edited by Shireen T. Hunter. Westport: Praeger, 2002.

Donnan, Hastings, and Thomas M. Wilson. *Borders: Frontiers of Identity, Nation and State.* Oxford: Berg, 2001.

Dorangricchia, A., and X. Itçaina. "Le répertoire de l'hospitalité: mobilisations catholiques et politisation de la question migratoire." Pp. 185-222 in *L'Europe du Sud face à l'immigration: Politique de l'Étranger*, edited by Évelyne Ritaine. Paris: Presses Universitaires de France, 2005.

Doresse, Jean. *L'empire du prêtre Jean. Vol. II.* Paris: Plon, 1957.

Drescher, Seymour. "Evolution of European Scientific Racism." Pp. 361-396 in *The Atlantic Slave Trade: Effects on Economics, Societies, and Peoples in Africa, the Americas, and Europe*, edited by Joseph E. Inikori and Stanley L. Engerman. Durham: Duke University Press, 1992.

Duberman, Martin Bauml. *Paul Robeson: A Biography.* New York: The New Press, 1995.

Dubet, François. *La galere. Jeunes en survie.* Paris: Seuil, 1987.

Due, Johnita P. "European Union Anti-Racism Policy Reaches Turning Point." A publication of The Center for Human Rights and Humanitarian Law at Washington College of Law, American University, 1996. http://www.wcl.american.edu/hrbrief/-v3i2/euro32.htm. (August 18, 1998).

Duffy, James. *Portuguese Africa.* Cambridge: Harvard University Press, 1959.

Dull, Jonathan R. *The French Navy and the Seven Years' War.* Lincoln: University of Nebraska Press, 2005.

Dumont, Gérard-François. "Les grands courants migratoires dans le monde au début du XXIe siècle." Pp. 11-36 in *Ces migrants qui changent la face de l'Europe,"* edited by Jacques Dupâquier and Yves-Marie Laulan. Paris: L'Harmattan, 2004.

Dunbar, Ernest, ed. *The Black Expatriates: A Study of American Negroes in Exile.* New York: Dutton, 1968.

Düvell, Franck. "Globalization of Migration Control: A Tug-of-War between Restrictionists and Human Agency?" Pp. 23-46 in *Crossing Over: Comparing Recent Migration in the United States and Europe,* edited by Holger Henke. Lanham, MD: Lexington Books, Inc., 2005.

Dupâquier, Jacques. "Facteurs démographiques: la croissance démographique differentielle." Pp. 37-56 in *Ces migrants qui changent la face de l'Europe,* edited by Jacques Dupâquier and Yves-Marie Laulan. Paris: L'Harmattan, 2004.

Durmelat, Sylvie. "Revisiting Ghosts: Louisette Ighilahriz and the Remembering of Torture." Pp. 142-159 in *Memory, Empire, and Postcolonialism: Legacies of French Colonialism,* edited by Alec G. Hargreaves. Lanham, MD: Lexington Books, 2005.

Duveyrier, H. *Les Touaregs du nord.* Paris: Challamel aîné 1864.

Earle, Peter. *Corsairs of Malta and Barbary.* London: Sidgwick & Jackson, 1970.

Edwards, Paul. "Introduction: Equiano's Narative." Pp. vii-xxxviii in *The Life of Olaudah Equiano,* edited by Paul Edwards. New York: Longman Publishers, 1988.

Edwards, Paul and James Walvin. "Africans in Britain, 1500-1800." Pp. 173-204 in *The African Diaspora: Interpretive* Essays, edited by Martin L. Kilson and Robert I. Rotberg. Cambridge: Harvard University Press, 1976.

Efron, John M. *Defenders of the Race: Jewish Doctors and Race Science in Fin-de-Siècle Europe.* New Haven: Yale University Press, 1994.

Ehrenkreutz, Andrew. "Strategic Implications of the Slave Trade between Genoa and Mamluk Egypt in the Second Half of the Thirteenth Century." Pp. 335-345 in *The Islamic Middle East: 700-1900, Studies in Economic and Social History,* edited by Abraham Udovitch. Princeton: Darwin press, 1981.

Ehret, Christopher. *Reconstructing Proto-Afroasiatic (Proto-Afrasian): Vowels, Tone, Consonants, and Vocabulary.* Berkeley: University of California Press, 1995.

Eichel, Marijean H., and Joan Markley Todd. "Notes and Discussions: A Note on Polybius' Voyage to Africa," *Classical Philology* 71 (1976): 237-243.

Eide, Asbjørn. "Racial and Ethnic Discrimination in Europe: Past, Present and Future." Pp. 13-34 in *Scapegoats and Social Actors: The Exclusion and Integration of Minorities in Western and Eastern Europe,* edited by Danièle Joly. New York: St. Martin's Press, Inc. 1998.

Ellis, Mark. "'Closing Ranks' and 'Seeking Honors': W. E. B. Du Bois in World War I." *The Journal of American History* 79 (1992): 96-124.

Emeagwali, Gloria. "On the Slavery Issue in Wonders of the African World." *West African Review* (2000). http://www.africahistory.net/westafricareview2000.htm (May 6, 2008).

Emmer, Pieter C. *Les Pays-Bas et la traite des Noirs.* Paris: Éditions Karthala, 2005.

English, P. "Cushites, Colchians, and Khazars," *Journal of Near Eastern Studies* 18 (1959): 49-53.

Equiano, Olaudah. *The Life of Olaudah Equiano, or Gustavus Vassa the African*, edited with "Introduction" by Paul Edwards. White Plains, NY: Longman, 1988.

Erickson, Peter. "Representations of Blacks and Blackness in the Renaissance." *Criticism* 35 (1993): 499-527.

———. "Representations of Race in Renaissance Art." *The Upstart Crow: A Sheakespeare Journal* 18 (1998a): 2-9.

———. "The Moment of Race in Renaissance Studies." *Shapespeare Studies* 26 (1998b): 27-36.

Erickson, Peter, and Clark Hulse, eds. *Early Modern Visual Culture: Representation, Race, Empire in Renaissance England*. Philadelphia: University of Pennsylvania Press 2000.

Erlmann, Vett. "'Spectatorial Lust': The African Choir in England, 1891-1893." Pp. 107-134 in *Africans on Stage: Studies in Ethnological Show Business*, edited by Bernth Lindfors. Bloomington: Indiana University Press, 1999.

Ersbøll, Eva. "Le droit de la nationalité en Scandinavie: Danemark, Finlande et Suède." Pp. 239-264 in *Nationalité et citoyenneté en Europe*, edited by Patrick Weil and Randall Hansen. Paris: Éditions la Découverte, 1999.

Esposito, John L. "The Muslim Diaspora and the Islamic World." Pp. 245-256 in *Islam, Europe's Second Religion: The New Social, Cultural, and Political Landscape*, edited by Shireen T. Hunter. Westport: Praeger, 2002.

Essed, Philomena. "Transnationality: The Diaspora of Women of Color in Europe," translated by Rita Gircour. Pp. 104-118 in *Diversity: Gender, Color, and Culture*. Amherst: University of Massachusetts Press, 1996.

Eze, Katherine Faull. "Self-Encounters: Two Eighteenth-Century African Memoirs from Moravian Bethlehem." Pp. 29-52 in *Crosscurrents: African Americans, Africa, and Germany in the Modern World*, edited by David McBride, Leroy Hopkins, and C. Aisha Blackshire-Belay. Columbia, SC: Camden House, Inc., 1998.

Fabre, Michel. *From Harlem to Paris: Black American Writers in France, 1840-1980*. Urbana, IL: University of Illinois Press, 1991.

Fanon, Frantz. *The Wretched of the Earth*. New York: Grove Press, Inc., 1965.

———. *Black Skin, White Masks*. New York: Grove Press, 1967.

Feigin, Leo. *Russian Jazz: New Identity*. London: Quartet Books, 1985.

Felouzis, Georges, Françoise Liot, and Joëlle Perroton. *L'Apartheid scholaire: Enquête sur la ségrégation ethnique dans les collèges*. Paris: Éditions du Seuil, 2005.

Ferraro, Gary, Wenda Trevathan, and Janet Levy. *Anthropology: An Applied Perspective*. Minneapolis: West Publications Co., 1994.

Field, Frank, and Patricia Haikin. *Black Britons*. Oxford University Press, 1971.

Fikes, Kesha D. "Santiaguense Cape Verdean Women in Portugal: Labor Rights, Citizenship and Diasporic Transformation." Ph.D. diss. University of California, Los Angeles, 2000.

Fikes, Kesha D., and Alaina Lemon. "African Presence in Former Soviet Spaces." *Annual Review of Anthropology* 31(2002): 497-524.

Finley, Moses I. *Ancient Slavery and Modern Ideology*, edited by Brent D. Shaw. Princeton, NJ: Markus Wiener Publishers, 1998.

Fletcher, Yaël Simpson. "Catholics, Communists, and Colonial Subjects: Working-Class Militancy and Racial Difference in Postwar Marseille." Pp. 338-350 in *The Color of Liberty, Histories of Race in France*, edited by Sue Peabody and Tyler Stovall. Durham: Duke University Press, 2003.

Fonseca, Jorge. "Black Africans in Portugal during Cleynaerts's Visit (1533-1538)." Pp. 113-121 in *Black Africans in Renaissance Europe*, edited by T. F. Earle and K. J. P. Lowe. Cambridge: Cambridge University Press, 2005.

Fortescue, John William. *A History of the Britain Army. Vol. 5.* London: Macmillan and Col, Ltd, 1899-1930.

Foss, John D. "A Journal, of the Captivity and Suffering of John Foss." Pp. 71-102 in *White Slaves, African Masters*, edited and "Introduction" by Paul Baepler. Chicago: The University of Chicago Press, 1999.

Fra-Molinero, Baltasar. "Juan Latino and His Racial Difference." Pp. 326-344 in *Black Africans in Renaissance Europe*, edited by T. F. Earle and K. J. P. Lowe. Cambridge: Cambridge University Press, 2005.

Freeman-Grenville, G. S. P. *Chronology of African History*. London: Oxford University Press, 1973.

Friedman, Ina R. *The Other Victims: First Person Stories of Non-Jews Persecuted by the Nazis*. Boston: Houghton Mifflin, 1995.

Friedman, Jonathan. "Global Crisis, the Struggle for Cultural Identity and Intellectual Porkbarrelling: Cosmopolitans versus Locals, Ethnics and Nationals in an Era of De-hegemonisation." Pp. 70-89 in *Debating Cultural Hybriadity: Multi-Cultural Identities and the Politics of Anti-Racism*, edited by Pnina Werbner and Tariq Modood. London: Zed Books, 2000.

Friedrichsmeyer, Sara, Sara Lennox, and Susanne Zantop, eds. *The Imperialist Imagination: German Colonialism and Its Legacy: Blacks, Germans, and The Politics of the Imperialist Imagination, 1920-1960*. Ann Arbor: University of Michigan Press, 1998.

Fryer, Peter. *Staying Power: The History of Black People in Britain*. London: Pluto Press, 1984.

Fuentes, Francisco Javier Moreno. "La migration et le droit de la nationalité espagnole." Pp. 117-144 in *Nationalité et citoyenneté en Europe*, edited by Patrick Weil and Randall Hansen. Paris: Éditions la Découverte, 1999.

Gallaher, John G. *General Alexandre Dumas, Soldier of the French Revolution*. Carbondale, IL: Southern Illinois University Press, 1997.

Gammage, R. G. *History of the Chartist Movement 1837-1854*. New York: Augustus M. Kelley, Publishers, 1969.

Garapon, Antoine, Hervé Hamon, Etienne Le Roy, et al. "La différence culturelle. Défi à la société française." Pp. 225-235 in *Face au racisme: Analyses, hypotheses, perspectives*, edited by Pierre-André Taguieff. Paris: Éditions la Découverte, 1991.

García, Bernabé López, and Ana I. Plane Contreras. "Islam in Spain." Pp. 157-174 in *Islam, Europe's Second Religion: The New Social, Cultural, and Political Landscape*, edited by Shireen T. Hunter. Westport: Praeger, 2002.

Garrigues, Emmanuel, and Gérard Lévy. *L'Ethnographie: n° 2- Villages noirs, Zoos humains*. Paris: L'entretemps, 2003.

Gaspard, Françoise, and Claude Servan-Schreiber. *La fin des immigrés*. Paris: Éditions du Seuil, 1985.

Geddes, Andrew. "The EU Migration Regime's Effects on European Welfare States." Pp. 195-208 in *Migration and the Externalities of European Integration*, edited by Sandra Lavenex and Emek Uçarer. Lanham, MD: Lexington Books, 2002.

Géroudet Noëlle, and Hélène Ménard. *L'Afrique romaine, De l'Atlantique à la Tripolitaine (69-439)*. Paris: Éditions Belin, 2005.

Gerzina, Gretchen Holbrook. *Black London: Life before Emancipation*. New Brunswick: Rutgers University Press, 1995.

―――. "Introduction." Pp. 1-8 in *Black Victorians, Black Victoriana*, edited by Gretchen Holbrook Gerzina. New Brunswick: Rutgers University Press, 2003.

Gewald, Jan-Bart. *Herero Heroes: Socio-Political History of Herero of Namibia, 1890-1923*. Oxford: James Currey, 1999.

Ghazli, Mourad. *Ne leur dites pas que je suis français, ils me croient arabe*. Paris: Presses de la renaissance, 2006.

Gibbon, Edward. *The History of the Decline and Fall of the Roman Empire* with notes by H. H. Milman. London: J. Murray, 1846.

Gilman, Sander L. *On Blackness Without Blacks: Essays on the Image of the Black in Germany*. Boston: G. K. Hall, 1982.

Giugni, Marco, and Florence Passy. "Introduction: Four Dialogues on Migration Policy." Pp. 1-21 in *Dialogues on Migration Policy*, edited by Marco Giugni and Florence Passy. Lanham, MD: Lexington Books, 2006a.

―――. "Influencing Migration Policy from Outside: The Impact of Migrant, Extreme-Right, and Solidarity Movements." Pp. 193-214 in *Dialogues on Migration Policy*, edited by Marco Giugni and Florence Passy. Lanham, MD: Lexington Books, 2006b.

Gnammankou, Dieudonné. "Entre la Russie et l'Afrique: Pouchkine, symbole de l'âme russe." http://www. gnammankou.com/diogene1.htm. (March 17, 2008).

Godbolt, Jim. *A History of Jazz in Britain, 1919-50*. London: Paladin Books, 1986.

―――. *A History of Jazz in Britain, 1950-70*. London: Quartet Books, 1989.

Goddard, Chris. *Jazz Away from Home*. New York: Paddington Press, 1979.

Godkin, Edwin Lawrence. *The History of Hungary and the Magyars*. New York: A. Montgomery, 1853.

―――. *The History of Hungary and the Magyars: From the Earliest Period to the Close of the Late War*. London: W. Kent, 1856.

Goldberg, Andreas. "Islam in Germany." Pp. 29-50 in *Islam, Europe's Second Religion: The New Social, Cultural, and Political Landscape*, edited by Shireen T. Hunter. Westport: Praeger, 2002.

Goodwin, Stefan. "Toward a Nonracial View of Human Evolution in Africa and Europe." *Association of Third World Anthropologists Research Bulletin* 2 (1980): 4-14.

―――. "Emergence of a Continent from 'Racial' Dismemberment: Anthropology's Responsibility toward Africa." *African Anthropology*, 6 (1999): 4-31.

―――. *Malta: Mediterranean Bridge*. Westport, CT: Greenwood Publishing, 2002.

―――. "Stone Age (Later) Nile Valley." *Encyclopedia of African History*. New York: Routeledge Reference, Taylor & Francis Books, Inc. 2004.

―――. *African Legacies of Urbanization: Unfolding Saga of a Continent*. Lanham: Lexington Books, 2006.

Gordon, Murray. *Slavery in the Arab World*. New York: New Amsterdam, 1992.

Gordon, Robert J. "'Bain's Bushmen': Sciences at the Empire Exhibition, 1936." Pp. 266-289 in *Africans on Stage: Studies in Ethnological Show Business*, edited by Bernth Lindfors. Bloomington: Indiana University Press, 1999.

Gosnell, Jonathan. "Mediterranean Waterways, Extended Borders, and Colonial Mappings: French Images of North Africa." Pp. 159-174 in *Images of Africa: Stereotypes and Realities*, edited by Daniel M. Mengara. Trenton, NJ: Africa World Press, Inc., 2001.

Gould, Stephen Jay. *The Mismeasure of Man*. New York: Norton, 1996.

Gray, Richard T. *About Face: German Physioganomic Thought from Lavater to Auschwitz*. Detroit: Wayne State University Press, 2004.

Green, Jeffrey P. "A Revelation in Strange Humanity: Six Congo Pygmies in Britain, 1905-1907." Pp. 156-187 in *Africans on Stage: Studies in Ethnological Show Business*, edited by Bernth Lindfors. Bloomington: Indiana University Press, 1999.

————. "Re-examining the Early Years of Samuel Coleridge-Taylor, Composer." Pp. 39-50 in *Black Victorians, Black Victoriana*, edited by Gretchen Holbrook Gerzina. New Brunswick: Rutgers University Press, 2003.

Green, Simon. "La politique de la nationalité en Allemagne. La predominance de l'appartenance ethnique sur la résidence?" Pp. 29-54 in *Nationalité et citoyenneté en Europe*, edited by Patrick Weil and Randall Hansen. Paris: Éditions la Découverte, 1999.

Groeneddijk, Kees, and Eric Heijs. "Immigration, immigrés et legislation sur la nationalité au Pays-Bas (1945-1998)." Pp. 145-176 in *Nationalité et citoyenneté en Europe*, edited by Patrick Weil and Randall Hansen. Paris: Éditions la Découverte, 1999.

Gronniosaw, James Albert Ukawsaw. *A Narrative of the Most Remarkable Particulars in the Life of James Albert Ukawsaw Gronnisaw, an African Prince, Written By Himself*. Bath, 1774. Prepared by TextBase, Inc. in consultation with David Seaman, University of Virginia Library Electronic Text Center. http://etext.Virginia.edu.readex/13311.html (March 1, 2007).

Guédé, Alain. *Monsieur de Saint-George, Virtuoso, Swordsman, Revolutionary: A Legendary Life Rediscovered*. New York: Picador, 2003.

Haas, Hein de. *Engaging Diasporas: How Governments and Development Agencies Can Support Diaspora Involvements in the Development of Origin Countries*. Oxford: Oxfam Novib, 2006.

Haavik, Kristof. "From Crusades to Colonies: Africa in French Literature." Pp. 127-136 in *Images of Africa: Stereotypes and Realities*, edited by Daniel M. Mengara. Trenton, NJ: Africa World Press, Inc., 2001.

Haddad, Saïd. "Les migrations africaines, enjeu géopolitique libyen." *Maghreb-Machrek* 185 (2005): 81-93.

Hagelund, Anniken. "A Matter of Decency? The Progress Party in Norwegian Immigration Politics." *Journal of Ethnic and Migrational Studies* 29 (2003): 47-65.

Hall, Catherine. *Civilising Subjects: Metropole and Colony in the English Imagination 1830-1867*. Chicago: The University of Chicago Press, 2002.

Hammond, Bryan, and Patrick O'Connor. *Josephine Baker*. Boston: Little, Brown and Company, 1988.

Haney, Lynn. *Naked at the Feast: A Biography of Josephine Baker*. New York: Dood, Mead, 1981.

Hansen, Randall. "Le droit de l'immigration et de la nationalité au Royaume-Uni. Des sujets aux citoyens." Pp. 71-94 in *Nationalité et citoyenneté en Europe*, edited by Patrick Weil and Randall Hansen. Paris: Éditions la Découverte, 1999.

Hansberry, William Leo. *Pillars in Ethiopian History:African History Notebook, Vol 1*, edited by Joseph E. Harris. Washington, D.C., 1981a.

————. *Africa and Africans as Seen by Classical Writers:African History Notebook. Vol 2*, edited by Joseph E. Harris. Washington, D.C., 1981b.

Hardill, Irene, David T. Graham, and Eleonore Kofman. *Human Geography of the UK, An Introduction*. London: Routledge, 2001.

Hargreaves, Alec G. "Half-Measures: Anti-discrimination Policy in France. Pp. 227-245 in *Race in France*, edited by Herrick Chapman and Laura L. Frader. New York: Berghahn Books, 2004.

Hargrove, Hondon B. *Buffalo Soldiers in Italy: Black Americans in World War II*. Jefferson, NC: McFarland, 1985.

Harney, Elizabeth. *In Senghor's Show: Art, Politics, and the Avant-Garde in Senegal, 1960-1995*. Durham: Duke University Press, 2004.

Harris, James E., and Kent R. Weeks. *X-Raying the Pharaohs*. New York: Charles Scribner's Sons, 1973.

Harris, Joseph E., ed. *Pillars in Ethiopian History: William Leo Hansberry, African History Notebook, Vol. 1.* Washington, D.C.: Howard University Press, 1981a.

———. *Africa and Africans as Seen by Classical Writers: William Leo Hansberry, African History Notebook, Vol. 2.* Washington, D.C.: Howard University Press, 1981b.

Harris, Marvin. *The Rise of Anthropological Theory: A History of Theories of Culture.* New York: Thomas Y. Crowell Co., 1968.

Haywood, Harry. 1978. *Black Bolshevik: Autobiography of an Afro-American Communist.* Chicago: Liberator Press, 1978.

Heffley, Mike. *Northern Sun, Southern Moon: Europe's Reinvention of Jazz.* New Haven: Yale University Press, 2005.

Heggoy, Alf Andrew. "Introduction." Pp. 1-6 in *Through Foreign Eyes: Western Attitudes Toward North Africa*, edited by Alf Andrew Heggoy. Lanham, MD: University Press of America, 1982.

Heine-Geldern, Robert. "One Hundred Years of Ethnological Theory in the German-Speaking Countries: Some Milestones." *Current Anthropology* 5 (Dec., 1964), 407-418.

Henderson, Mae Gwendolyn. "In Another Country: Afro-American Expatriate Novelists in France, 1946-1974." Ph.D. diss. Yale University, 1983.

Herbert, Eugenia W. *Red Gold of Africa: copper in Precolonial History and Culture.* Madison, WI: The University of Wisconsin Press, 1984.

Herzberger-Fofana, Pierrette. "Dominique Amigou Mendy (1909-2003), rescapé du camp de concentration de Neuengamme en Allemagne." June 23, 2005. http://www.afri-cultures.com/index.asp?menu=affiche_article&no=3868. (November 28, 2006).

Hicks, Mary. "The Coverage of World War I by the Radical Black Press, 1917-1919." *The Iowa Historical Review* 1 (2007): 57-82.

Hintze, Fritz. "Meroitic Chronology: Problems and Prospects," [Draft paper in the files of Sudan Antiquities Service] *Arkamani, Sudan Elecronic Journal of Archaeology and Anthropology*, Feb. 1-11, 2002. http://www.arkamani.org/arkamani-library/meroitic-/meroitic_chronology.htm (April 28, 2007).

Hochschild, Adam. *King Leopold's Ghost: A Story of Greed, Terror, and Heroism in Colonial Africa.* Boston: Houghton Mifflin Co., 1998.

Hodgen, Margaret T. *Early Anthropology in the Sixteenth and Seventeenth Centuries.* Philadelphia: University of Pennsylvania Press, 1971.

Holmes, C. *John Bull's Island: Immigration and British Society, 1871-1971.* Basingstoke: Macmillan, 1988.

Holte, Clarence L. "The Black in Pre-Revolutionary Russia." Pp. 261-275 in *African Presence in Early Europe*, edited by Ivan Van Sertima. New Brunswick: Transaction Books, 1985.

Honour, Hugh. *The Image of the Black in Western Art: From the American Revolution to World War I, Slaves and Liberators*, edited by Ladislas Bugner. *Vol. IV, Part 1.* Cambridge: Menil Foundation, Inc. and Harvard University Press, 1989a.

———. *The Image of the Black in Western Art: From the American Revolution to World War I, Black Models and White Myths*, edited by Ladislas Bugner. *Vol. IV, Part 2.* Cambridge: Menil Foundation, Inc. and Harvard University Press, 1989b.

Hopkins, Keith. *Conquerors and Slaves, Sociological Studies in Roman History.* Cambridge: Cambridge University Press, 1981.

Hopkins, Leroy. "Inventing Self: Parallels in the African-German and African-American Experience." Pp. 37-52 in *The African-German Experiences: Critical Essays*, edited by Carol Aisha Blackshire-Belay. Westport, CT: Praeger, 1996.

Hulst, Hans van. "A Continuing Construction of Crisis: Antilleans, Especially Curaçaoans, in the Netherlands." Pp. 93-122 in *Immigrant Integration: The Dutch Case*, edited by Hans Vermeulen and Rinus Penninx. Amsterdam: Het Spinhuis, 2000.

Hunter, Shireen T. "Conclusions and Outlook for European Union." Pp. 271-276 in *Islam, Europe's Second Religion: The New Social, Cultural, and Political Landscape*, edited by Shireen T. Hunter. Westport: Praeger, 2002.

Hunwick, J. O. "Black Africans in the Islamic World: An Understudied Dimension of the Black Diaspora." *Tarikh* 5 (1978): 27.

Hunwick, John. "Islamic Law and Polemics Over Race and Slavery in North and West Africa (16th-19th Century)." Pp. 43-68 in *Slavery in the Islamic Middle East*, edited by Shaun E. Marmon. Princeton: Markus Wiener Publishers, 1999.

———. "The Religious Practices of Black Slaves in the Mediterranean Islamic World." Pp. 149-172 in *Slavery on the Frontiers of Islam*, edited by Paul E. Lovejoy. Princeton: Markus Wiener, 2004.

Hunwick, John, and Eve Troutt Powell. *The African Diaspora in the Mediterranean Lands of Islam*. Princeton: Markus Wiener, 2002.

Hyttinen, Milla. "Racism in Finland." 2005. http://www.uta.fi/fast/fin/socpol/mhracis.-html (November 15, 2006).

Issac, Benjamin H. *The Invention of Racism in Classical Antiquity*. Princeton: Princeton University Press, 2004.

Itandala, Buluda. "European Images of Africa from Early Times to the Eighteenth Century." Pp. 61-81 in *Images of Africa: Stereotypes and Realities*, edited by Daniel M. Mengara. Trenton, NJ: Africa World Press, Inc., 2001.

Jasanoff, Jay H., and Alan Nussbaum. "Word Games: The Linguistic Evidence in Black Athena." Pp. 177-205 in *Black Athena Revisited*, edited by Mary R. Lefkowitz and Guy MacLean Rogers. Chapel Hill: The University of North Carolina Press, 1996.

Jehel, Georges. *La Médierranée médiévale de 350 à 1450*. Paris: Armand Colin, 1992.

Jileva, Elena. "Larger than the European Union: The Emerging EU Migration Regime and Enlargement." Pp. 75-90 in *Migration and the Externalities of European Integration*, edited by Sandra Lavenex and Emek Uçarer. Lanham, MD: Lexington Books, 2002.

Jobatey, Francine. "From *Toxi* to TV: Multiculturalism and the Changing Images of Black Germans." Pp. 29-36 in *The African-German Experiences: Critical Essays*, edited by Carol Aisha Blackshire-Belay. Westport, CT: Praeger, 1996.

Jobert, Timothée. *Champions noirs, racism blanc: La métropole et les sportifs noirs en context colonial (1901-1944)*. Grenoble: Presses universitaires de Grenoble, 2006.

Johnson, Samuel. *The Yale Edition of the Works of Samuel Johnson*. Volume 10. New Haven: Yale University Press, 1977.

Jones, Eldred D. *Othello's Countrymen: The African in English Renaissance Drama*. London: Oxford University Press, 1965.

———. *The Elizabethan Image of Africa*. Charlottsville: University Press of Virginia, 1971.

Johns, Jeremy. "Malik Ifriqiya: The Norman Kingdom of Africa and the Fatimids," *Libyan Studies* 29 (1998): 89-101.

———. *Arabic Administration in Norman Sicily: The Royal Dīwān*. Cambridge: Cambridge University Press, 2002.

Jordan, Annemarie. "Images of Empire: Slaves in the Lisbon Household and Court of Catherine of Austria." Pp. 155-180 in *Black Africans in Renaissance Europe*, edited by T. F. Earle and K. J. P. Lowe. Cambridge: Cambridge University Press, 2005.

Jordan, Winthrop D. *White Over Black: American Attitudes Toward the Negro, 1550-1812*. Chapel Hill: University of North Carolina Press, 1968.

Jules-Rosette, Bennetta. *Black Paris: The African Writers' Landscape*. Urbana: University of Illinois Press, 1998.

Julien, Ch.-Andre. *Histoire de l'Afrique du nord*. Paris, Payot, 1966.

Julien-Laferrière, François. "Les réactions européennes face à l'immigration." Pp. 245-252 in *Ces migrants qui changent la face de l'Europe*," edited by Jacques Dupâquier and Yves-Marie Laulan. Paris: L'Harmattan, 2004.

Kaplan, Paul H. D. "Isabella d'Este and Black African Women." Pp. 125-154 in *Black Africans in Renaissance Europe*, edited by T. F. Earle and K. J. P. Lowe. Cambridge: Cambridge University Press, 2005.

Kastoryano, Riva. "Relations interethniques et formes d'intégration." Pp. 167-177 in *Face au racisme: Analyses, hypotheses, perspectives*, edited by Pierre-André Taguieff. Paris: Éditions la Découverte, 1991.

Kater, Michael H. *Different Drummers: Jazz in the Culture of Nazi Germany*. New York: Oxford University Press, 1992.

Kayserling, Meyer. *Christopher Columbus and the Participation of the Jews in the Spanish and Portuguese Discoveries*, translated by Charles Gross. London: Longmans, Green, and Co., 1907.

Keaton, Trica. "Arrogant Assimilationism: Natinal Identity Politics and African-Origin Muslim Girls in the Other France." *Anthropology and Education Quarterly* 36 (2005): 405-423.

Kelman, Gaston. *Je suis noir et je n'aime pas le manioc*. Paris: Éditions Max Milo, 2004.

Kenny, Joseph. *The Catholic Church in Tropical Africa, 1445-1850*. Ibadan University Press and Dominican Publications, 1882. http://www.diafrica.org/kenny/ccta/-default.htm. (April 30, 2006a).

———. *The Catholic in Nigeria, 1486-1850: A Documentary History*. N. d. [A multilingual compilation of primary documents] http:www.diafrica.org/Kenny/Dhdefault.-htm. (April 30, 2006b).

Kepel, Gilles. "Les mouvements de 'réislamisation' de la société." Pp. 208-215 in *Face au racisme: Analyses, hypotheses, perspectives*, edited by Pierre-André Taguieff. Paris: Éditions la Découverte, 1991.

Kesting, Robert W. "Forgotten Victims: Blacks in the Holocaust." *Journal of Negro History* 77 (1992):30-36.

———. "Blacks Under the Swastika: A Research Note." *Journal of Negro History* 83 (1998a): 84-99.

———. "The Black Experience During the Holocaust." Pp. 358-365 in *The Holocaust and History: The Known, the Unknown, the Disputed, and the Reexamined*, edited by Michael Berenbaum and Abraham J. Peck. Bloomington: Indiana University Press, 1998b.

Khanga, Y. *Soul to Soul: A Black Russian American Family, 1865-1992*. New Yok: Norton, 1992.

Khellil, Mohand. *Maghrébins de France, De 1946 à nos jours: la naissance d'une communauté*. Paris: Editions Privat, 2004.

Kiernan, Victor G. *The Lords of Human Kind: Black Man, Yellow Man, and White Man in an Age of Empire*. New York: Columbia University Press, 1986.

———. *The Lords of Human Kind: European Attitudes to Other Cultures in the Imperial Age*. London: Serif, 1995.

Killingray, David. "Tracing Peoples of African Origin and Descent in Victorian Kent." Pp. 51-67 in *Black Victorians, Black Victoriana*, edited by Gretchen Holbrook Gerzina. New Brunswick: Rutgers University Press, 2003.

Killingray, David, and Willie Henderson. "Bata Kindai Ammgoza Ibn LoBagola and the Making of *An African Savage's Own Story*." Pp. 228-265 in *Africans on Stage: Studies in Ethnological Show Business*, edited by Bernth Lindfors. Bloomington: Indiana University Press, 1999.

King, Nicole. "'A Colored Woman in Another Country Pleading for Justice in Her Own': Ida B. Wells in Great Britain." Pp. 88-109 in *Black Victorians, Black Victoriana*, edited by Gretchen Holbrook Gerzina. New Brunswick: Rutgers University Press, 2003.

Kitchen, K. A. "The Land of Punt." Pp. 587-606 in *The Archaeology of Africa: Food, Metals and Towns*, edited by Thurstan Shaw, Paul Sinclair, Bassey Andah, and Alex Okpoko. London: Routledge, 1995.

Klaauw, Johannes van der. "European Asylum Policy and the Global Protection Regime: Challenges for UNHCR." Pp. 33-54 in *Migration and the Externalities of European Integration*, edited by Sandra Lavenex and Emek Uçarer. Lanham, MD: Lexington Books, 2002.

Kleinschmidt, Harald. *People on the Move: Attitudes toward and Perceptions of Migration in Medieval and Modern Europe*. Westport, CT: Praeger Publishers, 2003.

Kolb, Holger. "Germany's 'Green Card' in Comparative Perspective." Pp. 303-317 in *Crossing Over: Comparing Recent Migration in the United States and Europe*, edited by Holger Henke. Lanham, MD: Lexington Books, Inc., 2005.

Koos, Leonard R. "Colonial Culture as Francophone? The Case of Late Nineteenth-Century Algeria." Pp. 17-27 in *Francophone Post-Colonial Cultures*, edited by Kamal Salhi. Lanham, MD: Lexington Books, 2003.

Korhonen, Anu. "Washing the Ethiopian White: Conceptualising Black Skin in Renaissance England." Pp. 1-16 in *Black Africans in Renaissance Europe*, edited by T. F. Earle and K. J. P. Lowe. Cambridge: Cambridge University Press, 2005.

Krause, Elizabeth L. "'Empty Cradles' and the Quiet Revolution: Demographic Discourse and Cultural Struggles of Gender, Race, and Class in Italy." *Cultural Anthropology* 16 (2001): 576-611.

Kroissenbrunner, Sabine. "Islam in Austria." Pp. 141-156 in *Islam, Europe's Second Religion: The New Social, Cultural, and Political Landscape*, edited by Shireen T. Hunter. Westport: Praeger, 2002.

Kruyt, A., and J. Niessen. "Integration." Pp. 15-55 in *Immigrant Policy for a Multicultural Society: A Comparative Study of Integration, Language, and Religious Policy in Five Western European Countries*, edited by Hans Vermeulen. Brussels: Migration Policy Group, 1997.

Kuczynski, Liliane. *Les marabouts africains à Paris*. Paris: CNRS Éditions, 2002.

Kürti, László. "Globalisation and the Discourse of Otherness in the 'New' Eastern and Central Europe." Pp. 29-53 in *The Politics of Multiculturalism in the New Europe: Racism, Identity and Community*, edited by Tariq Modood and Pnina Werbner. London: Zed Books Ltd, 1997.

Lahon, Didier. "Black African Slaves and Freedmen in Portugal during the Renaissance: Creating a New Pattern of Reality." Pp. 261-279 in *Black Africans in Renaissance Europe*, edited by T. F. Earle and K. J. P. Lowe. Cambridge: Cambridge University Press, 2005.

Lai, Cheng-Chung. *Braudel's Historiography Reconsidered*. Lanham, MD: University Press of America, Inc., 2004.

Lallaoui, Mehdi. "Réfugiés, exilés et droits d'asile." Pp. 93-109 in *Un siècle d'Immigrations en France: 1845 à nos jours, Du chantier à la citoyenneté?*, edited by David Assouline and Mehdi Lallaoui. Paris: Diffusion Syros, 1997.

Landman, Nico. "Islam in the Benelux Countries." Pp. 97-120 Goldberg, Andreas. "Islam in Germany." Pp. 29-50 in *Islam, Europe's Second Religion: The New Social, Cultural, and Political Landscape*, edited by Shireen T. Hunter. Westport: Praeger, 2002.

Lane-Poole, Stanley. *A History of Egypt in the Middle Ages*. London: Frank Cass and Co., 1968.

———. *The Barbary Corsairs*. Westport, CT: Negro Universities Press, 1970.

———. *The Story of the Moors in Spain*. Baltimore: Black Classic Press, 1990.

Langley, J. Ayo. "Pan-Africanism in Paris, 1924-36." *The Journal of Modern African Studies* 7 (1969): 69-94.

Lapeyronnie, Didier. *"L'exclusion et le mépris."* *Les temps modernes* 545-546 (1992) 2-17.

Larson, Edward J. *Sex, Race, and Science: Eugenics in the Deep South*. Baltimore: The Johns Hopkins University Press, 1995.

Lavenex, Sandra. "EU Trade Policy and Immigration Control." Pp. 161-178 in *Migration and the Externalities of European Integration*, edited by Sandra Lavenex and Emek Uçarer. Lanham, MD: Lexington Books, 2002.

Lavenex, Sandra, and Emek Uçarer. "Introduction: The Emergent EU Migration Regime and Its External Impact." Pp. 1-14 in *Migration and the Externalities of European Integration*, edited by Sandra Lavenex and Emek Uçarer. Lanham, MD: Lexington Books, 2002.

———. "Conclusion." Pp. 209-221 in *Migration and the Externalities of European Integration*, edited by Sandra Lavenex and Emek Uçarer. Lanham, MD: Lexington Books, 2002.

Lawrance, Jeremy. "Black Africans in Renaissance Spanish Literature." Pp. 94-112 in *Black Africans in Renaissance Europe*, edited by T. F. Earle and K. J. P. Lowe. Cambridge: Cambridge University Press, 2005.

Leca, Jean. "La citoyenneté en question." Pp. 311-336 in *Face au racisme: Analyses, hypotheses, perspectives*, edited by Pierre-André Taguieff. Paris: Éditions la Découverte, 1991.

Leclant, Jean. "Egypt, Land of Africa: In the Greco-Roman World." Pp. 269-285 in *The Image of the Black in Western Art: From the Pharaohs to the Fall of the Roman Empire*, edited by Ladislas Bugner. *Vol. 1*. Cambridge: Menil Foundation, Inc. and Harvard University Press, 1976.

Le Gall, Michel. "Translation of Louis Frank's 'Mémoire sur le commerce des nègres au Kaire, et sur les maladies auxquelles ils son sujets en y arrivant' (1802) or Memoir on the Traffic in Negroes in Cairo and on the Illnesses to Which They are Subject Upon Arrival There." Pp. 69-88 in *Slavery in the Islamic Middle East*, edited by Shaun E. Marmon. Princeton: Markus Wiener Publishers, 1999.

Leininger-Miller, Theresa. *New Negro Artists in Paris: African American Painters and Sculptors in the City of Light, 1922-1934*. New Brunswick: Rutgers University Press, 2001.

Lester, Rosemarie K. "Blacks in Germany and German Blacks: A Little-Known Aspect of Black History." Pp.113-134 in *Blacks and German Culture: Essays*, edited by Reinhold Grimm and Jost Hermand. Madison: University of Wisconsin Press, 1986.

Leveau, Remy and Shireen T. Hunter. "Islam in France." Pp. 3-28 in *Islam, Europe's Second Religion: The New Social, Cultural, and Political Landscape*, edited by Shireen T. Hunter. Westport: Praeger, 2002.

Levine, Bruce. "'Against All Slavery, Whether White or Black': German-Americans and the Irrespressible Conflict." Pp. 53-64 in *Crosscurrents: African Americans, Africa, and Germany in the Modern World*, edited by David McBride, Leroy Hopkins, and C. Aisha Blackshire-Belay. Columbia, SC: Camden House, Inc., 1998.

Levine, Donald N. *Greater Ethiopia: The Evolution of a Multiethnic Society*. Chicago: The University of Chicago Press, 1974.

Lévi-Provençal, Évariste. *Histoire de l'Espagne musulmane: Califat umaiyade de Cordoue*. Paris: Maisonneuve et Larose, 1999.

———. *Séville musulmane au début du XIIe siècle*. Paris: Maisonneuve et Larose, 2001a.

———. *Histoire de l'Espagne musulmane: Historiens des Chorfa, La Fondation de Fès*. Paris: Maisonneuve et Larose, 2001b.

———. *Histoire de l'Espagne musulmane: L'Espagne musulmane au Xe siècle*. Paris: Maisonneuve et Larose, 2002.

Lewis, Bernard. *Istanbul and Civilization of the Ottoman Empire*. Norman: University of Oklahoma Press, 1963.

———. *The Muslim Discovery of Europe*. New York: W. W. Norton & Co., 1982.

———. *The Jews of Islam*. Princeton: Princeton University Press, 1984.

———. *Race and Slavery in the Middle East: An Historical Enquiry*. New York: Oxford University Press, 1990.

———. *Semites and Anti-Semites: An Inquiry into Conflict and Prejudice*. New York: W. W. Norton & Co., 1999.

———. "What Is an Arab?" Pp. 3-9 in *Peoples and Cultures of the Middle East*, edited by Ailon Shiloh. New York: Random House, 1969.

———. *What Went Wrong? Western Impact and Middle Eastern Response*. Oxford: Oxford University Press, 2002.

Lewis, Martin W., and Karen E. Wigen. *The Myth of Continents: A Critique of Metageography*. Berkeley: University of California Press, 1997.

Lewis, Mary Dewhurst. "The Strangeness of Foreigners, Policing Migration and Nation in Interwar Marseille." Pp. 77-107 in *Race in France*, edited by Herrick Chapman and Laura L. Frader. New York: Berghahn Books, 2004.

Lewis, Philip. "Arenas of Ethnic Negotiation: Cooperation and Conflict in Bradford." Pp. 126-147 in *The Politics of Multiculturalism in the New Europe: Racism, Identity and Community*, edited by Tariq Modood and Pnina Werbner. London: Zed Books Ltd., 1997.

Lewis, Shireen K. *Race, Culture, and Identity: Francophone West African and Caribbean Literature and Theory from Négritude to Créolité*. Lanham, MD: Lexington Books, 2006.

Liauzu, Claude. *Histoire des Migrations en Méditerranée occidentale*. Brussels: Éditions Complexe, 1996.

Liénard-Ligny, Monique. "Le droit de la nationalité en Belgique et au Luxembourg." Pp. 199-220 in *Nationalité et citoyenneté en Europe*, edited by Patrick Weil and Randall Hansen. Paris: Éditions la Découverte, 1999.

Lindfors, Bernth. "Charles Dickens and the Zulus." Pp. 62-80 in *Africans on Stage: Studies in Ethnological Show Business*, edited by Bernth Lindfors. Bloomington: Indiana University Press, 1999.

Linke, Uli. *German Bodies: Race and Representation After Hitler*. New York: Routledge, 1999.

Little, Jr., Monroe H. "The Black Military Experience in Germany: From the First World War to the Present." Pp. 177-196 in *Crosscurrents: African Americans, Africa, and Germany in the Modern World*, edited by David McBride, Leroy Hopkins, and C. Aisha Blackshire-Belay. Columbia, SC: Camden House, Inc., 1998.

Lloyd, Cathie. "Antiracist Mobilization in France and Britain in the 1970s and 1980s." Pp. 155-172 in *Scapegoats and Social Actors: The Exclusion and Integration of Mi-*

norities in Western and Eastern Europe, edited by Danièle Joly. New York: St. Martin's Press, Inc. 1998.

Lloyd, Christopher. *The Nile Campaign*. New York: Barnes & Noble Books, 1973.

Lloyd, Martin. *The Passport: The History of Man's Most Travelled Document*. Thrupp, UK: Sutton Publishing Ltd., 2003.

Loisy, Anne de. *Bienvenue en France! Six mois d'enquête clandestine dans la zone d'attente de Roissy*. Paris: Le Cherche-midi, 2005.

Loja, Fernando Soares. "Islam in Portugal." Pp. 191-204 in *Islam, Europe's Second Religion: The New Social, Cultural, and Political Landscape*, edited by Shireen T. Hunter. Westport: Praeger, 2002.

Lorimer, Douglas. *Colour, Class, and the Victorians: English Attitudes to the Negro in the Mid-Mineteenth Century*. Leicester: Leicester University Press, 1978.

————. "Reconstructing Victorian Racial Discourse: Images of Race, the Language of Race Relations, and the Context of Black Resistance." Pp. 187-207 in *Black Victorians, Black Victoriana*, edited by Gretchen Holbrook Gerzina. New Brunswick: Rutgers University Press, 2003.

Lotz, Rainer. *Black People: Entertainers of African Descent in Europe and Germany*. Birgit Lotz Verlag, 1997.

Lowe, Kate. "Introduction: The Black African Presence in Renaissance Europe." Pp. 1-16 in *Black Africans in Renaissance Europe*, edited by T. F. Earle and K. J. P. Lowe. Cambridge: Cambridge University Press, 2005a.

————. "The Stereotyping of Black Africans in Renaissance Europe." Pp.17-47 in *Black Africans in Renaissance Europe*, edited by T. F. Earle and K. J. P. Lowe. Cambridge: Cambridge University Press, 2005b.

Lucas, C. P. *A Historical Geography of the British Colonies. Vol. III. West Africa*. Oxford: The Clarendon Press, 1894.

Lusane, Clarence. *Hitler's Black Victims: The Historical Experiences of Afro-Germans, European Blacks, Africans, and African Americans in the Nazi Era*. New York: Routledge, 2003.

Luttrell, Anthony T. "Approaches to Medieval Malta." Pp. 1-70 in *Medieval Malta: Studies on Malta before the Knights*, edited by Anthony T. Luttrell. London: The British School at Rome, 1975.

————. "Girolamo Manduca and Gian Francesco Abela: Tradition and Invention in Maltese Historiography." *Melita Historica* 7 (1977): 105-132.

Ly, Abdoulaye. *La compagnie du Sénégal*. Paris: Karthala, 1993.

Lyon, Wenonah. "Defining Ethnicity: Another Way of Being British." Pp. 186-206 in *The Politics of Multiculturalism in the New Europe: Racism, Identity and Community*, edited by Tariq Modood and Pnina Werbner. London: Zed Books Ltd., 1997.

Maalouf, Amin. *Leo Africanus*, translated by Peter Sluglett. Chicago: New Amsterdam, Ivan R. Dee, Publisher, 1992.

Machado, F. L. "Des étrangers moins étrangers que d'autres? La régulation politico-institutionnelle de l'immigration au Portugal." Pp. 109-148 in *L'Europe du Sud face à l'immigration: Politique de l'Étranger*, edited by Évelyne Ritaine. Paris: Presses Universitaires de France, 2005.

MacMaster, Neil. *Racism in Europe: 1870-2000*. New York: Palgrave, 2001.

MacMichael, Harold Alfred. *A History of the Arabs in the Sudan and Some of the People Who Preceded Them and of the Tribes Inhabiting Dàrfur*. New York: Barnes and Noble, 1967.

Madden, John. "Slavery in the Roman Empire—Numbers and Origins." *Classic Ireland*" 3 (1996). http://home.mindspring.com/~decer/roman.htm (February 2, 2005).

Makanah, Toma J., and Mohamed Bailey. "Sierra Leone." Pp. 298-314 in *Urbanization in Africa: A Handbook*, edited by James D. Tarver. Westport, CT: Greenwood Press, 1994.

Mandaville, Peter P. "Muslim Youth in Europe." Pp. 29-50 in *Islam, Europe's Second Religion: The New Social, Cultural, and Political Landscape*, edited by Shireen T. Hunter. Westport: Praeger, 2002.

Mangin, Charles. *La force noire*. Paris: Hachette et cie, 1911.

Marie, Clalude-Valentin. "L'Europe: de l'empire aux colonies intérieures." Pp. 296-310 in *Face au racisme: Analyses, hypotheses, perspectives*, edited by Pierre-André Taguieff. Paris: Éditions la Découverte, 1991.

Mark, Peter. *Africans in European Eyes: The Portrayal of Black Africans in Fourteenth and Fifteenth Century Europe*. Syracuse: Syracuse University Press, 1974.

———. "European Perceptions of Black Africans in the Renaissance."Pp. 21-31 in *Africa and the Renaissance: Art in Ivory*, edited by Ezio Bassani and William B. Fagg. New York: Center for African Art, 1988.

Marlowe, John. *A History of Modern Egypt and Anglo-Egyptian Relations, 1800-1956*. Hamden,CT: Archon Books, 1965.

Marmon, Shaun E. "Domestic Slavery in the Mamluk Empire: A Preliminary Sketch." Pp. 1-24 in *Slavery in the Islamic Middle East*, edited by Shaun E. Marmon. Princeton: Markus Wiener Publishers, 1999.

Marques, M. M., N. Dias, and J. Mapril. "Le 'retour des caravelles' au Portugal: de l'exclusion des immigrés à l'inclusion des lusophones?" Pp. 149-184 in *L'Europe du Sud face à l'immigration: Politique de l'Étranger*, edited by Évelyne Ritaine. Paris: Presses Universitaires de France, 2005.

Martin, Maria. "History of the Captivity and Suffering of Mrs. Maria Martin." Pp. 147-158 in *White Slaves, African Masters*, edited and "Introduction" by Paul Baepler. Chicago: The University of Chicago Press, 1999.

Massaquoi, Hans J. *Destined to Witness: Growing Up Black in Nazi Germany*. New York: William Morrow, 1999.

Massing, Jean Michel. "The Image of Africa and Iconography of Lip-Plated Africans in Pierre Desceliers's World Map of 1550." Pp. 48-69 in *Black Africans in Renaissance Europe*, edited by T. F. Earle and K. J. P. Lowe. Cambridge: Cambridge University Press, 2005.

Matar, Nabil. *Turks, Moors and Englishmen in the Age of Discovery*. New York: Columbia University Press, 1999.

———. "Introduction: England and Mediterranean Captivity, 1577-1704." Pp. 1-52 in *Piracy, Slavery, and Redemption: Barbary Captivity Narratives from Early Modern England*, edited by Daniel J. Vitkus. New York: Columbia University Press, 2001.

Mather, Cotton. "The Glory of Goodness." Pp. 59-70 in *White Slaves, African Masters*, edited and "Introduction" by Paul Baepler. Chicago: The University of Chicago Press, 1999.

Matusevich, Maxim, ed. *Africa in Russia, Russia in Africa: Three Centuries of Encounters*. Trenton, NJ: Africa World Press, 2006.

Mayer, Nonna. "Racisme et antisémitisme dans l'opinion publique française." Pp. 64-72 in *Face au racisme: Analyses, hypotheses, perspectives*, edited by Pierre-André Taguieff. Paris: Éditions la Découverte, 1991.

Mazauric, Claude. "La Société des Amis des Noirs (1788-1799). Contribution à histoire de l'abolition de l'esclavage." *Annales historiques de la Révolution française*, 317 (April 10, 2006) http://ahrf.revues.org/document928.html (Dec. 28, 2006).

Mazón, Patricia M., and Reinhild Steingröver, eds. *Not So Plain as Black and White: Afro-German Culture and History, 1890-2000.* Rochester, NY: University of Rochester Press, 2005.

Mazrui, Ali A. "The German Factor in the Global Black Experience: From the Berlin Conference to the Berlin Wall." Pp. 240-251 in *Crosscurrents: African Americans, Africa, and Germany in the Modern World,* edited by David McBride, Leroy Hopkins, and C. Aisha Blackshire-Belay. Columbia, SC: Camden House, Inc., 1998.

McCloy, Shelby T. *The Negro in France.* Lexington: University of Kentucky Press, 1961.

McCormick, Michael. *Origins of the European Economy: Communications and Commerce, A.D. 300-900.* Cambridge: Cambridge University Press, 2001.

McEnnerney, Dennis. "Franz Fanon, the Resistance, and the Emergence of Identity Politics." Pp. 259-281 in *The Color of Liberty, Histories of Race in France,* edited by Sue Peabody and Tyler Stovall. Durham: Duke University Press, 2003.

McIntosh, Janet S. "Strategic Amnesia: Versions of Vasco da Gama on the Kenya Coast." Pp. 85-104 in *Images of Africa: Stereotypes and Realities,* edited by Daniel M. Mengara. Trenton, NJ: Africa World Press, Inc., 2001.

Médevielle, Nicolas P. A. "La Racialisation des africains: Récits commerciaux, religieux, philosophiques et littéraires, 1480-1880." Ph.D. diss. The Ohio State University, 2006.

Melotti, Umberto. "International Migration in Europe: Social Projects and Political Cultures." Pp. 73-92 in *The Politics of Multiculturalism in the New Europe: Racism, Identity and Community,* edited by Tariq Modood and Pnina Werbner. London: Zed Books Ltd, 1997.

Melucci, Alberto. "Difference and Otherness in a Global Society: Individual Experience and Collective Action." Pp. 39-58 in *Stranger or Guest? Racism and Nationalism in Contemporary Europe,* edited by Sandro Fridlizius and Abby Peterson. Stockholm: Almqvist & Wiksell International, 1996.

————. "Identity and Difference in a Globalized World." Pp. 58-69 in *Debating Cultural Hybriadity: Multi-Cultural Identities and the Politics of Anti-Racism,* edited by Pnina Werbner and Tariq Modood. London: Zed Books, 2000.

Messmer, Pierre. "Ouverture du colloque." Pp. 7-8 in *Ces migrants qui changent la face de l'Europe,* edited by Jacques Dupâquier and Yves-Marie Laulan. Paris: L'Harmattan, 2004.

Midiohowan, Guy O. "Samine Senghor (1889-1927), Precuseur de la Prose Nationalist Negro-Africane." Pp. 69-78 in *The Growth of African Literature: Twenty-Five Years after Dakar and Fourah Bay,* edited by Edris Makward, Thelma Ravell-Pinto, and Aliko Songolo. Durham: Duke University Press, 1998.

Miller, Aurie Hollingsworth. "One Man's View: William Shaler and Algiers." Pp. 7-56 in *Through Foreign Eyes: Western Attitudes Toward North Africa,* edited by Alf Andrew Heggoy. Lanham, MD: University Press of America, 1982.

Miller, Christopher L. *Blank Darkness, Africanist Discourse in French.* Chicago: University of Chicago Press, 1985.

————. *Nationalists and Nomads: Essays on Francophone African Literature and Culture.* Chicago: Chicago University Press, 1998.

Milner, Viscount. *England in Egypt.* London: Edward Arnold, 1926.

Minnen, Peter van. "Writing in Egypt under Greek and Roman Rule," 1995. http://scriptorjum.lib.duke.edu/papyrus/texts/rule.html (12 June 2004).

Minnich, Nelson H. "The Catholic Church and the Pastoral Care of Black Africans in Renaissance Italy." Pp. 280-300 in *Black Africans in Renaissance Europe,* edited by T. F. Earle and K. J. P. Lowe. Cambridge: Cambridge University Press, 2005.

Modood, Tariq. "Introduction: The Politics of Multiculturalism in the New Europe." Pp. 1-26 in *The Politics of Multiculturalism in the New Europe: Racism, Identity and Community*, edited by Tariq Modood and Pnina Werbner. London: Zed Books Ltd., 1997.

————. "'Difference,' Cultural Racism and Anti-Racism." Pp. 154-172 in *Debating Cultural Hybridity: Multi-Cultural Identities and the Politics of Anti-Racism*, edited by Pnina Werbner and Tariq Modood. London: Zed Books Ltd., 2000.

Montagu, Ashley "The Concept of Race in the Human Species in the Light of Genetics." Pp. 1-11 in *The Concept of Race*, edited by Ashley Montagu. New York: Collier Books, 1969.

————. *Man's Most Dangerous Myth: The Fallacy of Race*. New York: Oxford University Press, 1974.

Montana, Ismael Musah. "Ahmad ibn al-Wadi al-Timbuktawi on the Bori Ceremonies of Tunis." Pp. 173-198 in *Slavery on the Frontiers of Islam*, edited by Paul E. Lovejoy. Princeton: Markus Wiener, 2004.

Morsy, Soheir A. "Beyond the Honorary 'White' Classification of Egyptians: Societal Identity in Historical Context." Pp. 175-198 in *Race*, edited by Steven Gregory and Roger Sanjek. New Brunswick: Rutgers University Press, 1996.

Mosse, George L. *Toward the Final Solution: A History of European Racism*. New York: Howard Fertig, Inc., Publisher, 1985.

Mudimbe, V. Y. *The Idea of Africa*. Bloomington: University of Indiana Press, 1994.

Mullard, Chris. *Black Britain*. London: George Allen & Unwin Ltd., 1973.

Murdock, George Peter. *Africa: Its Peoples and Their Culture History*. New York: McGraw-Hill Book Company, 1959.

Musbaben, Joyce Marie. "More Than Just a Bad-Hair Day: The Head-Scarf Debate as a Challenge to Euro-National Identities." Pp. 182-234 in *Crossing Over: Comparing Recent Migration in the United States and Europe*, edited by Holger Henke. Lanham, MD: Lexington Books, Inc., 2005.

NAACP. *Papers of the NAACP*. Bethesda, MD: University Publications of America, 1993.

Naumann, Christine. "African American Performers and Culture in Weimar Germany." Pp. 96-114 in *Crosscurrents: African Americans, Africa, and Germany in the Modern World*, edited by David McBride, Leroy Hopkins, and C. Aisha Blackshire-Belay. Columbia, SC: Camden House, Inc., 1998.

Nelissen, Carien, and Frank J. Buijs. "Between Continuity and Change: Moroccans in the Netherlands." Pp. 178-201 in *Immigrant Integration: The Dutch Case*, edited by Hans Vermeulen and Rinus Penninx. Amsterdam: Het Spinhuis, 2000.

Niekerk, Mies van. "Paradoxes in Paradise: Integration and Social Mobility of the Surinamese in the Netherlands." Pp. 64-92 in *Immigrant Integration: The Dutch Case*, edited by Hans Vermeulen and Rinus Penninx. Amsterdam: Het Spinhuis, 2000.

————. *Premigration Legacies and Immigrant Social Mobility: The Afro-Surinamese and Indo-Surinamese in the Netherlands*. Lanham, MD: Lexington Books, 2002.

Niessan, Jan, and Yongmi Shibel. "Towards an European Common Policy on Immigration." Pp. 27-46 in *Europe des migrations/Europe de développement*, edited by Reynald Blion and Nedjma Meknache Boumaza. Paris: Institut Panos Paris-Karthala, 2004.

Noiriel, Gérard. *Atlas de l'immigration en France*. Paris: Éditions Autrement, 2002.

Nordin, Dennis Sven. *A Swedish Dilemma: A Liberal European Nation's Struggle with Racism and Xenophobia, 1990-2000*. Lanham, MD: University Press of America, Inc., 2005.

Northrup, David. *Africa's Discovery of Europe: 1450-1850*. New York: Oxford University Press, 2002.

Norton, Robert E. "Bernal, Herder, and the German Appropriation of Greece." Pp. 403-410 in *Black Athena Revisited*, edited by Mary R. Lefkowitz and Guy MacLean Rogers. Chapel Hill: The University of North Carolina Press, 1996.

O'Connor, David. *Ancient Nubia: Egypt's Rival in Africa*. Philadelphia: University of Pennsylvania Press, 1993.

Ohaegbulam, F. Ugboaja. *West African Responses to European Imperialism in the Nineteenth and Twentieth Centuries*. Lantham, MD: University Press of America, Inc., 2002.

Oliver, Roland, and Anthony Atmore. *The African Middle Ages, 1400-1800*. Cambridge: Cambridge University Press, 1981.

Oliver, Roland, and Brian M. Fagan. *African in the Iron Age: c.500 B.C. to A.D. 1400*. Cambridge: Cambridge University Press, 1975.

Onana, Charles. *Joséphine Baker contre Hitler, La Star Noire de la France Libre*. Paris: Éditions Duboiris, 2006.

Opitz, May. "African and Afro-German Women in the Weimar Republic and under National Socialism." Pp. 41-55 in *Showing Our Colors: Afro-German Women Speak Out*, edited by May Opitz, Katharina Oguntoye, and Dagmar Schultz. Amherst: The University of Massachusetts Press, 1992.

O'Riley, Michael. "On Earthquakes and Cultural Sedimentation: The Origins of Postcolonial Shock Waves in Azouz Begag's *Zenzela*." Pp. 296-307 in *Francophone Post-Colonial Cultures*, edited by Kamal Salhi. Lanham, MD: Lexington Books, 2003.

Orlando, Valerie. "Transposing the Political and the Aesthetical: Eugene Fromentin's Contributions to Oriental Stereotypes." Pp. 175-191 in *Images of Africa: Stereotypes and Realities*, edited by Daniel M. Mengara. Trenton, NJ: Africa World Press, Inc., 2001.

Ottlely, Roi. *No Green Pastures*. New York: Scribner, 1951.

Padmore, George. *Pan-Africanism or Communism? The Coming Struggle for Africa*. New York: Roy Publishers, 1955.

Pakenham, Thomas. *The Scramble for Africa: White Man's Conquest of the Dark Continent From 1876 to 1912*. New York: Perennial, 2003.

Palter, Rober. "Eighteenth-Century Historiography." Pp. 349-402 in *Black Athena Revisited*, edited by Mary R. Lefkowitz and Guy MacLean Rogers. Chapel Hill: The University of North Carolina Press, 1996.

Pandian, Jacob. *The Making of India and Indian Traditions*. Englewood Cliffs, NJ: Prentice Hall, 1995.

Panton, Clifford D., Jr. *George Augustus Polgreen Bridgetower, Violin Virtuoso and Composer of Color in Late 18th Century Europe*. Lewiston, NY: E. Mellen Press, 2005.

Papastergiadis, Nikos. "Tracing Hybridity in Theory." Pp. 257-281 in *Debating Cultural Hybridity: Multi-Cultural Identities and the Politics of Anti-Racism*, edited by Pnina Werbner and Tariq Modood. London: Zed Books Ltd., 2000.

Paravisini-Gebert, Lizabeth. "Mrs. Seacole's Wonderful Adventures in Many Lands and the Consciousness of Transit." Pp. 71-87 in *Black Victorians, Black Victoriana*, edited by Gretchen Holbrook Gerzina. New Brunswick: Rutgers University Press, 2003.

Parker, Grant. *The Agony of Asar, A Thesis on Slavery by the Former Slave*. Princeton: Markus Wiener Publishers, 2001.

Parsons, Neil. "'Clicko': Franz Taaibosch, South African Bushman Entertainer in England, France, Cuba and the United States, 1908-1940." Pp. 203-227 in *Africans on Stage: Studies in Ethnological Show Business*, edited by Bernth Lindfors. Bloomington: Indiana University Press, 1999.

———. "'No Longer Rare Birds in London': Zulu, Ndebele, Gaza, and Swazi Envoys to England, 1882-1894." Pp. 110-141 in *Black Victorians, Black Victoriana*, edited by Gretchen Holbrook Gerzina. New Brunswick: Rutgers University Press, 2003.

Pastor, Ana Maria Relaño, and Guillermo Alonso Meneses. "Latino Diaspora in Chula Vista, San Diego, and Ciutat Vella, Barcelona: Comparative Approaches." Pp. 257-276 in *Crossing Over: Comparing Recent Migration in the United States and Europe*, edited by Holger Henke. Lanham, MD: Lexington Books, Inc., 2005.

Pastore, Ferruccio. "Droit de la nationalité et migrations internationals: Le cas italien." Pp. 95-116 in *Nationalité et citoyenneté en Europe*, edited by Patrick Weil and Randall Hansen. Paris: Éditions la Découverte, 1999.

———. "Aeneas's Route: Euro-Mediterranean Relations and International Migration." Pp. 105-124 in *Migration and the Externalities of European Integration*, edited by Sandra Lavenex and Emek Uçarer. Lanham, MD: Lexington Books, 2002.

Patterson, Sheila. *Immigration and Race Relations in Britain, 1960-1967*. London: Oxford University Press, 1969.

Paul, Kathleen. *Whitewashing Britain: Race and Citizenship in the Postwar Era*. Ithaca: Cornell University Press, 1997.

Peabody, Sue. *"There Are No Slaves in France": The Political Culture of Race and Slavery in the Ancien Régime*. Oxford: Oxford University Press, 1996.

Peacock, Shane. "Africa Meets the Great Farini." Pp. 81-106 in *Africans on Stage: Studies in Ethnological Show Business*, edited by Bernth Lindfors. Bloomington: Indiana University Press, 1999.

Pearson, Michael N. *Port Cities and Intruders: The Swahili Coast, India, and Portugal in the Early Modern Era*. Baltimore: The Johns Hopkins University Press, 1998.

Perdicaris, Ion H. "In Raissuli's Hands." Pp. 285-302 in *White Slaves, African Masters*, edited and "Introduction" by Paul Baepler. Chicago: The University of Chicago Press, 1999.

Perrin, Delphine. "Le Maghreb sous influence: le nouveau cadre juridique des migrations transsahariennes." *Maghreb-Machrek* 185 (2005): 59-80.

Perrineau, Pascal. "Le Front national: du désert à l'enracinement." Pp. 83-104 in *Face au racisme: Analyses, hypotheses, perspectives*, edited by Pierre-André Taguieff. Paris: Éditions la Découverte, 1991.

Peterson, Abby. "Introduction." Pp.1-20 in *Stranger or Guest? Racism and Nationalism in Contemporary Europe*, edited by Sandro Fridlizius and Abby Peterson. Stockholm: Almqvist & Wiksell International, 1996.

Pétrissans-Cavaillès, Danielle. *Sur les traces de la traite des Noirs à Bordeaux*. Paris: L'Harmattan, 2004.

Phillips, Alan. "Minority Rights: Some New Intergovernmental Approaches in Europe." Pp. 112-136 in *Scapegoats and Social Actors: The Exclusion and Integration of Minorities in Western and Eastern Europe*, edited by Danièle Joly. New York: St. Martin's Press, Inc., 1998.

Phillipson, David W. *African Archaeology*. Cambridge: Cambridge University Press, 1985.

Pialoux, Michel. "Jeunesse sans avenir et travail intérimaire." *Actes de la recherche en sciences sociale* 26 (1979): 19-47.

Pickering, Michael. "The Blackface Clown." Pp. 159-174 in *Black Victorians, Black Victoriana*, edited by Gretchen Holbrook Gerzina. New Brunswick: Rutgers University Press, 2003.

Pieterse, Jan Nederveen. *White on Black: Images of Africa and Blacks in Western Popular Culture*. New Haven: Yale University Press, 1992.

Piggott, Stuart. *Ancient Europe: From the Beginnings of Agriculture to Classical Antiquity*. Chicago: Aldine Publishing Co., 1965.

Pignet, Etienne. "Economy versus the People? Swiss Immigration Policy between Economic Demand, Xenophobia, and International Constraint." Pp. 67-89 in *Dialogues on Migration Policy*, edited by Marco Giugni and Florence Passy. Lanham, MD: Lexington Books, 2006.

Pina, Rui de. *Chronica d'El-Rei D. Affonso III*. Lisbon: Escriptorio, 1907. Etext-No. 15674.

———. *Chronica d'el rei D. Diniz, Vol II*. Lisbon: Escriptorio. 1912. Etext-No. 18167.

Pina, Ruy de. "The Discovery of the Kingdom of Benin." Pp. 78-79 in *Europeans in West Africa, 1450-1560*, translated and edited by John William Blake. London: The Hakluyt Society, 1942.

———. "Discovery of Benin." In *Church in Nigeria*, compiled by Joseph Kenny from *Chronica del Rey João II*, ch. 24 (MMA, I, 52; Coimbra, 1950, pp. 74-5). A compilation of primary documents. http://www.diafrica.org/nigeriaop/kenny/DH-01.htm. [Portuguese] (February 21, 2006).

Pitte, Jean Robert. "Conclusion." Pp. 253-260 in *Ces migrants qui changent la face de l'Europe*, edited by Jacques Dupâquier and Yves-Marie Laulan. Paris: L'Harmattan, 2004.

Pommerin, Reiner. "The Fate of Mixed Blood Children in Germany." *German Studies Review* 5 (1982): 315-323.

Popovic, Alexandre. *The Revolt of African Slaves in Iraq in the 3rd/9th Century*. Princeton: Markus Wiener Publishers, 1999.

Poulain, Michel. "Les flux migratoires vers l'Europe: où sont-ils et combine sont-ils?" Pp. 83-94 in *Ces migrants qui changent la face de l'Europe*," edited by Jacques Dupâquier and Yves-Marie Laulan. Paris: L'Harmattan, 2004.

Pred, Allan. *Even in Sweden: Racisms, Racialized Spaces, and the Popular Geographical Imagination*. Berkeley: University of California Press, 2000.

———. *The Past Is Not Dead: Facts, Fictions, and Enduring Racial Stereotypes*. Minneapolis: University of Minnesota Press, 2004.

Prince, Nancy. *A Black Woman's Odyssey through Russia and Jamaica*. "Introduction" by Ronald G. Walters. Princeton: Markus Wiener, 1990.

Pulgar, Hernando del. "A Castilian Account of the Discovery of Mina, c. 1474." Extracted from *Crónica de los senores reyes católicos Don Fernando y Dona Isabel* (*Bibliotecha de autores espanoles*, vol. 70; 1923) 0, pt. 2, ch. 62. Pp. 205-207 in *Europeans in West Africa, 1450-1560*, translated and edited by John William Blake. London: The Hakluyt Society, 1942a.

———. "A Flemish-Castilian Voyage to Mina. 1475." Extracted from *Crónica de los senores reyes católicos Don Fernando y Dona Isabel* (*Bibliotecha de autores espanoles*, vol. 70; 1923) 0, pt. 2, ch. 62. Pp. 207-208 in *Europeans in West Africa, 1450-1560*, translated and edited by John William Blake. London: The Hakluyt Society, 1942b.

Raphael-Hernandez, Heike. *Blackening Europe: The African American Presence*. New York: Routledge, 2004.

Ramadan, Tariq. "Europeanization of Islam or Islamization of Europe?" Pp. 207-218 in *Islam, Europe's Second Religion: The New Social, Cultural, and Political Landscape*, edited by Shireen T. Hunter. Westport: Praeger, 2002.

Ramos, Rui Manuel Moura. "Mouvements migratoires et droit de la nationalité au Portugal." Pp. 221-238 in *Nationalité et citoyenneté en Europe*, edited by Patrick Weil and Randall Hansen. Paris: Éditions la Découverte, 1999.

Randers-Pehrson, Justine Davis. *Barbarians and Romans: The Birth Struggle of Europe, A.D. 400-700*. Norman: University of Oklahoma, 1983.

Ray, William. "Horrors of Slavery." Pp. 187-204 in *White Slaves, African Masters*, edited by Paul Baepler with "Introduction." Chicago: The University of Chicago Press, 1999.

Reader, John. *Africa: A Biography of the Continent*. New York: Vintage Books, 1997.

Régent, Frédéric. *La France et ses esclaves de colonization aux abolitions (1620-1848)*. Paris: Éditions Bernard Grasset, 2007.

Reiprich, Doris and Erika N'Gambi. "Our Father was Cameroonian, Our Mother East Prussian, We Are Mulattoes" Pp. 56-76 in *Showing our Colors, Afro-German Women Speak Out*, edited by May Optiz, Katharina Oguntoye and Dagmar Schultz. Translated by Anne V. Adams. Amherst: The University of Massachusetts Press, 1992.

Rex, John. "Islam in the United Kingdom." Pp. 51-76 in *Islam, Europe's Second Religion: The New Social, Cultural, and Political Landscape*, edited by Shireen T. Hunter. Westport: Praeger, 2002.

———. "The Nature of Ethnicity in the Project of Migration." Pp. 121-136 in *Dialogues on Migration Policy*, edited by Marco Giugni and Florence Passy. Lanham, MD: Lexington Books, 2006.

Ribbe, Clalude. *Alexandre Dumas, le dragon de la reine*. Monaco: Éditions du Rocher, 2002.

———. *Les Nègres de la République*. Monaco: Éditions Alphée, 2007.

Richardson, James. *Travels in the Great Desert of the Sahara, in the Years of 1845 and 1846. Vol 1*. London: R. Bentley, 1848.

Ringold, Dena. *Roma and the Transition in Central and Eastern Europe: Trends and Challenges*. Washington, D.C.: The World Bank, 2000.

Ritaine, É. "Introduction – Quand parler de l'Autre, c'est parler de Soi." Pp. 1-28 in *L'Europe du Sud face à l'immigration: Politique de l'Étranger*, edited by Évelyne Ritaine. Paris: Presses Universitaires de France, 2005a.

———. "L' Étranger et le Populiste en Italie: liaisons dangereuses." Pp. 29-70 in *L'Europe du Sud face à l'immigration: Politique de l'Étranger*, edited by Évelyne Ritaine. Paris: Presses Universitaires de France, 2005b.

———. "Conclusion – Miroir, mon beau miroir. . ." Pp. 259-262 in *L'Europe du Sud face à l'immigration: Politique de l'Étranger*, edited by Évelyne Ritaine. Paris: Presses Universitaires de France, 2005c.

Robbins, Sarah. "Gendering the debate over African Americans' education in the 1880s: Frances Harper's reconfiguration of Atticus Haygood's Philanthropic model." *Legacy: A Journal of American Women Writers* 19 (2002): 81-89.

Roberts, J. M. *The Penguin History of Europe*. London: Penguin Books, 1997.

Robinson, Donald L. *Slavery in the Structure of American Politics, 1765-1820*. New York: Harcourt Brace Jovanovich, Inc., 1971.

Rogers, J. A. *Nature Knows No Color-Line*. New York: Helga M. Rogers, 1952.

———. *Sex and Race: The Old World. Vol 1*. New York: Helga M. Rogers, 1967.

———. *Sex and Race: The Old World. Vol II*. New York: Helga M. Rogers, 1972.

Rosen, Christine. *Preaching Eugenics: Religious Leaders and the American Eugenics Movement.* New York: Oxford University Press, 2004.

Rosenberg, Clifford. "Albert Sarraut and Republican Racial Thought." Pp. 36-83 in *Race in France*, edited by Herrick Chapman and Laura L. Frader. New York: Berghahn Books, 2004.

Rotman, Youval. *Les Esclaves et l'Esclavage: De la Médierranée antique à la Médierranée médiévale, VIe-XIe siècles.* Paris: Les Belles Lettres, 2004.

Rouadjia, Ahmed. *Les enfants illégitimes de la République.* Paris: Maisonneuve & Larose, 2004.

Rousseau, Theodore. "Juan de Pareja by Diego Velazquez: An Appreciation of the Portrait." *The Metropolitan Museum of Art Bulletin*, New Series 29 (1971): 449-451.

Rout, Jr., Leslie B. *The African Experience in Spanish America: 1502 to the Present Day.* London: Combridge University Press, 1976.

Rozakis, Christos L. "Le droit de la nationalité en Grèce." Pp. 177-198 in *Nationalité et citoyenneté en Europe*, edited by Patrick Weil and Randall Hansen. Paris: Éditions la Découverte, 1999.

Rudder, Véronique de. "'Seuil de tolérance' et cohabitation pluriethnique." Pp. 154-166 in *Face au racisme: Analyses, hypotheses, perspectives*, edited by Pierre-André Taguieff. Paris: Éditions la Découverte, 1991.

Ruhlen, Merritt. *A Guide to the World's Languages. Volume I: Classification.* Stanford: Ctanford University Press, 1987.

Rydell, Robert W. "'Darkest Africa': African Shows at America's World's Fairs, 1893-1940." Pp. 135-155 in *Africans on Stage: Studies in Ethnological Show Business*, edited by Bernth Lindfors. Bloomington: Indiana University Press, 1999.

Sahlins, Peter. *Unnaturally French: Foreign Citizens in the Old Regime and After.* Ithaca: Cornell University Press, 2004.

Said, Edward W. *Orientalism.* New York: Vintage Books, 1994.

Samad, Yunas. "The Plural Guises of Multiculturalism: Conceptualising a Fragmented Paradigm." Pp. 240-260 in *The Politics of Multiculturalism in the New Europe: Racism, Identity and Community*, edited by Tariq Modood and Pnina Werbner. London: Zed Books Ltd, 1997.

Samples, Susann. "African Germans in the Third Reich." Pp. 53-69 in *The African-German Experience: Critical Essays*, edited by Carol Aisha Blackshire-Belay. Westport, CT: Praeger, 1996.

Sanford, Eva Matthews. *The Mediterranean World in Ancient Times.* New York: The Ronald Press Company, 1938.

Saunders, A. C. de C. M. *A Social History of Black Slaves and Freedmen in Portugal, 1441-1555.* Cambridge: Cambridge University Press, 1982.

Scheck, Raffael. "'They Are Just Savages': German Massacres of Black Soldiers from the French Army in 1940." *Journal of Modern History* 77 (June 2005): 325-344.

———. *Hitler's African Victims: The German Army Massacres of Black French Soldiers in 1940.* New York: Cambridge University Press, 2006.

Schiffauer, Werner. "Islam as a Civil Religion: Political Culture and the Organisation of Diversity in Germany." Pp. 147-166 in *The Politics of Multiculturalism in the New Europe: Racism, Identity and Community*, edited by Tariq Modood and Pnina Werbner. London: Zed Books Ltd., 1997.

Schneer, Jonathan. "Anti-Imperial London: The Pan-African Conference of 1900." Pp. 175-186 in *Black Victorians, Black Victoriana*, edited by Gretchen Holbrook Gerzina. New Brunswick: Rutgers University Press, 2003.

Schneider, I. "A Negro Citizen of Soviet Georgia." *Soviet Russia Today* 10 (1942): 24-26.

Schneider, Jens. "Discourses of Exclusion: Dominant Self-Definitions and the 'The Other' in German Society." *Journal of the Society for the Anthropology of Europe.* 2 (2002): 13-21.

Schneider, William H. *An Empire for the Masses: The French Popular Image of Africa, 1877-1900.* Westport, CT: Greenwood, 1982.

Schor, Ralph. *Histoire de l'immigration en France de la fin du XIXe siècle à nos jours.* Paris: Armand Colin/Masson, 1996.

Schumann, Reinhold. *Italy in the Last Fifteen Hundred Years.* 2nd ed. Lanham, MD: University Press of America, 1992.

Sciortino, G. "La politique migratoire européenne: une orthodoxie restrictive." Pp. 223-258 in *L'Europe du Sud face à l'immigration: Politique de l'Étranger,* edited by Évelyne Ritaine. Paris: Presses Universitaires de France, 2005.

Seck, Assane. *Dakar: Métropole Ouest-Africaine.* Dakar: Institut Fondamental d'Afrique Noire, 1970.

Seelig, Lorenz. "Christoph Jamnitzer's 'Moor's Head': a Late Renaissance Drinking Vessel." Pp. 181-209 in *Black Africans in Renaissance Europe,* edited by T. F. Earle and K. J. P. Lowe. Cambridge: Cambridge University Press, 2005.

Segal, Ronald. "Blacks in Britain." Pp. 263-286 in *The Black Diaspora: Five Centuries of the Black Experience Outside Africa.* New York: Farrar, Straus and Giroux, 1995.

———. *Islam's Black Slaves: The Other Black Diaspora.* New York: Farrar, Straus and Giroux, 2001.

Selm, Joanne van. "Immigration and Asylum or Foreign Policy: The EU's Approach to Migrants and Their Countries of Origin." Pp. 143-160 in *Migration and the Externalities of European Integration,* edited by Sandra Lavenex and Emek Uçarer. Lanham, MD: Lexington Books, 2002.

Seng, Yvonne J. "A Liminal State: Slavery in Sixteenth-Century Istanbul." Pp. 25-42 in *Slavery in the Islamic Middle East,* edited by Shaun E. Marmon. Princeton: Markus Wiener Publishers, 1999.

Sephocle, Marilyn. "Black Germans and Their Compatriots." Pp. 13-28 in *The African-German Experiences: Critical Essays,* edited by Carol Aisha Blackshire-Belay. Westport, CT: Praeger, 1996.

Sepinwall, Alyssa Goldstein. "Eliminating Race, Eliminating Difference: Blacks, Jews, and the Abbé Grégoire." Pp. 28-41 in *The Color of Liberty, Histories of Race in France,* edited by Sue Peabody and Tyler Stovall. Durham: Duke University Press, 2003.

Shack, William A. *Harlem in Montmartre: A Paris Jazz Story between the Great Wars.* Berkeley: University of California Press, 2001.

Sharp, William Frederick. *Slavery on the Spanish Frontier: The Colombian Chocó, 1680-1810.* Norman: The University of Oklahoma Press, 1976.

Sherwin-White, A. N. *Racial Prejudice in Imperial Rome.* Cambridge: Cambridge University Press, 1967.

Shinnie, P. L. *Medieval Nubia.* Khartoum: Sudan Antiquities Service, 1954. [Electronic version] http://rum.atkilise.org/nubia.htm (June 6, 2004).

Shyllon, F. O. *Black People in Britain, 1555-1833.* London: Oxford University Press, 1977.

Silverman, Max. "Encounters in the City." Pp. 95-107 in *Stranger or Guest? Racism and Nationalism in Contemporary Europe,* edited by Sandro Fridlizius and Abby Peterson. Stockholm: Almqvist & Wiksell International, 1996.

Silvestri, Sara. "The Situation of Muslim Immigrants in Europe in the Twenty-first Century: The Creation of National Muslim Councils." Pp. 101-129 in *Crossing Over:*

Comparing Recent Migration in the United States and Europe, edited by Holger Henke. Lanham, MD: Lexington Books, Inc., 2005.

Simola, Raisa. "Notion of Hybridity in the Discourse of Some Contemporary West African Artists." *Nordic Journal of African Studies* 16(2007): 197-211.

Simon, Jacques. *L'Immigration Algérienne en France des origins à l'indépendance*. Paris: Éditions Paris-Méditerranée, 2000.

Simon, Patrick, and Claude Tapia. *Le Belleville des Juifs tunisiens*. Paris: Éditions Autrement, 1998.

Small, Stephen. "Racism, Black People, and the City in Britain." Pp. 357-377 in *Globalization and Survival in the Black Diaspora: The New Urban Challenge*, edited by Charles Green. Albany: State University of New York Press, 1997.

Smedley, Audrey. *Race in North America, Origins and Evolution of a Worldview*. Boulder, CO: Westview Press, 2007.

Smith, Andrea Llynn. "The Colonial in Postcolonial Europe: The Social Memory of Maltese-Origin Pieds-Noirs." Ph.D. diss. University of Arizona, 1998.

Smith, Denis Mack. *A History of Sicily, Medieval Sicily: 800-1713*. London: Chatto and Windus, 1968.

Smith, Preserved. *The Enlightenment, 1687-1776*. New York: Collier Books, 1962.

Smith, Walter E. *The Black Mozart, Le Chevalier de Saint-Georges*. Bloomington, IN: AuthorHouse, 2005.

Snowden, Jr., Frank M. *Blacks in Antiquity: Ethiopians in the Greco-Roman Experience*. Cambridge: Harvard University Press, 1970.

———. "Iconographical Evidence on the Black Populations in Greco-Roman Antiquity." Pp. 133-245 in *The Image of the Black in Western Art: From the Pharaohs to the Fall of the Roman Empire*, edited by Ladislas Bugner. Vol 1. Cambridge: Harvard University Press, 1976.

———. *Before Color Prejudice: The Ancient View of Blacks*. Cambridge: Harvard University Press, 1983.

Soemmerring, Samuel Thomas von. *Über die körperliche Verschiedenheit des Negers vom Europäer*. Frankfurt: Bey Varrentrapp Sohn und Wenner, 1785.

Solé, Carlota and Sònia Parella. "Immigrant Women in Domestic Service: The Care Crisis in the United States and Spain." Pp. 235-256 in *Crossing Over: Comparing Recent Migration in the United States and Europe*, edited by Holger Henke. Lanham, MD: Lexington Books, Inc., 2005.

Solsten, Eric, and Sandra W. Meditz, eds. *Finland, A Country Study*, Washington, D.C.: United States Government, 1990.

Soulamas, Nacira Guénif. *Des 'beurettes' aux descendants d'immigrants nord-africains*. Paris: Éditions Grasset & Fasquelle, 2000.

Sowards, Steven W. "Twenty-Five Lectures on Modern Balkan History: The Balkans in the Age of Nationalism." 1996. http://www.lib.msu.edu/sowards/balkan/. (September 30, 2002).

Stanford, Eva Matthews. *The Mediterranean World in Ancient Times*. New York: The Ronald Press Co., 1938.

Stenberg, Lief. "Islam in Scandinavia." Pp. 121-140 in *Islam, Europe's Second Religion: The New Social, Cultural, and Political Landscape*, edited by Shireen T. Hunter. Westport: Praeger, 2002.

Steward, T. G. *The Colored Regulars in the United States Army*. Philadelphia: A. M. E. Concern, 1904.

Stora, Benjamin. "L'intégrisme islamique en France: entre fantasmes et réalités." Pp. 216-222 in *Face au racisme: Analyses, hypotheses, perspectives*, edited by Pierre-André Taguieff. Paris: Éditions la Découverte, 1991.

————. "Les Algeriens en France: 1945-1975." Pp. 111-135 in *Un siècle d'Immigrations en France: 1845 à nos jours, Du chantier à la citoyenneté?*, edited by David Assouline and Mehdi Lallaoui. Paris: Diffusion Syros, 1997.

Stora, Brigitte, and Samia Messaoudi. "Les années citoyennes." Pp. 31-47 in *Un siècle d'Immigrations en France: 1845 à nos jours, Du chantier à la citoyenneté?*, edited by David Assouline and Mehdi Lallaoui. Paris: Diffusion Syros, 1997.

Stovall, Tyler. "From Red Belt to Black Belt: Race, Class, and Urban Marginality in Twentieth-Century Paris." Pp. 351-369 in *The Color of Liberty, Histories of Race in France*, edited by Sue Peabody and Tyler Stovall. Durham: Duke University Press, 2003.

Strother, Z. S. "Display of the Body Hottentot." Pp. 1-61 in *Africans on Stage: Studies in Ethnological Show Business*, edited by Bernth Lindfors. Bloomington: Indiana University Press, 1999.

Stuart, Susan. "Linguistic Profit, Loss and Betrayal in *Paris-Athènes*." Pp. 284-295 in *Francophone Post-Colonial Cultures*, edited by Kamal Salhi. Lanham, MD: Lexington Books, 2003.

Stuurman, Siep. "François Bernier and the Invention of Racial Classification." *History Workshop Journal* 50 (2000): 1-21.

Sweet, James H. "Collective Degradation: Slavery and the Construction of Race." http://www.yale.edu/glc/events/race/Sweet.pdf (August 31, 2006).

Symmons, Clive. "Le droit de la nationalité en Irlande." Pp. 307-328 in *Nationalité et citoyenneté en Europe*, edited by Patrick Weil and Randall Hansen. Paris: Éditions la Découverte, 1999.

Taguieff, Pierre-André. "Les métamorphoses idéologiques du racisme et la crise de l'antiracisme." Pp. 13-63 in *Face au racisme: Analyses, hypotheses, perspectives*, edited by Pierre-André Taguieff. Paris: Éditions la Découverte, 1991.

Tandonnet, Maxime. *Migrations, La nouvelle vague*. Paris: L'Harmattan, 2003.

Temperley, Howard. "The Ideology of Antislavery." Pp. 21-36 in *The Abolition of the Atlantic Slave Trade*, edited by David Eltis and James Walvin. Madison: The University of Wisconsin Press, 1981.

Thomas, Dominic. *Black France: Colonialism, Immigration, and Transnationalism*. Bloomington: Indiana University Press, 2007.

Thomas, Hugh. *The Slave Trade, The Story of the Atlantic Slave Trade: 1440-1870*. New York: Touchstone, 1997.

Thompson, Lloyd A. *Romans and Blacks*. Norman: University of Oklahoma Press, 1989.

Thornton, John. *Africa and Africans in the Making of the Atlantic World, 1400-1800*. 2nd ed. Cambridge: Cambridge University Press, 1998.

————. "Mbanza Kongo/São Salvador: Kongo's Holy City." Pp. 67-84 in *Africa's Urban Past*, edited by David M. Anderson and Richard. Oxford: James Currey, 2000.

Tinhorão, José Ramos. *Os Negros em Portugal*. Lisbon: Edicões Caminho, 1998.

Tobo, Bassa. *Arab Nationalism: Between Islam and the Nation-State*. New York: St. Martin's Press, 1997.

Tognetti, Sergio. "The Trade in Black African Slaves in Fifteenth – Century Florence." Pp. 213-224 in *Black Africans in Renaissance Europe*, edited by T. F. Earle and K. J. P. Lowe. Cambridge: Cambridge University Press, 2005.

Toledano, Ehud R. *Slavery and Abolition in the Ottoman Middle East*. Seattle: University of Washington Press, 1998.

Torpey, John. *The Invention of the Passport: Surveillance, Citizenship, and the State*. Cambridge: Cambridge University Press, 2000.

Trento, Giovanna. "Lomi and Totò: An Ethiopian-Italian Colonial or Postcolonial 'Love Store'?" *Conserveries mémorielles*, 2007. No. 2. http://www.celat.ulaval.ca/histoire.-memoire/revuefiles/cm2_tento.pdf (May 11, 2007).

Triadafilopoulos, Triadafilos, and Andrej Zaslove. "Influencing Migration Policy from Inside: Political Parties." Pp. 171-191 in *Dialogues on Migration Policy*, edited by Marco Giugni and Florence Passy. Lanham, MD: Lexington Books, 2006.

Tribalat, Michèle. "Intégration/assimilation en France: qu'en sait-on?" Pp. 195-222 in *Ces migrants qui changent la face de l'Europe*, edited by Jacques Dupâquier and Yves-Marie Laulan. Paris: L'Harmattan, 2004.

Trimingham, J. Spencer. *Islam in Ethiopia*. Oxford: Geoggrey Cumberlege for the University Press, 1952.

———. *Christianity among the Arabs in pre-Islamic Times*. London: Longman, 1979.

Tudor House Museum. "Bought and Sold – Southampton's Links with the Slave Trade." Exhibition, 2002.

Turner, John M. "Pablo Fanque, Black Circus Proprietor." Pp. 20-38 in *Black Victorians, Black Victoriana*, edited by Gretchen Holbrook Gerzina. New Brunswick: Rutgers University Press, 2003.

Uçarer, Emek M. "Guarading the Borders of the European Union: Paths, Portals, and Prerogatives." Pp. 15-32 in *Migration and the Externalities of European Integration*, edited by Sandra Lavenex and Emek Uçarer. Lanham, MD: Lexington Books, 2002.

Vatican Library, The. "The Study of Eastern Languages." http://www.ibiblio.org/expo/-vatican.exhibitg/exhib/h-oreint_to_rome/Eastern_lang.html#oriento5 (September 17, 2007).

Veer, Peter van der. "'The Enigma of Arrival': Hybridity and Authenticity in the Global Space." Pp. 90-105 in *Debating Cultural Hybridity: Multi-Cultural Identities and the Politics of Anti-Racism*, edited by Pnina Werbner and Tariq Modood. London: Zed Books Ltd., 2000.

Vella, Andrew P. "The Order of Malta and the Defence of Tripoli 1530-1551." *Melita Historica* 6 (1975): 362-381.

Vercoutter, Jean, Jean Leclant, Frank M. Snowden, Jr., and Jehan Desanges. *The Image of the Black in Western Art: From the Pharaohs to the Fall of the Roman Empire*, edited by Ladislas Bugner. Cambridge: Menil Foundation, Ind. And Harvard University Press, 1991.

Verlinden, Charles. *L'Esclavage dans l'Europe médiévale*. Brugge: De Tempel, 1955.

Vermeulen, Hans, and Rinus Penninx. "Introduction." Pp. 1-35 in *Immigrant Integration: The Dutch Case*, edited by Hans Vermeulen and Rinus Penninx. Amsterdam: Het Spinhuis, 2000a.

———. "Conclusion." Pp. 202-232 in *Immigrant Integration: The Dutch Case*, edited by Hans Vermeulen and Rinus Penninx. Amsterdam: Het Spinhuis, 2000b.

Vimont, Claude. "Conséquences économiques dans les pays d'accueil." Pp. 125-134 in *Ces migrants qui changent la face de l'Europe*, edited by Jacques Dupâquier and Yves-Marie Laulan. Paris: L'Harmattan, 2004.

Vink, Markus. "'The World's Oldest Trade': Dutch Slavery and Slave Trade in the Indian Ocean in the Seventeenth Century." *Journal of World History*. June 2003. http://www.historycooperative.org/journals/jwh/14.2/vinkhtml (April 14, 2004).

Vioque, G. G. *Martial, Book VII: A Commentary*, translated by J. J. Zoltowski. Leiden: Brill, 2002.

Vitkus, Daniel J., ed. *Piracy, Slavery, and Redemption: Barbary Captivity Narratives form Early Modern England*. New York: Columbia University Press, 2001.

Wacquant, Loïc J. D. "Urban Outcasts: Sigma and Division in the Black American Ghetto and the French Urban Periphery." Pp. 331-356 in *Globalization and Survival in the*

Black Diaspora: The New Urban Challenge, edited by Charles Green. Albany: State University of New York Press, 1997.

Wal, Jessika ter, ed. *Racism and Cultural Diversity in the Mass Media*. Vienna: European Monitoring Centre on Racism and Xenophobia, 2002.

Walbank, Frank W. *Polybius, Rome and the Hellenistic World*. Cambridge: Cambridge University Press, 2002.

Walvin, James. *The Black Presence: A Documentary History of the Negro in England, 1555-1860*. New York: Schocken Books, 1972.

———. *Black and White: The Negro and English Society, 1555-1945*. London: Allen Lane the Penguin Press, 1973.

———. *England, Slaves, and Freedom, 1776-1838*. Jackson: University of Mississippi, 1986.

———. *Black Ivory: A History of British Slavery*. Oxford: Blackwell Publishers, 2001.

———. "Introduction." Pp. 1-8 in *Black Victorians, Black Victoriana*, edited by Gretchen Holbrook Gerzina. New Brunswick: Rutgers University Press, 2003.

Warmington, B. S. *The North African Provinces from Diocletian to the Vandal Conquests*. Westport, CT: Greenwood Press, Publishers, 1971.

Watson, Waltraud Nicole. "Afro-Germans in Germany: A Private Perspective." Pp. 233-239 in *Crosscurrents: African Americans, Africa, and Germany in the Modern World*, edited by David McBride, Leroy Hopkins, and C. Aisha Blackshire-Belay. Columbia, SC: Camden House, Inc., 1998.

Watt, Richard. *Packaging Post/Coloniality: The Manufacture of Literary Identity in the Francophone World*. Lanham, MD: Lexington Books, 2005.

Weil, Patrick. "Le logement des travailleurs immigrés: detournements et impasses d'une politique." Pp. 178-188 in *Face au racisme: Analyses, hypotheses, perspectives*, edited by Pierre-André Taguieff. Paris: Éditions la Découverte, 1991.

———. "L'histoire de la nationalité française: une leçon pour l'Europe." Pp. 55-70 in *Nationalité et citoyenneté en Europe*, edited by Patrick Weil and Randall Hansen. Paris: Éditions la Découverte, 1999.

———. *La France et ses étrangers: L'aventure d'une politique de l'immigration de 1938 à nos jours*. Paris: Éditions Gallimard, 2004.

Weil, Patrick, and Randall Hansen. "Introduction: Citoyenneté, immigration et nationalité ver la convergence européeanne?" Pp. 9-28 in *Nationalité et citoyenneté en Europe*, edited by Patrick Weil and Randall Hansen. Paris: Éditions la Découverte, 1999.

Wellard, James Howard. *Desert Pilgrimage: Journeys to the Egyptian and Sina Deserts, Completing the Third of the Trilogy of Saharan Explorations*. London: Hutchinson, 1970.

Wenden, Catherine Wihtol de. *Atlas des migrations dans le monde, Réfugiés ou migrants volontaires*. Paris: Éditions Autrement, 2005.

Wenke, Robert J. *Patterns in Prehistory: Mankind's First Three Million Years*. New York: Oxford University Press, 1980.

Werbner, Pnina. "Afterword: Writing Multiculturalism and Politics in the New Europe." Pp. 261-267 in *The Politics of Multiculturalism in the New Europe: Racism, Identity and Community*, edited by Tariq Modood and Pnina Werbner. London: Zed Books Ltd, 1997.

———. "Introduction: The Dialectics of Cultural Hybridity." Pp. 1-28 in *Debating Cultural Hybridity: Multi-Cultural Identities and the Politics of Anti-Racism*, edited by Pnina Werbner and Tariq Modood. London: Zed Books, 2000a.

————. "Essentialising Essentialism, Essentialising Silence: Ambivalence and Multiplicity in the Constructuions of Racism and Ethnicity." Pp. 226-256 in *Debating Cultural Hybridity: Multi-Cultural Identities and the Politics of Anti-Racism*, edited by Pnina Werbner and Tariq Modood. London: Zed Books Ltd., 2000b.

Wettinger, Godfrey. *Slavery in the Islands of Malta and Gozo, ca. 1000-1812.* San Gwann, Malta: PEG Ltd., 2002.

Wicker, Hans-Rudolf. "From Complex Culture to Cultural Complexity." Pp. 29-45 in *Debating Cultural Hybridity: Multi-Cultural Identities and the Politics of Anti-Racism*, edited by Pnina Werbner and Tariq Modood. London: Zed Books, 2000.

Wieviorka, Michel. "L'expansion du racisme populaire." Pp. 73-82 in *Face au racisme: Analyses, hypotheses, perspectives*, edited by Pierre-André Taguieff. Paris: Éditions la Découverte, 1991.

————. "Populism and Nationalism in Contemporary Europe." Pp. 21-38 in *Stranger or Guest? Racism and Nationalism in Contemporary Europe*, edited by Sandro Fridlizius and Abby Peterson. Stockholm: Almqvist & Wiksell International, 1996.

————. "Is It So Difficult to be an Anti-Racist?" Pp. 139-153 in *Debating Cultural Hybridity: Multi-Cultural Identities and the Politics of Anti-Racism*, edited by Pnina Werbner and Tariq Modood. London: Zed Books, 2000.

Wilder, Gary. "Panafricanism and the Republican Political Sphere." Pp. 237-258 in *The Color of Liberty, Histories of Race in France*, edited by Sue Peabody and Tyler Stovall. Durham: Duke University Press, 2003.

Williams, Daniel. "From Russia With Hate: Africans Face Racism." Washington Post Foreign Service, January 12, 1998. http://www.washingtonpost.com/wpsrv/inati/-longterm.russiagov/stories/racism011298.htm. (February 18, 2000).

Williams, Francee Greer. *The Abyssinian Prince: The True Life Story of George Polgreen Bridgetower*. Lincoln, NE: Writers Club Press, 2001.

Wilson, Carlton Eugene. "A Hidden History: The Black Experience in Liverpool, England, 1919-1945." Ph.D. diss. University of North Carolina, 1993.

Wood, Ean. *The Josephine Baker Story*. London: Sanctuary, 2000.

Woodard, Helena. *African-British Writings in the Eighteenth Century: The Politics of Race and Reason.* Westport, CT: Greenwood Press, 1999.

Wren, Melvin C. *The Course of Russian History*. New York: The Macmillan Co., 1958.

Yalçun-Heckmann, Lale. "The Perils of Ethnic Associational Life in Europe: Turkish Migrants in Germany and France." Pp.95-110 in *The Politics of Multiculturalism in the New Europe: Racism, Identity and Community*, edited by Tariq Modood and Pnina Werbner. London: Zed Books Ltd, 1997.

Ylänkö, Maaria. "Le droit de la nationalité finlandaise." Pp. 281-306 in *Nationalité et citoyenneté en Europe*, edited by Patrick Weil and Randall Hansen. Paris: Éditions la Découverte, 1999.

Yuval-Davis, Nina. "Ethnicity, Gender Relations and Multiculturalism." Pp. 193-208 in *Debating Cultural: Multi-Cultural Identities and the Politics of Anti-Racism*, edited by Pnina Werbner and Tariq Modood. London: Zed Books Ltd., 2000.

Zeine, Zeine N. *Arab-Turkish Relations and the Emergence of Arab Nationalism*. Westport, CT: Greenwood Press, 1981.

Zanten, Agnès van. "Schooling Immigrants in France in the 1990s: Success or Failure of the Republican Model of integration?" *Anthropology & Education Quarterly* 28 (1997): 351-374.

Zemni, Sami and Christopher Parker. "Islam, the European Union, and the Challenge of Multiculturalism." Pp. 231-244 in *Islam, Europe's Second Religion: The New Social, Cultural, and Political Landscape*, edited by Shireen T. Hunter. Westport: Praeger, 2002.

Index

About the Author

Stefan Goodwin holds a B.A. degree in French, an M.A. in international relations, an M.A. in anthropology, and a Ph.D. in anthropology from Northwestern University. His scholarly maturation has unfolded on several continents. Beginning his long career in higher education on the faculty of Wayne State University, Goodwin continues educating people for global citizenship by encouraging them to draw on human experience in its broadest context. In addition to his articles in books, journals, and encyclopedias that range over subjects from Egyptian prehistory to European folklore, Goodwin has produced a number of volumes.

Using the Maltese Islands as a prism, his *Malta, Mediterranean Bridge* (2002) examined historical, cultural, ecological, and social relationships among Mediterranean peoples. His *Africa's Legacies of Urbanization: Unfolding Saga of a Continent* (2006) focused on the centrality of Africa to a broad understanding of the urbanization process. Inspired by his deep interest in how perceived frontiers and social identities impact our ability to survive as a single species in a globalized village, Goodwin now posits *Africa in Europe* in two volumes. Bringing decades of research and travel to this reexamination of the mythical opposition between Europeans and Africans, the author doubts that any serious readers will come away from these volumes thinking about self and human "otherness" exactly as in the past.